MW01000618

LEGAL DRAFTING

LITIGATION DOCUMENTS, CONTRACTS, LEGISLATION, AND WILLS

■ ■ ■

By

Margaret Temple-Smith

Senior Legal Skills Professor
University of Florida

Deborah Cupples

Senior Legal Skills Professor
University of Florida

AMERICAN CASEBOOK SERIES®

A Thomson Reuters business

Mat #41063786

American Casebook Series is a trademark registered in the U.S. Patent and Trademark Office.

© 2013 Thomson Reuters

610 Opperman Drive
St. Paul, MN 55123
1-800-313-9378

Printed in the United States of America

ISBN: 978–0–314–26799–3

ACKNOWLEDGMENTS

We acknowledge Barbara Child as a pioneer in the field of legal drafting and as the founder of the University of Florida's legal drafting program.

We are grateful for the editorial or research-related assistance provided by the following (listed in chronological order of contributions):

Gregory Kwok

Katherine Thomason

Hanna Edeback

Nicholas Temple-Smith

Cami L. Cupples

Emily Frazier

Dr. Kendra Siler-Marsiglio

For his advice and support, we are grateful to Larry Keith Southerland, Esq.

We are grateful to the following for other forms of help or support:

Caroline Moss Emanuel, Victorina Basauri, William Cupples, C. Douglas Miller, Susan Carr, Nancy Wilcox, Dr. Wayne Losano, Nancy Baldwin, Fletcher Baldwin, Chris Morris, Louis Higgins, Bonnie Karlen, Greg Olson, Laura Holle, Karen Kays, and Kent N. Wenger.

Our colleagues at the University of Florida's Levin College of Law: Anne Rutledge, Gaylin Soponis, Leslie Knight, Sylvia Menendez, Diane Tomlinson, Leanne Pflaum, and Teresa Reid.

SUMMARY OF CONTENTS

ACKNOWLEDGMENTS --- iii

Legal Drafting: An Introduction ------------------------------------- **1**
   I.   Purpose of the Course ------------------------------------- 1
   II. Focuses of the Course ------------------------------------- 1
   III. Collaboration with the Client ------------------------------- 3

PART 1.   LITIGATION DOCUMENTS

1. **General Introduction to Litigation–Related Documents** - **6**
   I.   Pleadings Requesting Affirmative Relief -------------------- 6
   II. Defensive Pleadings --- 7
   III. Requirements Regarding Pleadings, Motions, and Other
          Papers --- 8
   IV. Federal Rule 11: Purpose, Requirements and Sanctions --- 11

2. **The Initial Pleading** -- **14**
   I.   Purpose of the Initial Pleading ----------------------------- 14
   II. Drafting a Legally Sufficient Pleading ---------------------- 14
   III. Procedural Matters Addressed in the Pleading ----------- 17
   IV. Fundamentals of Drafting a Complaint -------------------- 23
   V. Drafting Multi–Count Complaints ------------------------- 33
   VI. Pleading Pursuant to Statute ------------------------------- 35

3. **Answers (Defensive Pleadings)** -------------------------------- **43**
   I.   Purpose of the Answer -------------------------------------- 43
   II. Time for Responding by Answer ----------------------------- 43
   III. Failure of Defendant to Respond (Default) ---------------- 43
   IV. Responses to the Allegations ------------------------------- 44
   V. Pleading Affirmative Defenses ------------------------------ 50
   VI. Responding to the Answer Via Reply ---------------------- 53
   VII. Defenses Relating to Certain Special Matters ------------- 54
   VIII. Motion to Strike a Legal Defense -------------------------- 54

4. **Motions** --- **56**
   I.   Introduction to Motions ------------------------------------ 56
   II. Motion Practice Generally ----------------------------------- 56
   III. Pre–Answer Motions -- 60
   IV. Motions for Summary Adjudication -------------------------- 67

5. **Exercises for Part 1: Pleadings** ------------------------------------ **75**

PART 2. CONTRACTS

6. **Introduction to Contract Drafting** ---------------------------- **96**
    I.   The Contract Drafter as "Lawmaker" ----------------------- 96
    II.   The Contract Drafter's Role as an Advocate --------------- 96
    III. Some Preliminary Considerations --------------------------- 97
    IV.   Typical Contract Provisions ------------------------------ 98
    V.   Articulation of the Contract ----------------------------- 98
    VI.   Invalid Contracts or Provisions ------------------------- 105

7. **Contract Components: Preliminary Matters, Core Trans-
    action, and Subsidiary Agreements** ------------------------ **108**
    I.   Title and Exordium --------------------------------------- 108
    II.   Provisions Dealing With Preliminary Matters ------------ 109
    III. Articulating the Core Obligations ---------------------- 115
    IV.   Identifying and Articulating the Subsidiary Agreements -- 118

8. **Limitation or Exclusion of Liability** -------------------------- **123**
    I.   Purpose of Provisions Addressing Liability ---------------- 123
    II.   Excuse Based on Inability to Perform --------------------- 123
    III. Exculpatory Clauses ------------------------------------- 126
    IV.   Clauses Used to Limit Damages or Remedies ------------- 131
    V.   Limiting or Excluding Warranties Under the UCC ------- 134
    VI.   Agreements to Indemnify --------------------------------- 136
    VII. Agreement to Defend ------------------------------------ 139

9. **Contract Components: Termination, Breach, and
    Remedies** -- **140**
    I.   Termination of Contractual Obligations ------------------- 140
    II.   Breach of Contract ------------------------------------ 144

10. **Contract Components: Winding–Up, Non–Compete,
    Severance, Integration, and Dispute–Resolution
    Provisions** --- **149**
    I.   Winding up the Contractual Relationship ----------------- 149
    II.   Covenants that Protect Business Interests after Relation-
          ship Ends --- 149
    III. Severance of an Unenforceable Provision ----------------- 152
    IV.   Integration (or Merger) Clauses ------------------------ 153
    V.   Dispute Resolution ------------------------------------ 154

11. **Contract Components: Modification, Execution, and
    Effective Date** --- **163**
    I.   Modification Provisions -------------------------------- 163
    II.   Execution of the Contract ----------------------------- 164

12. How Courts Read and Construe Contracts ------------------ **168**
     I.   Why a Drafter Needs to Know How Courts Construe ---- 168
     II.   Questions for Which a Drafter Needs Answers ----------- 168
     III.   Goal of Construction ------------------------------------- 169
     IV.   Approaches to Construction --------------------------------- 169

13. Exercises for Part 2: Contract Drafting ---------------------- **176**

PART 3.   LEGISLATIVE DRAFTING: PUBLIC AND PRIVATE RULE–MAKING DOCUMENTS

14. Introduction to Legislative Drafting: Public and Private Rule–Making Documents ------------------------------------- **188**
     I.   Public and Private Rule–Making Documents ------------- 188
     II.   Organization of a Rule–Making Document ---------------- 188
     III.   Articulating Legislative Statements ------------------------ 189
     IV.   Drafting Style for Rule–Making Documents ---------------- 191

15. Drafting Private Rule–Making Documents ------------------ **195**
     I.   Drafting Process for Private Rule–Making Documents --- 195
     II.   Documents for Property Owner Associations -------------- 195
     III.   Documents Relating to Corporations ----------------------- 198
     IV.   Documents Relating to Limited–Liability Companies ----- 200
     V.   Other Documents That Regulate Conduct ----------------- 200

16. Drafting Public Legislation --------------------------------- **201**
     I.   Preparing to Draft Public Legislation ---------------------- 201
     II.   Basics About Bills -- 202
     III.   Drafting Local Ordinances --------------------------------- 210

17. How Courts Construe Statutes and Other Public Rule–Making Documents --- **212**
     I.   Introduction to Statutory Construction --------------------- 212
     II.   Goal of Courts in Construing a Statute -------------------- 212
     III.   Process of Statutory Construction -------------------------- 213
     IV.   Use of Canons of Construction ------------------------------ 214
     V.   Extrinsic Aids to Construction ------------------------------ 218
     VI.   Strict Versus Liberal Construction -------------------------- 219

18. Exercises for Part 3: Rule–Making Documents ------------ **220**

PART 4. GENERATING AND ORGANIZING CONTENT OF A CONTRACT OR RULE–MAKING DOCUMENT

19. **Generating Your Document's Content** ----------------------- **236**
   I.   Researching the Document's Legal Background ----------- 236
   II.   Researching the Document's Factual Background --------- 236
   III. Assessing the Client's Needs -------------------------- 237
   IV.   Generating a Master Term Sheet and Client Question-
         naire --- 238

20. **Creating an Outline for Your Document** --------------------- **244**
   I.   Overview of Document Organization ---------------------- 244
   II.   Generating an Outline --------------------------------- 244
   III. Sequencing Sections and Subsections of Your Outline ---- 251
   IV.   Basic Format Design for the Document -------------------- 254

21. **Refining the Draft's Organizational Scheme** --------------- **258**
   I.   Reassessing the Drafted Document's Organization -------- 258
   II.   Common Problems --------------------------------------- 258
   III. Using Cross–Referencing (if needed) ------------------- 264

22. **Exercises for Part 4: Generating Content and Creating
      an Organizational Scheme** ----------------------------------- **266**

PART 5. WILLS

23. **Background for Drafting a Will** ----------------------------- **276**
   I.   Preparation for Drafting a Will: An Overview ------------- 276
   II.   Nomination and Duties of an Executor --------------------- 278
   III. Requisites for a Valid Will --------------------------- 279
   IV.   Changes to the Will -------------------------------------- 284

24. **Drafting and Executing the Will** ----------------------------- **286**
   I.   Organizing the Components of a Simple Will ------------- 286
   II.   Choosing Your Language -------------------------------- 289
   III. Nomination and Powers of Executor and Related Issues -- 293
   IV.   Basics for Drafting Simple Dispositive Provisions -------- 294
   V.   Setting Up an Execution Ceremony ----------------------- 301
   VI.   How Courts Read Wills -------------------------------- 302

25. **Exercises for Part 5: Wills** ---------------------------------- **304**

PART 6. ARTICULATING CONTENT

26. **Choosing Language** --- **310**
   I.   Precise Drafting as Preventive Law ---------------------- 310

II. Choosing Your Words ------------------------------------ 310
III. Delineating the Scope of a Provision ------------------ 314

27. Drafting Definitions ----------------------------------- **325**
I. When to Use Definitions ------------------------------ 325
II. Stipulated Definitions ------------------------------- 325
III. Setting Out Definitions in the Document ------------ 329
IV. Common Errors -- 332

28. Eliminating Ambiguity ----------------------------------- **335**
I. Recognizing Ambiguity -------------------------------- 335
II. Ambiguity Caused by Modifier Placement Problems ------ 335
III. Ambiguity Caused by Pronouns ------------------------ 340
IV. Ambiguity Caused by Plurals -------------------------- 341
V. Ambiguity Caused by Word Choice ----------------------- 341
VI. Ambiguity Caused by Inconsistency -------------------- 345
VII. Ambiguity Caused by Punctuation Usage --------------- 346

29. Time Clauses and Conditional Statements --------------- **347**
I. Drafting Time Clauses -------------------------------- 347
II. Conditional Statements ------------------------------- 360

**30. Exercises for Part 6: Word Choice, Ambiguity, and Time
Clauses** -- **364**

PART 7. GRAMMAR, PUNCTUATION, AND STYLE

31. Some Basics About Grammar ----------------------------- **372**
I. The Importance of Grammar Handbooks ------------------ 372
II. Refresher: Some Key Grammatical Terms --------------- 372
III. A Bit About Verbs ---------------------------------- 377
IV. A Bit About Pronouns -------------------------------- 384
V. Parallel Structure ----------------------------------- 389
VI. Avoiding Problems With Modifiers --------------------- 391
VII. Deal–Breaking Grammatical Errors -------------------- 394

32. Some Basics About Punctuation ----------------------------- **395**
I. The Importance of Punctuation ------------------------ 395
II. Commas -- 395
III. Semicolons --- 399
IV. Colons -- 400
V. Apostrophes -- 401
VI. Dashes --- 403
VII. Hyphens --- 404
VIII. Punctuating Quoted Language ----------------------- 405
IX. Parentheses: Does the Period Go Inside or Outside? ------ 406

33. Style --- **407**

    I.   Style Handbooks -- 407

    II.   Write Concisely --- 407

    III.   Avoid Passive Voice Unless You Need It -------------------- 409

    IV.   Refrain From Overloading Sentences ---------------------- 410

    V.   Strive for Simplicity ------------------------------------- 411

    VI.   Omit Needless Legal Jargon ------------------------------- 412

    VII. Indented Lists -- 413

    VIII. Use Gender–Neutral Nouns and Pronouns ---------------- 413

34. Exercises for Grammar, Style, and Punctuation ----------- **415**

ENDNOTES --- 423

INDEX -- 495

TABLE OF CONTENTS

ACKNOWLEDGMENTS --- iii

PART 1. LITIGATION DOCUMENTS

Legal Drafting: An Introduction ------------------------------------- **6**
   I.   Purpose of the Course --------------------------------- 1
   II.   Focuses of the Course --------------------------------- 1
        A. Skills Practiced in Drafting --------------------------- 1
        B. The Focus on Users of Documents --------------------- 2
   III. Collaboration with the Client ------------------------- 3

1. **General Introduction to Litigation–Related Documents** -- **6**
   I.   Pleadings Requesting Affirmative Relief ------------------ 6
        A. Affirmative Relief ------------------------------------ 6
        B. Types of Pleadings Seeking Affirmative Relief -------- 6
   II.   Defensive Pleadings ----------------------------------- 7
   III. Requirements Regarding Pleadings, Motions, and Other
        Papers --- 8
        A. Caption -- 8
           1. Content of the Caption ----------------------- 8
           2. Basic Caption Format ------------------------ 8
           3. Local Rules Addressing Captioning ---------------- 9
        B. Format Requirements for Pleadings, Motions, and
           Other Papers ------------------------------------ 9
           1. In the Federal Courts ------------------------ 9
           2. In the State Courts -------------------------- 9
        C. Incorporation of Exhibits Into Pleadings or Motions -- 9
           1. In Federal Court ----------------------------- 9
           2. In State Courts ------------------------------- 10
        D. Verification of Pleadings, Motions, or Other Papers -- 10
        E. Electronic Filing Requirements ------------------------ 10
           1. In Federal Court ----------------------------- 10
           2. In State Court ------------------------------- 10
        F. Service of Pleadings and Motions --------------------- 11
   IV. Federal Rule 11: Purpose, Requirements and Sanctions -- 11
        A. Purpose of Federal Rule 11 --------------------------- 11
        B. Effect of Presenting a Document to the Court -------- 12

       C. Sanctions for Violation of Federal Rule 11 ------------   12
       D. Specifications for Signing -------------------------------   12
       E. Federal Rule 11's Impact on the State Courts --------   13

2.   The Initial Pleading --   **14**
   I.   Purpose of the Initial Pleading ----------------------------   14
   II.   Drafting a Legally Sufficient Pleading ---------------------   14
       A. Requirement of Legal Sufficiency ----------------------   14
       B. Standards in Federal Court ----------------------------   15
       C. Standards in State Court ------------------------------   16
          1. Notice and Plausibility Standards -----------------   16
          2. Fact Pleading --   17
   III. Procedural Matters Addressed in the Pleading -----------   17
       A. Pleading Jurisdiction ----------------------------------   17
          1. Pleading Subject–Matter Jurisdiction -------------   17
          2. Pleading Personal Jurisdiction --------------------   19
       B. Pleading Venue --   20
       C. Pleading "Special Matters" ----------------------------   21
       D. Demand for Judgment --------------------------------   22
       E. Exhibits to the Pleading ------------------------------   23
   IV.   Fundamentals of Drafting a Complaint --------------------   23
       A. Format and Presentation Requirements --------------   23
       B. Identifying and Referring to the Parties --------------   23
       C. Four Types of Allegations ------------------------------   24
          1. Description of Types of Allegations ----------------   24
          2. Use of Types of Allegations in a Pleading ---------   25
       D. Framing Allegations ------------------------------------   26
          1. Making Allegations Plain, Concise, and Direct ---   26
          2. Focusing on the Parties ---------------------------   26
          3. Alleging Time and Place ---------------------------   27
          4. Pleading Strategically -----------------------------   28
       E. Organizing the Allegations ----------------------------   30
          1. Sequence of Allegations ----------------------------   30
          2. Grouping Facts Into Paragraphs -------------------   32
          3. Numbering Paragraphs ----------------------------   33
          4. Cross–Referencing Between Paragraphs ----------   33
   V.   Drafting Multi–Count Complaints --------------------------   33
       A. Dividing a Pleading Into Counts ----------------------   33
       B. Re–Allegation and Incorporation by Reference -------   34
       C. Demand for Judgment Following Each Count --------   34
       D. Headings for Each Count ------------------------------   35
   VI.   Pleading Pursuant to Statute -------------------------------   35
       A. Statutory Causes of Action Generally -----------------   35
       B. Identifying the Elements of the Statutory Cause of
           Action --   35
          1. Understanding the Statute's Structure ------------   35
          2. Analyzing the Statute ------------------------------   36

        C. Pleading the Statutory Cause of Action ---------------- 38
            1. Identifying the Statute and Adopting a Short
               Form -- 38
            2. Organizing the Allegations -------------------------- 38
            3. Tracking Statutory Language When Framing
               Allegations of Fact --------------------------------- 38
            4. Identifying the Violated Sections and Subsections - 39
        D. Requesting Relief ------------------------------------- 41
        E. Template for Pleading Statutory Cause of Action ---- 41

3. Answers (Defensive Pleadings) ---------------------------------- **43**
    I.   Purpose of the Answer ------------------------------------- 43
    II.   Time for Responding by Answer --------------------------- 43
    III. Failure of Defendant to Respond (Default) ----------------- 43
    IV. Responses to the Allegations ------------------------------- 44
        A. Allowable Responses in State and Federal Court ---- 44
        B. Drafting Responses in Federal or State Court -------- 45
            1. Articulating the Three Basic Responses ----------- 45
            2. Admitting an Allegation in Part -------------------- 46
            3. Avoiding Evasive Responses ------------------------ 48
            4. Responding to Conclusory Allegations ------------- 49
            5. Responding to Allegations Relating to Another
               Defendant --- 49
    V.   Pleading Affirmative Defenses ----------------------------- 50
        A. Characteristics of an Affirmative Defense ------------- 50
        B. Typical Affirmative Defenses -------------------------- 50
            1. Affirmative Defenses Listed in Procedural Rules - 50
            2. Other Affirmative Defenses ------------------------ 51
        C. Drafting an Affirmative Defense ----------------------- 51
            1. Sufficiency of Defense ------------------------------ 51
            2. Pleading Inconsistently, Hypothetically, and
               Alternatively ------------------------------------- 53
            3. Formatting Affirmative Defenses ------------------- 53
    VI. Responding to the Answer Via Reply ----------------------- 53
    VII. Defenses Relating to Certain Special Matters ------------- 54
        A. Challenges to Capacity -------------------------------- 54
        B. Non–Occurrence or Non–Performance of Conditions
            Precedent --- 54
        C. Defense Based on Fraud or Mistake ------------------- 54
    VIII. Motion to Strike a Legal Defense --------------------------- 54

4. Motions -- **56**
    I.   Introduction to Motions ------------------------------------ 56
    II.   Motion Practice Generally ---------------------------------- 56

A. In Federal Court -- 56
    1. Requirements for Filing a Motion ------------------ 56
    2. Availability of Oral Hearing on a Motion --------- 58
    3. Notice of Motion --------------------------------- 59
    4. Opposition to Motion ----------------------------- 59
B. Motion Practice in State Court ------------------------ 59
III. Pre–Answer Motions --------------------------------------- 60
  A. Objections and Defenses Usually Raised by Motion -- 60
    1. Overview of Rule 12(b) Defenses ------------------- 60
    2. Consolidation and Waiver of Rule 12(b) Defenses - 61
  B. Rule 12 Defenses That Address Defects in the Pleading -- 61
    1. Motion Challenging Legal Sufficiency of Pleading Requesting Affirmative Relief -------------------- 61
    2. Motion for More Definite Statement -------------- 64
    3. Motion to Strike -------------------------------- 66
IV. Motions for Summary Adjudication ----------------------- 67
  A. Summary Judgment ------------------------------------ 67
    1. In Federal Court -------------------------------- 67
    2. In State Court ---------------------------------- 71
  B. Judgment on the Pleadings --------------------------- 72
    1. In Federal Court -------------------------------- 72
    2. In State Court ---------------------------------- 74

5. **Exercises for Part 1: Pleadings** ---------------------------- 75

PART 2. CONTRACTS

6. **Introduction to Contract Drafting** --------------------------- 96
I. The Contract Drafter as "Lawmaker" ---------------------- 96
II. The Contract Drafter's Role as an Advocate -------------- 96
III. Some Preliminary Considerations ------------------------- 97
  A. Applicable Law -------------------------------------- 97
  B. Level of Detail Required ---------------------------- 97
  C. Implied Covenant of Good Faith and Fair Dealing --- 97
IV. Typical Contract Provisions ---------------------------- 98
V. Articulation of the Contract -------------------------- 98
  A. General Principles ---------------------------------- 98
  B. Drafting Contract Statements ------------------------ 98
    1. Recommended Verbs ------------------------------- 98
    2. Statement of an Obligation --------------------- 99
    3. Statement of a Policy -------------------------- 100
    4. Statement of a Right --------------------------- 101
    5. Statement of a Requirement or Condition -------- 102
    6. Recitals --------------------------------------- 102

        C. Articulating the Scope of a Promise ------------------- 103
            1. Choosing Precise Verbs ----------------------------- 103
            2. Expressing a Promise Narrowly ------------------- 104
   VI. Invalid Contracts or Provisions ---------------------------- 105
        A. Courts' Preference for Enforcement Over Invalidity - 105
        B. Invalid Contracts ------------------------------------- 105
            1. Contracts That Contravene Law or Public Policy - 105
            2. Unconscionable Contract or Provision ------------- 106

7. Contract Components: Preliminary Matters, Core Transaction, and Subsidiary Agreements ------------------------ **108**
   I. Title and Exordium --------------------------------------- 108
   II. Provisions Dealing With Preliminary Matters ------------- 109
        A. Defining Words and Phrases ------------------------- 109
        B. Drafting Background Recitals ------------------------- 110
        C. Identifying and Describing the Contract's Subject Matter -- 110
        D. Performance Due at or Before Signing ---------------- 112
        E. Dealing With Duration ------------------------------- 113
            1. Stipulating Duration of Obligations to Perform -- 113
            2. Contracts Lacking a Specified Performance Period -- 114
   III. Articulating the Core Obligations ------------------------- 115
        A. The Basic Bargain ----------------------------------- 115
        B. Thing of Value Exchanged for Payment --------------- 115
        C. Thing of Value Exchanged for Another Thing of Value --- 117
   IV. Identifying and Articulating the Subsidiary Agreements - 118
        A. Purpose of Subsidiary Agreements --------------------- 118
        B. Types of Subsidiary Agreements ----------------------- 119
            1. Subsidiary Agreements Regarding Maintenance of Subject–Matter ------------------------------- 119
            2. Subsidiary Agreements Regarding Use of Subject–Matter --------------------------------- 119
            3. Insurance Provisions ----------------------------- 119
            4. Subsidiary Agreement Regarding Other Conduct - 121

8. Limitation or Exclusion of Liability ------------------------ **123**
   I. Purpose of Provisions Addressing Liability --------------- 123
   II. Excuse Based on Inability to Perform --------------------- 123
        A. Excuse Provided by Law ------------------------------ 123
        B. Excuse Based on Contract ---------------------------- 124
            1. The *Force Majeure* Clause ------------------------ 124
            2. Drafting *Force Majeure* Language ---------------- 125
   III. Exculpatory Clauses --------------------------------------- 126
        A. Purpose of Exculpatory Clause ----------------------- 126
        B. Limits on Enforceability ----------------------------- 127

C. Drafting an Exculpatory Clause ------------------------ 128
    1. Use Language That Is "Clear and Unequivocal" -- 128
    2. Identify Persons to Whom the Exculpatory Clause
        Applies --- 129
    3. Articulate the Scope of an Exculpatory Clause --- 129
    4. Conspicuousness of Provision ---------------------- 130
IV. Clauses Used to Limit Damages or Remedies ------------- 131
    A. Limitation-of-Damages Clauses ----------------------- 131
        1. Characteristics of a Limitation-of-Damages
            Clause -- 131
        2. Enforceability of a Limitation-of-Damages
            Clause -- 132
    B. Limitation-of-Remedies Clauses ---------------------- 132
        1. Characteristics of a Limitation-of-Remedies
            Clause -- 132
        2. Enforceability of a Limitation-of-Remedies
            Clause -- 133
V. Limiting or Excluding Warranties Under the UCC ------- 134
    A. Express Warranties --------------------------------- 134
    B. Implied Warranties --------------------------------- 135
        1. Types of Implied Warranties ------------------- 135
        2. Exclusion of Implied Warranties -------------- 135
        3. The Requirement of Conspicuousness ---------- 136
VI. Agreements to Indemnify ------------------------------- 136
    A. Purpose of Indemnity Agreements ------------------- 136
    B. Construction and Enforceability of Indemnity Agree-
        ments -- 137
    C. Some Crucial Considerations Regarding Drafting ---- 138
VII. Agreement to Defend ---------------------------------- 139

9. Contract Components: Termination, Breach, and
    Remedies -- 140
I. Termination of Contractual Obligations -------------- 140
    A. Purpose and Effect of Termination Provision -------- 140
    B. When a Termination Right May Be Necessary -------- 141
    C. Enforcement of Termination Provision --------------- 141
        1. Unilateral Right of Termination ---------------- 141
        2. Termination-for-Convenience Clause ------------- 142
        3. Termination Clause in a Contract With a Fixed
            Duration -- 142
    D. Procedural Requirements for Termination ------------ 142
II. Breach of Contract ----------------------------------- 144
    A. Elements of Breach Action ------------------------- 144
    B. Party's Recovery for Breach ----------------------- 144
        1. Remedies Provided by Law ---------------------- 144
        2. Remedies Provided by the Contract ------------- 146

10. Contract Components: Winding–Up, Non–Compete, Severance, Integration, and Dispute–Resolution Provisions -- 149
    I.   Winding up the Contractual Relationship ------------------ 149
    II.   Covenants that Protect Business Interests after Relationship Ends -- 149
          A. Types of Activities Restricted ---------------------------- 149
          B. Enforcement of Covenants ------------------------------ 150
          C. Factors to Consider When Drafting --------------------- 151
              1. Factors That May Affect Enforceability ----------- 151
              2. Reformation of Overbroad Covenant -------------- 152
    III. Severance of an Unenforceable Provision ------------------ 152
    IV.   Integration (or Merger) Clauses --------------------------- 153
    V.   Dispute Resolution --------------------------------------- 154
          A. Forum–Selection Clause ------------------------------- 154
              1. Purpose and Effect of Forum–Selection Clause -- 154
              2. Enforceability of Forum–Selection Clause --------- 155
              3. Drafting a Presumptively Valid Forum–Selection Clause --- 155
          B. Choice-of-Law Clauses -------------------------------- 157
              1. Purpose and Enforceability of Choice-of-Law Clause --- 157
              2. Construction of Choice-of-Law Clause ------------ 157
          C. Provisions Allowing Attorney's Fees ------------------- 159
          D. Arbitration Agreements ------------------------------- 160
              1. Purpose and Effect of Arbitration ----------------- 160
              2. Federal Arbitration Act --------------------------- 160
              3. Drafting Arbitration Agreements ----------------- 161
              4. "Clear and Unequivocal" Language --------------- 162

11. Contract Components: Modification, Execution, and Effective Date --- 163
    I.   Modification Provisions ------------------------------------ 163
    II.   Execution of the Contract --------------------------------- 164
          A. Signatures of the Parties ------------------------------ 164
          B. Effective Date of Contract ----------------------------- 166

12. How Courts Read and Construe Contracts ------------------ 168
    I.   Why a Drafter Needs to Know How Courts Construe ---- 168
    II.   Questions for Which a Drafter Needs Answers ----------- 168
    III. Goal of Construction ------------------------------------- 169
    IV.   Approaches to Construction -------------------------------- 169
          A. Basics About Approaches to Construction ------------- 169
          B. Use of Extrinsic Evidence ----------------------------- 170

C. Use of Canons of Construction -------------------------- 171
   1. Role of the Canons in Promoting Fair Dealing --- 171
   2. Canons That Guide the Court in Reading the Contract -- 171
   3. Canons Used to Resolve Uncertain Meaning ----- 172
   4. Canons for Choosing Between Conflicting Provisions -- 173
   5. Ambiguity Construed Against Drafter ------------- 174
   6. Types of Provisions That Tend to Be Strictly Construed -- 174

13. Exercises for Part 2: Contract Drafting ---------------------- **176**

PART 3. LEGISLATIVE DRAFTING: PUBLIC AND PRIVATE RULE–MAKING DOCUMENTS

14. Introduction to Legislative Drafting: Public and Private Rule–Making Documents ------------------------------------- **188**
  I. Public and Private Rule–Making Documents -------------- 188
  II. Organization of a Rule–Making Document ---------------- 188
  III. Articulating Legislative Statements ------------------------ 189
    A. Recommended Verbs -------------------------------------- 189
    B. Stating a Duty or Prohibition -------------------------- 189
    C. Stating a Right -- 190
    D. Stating a Right–Related Requirement or Condition Precedent -- 190
    E. Stating a Legislative Policy --------------------------- 191
    F. Stating a Fact -- 191
  IV. Drafting Style for Rule–Making Documents -------------- 191
    A. Verb Tense -- 191
    B. Concise Language -- 191
    C. Positive Versus Negative Statements ------------------- 192
    D. Active Versus Passive Voice ---------------------------- 193
    E. Singular Versus Plural Nouns ------------------------- 193
    F. Needless Synonyms --------------------------------------- 194
    G. Needless Legal Jargon --------------------------------- 194
    H. Using "And," "Or," and "And/Or" --------------------- 194

15. Drafting Private Rule–Making Documents ------------------ **195**
  I. Drafting Process for Private Rule–Making Documents -- 195
  II. Documents for Property Owner Associations -------------- 195
    A. Declaration of Covenants -------------------------------- 195
      1. Purpose of Declaration ----------------------------- 195
      2. Drafting the Declaration --------------------------- 197
    B. By–Laws for Property Owners Association ------------ 197

III.   Documents Relating to Corporations ----------------------- 198
    A.   Articles of Incorporation -------------------------------- 198
    B.   Corporate By–Laws ----------------------------------- 199
IV.   Documents Relating to Limited–Liability Companies ---- 200
    A.   Articles of Organization -------------------------------- 200
    B.   Members Operating Agreement ------------------------ 200
V.   Other Documents That Regulate Conduct ---------------- 200

16.   Drafting Public Legislation ------------------------------- 201
I.   Preparing to Draft Public Legislation ---------------------- 201
    A.   Understanding the Legislative Process ----------------- 201
    B.   Consulting State Legislative Drafting Manuals ------ 201
    C.   Checking Legal and Factual Background ------------- 201
II.   Basics About Bills --- 202
    A.   Single Subject Rule ------------------------------------- 202
    B.   Typical Components of a Bill -------------------------- 203
      1.   Identifying Information and Title ------------------ 203
      2.   The Enacting Clause -------------------------------- 204
      3.   Preamble Section ------------------------------------- 204
      4.   Purpose or Intent Section -------------------------- 205
      5.   Legislative Findings Section ----------------------- 205
      6.   Short Title Section ---------------------------------- 206
      7.   Definitions Section ---------------------------------- 207
      8.   Body of the Bill ------------------------------------- 207
      9.   Some Technical Provisions ------------------------- 207
III.   Drafting Local Ordinances ---------------------------------- 210
    A.   Authority of City or County to Legislate ------------- 210
    B.   Preparing to Draft an Ordinance ---------------------- 211
      1.   Researching Existing Law ------------------------- 211
      2.   Consulting a Drafting Manual --------------------- 211

17.   How Courts Construe Statutes and Other Public Rule–Making Documents --- 212
I.   Introduction to Statutory Construction -------------------- 212
II.   Goal of Courts in Construing a Statute -------------------- 212
III.   Process of Statutory Construction ------------------------- 213
    A.   Circumstances in Which Construction is Required --- 213
    B.   Varying Approaches to Statutory Construction ------- 213
IV.   Use of Canons of Construction ----------------------------- 214
    A.   Nature and Purpose of Canons ------------------------ 214
    B.   Certain Canons of Interest to the Drafter ------------ 215
      1.   Canons Favoring One Reading Over Another ---- 215
      2.   Use of a Statute's Components --------------------- 216
      3.   Determination of a Term's Meaning or Application --- 217

V.   Extrinsic Aids to Construction ---------------------------- 218
     A. Use of Extrinsic Aids to Determine Meaning --------- 218
     B. Types of Extrinsic Aids --------------------------------- 218
VI. Strict Versus Liberal Construction ------------------------- 219

18. **Exercises for Part 3: Rule–Making Documents** ------------ **220**

PART 4.   GENERATING AND ORGANIZING CONTENT OF A CONTRACT OR RULE–MAKING DOCUMENT

19. **Generating Your Document's Content** ------------------------ **236**
    I.   Researching the Document's Legal Background ----------- 236
    II.   Researching the Document's Factual Background -------- 236
          A. For Contracts and Private Rule–Making Documents - 236
          B. Impact of the Negotiating Context --------------------- 237
    III. Assessing the Client's Needs ------------------------------- 237
          A. Regarding Contracts and Private Rule–Making
              Documents -- 237
          B. Regarding Public Legislation --------------------------- 238
    IV.   Generating a Master Term Sheet and Client Question-
          naire --- 238
          A. What a "Master Term Sheet" Is ----------------------- 238
          B. Steps for Preparing a Master Term Sheet ------------ 239
          C. Creating a Client Questionnaire From the Master
              Term Sheet --- 241

20. **Creating an Outline for Your Document** --------------------- **244**
    I.   Overview of Document Organization ----------------------- 244
    II.   Generating an Outline -------------------------------------- 244
          A. Dividing the Master Term Sheet into Major Sections - 244
          B. Creating Headings --- 245
              1. Purpose of Headings --------------------------------- 245
              2. Using a Template to Generate Headings ---------- 246
              3. Some Heading Formats to Avoid ------------------- 247
          C. Subdividing Major Sections and Subsections ---------- 248
          D. Common Errors in Subdivision Schemes -------------- 249
              1. The Single–Subsection Error ---------------------- 249
              2. The Organization-by-Party Error ------------------ 250
              3. The Overlapping–Headings Error ----------------- 251
    III. Sequencing Sections and Subsections of Your Outline --- 251
          A. Templates for Creating an Initial Sequencing
              Scheme --- 251
              1. Template for Contracts ------------------------------ 251
              2. Template for Rule–Making Documents ----------- 253
          B. Tweaking the Initial Sequencing Scheme ------------- 254

IV.   Basic Format Design for the Document -------------------- 254

    A.   Traits of an Informative and Reader–Friendly Format -- 254

    B.   Designing an Informative and Reader–Friendly Format --- 255

       1.   Form of Headings ------------------------------------ 255

       2.   Lettering and Numbering of Headings ----------- 255

       3.   Spacing Between Provisions ----------------------- 255

       4.   Indenting Certain Text ---------------------------- 255

       5.   Page Numbering -------------------------------------- 256

       6.   Examples of Formats ------------------------------- 256

21. Refining the Draft's Organizational Scheme --------------- **258**

    I.   Reassessing the Drafted Document's Organization ------- 258

    II.   Common Problems -- 258

      A.   The Wall of Text --------------------------------------- 258

      B.   The "Displaced Text" Error ------------------------------ 260

      C.   The Heading–Replacing–Content Error --------------- 261

      D.   Overlapping Sentences --------------------------------- 262

        1.   Redundant Sentences ------------------------------- 262

        2.   Conflicting Sentences ------------------------------ 262

    III.   Using Cross–Referencing (if needed) ---------------------- 264

      A.   When to Use Cross–Referencing ------------------------ 264

      B.   How to Write Useful Cross–References --------------- 264

22. Exercises for Part 4: Generating Content and Creating an Organizational Scheme ---------------------------------- **266**

PART 5.   WILLS

23. Background for Drafting a Will -------------------------------- **276**

    I.   Preparation for Drafting a Will: An Overview ------------ 276

      A.   Limited Scope of This Discussion ---------------------- 276

      B.   The Basics -- 277

        1.   What Is the Purpose of a Will? --------------------- 277

        2.   What Property Can Pass by Will? ----------------- 278

        3.   Who Can Make a Will? ----------------------------- 278

        4.   Who Can Be Beneficiaries of a Will? -------------- 278

    II.   Nomination and Duties of an Executor -------------------- 278

    III.   Requisites for a Valid Will ------------------------------- 279

      A.   Requirement of Testamentary Intent ------------------ 279

      B.   Compliance with the Wills Act Formalities ----------- 280

        1.   Purpose of Wills Act Formalities ------------------- 280

        2.   Formalities for Attested Wills ---------------------- 280

        3.   Degree of Compliance with the Wills Act Formalities --- 282

IV.   Changes to the Will -------------------------------------- 284
       1. Codicils -- 284
       2. Replacement Wills ---------------------------------- 285
       3. Effect of Changed Circumstances ------------------ 285

24. Drafting and Executing the Will ----------------------- **286**
    I.   Organizing the Components of a Simple Will ------------- 286
          A. Organizational Issues Specific to Wills ---------------- 286
          B. Components of the Will -------------------------------- 286
             1. Components Conventionally Set Out at the
                 Beginning -------------------------------------- 286
             2. Components Set Out at the End ------------------- 287
             3. Other Components (Sequence Varies) ------------- 288
    II.   Choosing Your Language ---------------------------------- 289
          A. Types of Statements ---------------------------------- 289
             1. Expressing a Disposition --------------------------- 289
             2. Expressing a Right or Power ---------------------- 289
             3. Imposing a Duty --------------------------------- 290
             4. Stating Facts (Declarations) ---------------------- 290
          B. Word Choice -- 290
             1. Importance of Understanding the Scope of Words
                 and Phrases ------------------------------------ 290
             2. Checking the Meaning of Words ------------------ 291
             3. Creating Definitions ----------------------------- 292
    III. Nomination and Powers of Executor and Related Issues - 293
    IV.   Basics for Drafting Simple Dispositive Provisions -------- 294
          A. Types of Provisions Addressed ----------------------- 294
          B. Certain Consequences of a Legacy's Characteriza-
             tion -- 295
             1. Ademption of Specific Legacies -------------------- 295
             2. Abatement of Legacies --------------------------- 296
             3. Other Consequences ----------------------------- 297
          C. Drafting Legacies ------------------------------------ 297
             1. Specific Legacy ---------------------------------- 297
             2. General Legacy ---------------------------------- 298
             3. Demonstrative Legacy --------------------------- 298
             4. Residuary Legacy -------------------------------- 298
          D. Preventing Lapse of Legacies ------------------------ 299
          E. Dealing With Simultaneous Death -------------------- 300
    V.   Setting Up an Execution Ceremony ----------------------- 301
    VI.   How Courts Read Wills --------------------------------- 302

25. Exercises for Part 5: Wills ---------------------------- **304**

PART 6.   ARTICULATING CONTENT

26. Choosing Language -- **310**

I.   Precise Drafting as Preventive Law ----------------------- 310

II.   Choosing Your Words ------------------------------------- 310

A. Know the Meaning of the Words You Choose --------- 310

1. When Choosing Key Words, Reach for the Dictionary -- 310

2. Technical Language or Terms of Art ---------------- 311

B. Choose the Right Word ----------------------------------- 313

III. Delineating the Scope of a Provision ----------------------- 314

A. Determining the Scope of a Provision ------------------ 314

B. Choosing Language to Delineate the Scope of a Provision --- 316

1. Creating Flexible Provisions ------------------------ 316

2. Drafting to Achieve Definiteness ------------------- 320

C. Canons of Construction Relating to Word Choice ----- 321

1. Relevance of Canons --------------------------------- 321

2. Common Canons of Construction ------------------- 321

27. Drafting Definitions -- **325**

I.   When to Use Definitions --------------------------------------- 325

II.   Stipulated Definitions --------------------------------------- 325

A. When to Stipulate a Definition ------------------------ 325

1. In Contracts and Statutes --------------------------- 325

2. In Wills --- 326

B. Framing a Definition ------------------------------------- 327

1. Redefining a Term ----------------------------------- 327

2. Narrowing the Ordinary Meaning of a Term ----- 328

3. Broadening the Ordinary Meaning of a Term ---- 329

III. Setting Out Definitions in the Document ----------------- 329

A. Placement and Format --------------------------------- 329

B. Definitions Sections ------------------------------------- 330

1. Single Definitions Section for Entire Document -- 330

2. Placement of Definition of Term That Appears Only Once --- 330

3. Creation of Multiple Definitions Section --------- 331

IV.   Common Errors --- 332

A. Check the Grammar of Your Definition --------------- 332

B. Avoid Burying Rules in Definitions -------------------- 333

C. Strained Definitions ------------------------------------- 333

28. Eliminating Ambiguity --- **335**

I.   Recognizing Ambiguity --------------------------------------- 335

II.   Ambiguity Caused by Modifier Placement Problems ----- 335

A. Importance of Modifier Placement -------------------- 335

B. Examples: Common Modifier–Placement Problems -- 336
1. Imprecise Use of Percentages ---------------------- 336
2. Ambiguous Maximum (or Cap) --------------------- 337
3. Ambiguous Price and Quantity Provisions -------- 338
4. Ambiguity Arising From "Squinting Modifier" ---- 339
III. Ambiguity Caused by Pronouns ----------------------------- 340
IV. Ambiguity Caused by Plurals ----------------------------- 341
V. Ambiguity Caused by Word Choice ------------------------ 341
A. Words and Phrases With More Than One Meaning -- 341
B. Common Examples ------------------------------------- 341
1. "Subject to" ------------------------------------- 341
2. "Term" --- 342
3. "And" and "Or" ---------------------------------- 343
4. "Is Responsible ..." and "Has the Responsibili-
ty ..." --- 345
VI. Ambiguity Caused by Inconsistency ----------------------- 345
VII. Ambiguity Caused by Punctuation Usage ----------------- 346

29. **Time Clauses and Conditional Statements** ------------------- **347**
I. Drafting Time Clauses ------------------------------------- 347
A. The Importance of Ambiguity–Free Time Clauses ---- 347
B. Types of Time Clauses --------------------------------- 347
C. Drafting Time Clauses Stating a Due Date, Deadline
or Cut-off --- 348
1. Due Dates, Deadlines and Cut-offs with Specified
Dates --- 348
2. Due Dates, Deadlines, and Cut-offs with Unspeci-
fied Dates --- 349
D. Drafting Time Clauses That State a Duration Period - 351
1. Duration Periods With Specified Dates ------------ 351
2. Duration Periods With Unspecified Dates --------- 352
3. Drafting a Renewable or Extendable Performance
Period -- 353
E. Placement of Time Clauses Within a Sentence ------- 355
F. Avoid Potentially Ambiguous Phrasing ----------------- 356
1. Avoid "Upon," "When," and "Once" ---------------- 356
2. Avoid "Between" When Setting a Date Range ---- 357
3. Avoid "Within" When Drafting a Due Date, Deadline, or Cut-off --------------------------------------- 357
4. Avoid "To," "Until," and "By" to Signify an End
Date --- 358
5. Avoid "Month" to Stipulate a Range of Days ------ 358
6. Avoid "Week" to Stipulate a Range of Days ------- 359
7. Avoid "Midnight" to Express a Deadline ----------- 359
G. Drafting Time Clauses in Your Jurisdiction ----------- 359

II.   Conditional Statements ------------------------------------- 360
    A.   Articulating Conditional Statements ------------------- 360
    B.   Placement of Conditional Statement in Sentence ---- 361

30. Exercises for Part 6: Word Choice, Ambiguity, and Time Clauses --- **364**

PART 7. GRAMMAR, PUNCTUATION, AND STYLE

31. Some Basics About Grammar --------------------------------- **372**
  I.   The Importance of Grammar Handbooks ------------------- 372
  II.   Refresher: Some Key Grammatical Terms ----------------- 372
    A.   The Eight Parts of Speech ------------------------------ 372
    B.   Other Key Grammatical Terms ------------------------- 375
  III.   A Bit About Verbs -- 377
    A.   Voice of Verbs --- 377
      1.   Determining Whether Verbs Have Voice ----------- 377
      2.   The Voices: Active and Passive --------------------- 378
    B.   Verb Tense --- 379
    C.   Verb Mood --- 382
  IV.   A Bit About Pronouns ------------------------------------- 384
    A.   Overview of Pronouns ------------------------------------ 384
    B.   Pronoun Case -- 385
      1.   The Three Cases --------------------------------------- 385
      2.   Choosing Between Subjective and Objective Case - 385
      3.   Possessive Case --- 386
    C.   Pronoun Number and Gender -------------------------- 387
    D.   Avoiding Ambiguous Pronoun Usage ------------------ 388
  V.   Parallel Structure -- 389
  VI.   Avoiding Problems With Modifiers ------------------------- 391
    A.   Placement of Modifiers ---------------------------------- 391
    B.   Phrasing of Modifiers ----------------------------------- 393
  VII.   Deal–Breaking Grammatical Errors ----------------------- 394

32. Some Basics About Punctuation ----------------------------- **395**
  I.   The Importance of Punctuation ---------------------------- 395
  II.   Commas --- 395
    A.   The Comma's Impact on Meaning --------------------- 395
    B.   Some Basic Comma–Usage Rules --------------------- 396
      1.   Commas in a Series ---------------------------------- 396
      2.   When to Use and Not Use Commas With Conjunctions --- 396
      3.   Commas and Restrictive vs. Non–Restrictive Modifiers --- 397
      4.   Commas and Introductory Elements -------------- 399

III.   Semicolons --- 399

     A. Semicolons in a Series ---------------------------------- 399

     B. Semicolons Separating Independent Clauses ---------- 400

IV.   Colons -- 400

V.   Apostrophes --- 401

     A. Showing Possession of Nouns ---------------------------- 401

     B. Plurals of Numerals, Letters, and Words -------------- 402

     C. Signifying a Contraction or Omission ------------------ 403

VI.   Dashes --- 403

     A. Typing the Dash -- 403

     B. Creating Emphasis -------------------------------------- 403

     C. Inserting a Series of Modifying Words or Phrases --- 404

     D. Introducing or Explaining a List ---------------------- 404

VII.   Hyphens --- 404

     A. Typing the Hyphen -------------------------------------- 404

     B. Usage With Some Prefixes and Compound Words ---- 404

     C. Usage With Compound Adjective ---------------------- 405

VIII.   Punctuating Quoted Language ----------------------------- 405

     A. Periods and Commas ------------------------------------ 405

     B. Colons and Semicolons --------------------------------- 406

     C. Question Marks --- 406

IX.   Parentheses: Does the Period Go Inside or Outside? ----- 406

33. Style --- **407**

I.   Style Handbooks --- 407

II.   Write Concisely -- 407

III.   Avoid Passive Voice Unless You Need It ------------------- 409

IV.   Refrain From Overloading Sentences --------------------- 410

V.   Strive for Simplicity -- 411

VI.   Omit Needless Legal Jargon -------------------------------- 412

VII.   Indented Lists -- 413

VIII.   Use Gender–Neutral Nouns and Pronouns ---------------- 413

34. Exercises for Grammar, Style, and Punctuation ----------- **415**

ENDNOTES -- 423

INDEX --- 495

LEGAL DRAFTING

LITIGATION DOCUMENTS, CONTRACTS, LEGISLATION, AND WILLS

LEGAL DRAFTING: AN INTRODUCTION

■ ■ ■

I. Purpose of the Course

The purpose of a course in legal drafting is to give you practical experience doing tasks that are a major part of any attorney's work: writing and reading documents. The goal is to be the client's advocate.

In litigation, being the advocate means presenting the client's case in a way that will get the case past the initial stages and to a point where the client has a reasonable chance of obtaining a resolution (through settlement, arbitration, mediation, or trial).

In contract drafting, being the advocate means setting out a planned transaction in words that will protect the client's interests and implement the client's intentions. A contract drafter creates the law of the transaction.

In legislative drafting, the goal is the same: the only difference is that in some instances, the client is a governmental entity and the law of the transaction becomes the actual law. In drafting a will, the drafter and the client create the law for the distribution of the client's property through a probate court.

At some point, an attorney must deal with the types of documents discussed in this book. Litigators litigate over the meaning of contracts. Contract drafters, estate planners, and drafters of rule-making documents draft to avoid later litigation (and must be aware in advance of how a document can be attacked). Every attorney, regardless of practice area, benefits from understanding the nuts and bolts of drafting documents that most attorneys must sometimes use or challenge.

II. Focuses of the Course

A. Skills Practiced in Drafting

A legal drafting course focuses on the following skills:

- Reading documents closely and analyzing them critically.

1

- Analyzing a body of facts for key issues and identifying questions that the drafter needs to answer.

- Making *appropriate* use of form documents.

- Identifying the basic elements of a document and determining how to present them systematically.

- Articulating meaning with the maximum precision possible and with extraordinary attention to consistency and to the relationship between each component of the document.

- Editing to ensure that the document's meaning is plain on the document's face.

- Identifying ambiguous language.

- Correcting grammar and punctuation.

- Choosing between competing words and phrases to determine those that best reflect your meaning.

- Defining terms.

- Creating an organizational scheme with useful headings and subheadings.

- Creating an easily readable format.

As the list above shows, there is more to drafting than simply moving words around on paper until you get something that looks like a legal document (though, sadly, some attorneys approach the task in that way).

Because the goal of drafting is to be the client's advocate, every phase of drafting requires the drafter to think strategically. The drafter is constantly looking ahead to anticipate (and either avoid or overcome) any looming hurdles. Each word that the drafter writes should reflect the drafter's strategy for the particular circumstance.

B. The Focus on Users of Documents

A drafter must learn to write in a way that gets across the drafter's meaning to a range of potential users of the document. The potential audience includes judges and other attorneys (generally opposing counsel, looking for a weakness to exploit); the client; and anyone else who is likely to refer to the document for guidance.

A drafter must therefore learn to write and present information in a way that is immediately understandable by people who have varying degrees of understanding and different points of view. Some documents have a long life expectancy (e.g., long-term contracts, most public legislation, and private rule-making documents such as articles of incorporation). Long after the drafting task is over, the document will continue to govern the actions of real persons in the real world, whom the drafter cannot possibly know at the outset.

A drafter must therefore anticipate who the audience is and design texts to foster real-world actions without giving rise to disputes over meaning between potential classes of future users.

III.   Collaboration with the Client

Drafting is a collaborative process. To be an advocate for the client, the drafter must understand the client's goals and needs. Though ultimately the job is to understand those goals and needs better than the client does, the process begins with the drafter's finding out from the client the essential facts underlying the client's desire for legal assistance.

Many clients have only a rough idea of what they need. Others may have very specific ideas, some of which may be legally unfeasible. The attorney helps the client understand which outcomes are achievable in the particular context. To bring about those outcomes, the attorney must also help the client understand how to help the attorney.

Ultimately, it is the client who chooses the policies that the attorney implements. Though the attorney cannot take over the client's decision-making, the attorney must advise the client and participate in refining the client's understanding of the law and its limits. The most successful drafting occurs when attorneys and clients work together, each contributing their own expertise to the process.

Part 1

Litigation Documents

■ ■ ■

- Chapter 1.   Introduction to Litigation-Related Documents
- Chapter 2.   The Initial Pleading
- Chapter 3.   Answers (Defensive Pleadings)
- Chapter 4.   Motions
- Chapter 5.   Exercises for Part 1

CHAPTER 1

GENERAL INTRODUCTION TO LITIGATION–RELATED DOCUMENTS

■ ■ ■

I. Pleadings Requesting Affirmative Relief

A. Affirmative Relief

Generally, a plaintiff initiates a lawsuit because the plaintiff has suffered harm and wants a court to provide affirmative relief (the remedy). The nature of the available remedy depends on the nature of the harm and the applicable law. Typical common-law remedies include damages to compensate the plaintiff, a declaratory judgment, or an order enjoining the defendant to act or to refrain from acting. If a contract, rule or statute authorizes it, the plaintiff might also receive an award of attorney's fees and the plaintiff's costs.

B. Types of Pleadings Seeking Affirmative Relief

At the beginning of a lawsuit or action, there are two parties: (1) the plaintiff (in some states called "petitioner"), who seeks affirmative relief; and (2) the defendant, against whom the plaintiff files suit and from whom the plaintiff seeks affirmative relief. Most lawsuits begin with an **initial pleading**, typically called a "complaint," though the nomenclature varies depending on the jurisdiction. For example, in Iowa,[1] Louisiana,[2] Missouri,[3] and Texas,[4] the initial pleading is known as a "petition." In Florida, the initial pleading is generally called a "complaint" unless a rule or statute designates it as a "petition."[5]

Depending on the jurisdiction, the initial pleading typically states the plaintiff's "claim" or "cause of action." The initial pleading sets out the grounds on which the plaintiff requests relief from the court. The purpose of the initial pleading is to provide the defendant with (1) notice of the plaintiff's claim and (2) the grounds on which the claim rests.[6] The principles for drafting an initial pleading are set out in Chapter 2.

The initial pleading is not the only the only type of pleading that seeks affirmative relief. Other types are set forth below.

Types of Pleadings Seeking Affirmative Relief	
• **Initial Pleading** (Complaint or Petition):	Plaintiff files against Defendant.
• **Counter-claim**:	Defendant files against Plaintiff.
• **Cross-claim**:	Defendant files against co-Defendant or Plaintiff files against co-Plaintiff.
• **Third-party complaint**:	Defendant files against someone not yet named as a defendant.

A defendant in a lawsuit may request affirmative relief from the plaintiff by filing suit against the plaintiff in a pleading typically called a **counter-claim**. The nomenclature varies among jurisdictions. For example, California has abolished the "counter-claim": instead, any claim that a defendant makes against a plaintiff is asserted by a "cross-complaint."[7] In an action that has multiple plaintiffs or defendants, a party might seek to recover affirmative relief from a co-party through a **cross-claim**.

If appropriate given the facts of a case and the relevant law, a defendant might file a **third-party complaint** to bring into the suit someone who was not named as a defendant in the plaintiff's initial pleading. A third-party complaint alleges that the third party may be liable for some of the damages that the plaintiff is trying to recover from the defendant.

The counter-claim, cross-claim, and third-party complaint have the following in common: (1) they all seek some form of affirmative relief, (2) they all give notice to the other party of the nature of the claims, and (3) they all are drafted according to the same principles as the initial pleading.

II. Defensive Pleadings

Defensive pleadings do not seek affirmative relief. A defensive pleading (1) responds to the allegations in a pleading that requests affirmative relief and (2) sets out any affirmative defenses. In many jurisdictions, the defensive pleading to *any* pleading seeking affirmative relief is called an answer[8] (though in some jurisdictions the response to a counter-claim is called a "reply").[9] The principles for drafting a defensive pleading are set out in Chapter 3.

III. Requirements Regarding Pleadings, Motions, and Other Papers

A. Caption

1. Content of the Caption

Pleadings, motions, and other papers typically begin with a caption that sets out certain information. Federal Rule of Civil Procedure 10(a)[10] states that every pleading must have a caption. Federal Rule 7(b)(2) makes the rules that apply to pleadings generally applicable to motions and other papers. In other words, those documents must be captioned as well.

The caption is necessary so that the court (and the attorneys representing the parties) can track documents tendered to the court during the course of an action. According to Federal Rule 10(a), the caption must contain the following:

- The name of the court in which the action was filed.

- The title.

- The file number.

- A "designation" identifying the type of pleading.

The title of the initial pleading must name all parties on each side, but pleadings filed *after* the initial pleading may name only the first party on each side and should refer generally to the other parties (typically by using "et al." to signify "and others").[11] State rules of civil procedure impose similar requirements for captioning.[12]

2. Basic Caption Format

There may be differences among jurisdictions, but the caption format prescribed for most jurisdictions is similar to the example shown below.

```
                    United States District Court for the
                         Northern District of Florida

        William Cupples, Plaintiff  )
                                     )
        v.                           )
                                     )   Civil Action No. _____
        Emanuel Industries, Inc.,    )
        a Delaware Corporation,      )
        Defendant                    )



                    Complaint for Patent Infringement
```

3. Local Rules Addressing Captioning

A local rule is a court-generated rule that applies in a particular court.[13] Many federal district courts and state courts have promulgated local rules addressing captions. Failing to follow the local rules of a court will not endear you to either the judge or the clerk of court. Some courts have very specific requirements for caption format and content: e.g., centering, indentation, or specific information to be included.

B. Format Requirements for Pleadings, Motions, and Other Papers

1. In the Federal Courts

Many federal district courts have local rules regulating the format of pleadings, motions, and other papers. These rules may specify a document's margins, spacing, or font size.[14] The specifications can be quite precise, and an attorney should diligently follow them (though Federal Rule 5(d)(4) states, "the clerk must not refuse to file a paper solely because it is not in the form prescribed by these rules or by a local rule or practice").

2. In the State Courts

Even if a state's general rules of procedure address document formatting, an attorney should make sure to check the local rules and any administrative orders. Some states (such as Connecticut,[15] Colorado,[16] and Utah[17]) set out formatting requirements in the rules of procedure. Other states set out the requirements in other places.

Those requirements can be very specific. For example, Florida's Rule of Judicial Administration section 2.520 requires that all papers be filed on letter-sized, recycled paper (i.e., paper containing "a minimum content of 50% waste paper").[18] The rule further states that an attorney must resubmit non-complying documents if the clerk of the court so requests.[19]

C. Incorporation of Exhibits Into Pleadings or Motions

1. In Federal Court

Federal Rule 10(c) provides that a document that is an exhibit to a pleading is part of that pleading for all purposes. Since Federal Rule 7(b)(2) makes the rules regarding the form of pleadings also applicable to motions, the same rule applies to an exhibit to a motion. Though the rule does not require that an attorney attach an exhibit to a pleading or other paper, the attorney will typically want to include any exhibit that is integral to the claim or defense.

Local rules may impose specific guidelines for the filing of exhibits. In one federal district in North Carolina, for example, a local rule provides that a particular exhibit can be filed only *once*; that it should be filed as a "separate attachment"; and that the exhibit's pages must be numbered so that they can be cross-referenced in later documents by the docket entry, exhibit number, and page number.[20]

2. In State Courts

Many states, particularly those whose rules are modeled on Federal Rule 10(c), deal with exhibits in the same fashion: i.e., by treating an exhibit to a pleading as incorporated in the pleading for all purposes.[21] Some states may require a party to attach to a pleading an exhibit that is integral to a claim or defense unless the party incorporates the relevant information into the pleading.

State courts, like federal courts, may promulgate local rules addressing the format and attachment of exhibits. For example, a local rule in a New Mexico court restricts the length of an exhibit to 25 pages (unless the court allows otherwise) and prohibits the attachment of "clinical records," such as medical or psychological records.[22]

D. Verification of Pleadings, Motions, or Other Papers

Federal Rule 11(a) states, "Unless a rule or statute specifically states otherwise, a pleading need not be verified or accompanied by an affidavit."[23] States typically do not require verification of pleadings and motions in the absence of a rule or statute requiring it.[24]

When verification is required by a rule or statute, an attorney must verify the document. A document verification might look like this:

> "Under penalty of perjury, I declare that I have read the foregoing, and the facts alleged in it are true and correct to the best of my knowledge and belief."[25]

E. Electronic Filing Requirements

1. In Federal Court

Most federal courts now have rules regulating electronic filing. In some federal districts, electronic filing is mandatory by local rule or order in most types of cases, with limited exceptions (e.g., for pro se plaintiffs). Examples of federal courts that in most cases require electronic filing include the district courts in Florida,[26] New Jersey,[27] and New Mexico;[28] the Western District of Oklahoma;[29] and the Western District of Washington.[30]

2. In State Court

An increasing number of states permit or require electronic filing. The source of authority (e.g., rules or statutes) differs from state to state, and an attorney may need to look to more than one source to get the full picture.

F.   Service of Pleadings and Motions

So that all defendants are on notice of an action, Federal Rule 4 requires that the initial pleading be served on each defendant in a pre-scribed manner and with a summons.[31] The federal rules set out specific requirements regarding what a summons should contain.[32] The following is an example.

Summons

[Caption]

To Nicholas Temple–Smith:

A lawsuit has been filed against you in the Federal District Court for the Northern District of Florida.

No later than the 21st day after service of this summons on you (excluding the day you received it), you are required to serve on Plaintiff either an answer to the complaint or a motion pursuant to Federal Rule of Civil Procedure 12. You must serve the answer or motion on the court and on Plaintiff's attorney, Victorina Basauri, whose address is 115 Main Street, Gainestown, Florida, 32601.

If you fail to serve a motion or answer on Plaintiff, judgment by default for the relief requested in the complaint will be entered against you.

December 29, 2011
Stanley Roberts, Clerk of Court
[Court Seal]

After the initial pleading is served, Federal Rule 5(a) requires subsequent documents to be served on every party, absent a contrary order by the court.[33] State courts have similar rules for service of documents subse-quent to the initial pleading and summons. Any attorney who files or serves documents electronically must understand the applicable rules for electronic service. For the requirements in your state, check your state's rules of civil procedure.

IV.   Federal Rule 11: Purpose, Requirements and Sanctions

A.   Purpose of Federal Rule 11

According to the federal district court for the District of Columbia, Federal Rule 11 protects *the court* from frivolous and baseless filings.[34] As the Advisory Committee's notes to the rule suggest, the rule requires liti-gants to pause for reflection before making legal or factual contentions.[35]

B.   Effect of Presenting a Document to the Court

To comply with Rule 11, an attorney must make a reasonable inquiry into the law and facts before signing a litigation document or presenting it to the court.[36] An attorney "presents" a paper to a court by signing it, filing it, submitting it, or advocating it. By presenting a paper to the court, an attorney represents and *certifies* to the court that to the best of the attorney's knowledge, information, and belief—formed after an inquiry reasonable under the circumstances—all of the following are true:

- The attorney is not presenting the signed document for an improper purpose.

- The attorney's legal contentions are either warranted by existing law or by a *nonfrivolous* argument for modifying existing law or establishing new law.

- The attorney's factual contentions are supported by evidence or are likely to be supported by evidence the attorney expects to uncover.

- The attorney's denial of an opponent's factual contentions are either warranted by evidence or reasonably based on belief or lack of information.[37]

C.   Sanctions for Violation of Federal Rule 11

A court may impose sanctions on a party who violates Rule 11, though Federal Rule 11(c)(2) provides "a 21–day 'safe harbor' period." Possible sanctions for a district court to impose under Federal Rule 11(c) now include the following:

- Non-monetary directives (e.g., ordering the attorney to take a legal ethics course).

- Payment of a penalty to the court.

- Payment of the movant's attorney's fees and expenses resulting from the violation.

Appropriate sanctions can be imposed on *both* the attorney who presented the document to the court and on the attorney's law firm.[38]

D.   Specifications for Signing

Federal Rule 11(a) requires that every pleading, motion, or other paper be signed by at least one attorney of record and that the signer's mailing address, email address, and phone number be included. The court must strike an unsigned paper unless the omission is promptly corrected after being called to the attorney's or party's attention.

While some district courts are satisfied with the signature requirements of Federal Rule 11(a), others have imposed additional signature requirements.[39] An attorney should check for special signature requirements beyond those imposed by Federal Rule 11(a). If a district court allows or mandates electronic filing, it may implement requirements for signing a document tendered electronically.[40]

E. Federal Rule 11's Impact on the State Courts

Federal Rule 11 has had a substantial influence on the signing requirements in effect in the state courts. Many jurisdictions' signature rules incorporate language mirroring the key provisions of the current version of Rule 11, though often with variations (e.g., California,[41] Hawaii,[42] South Dakota,[43] Utah,[44] and West Virginia[45]). Some states have signature rules modeled on, or incorporating key language from, earlier versions of Rule 11.[46] It seems likely that the number of states that follow the current Rule 11 will increase in the future.

Still other states have adopted their own unique procedures for dealing with the type of misconduct addressed by Rule 11. For example, Florida addresses the effect of a signature in the state's Rules of Judicial Administration (instead of the Rules of Civil Procedure).[47] Florida has also enacted legislation that permits courts to sanction parties and attorneys for improperly filing a claim or defense.[48]

Variations among states' signature rules can result in variations in the consequences of failure to comply with those rules. Thus, before filing a paper in a state court, an attorney must fully understand the particular state's signature rules.

CHAPTER 2

THE INITIAL PLEADING

■ ■ ■

I. Purpose of the Initial Pleading

In all jurisdictions, the initial pleading *at a minimum* notifies each defendant of the plaintiff's claim and of the relief the plaintiff is seeking, preventing unfair surprise.[1] The initial pleading thus enables the defendant to prepare a response.[2] Due process demands it.

Beyond the minimum, courts differ regarding the amount of detail that they require the initial pleading to convey. Thus, to draft a legally sufficient pleading, an attorney must be acquainted with the standards for determining sufficiency in the jurisdiction where he or she intends to practice.

II. Drafting a Legally Sufficient Pleading

A. Requirement of Legal Sufficiency

A complaint is based on a legal theory, often called a "cause of action." A cause of action is identified by its characteristic elements. For example, a cause of action for negligence is identified by the following elements: (1) the defendant owes a legal duty to the plaintiff to exercise reasonable care to protect the plaintiff, (2) the defendant has breached the duty of reasonable care, (3) the breach proximately caused harm to the plaintiff, and (4) actual damages resulted.[3]

To establish a plaintiff's entitlement to relief, the attorney must set out in the pleading *allegations* sufficient to show the existence of a claim or (in some states) a cause of action. An allegation is a party's assertion concerning a factual matter. To survive a motion to dismiss, a pleading must be legally sufficient according to the standards of the court in which it is filed. To understand how much factual detail is required in a complaint, you must understand the standards by which courts determine sufficiency.

B.   Standards in Federal Court

Traditionally, federal courts followed a system of "notice pleading," requiring only that the pleading give notice to the defendant of the claim and the relief requested. The theory underlying notice pleading is that the parties use the pleadings to present their contentions to the court and to limit the issues for trial; exploration of the underlying facts is left to the discovery process.

Federal Rule of Civil Procedure 8(a) provides that a pleading that states a claim for relief must contain "a short and plain statement of the claim showing that the pleader is entitled to relief."[4] On its face, Rule 8(a) does not address the level of detail required to state a claim. Notice pleading—which requires minimal detail—became the rule in federal courts when the U.S. Supreme Court decided *Conley v. Gibson* in 1957.[5]

For as long as it lasted, *Conley* stood for the principle that a complaint should not be dismissed "unless it appears beyond doubt that the plaintiff can prove no set of facts in support of his claim which would entitle him to relief."[6] The minimal standard of *Conley* remained the rule for federal pleading until the 2007 Supreme Court case, *Bell Atlantic Corporation v. Twombly.*[7]

The *Twombly* decision retired the *Conley* rule.[8] Together with its 2009 successor, *Ashcroft v. Iqbal*,[9] the *Twombly* decision has created shock-waves throughout the federal court system. In *Twombly*, the Court held that a complaint should survive a motion to dismiss for failure to state a claim *only if* the pleading contains sufficient factual matter, accepted by the court as true, to state a claim for relief **that is plausible on its face.**[10] In the *Iqbal* decision, the Court held that the plausibility standard applies to all civil actions in federal court.[11]

Under *Iqbal* and *Twombly*, a two-pronged analysis is required to decide whether a pleading states a claim. First, the court must identify and disregard factual allegations that are no more than legal conclusions, legal conclusions presented as factual allegations, or unwarranted inferences.[12] Second, to determine sufficiency, the Court must evaluate the well-pleaded factual allegations to determine whether the complaint states a plausible claim.[13]

In *Iqbal*, the Court said that factual allegations must be sufficient "to raise a right to relief above the speculative level."[14] For that threshold to be reached, the plaintiff must plead sufficient facts to allow the Court to draw a reasonable inference that the defendant is liable for the alleged misconduct.[15] According to the D.C. Circuit Court of Appeals, a complaint has enough "factual heft" to show entitlement to relief if it alleges sufficient facts "to nudge the claim for relief across the line from conceivable to plausible."[16]

The law at present is in a state of flux, with some federal courts interpreting *Twombly* and *Iqbal* in a way that narrows the courthouse doorways.[17] Depending on how a court applies it, the plausibility standard may impose a heavy burden on plaintiffs, particularly in cases in which the defendants have possession of the bulk of the evidence.[18] For example, in price-fixing cases, the ability to state a claim may depend on the plaintiff's being allowed to rely on inferences from circumstantial evidence.[19] The same is true of federal discrimination claims.[20]

Explanations of the plausibility standard vary greatly. For example, the Sixth Circuit Court of Appeals stated that the plausibility standard requires a plaintiff to plead sufficient specific facts to raise a reasonable expectation that discovery will reveal evidence—a hard row to hoe for a plaintiff.[21] In contrast, the Tenth Circuit characterized the plausibility standard as a "refined standard": a "middle ground between heightened fact pleading, which is expressly rejected, and allowing complaints that are no more than labels and conclusions."[22] The Seventh Circuit stated that a complaint must actually *suggest* that the plaintiff has a right to relief by providing allegations that raise a right to relief above the speculative level.[23]

It remains unsettled how far "*Twombly* and *Iqbal*" have shifted the standard from notice pleading to a significantly heightened standard. Until the U.S. Supreme Court provides further guidance, a practitioner who needs to determine the level of specificity required to achieve "plausibility" must consult the case law in the relevant circuit as well as the position of the particular district court where the action is filed.

C. Standards in State Court

1. Notice and Plausibility Standards

As previously stated, Federal Rule of Civil Procedure 8(a) provides that a pleading that states a claim for relief must contain "a short and plain statement of the claim showing that the pleader is entitled to relief." Many states have modeled their rules of procedure on the federal rules.[24] Courts in these states often emphasize that the function of the pleading is merely to give notice to the opposing party.[25] Many cite the Supreme Court's decision in *Conley* as the basis of their standard. For example, the Vermont Supreme Court said that the Vermont rule requires only a "bare bones statement" sufficient to put the defendant on notice of the claim.[26]

The Washington Supreme Court and the Tennessee Supreme Court have declined to apply the plausibility standard.[27] In rejecting the standard, the Washington Supreme Court characterized it as a "drastic change."[28] The Tennessee Supreme Court commented that the plausibility standard was a substantial departure from the liberal notice pleading standard recognized in *Conley*[29] and concluded that to apply the plausibility standard would require a court to evaluate and determine—at the *earliest stage* of the proceedings—the likelihood that the plaintiff will succeed on the merits.[30]

In contrast, the Nebraska Supreme Court adopted the *Twombly–Iqbal* standard and concluded that the plausibility standard is a "balanced approach" (while expressing reservations about the way some federal courts have applied it).[31]

Regardless of the label a state applies to its standard, a particular notice-pleading state might require more factual detail than another state that has adopted the plausibility standard. For example, both Wisconsin and North Carolina courts characterize their standard as "notice pleading" though their Rule 8 equivalents require the pleading to give notice of the transaction or occurrence out of which the claim arose (which seems to require factual allegations).[32] To understand the level of specificity required under your state's standards, you must consult the case law.

2. Fact Pleading

Some states require the pleading of some facts in order for a complaint to be legally sufficient.[33] Many fact-pleading jurisdictions require the pleading of facts sufficient to state a cause of action.[34] Stating a cause of action typically means that the pleader must allege facts to support each element of at least one cause of action. Standards for stating a cause of action might or might not require significantly more detail than pleading under a notice pleading or plausibility standard.

Case law in fact-pleading jurisdictions provides insight into courts' expectations concerning the level of detail the state's rules of procedure require. For example, Maryland's rules of procedure require that a pleading contain only such statements of fact as may be necessary to show the pleader's entitlement to relief or a ground of defense.[35] Maryland's Court of Special Appeals said that a complaint is sufficient to state a cause of action if it contains "just the facts" necessary to establish the elements.[36]

The South Carolina rule, like the federal rule, requires "a short and plain statement of the facts showing that the pleader is entitled to relief."[37] The South Carolina Court of Appeals interpreted the rule to require that the pleader state "ultimate facts."[38] Ultimate facts are discussed in Section IV–C–1 of this chapter.

An attorney in a fact-pleading state who wants to know how much detail is required for legal sufficiency must check state law.

III. Procedural Matters Addressed in the Pleading

A. Pleading Jurisdiction

1. Pleading Subject–Matter Jurisdiction

To have power to hear a case, a court must have subject-matter jurisdiction. Federal Rule 8(a)(1) requires that an initial pleading include "a short and plain statement of the grounds for the court's jurisdiction." If the necessary allegation is missing, a federal court probably will dismiss the action for lack of subject-matter jurisdiction.[39]

Among the grounds for federal court jurisdiction are diversity jurisdiction[40] and federal-question jurisdiction.[41] For diversity jurisdiction to apply, the case must meet the amount-in-controversy requirement (currently in excess of $75,000 exclusive of interest and costs) and the parties must be citizens of different states (in circumstances not involving a foreign state or a citizen of a foreign state).[42]

**Examples: Pleading the Basis
of Diversity Jurisdiction**

- Plaintiff is a citizen of the state of Illinois and a resident of Cook County.

- Defendant is a corporation incorporated under the laws of Delaware with its principal place of business in the State of Florida.

- This court has jurisdiction pursuant to 28 U.S.C. § 1331. The parties are diverse. The plaintiff seeks damages in excess of $75,000.

For federal-question jurisdiction to apply, the action must arise under the Constitution, laws, or treaties of the United States. In federal question cases, the complaint must establish that there is, in fact, a federal question.[43]

**Example: Pleading the Basis of
Federal Question Jurisdiction**

This action is for trademark infringement and unfair competition under 15 U.S.C. § 1125(a) and for cyber-piracy under 15 U.S.C. § 1125(d).

The format for pleading subject-matter jurisdiction differs among federal courts according to local rules or practice.

In many states, the rules of procedure do not require the pleading to state the basis of subject-matter jurisdiction because the states' courts are courts of general jurisdiction. In states with a different type of system, the rules of procedure may require the pleading of facts sufficient to establish subject-matter jurisdiction. Examples of such states include Arizona,[44] Colorado (if the court is of limited jurisdiction),[45] Florida,[46] Idaho (if the court is of limited jurisdiction),[47] South Carolina,[48] and Wyoming.[49] If your state requires factual allegations to establish the basis of subject-matter jurisdiction, check state law and local practice to determine the necessary allegations and the manner of pleading them.

2. Pleading Personal Jurisdiction

To have power to subject a defendant to its judicial processes, a court must have personal jurisdiction over the defendant, and the defendant must have received notice (typically by service of process). Federal Rule 4(k) addresses the territorial limits of effective service. The burden is on the plaintiff to establish the court's personal jurisdiction over each defendant.[50]

A state court has personal jurisdiction over an individual who is domiciled in the state or a corporation that is incorporated in the state.[51] A state court may also exercise personal jurisdiction over a non-resident defendant who is validly served with process while present in the forum state or who consents to personal jurisdiction. Otherwise, a court may exercise jurisdiction over a nonresident defendant only if (1) the state's long-arm statute authorizes it,[52] and (2) federal due process requirements are satisfied.[53]

State long-arm statutes generally fall into two categories: (1) statutes, such as Florida's, that specify the types of contacts that provide the basis for long-arm jurisdiction (e.g., committing a tort within the forum state[54]); and (2) statutes, such as California's, that extend the state's long-arm jurisdiction to state and federal constitutional limits.[55] A long-arm statute enables a court to exercise personal jurisdiction over a non-resident defendant who has had sufficient minimum contacts with the forum state.

The minimum contacts rule is intended to ensure that a defendant cannot be subjected to a state's judicial processes if the defendant had no substantial, systematic,[56] or purposeful[57] connection to the state. Discussion of minimum contracts is beyond the scope of this textbook, but an attorney filing a claim against a non-resident defendant must determine whether the circumstances would support exercise of personal jurisdiction in light of current state and federal law.[58] The law is complex, and multiple factors must be considered.

Except in some federal question cases, federal courts generally look to the forum state's long-arm statutes for authority to exercise personal jurisdiction[59] and to federal law to determine whether the minimum contracts requirement is met.[60] Many federal complaints address personal jurisdiction, often under a section labeled "Parties," which presents information establishing subject-matter jurisdiction (e.g., diversity or federal question), personal jurisdiction, and the appropriateness of the forum choice. The following is an example, though attorneys in different districts follow different practices.

> **Example: "Parties" Section in a**
> **Case Filed in North Carolina**
>
> II. Parties
>
> 3. Plaintiff is an individual citizen and resident of the State of North Carolina.
>
> 4. Defendant is a Delaware Corporation. **[diversity]** Defendant does substantial business in North Carolina and operates a factory in this district **[personal jurisdiction under long-arm statute].** A substantial part of the events giving rise to the claim occurred in this district **[appropriate venue under 28 U.S.C. § 1391 (2012)].**

If the state's long-arm statute lists the circumstances in which the court can exercise personal jurisdiction, the pleading may need to allege facts to show that the state's long-arm statute applies. In Florida, for example, the initial pleading must allege sufficient jurisdictional facts to bring the pleading "within the ambit" of the state's long-arm statute.[61] Below is an example of how one might allege the applicability of the long-arm statute in Florida:

> **Example: Alleging Applicability of Long Arm Statute**
>
> At all times relevant to this cause of action, Defendant, a Delaware corporation, had an office in Alachua County, Florida. Defendant engaged in its manufacturing business in Florida. These actions fall within the ambit of section 48.193(1)(a) of the Florida Statutes.

B. Pleading Venue

After determining which court has power to decide the case, an attorney must determine in which geographic location (venue) to file the action. There are federal district courts all over the country. In any state, there will be more than one trial court.

Federal Rule 8 does not require the pleading of venue, but many lawyers prefer to plead the facts establishing the basis of the selected venue. Though the format for pleading venue differs among federal courts, the following is an example of an allegation from a pleading filed in a federal district court in Colorado:

> **Example: Alleging Venue in Federal Court**
>
> Venue is proper in this judicial district under 28 U.S.C. §§ 1391(a)(2). A substantial part of the events giving rise to the claims occurred in this district, and all parties reside in the State of Colorado.

Venue rules differ among states. Some states may require that the plaintiff allege the basis of venue in the initial pleading.[62] In Florida, where there is case law indicating that the plaintiff should plead the basis of the venue choice,[63] the allegation might be framed as follows:

> **Example: Alleging Venue in a State Court**
>
> Venue is proper pursuant to section 47.051 of the Florida Statutes because the cause of action accrued in Dade County.

Many states do not require that the initial pleading allege the grounds for the plaintiff's venue choice, but attorneys sometimes plead the grounds anyway. To know whether to address the basis of venue choice in a pleading, an attorney should consult the state's procedural law and the pleading practice in the jurisdiction.

If an attorney bases a cause of action on the violation of a statute, the correct venue for filing the action may be specified in the statute. If an attorney files an action based on a contract, the venue specified in the contract's forum-selection provision may determine the venue choice. Forum-selection clauses in contracts are discussed in Chapter 9.

C.   Pleading "Special Matters"

In most jurisdictions, special pleading rules apply to the pleading of "special matters." Below are a few examples of "special matters" that are listed in Federal Rule 9:

- Capacity or authority to sue.

- Fraud or mistake.

- Condition of mind (e.g., malice, intent, or knowledge).

- Satisfaction of conditions precedent.

- Special damages.

Before pleading a "special matter" in federal court, an attorney must be familiar with how and when the matter must be pleaded. For example, Federal Rule 9 states that fraud must be pleaded with particularity; thus, a heightened pleading standard applies to fraud. The rule also requires the pleading of special damages.

Most states have an equivalent to Federal Rule 9,[64] though an attorney must look to state law to see which matters are considered "special." For example, North Carolina's version of Rule 9 covers some matters not addressed in the federal rule, such as pleading rules that are applicable to libel and slander, medical malpractice, and punitive damages.[65] North Dakota's version includes a rule for pleading the name of an unknown party.[66] West Virginia's version covers pleading eminent domain.[67] An attorney must be familiar with the applicable "special matters" rules.

D. Demand for Judgment

Pleadings typically include a clause called the "demand for judgment," "prayer for relief," or "ad damnum clause." This clause is typically required in a pleading that requests affirmative relief. Federal Rule 8(a)(3), for example, requires that a pleading for affirmative relief include "a demand for the relief sought, which may include relief in the alternative or different types of relief." State rules of procedure likewise require the complaint to include a demand for judgment.[68]

These clauses are generally introduced by the word "Wherefore," a convention that we recommend you follow (depending on your state's practice). Below are examples of demands for judgment.

Examples: Demands for Judgment

Negligence Case:

Wherefore, Plaintiff requests that the court give judgment against Defendant awarding damages.

Statutory Cause of Action:

Wherefore, Plaintiff, pursuant to section 501.625 of the Florida Telemarketing Act, requests that the court give judgment against Defendant awarding damages, attorney's fees and costs.

Different states have different rules regarding the inclusion of the amount of damages in the demand for judgment. For example, Indiana's rule provides "In any complaint seeking damages for personal injury or death, or seeking punitive damages, no dollar amount or figure shall be included in the demand."[69] New Mexico's rule states: "Unless it is a necessary allegation of the complaint, the complaint shall not contain an allegation for damages in any specific monetary amount."[70]

Attorney's fees are generally available only if a contract provision, rule, or statute authorizes them. In federal court, attorney's fees are usually viewed as special damages and must be pleaded for the plaintiff to recover them.[71] State courts also might refuse to allow a plaintiff to recover attorney's fees if the plaintiff fails to mention or demand attorney's fees in the pleading.[72] Check the applicable law in your jurisdiction.

E. Exhibits to the Pleading

Federal Rule 10(c) provides that a document or instrument attached to a pleading (i.e., an exhibit) becomes a part of the pleading *for all purposes*. If any information in the exhibit contradicts the allegations of the pleading, then the information in the exhibit prevails.[73]

State rules concerning exhibits vary.[74] A few states require an attorney to attach to a pleading any document or instrument on which the pleading is based. For example, the Arkansas rule states, "A copy of any written instrument or document upon which a claim or defense is based shall be attached as an exhibit to the pleading in which such claim or defense is averred unless good cause is shown for its absence in such pleading."[75] Illinois and Mississippi have similar rules.[76] In contrast, Michigan's rule lists the circumstances in which it is *not* necessary to attach a copy of the exhibit: for example, if the instrument is in the possession of the adverse party and the pleading so states.[77] Tennessee has a similar rule.[78]

Regarding exhibits, an attorney should check both the rules of civil procedure and any local rules regulating attachments to the pleading. If your state's rule of procedure relating to exhibits is vague or there is no rule, check local rules.

IV. Fundamentals of Drafting a Complaint

A. Format and Presentation Requirements

Before drafting a pleading, an attorney should review the local rules of the jurisdiction and look at pleadings filed in the same court. As Chapter 1 explains, some courts may have rules regarding paper size, margins, font, spacing, the caption, and the signature block.

As well as formatting requirements, some courts have requirements relating to the presentation of an initial pleading. For example, Pennsylvania's rule of civil procedure 1018.1 requires the plaintiff to attach to the initial pleading a document called a "notice to defend." Some states may require that an attorney attach to the complaint a document called a "civil cover sheet."[79]

B. Identifying and Referring to the Parties

Initial pleadings typically begin with an introductory clause called a "commencement." The commencement states that Plaintiff X is suing Defendant Y. If there is more than one defendant or plaintiff and it is necessary to distinguish the parties in the body of the pleading, the commencement is usually the best place to stipulate how you intend to refer to the various plaintiffs or defendants.

To prevent reader confusion, we recommend that you refer to parties by their party designation (i.e., *Plaintiff* or *Defendant*). If you have only one plaintiff and one defendant, refer to them as "Plaintiff" and "Defendant," using the party designations as name substitutes. If you have multiple parties on each side and have to refer to some of them by name in the pleading, create shorthand forms that include the party designation. Below are examples.

Examples: Referring to Multiple Parties on One Side

Plaintiff Jordan Smith sues Defendants Mark Reed (Defendant Reed), SNZ of Florida Convenience Stores, Inc. (Defendant SNZ), and Hogtown Machinery, Inc. (Defendant Hogtown) and alleges the following:

Note the absence of needless legal jargon in the example above (e.g., "Comes now the plaintiff," "by and through his undersigned attorney," or "hereinafter referred to as"). Unless your jurisdiction requires otherwise, we recommend that you omit needless legal jargon, as it simply takes up space on the page.

C. Four Types of Allegations

1. Description of Types of Allegations

An **allegation** is a party's assertion concerning a factual matter. There are four types of allegations: (1) legal conclusion, (2) ultimate fact, (3) evidentiary fact, and (4) extraneous detail.

A **legal conclusion** expresses—without inclusion of supporting facts—the pleader's opinion about how the law operates or should operate. Consider, for example, a negligence case arising out of a car accident. One legal conclusion that the plaintiff would want the court to draw is that the defendant owed the plaintiff a duty of care (i.e., one element of a negligence cause of action).

An **ultimate fact** is a fact that is necessary to establish an element of a cause of action. In the car-accident hypothetical, ultimate facts would include that the defendant owned and was driving the car (the defendant's ownership and driving of the car gave rise to the defendant's duty of care to the plaintiff).

An **evidentiary fact** is a fact that provides evidence in support of the existence of some other fact. In the car-accident hypothetical, an evidentiary fact would be that the defendant's name was on the title to the car. This fact is evidence of the *ultimate fact* that the defendant owned the car.

An **extraneous detail** is one that merely takes up space on the page. It neither helps establish an element of a cause of action nor supports a legal conclusion. Whether a detail is extraneous depends on the nature of the cause of action. In the car-accident hypothetical, if the car and its ownership are not in dispute, the color of the car could be irrelevant.

Below are examples of each of the four types of allegations:

Examples: Allegations

Legal Conclusion: Defendant owed Plaintiff a duty of care.

Ultimate Facts: On or about December 1, 2011, Defendant was driving on Main Street a car that Defendant owned.

Evidentiary Fact: At all times relevant to this action, Defendant's name was on the title to the car.

Extraneous Details: On or about December 1, 2011, Defendant owned a blue car that had a leather interior.

---

2.   Use of Types of Allegations in a Pleading

(a) Use of Ultimate Facts

At the initial stage of litigation, the court mainly wants to ascertain whether there is enough of a case to go forward. A pleading will usually give adequate notice to the other party if the complaint contains sufficient information to *outline* the elements of the claim or to permit the court to draw inferences that those elements exist.[80] In a recent case interpreting the "plausibility" standard, the U.S. Tenth Circuit Court of Appeals commented that the elements of a cause of action help to determine whether the plaintiff has set forth a plausible claim.[81] Matching facts to elements (whenever possible) makes it clear that the complaint states a claim (or, in a fact-pleading state, a cause of action). Unless your state requires otherwise, we recommend that you support each element of the cause of action with ultimate facts.

(b) Use of Legal Conclusions

When determining whether a pleading states a claim or cause of action, courts generally disregard a party's conclusions of law, inferences, and expressions of opinion.[82] Some courts do not object to inclusion in the pleading of some legal conclusions *if* the conclusions are supported by sufficient factual allegations. In *Iqbal*, the U.S. Supreme Court said that legal conclusions can provide "the framework of a complaint" if the conclusions are supported by factual allegations.[83]

Some state courts strongly discourage conclusions of law or conclusory language in a pleading. For example, a Pennsylvania court stated, "A conclusion of law has no place in a pleading."[84] Similarly, the Illinois Court of Appeals said, "Not only are allegations of law or conclusions not required, they are improper."[85] Some states may be more lenient.[86]

(c) Use of Evidentiary Facts and Extraneous Details

At the outset of a lawsuit, the facts are still undeveloped because discovery has not yet occurred. Courts in some jurisdictions sometimes consider evidentiary facts to be harmless, but most courts agree that such information is not necessary.[87]

Courts in fact-pleading jurisdictions typically do not require the pleading of evidentiary facts. For example, an Illinois court said, "Though Illinois is a fact-pleading jurisdiction..., the plaintiff is not required to prove his or her case at the pleading stage."[88] In some states, courts strongly discourage pleading evidentiary facts. For example, the Connecticut Supreme Court, which requires the pleading of material facts, recently wrote that inclusion of evidence in a complaint is a violation of state rules of practice.[89] Some other fact-pleading states agree.[90]

In addition to omitting evidentiary facts, we also suggest that you omit extraneous details. Courts dislike wordy and convoluted pleadings. A court might even require such a complaint to be amended to conform to the state's pleading rules. For example, the New Hampshire Supreme Court said, "When faced with an excessively burdensome and muddled pleading, the trial court may require the submitting party to file a more orderly and concise pleading."[91]

D. Framing Allegations

1. Making Allegations Plain, Concise, and Direct

The typical requirements that allegations in an initial pleading be "plain" and "direct" indicate that an attorney should write so that an ordinary or extremely busy person (such as a judge) can easily understand the pleading in a single reading. Every sentence an attorney writes should be understandable on one reading.

The requirement that the pleading be "concise" means that the attorney should use no more words than are necessary to make the point. As discussed in Chapter 33, "concise" does not necessarily mean short; pleadings in complex litigation are often lengthy. "Concise" means that each sentence is no longer than it needs to be. Thus, we recommend that you devote at least one phase of editing to eliminating unnecessary words and shortening wordy phrases.

2. Focusing on the Parties

A pleading is a story about a relationship between parties, the actions of the parties, and the wrongful actions of one or more of the parties. It is about responsibility for consequences. Courts do not like allegations that provide an incomplete, partially developed picture. As you draft a pleading, be clear about who did what.

To keep the reader focused on the parties, the subject of most sentences in a pleading should be the name of the relevant party or parties. In other words, draft most sentences in active voice. Instead of stating that the plaintiff's car "was hit," frame the allegation to state that the *defendant hit* the plaintiff's car. Active voice is discussed in Chapters 31 and 33. Stick with active voice unless you have a strategic reason for doing otherwise (e.g., framing allegations to elicit admissions, as addressed in Section III–D–4–[a]).

If there are multiple defendants, some or all may have acted jointly: make it clear that *each* of those defendants engaged in the wrongful conduct. If all defendants acted together, refer to them collectively as "Defendants." If some but not all of them acted together, specify which of the defendants engaged in the action. If you do not know which one did the relevant action, you may refer to "Defendant Smith or Defendant Jones."

Below are examples of allegations from a complaint against three defendants based on a statute regulating vehicle repair shops:

Examples: Allegations

12.   On or about May 10, 2012, Defendant Carr failed to provide Plaintiff with a written estimate of repair costs.

13.   On that date, Defendant Alford or Defendant Bailey failed to comply with the vehicle inspection requirements set out in section 90.345(a) of the statute.

14.   By their actions alleged in paragraphs 12–13, Defendants violated section 90.345(a) and (b) of the statute.

---

3. Alleging Time and Place

Federal Rule 9(f) and many states' rules of procedure state that allegations regarding time and place are material for purposes of testing the sufficiency of a pleading.[92] Omitting these allegations is not necessarily fatal to a cause of action, but a complaint or petition lacking this information may be too vague to provide notice to the other party or to enable the other party to respond. Omission of information identifying the time or place could lead to the court's granting the other party a motion to dismiss or a request for a more definite statement.

If certain of the precise date, you can provide it or you can leave yourself some wiggle room by using one of the following:

•   On approximately June 1, 2010 …

- On or about June 1, 2011 …

- During the first week of June 2012 …

- During a period beginning on approximately June 1, 2012 and continuing through June 15, 2012.…

Dates are only one type of time statement. The following are some other types that keep the reader's sense of time on track:

- While Plaintiff was still on the premises …

- While Defendant's employees were unloading the truck …

- After Defendant completed the presentation.…

Setting out time statements at the beginning of sentences creates a time line that the reader can easily track throughout the pleading. Thus, for the reader's convenience, we recommend that you put dates or other time statements **at the beginning of the sentence**.

As stated above, the place where the alleged circumstance occurs should also be included. If a shift from one place to another occurs, the pleading should notify the reader of the shift, as in the following examples:

- On July 10, 2010, when Plaintiff returned home from vacation …

- After Defendant returned to the warehouse with the shipment …

- Before Defendant arrived at the restaurant.…

4. Pleading Strategically

(a) Framing Allegations to Elicit Admissions

Remember that the defendant responds to a complaint in an answer. Under Federal Rule 8(b), the defendant has the following options for responding to allegations:

- Admit the allegation.

- Deny the allegation.

- State that the defendant lacks sufficient knowledge to form a belief as to the truth of the allegation.

- Admit the allegation in part and deny the allegation in part (or plead insufficient knowledge as to the truth of part of the allegation).

An allegation framed to elicit an admission can render valuable information concerning the defendant's position regarding underlying facts, even if the defendant denies the allegation. If you do not frame the allegation to elicit an admission, you will not learn as much.

To get meaningful responses from a defendant, frame allegations of ultimate fact neutrally, objectively, and with precision. A **neutrally framed** allegation sets out the facts free of the drafter's conclusions, arguments, beliefs, and factual inferences. An **objective** allegation is one that focuses on the observable facts instead of on what the party subjectively perceived or concluded about the facts. A **precise** allegation is one that sufficiently identifies the key issues of who, when, what, and where.

Assume that a plaintiff slipped and fell in a convenience store and is suing the store's owner. When drafting the complaint, the attorney could choose to frame the allegations in either a conclusory or a neutral way, as illustrated by the following examples.

Examples: Conclusory versus Neutral Allegations

Conclusory:
On or about June 9, 2012, <u>Defendant negligently failed</u> to remove spilled water or some other liquid that was on the floor of Defendant's store.

Neutral:
On or about June 9, 2012, there was <u>water or some other liquid</u> on the floor of Defendant's store.

If the plaintiff's attorney frames the allegation in the conclusory way shown above and if the defendant's attorney believes that the defendant was not negligent, the defendant's attorney might deny the entire allegation. Thus, the plaintiff's attorney would learn nothing from the denial about whether the defendant's attorney believes that there was water on the floor. By framing the allegation in a neutral way, the plaintiff's attorney forces the defendant to address the crucial fact of whether there was water on the floor.

Framing allegations objectively (instead of subjectively) may draw out admissions. Suppose the following allegations are true. How would the defendant's response to each differ?

Examples: Subjective versus Objective

Subjective:
Plaintiff <u>became interested</u> in buying canning equipment when <u>Plaintiff learned</u> from an advertisement in the July 1, 2011 edition of *Crosstown Deals* that Defendant sold home-canning kits.

> **Examples: Subjective versus Objective** (cont.)
>
> **Objective:**
> Defendant's advertisement appeared in the July 1, 2011 edition of *Crosstown Deals*. <u>In its advertisement, Defendant stated that it sold home-canning kits.</u>

If the plaintiff's attorney uses the subjective language, the defendant would be without actual knowledge concerning the truth of the allegations that "plaintiff became interested" and "plaintiff learned from an advertisement" and might respond accordingly. If the plaintiff's attorney frames the allegation so that it is about the defendant (i.e., that the defendant placed the ad), then the defendant is in a position to respond.

(b) Pleading Alternatively or Inconsistently

Federal Rule 8(d) provides, "A party may set out 2 or more statements of a claim or defense alternatively or hypothetically, either in a single count or defense or in separate ones. If a party makes alternative statements, the pleading is sufficient if any one of them is sufficient."[93]

States generally have similar rules.[94] As a California court said, "when a pleader is in doubt about what actually occurred or what can be established by the evidence, the modern practice allows that party to plead in the alternative and make inconsistent allegations."[95] A Massachusetts court explained that the court may grant relief if one of the alternative grounds is sufficient, despite the insufficiency of any other alternative grounds.[96]

For example, if the plaintiff was badly injured by the defendant's escaped horse, the attorney does not have to know at the pleading stage exactly how the horse escaped. If addressing the means of escape is essential, the attorney could allege multiple alternatives: e.g., that the defendant (1) negligently left the gate to the pasture open so that the horse escaped, <u>or</u> (2) negligently failed to maintain the pasture fence in sufficient repair to prevent the horse from escaping, <u>or</u> (3) negligently failed to otherwise prevent the horse from escaping.

In addition to pleading alternative facts, a plaintiff may plead alternative and inconsistent theories.[97] For example, a plaintiff's attorney may plead based on the same set of circumstances both that the defendant negligently injured the plaintiff and that the defendant committed an intentional tort.

A party may also ask for alternative or inconsistent remedies, though the plaintiff would be entitled to only one recovery for the same injury.

E.   Organizing the Allegations

1.   Sequence of Allegations

The elements of most causes of action (whether laid out by a court or in a statute) typically fit into four key categories:

1) The law imposes a legal duty on the defendant (e.g., based on a contract or statute);

2) The defendant engaged in wrongful conduct (e.g., by breaching the contract or violating the statute);

3) There is a causal connection between the defendant's wrongful conduct and the resulting harm to the plaintiff (e.g., physical injury, economic loss, or property damage);

4) Compensable damage or loss resulted from the wrongful conduct.

We recommend that you use the four key categories as a guide to sequencing your factual allegations. To prepare a rough draft of a complaint, we recommend that you (1) list the four key categories; and (2) under each listed category, set out each fact that establishes the related element of the cause of action. Below is an example of what such a list might look like.

Example: Sequencing Allegations
(Premises Liability case)

1.   Basis of Defendant's Duty

- Defendant owned and operated a grocery store located at 111 Main Street, Smith, Georgia.

- On June 5, 2011, Plaintiff was a customer at Defendant's store.

2.   Defendant's Wrongful Conduct

- On that date, water or some other liquid had spilled on the floor of Defendant's store.

- Defendant knew about the liquid on the floor or had sufficient time to become aware of it.

- Defendant negligently failed to remove the liquid from the floor.

3.   Causal Connection Between Wrongful Conduct and Harm

- Plaintiff stepped into the liquid, slipped and fell backward.

- The fall caused Plaintiff to suffer a fractured skull.

Example: Sequencing Allegations (cont.)

4.   **Compensable Damage or Loss Resulting from Wrongful Conduct**

   • Plaintiff endured pain and suffering, emotional distress, disability, humiliation, and loss of enjoyment of life.

   • Plaintiff incurred medical expenses, including expenses for hospitalization and physical therapy.

   • Plaintiff lost the income that she earned through her work.

---

2.   Grouping Facts Into Paragraphs

Federal Rule 10(b) requires that the plaintiff set out a claim in numbered paragraphs and that each paragraph be limited "as far as practicable" to a single set of circumstances. Most states' rules on paragraph design are similar.[98]

Unless your jurisdiction requires otherwise, we recommend that each paragraph address no more than one element of the cause of action. For example, do not set out facts relating to the defendant's wrongful conduct (breach of duty) in the same paragraph as facts showing the basis of the duty or in the same paragraph as facts showing causation. The reason for that recommendation is to increase the chances that the defendant will respond systematically regarding each element, rather than give a global response to a mixed cluster of allegations. Below is an example of allegations that are organized into paragraphs.

Example: Organizing the Allegations into Paragraphs
(Premises Liability case)

2.   At all time relevant to this action, Defendant owned and operated a grocery store located at 111 Main Street, Smith, Georgia.

3.   On June 5, 2011, Plaintiff was a customer at Defendant's store.

4.   On that date, water or some other clear liquid had spilled onto the floor of Defendant's store.

5.   Defendant knew about the liquid on the floor or had sufficient time to become aware of it. Defendant negligently failed to remove the liquid from the floor.

> **Example: Organizing the Allegations into
> Paragraphs** (cont.)
>
> 6.   While Plaintiff was in Defendant's store, Plaintiff
> stepped into the liquid, slipped, and fell backward to the
> floor. Defendant's negligence caused Plaintiff to suffer
> injury, including a fractured skull.
>
> 7.   As a result of Defendant's negligence, Plaintiff endured
> pain and suffering, emotional distress, disability, humilia-
> tion, and loss of enjoyment of life. Plaintiff incurred medi-
> cal expenses, including expenses for hospitalization and
> physical therapy. Plaintiff lost the income that Plaintiff
> earned through working as a waitress.

We also recommend that you keep paragraphs concise. If a paragraph exceeds three or four reasonably short sentences, consider breaking it into two paragraphs. Keeping the length manageable will yield more useful responses (i.e., responses that genuinely identify the facts that are in dispute). On the other hand, overuse of one-sentence paragraphs may cause the allegations to seem disconnected and difficult to follow.

3.   Numbering Paragraphs

Typically, paragraphs are consecutively numbered throughout the pleading, though there are exceptions. Connecticut, for example, requires that paragraphs set out under separate counts "be numbered separately beginning in each count with the number one."[99]

4.   Cross–Referencing Between Paragraphs

Most states permit cross-referencing from one paragraph into another: e.g., "Defendant negligently failed to remove or repair the condition described in paragraph 8." Limit cross-referencing to the minimum amount necessary to prevent serious redundancy or prolixity problems. Do not force the reader to jump back and forth between paragraphs more than is necessary.

V.   Drafting Multi–Count Complaints

A.   Dividing a Pleading Into Counts

Contrary to the common practice, most jurisdictions' rules of procedure regarding division of a pleading into counts do not expressly require each count to be based on a separate legal theory (e.g., breach of contract or violation of a statute). Federal Rule 10(b) states that each claim founded on a separate transaction or occurrence should be stated in a separate count if doing so would promote clarity.

Generally, state rules are similar.[100] Oregon is one of the exceptions: "Within each claim alternative theories of recovery shall be identified as separate counts."[101] This is what most lawyers do and what we recommend.

Typically, multiple counts are not required if multiple defendants engaged in the same type of wrongful conduct covered by the same legal theory or if one defendant engaged in multiple instances of the same sort of wrongful conduct (e.g., if the defendant violated eight provisions of the same statute). Check the rules and practice conventions in your state.

B. Re–Allegation and Incorporation by Reference

Avoiding redundancy in a pleading is an important objective. To avoid redundancy, an attorney can re-allege a paragraph containing a previously alleged fact or incorporate the material by reference. Federal Rule 10(c) states, "A statement in a pleading may be adopted by reference elsewhere in the same pleading or in any other pleading or motion." Many state courts have similar rules.[102] Below are examples of re-allegation and incorporation by reference.

Examples: Re-allegation and Incorporation by Reference

Re-allegation:
Plaintiff re-alleges paragraphs 3, 7, and 12 from Count I.

Incorporation by Reference:
As alleged in paragraph 10, Defendant did not obtain the required authorization.

Beware of wholesale incorporation of allegations from one count into another if the allegations contain language that is inconsistent with the legal theory on which the count is based. For example, do not incorporate a paragraph containing the word "negligence" into a count addressing breach of contract, even if the underlying fact was the same for both.

Avoid what some federal courts call "shotgun pleading."[103] One court described a shotgun pleading as containing "several counts, each one incorporating by reference the allegations of its predecessors, leading to a situation where most of the counts (i.e., all but the first) contain irrelevant factual allegations and legal conclusions."[104] Check your state's rules regarding re-allegation and incorporation by reference.

C. Demand for Judgment Following Each Count

We generally recommend placing a demand for relief at the end of each count so that the reader can easily understand what remedies the plaintiff is seeking based on the particular legal theory supporting the count. As always, check applicable law and practice conventions.

D. Headings for Each Count

We recommend that each count in a multi-count pleading be assigned a number and a heading. Below are two pairs of examples:

Examples: Headings for a Two–Count Complaint

Example 1:

Count 1: Negligence

Count 2: Breach of Contract

Example 2:

First Count—Negligence

Second Count—Breach of Contract

VI. Pleading Pursuant to Statute

A. Statutory Causes of Action Generally

Many federal and state statutes provide a party with a right to file an action against persons to whom the statute applies if those persons inflict injury on the party by violating the statute. Many of those statutes allow the party to recover not only damages or injunctive relief, but also attorney's fees. Pleading pursuant to a statute is similar to pleading based on a common-law theory. Generally, the statute will tell you what to plead.

B. Identifying the Elements of the Statutory Cause of Action

1. Understanding the Statute's Structure

To plead pursuant to a statute, an attorney must discern the elements of the statutory cause of action. A systematic approach is useful. Before beginning a close reading of the statute, scan it to get familiar with its overall structure, including its headings. Notice whether the statute sets forth the statute's purpose and application. Notice *where* in the statute the legislature has addressed the following:

- Definitions.

- Identity of the government agency that enforces the statute.

- Regulatory provisions (e.g., requirements applying to persons the statute regulates).

- Administrative provisions (e.g., how the enforcing authority obtains relief).

- Remedies and penalties (including a private right of action).

- Exemptions and exclusions.

By scanning the statute in advance, you may be able to weed out irrelevant sections.

2. Analyzing the Statute

To analyze a statute, make a list addressing the following issues and questions (be precise, or the list will not be useful):

Checklist for Analyzing a Statute

1.   Purpose of Statute

If the statute contains a purpose clause, what is the purpose?

2.   Existence of Remedy

- Does the statute grant to a party a private right of action?

- If so, what remedies does it provide (e.g., damages or attorney's fees)?

3.   Defendant's Duty to Plaintiff

a.   Questions relating to Plaintiff:

- What classes of persons is the statute designed to *protect*?

- Are these classes listed in the "Definitions" section?

- If so, what are the criteria for qualifying as a member of the class?

- Does Plaintiff fit into one or more protected classes?

b.   Questions relating to Defendant:

- Which classes of persons is the statute designed to *regulate*?

- Are the classes listed in the "Definitions" section?

- If so, what are the criteria for qualifying as a member of the class?

Checklist for Analyzing a Statute (cont.)

- Does Defendant fit into one or more regulated classes?

c. <u>Questions relating to the transaction or circumstances:</u>

- To what type of transaction or circumstances does the statute apply?

- Does the statute name the transaction or circumstances (e.g., "health maintenance contract" or "excavation of protected lands")?

- If so, is that name defined in the statute?

- If so, what are the criteria for meeting the definition?

4. Violations of the Statute

- Which sections or subsections do you believe each defendant violated?

- Which conduct by each defendant qualifies as a violation?

- Note: it is generally *not* possible for a party to violate a definition or a purpose clause. To establish a violation, you must identify a prohibition, requirement, or provision imposing liability.

5. Causation Issues

- Does the statute require you to allege a causal connection between Defendant's actions and the harm that Plaintiff suffered (e.g., does the statute provide a remedy only if harm "results from" or "is caused by" the violation)?

- If so, then use the statutory language in pleading a causal connection.

6. Remedies

- Which injuries, losses, and other harms are compensable under the statute?

- Does the statute authorize attorney's fees?

- If so, make it clear that Plaintiff incurred reasonable attorney's fees

---

C. Pleading the Statutory Cause of Action

1. Identifying the Statute and Adopting a Short Form

Identify at the beginning of the count (or the beginning of the pleading if you have only one legal theory) the statute on which the cause of action is based. If doing so is not contrary to local practice and if it would help your reader, you can adopt a short form for referring to the statute. The short form could be an acronym or the name by which the statute is popularly known. Below is one possible approach:

> This action is pursuant to Title 10, Chapter 401, Part II, sections 401.10 through 401.20, "The Floregon Membership Facilities Act" (<u>FMFA</u>).

2. Organizing the Allegations

In a statute-based pleading, we recommend that you set out allegations in the following order:

1) Facts establishing defendant's duty.

2) Defendant's wrongful conduct (statutory violations).

3) Causal connection between violations and harm.

4) Damages.

One of the court's first questions is whether the statute applies to the parties. Therefore, it makes sense to establish duty-related facts up front. These include facts that (1) introduce the defendant, (2) show that the defendant qualifies as a potential violator of the statute, and (3) show that the plaintiff fits within the class of persons the statute is intended to protect or benefit.

After setting out the basis of the statutory duty, address the wrongful conduct (i.e., the conduct that violates the statute). After setting out all violations in the order in which they occurred, address causation and then damages.

This organizational approach does not result in a mere relation of the events in the order that they occurred. Instead, it groups facts together according to their relationship to the four categories discussed in Section IV–E–1.

3. Tracking Statutory Language When Framing Allegations of Fact

To the extent possible, frame the facts in the language of the statute. Doing so is called "tracking" the statute. "Tracking" does not mean quoting the statute (which generally should not be done). Tracking means incorporating *only the relevant words* from the statute.

Suppose that you want to show that the defendant is a "health studio" under the statutory definition of that term. Below is an example of a statutory definition and an allegation that tracks the language of that definition (relevant words are underlined).

Example: Tracking Statutory Language

Statutory Definition:
"Health Studio" means a <u>facility</u> where an <u>individual patron</u> can obtain <u>instruction</u>, <u>training</u>, or <u>assistance</u> by <u>contract</u> for the following: physical culture, body building, exercising, dancing, martial arts, or any other such similar activity.

Allegation Tracking the Statutory Definition:
"At all times relevant to this cause of action, Defendant Quantum Physiques was a <u>facility</u> located at 2200 University Avenue, Micanopia, Temple County, Floregon. <u>Individual patrons</u> contracted with Defendant for <u>instruction</u>, <u>training</u>, or <u>assistance</u> in <u>body building</u>. On February 2, 2012, Plaintiff signed a <u>contract</u> with Defendant for membership in its facility.

---

4.   Identifying the Violated Sections and Subsections

After alleging *facts* showing that the defendant violated the statute, identify the violated sections and subsections (1) as a courtesy to the court and (2) to assist the defendant in responding.

Consider Floregon's "Membership Facilities Act," which regulates certain health clubs. Sections 2301(a) and (b) provide the following:

2301(a). A membership facility that operates as a health studio shall regularly inspect its machines for defects. If a machine is defective, the membership facility shall promptly disable the machine and post a notice stating that the machine is out of order.

2301(b). A membership facility that operates as a health studio shall ensure that any service to a defective machine is made by a service agent who is authorized by the manufacturer to make such repairs.

When alleging that a defendant violated Floregon's Membership Facilities Act, we recommend that you take one of two approaches: either the chronological approach or the fact-violation approach.

To use the chronological approach, first set out allegations relating to the defendant's conduct in the order that the conduct occurred. Next identify the violated sections or subsections. Below is an example.

Example: Chronological Approach

6. Defendant failed to regularly inspect the Yogamagic machine for defects. On February 10, 2012, when Plaintiff was using Defendant's facility, Defendant had not disabled the Yogamagic and had not posted a notice stating that the Yogamagic was out of order.

7. Defendant's employee had attempted to repair the machine. On information and belief, the employee was not a service agent whom the manufacturer had authorized to make such repairs.

8. Defendant violated FMFA section 2301(a) by failing to inspect the Yogamagic for defects or malfunctions and by failing to promptly disable or remove the malfunctioning machine from service.

9. Defendant violated FMFA section 2301(b) by failing to ensure that service to the defective or malfunctioning machine was made by a service agent authorized by the manufacturer to make such repairs.

To use the fact-violation approach, first set out the paragraph alleging conduct that violated the statute. Immediately after that paragraph, set out the allegation identifying the violated section or subsection. Below is an example.

Example: Fact–Violation Approach

6. Defendant failed to regularly inspect the Yogamagic machine for defects. On February 10, 2012, when Plaintiff was using Defendant's facility, Defendant had not disabled the Yogamagic and had not posted a notice stating that the Yogamagic was out of order.

7. Defendant violated FMFA section 2301(a) by failing to inspect the Yogamagic for defects or malfunctions and by failing to promptly disable or remove the malfunctioning machine from service.

8. Defendant employee had attempted to repair the machine. On information and belief, Defendant employee was not a service agent whom the manufacturer had authorized to make such repairs.

9. Defendant violated FMFA section 2301(b) by failing to ensure that service to the defective or malfunctioning machine was made by a service agent authorized by the manufacturer to make such repairs.

If you prefer a shorter pleading, you could dispense with the individual paragraphs that identify the violations and simply list all of the violated sections in a single paragraph without elaboration: e.g., "Defendant violated FMFA sections 2301(a) and (b)."

D.   Requesting Relief

In the demand for judgment, set out all the relief to which the plaintiff is entitled under the statute. Even if your jurisdiction does not require it, we recommend that you identify the statutory provision authorizing each item of relief. In some instances, a tabulated sentence may be useful. Below is an example.

Example: Demand for Judgment

Wherefore, Plaintiff requests that the court award to Plaintiff the following:

a)   treble damages, as authorized by FMFA section 2509(a); and

b)   attorney's fees and costs, as authorized by FMFA section 2509(c).

E.   Template for Pleading Statutory Cause of Action

Below is a template that may be useful for pleading a statutory cause of action.

Template for Pleadings

Caption

• Identify the court and venue.

• Name all parties on each side.

• Identify the pleading as a complaint or petition.

• Include other information required by relevant rules.

Commencement

• Follow local conventions.

• Stipulate short forms for the parties if desired.

Procedural Issues (if required)

• Establish the court's subject-matter jurisdiction.

• Establish the court's personal jurisdiction over each defendant.

• Establish venue.

Template for Pleadings (cont.)

Body of Pleading

<u>First or Only Count</u>

- Identify the statute (if the pleading is based on a statute).

- Allege facts showing the basis of each defendant's legal duty.

- Allege facts showing each defendant's wrongful conduct.

- Set out causal nexus between wrongful conduct and harm to Plaintiff.

- Set out the resulting items of damage.

- Set out as an <u>un</u>-numbered allegation the demand for judgment, stating all requested relief.

<u>Subsequent Counts</u>

- Same as for first count.

- Use re-allegation selectively: if you use an initial re-allegation clause, choose only facts that fit the theory of the subsequent count.

Signature Block

CHAPTER 3

ANSWERS (DEFENSIVE PLEADINGS)

■ ■ ■

I. Purpose of the Answer

In the answer, the defendant identifies which issues are genuinely in dispute by responding to the allegations in the plaintiff's complaint. The defendant also raises any available affirmative defenses in the answer.

The principles that apply to drafting an answer to a complaint generally apply to *any* responsive pleading, including an answer (or reply) to a counter-claim, an answer to a cross-claim, and so on.

II. Time for Responding by Answer

Federal Rules 12(a) and 12(b) address the timing-related rules for the defendant's response. If practicing in federal court, an attorney must become familiar with the timing requirements for filing an answer. There are many time periods to keep straight, and the defendant must be alert to deadlines set by various rules of procedure, local rules, and court orders.

State courts have their own rules governing the time for filing the answer and for presenting a state's equivalent to the Rule 12 defenses.[1]

III. Failure of Defendant to Respond (Default)

If a defendant does not file a pre-answer motion, then the defendant must file an answer. What happens if the defendant, for whatever reason, simply does not respond at all?

Federal Rule of Civil Procedure 55 states that the clerk of court must enter the party's default if a party against whom a judgment for affirmative relief is sought fails to plead or defend and if the other party produces affidavits to establish the failure.[2] Depending on the circumstances, the clerk may be able to enter a default judgment[3] or the plaintiff may apply to the court for a default judgment.[4] If the defendant never appears and the plaintiff provides adequate support for the relief Plaintiff seeks, the court may enter judgment against the defendant.[5]

In general, federal law does not favor default judgments,[6] and Federal Rule 55(c) gives a court broad discretion to set aside a default judgment. Grounds for doing so are set out in Federal Rule 60(b) and include "mistake, inadvertence, surprise, or excusable neglect." To understand the facts that influence a court to set a default judgment aside you must look to the case law.

Guidance from the federal circuits varies. For example, the U.S. Ninth Circuit Court of Appeals stated that judgment by default is a "drastic step appropriate only in extreme circumstances."[7] The Second Circuit Court of Appeals, emphasizing the great weight given to resolution of cases on their merits,[8] said that default judgments are reserved for rare occasions.[9] In contrast, the Seventh Circuit Court of Appeals said in a 1995 case that the Seventh Circuit court does *not* disfavor default judgment, "though a default judgment should not be considered a ready response to all litigant misbehavior."[10]

State courts, like some federal courts, may disfavor default judgments.[11] For example, the Georgia Court of Appeals said that default judgment is a "drastic sanction" that a court should apply only in extreme situations.[12] A Wisconsin court said that a default judgment is appropriate only if the party on whom the sanction is imposed has engaged in "egregious conduct."[13] As in federal court, you must consult the case law to understand the actual practice.

IV. Responses to the Allegations

A. Allowable Responses in State and Federal Court

Federal Rule 8(b) gives a defendant the following options for responding to an allegation in a pleading that requests affirmative relief:

- Admit the allegation.

- Deny the allegation.

- State that Defendant lacks sufficient knowledge to form a belief concerning the truth of the allegation.

- A combination response, such as stating that Defendant admits certain stipulated allegations and denies the remainder (or lacks sufficient knowledge to form a belief concerning the truth of the remaining allegations).

If the defendant admits the allegation, the matter is treated as established. If the defendant responds to an allegation with a denial or with a statement that the defendant lacks knowledge, the matter remains in dispute. Most state equivalents to Rule 8(b) are similar to the federal rule regarding available responses.[14]

An attorney should use the response that the defendant lacks sufficient knowledge only when the defendant *truly* lacks sufficient knowledge.[15] For example, it would be unwise for a building contractor who was operating without a license to respond "without knowledge" to an allegation that the contractor was, in fact, operating without a license.[16] As a federal court in the District of Columbia pointed out, a party must comply with the requirement of honesty in pleading.[17]

Moreover, a party may have a duty to make reasonable efforts to obtain knowledge of a fact.[18] Some states' rules of procedure address this issue. For example, in Pennsylvania a party claiming insufficient knowledge or information to form a belief as to an allegation's truth must state that the party has made a reasonable investigation.[19]

If a defendant fails to respond to an allegation (other than one relating to the amount of damages), the allegation is deemed admitted.[20] To avoid unintentional omissions—which under Federal Rule 8(b)(6) and its state equivalents turn into unintended *admissions*—we advise you to respond systematically to each individual allegation, paragraph by paragraph.

A general denial is an across-the-board denial disputing *all* of the pleading's material issues. A general denial is permitted in appropriate circumstances under the federal rule if the party, *in good faith*, intends to deny all of a pleading's allegations (including jurisdictional grounds).[21] Otherwise, as stated in Rule 8(b)(3), a party who does not intend to deny all the allegations must either specifically deny designated allegations or generally deny all allegations except those that the party specifically admits.

Some states prohibit a general denial. For example, New Jersey's rule requires that the defendant "make the denials as specific denials of designated allegations or paragraphs."[22] Missouri's rule regarding general denials is similar.[23] Pennsylvania's rule states that a general denial has the effect of an *admission*.[24] Know where your state stands on general denials.

B.　Drafting Responses in Federal or State Court

1.　Articulating the Three Basic Responses

If you intend to admit or deny an entire paragraph, state your intention accordingly. Below are examples of how one might sufficiently frame an admission and a denial:

Examples: Admission and Denial

3.   Defendant admits each allegation in paragraph 3 of the complaint.

4.   Defendant denies each allegation in paragraph 4 of the complaint.

One way to frame an allegation of insufficient knowledge is simply to track the language of the applicable rule of procedure. Using Federal Rule 8(b)(5) as our guide, we recommend the following response:

Example: Allegation of Insufficient Knowledge

7.   Defendant lacks knowledge sufficient to form a belief concerning the truth of each allegation set forth in paragraph 7.

A careful, systematic response to each allegation of each paragraph is likely to save you time and your client legal fees in the long run. If possible, each paragraph should be numbered to correspond with the paragraph to which it relates, as shown in the example below.

Examples: Corresponding Paragraph Numbers

1.   Defendant admits each allegation in paragraph 1 of the complaint for jurisdictional purposes only.

2.   Defendant denies each allegation in paragraph 2 of the complaint.

3.   Defendant lacks sufficient knowledge to form a belief concerning the truth or falsity of each allegation in paragraph 3 of the complaint.

While many attorneys prefer the terse "admit," "deny," and "insufficient knowledge to form a belief as to truth," failing to specify in your responses the paragraph to which you are responding could lead to trouble if you accidentally skip a paragraph in a pleading containing numerous paragraphs.

Another way to run into trouble is using an approach such as the following: "Defendant denies all allegations in all paragraphs of the pleading except for paragraphs 2–4, 11, 17–18, 30–36, 45, and 52–56, which Defendant admits." When using such an approach, it is very easy to admit an allegation unintentionally.

2.   Admitting an Allegation in Part

If you believe in good faith that only some allegations in a paragraph are true, Federal Rule 8(b)(3) and its state equivalents require that you identify those that you intend to admit and deny the remainder. To ensure that you are admitting only those facts that you intend to admit, we strongly recommend that you track *all* of the language of the original allegation, even if you end up repeating most of the paragraph you are answering. Having done so, make sure to deny (or allege lack of sufficient knowledge of) the remainder of the allegation.

We strongly recommend that you do not reframe the language of the original allegation because doing so may cause you to inadvertently admit an allegation that is not even in the complaint. Suppose that an original allegation in a complaint reads as follows:

Example: Allegations in a Paragraph of a Complaint

3.   From approximately January 1, 2005 to the time of filing this complaint, Defendant, through its laboratories, manufactured a lozenge known as "Kwit–Kwik" that was intended to be used by members of the public who wished to stop smoking. Defendant marketed "Kwit–Kwik" to the public through a national advertising campaign and distributed the drug through its agents. In addition, Defendant manufactured a more potent version of the lozenge, known as "Tar–Ban," made available only by prescription.

Suppose that your client is not in a position to deny any part of the paragraph except the final sentence. To ensure that you admit only the parts of this paragraph that you intend to admit, even if this amounts to a substantial part of the paragraph, you might respond as follows:

**Example: Partial Admission of Allegations
in a Paragraph**

3.   Defendant denies each allegation in paragraph 3, except that Defendant admits the following:

(a) From approximately January 1, 2005 to the time the complaint was filed, Defendant, through its laboratories, manufactured a lozenge known as "Kwit–Kwik" that is intended to be used by members of the public who wished to stop smoking.

(b) Defendant markets "Kwit–Kwik" to the public through a national advertising campaign and distributes the drug through its agents.

You could instead respond in the opposite order: first admitting the specific allegations and then denying the remainder. Either way would comply with Federal Rule 8(b)(3) and its equivalents. While not required, indented format makes it easy for the court to determine which issues the defendant is admitting (and taking off the table).

Note that a response such as the one above identifies for the court the *exact* allegations that the defendant is prepared to admit. We recommend that you do not specify the allegations that you intend to deny: if you inadvertently omit one, that allegation would be deemed admitted.

3. Avoiding Evasive Responses

Federal Rule 8(b)(2) and many states' rules require that a denial "fairly" respond to the substance of the plaintiff's allegations. Though rules of procedure typically do not spell out the exact form and words to be included in a response, the trial court will see through an evasive response. The following is a classic evasive response:

Example: Evasive Response

3. Defendant neither admits nor denies the allegations in paragraph 3 but puts Plaintiff to her proof.

Some federal courts have said that such a refusal to take a position is not acceptable. One federal court stated that such a refusal violates Federal Rule 8(b), which requires a defendant to respond to *all* allegations.[25] The states' treatment of such refusals may vary. An attorney should check the state law because the consequences of unfamiliarity could be detrimental to the case: for example, Pennsylvania's rule relating to responses states that a mere demand for proof "shall have the effect of an *admission*."[26]

Another evasion tactic is to state that a document on which the plaintiff's allegation relies "speaks for itself," as illustrated below:

6. Regarding paragraph 6, Defendant is without knowledge or information sufficient to form a belief as to the truth or falsity of each allegation contained in paragraph 6, except that the Lease speaks for itself.

A federal district court in Illinois clearly rejected that form of evasiveness:

This Court has been attempting to listen to such written materials for years (in the forlorn hope that one will indeed give voice) but until some such writing does break its silence, this Court will continue to require pleaders to employ one of the three alternatives that *are* permitted by Rule 8(b) in response to all allegations about the contents of documents.[27]

We recommend that you respond candidly to the allegations in the complaint. Since allegations that are not denied are deemed admitted, an evasive or disingenuous response could be deemed by the court to be an admission. Furthermore, if you fail to plead candidly and in good faith, you might end up in violation of Rule 11 or its state equivalent.

"Strategy" is not a good reason for evading the truth. Furthermore, it is not good strategy to keep in dispute matters on which your client cannot prevail. Doing so undermines your credibility with the court and increases the time and cost required to resolve matters that are legitimately in dispute.

4.   Responding to Conclusory Allegations

An attorney who represents a defendant in federal court is likely to encounter allegations containing some conclusions of law, as Rule 8(a) does not prohibit them. As federal courts have pointed out, legal conclusions are an "integral part of the federal notice pleading regime."[28] Federal Rule 8(b) and most states' rules do not specifically address how you should respond to an allegation that is wholly conclusory. However, it may be risky to leave a conclusory statement unaddressed because Rule 8(b) says that if an allegation requires a response and is not denied, it is deemed admitted. For example, a federal court in New Mexico stated that a defendant must respond to a legal conclusion in one of the three ways that Rule 8 authorizes.[29]

Many state courts may agree, but not all of them do. In a Pennsylvania case, for example, the court said that conclusions of law (i.e., statements of a legal duty that do not state the facts from which the duty arises) do not compel a response.[30]

If you practice in a court that requires a response to legal conclusions and you receive a pleading that contains both legal conclusions and factual allegations, it may be difficult to decide how to respond to the legal conclusions. Suppose that the pleading says the following: "Defendant Cupples owed a duty of reasonable care to Plaintiff."

Assuming that you are prepared to admit the underlying facts that establish a duty of reasonable care, how do you respond? How do you respond if you are not prepared to admit the underlying facts? If the matter of duty is in dispute, you can deny the allegation. If it is not in dispute and if it would save time and expense to get the issue off the table, you might consider admitting it. Check the practice conventions in your area.

5.   Responding to Allegations Relating to Another Defendant

If there are several named defendants in an action, the question arises whether a defendant must respond to the paragraphs that do not apply to that defendant (and if so, how that defendant should respond). In one case, a federal district court said that the defendant's failure to respond to allegations relating to other defendants violated federal pleading standards. Pointing out that Federal Rule 8(b) requires that a defendant answer *all* allegations, the court said that no attorney or party has authority under the rule to decline to answer such an allegation.[31]

If the allegation is true and if you know that it is true, you may admit it. If you sincerely are unable to answer, you might try providing a sincere response that meets the requirements of the rule, such as the following:

3. The allegations of paragraph 3 do not apply to Defendant. Defendant therefore lacks sufficient knowledge and information to form a belief about the truth of the allegation as applied to the other defendant.

V. Pleading Affirmative Defenses

A. Characteristics of an Affirmative Defense

An affirmative defense consists of new facts (i.e., facts not addressed in the plaintiff's pleading) that the defendant may raise in the answer. A federal court in New Mexico recently described an affirmative defense as a defense that does not negate the elements of the plaintiff's claim but instead precludes liability, even if all of the elements of the plaintiff's claim are proven.[32] An affirmative defense "avoids" liability, either wholly or partly, by alleging new grounds of excuse, justification or other negating matter.[33] Whereas the plaintiff has the burden of proof regarding the plaintiff's cause of action, the defendant has the burden of proof regarding affirmative defenses.[34]

A defendant might waive an affirmative defense by failing to timely plead it.[35] Thus, defendants' attorneys must be vigilant in assessing available affirmative defenses and in timely raising them.[36]

Unless a court orders a reply to the answer (an unusual circumstance in federal court), the plaintiff does not have to respond to the allegations in the affirmative defenses. Under the federal rule, and in most states, allegations in a pleading to which no responsive pleading is required or permitted are deemed denied.[37]

B. Typical Affirmative Defenses

1. Affirmative Defenses Listed in Procedural Rules

Federal Rule 8(c) lists certain affirmative defenses, though the list is not intended to be exhaustive:

1.	accord and satisfaction	10.	injury by fellow servant
2.	arbitration and award	11.	laches
3.	assumption of risk	12.	license
4.	contributory negligence	13.	payment
5.	duress	14.	release
6.	estoppel	15.	res judicata
7.	failure of consideration	16.	statute of frauds
8.	fraud	17.	statute of limitations
9.	illegality	18.	waiver

Most states have similar or identical rules enumerating certain common affirmative defenses.[38]

2.   Other Affirmative Defenses

Other affirmative defenses exist besides those listed in the federal rule. For example, Colorado's rule listing affirmative defenses states that a pleader must affirmatively plead "any mitigating circumstances to reduce the amount of damage."[39] The Illinois rule requires the pleading of *any* facts that seek "to avoid the legal effect of or defeat the cause of action set forth in the complaint."[40] The Wright & Miller treatise lists some of the affirmative defenses that the federal courts have recognized and provides a useful discussion.[41]

Though most lawyers raise their Rule 12(b) defenses by motion, a lawyer in federal court who does not file a Rule 12 motion can raise in the answer any Rule 12(b) defense as an affirmative defense.[42] The same is true in most states. If you raise such a defense in your answer, we recommend that you state the grounds for the defense (just as you would if filing a motion) to apprise the court and notify the plaintiff of the defect.[43]

C.   Drafting an Affirmative Defense

1.   Sufficiency of Defense

Federal Rule of Civil Procedure 8(d) requires all pleadings to be simple, direct, and concise. Although some affirmative defenses seem to require some degree of factual detail (e.g., contributory negligence), many common affirmative defenses can be alleged concisely while still incorporating the necessary factual support, as shown in the following examples.

Examples: Concise, Fact–Driven Affirmative Defenses

Release:
On May 22, 2012, Plaintiff signed a release, in return for a payment of $20,000, which discharged Defendant from any further obligations to Plaintiff arising from the circumstances alleged in the complaint. The release is attached.

Accord and Satisfaction:
On November 11, 2011, Defendant delivered to Plaintiff a check for $16,000. The parties had agreed that Plaintiff would accept this amount in full satisfaction of Plaintiff's claim.

Statute of Limitations:
Plaintiff's claim for negligence accrued on December 30, 2008. When Plaintiff filed the complaint (January 1, 2012), the 2–year statute of limitations for a negligence action had run. The claim is therefore time-barred.

At present, federal courts are grappling with the question whether the plausibility standard of *Twombly* and *Iqbal* (discussed in Chapter 2) applies to affirmative defenses. Before those decisions, most federal circuits required very little to establish an affirmative defense. For example, the Fifth Circuit Court of Appeals had suggested that merely pleading the name of the affirmative defense would be sufficient.[44] Similarly, in one case, the Sixth Circuit Court of Appeals had stated that the following was a sufficient statement of a defense based on res judicata: "Plaintiffs' claims are barred by the doctrine of res judicata."[45]

At the time of this writing (after *Twombly* and *Iqbal*), no federal Court of Appeals has ruled on whether the plausibility standard applies to affirmative defenses.[46] Meanwhile, a sea change is occurring in some federal districts.[47]

As of the time of this writing, most of the federal district courts that have considered the issue hold that the plausibility does apply to affirmative defenses.[48] In district courts where the plausibility standard is applied, the courts may now require more facts to establish affirmative defenses. Just identifying the defense might not do. Check the practice in federal district courts in your state.

Note that application of a plausibility standard to affirmative defenses presumably would eliminate or significantly curtail the practice, common in some jurisdictions, of incorporating in the answer a list of so-called "boilerplate" defenses. In alleging boilerplate defenses, the attorney lists in the answer all affirmative defenses that the attorney can think of, whether applicable or not, to avoid a waiver.[49]

While some courts apparently tolerate this practice, a federal judge in Michigan pointed out that boilerplate defenses simply clutter the docket and create unnecessary work;[50] furthermore, they are unnecessary since Rule 15 allows amendments to the answer and "counsel should therefore feel no need in this court to window-dress pleadings early for fear of losing defenses later." Applying the plausibility standard to affirmative defenses, the court said that it would require attorneys to accept a continuing obligation to eliminate unnecessary boilerplate from their pleadings.[51]

Some federal district courts have concluded that the plausibility standard does not apply to affirmative defenses.[52] For example, a federal court in New Mexico contends that the plausibility standard applies only to pleadings in complaints drafted pursuant to Rule 8(a), not to affirmative defenses raised in an answer.[53]

Until the governing Circuit Court has stepped in, a defendant in federal court must determine the law in the particular district because district courts in the same circuit have sometimes been unable to agree.

Most states' rules of procedure relating to affirmative defenses are similar to the federal rule, though as of the time of this writing, state courts do not generally apply a plausibility standard to affirmative defenses. The tolerance of state court judges for "boilerplate defenses" may vary.

2.   Pleading Inconsistently, Hypothetically, and Alternatively

Federal Rules 8(d)(2) and (3) and their state equivalents authorize a party to plead inconsistently, hypothetically, and alternatively. According to the rules, the defendant's responses to the plaintiff's allegations need not be factually consistent with the defendant's affirmative defenses.

Suppose that a defendant owns an apartment building that has two stairways. The lights for one stairway are not working, but the lights for the other stairway are. One evening, the plaintiff falls while using the poorly lighted stairway.

In the complaint, the plaintiff alleges that the stairs were inadequately lighted. The defendant could plead inconsistently and hypothetically. For example, the defendant could deny that the stairs were inadequately lighted and could also raise the affirmative defense of contributory negligence (by alleging that *if* the stairs were inadequately lighted, the plaintiff was contributorily negligent for descending the inadequately lighted stairs). Pleading alternatively, the defendant might allege either that the plaintiff ran down the stairs in order to start a fight or that the plaintiff descended the stairs while intoxicated.

3.   Formatting Affirmative Defenses

Federal Rule 10(b) applies to defenses as well as to claims and causes of action. That rule and its equivalents require that a party state defenses in numbered paragraphs, each limited as far as practicable to a single set of circumstances. We recommend that you draft separate headings for each affirmative defense, as illustrated below:

- First Affirmative Defense: Contributory Negligence.

- Second Affirmative Defense: Accord and Satisfaction.

In some federal and state courts, the responses and affirmative defenses are numbered consecutively from start to finish (i.e., the answer would not contain two paragraphs numbered "1"). The practice in state courts and among federal courts regarding the numbering of paragraphs may vary; consult the applicable rules.

VI.   Responding to the Answer Via Reply

Typically, the pleadings close after the claim for affirmative relief is answered. For this reason, no further pleading is usually permitted or required. The plaintiff is usually deemed to have denied the allegations in the answer, including affirmative defenses. There are exceptions to this general practice. For example, Federal Rule 7(a)(7) permits the court to order a plaintiff to reply to an answer if the answer raises a new matter that the court determines requires a specific response. If the court orders a reply, the plaintiff must respond as ordered.

VII. Defenses Relating to Certain Special Matters

A. Challenges to Capacity

In federal court and in most states, the plaintiff is not required to allege the capacity of a named party to sue and be sued.[54] If the defendant wishes to raise the issue of capacity, Federal Rule 9(a)(2) requires that the defendant do so by a "specific denial." In short, the defendant's lawyer must plead lack of capacity as a defense.

B. Non–Occurrence or Non–Performance of Conditions Precedent

Under Federal Rule 9(c), and in many states, the plaintiff can allege in general terms that all conditions precedent to the filing of the action have occurred or been satisfied. In a recent case, a federal court in Florida said that a plaintiff sufficiently meets this standard by stating in the complaint that "all conditions precedent to the filing of this action have either occurred or been waived."[55] In an insurance case, a federal court in California determined that the following statement was sufficient: "At all times herein mentioned, Plaintiff paid all premiums on the policy as they became due and payable, *and has otherwise performed all the required terms and conditions of the policy.*"[56]

While a plaintiff can allege in general terms the occurrence or performance of conditions precedent, a defendant in federal court who wishes to challenge the allegation must allege with particularity in the answer the non-occurrence or non-performance of the condition precedent.[57] Otherwise, a court could treat the plaintiff's allegation as admitted.[58] Check applicable law.

C. Defense Based on Fraud or Mistake

Federal Rule 9(b) requires fraud or mistake to be pleaded with particularity, and the rule applies to defensive pleadings as well as to pleadings seeking affirmative relief. If you must plead a defense based on mistake or fraud (or "sounding in" fraud), the safest approach is to plead facts in support of each element with the maximum amount of specificity possible.[59] As a federal court in Georgia remarked, Federal Rule 9(b) requires "the who, what, when, where, and how" of the circumstances constituting any misrepresentation.[60]

VIII. Motion to Strike a Legal Defense

After a defendant files the answer, Federal Rule 12(f) permits the plaintiff to move to strike any insufficient defense. As a federal court in

California pointed out, a Rule 12(f) motion might be useful for excising improper materials from pleadings but is typically disfavored because of its potential for use as a delaying tactic and because of the strong policy favoring resolution of cases on the merits.[61] Below is an example of a motion to strike a defense in a state pleading.

Plaintiff's Motion to Strike Affirmative Defenses

Plaintiff, Hanna Kwok, respectfully moves this court, for reasons explained in the attached memorandum, to strike from the answer the following affirmative defenses to Plaintiff's action based on the Calibama Deceptive and Unfair Trade Practices Act (CDUTPA):

    (1)   Defendant's Second Defense (Contributory Negligence). This defense is unsupported by factual allegations and is inapplicable to Plaintiff's action for violation of CDUPTA.

    (2)   Defendant's Third Defense (Assumption of Risk). This defense is unsupported by factual allegations and is inapplicable to Plaintiff's action for violation of CDUTPA.

The listed defenses are mere boilerplate extracted from a list of boilerplate defenses commonly attached to answers by some lawyers in this jurisdiction. For reasons stated in the attached memorandum, these boilerplate defenses have no application here. Accordingly, Plaintiff asks that the court strike these defenses.

For procedure in your jurisdiction regarding motions to strike, consult the applicable rules.

CHAPTER 4

MOTIONS

■ ■ ■

I. Introduction to Motions

A motion is a request to the court for an order. For strategic reasons, many lawyers file one or more motions before filing an answer. The range of potential motions is as extensive as the range of potential orders that the attorney is prepared to request from a court. Below are a few common motions:

- Motion for more definite statement.

- Motion for extension of time.

- Motion to dismiss for failure to state a claim.

- Motion to compel discovery.

- Motion for summary judgment.

- Motion to set aside judgment.

- Motion for new trial.

- Motion for attorney's fees.

Case law, statutes, rules of procedure, local rules, and other law may all serve as a basis for motions.

II. Motion Practice Generally

A. In Federal Court

1. Requirements for Filing a Motion

(a) Preparation of the Motion

Federal Rule 7(b)(1) requires that every application to a district court for an order be made by *written* motion unless the motion is made during a hearing or trial. Because many federal district courts have implemented local rules for motion practice, an attorney must be familiar with a court's relevant local rules. It is probably safe to assume that most courts require a concise and straightforward account of exactly what you want the court to do, your reasons for requesting the action, and legal authority.

The motion itself is usually simple to draft. The bulk of the work for a motion (or for opposition to a motion) goes into the supporting documents: e.g., the supporting memorandum discussed in the next section. Useful forms for drafting motions exist, and we encourage you to make use of them. As of this writing, for example, the federal court system's website (www.uscourts.gov) has a collection of forms.

Be sure that you are familiar with local rules for filing a motion. For example, one Federal District Court imposes on a party who wishes to file most types of motions the following duties:

- to confer or attempt to confer with opposing counsel,

- to attempt in good faith to resolve the matter contained in the motion, and

- to include in the motion an affirmation that he or she has complied with this requirement.[1]

Federal Rule 7(b)(2) and its state equivalents require that a motion meet the same formal requirements as a pleading. As discussed in Chapter 1, a court may develop its own rules for the captioning of documents. For example, a local rule for the Federal District Court for Rhode Island requires every motion to bear a title identifying the party filing it and the precise nature of the motion.[2] A federal district court in Vermont states that it will not consider any motion unless the word "motion" appears in the title.[3] Absent a more specific requirement, it is a good idea to identify in your caption the purpose of the motion and the party from whom it originates: e.g., "Defendant's Motion for Summary Judgment." Check your court's captioning requirements before you begin to draft your motion.

The signature requirements of Federal Rule 11 apply to motions, as well as pleadings.[4] By signing a motion, the attorney certifies (among other things) that the motion is not presented for any improper purpose, such as to harass, cause unnecessary delay, or needlessly increase the cost of litigation.

Local rules may address the consequences of filing baseless motions or of filing for an improper purpose. For example, a local rule of the U.S. District Court of South Carolina states: "Where the Court finds that a motion is frivolous or filed for delay, sanctions may be imposed against the party or counsel filing such motion."[5]

(b) Documents Filed in Support of the Motion

In support of the motion, an attorney in federal court will usually submit a memorandum of law setting out the attorney's legal arguments and supporting authorities. The document may have different names in different jurisdictions. For example, in the Western District of Missouri, the District Court refers to a written statement in support of a motion as a "suggestion."[6] In Nebraska, it is called a "brief."[7] In other courts, it is called a memorandum of points and authorities. Whatever the document is called in a particular jurisdiction, if you fail to file a memorandum of law when one is required, the court may deny or refuse to consider the motion.

There is some variation among federal courts as to whether a supporting memorandum is required. For example, the district courts for the Eastern and Western Districts of Kentucky require memoranda of law for all motions other than routine motions (such as motions for extensions of time).[8] The district court for the Northern District of Florida requires a memorandum for all motions *except* as specified in its rule.[9] An attorney must be familiar with the applicable rules.

Many courts set page limits for supporting memoranda. In the Southern District of West Virginia, for example, the page limit is 20 double-spaced pages. A memorandum exceeding that length is an "oversized memorandum." A party must file a motion to receive permission to exceed the page limit.[10]

A motion may be supported by affidavits or other exhibits. Federal Rule 6(c)(2) provides that affidavits in support of a motion must be served with the motion. Pursuant to local rules, some courts require the attorney to submit with the motion all documentary evidence that the party intends to submit in support of the motion.[11] (Be attentive also to the time guidelines in Federal Rule 6(c)(1)).

Courts also may require an attorney to include with the motion a proposed order (i.e., the order that the attorney is requesting the court to issue).[12] (From a tactical standpoint, it is a good idea to draft a proposed order, as it is a timesaver for the court and may incline the court to grant your motion as you drafted it.)

Make sure that you understand exactly which documents the court requires you to attach to the motion. Courts that still accept paper filings may have specific requirements about which documents should be attached to motions and which should be submitted to the court separately.

2. Availability of Oral Hearing on a Motion

Federal Rule 78(b) states that a court may, by rule or order, provide for a motion to be determined on written briefs *without* an oral hearing, though a court may allow the party to request an oral hearing.

Procedures for obtaining a hearing vary. For example, the local rule for the Southern District of California states that motions "must" be decided on oral argument but gives the judge the discretion to decide the motion without oral argument.[13] In other courts, oral argument is the exception to the general practice. For example, a local rule from Nebraska states that the court generally does not permit oral argument or evidentiary hearings on motions.[14] A party who is requesting an oral hearing must explain why it is necessary and must provide an estimate of the time the party expects it to take.[15] Similarly, the Middle District of North Carolina provides that motions are usually decided on the motion papers and briefs without an oral hearing, though counsel can alert the court to any special considerations warranting a hearing.[16] Some courts may allow oral argument on a motion to be conducted by telephone.[17]

3.   Notice of Motion

Typically, a motion is filed along with a separate document: a notice stating the party's intention to present the motion and the date of any applicable hearing (check your local rules). Below is an example of such a notice:

[Caption]

To: Deborah Cupples, Attorney for Heath Technologies, Inc.

Please take notice that I will be bringing this motion for hearing before the Honorable Barbara Morton at 2601 Federal Plaza, Gatortown, Florida, on February 28, 2011, at 3:00 pm of that day or as soon afterwards as the motion can be heard.

February 11, 2011

Nicholas Temple-Smith

Nicholas Temple-Smith, Counsel for Defendant
1100 NW 6th Street, Suite 4-A
Gatortown, Florida 32000
(555) 555-5555
Templesmith@TempleSmith.org
Florida Bar Attorney Number: 000000

---

4.   Opposition to Motion

If you file a written motion to which the other party objects, the other party is entitled to file a written response. After receiving the response, an attorney may be permitted to file a reply. The content of the reply may be restricted to discussing only new matters that were raised in the response.[18] In federal court, local rules govern the procedure.

B.   Motion Practice in State Court

Though overall motion practice among the states may be similar, the specifics may vary. You will have to learn the rules in force in the state where you practice. Rules governing motion practice may appear in sources other than the state's rules of procedure, such as in the rules of practice for a particular court or in local rules.

III. Pre–Answer Motions

A. Objections and Defenses Usually Raised by Motion

1. Overview of Rule 12(b) Defenses

Federal Rule 12 and many of its state equivalents[19] provide that every defense to any claim in the initial pleading can be raised in the responsive pleading (usually called an "answer"). Nevertheless, the defendant can raise certain defenses and objections by a pre-answer motion. Defenses available under Rule 12 or its equivalents address preliminary matters that courts want you to take care of as early as possible.

Under Federal Rule 12(b), you may use the pre-answer motion to attack procedural defects in the initial pleading. The 12(b) defenses are as follows:

1) the court lacks subject matter jurisdiction.

2) the court lacks personal jurisdiction over the defendant.

3) the venue (location) of the action is improper.

4) the process served on the defendant was insufficient.

5) the service of the process was insufficient.

6) the plaintiff failed to state a claim on which relief can be granted.

7) an indispensable party is missing from the action.

Some states authorize the defendant to raise other defenses by a pre-answer motion. For example, Wisconsin's version of Rule 12 allows the defendant to raise by pre-answer motion the defenses of res judicata and statute of limitations.[20] California, Wisconsin and Missouri allow the defendant to raise the defense that the plaintiff lacks capacity to sue.[21] Missouri also allows the defendant to raise the defense of improper joinder of claims.[22]

If a defendant chooses *not* to file a pre-answer motion, Federal Rule 12 and most state equivalents permit the defendant to raise these defenses in the answer instead. However, in some jurisdictions, the defendant *must* raise by pre-answer motion any defense that is based on the court's lack of personal jurisdiction, on insufficient process, or on insufficient service of process; otherwise, the defense is waived.[23] As always, make sure that you know your own jurisdiction's rules.

2. Consolidation and Waiver of Rule 12(b) Defenses

Some Federal Rule 12(b) defenses focus on threshold procedural matters: i.e., the court's lack of personal jurisdiction, improper venue, improper process, and improper service of process. If the party chooses not to file a motion raising any Rule 12 defense, the party preserves the threshold defenses for the answer. On the other hand, a party who *does* file a motion under Rule 12 must raise in the motion certain Rule 12 defenses (i.e., the threshold defenses) if they are available at the time of filing. If a party makes a Rule 12 motion, the party cannot make another motion that raises one of the threshold Rule 12 defenses if that defense was available when the party made the earlier Rule 12 motion. Those defenses not raised in the initial motion are waived.[24]

Some defenses are not waived by a failure to consolidate them in a Rule 12 motion. The defense of lack of subject-matter jurisdiction is never waived; it can be raised at any time, even on appeal.[25] The defenses of failure to join a party and of failure to state a claim can be raised in a pleading that the court orders or allows, by a motion for judgment on the pleadings, or at trial.[26]

Check your state's Rule 12 equivalent to understand how and when to raise defenses to which the rule applies.

B. Rule 12 Defenses That Address Defects in the Pleading

1. Motion Challenging Legal Sufficiency of Pleading Requesting Affirmative Relief

(a) In Federal Court

A motion based on Rule 12(b)(6) tests the legal sufficiency of a complaint. The question that such a motion raises is whether the complaint contains sufficient substance for the court to allow the complaint to go on to the next stage of litigation. The purpose of the rule is to eliminate cases that are destined to fail due to fatal flaws in their legal premises.[27]

To get past a Rule 12(b)(6) attack, a complaint must state at least one claim. The question raised by a Rule 12(b)(6) defense is *not* whether the plaintiff is likely to prevail; it may even appear to the court that recovery is very unlikely.[28] On a motion to dismiss for failure to state a claim, the court is asking whether the court can discern the outlines of a situation for which the law grants a right to a remedy. All that the plaintiff needs is *one* cognizable claim. If the plaintiff pleads 10 counts and the court dismisses nine of them for not stating a claim for which relief can be granted, the one remaining claim can go forward.

As Chapter 2 explains, federal courts now use a two-part plausibility analysis. Because the case law under *Twombly* and *Iqbal* is still evolving, defendants who wish to challenge the sufficiency of pleadings under Rule 12(b)(6) are still struggling with the plausibility standard.

Since the question on a Federal Rule 12(b)(6) challenge is whether the claim is *legally sufficient* (not whether the plaintiff could prevail on the merits), a court generally should not consider the defendant's potential affirmative defenses.[29] There is an exception to this principle: if the defense appears on the face of the complaint, the defendant may attack the pleading via a motion to dismiss. If, for example, the plaintiff included facts in the pleading showing that the action is barred by a valid release, the inclusion of these facts undercuts the plaintiff's claim. In such a case, the defendant could challenge the pleading under Rule 12(b)(6) for failure to state a claim.[30] Thus, it is possible for a plaintiff's attorney to inadvertently "plead a client right out of court."[31]

A successful Rule 12(b)(6) motion cuts the plaintiff off at the threshold of the courthouse.[32] For this reason, a court granting a defendant's motion to dismiss almost always gives the plaintiff leave to re-plead.[33] Federal Rule 15 mandates a liberal amendment policy. Also, the U.S. Supreme Court has held that courts should freely give leave to amend.[34] The court may deny the motion (1) if granting the motion would cause undue delay or undue prejudice to the other party; (2) if the party seeking leave to amend is acting in bad faith, has dilatory motives, has had previous opportunities to amend and has failed to cure the deficiency; or (3) if amendment would be futile.[35]

Typically, a court allows the plaintiff to amend the complaint the first time its sufficiency is challenged, unless there is a valid basis for dismissing it without leave to amend.[36] For example, a court might dismiss the pleading without leave to amend if the pleading shows on its face that it was filed after the statute of limitations had run. Below is an example of a motion to dismiss in a federal diversity case.

[Caption]*

Defendant's Motion to Dismiss the Complaint

Defendant Stop-&-Go Stores, Inc. (Defendant) moves that this Court dismiss Plaintiff's Complaint on the following grounds.

As reflected in the attached Memorandum of Points and Authorities, Plaintiff has failed to state a plausible claim for relief. Plaintiff's complaint shows on its face that all the events on which this cause of action is based occurred on December 30, 2006. As such, this action is time-barred by the four-year limitations period for negligence set out in Fla. Stat. § 95.11(3)(a) (2011). This complaint should therefore be dismissed pursuant to Rule 12(b)(6).

[signature]*

(* Chapter 1 discusses captions and signatures)

In determining whether to grant a motion to dismiss for failure to state a claim, courts are confined to "the four corners of the complaint"[37] without reference to any evidence developed by the parties or to the defendant's possible defenses.

The "four corners" rule does not prevent the court from looking at an attached exhibit since the exhibit is part of the complaint. In addition, district courts have held that they can consider the record of the case,[38] public records,[39] and matters of which the court takes judicial notice (facts that are generally known).[40] Federal courts have also looked at documents that are *not* attached to the complaint but that are referenced or incorporated in the complaint. Some federal courts may consider unattached documents that are integral to the plaintiff's claim.[41] Other courts have extended the "four corners" rule even further.

(b) In State Court

(i) Differing Standards Among the States

Though many states have modeled their pleading standard on Federal Rule 8(a) and have in place an equivalent to Rule 12(b), most of those states have not adopted the "plausibility" standard used in federal court. To know how a particular state court determines the sufficiency of a claim, you must be familiar with the jurisdiction's pleading standards and its practice under its Rule 12(b) equivalent.

Regardless of the standard applied, state courts generally apply a liberal amendment policy to a pleading that is legally insufficient.[42] However, the standard for determining the sufficiency of a pleading varies among states, and the authors of this textbook want to make it clear that the attorney filing a motion to dismiss should not rely on classifications such as "notice pleading," "fact-pleading," or "plausibility standard."

Knowing how the courts label their pleading standards is no substitute for knowing what the courts *actually do* when applying their standards. The following subsections illustrate three states' differently labeled pleading standards. Despite the difference in labels, do the three courts actually require very different levels of factual detail? For a definitive answer, you must look to the case law or other resources, such as local practice manuals or bar journal articles.

(ii) Notice–Pleading Standard in State Court

Arizona is an example of a notice-pleading jurisdiction. Arizona's version of Rule 8 states that a pleading must contain a "short and plain statement of the claim showing that the pleader is entitled to relief."[43]

In 2008, the Arizona Supreme Court rejected the plausibility standard. The Court stated that because Arizona courts evaluate only the well-pleaded allegations, they do not consider mere conclusory statements; thus, if the complaint states only legal conclusions without supporting facts, Arizona's notice-pleading standard is not satisfied.[44] The Arizona Supreme Court pointed out that the federal notice-pleading standard has always been broader than Arizona's.[45]

(iii) Plausibility Standard in State Court

Nebraska, formerly a notice-pleading state,[46] recently adopted the *Twombly–Iqbal* plausibility standard.[47] Thus, a plaintiff in Nebraska must allege sufficient facts to state a claim that is plausible on its face.[48] What makes a claim plausible in Nebraska? According to the Nebraska Supreme Court, a court should accept the factual allegations as plausible "if they suggest the existence of the element and raise a reasonable expectation that discovery will reveal evidence of the element or claim."[49]

How much detail is required for a pleading to achieve plausibility in Nebraska? Apparently, the plaintiff must allege enough facts to "suggest" to the court that the elements of a cause of action are all present.[50] Furthermore, for the "suggestion" to be sufficient, the court must conclude that it is reasonable to expect that the facts will be backed up through discovery.[51]

(iv) Fact–Pleading Standards in State Court

Maryland is a fact-pleading jurisdiction. Maryland's rule requires that each averment be simple, concise, and direct and that the pleading contain "only such statements of fact as may be necessary to show the pleader's entitlement to relief," without "argument, unnecessary recitals of law, evidence, or documents, or any immaterial, impertinent, or scandalous matter."[52] At the same time, Maryland's rules also require that the pleading "shall contain a clear statement of the facts necessary to constitute a cause of action."[53]

How much detail is required? As a Maryland appellate court stated, "Essentially, a complaint is sufficient to state a cause of action even if it relates 'just the facts' necessary to establish its elements."[54] The Maryland Supreme Court stated that the allegations of fact necessary to state a cause of action in a simple factual situation are not the same as those necessary in a more complex factual situation.[55]

2. Motion for More Definite Statement

(a) In Federal Court

Sometimes a pleading may be so poorly written that the respondent does not know how to answer it. Under such circumstances, the party can move pursuant to Federal Rule 12(e) for a more definite statement. If the court grants the motion, the party ordered to provide the more definite statement must do so; otherwise, the court could strike that party's pleading or take other action.

Granting a more definite statement amounts to telling the party to spend more time polishing the pleadings. A federal court typically will not permit a defendant to use this device to force the plaintiff to supply in the complaint more details than the federal pleading standard requires[56] or information that may come out in discovery.[57] A federal district court typically grants a motion for more definite statement only for complaints that are so vague or ambiguous that the party cannot respond in good faith and without the risk of serious prejudice.[58]

The following is an example of a motion for more definite statement.

[caption]

Defendant's Motion for More Definite Statement

Pursuant to Federal Rule of Civil Procedure 12(e), Defendant Hotel Hogtown, Inc. (Defendant) moves the court for an order requiring Plaintiff to provide Defendant with a more definite statement of the allegations in the complaint for premises liability negligence.

1.   As explained in the attached memorandum of points and authorities, Plaintiff has not provided Defendant with sufficient information to enable Defendant to determine the date of the alleged incident or to identify which of Defendant's eight Alachua County motels was the location of the alleged incident. Without such information, Defendant is unable to respond to the complaint.

2.   For reasons set out in the attached memorandum of points and authorities, the allegations as to the nature and location of the alleged hazard are so vague and ambiguous as to be unintelligible. Defendant is unsure what the complaint is alleging as to the so-called "hazardous condition" and is unable to frame a response.

3.   Accordingly, the Court should grant this motion for more definite statement.

[signature]

(b) In State Court

Most states allow a party who is required to answer a complaint to move for a more definite statement; most use language that is based on or similar to that of Federal Rule 12(e).[59]

Be aware of variations in language, even if the state's rule is similar to the federal rule. Even if the state's rule is identical to the federal rule, a practitioner would need to consult case law to know how the rule is actually applied.

3. Motion to Strike

(a) In Federal Court

Rule 12(f) permits a district court, either on its own or on a party's motion, to strike from a pleading any "redundant, immaterial, impertinent, or scandalous matter." The function of the rule is to avoid expenditure of money and time resulting from litigation of spurious issues that can be dispensed with before trial.[60]

Motions to strike are disfavored. Pleadings in federal court are not intended to test an opponent's case,[61] and federal courts dislike delays that result in a party's merely "polishing the pleadings."[62] For this reason, federal courts may err on the side of denying the motion if there is doubt as to the possible relevance of the language that the movant seeks to eliminate.[63] The following is an example of a motion to strike.

[caption]

Defendant's Motion to Strike Scandalous Allegations from the Complaint

Pursuant to Federal Rule 12(f), Defendant Byers, Inc. (Defendant DBI) moves this court for an order

(1) Striking the third sentence of paragraph 7 of the complaint,

(2) Striking the first and last sentences of paragraph 15 of the complaint, and

(3) Striking the first and final sentence of paragraph 22 of the complaint.

Defendant DBI requests this relief because each of these sentences is untrue and therefore defamatory, inflammatory, and prejudicial to Defendant DBI. None of these sentences is relevant to Plaintiff's cause of action for negligent manufacture of Defendant DBI'S product (Count 1) or for breach of implied warranty of merchantability (Count 2), and none is supported by evidence. Furthermore, no evidence in support of any of these statements would be admissible in court. Finally, these remarks are an affront to this Court.

On these grounds, Defendant DBI respectfully requests an order striking the allegations and requiring Plaintiff to comply with this Court's Local Rule 82.02, which imposes on counsel and all parties the duty to conduct themselves civilly and in a manner tending to protect the dignity of the individuals who are before this Court.

[signature]

To grant a motion to strike allegations under Federal Rule 12(f), a court may require a showing that the movant is prejudiced by the inclusion in the pleading of the allegations *and* that the allegations are clearly not supported by admissible evidence or are immaterial.[64]

Allegations in a pleading are **redundant** if they are needlessly repeated;[65] counts are redundant if they are unnecessarily duplicative.[66]

An allegation is **immaterial** if it either has no bearing on the controversy[67] or is non-essential or unimportant to the controversy.[68] Courts have said that allegations are *not* immaterial unless they would be irrelevant "under any state of facts which could be proved in support of the claims being advanced" (i.e., if they have no possible bearing on the litigation).[69] Immateriality could be a ground for striking verbose, conclusory, or evidentiary allegations if their presence is prejudicial to the party moving to strike.[70]

Impertinent allegations are statements that are neither responsive nor relevant to the issues involved in the action.[71] As a federal district court in New York explained, a court usually will not grant a motion to strike an allegation as impertinent unless the movant can show that no evidence supporting the allegation would be admissible.[72]

Scandalous allegations are the most likely to be prejudicial to a party. A federal bankruptcy court defined *scandalous allegations* as statements that would cause a reasonable person to alter his or her opinion of a party when the statements are read in context.[73] For a federal court to strike an arguably scandalous allegation, the allegation must be irrelevant to the claims alleged and not supported by admissible evidence.[74] A party's offended feelings are not enough to get allegations stricken from a pleading if the allegations are relevant to the action.[75]

(b) In State Court

Most states have a rule of procedure that is similar to Federal Rule 12(f), allowing a court to strike from the pleading any redundant, immaterial, impertinent, or scandalous matter.[76] A few states' rules vary. For example, the Oregon rule provides that "the court may order stricken: (1) any sham, frivolous, or irrelevant pleading or defense or any pleading containing more than one claim or defense not separately stated; (2) any insufficient defense or any sham, frivolous, irrelevant, or redundant matter inserted in a pleading."[77] An attorney must check case law in the relevant jurisdiction to know what qualifies as *redundant, immaterial, impertinent,* or *scandalous.*

IV. Motions for Summary Adjudication

A. Summary Judgment

1. In Federal Court

(a) Purpose of Summary Judgment

According to the U.S. Supreme Court, a motion for summary judgment raises the threshold question of whether the case needs to go to trial.[78] A grant of a motion for summary judgment results in a judgment on the merits of the case. Through a motion for summary judgment, either party could conceivably bring about a full adjudication of the lawsuit without a trial.

Summary judgment is addressed by Federal Rule 56, which was recently revised. The U.S. Supreme Court said that a principal purpose of summary judgment is to isolate and dispose of factually unsupported claims or defenses.[79] The Second Circuit Court of Appeals said that summary judgment puts "a swift end to meritless litigation."[80] By disposing of unsupported or frivolous claims or defenses, summary judgment conserves public and private resources.

(b) Determination of a Motion for Summary Judgment

For a court to grant a motion for summary judgment, the moving party must demonstrate and the court must determine that there is no genuine dispute regarding a material fact.[81] As a district court in Illinois put it, summary judgment is "put up or shut up time" for the non-moving party, who must "show what evidence it has that would convince a trier of fact to accept its version of the events."[82]

The district court's task is to determine whether the evidence indicates sufficient disagreement to merit submission of the case to a jury or whether it is so one-sided that one party would prevail as a matter of law.[83] According to the U.S. Supreme Court, the question on summary judgment is not whether a jury *would* decide in favor of the non-moving party but whether "a fair-minded jury" *could* reasonably return a verdict for the non-moving party based on the evidence presented.[84]

Disputes as to material facts preclude the entry of summary judgment. The U.S. Supreme Court defined "material facts" as "facts that might affect the outcome of the suit under the governing law."[85] In determining whether there is a dispute as to any material fact, the court must treat the non-movant's evidence as true and must draw all reasonable inferences in the non-movant's favor.[86] A court may refuse to grant summary judgment if there is a dispute not as to the facts but as to the conclusions to be drawn from them.[87]

If the court determines that the material facts are undisputed and do *not* give rise to competing inferences, the court must apply the law to the facts to determine whether the moving party is entitled to summary judgment as a matter of law. If so, the court should grant the motion.

While a grant of a motion for summary judgment results in a final adjudication of the case on the merits, a *denial* of the motion does not. A denial of a motion for summary judgment does not settle, even tentatively, the merits of the case, since it results in a pretrial order that decides only one thing—that the case is to go to trial.[88]

(c) Procedures Related to Summary Judgment

(i) Time for Filing the Motion

Federal Rule 56(b) provides that "Unless a different time is set by local rule or the court orders otherwise, a party may file a motion for summary judgment at any time until 30 days after the close of all discovery."[89] Some local rules might supplement Rule 56(b); thus, you will need to consult local rules.

(ii) Materials in Support of the Motion

Some courts have adopted rules concerning the materials to be filed in support of a motion for summary judgment. For example, a local rule of a federal district court in Illinois requires that the moving party submit with the motion the following materials: (1) a supporting memorandum of law, (2) any affidavit or other material described in Rule 56(c), (3) a statement of material facts as to which there is no genuine issue and that entitle the party to judgment as a matter of law, (4) a description of the parties, and (5) all facts supporting venue and jurisdiction in the court.[90] Furthermore, the statement of facts is limited to no more than 80 short, separately numbered paragraphs.[91]

Federal Rule 56(c) provides that a party can support its contention that a fact is not in dispute by citing to particular parts of materials in the record. Such materials may include depositions, documents, electronically stored information, affidavits or declarations, stipulations, admissions, interrogatory answers, or other materials.

A careful drafter will ensure that any references to the record are supported by exact citations so that the court need not "ferret through" the record looking for support.[92] In a recent case, the U.S. Ninth Circuit Court of Appeals said that a party had waived its trade secret claims "by citing to two sets of exhibits, one totaling 57 pages in length and the other 141 pages in length … without providing explanation or specific line or page references."[93] As the Seventh Circuit Court of Appeals explained, "Judges are not like pigs, hunting for truffles buried in briefs."[94]

Alternatively, a party may support the assertion that a fact is or is not in dispute by showing (1) that the cited materials do not establish the absence or presence of a genuine dispute or (2) that the adverse party cannot produce admissible evidence to support the fact. In short, a party can point out to the court that the other party cannot back up its case with evidence.[95]

Below is an example of a motion for summary judgment.

[caption]

DEFENDANT'S MOTION FOR SUMMARY JUDGMENT

Defendant, Heath Equipment, Inc. (Defendant), submits this motion pursuant to Federal Rule of Civil Procedure 56 for summary judgment against Plaintiffs Mark Melbourne and Melbourne Farms, Inc.

As shown by the attached memorandum of law, record of the case, and affidavits, there is no genuine issue as to any material fact, and Defendant is entitled to judgment as a matter of law.

Pursuant to Local Rule 76.19(a), Defendant has incorporated within this motion Defendant's statement of the undisputed facts of the case and Defendant's supporting brief. Pursuant to Local Rule 55.01(c), Defendant has attached to this document a tabbed appendix containing supporting documents.

[DEFENDANT'S STATEMENT OF
UNDISPUTED FACTS]

[DEFENDANT'S SUPPORTING BRIEF]

Nicholas Temple, Counsel for Plaintiff
Temple and Southerland
2601 Brookwood Terrace
Gatortown, Florida 32000
Phone: (555) 555–5555
Email: Southerland@TemplesSoutherland.com

[certificate of service]

ATTACHED: APPENDIX OF EXHIBITS

Tab A: Contract for Lease of Used Combine

Tab B: Affidavit of Jeff Coates, Defendant's CEO)

Tab C: Affidavit of Nicholas Grafton, Defendant's warehouse manager

Tab D: Excerpts from Deposition of Plaintiff Mark Melbourne

A party filing or responding to a summary judgment motion can present testimony of witnesses by affidavit.[96] An affidavit must meet the standard of Rule 56(c)(4): i.e., the affidavit must be made on personal knowledge, it must set out facts that would be admissible, and it must show that the affiant is competent to testify regarding the matters to which the affidavit relates.

A sworn affidavit is no longer required: pursuant to 28 U.S.C. § 1746, unsworn declarations may be used under any rules that require a matter to be supported by a sworn statement if the unsworn declaration is made under penalty of perjury, and is written, subscribed, dated, and substantially in the following form:

> "I declare (or certify, verify, or state) under penalty of perjury that the foregoing is true and correct. Executed on (date). (Signature)."[97]

Federal Rule 56(h) provides for sanctions against a party who submits an affidavit or declaration "in bad faith or solely for delay." Pursuant to Rule 56(h), the court can order the party to pay reasonable expenses (including attorney's fees) that the other party incurred as a result. The rule also provides that the court can hold "an offending party or attorney" in contempt or can impose other sanctions.

(iii) Discovery Under Rule 56

Traditionally, courts have had wide latitude in controlling the scope of discovery.[98] According to the U.S. First Circuit Court of Appeals, parties are expected to use due diligence in pursuing discovery.[99] Courts have refused to allow additional discovery if the party's intent is to conduct a fishing expedition.[100]

2.   In State Court

The philosophy underlying state rules relating to summary judgment is similar to the philosophy underlying the federal rules. For example, a Kentucky court stated that the function of summary judgment is to terminate litigation when, as a matter of law, it appears that it would be impossible for the respondent to produce evidence at the trial warranting a judgment in his or her favor.[101] An Indiana court stated that the purpose of summary judgment is "to end litigation about which there can be no factual dispute and which may be determined as a matter of law."[102]

State courts recognize that some cases are not appropriate for summary judgment. For example, a Louisiana court pointed out that summary judgment is rarely appropriate in cases requiring judicial determination of subjective facts such as motive, intent, good faith or knowledge since a court on summary judgment cannot consider an issue's merits, make credibility determinations, evaluate testimony or weigh evidence.[103] The substantive and procedural requirements for filing a motion may differ from state to state.

Discussion of the varying substantive and procedural requirements for summary judgment in the state courts is beyond the scope of this textbook. To understand the standards and procedures that apply to summary judgment in your jurisdiction, consult your state's equivalent to Federal Rule 56.

B. Judgment on the Pleadings

1. In Federal Court

(a) Purpose and Effect of Motion Pursuant to Rule 12(c)

A motion for judgment on the pleadings, pursuant to Federal Rule 12(c), is another means for obtaining a summary adjudication of a case at the pre-trial stage. By issuing judgment on the pleadings, the court renders a judgment on the merits based on the contents of the pleadings.[104] Because a judgment on the pleadings resolves a case at a very early stage in the litigation, federal courts require that no material issue of fact remains and that the moving party be clearly entitled to the judgment.[105]

Either party can move for judgment on the pleadings, and the motion is available at the close of the pleadings.[106] "The close of pleadings" means the time at which all required or permitted pleadings have been served and filed.[107] The pleadings usually close after both the complaint and answer have been filed,[108] though if the defendant files a counter-claim or a cross-claim, the pleadings will not close before the responding party has had time to respond.[109]

In determining the motion, the court assumes that the well-pleaded factual allegations in the non-movant's pleadings are true and that all contravening allegations in the movant's pleadings are false.[110] The court will construe in the light most favorable to the non-movant the non-movant's factual allegations and the inferences reasonably drawn from them.[111]

Federal Rule 12(h)(2) permits a party to raise the issue of failure to state a claim via a Rule 12(c) motion for judgment on the pleadings. In instances in which the defendant waited too long to file a Rule 12(b)(6) motion, federal courts have treated motions for judgment on the pleadings as functionally equivalent to a Rule 12(b)(6) motion to dismiss.[112] In such cases, courts have stated that the distinction between Rule 12(b)(6) and Rule 12(c) is "purely formal," since courts analyze a motion for judgment on the pleadings according to the same standard as a motion to dismiss.[113] A Georgia bankruptcy court said, "The distinction is simply one of timing."[114]

In cases in which a motion for judgment on the pleadings is used to attack the sufficiency of a pleading, courts have applied the *Twombly–Iqbal* plausibility standard.[115]

Below is an example of a motion for judgment on the pleadings.

[caption]

DEFENDANT'S MOTION FOR JUDGMENT ON THE PLEADINGS

Defendant, Edward Swann, through his undersigned attorney, William Cupples, 2601 Federal Plaza, Suite 224, Gatortown, Florida 32001, 555–555–5555, email Cupples@Gatorpond.com, moves pursuant to Federal Rule of Civil Procedure 12(c) for a judgment on the pleadings. A copy of Defendant's proposed order is attached.

Defendant files this Rule 12(c) motion on the ground that the complaint shows on its face that it is barred as a matter of law. The complaint alleges facts showing that the matter is barred by both res judicata and the statute of limitations. Defendant Swann is therefore entitled to judgment as a matter of law.

Pursuant to Local Rule 98.01(b) governing dispositive motions, Defendant Swann's statement of the relevant facts follows. Pursuant to Local Rule 15.1(a), Defendant has separately filed a brief setting forth supporting points and authorities.

[STATEMENT OF RELEVANT FACTS]

[INCORPORATED MEMORANDUM OF LAW]

[signature/certificate of service]

(b) Conversion of Rule 12(c) Motion to Summary Judgment Motion

Under some circumstances, a federal district court may treat a motion for judgment on the pleadings as a motion for summary judgment. If the party submits matter that is "outside the pleadings" and the court decides to consider it, Federal Rule 12(d) requires the court to treat the motion as one for summary judgment. If outside matters are admitted, the court must ensure that all the parties get "a reasonable opportunity to present all the material pertinent to the motion."[116]

In determining motions pursuant to Rule 12(c), the court cannot consider materials "outside the pleadings." Various federal courts have determined that the following materials are not "outside the pleadings": (1) documents that are incorporated by reference in or that are integral to the pleadings,[117] (2) "indisputably authentic" documents that are attached to the motion to which neither party objects,[118] (3) public records,[119] and (4) any information that the court can judicially notice (facts that are generally known).[120]

The court has discretion whether to consider or exclude matters that are outside the pleadings.[121] The court therefore has discretion to determine whether to convert a Rule 12(c) motion to a motion for summary judgment.

2. In State Court

Not all states have a procedure for judgment on the pleadings, but most do. Many states' rules are identical or very similar to the federal rule. A number of states have procedures based on or similar to those under Federal Rule 12(c).[122]

To understand how judgment on the pleadings operates within a particular state, you must familiarize yourself with the applicable case law of that state. For example, the Supreme Court of North Dakota said that North Dakota courts may not grant judgment on the pleadings unless "it appears beyond doubt that the plaintiff can prove no set of facts in support of his claim which would entitle him to relief."[123]

Like the federal courts, state courts may require conversion of a motion for judgment on the pleadings to one for summary judgment if the trial court considers materials outside the pleadings.[124] The types of documents or other information considered to be "within" the pleadings varies. In Alabama, for example, a court can consider—without going "outside" the pleadings—documents attached to the complaint if their identity and authenticity are not in dispute.[125] A Colorado court reached a similar conclusion.[126]

Some states restrict their trial courts to the pleadings and their attachments when determining a motion for judgment on the pleadings. For example, Florida's Rule 12(c) equivalent omits the language permitting the court to convert the motion for judgment on the pleadings to one for summary judgment.[127] Florida courts have held that the omission of this language from the rule prohibits the court from going outside the pleadings when considering a motion for judgment on the pleadings; if the motion cannot be decided based on the pleadings, the court must deny it.[128] Ohio's Rule 12(c) equivalent similarly omits the conversion language.[129]

CHAPTER 5

EXERCISES FOR PART 1: PLEADINGS

■ ■ ■

Project 1. Slip-and-Fall (Premises Liability) Complaint

You are a first-year associate at the firm of Romford, Guilford, and Colchester in the city of Oberon, Penntucky. Read *only one* of the two fact patterns below (whichever your teacher assigns) and the memorandum that follows. The assignments are set out afterward.

Complaint Fact Pattern 1 (Portia Pond)

Your client, Portia Pond, doing business as "Oldtown Commercial Cleaning," was injured while performing janitorial services at a jewelry store owned by Grantham's Jewelry. The incident occurred on November 11 of last year. The following are the facts, as your paralegal stated them after interviewing Ms. Pond:

(a) She slipped and fell when she went into the store's employee break room to clean the room's linoleum floor. Someone had left a five-gallon drum containing jewelry-cleaning solution in the area near the sink, and the bucket had either leaked onto the floor or a spigot attached to the bucket had been left in a position that permitted fluid to drip onto the floor.

(b) There is evidence that the store's owner had notice of the condition. On at least two occasions, Pond told the manager or an employee that Pond had cleaned up fluid from the area around the bucket. The area is under the exclusive control of Grantham's employees.

(c) Pond was severely injured. Apparently, Pond lay unconscious on the floor with a broken hip and serious head and neck injuries for as long as two hours before anyone came to her assistance. The incident occurred sometime after 7 AM. She suffered brain damage resulting in a severe seizure disorder. She had several surgeries. She has speech and memory difficulties. She can no longer carry on her business and is totally disabled.

(d) Grantham's Jewelry, a sole proprietorship operated by Philip A. Grantham, is located at 212 Tennant Street, Oldtown, Penntucky (Oldtown is in Caledonia County). The building's owner is Golden Trace Properties, Inc., a corporation registered in the state of Idaware. Golden Trace owns several apartment buildings and commercial properties all over Caledonia County, and its main office is located at 905 1st Street, Oberon, Penntucky (Oberon is in Caledonia County).

Complaint Fact Pattern 2 (Bernard Whistler)

Your client, Bernard Whistler, fell when he was descending the stairs in the stairwell in his apartment building (Maple Grove Apartments, located at 430 E Austen Drive, College Heights in Caledonia County, Penntucky). The incident occurred on August 8 of last year. The following are the facts, as your paralegal stated them after interviewing Mr. Whistler:

(a) The lights at the top of the stairs were not working on the night he fell. He says that they had not been working for more than a week. The top of the stairs was dim but not dark. The window lower down let in some light from the street lamp just outside.

(b) Apparently, a maintenance worker left a wrench on the edge of the third step from the top, next to the banister. Whistler tripped on the tool and fell to the bottom of the stairs. The results were two broken ribs and a compound fracture of the shin. The stairwell stairs are the only means by which tenants on the second floor have access to the ground floor.

(c) Whistler's roommates back up his story. They say that they complained twice to the apartment manager (an employee of Silvershoe Property Management): once by email and once by text-messaging. The roommates were told that the problem would be fixed but nothing was done. Whistler himself has not complained. Whistler says that the property-management company is "basically a bunch of slackers" who are always leaving cleaning materials and tools around the stairs. One of Whistler's roommates photographed the wrench with her cell phone.

(d) Golden Trace Properties, Inc. is a corporation registered in the state of Idaware. It owns several apartment buildings and commercial properties all over Caledonia County, Penntucky. Golden Trace's main office is located at 905 1st Street, Oberon, Penntucky (Oberon is in Caledonia County). Silvershoe Property Management is a sole proprietorship operated by Julia Silvershoe. Its offices are located at 700 1st Street, Oberon, Penntucky.

Memorandum: Practical Effect of Penntucky Rules of Civil Procedure

1. Pleading Practice

Penntucky is a fact-pleading state. Penntucky Rule of Procedure 8(a) provides that the complaint must allege sufficient ultimate facts to support each element of a cause of action. According to the case law, a plaintiff who does not have first-hand knowledge of the facts can base an allegation "on information and belief." Conclusory allegations should not be included in the complaint.

The ultimate facts rule does not apply to certain allegations covered by Penntucky Rule 9(b). That rule provides that "Malice, intent, knowledge, and other conditions of a person's mind may be alleged generally." Thus, if the defendant's knowledge needs to be pleaded, it may be averred generally.

2. Jurisdiction of Courts

The Penntucky Superior court has jurisdiction over cases involving damages in excess of $20,000. If the amount of damages is more than $5000 but not more than $20,000, jurisdiction is in the District Court. If the amount is less than $5000, it is in the Small Claims Division of the District Court. The Penntucky rules require the plaintiff to plead the grounds for jurisdiction.

The Penntucky long-arm statute provides that any person, whether or not a citizen, submits to the jurisdiction of the state courts by "operating, conducting, engaging in, or carrying on a business venture in this state or having an office or agency in this state." Penntucky case law requires that a plaintiff who is suing a foreign corporation allege the basis for long-arm jurisdiction by tracking the relevant language from the statute in the complaint (e.g., Defendant was doing business in the state of Penntucky).

3. Venue

Venue is proper in the county where the defendant resides, where the cause of action accrued, or where the property that is the subject of the action is located. An action may be brought against a domestic corporation only in the county where such corporation has, or usually keeps, an office for transaction of its customary business, where the cause of action accrued, or where the property in litigation is located.

Actions against foreign corporations can be brought in a county where the corporation has an agent or other representative, where the cause of action accrued, or where the property in litigation is located.

4. Damages

Penntucky law prohibits (1) stating the amount of general damages in the complaint and (2) pleading punitive damages in the initial complaint.

5. **Signing and Caption**

A local rule of the Caledonia Superior Court requires that the signature contain the following information: attorney's name and Penntucky State Bar number, attorney's firm if the attorney is employed by a law firm, address of offices, telephone number and email. This rule has been in effect since 2009.

In addition, the caption must identify the case number and judge (information that the Clerk of Court fills in but that the drafter should leave space for on the right-hand side of the page).

6. **Elements of Premises Liability Action**

In Penntucky, a person who owns or is in control or possession of premises has a duty to use reasonable care to make the premises safe for a business invitee (i.e., a person whom a commercial entity invites onto its premises in the hope of gaining that person's patronage). The following is an outline of the elements:

(1) The existence of a duty of reasonable care arising from the defendant's possession or control of the relevant premises.

(2) Breach of the duty, consisting of <u>both</u> of the following:

(a) Existence of a (latent) hazardous condition that the defendant either knew of or had sufficient time to become aware of; and

(b) Defendant failed to remove, repair, or otherwise correct the condition or failed to make reasonable efforts to warn the plaintiff.

(3) The breach proximately caused personal injury to the plaintiff.

(4) As a result of the breach, the plaintiff suffered damages.

Assignment A.   Assess the Cause of Action: List Facts With Elements

After reading the memorandum and the facts above, answer the following questions:

(1) Do think you have sufficient facts to establish a cause of action in Penntucky (a fact-pleading jurisdiction)?

(2) Which court would have subject-matter jurisdiction over the action? Why? Can the action be filed in Caledonia County?

(3) How many potential defendants do you have? What was the basis of each potential defendant's duty? What was the nature of each defendant's breach? Regarding the breach, were the defendants acting together or separately?

(4) What are the ultimate facts that support each element of the cause of action, and on what dates did they arise or occur?

(5) What weaknesses do you notice in the facts?

Assignment B. *Critique Premises Liability Complaints*

You find a premises liability complaint in your firm's files (set out below). Review the list of elements set out in the memorandum, review Chapter 1 regarding procedural matters affecting the complaint, and review Chapter 2 regarding the components of a complaint. Based on those materials, answer the following questions:

(1) Does the complaint contain a proper caption and jurisdictional statement?

(2) Is there a proper commencement, and is it properly signed?

(3) Is the jurisdictional allegation correct for the court?

(4) Does each paragraph deal with a *single* element?

(5) Is each paragraph consecutively numbered (except the commencement and demand for judgment)?

(6) Does each sentence set out ultimate facts? Does any sentence contain evidentiary detail, extraneous details, or conclusory language?

(7) Is the language in each paragraph clear? Is it free of needless legal jargon?

(8) Do the sentences focus on the actor, except when strategic considerations require a different focus?

(9) Are time and place sufficiently clear for each paragraph?

(10) Does each paragraph address a single set of facts and circumstances?

(11) Is the terminology in the complaint used consistently?

Sample Complaint to be Evaluated

IN THE SUPERIOR COURT
CALEDONIA, PENNTUCKY

Susan Braintree, Plaintiff

v.

Blue Lake Health Club, Inc.,   Case No. 1997–345A
a Penntucky Corporation,   Judge: Earhart
Defendant.

COMPLAINT

COMES NOW THE PLAINTIFF, Susan Braintree (Braintree), complaining of Defendant, Blue Lake Health Club, Inc., a Penntucky Corporation (Blue Lake), alleging:

1) This action is for damages. The matter in controversy is for damages in excess of $15,000. Pursuant to § 28.01(a), Pennt. Stat., this court has jurisdiction of the matter.

2) At all times relevant to this cause of action, Blue Lake was in possession and control of a building located at 2300 N.E. Boulevard, Oberon, Caledonia, Penntucky. At the said location, defendant operated a health club known as "Blue Lake Health Club."

3) On September 9, 2003, and in that location, defendant had suffered a film of soap and water to be and remain upon the tile floor of the women's changing room in the area beside the locker where Blue Lake's staff had been mopping the floor. On information and belief, Defendant knew or had sufficient time to become aware of the aforesaid hazardous condition of the tile floor and to remove or warn of the film of soap and water. Blue Lake's negligence caused her to slip, fall, and suffer severe injury, though Plaintiff was using reasonable care.

4) Blue Lake negligently failed to post any sign in the changing room of the hazardous condition of the tile floor near the lockers.

5) Plaintiff slipped, fell, and was severely injured. Among other injuries she suffered, she broke both legs.

6) As a direct and proximate result of the defendant's breach of the duty of reasonable care, Braintree suffered physical injury, disability, pain and suffering, emotional distress, humiliation, and loss of enjoyment of life. She also incurred medical expenses in the treatment of her injuries. She has had to pay costs for extensive hospitalization, physical therapy, and other injuries. She has lost wages, as she is presently totally disabled and will lose wages in the future.

WHEREFORE, the plaintiff demands judgment against the defendant named hereinabove.

Adam Colchester

Adam Colchester, Attorney for Plaintiff
Romford, Guilford, and Colchester
2300 Downtown Plaza, Suite B-2
Oberon, Penntucky 21000
Tel. 000-000-0000
Penntucky Bar Number 9870-00

Assignment C.   Draft a Complaint

Review the pleading set out in Assignment B, the facts, and the memorandum. Review Chapters 1 and 2. Draft a one-count premises liability complaint that meets the requirements of Penntucky law.

Project 2.   Answer to Premises Liability Complaint

You are a first-year associate at the firm of Tennison, Hathaway, and Barnaby in the city of Oberon, Penntucky. Read *only one* of the two fact patterns below (the one that your teacher assigns to you). After reading the assigned fact pattern, do the assignment that follows.

Answer Based on Fact Pattern 1 (Portia Pond)

Your client is Philip A. Grantham, owner of Grantham's Jewelry, a sole proprietorship. The store is located at 212 Tennant Street, Oldtown, Caledonia county. The following is a summary of the facts prepared by your paralegal, based on your interviews with the client:

(a) Grantham says that he was "personally devastated" by Pond's accident. Shortly after Pond was injured (while she was still in the hospital), he offered to pay her full expenses ($35,000) in exchange for a release. She agreed.

(b) Grantham and the then-manager, Andrew Bell (no longer employed at Grantham's), conceded that there might have been leaked jewelry cleaner on the floor of the employee break room. One of the drums containing the jewelry-cleaning solution was defective: the spigot dripped.

(c) Though Pond's complaint states otherwise, the employees had posted a notice that the fluid was leaking. They had placed the canister on plastic sheeting in an alcove and had put a computer-printed sign on the wall, in large font, that said "WARNING! LEAKING FLUID!!!! WET FLOOR!!!" They also placed a WET FLOOR post in the area.

(d) Bell emailed Pond personally to tell her that they had received her note about the leaking drum of fluid and had attempted to fix the dripping spigot. Grantham assumes that she did not get the note. To be on the safe side, they put the drum in the employee break-room so that it would be out of the way and put towels around the floor to soak up any excess fluid.

Answer Based on Fact Pattern 2 (Bernard Whistler)

Your client is Julia Silvershoe of Silvershoe Property Management, a sole proprietorship with an office located at 700 1st Street in Oberon. She is being sued by Bernard Whistler, formerly a tenant in her Maple Grove Apartment Building (located at 430 E Austen Drive, College Heights in Caledonia County, Penntucky). The following is a summary of the facts prepared by your paralegal, based on your interviews with the client:

(a) Silvershoe has had no personal contact with Whistler. The Maple Grove Building, where he used to be a tenant, is managed by an employee, Hiram Valadon.

(b) Valadon says that Whistler and his roommates have been nothing but trouble since they moved in. On the day of the accident, Valadon had just informed Whistler and his three roommates that their lease would not be renewed. On at least four occasions, police had been summoned to the premises because of drunken brawling. Apparently, Whistler and his roommates are engaged in some sort of feud with the downstairs tenants, a middle-aged couple (the Matisses).

(c) According to the police report, Whistler fell down the stairs during a screaming match with Mark Matisse. Both Matisses described Whistler as "drunk" and "out of control."

(d) Valadon concedes that the 50–year old apartment building had some "issues." However, she has documentation showing that on the day of the incident she sent an employee to the premises to fix the lights. The employee told her that he was unable to get the lights working and that she would need to call an electrician, which she did immediately via email.

(e) The employee, Gilbert Hillier, denies that he left a wrench on the stairs. He has seen the photo that Whistler's roommate took of the wrench on the stairs. He states that the wrench does not belong to him: the company provides him with professional-quality tools, and the wrench shown in the photograph is a cheap brand not suited for his type of work. Hillier thinks that the plaintiff's friends put it there after the fact. Valadon says that Hillier has worked for the company for 15 years and has always been reliable.

Memorandum Excerpt: Defenses in Premises Liability Case

Penntucky is a comparative negligence state. The elements of a contributory negligence defense are as follows:

(a) Plaintiff failed to act with reasonable care for his or her own safety (i.e., was negligent).

(b) Plaintiff's negligence caused or contributed to Plaintiff's injuries and the resulting damages.

Under Penntucky law, a defendant owes a duty of care regarding any part of the premises that were under the defendant's control. Potential defendants include the owner, a tenant or other person in possession, or a person performing work (such as construction) in a particular area.

A defendant owes no duty of care to a person who "exceeds the scope of the invitation" by entering an area not generally open to members of the public. In one case, the Court of Appeals held that an independent contractor performing construction in a mall exceeded the scope of his invitation when he entered an area set aside for mall employees (instead of the public restroom). The mall's owner therefore owed him no duty of care.

According to Penntucky law, a defendant must plead sufficient facts in the answer to give the other party notice of any facts on which the defendant intends to rely. The defendant can allege facts on "information and belief" where appropriate.

The defense of implied assumption of risk is no longer recognized in Penntucky as a defense to negligence. The defense is said to be "merged" into contributory negligence.

If a defense is based on a contract such as a release, Penntucky's equivalent to Federal Rule 10(c) states that the defendant *must* attach the contract to the answer. It further states that the pleading should *not* unnecessarily recite language from the document; if the document is attached, it is incorporated by reference for all purposes.

In March of last year, the Penntucky Supreme Court stated that "boilerplate" defenses are improper and that only those defenses that are available based on the facts should be pleaded. The Court's opinion states that (1) unnecessary boilerplate defenses will be stricken, and (2) the attorney who files them (and possibly the client) may be sanctioned for filing them.

Assignment. Draft an Answer to the Complaint

Study the answer below, and take note of any drafting-related flaws (there are plenty of flaws). Review the following materials:

- Chapter 3.

- The relevant fact pattern for the answer.

- The memo about defenses in a premises liability case (in Project 2).

- The memo about Penntucky's rules of procedure (in Project 1).

Based on the listed materials, draft an answer to the complaint that incorporates all affirmative defenses suggested by the materials. Assume that the procedural rules that apply in Penntucky are identical to the federal court rules discussed in Chapter 3.

Sample Answer Filed in a Previous Case

IN THE SUPERIOR COURT
CALEDONIA, PENNTUCKY

Marianne Dawlish, *et al.*
Plaintiff

Case No. 2004–456A
v.
Judge: Harbottle

Ciaran Hodson d/b/a
"Davey's Irish Pub," *et al.*

Defendants.

ANSWER OF DEFENDANT BIEHL INVESTMENT
PROPERTIES, INC.

Defendant Biehl Investment Properties (Defendant Biehl) answers the complaint and says:

1. Defendant Biehl admits the allegations in paragraph 1 for jurisdictional purposes only.

2. The allegations in paragraph 2 do not apply to Defendant Biehl. Defendant Biehl lacks sufficient information to form a belief concerning the truth of the allegations set forth in paragraph 2.

3. Defendant Biehl admits the allegations set forth in paragraph 3.

4. Defendant Biehl admits that Plaintiff was present on the premises on the said date and at the said time. Defendant Biehl denies the remainder of paragraph 4 to the extent that it applies to Defendant Biehl and is unable to form a belief concerning the truth of the remaining allegations.

5. Defendant Biehl lacks sufficient information to form a belief concerning the truth of the allegations set forth in paragraph 5.

6. Defendant Biehl denies that its negligence caused Plaintiff's injuries. Defendant Biehl lacks sufficient information to form a belief concerning the truth of the remaining allegations set forth in paragraph 6.

7. Defendant Biehl admits that Plaintiff fell as she was exiting the pub. Defendant Biehl lacks sufficient information to form a belief concerning the truth of the remaining allegations set forth in paragraph 7.

FIRST AFFIRMATIVE DEFENSE: RELEASE

8. On July 23, 2004, Plaintiff and Defendant Biehl executed the following settlement and release set out hereinbelow:

> For the sole consideration of $65,000 to me in hand paid, the receipt of which is hereby acknowledged, I, Releasor, being over 18 years of age, do hereby release and forever discharge Biehl Investment Properties, Inc. (Releasee) and all other persons, firms, corporations, subsidiaries, successors, parents, officers, directors, and other agents of Releasee from any and all actions, causes of action, claims, rights, lawsuits, liabilities, or demands for damages, costs, loss of use, loss of services, expenses, compensation, consequential damages, or any other thing whatsoever on account of, originating from, arising out of, or in any way growing out of any and all personal injuries (and consequences thereof, including death, and specifically including also any injuries which may exist, but which at this time are unknown and unanticipated and which may develop at some time in the future, and all unforeseen developments arising from known injuries) and any and all property damage resulting from or to result from the occurrence that happened on or about September 30, 2003 at "Davey's Pub" at 265 1st Street, Oberon, Penntucky.

Via this document, which is attached to this answer, Defendant is forthwith released from any liability to Plaintiff based on these circumstances.

SECOND AFFIRMATIVE DEFENSE: CONTRIBUTORY NEGLIGENCE

9. On information and belief, Plaintiff entered the premises in order to engage in a fight with one of Defendant Hodson's cus-

tomers. She threw a full pint of beer in the customer's face and the two of them were pushing and shoving in the resultant spill. She also knocked over the customer's plate of food and on information and belief stepped in the spilled food. She was asked to leave because of the aforesaid threats and battery. She slipped due to the slippery condition of her feet on information and belief, as she was exiting the premises at the request of Defendant Hodson's bouncers. Plaintiff acted without reasonable care for her own safety.

10. Plaintiff's own lack of reasonable care caused or contributed to the injuries she allegedly suffered.

Tennison, Hathaway, and Barnaby

By: *Christobel Barnaby*

CHRISTOBEL BARNABY, Penntucky Bar Number 7639-78
Attorney for Defendant Biehl Investment Properties, Inc.
Downtown Plaza, Skyway Building Floor 23
Oberon, Penntucky 21000
Tel. 000-000-0000, barnaby@ashgrove.web

(Certificate of Service)

Project 3. Pleading and Motion based on Wandering Livestock Statute

You are a first-year associate at the prestigious firm of Thomason, Kwok, and Edeback. You represent James Ortiz, who was injured in a bizarre accident. After reading the following materials, do the assignments.

Fact Pattern

The following are notes taken by your paralegal, Maggie Schmid, during a client interview:

(a) James Ortiz owns a horse farm at 1100 S.R. 19, Micanopia, Ottokar County, Floregon. His accident occurred when he was driving home one night along State Road 19. As he was about to turn right onto the private road that belongs to his farm, a llama "appeared out of nowhere" directly in the path of his car. He swerved left to avoid hitting the llama and ended up in the pond on the other side of his private road. He did not see what happened to the llama.

(b) The car was a total loss. Deployment of the airbag broke two of Ortiz's ribs. He also suffered exacerbation of a chronic back condition. He has had to have extensive physical therapy and is unable to ride horses, care for the horses, give riding lessons, drive, or do any strenuous task of any kind. He had to hire two employees to cover his work and had to suspend his riding school indefinitely.

(c) Rowena Sweeney, one of Ortiz's employees, was just about to pull out onto the state road when the accident occurred. She saw the llama and saw Ortiz swerve to avoid it. She telephoned Ortiz's wife and an ambulance.

(d) The llama, which ended up grazing in Ortiz's pasture, belongs to Joseph and Lula McKern, lessees of Bailey Farm. Bailey Farm is located at 1195 S.R. 19, Micanopia (across the highway from the Ortiz farm). The McKerns make extra money from running a petting zoo. Everyone in town knows that the llama has escaped on at least two occasions. It seems to be escaping through a gap in the pasture fence.

(e) The owner of Bailey Farm, Aubrey Bailey, lives on a neighboring farm. He says that he has notified the Baileys in writing that under the terms of their lease, they are obligated to pay all repair costs for maintaining the pasture and to make any necessary repairs. He has reminded them of their obligation under the lease to keep all livestock confined to the land. The McKerns maintain that the llama is a pet, not livestock. Bailey's address is 1520 Sweetbranch Road, Micanopia, Ottokar County.

(f) The McKerns state that they did not repair the fence because Bailey, the owner, refused to pay any portion of the repairs. They say that the llama is not their property but is merely on loan to them from their daughter (who lives 600 miles away) and that Ortiz should sue her.

Memorandum Excerpts: Relevant Floregon Law

1. Pleading Standard. In 2012, the Floregon Supreme Court abandoned the previous notice pleading standard and adopted a "plausibility standard" that requires "sufficient factual allegations to indicate to the court the existence of a cognizable theory." No one knows yet what this change means.

2. Subject-matter Jurisdiction. Under Floregon law, the Circuit Court has jurisdiction of cases involving damages exceeding $15,000. If the amount of damages is more than $5000 but not more than $15,000, jurisdiction is in the County Court. If the amount is $5000 or less, jurisdiction is in the Magistrate's Division of the County Court.

3. Venue. Venue is proper in the county where the defendant resides, where the cause of action accrued, or where the property that is the subject of the action is located.

4. Wandering Livestock. Section 79–9–23 of the Floregon statutes provides:

Every owner of livestock who intentionally, willfully, carelessly, or negligently suffers or permits such livestock to run at large upon or stray upon the public roads of this state shall be liable in damages for all injury and property damage sustained by any person by reason thereof.

"Livestock" is defined as follows by Flo. Stat. § 79–9–23, which was amended in 2012 to include the underlined language;

(E) "Livestock" shall include all animals of the equine, bovine, or swine class, including goats, sheep, mules, horses, hogs, cattle, ostriches, llamas, and other grazing animals.

Other relevant definitions from Flo. Stat. § 79–9–20 are as follows:

(B) "Owner" means any individual, person, association, firm, or corporation that has custody or charge of livestock.

(C) "Running at large or straying" means being found on land, including a public road, belonging to a person other than the owner, without the permission of the landowner and posing a threat to public safety.

(D) "Public road" means any road in the state that is maintained by the state or a political subdivision of the state, or a municipality.

5. Requirements for Stating a Cause of Action. To state a cause of action under the statute, the plaintiff must

(1) establish that the statute applies to the parties and circumstances, and

(2) allege an act of negligence or a willful act by the "owner" by failing to use reasonable care to confine the animal to the owner's property.

Note: the case law suggests that for the plaintiff to establish negligence, the plaintiff must show that the defendant had reasonable notice that the animal could escape.

Assignment A. *Draft a Complaint*

Based on the materials above and on a review of Chapter 2, draft a one-count complaint on behalf of James Ortiz based on the statute.

Assignment B. *Draft a Summary Judgment Motion*

Review Chapter 4 (motions). You are an associate of the law firm of Templesmith & Emanuel. You represent the owner of Bailey Farm, Aubrey Bailey. Reviewing the case law, you found an old Court of Appeals case (1978) stating that a lessor of land from which livestock has wandered has no obligation to a person injured by the livestock if both of the following apply:

(a) The lessor has no ownership interest or right to custody or control of the livestock; and

(b) By the terms of the lease, the landowner has no obligation to repair or pay for repairs to the fence in which the livestock is confined.

After examining the complaint (your own or one provided by your teacher), draft a motion for summary judgment.

PROJECT 4. MULTI–COUNT PLEADING BASED ON STATUTE

You are an associate at the prestigious firm of Thomason, Kwok, and Edeback. You represent Miguel and Amarantha Raeburn, who want to sue the moving company that recently handled their move from one city to another.

Memorandum Regarding Facts

Miguel and Amarantha Raeburn want you to sue the moving company for anything you can get. The following are the facts that your paralegal compiled after you interviewed the clients.

(a) The Raeburns' address is 56 Herman Street, Port Lochloosa, Floregon.

(b) Miguel and Amarantha hired a moving company to handle their move from Wedderburn, Floregon to Port Lochloosa, a distance of about 45 miles.

(c) The company that handled the move was Floregon Statewide Movers, Inc., which has a Port Ottokar office at 43 Commerce Plaza, Ottokar Beach, Floregon.

(d) The relevant provisions from the Raeburns' contract with the moving company are set out as follows:

> **Sec. 5(a).** Movers shall arrive at 670 Byatt Street, Wedderburn, Floregon at 8:30 AM on September 1 to begin their packing. They shall leave the location no later than 6 PM on that date in order to arrive at the destination at 56 Herman Street, Port Lochloosa, Floregon no later than 8:30 PM. They shall have completed the delivery by 10:30.

> **Sec. 5(b).** Movers shall pack Customer's household items for transport to destination. Customer has arranged with Movers for specialty packing for fragile/antique/valuable items in manner stated in attachment. Movers shall load the packed goods into truck, shall transport the goods to the destination, and shall unload

and place the items inside the customer's dwelling in the stipulated place.

Sec. 6(b) The total cost of these services is $900, including the cost of basic transport and loading service ($400), packing of goods ($300), specialty goods packing ($200). Customer shall pay in full by check or Visa credit card, payment to be rendered at time of completion of delivery to the driver or other person in charge of operation. This amount is based on an estimate performed by Moving Company after assessing the goods to be packed and transported.

Sec. 9. Company shall not be liable for any delay that is based on Customer's misrepresentation of the amount of goods to be packed or moved. Customer may be liable for additional charges if such a delay occurs. Customer understands that the times stated in Sec. 5(a) are estimates and that delays occur.

(e) On September 1, the movers did not arrive until noon. The foreman, Bill Fairley, stated that they had been delayed by heavy traffic on the way back from a delivery to another city. Miguel feels that the movers did a rushed job of packing up the family's goods. Miguel got into a heated argument with Fairley about the "specialty packing" of his collection of early 20th Century jazz records and his wife's Wedgewood china collection.

(f) The movers did not finish packing until nearly 9:00 PM. They did not arrive in Port Lochloosa until 10:30 PM. The crew unloaded one item: an antique sofa. At that point, Fairley demanded that the Raeburns pay the full amount due plus an additional $100 to cover "overtime" since the work was obviously going to go on well past midnight. When the Raeburns refused, Fairley said that the movers would not do further work unless they were paid in advance.

(g) Fairley accused the Raeburns of "scamming" the company by misrepresenting to the company "how much stuff" they had. He claimed that the itemized statement was misleading (in fact, the second page of the "1 of 3" was not attached to his work order). He said he would accept payment up front only and by Visa only. When Amarantha said that she had only her checkbook, he told her that he would not take her "worthless check." The Raeburns, who try to avoid paying anything by credit card, had packed up their Visa cards with their financial records (which were in the moving truck).

(h) Miguel offered to drive to an ATM, but Fairley and his crew got in the truck and drove off, leaving the living room sofa sitting on the lawn. In the truck were toys belonging to the Raeburns' three children and one child's essential medications. The Raeburns had to rush to the nearest all-night drugstore to buy replacement medication. Because they had already purchased the maximum number of pills they were allowed per month by their insurance, they had to pay the full cost of $800 for the pills.

(i) Miguel and Amarantha were unable to move the sofa into the house. When it began to rain heavily the next morning, the sofa (valued at $8000) was ruined.

(j) The Raeburns were unable to reach anyone from the company over the weekend. Because they had no furniture and no cooking utensils, they had to take their three children to an "Apartment Inn," which cost $50 a night. They ate out for every meal: the total cost was $400.

(k) On Monday, Amarantha drove to the company's office in Ottokar Beach. The manager promised to have Fairley fired (which has been done). The manager would not agree to pay for the damage to the Raeburns' property and other expenses. Later, when the crew turned up with the property, the Raeburns found that 12 of Miguel's jazz records were broken ($800) and an antique mirror was cracked that will cost $400 to repair.

Elements for Breach of Contract Action

In Floregon, the elements of an action for breach of contract are as follows:

    (1) the existence of a valid and binding contract;

    (2) breach of the contract by the defendant; and

    (3) money damages suffered by the plaintiff.

In Floregon, a document on which a cause of action is based may be incorporated in the complaint by reference.)

Moving Services Act

The Floregon legislature recently passed the "Floregon Moving Services Act" (Title 1, Chapter 301, Part 26, sections 1–16). No case law currently exists. The Act contains the following provisions:

Flo. Stat. § 301–26–1(a). "Mover" means any firm, corporation, individual, or entity that contracts to perform intrastate moving or related services (such as packing or shipping) in the state of Floregon.

Flo. Stat. § 301–26–1(b). "Shipper" means a person who contracts with a mover for moving services.

Flo. Stat. § 301–26–6. Violations

It is a violation of this chapter for a mover to do any of the following:

(3) Demand overtime charges not reflected in the itemized costs set out in the contract.

(4) Fail to reasonably comply with promises concerning times for arrival, departure, or performance of services unless the provision includes in boldface 12–point type this statement: **Customer understands that the times stated in this provision are only approximate and that the actual times may vary substantially from those stated.**

(5) Demand payment for services not performed.

(10) Refuse to accept payment when tendered in a form authorized in the contract.

(12) Withhold delivery of household goods or in any way hold goods in storage against the expressed wishes of the shipper if payment has been made as delineated in the estimate or contract for services.

Flo. Stat. § 301–26–7. Delivery of household goods

(a) A mover must relinquish household goods to a shipper and must place the goods inside a shipper's dwelling ... unless the shipper has not tendered payment in the amount specified in a written contract or estimate signed and dated by the shipper. A mover may not refuse to relinquish prescription medicines and goods for use by children, including children's furniture, clothing, or toys, under any circumstances.

(b) A mover may not refuse to relinquish household goods to a shipper or fail to place the goods inside a shipper's dwelling based on the mover's refusal to accept an acceptable form of payment. A mover who violates this section shall be liable for treble damages.

Flo. Stat. § 301–26–12. Remedies

If a shipper suffers losses caused by a mover's violation of this Act, the shipper shall be entitled to recover actual damages and attorney fees. In addition, the shipper shall recover statutory damages of $100 for each violation.

Assignment. Draft a Complaint

After reading the materials above, review Chapter 2 regarding drafting a statutory complaint. On behalf of the Raeburns, draft a two-count complaint based on breach of contract and violation of the Floregon Moving Services statute.

PART 2

CONTRACTS

■ ■ ■

- Chapter 6.   Introduction to Contract Drafting
- Chapter 7.   Contract Components: Preliminary Matters, Core Transaction, and Subsidiary Agreements
- Chapter 8.   Limitation or Exclusion of Liability
- Chapter 9.   Contract Components: Termination, Breach, and Remedies
- Chapter 10. Contract Components: Winding-up, Non-compete, Severance, Integration, and Dispute-Resolution Provisions
- Chapter 11. Contract Components: Modification, Execution, and Effective Date
- Chapter 12. How Courts Read and Construe Contracts
- Chapter 13. Exercises for Part 2

CHAPTER 6

INTRODUCTION TO CONTRACT DRAFTING

■ ■ ■

I. The Contract Drafter as "Lawmaker"

When you draft a contract, you create the rules that govern the parties' interactions. Essentially, the parties create their own law of the transaction. A California court explained it as follows:

> When two parties make a contract, they agree upon the rules and regulations which will govern their relationship; the risks inherent in the agreement and the likelihood of its breach. The parties to the contract in essence create a mini-universe for themselves, in which each voluntarily chooses his contracting partner, each trusts the other's willingness to keep his word and honor his commitments, and in which they define their respective obligations, rewards and risks.[1]

Some contracts address a single transaction (e.g., sale of a new car). Some contracts govern the relationship of the parties over an extended period of time.[2] To draft provisions that will continue to function effectively over time requires you to envision how each party's performance will unfold against a background of events that are still evolving and that are only partly within the parties' control. You must think ahead, speculate, and picture how potential disputes and problems could arise over time—and you must address them in the present.

A fundamental purpose of getting a contract in writing is to *prevent disputes*. The goal is to draft every sentence so that there is only one possible interpretation and that it is the exact interpretation that the drafter intends. That mark may be difficult to hit, but you should strive to hit it every time.

II. The Contract Drafter's Role as an Advocate

As your client's lawyer and advocate, another goal is to draft so as to ensure that *if* a dispute arises, the client's interests are protected to the fullest extent possible.

People who go to lawyers for their contracts often do not know what they need. They expect the lawyer to know. Few clients will have fully thought through all the angles and their ramifications. As your client's advocate, part of your job is to envision how the contract will function in real life and to address any problems that the client has not anticipated.

To do this, you must know how to get information from the client, including information that the client does not know you need. Chapter 19 addresses the process.

III.   Some Preliminary Considerations

A.   Applicable Law

Applicable laws in existence at the time of a contract's execution are impliedly incorporated into the contract without any statement to that effect.[3] Those laws are as much a part of the contract as if they were expressly referred to within the contract. A contract therefore need not cover every possible aspect of the parties' relationship.

B.   Level of Detail Required

Many contracts do not deal in detail with every aspect of the transaction. In some settings, a contract that controls every detail strips the parties of any discretion and flexibility. In other settings, the parties' relationship may necessitate greater specificity and tighter controls in the contract. A conscientious attorney adapts the level of detail to the requirements of the contract, the client, and the situation.

C.   Implied Covenant of Good Faith and Fair Dealing

To advise a client effectively, a drafter must be aware of the covenant of good faith and fair dealing that most courts consider to be implied in every contract.[4] The Oklahoma Supreme Court said that the covenant encompasses a party's duty to act reasonably (the "fair dealing" component) and diligently (the "good faith" component).[5] A party breaches the implied covenant of good faith and fair dealing by evading the spirit of the contract, willfully rendering imperfect performance, or interfering with the other party's performance.[6]

When a contract gives a party broad discretion in terms of how to perform, the doctrine of good faith and fair dealing requires the party to exercise its discretion reasonably rather than arbitrarily, capriciously, or in a manner that is inconsistent with the parties' reasonable expectations.[7] However, as the Utah Supreme Court pointed out, the covenant does not establish new or independent rights or duties under the contract or compel one party to act to its own detriment for the purpose of benefiting the other.

IV.   Typical Contract Provisions

Chapters 7 through 11 contain discussions of certain types of provisions. Chapter 20 contains a template that summarizes typical types of contract provisions.

V.   Articulation of the Contract

A.   General Principles

To write an effective contract, you must apply the principles discussed in Parts VI and VII of this book (which address phrasing, grammar, punctuation, and style).

To control the effect of your provisions, you must consider the exact meaning of the words you choose, as discussed in Chapter 26. The only way to ensure that the contract will operate as you intend is to design provisions to be as flexible as the circumstances require and as definite as the circumstances permit.

If you create a short-hand phrase to cover a complex concept or are using a word or phrase in a sense that differs from its ordinary meaning, you may need to create a definition. Chapter 27 explains when and how to create definitions.

Ambiguity is a lurking danger for every drafter. Chapter 28 discusses some common causes and illustrates their resolution. Chapter 29 discusses drafting time clauses and conditional statements. You must also familiarize yourself with the rules of construction discussed in Chapter 12, since the application of a rule of construction could affect how a court (or another lawyer) would read your document.

B.   Drafting Contract Statements

1.   Recommended Verbs

Generally speaking, there are no magic words that are essential to the creation of a contract. Reasonable minds may differ as to the best words to convey certain intentions. Below are some suggestions for you to consider.

Recommended Language for Contracts	
• Obligation to Act	Shall (or will) + verb
• Obligation to Refrain from acting	Shall not (or will not) + verb
• Right to Act	May + verb
• Requirement for exercising a right	Must + verb
• Condition precedent	Must + verb
• Policy effective at signing	Present tense
• Recitals of fact	Present or Past tense

Once you have decided on the terminology, we recommend that you stick to it consistently throughout the contract. If you vary the words used to express a particular *type* of statement, you automatically lead the reader to think that the change in language signals a change in intended effect.

2.   Statement of an Obligation

An obligation is a promise by a party—for the other party's benefit—to do an action or refrain from doing an action. An obligation applies only after the contract between the parties becomes effective.

In the authors' opinion, the best words for conveying the idea of a future obligation are the auxiliary verbs "shall" or "will" paired with a verb expressing the promised action. If you wish to emphasize the voluntary and consensual nature of the promised performance, use "will." If you wish to emphasize the imperative nature, use "shall."

Many attorneys prefer "shall" to "will." A number of cases have discussed the use of "shall" in contracts and its interpretation by courts as imperative.[8] Whichever you decide to use, make sure that "shall" or "will" statements apply only to a party—not to the performance period, not to the contract, and not to any other person or thing to which the contract refers.

Examples: Obligations to Act or Refrain from Acting

1(a)   TreeHabitat shall construct the tree house in accordance with the attached plans.

1(b)   TreeHabitat will construct the tree house in accordance with the attached plans.

2(a)   Employee will not disclose to any third party any confidential information.

2(b)   Employee shall not disclose to any third party any confidential information.

Do not use "shall" or "will" to express a right of a party to do something that is the reverse of beneficial to the other. Below are examples.

Examples: Right Improperly Framed as an Obligation

- If Buyer fails to timely pay the remaining balance, Seller ~~shall~~ may charge a late fee equal to 5% of the total price of the product.

- Lessee ~~will~~ may keep one approved pet in the apartment.

We recommend that you avoid the phrase "responsible for" because the phrase tends to be ambiguous when used to express a future obligation.

Examples: Multiple Meanings of "Responsible For"

Throughout the period of tenancy, Heath <u>is responsible for</u> maintaining Landlord's property <u>in a clean and sanitary</u> condition.

The example above might be interpreted as stating an obligation of Heath to take action, but that is not the only possible interpretation. It could also mean that it is up to Heath to do the maintenance *if* Heath wants it done.

3. Statement of a Policy

Most contracts contain statements setting out rules or policies that become effective at the moment the contract becomes effective and binding. By signing the contract, the parties assent to these rules. After the contract is signed, there is nothing further for either party to do; the Rules apply, and that is that.

There is no particular word or phrase that expresses "contract policy." Instead, we recommend that you state rules and policies *in present tense*. Many policy statements relate to the contract itself. Some relate to a particular aspect, such as the effective date of a termination or the duration of the relevant performance.

Examples: Policy Statements Relating to the Contract or Contract Period

- This contract <u>expresses</u> the complete agreement of the parties.

- The employment period <u>begins</u> on January 1, 2013. Unless Heath <u>terminates the</u> employment pursuant to paragraph 12 or Employee quits Heath's employment, the employment period <u>ends</u> on January 1, 2015.

- Termination of these obligations <u>becomes</u> effective on the 30th day after the date <u>set forth</u> in the termination notice.

Some policy statements relate directly to the parties. For example, a policy statement by which one party releases the other from liability becomes effective at the moment the contract does. Below is an example.

Example: Policy Statement Relating to the Parties

Temple–Smith <u>releases</u> Heath from any future liability to Temple–Smith for any claim by Temple–Smith for personal injury, property damage, or other loss resulting from Heath's performance of Heath's contractual obligations.

By executing the contract, the parties make that rule effective; no further action is required after the contract becomes effective.

4. Statement of a Right

A statement conferring a right to act permits, but does not obligate, a party to act for the party's own benefit. Unless the text indicates that the right does not come into being until some later event, rights become effective when the contract becomes effective. The case law indicates that "may" is most often read by courts to be permissive or discretionary,[9] unless the context indicates that a different meaning was intended.[10]

"May" is an all-purpose auxiliary verb that can express a number of ideas: e.g., that the party has the option, choice, or discretion to act; is entitled to act; has, retains, or reserves the right to act; or has the power or authority to act. While consistency in expressing rights is desirable, we recognize that occasionally one of the other phrases set out in the prior sentence might more precisely express the drafter's intention. Use good judgment as to whether "may" expresses your intention with sufficient precision. If you use one of the substitute phrases, draft it as a present-tense policy statement.

Examples: "May" Statement versus Policy Statement

1(a)   The attorney-in-fact <u>may take</u> any action that she deems necessary to <u>protect</u> Temple–Smith's financial interests.

1(b)   The attorney-in-fact <u>has discretion to take</u> any action that she deems necessary to protect Temple–Smith's financial interests.

2(a)   For as long as Promoter retains ownership of the common areas, Promoter <u>may appoint</u> one individual of Promoter's choosing to membership on the Rules Committee and the Membership Review Board.

2(b)   For as long as Promoter retains ownership of the common areas, Promoter <u>has the authority to appoint</u> one individual of Promoter's choosing to membership on the Rules Committee and the Membership Review Board.

---

5. Statement of a Requirement or Condition

Sometimes a drafter may want to impose a requirement or condition on a party's ability (1) to exercise a right or to obtain some benefit from the other party; or (2) to avoid some adverse consequence (e.g., paying a late fee). To set out a requirement or condition, use "must." To prevent any confusion about whether the action is an obligation, state the related condition *in the same sentence*. Unless you are certain that a reader will understand the effect of noncompliance with the requirement, you should state that as well.

Examples: Requirement or Condition for Exercising a Right or Procuring a Benefit

- To order additional supplies, Sales Representative must submit the order through Company's website. Otherwise, Company cannot fulfill the order.

- The parties may modify the contract by executing a supplemental written agreement. To modify the contract, both parties must sign it. In addition, the parties must identify in the supplemental agreement the exact section of the contract and the exact language to which the modification pertains. If the parties fail to comply with these requirements, the supplemental agreement is not effective to modify the contract.

Example: Requirement for Avoiding an Adverse Consequence

To avoid a late fee, Heath must pay the full monthly service charge by 5 pm of the final day of the grace period.

---

6. Recitals

Recitals are statements of fact, intention, understanding, or status. Though recitals often appear at the beginning of a contract, recitals can appear wherever the drafter needs to state a fact or explain a policy or other operative provision. Recitals are non-operative statements drafted in present or past tense.

Examples: Recitals

1. Tenant understands that Landlord does not carry insurance to cover Tenant's personal property that is located on the premises. Landlord does not require Tenant to carry Renter's Insurance but strongly recommends that Tenant do so.

Examples: Recitals (cont.)

2. Before signing this lease, Lessee <u>inspected</u> the premises and <u>determined</u> that they are acceptable for Lessee's purposes.

3. FishClub <u>has provided</u> Landowner with a complete and accurate <u>list of all</u> members to whom the license to use the land applies.

As the examples above illustrate, recitals have a number of uses. The first example is a statement that could not be framed *except* as a recital of fact. In the second example, inclusion of the recital preempts any issue concerning Lessee's inspection and acceptance of the premises. In the third example, the recital reflects that FishClub has performed, prior to signing, a condition precedent to the contract's becoming effective.

A drafter should not recite as a fact any information that does not accurately reflect the facts or the parties' true intentions. In general, it is best to use recitals only when you have good reason to do so.

Make sure that your factual statements could not be interpreted as a warranty or guarantee when that is not the client's intention. Consider the following recitals:

Examples: Recitals that Might be Interpreted as Warranties

1. Buyer <u>has chosen</u> to purchase hens from Farmer Heath <u>because</u> Farmer Heath's hens produce some of the highest quality eggs in the market.

2. Play–Day Play School <u>provides</u> the best-equipped child-care facilities in <u>Gainesville</u>, Florida.

Would a buyer regard the first example as warranting the quality of the eggs? Similarly, would a parent interpret the second example as guaranteeing that the facility is indeed the best equipped? Why include such a provision if it increases the risk of dispute?

C. Articulating the Scope of a Promise

1. Choosing Precise Verbs

The scope of the verb that you choose when articulating a promise determines the conduct that the duty requires. A verb may be too broad to create a clear picture of the required conduct. For example, what conduct is required by the following sentence?

Lessee shall <u>maintain</u> the pasture.

Is Lessee required to mow the grass? Trim the trees? Repair the fence?

Suppose that you represent Heath Cliff, a famous creator of insanely expensive custom-designed and custom-built dollhouses for wealthy adults who collect antique doll-furniture. In the sentences below, which verbs require Heath to do the work himself?

1(a) Heath shall <u>design</u> a custom dollhouse for Cupples.

1(b) Heath shall <u>furnish</u> a design for a custom dollhouse to Cupples.

2(a) Heath shall <u>construct</u> a dollhouse for Cupples.

2(b) Heath shall <u>provide</u> a dollhouse for Cupples.

In sentences 1(a) and 2(a), Health clearly has to do the work himself. In sentences 1(b) and 2(b), all he has to do is make sure that Cupples receives a design or a dollhouse, but another person (e.g., an apprentice) could actually create the design or build the dollhouse.

2. Expressing a Promise Narrowly

To prevent disputes and ensure that the transaction goes smoothly, make sure that you understand what each party is promising to give, do, or refrain from doing. Make sure that any language obligating a party or conferring a right is only as broad as the parties intend. Some drafters might draft broad promises and then try to protect the client from risk if circumstances beyond the client's control prevent performance. However, drafting an excuse (discussed in Chapter 8) is an unreliable way to prevent a dispute.

Therefore, you should nail down the exact scope of the promises so that the parties will not "fall out" over an expectation that does not materialize. To achieve this objective, you may combine promissory language with recitals or other types of statements that are addressed in this chapter. Below are examples of narrowly drafted promises.

Examples: Narrowly Drafted Promises

<u>If Templesmith's supplier continues to provide components to Templesmith at the supplier's current price</u>, Templesmith will provide Kwokworks with the components at the price that is stated in the attachment. <u>If Templesmith's supplier fails to deliver components to Templesmith at the current price</u>, Kwokworks and Templesmith will negotiate in good faith a new price.

VI.　Invalid Contracts or Provisions

A.　Courts' Preference for Enforcement Over Invalidity

Freedom of contract is a vital public policy to which courts give great deference.[11] Consequently, courts generally seek to enforce contracts rather than to set them aside.[12] If the requirements for a valid contract are met, the law generally gives the parties wide latitude in coming up with their own arrangements.

As the Nevada Supreme Court said, "parties are free to contract, and the courts will enforce their contracts if they are not unconscionable, illegal, or in violation of public policy."[13] Even if a provision is illegal, in violation of public policy, or unconscionable, the presence of an invalid provision does not necessarily make the entire contract unenforceable. As Chapter 10 explains, the court can in some circumstances sever the invalid provision and enforce the remaining provisions.

B.　Invalid Contracts

1.　Contracts That Contravene Law or Public Policy

"Illegal" contracts or provisions are those that contravene the law or public policy.[14] For example, a contract is illegal if it rests on illegal consideration: that is, on any act or forbearance that is contrary to law.[15] If the formation of the contract is illegal[16] or its subject-matter or purpose is illegal[17] so that it cannot be performed without a violation of the law,[18] a court will not enforce it.[19] If the illegality is only tangential to the contract, the contract is not necessarily void.[20]

If the legislature expressly makes void a contract that violates a statute, the contract is illegal and a court will not enforce it.[21] However, the rule that violation of a statute makes a contract unenforceable is riddled with exceptions.[22]

Courts often refuse to enforce illegal contracts but instead choose to leave the parties where they found them.[23] For example, the Wisconsin Court of Appeals refused to enforce a contract between two brothers that was intended to hide real estate from one brother's wife in a divorce proceeding.[24] As the Supreme Court of Illinois explained, enforcement of an illegal contract makes the court an indirect participant in the wrongful conduct.[25]

Courts do not apply this principle inflexibly. If the parties are not equally guilty of wrongdoing or if the illegality is slight and forfeiture would be harsh, the court may refuse to treat the entire contract as unenforceable.[26]

Courts will not enforce a contract that violates a state's public policy.[27] In Tennessee, for example, the principle of freedom of contract yields to the state's interest in preserving public health, safety, morals, or general welfare.[28]

For a court to invalidate a contract on public policy grounds, the court must be able to identify a clear public interest that the courts have a duty to protect. To determine whether a public policy exists, courts typically look to state and federal constitutions, state and federal statutes, and judicial decisions,[29] not to general notions of public policy. For example, Maine requires that any public policy consideration be "a well-defined and dominant policy that may be ascertained from the law and legal precedent."[30]

Courts do not lightly exercise the power to void a contract on public policy grounds.[31] In determining that public policy considerations prevail over freedom of contract, the courts generally attempt to "wield a scalpel rather than a sledgehammer."[32]

2. Unconscionable Contract or Provision

The doctrine of unconscionability protects the weaker party to a transaction against oppression and unfair surprise.[33] Generally speaking, a court may find unconscionability when there is (1) an absence of meaningful choice on the part of one of the parties to a contract and (2) contract terms that are unreasonably favorable to the other party.[34] In determining whether a contract or provision is unconscionable, many courts apply an analysis that evaluates two aspects of unconscionability: procedural and substantive unconscionability.[35]

Procedural unconscionability relates to unfairness in the contract's formation. To determine whether a contract is procedurally unconscionable, courts typically consider the voluntariness of the weaker party's assent.[36] Factors showing lack of voluntariness include the following:

- A great disparity in bargaining power.

- High-pressure tactics.

- Use of a contract of adhesion.

- The weaker party's lack of knowledge of a contract's or provision's effect.

- The weaker party's age or lack of education, business sophistication, or legal representation.[37]

- Fine print, deliberate ambiguity, over-vagueness, or complex "lawyer-speak."

Typically, procedural unconscionability on its own is not sufficient to show that a contract is unconscionable: the contract must also be **substantively unconscionable**. Though courts have articulated a range of standards for determining whether a contract is substantively unconscionable,[38] it seems safe to say that substantive unconscionability typically arises if the contract is unreasonably and blatantly harsh and unfair to the weaker party and unreasonably favorable to the stronger party.

In states that require both procedural and substantive unconscionability to determine that a contract is unconscionable, many courts apply a so-called "sliding scale." According to this approach, the more substantively oppressive the contract, the less evidence of procedural unconscionability the court will require to determine that a contract or provision is unconscionable, and vice versa. Check your jurisdiction's law.

Though many courts have stated that a contract is unconscionable only if it is *both* procedurally and substantively unconscionable,[39] not all courts agree. In Illinois, for example, a determination of unconscionability can be based on either procedural or substantive unconscionability or on both.[40] Oregon courts give greater weight to substantive unconscionability in determining whether a contract is unconscionable.[41]

Note: a **contract of adhesion** is a standardized form contract that is drafted by the party with the greater bargaining power and offered on a take-or-leave-it basis, without the opportunity for the weaker party to bargain.[42] As such, it is invariably one-sided. Nevertheless, a contract of adhesion is not necessarily unconscionable. Mere one-sidedness does not necessarily make a contract substantively unconscionable, though the cumulative effect of many one-sided provisions may edge the contract closer to the unconscionability line. Check your state's law.

CHAPTER 7

CONTRACT COMPONENTS: PRELIMINARY MATTERS, CORE TRANSACTION, AND SUBSIDIARY AGREEMENTS

■ ■ ■

I. Title and Exordium

A contract should have a title. We recommend that the title begin with the words "Contract For ..." and identify the nature of the contract: e.g., "Contract for Employment" or "Contract for the Lease of Equipment." A contract should begin with an un-headed introductory paragraph (also known as an "exordium clause"). We recommend that you draft the exordium as a concise paragraph in complete sentences, free of needless legal jargon. Let the person who refers to the contract see from the outset that the contract is written in ordinary English that means exactly what it says. The exordium should do the following:

- Identify the effective date.

- Identify the parties (including legal status—e.g., a corporation).

- Establish a short form for referring to each party.

- Express the nature of the parties' agreement.

- Express their intention to be bound by the contract's provisions.

That is generally all the information that the exordium should contain. More specific information concerning the transaction belongs in the body of the contract.

Examples: Exordium Clauses

- Effective on the date set out in the signature clause, Kwok Properties, LLC (Kwok) and _____ (Lessee) enter this contract for the lease of commercial properties. The parties agree to the following provisions:

- Effective on _____, Siler Farms, LLC (Seller) and Clovis Farms, Inc. (CFI) enter this contract for the sale of farm equipment. The parties assent to and agree to be bound by the following:

If you are drafting a form contract for your client, you will not know the identity of the party on the other side at the time you draft; thus, you would need to leave blanks for the other party's identifying information.

If you use a short form to refer to a party, you may stipulate the short form in parentheses immediately after the party's full name. It is not necessary to use "hereinafter referred to as ..." or other legalese. If you know the party's name, the short form may be the party's surname, a key word from the party's company name, or the initials of the company name. If you are drafting a form contract, you can refer to the other party by contractual role: e.g., "Tenant," "Buyer," "Purchaser." Some drafters prefer to use role names to refer to both parties.

Consistency is key: once you have set up a short form, stick to it.

Some attorneys embed the parties' contact information within the exordium. If the contact information includes a phone number and email address, placing it in the exordium will make the exordium less concise than it could be. It is probably better to set out the contact information in the signature clause under the party's name.

Some drafters like to include in the exordium the date on which the contract becomes effective. Rather than set out the date in two places—which opens up the possibility of conflicting dates—we suggest that you simply state in the exordium that the contract becomes effective on "the date set out in the signature clause."

In the exordium's second sentence, clearly express in present tense the parties' mutuality of agreement. Once the mutual agreement is expressed, the drafter is spared any need to repeat throughout the contract that "Party A agrees" to do this and "Party B agrees" to do that.

II. Provisions Dealing With Preliminary Matters

A. Defining Words and Phrases

In certain circumstances, you may need to create definitions for certain words or phrases that you use in your document. If so, draft your definitions in accordance with the guidelines set out in Chapter 27.

B. Drafting Background Recitals

You may have encountered contracts that open with a string of statements introduced by the word WHEREAS (initial recitals). These initial recitals typically set forth background information concerning the history of and reasons for the transaction, the basic assumptions of the parties, and other foundational matters.

Thoughtfully drafted recitals can be useful. Chapter 6 discusses the proper framing of recitals. Given the preference of courts for plain and concise language, some commentators recommend using ordinary English to express recitals, and we are among them.[1]

The background-recitals section should have a heading and should be lettered like any other section. If the section contains distinct subtopics, it should be subdivided, as explained in Chapter 20.

Examples: Headings for Background–Recitals Section

- Background of Contract

- Intention of Parties to Form a Partnership

- History of Transaction

- Fundamental Assumptions of the Parties

- Understandings of Smith Regarding Scope of Services

C. Identifying and Describing the Contract's Subject Matter

It is often necessary for a contract to contain a paragraph that describes the subject matter of the contract (e.g., a piece of land to be leased or purchased). Identifying the subject matter early on can make it easier for the parties to understand the provisions that follow. For this reason, drafters frequently provide a description of the contract's subject matter before they address the parties' promises regarding the subject matter.

Examples: Provisions Identifying Subject Matter

- This contract is for one framed 36″ x 24″ oil painting of Murdoch's cat, "Tobermory."

- This contract is for maintenance of the computers, server, and other equipment listed in the attachment. The contract does not apply to any item that is not listed in the attachment.

If you need to include a detailed description (or if the contract is a form contract that could apply to multiple items), you could handle the description in an attachment. To prepare such an attachment, you would need input from the client. For example, if your client is in the business of leasing equipment to commercial cleaners, you could create an attachment that your client could use with multiple customers.

Your client could specify in the attachment the items of equipment—whether one or a dozen—that each customer wishes to lease. The contract could simply state the following: "This contract applies to each item of equipment listed in the attachment." Below is an example of an attachment.

McHering Equipment Rentals				
Description of Equipment	Manufacturer	Year of Manufacture	Monthly Rent	Rent for Lease Period
1. Model 1500 Carpet Cleaner	CME Industries	2012	$100	$600
2. Model 1200 Vacuum	COS-Somersby	2012	$50	$300
3. Model WX Window Washer	CME Industries	2011	$50	$300
Total Rent Due			$200	$1200

Problems can arise if you are hazy about the scope of the contract's subject matter. Suppose that your client provides I-T services to small companies. If you are not clear about what the services apply to, your client could end up with more work than your client had wanted.

Examples: Descriptions of Varying Scope

- This contract is for maintenance of Henderson & Winslow's computer system.

- This contract is for maintenance of the computer system, server, and related equipment that Henderson & Winslow owned on the date on which this contract becomes effective.

- This contract is for maintenance of the computers, server, and other equipment listed in the attachment. The contract does not apply to any item that is not listed in the attachment.

If a contract's subject matter consists of services or of something that a party must design or construct, you could phrase the subject-matter description as a promise or a policy statement.

Examples: Differently Phrased Subject–Matter Descriptions

- Phrased as Policy Statement:

  This contract is for six 8″ x 10″ pen and ink illustrations (one per chapter) by Kwok for George Hampshire's book, *Nicholas Temple–Smith, Boy Barrister.*

- Phrased as Promise:

  Kwok will design six 8″ x 10″ pen and ink illustrations (one illustration per chapter) of George Hampshire's book, *Nicholas Temple–Smith, Boy Barrister.*

D. Performance Due at or Before Signing

A contract may contain a provision requiring some form of performance that must be completed at or before the signing of the contract: e.g., a disclosure of information, a security deposit, or a down payment.

Examples: Provisions Addressing Performance Due at Signing

- For the contract to become effective, Tenant <u>must pay</u> Landlord a security deposit of $___. Landlord will hold the deposit in an escrow account in a non-interest bearing account at Kwok Bank and will provide Tenant with the account number. After the lease period ends, Landlord determines pursuant to paragraph 12 whether any refund is due to Tenant.

- At the time of signing the contract, Tenant <u>paid</u> Landlord a security deposit of $___. Landlord will hold the deposit in an escrow account in a non-interest bearing account at Kwok Bank and will provide Tenant with the account number. After the lease period ends, Landlord determines pursuant to paragraph 12 whether any refund is due to Tenant.

Many drafters prefer to set out at the beginning of the contract the total prepayments due. If you do that, you may have to adjust provisions in a different section. If, for example, you state in an initial provision that a party must make a down payment before signing a sales contract, your main payment provision will be incomplete unless you adjust it to reflect that the down payment is covered in another part of the document. This issue can be handled by effective cross-referencing, as explained in Chapter 21.

A security deposit has a prepayment aspect but also involves obligations that do not apply until after the party's primary obligations end. It therefore has ramifications both at the beginning of the transaction and during its winding-up phase. There are pros and cons to either placement, so you must use your own judgment.

In drafting these provisions, consider whether the parties intend for the prepayments to be conditions precedent to the document's becoming effective. Courts disfavor conditions precedent,[2] so if you intend for a provision to be treated as such, draft it clearly and unequivocally.[3] Words such as "if" or "on condition that" indicate that a provision is a condition precedent.[4]

We recommend that you state in the provision exactly the outcome that you intend. If your client decides not to require the payment before signing the contract, the client may waive the condition precedent.[5]

Examples: Differently Phrased Prepayment Provisions

• Phrased as Condition Precedent

For the contract to become effective, Tenant must pay to Lessor—on or before the date of signing—a security deposit in the amount of one month's rent. This payment is a condition precedent to formation of the contract.

• Phrased as Recital

On the date of signing, Tenant paid Lessor a security deposit in the amount of $___.

E. Dealing With Duration

1. Stipulating Duration of Obligations to Perform

Certain types of contracts (e.g., a lease) typically contain a specified period during which the parties are to perform their core obligations. We recommend that you articulate the duration of performance if doing so would enhance clarity. The core obligations last for as long as the performance period, while some supporting obligations may extend beyond the performance period. Principles for drafting a time clause are discussed in Chapter 29.

Examples: Duration Provisions

Obligations Lasting Through Performance Period:

• For as long as the rental period is in effect, Thomason, Inc. grants to Tenant the right to occupy and use the office suite in accordance with this contract.

Examples: Duration Provisions (cont.)

- Throughout the rental period, Tenant will pay to Thomason, Inc. rent of $1200 each month.

Obligations Extending Beyond Performance Period:

- Throughout the rental period and at all additional times during which Gallery remains in possession of the sculpture, Gallery will ensure that no employee or other person acting on Gallery's behalf removes the sculpture from the location where Artist originally installed it.

- Throughout the employment period and for a period of five years following the last day on which Employee remains on Workbench's payroll, Employee will not reveal to any third party any information relating to Project J.

---

2. Contracts Lacking a Specified Performance Period

(a) Performance Pursuant to a Time Line

In some contracts, there are no specified dates for when performance begins and ends. Instead, the parties' performance occurs in predetermined steps, stages, or phases that are worked out in advance in the contract or in an attached schedule. Some contracts have simple performance time lines: e.g., one party performs, then the other pays. Those contracts are the sort that laypersons are least likely to bring to a lawyer.

The performance time-line for some arrangements can be complex, with performance dates hinging on contingencies whose timing the drafter does not know in advance but must allow for in the contract. For example, suppose that a website designer undertakes an extensive project for a business owner who wants to be involved in the process at every step. The contract could be designed so that each time the designer completes a project stage, the designer must obtain the business owner's approval; if the business owner does not approve, the designer must re-do the preceding step. In that case, the drafter would not know the due dates in advance and would have to provide that the due date occurs a certain number of days after the completion of a stage.

Examples: Due Date Contingent on Preceding Stage

- No later than the 10th day after the date that Farmer completes the harvest, Farmer shall notify Buyer to prepare for delivery.

- On or before the 30th day after the date that Customer receives the portrait, Customer shall pay Artist the balance due for the portrait.

Developing such a performance time-line can require careful planning. The time-line becomes even more complex if the business owner is required to pay a portion of the total price at each completed stage. If you are creating a time line for performance, be sure that the time line works.

(b) Performance Without Definite Duration

Sometimes, it might not make sense to limit the parties' obligations to a fixed period. Instead, the parties might want the performance of services (and the reciprocal promise to pay) to be ongoing until one party decides to terminate.

In such a contract, the parties' obligations would come into being on the effective date of the contract (unless you set a later date). If you draft such a contract, you will need to consider the means by which the parties can end their ongoing obligations. Chapter 9 deals with the drafting of termination clauses.

Courts do not favor perpetual-duration provisions.[6] For example, a Missouri court stated that it would construe a contract as providing for perpetual duration only if its unequivocal language compels that construction.[7] If they cannot determine the intended duration, some courts may treat a contractual relationship as terminable at will by either party's giving reasonable notice.[8] Some courts hold such contracts to be enforceable for a reasonable period of time and subsequently terminable by reasonable notice.[9] Check state law.

III. Articulating the Core Obligations

A. The Basic Bargain

At the core of every contract is a basic bargain: the parties' obligations to exchange something of value in return for a payment or for another thing of value: e.g., a contract to sell micro-widgets or a contract to exchange use of vacation homes. When preparing to draft a contract, be sure that you understand what each party is entering the contract to get.

Once you understand what the thing of value is, consider the details of when, where, and how. How does the thing of value get from the person providing it to the person who bargained for it? Where and how will delivery take place? Who pays for transportation costs if applicable?

B. Thing of Value Exchanged for Payment

Payment provisions make sense only if you understand what the payment is for. Thus, we recommend that you set forth the promise to provide the thing of value before setting forth the promise to pay. The following are examples of different types of payment arrangements:

- Payment of purchase price (sometimes in installments).

- Payment of a fixed recurring amount, such as monthly rent.

- Compensation for services (salary, commission or both).

- Payment or reimbursement of the expenses for designing or producing the thing of value plus an additional fee for services.

- Payment for the granting or relinquishing of a right.

- Payment for a royalty, or a licensing fee.

A payment provision may have one component (rent), two components (salary and commission), or more.

Example: Payment with Two Components

Section 3.   Compensation to Trainer for Services

     A. Payment of Salary for Animal–Training Services

     B. Payment of Percentage of Ticket Sales from Shows

If a contract involves more than one thing of value, make sure that it is clear which type of payment arrangement applies to which thing of value.

Examples: Payment for Two Separate Things of Value

Section 2.   Installation of Burglar Alarm System

     A. Arrangements for Installation

     B. Payment for Installation

Section 3.   Servicing of Burglar Alarm System

     A. Monthly Service Calls

     B. Payment for Service Calls

Each type of payment clause raises the same types of issues: how much, when, and how. The following example reflects those issues for a fixed, recurring payment.

Example: Fixed, Recurring Payment

Section 4.   Payment of Rent

     A. Amount of Rent

     B. Time for Payment

     C. Method of Payment

Often, payment for a single thing of value is broken into multiple payments that are due on different dates, such as when a down payment is involved.

Example: Multiple Payments for One Thing of Value

Section E.   Payment for Playhouse

    1. Down Payment for Playhouse

    2. Balance Due on Delivery Date

A payment is always *to someone* in exchange for some benefit. The reader should not have to work to understand what the payment is for or to whom it will be made. Thus, we recommend that you draft all payment provisions to articulate these elements clearly.

Examples: Clarifying the To–Whom and For–What

- In return for Consultant's basic service package, which is described in the attachment, Company will pay to Consultant a one-time service fee of $___.

- For each variety of rose listed in section B(1), Buyer will pay to Gardening Center $___ per plant, for a total payment of $___ for all the plants listed in section B(1).

When you draft a payment provision, make sure that your numbers and dates work. If you are drafting a form contract, prepare a time-line to check your dates. Test any formula for determining costs by plugging in amounts.

If you write numbers, we recommend that you use digits *instead of words*. It is easier for a person to read and process $1159.95 than it is to read and process "Eleven hundred and fifty-nine dollars and ninety-five cents." It is also easier for the drafter to check the accuracy of numbers. If you prefer to use both digits and words, make sure that they match.

When drafting a contract, keep your client's priorities in mind. Since your client is paying you to draft the contract, it would be nice (if possible) for you to set out *first* what your client is getting in the bargain and then to set out what the other party is getting.

C.   Thing of Value Exchanged for Another Thing of Value

When two parties agree to exchange things of value (i.e., when there is no payment of money), there are two ways to sequence the exchange: (1) in chronological order or (2) in the order that reflects the Client's priorities.

Examples: Sequencing of Exchanges

Example 1: Chronological Sequence

Section 3.   Company's Agreement to Maintain Confidentiality

Section 4.   Submission of New Technology to Company

Section 5.   Company's Evaluation of Feasibility of Use of Technology

Section 6.   Negotiation of Licensing Arrangement if Use is Feasible

Example 2: Sequence Mirroring Client's (Cupples') Priorities

Section 11.   Release of Claims

    A. Temple–Smith's Release of Claim to Interest in Film Script

    B. Cupples' Release of Claims Against Temple–Smith for Defamation

---

IV.   Identifying and Articulating the Subsidiary Agreements

A.   Purpose of Subsidiary Agreements

In addition to the core obligations, a contract may contain subsidiary agreements that otherwise regulate the parties' conduct. Below are some examples:

- Agreement to pay a fee for keeping a pet in an apartment.

- Agreement to maintain a leased car (e.g., oil changes).

- Agreement to pay ad valorem taxes on leased property.

- Agreement of an employee to comply with company rules.

- Agreement of a consultant to keep information confidential.

- Agreement of a building contractor to obtain liability insurance.

Usually, these provisions need to apply for as long as the core obligations apply. In many instances, they need to apply for even longer: for example, to a tenant who holds over past the date when the tenant should have vacated an apartment. When you draft a contract, consider the duration of your subsidiary agreements.

B. Types of Subsidiary Agreements

1. Subsidiary Agreements Regarding Maintenance of Subject–Matter

Subsidiary agreements requiring the maintenance of the contract's subject-matter include promises to provide routine upkeep, to repair any damage, or to refrain from making physical alterations. Usually, such agreements apply to leased property (e.g., an apartment) or property that is paid for in installments (e.g., a car that is financed).

The question of who has the duty to maintain and repair the subject-matter often is a matter of negotiation between the parties, since the costs of maintenance and repair can be significant.

2. Subsidiary Agreements Regarding Use of Subject–Matter

Many contracts contain provisions that prohibit or otherwise restrict certain uses of the contract's subject-matter. For purposes of this discussion, a prohibition disallows certain conduct; while a restriction merely limits conduct in some way. Below are examples.

Examples: Prohibitions and Restrictions

Prohibitions:

- Customer shall not store any toxic substance in the storage unit.

- Employee will not make personal phone calls using Company's phone.

Restrictions:

- Lessee may paint the apartment's walls only if Landlord approves of the color.

- Consultant shall not remove computer equipment from the office unless Consultant receives approval from the office manager.

Prohibitions and restrictions may include supporting recitals or other information, such as the consequences of non-compliance.

3. Insurance Provisions

In some circumstances, the parties will bargain for one party or the other to carry insurance. If you want to ensure that the other party has insurance sufficient to indemnify your client against losses, you could include in the contract a requirement that the other party maintain its insurance for as long as the risk to your client continues.

A promise by one party to procure insurance typically identifies the types of insurance required and the amount of coverage. It may require the party who purchases the insurance to name the other party as a beneficiary. It may require the party to furnish proof of insurance. The following is adapted from a provision that was litigated in a Colorado case:

> Party A shall provide insurance in the amounts and coverages specified in Section 5B. Insurance covering personal injuries or death must be in a sum of at least $250,000 for one person and at least $500,000 for a single accident. Party A shall provide written proof satisfactory to Party B of compliance with this section before Party B undertakes any work under this Subcontract.[10]

A transactional lawyer must become familiar with the types of insurance available to protect a client against certain risks involved in doing business. In some areas, industry practice will have created the expectation that the client will carry certain types of insurance; with respect to some trades or professions, the law may require it. Below is a list of various types of available insurance.

Business interruption insurance: protects against losses resulting from an event that causes the business to shut down temporarily.

Business overhead insurance: reimburses overhead expenses while the owner of the business is temporarily disabled.

Commercial vehicle insurance: covers commercial vehicles.

Cyber insurance: protects against losses resulting from the failure of a company's computer system due to the causes covered by the policy, losses due to claims by a third party for damages, and liability for a website's content.

Fidelity insurance: protects against losses due to dishonest acts of employees (e.g., embezzlement, computer fraud, theft).

"Key person" life insurance: protects against the consequences of the death or disability of an indispensable employee.

Liability insurance: protects against claims and lawsuits that fall within the scope of the policy (e.g., environmental, automobile, or malpractice) by creating a duty on the part of the insurer to indemnify a third party to whom the insured is legally liable.

Property insurance: extends typically to property at the insured location, can extend to property of others that are present at the location, and may be limited to a specific type of risk (e.g., fire, flood, hurricane).

Public liability insurance: protects against claims by a third party (e.g., a customer) who suffers injury while on the insured premises.

Shipping, cargo, freight, moving, container, or transit insurance: insures goods while in transit.

Surety bond insurance: is not really insurance but is a guarantee by a surety company (via a performance bond) to a party to a contract that the other party will perform as promised.

Theft insurance: protects against burglary, robbery, or other theft.

Worker's compensation insurance: protects against losses due to on-the-job injuries to an employee (usually required by state law).

Some types of policies are designed to cover a range of risks peculiar to particular occupations. The following is a small sampling:

Builder's risk insurance: protects the builder against loss or damage due to a cause covered by the policy (typically including fire, hail, vandalism, or windstorm) to the builder's equipment or materials.

Crop insurance (a type of federally subsidized insurance): protects farmers against losses due to insects, disease, weather, or natural disasters.

Lessor's risk insurance: typically covers the leased buildings and liability for third party claims (such as the claims of a tenant's guest against the lessor).

Pest control insurance: can protect persons in the pest control business against such loss due to such causes as errors and omissions, the costs of cleaning for "job site pollution," and liability to clients for personal injury or property damage.

Professional indemnity insurance: protects professionals from liability for third-party claims for negligence (e.g., malpractice of doctors and lawyers) or "errors and omissions" of other professionals (e.g., architects, IT professionals and engineers).

Agreements by the parties to a contract to procure insurance are enforceable, and a party who breaches such an agreement is liable for damages resulting from the failure to obtain the promised insurance.

4.   Subsidiary Agreement Regarding Other Conduct

Subsidiary agreements may regulate even parties' conduct other than conduct discussed in the previous subsections. Examples include an employee's promise to not compete during the employment period, a consultant's promise to keep information confidential, or a lessee's promise to comply with zoning regulations.

Two common prohibitions or restrictions in contracts relate to the assignment of a party's contractual rights and the delegation of the party's duties. Because these concepts overlap to some extent, drafters and courts often conflate them. If you wish to prohibit or restrict either assignment or delegation, check the applicable law.

An "assignment" is a transfer of a right or interest from one person to another that causes the right or interest to vest in the other person.[11] When a party assigns its right or interest, the assignee "steps into the shoes" of the original party, and the assignment extinguishes the right of the person who makes the assignment.[12]

A party can usually freely assign its right or interest to a third party in the absence of an agreement to the contrary,[13] though some exceptions typically apply. For example, a party cannot assign contractual rights if the assignment would offend public policy[14] or violate a statute. Typically, a party cannot transfer the right to recover for personal injuries.[15]

A party cannot assign rights to personal services.[16] This principle generally applies to any contract if a party has agreed to provide any personal service requiring special qualifications or skill,[17] including a contract for professional services.[18] To determine whether the contract is a personal services contract, courts look at the "overall tenor" of the contract.[19] Check state law.

A party "delegates" its duties by arranging for a third party to perform them. Unless the contract is for personal services[20] or expressly prohibits delegation, a party can usually delegate its duties without the other's consent, though certain exceptions apply to delegation: a delegation is not permissible if it violates public policy[21] or breaches an express provision of the party's contract[22] or if the contract is for personal services or the other party had a "substantial interest" in having the promisor perform.[23] In contrast to a party who assigns its contractual rights, the party who delegates its duties remains "on the hook" and therefore liable for a breach.[24]

Even if a right or interest would generally be non-assignable or a duty non-delegable, the parties can contractually agree to the assignment or delegation. They can also agree that an assignment or delegation by one party is prohibited unless the other party consents. To understand the legal limitations on assignment or prohibition of assignment, check state law.

CHAPTER 8

LIMITATION OR EXCLUSION OF LIABILITY

■ ■ ■

I. Purpose of Provisions Addressing Liability

Even if two parties have signed a contract, things sometimes go wrong. One of the parties may negligently injure the other, causing personal injury, property damage, or other loss. Goods to which the contract applies may not conform to the other party's expectations. Circumstances may occur that prevent a party from performing. Unless the contract provides for a different outcome, any of these circumstances could result in liability for the client—sometimes liability far exceeding the value of the contract.

A drafter can expressly eliminate or limit a client's liability through certain types of provisions that restrict the extent to which the client is "on the hook" if things go wrong. In drafting such provisions, the drafter must bear in mind that a court's decision to enforce these types of provisions will depend largely on the circumstances of the case. The best you can do for your client is to study the applicable state law (both statutory and case law) relating to enforceability.

Some of the most common types of liability-limiting provisions are discussed below. Caveat: to illustrate these provisions, we have taken some examples from case law. We do *not* offer these examples as guidance as to the proper way of drafting an exculpatory clause in your state: (1) practice varies among courts and (2) these provisions do not comply with the drafting principles discussed in Chapter 6 and Part VI of this book.

For each type of liability-limiting clause discussed, we make one recommendation that applies to all types: rather than rely on boilerplate language, state precisely the outcome that you wish to obtain.

II. Excuse Based on Inability to Perform

A. Excuse Provided by Law

What happens if an event occurs that makes it extremely difficult and actually detrimental for one of the parties to a contract to perform? If the event is one that the party should have foreseen and dealt with in the contract, courts tend to determine that any loss or detriment should fall on the party who assumed the risk rather than on the other party. If the party who cannot perform brought about the event that prevented the performance, courts generally will not shift the loss or detriment to the other party.

One risk that a party assumes is that its financial condition or market conditions may change and that what appeared to be a good bargain may turn out to be a very bad one. A party's mistaken belief that existing conditions will not change is not an excuse for that party's failure to perform. In a recent Georgia case, for example, the court held that a defense that performance had become impossible failed as a matter of law where it was predicated on the party's financial inability.[1]

Typically, a party is not excused for inability to obtain a third party's cooperation on which that party's performance depends.[2] At the time of making the contract, that party should anticipate and address the possibility that the third party will fail to cooperate.

Nevertheless, the law of contracts recognizes that in certain narrow circumstances a party should be excused from performance. The following doctrines may excuse a party from performing:

(1) impossibility of performance.[3]

(2) impracticability of performance.[4]

(3) frustration of purpose.[5]

Courts typically apply these doctrines only in certain circumstances involving events that fall outside the scope of the risks that the party assumed in entering the contract.

Another doctrine that may excuse performance is the "prevention doctrine." The prevention doctrine excuses performance if the party's performance was prevented or impeded by the other party.[6]

B. Excuse Based on Contract

1. The *Force Majeure* Clause

One way to address circumstances that may prevent a party from performing is through a *force majeure* clause. Such a clause covers certain types of events that a party cannot prevent or control, including certain types of actions by third parties.

Typically, a *force majeure* clause addresses so-called "acts of God" (e.g., certain uncontrollable and, in some states, catastrophic circumstances, such as a hurricane, epidemic, blizzard, or serious emergency). It might also cover actions of one or more third parties if the actions were beyond the control of the party who was prevented from performing (e.g., sabotage, riot, labor disputes, or criminal damage). It might address governmental action that prevents performance (e.g., a declaration of war or—if the circumstance could not have been foreseen and addressed in the contract—a law or regulation).

A *force majeure* clause might excuse performance altogether, allowing a party to terminate the arrangement if a *force majeure* event occurs. If the clause allows for termination, it might deal with notice and consequences. The clause might address delay instead of nonperformance (or might address both). If the clause covers delay, it might require the excused party to provide notice describing the *force majeure* event and its expected duration.[7]

Caveat: do not rely on a *force majeure* clause to shield the client from the normal risks associated with a contract that the contract does not specifically address.[8] A court might refuse to extend a *force majeure* clause to failure to perform due to economic factors, which are inherent in business transactions and are not generally unforeseeable.[9]

2.   Drafting *Force Majeure* Language

In the absence of contrary authority, it is safest to draft a *force majeure* clause on the assumption that it will be narrowly construed. We recommend that the drafter refrain from blindly incorporating boilerplate language into a *force majeure* clause. Instead, the drafter (1) should think through the circumstances that *the client* needs the provision to cover and (2) should precisely articulate them. Because these clauses tend to be narrowly construed, the drafter should be specific regarding any type of *force majeure* event that the drafter wants to cover.

In addition to a list of *force majeure* events, a typical *force majeure* clause contains catchall language intended to broaden the scope of the clause to events that are not actually listed. For example, the drafter might list specifics followed by a general statement that the clause applies to "any other occurrence that was beyond the parties' control or that could not have been prevented by the exercise of diligence."[10] Catchall clauses tend to be narrowly construed.[11] In determining the scope of the catchall clause, the court might apply the rule of construction *ejusdem generis* to limit the clause to events of the same kind as the events specified in the list of *force majeure* events.[12]

The following is an example of a *force majeure* clause, containing a catchall clause, that was litigated in a New York court:

> If either party to this Lease shall be delayed or prevented from the performance of any obligation through no fault of their own by reason of labor disputes, inability to procure materials, failure of utility service, restrictive governmental laws or regulations, riots, insurrection, war, adverse weather, Acts of God, <u>or other similar causes beyond the control of such party</u>, the per-

formance of such obligation shall be excused for the period of the delay.[13]

The provision did not help the party because it did not specifically cover the event that prevented the party's performance (inability to procure and maintain insurance). The court stated that the catchall clause ("other similar causes...") also did not cover the circumstance, because the principle of interpretation that applies to such clauses is that they are confined to things of the same kind or nature as the particular matters mentioned.[14]

In general, the drafter should not rely on a *force majeure* clause to excuse failure to perform an unqualified or broadly phrased promise Instead, the drafter should precisely articulate the scope of the promise using qualifying language, as discussed in Chapter 6. Though we regard *force majeure* clauses as useful fallbacks, we recommend that the drafter address—when setting out the scope of performance—any contingencies that could impede or prevent performance.

III.   Exculpatory Clauses

A.   Purpose of Exculpatory Clause

Though courts differ in their definitions of "exculpatory clause," it can generally be defined as a clause that either exempts a party from liability for a wrongful (usually negligent) act or that limits liability for such an act. In this chapter, we use "exculpatory clause" to mean a clause that *completely exempts* a party from liability.

Examples of such clauses include a release of liability, waiver of claims, and express assumption of risk. A **release** is a provision through which one party releases the other party from liability to the releasing party for certain claims (e.g., personal injury or other loss). A **waiver** is a provision through which a party waives its claims for personal injury, property damage, or other loss against the party in whose favor the waiver operates. An **assumption of risk** clause is a provision through which a party assumes certain risks described in the provision.

To get a sense of typical exculpatory language, consider the following *litigated* (poorly drafted) provision adapted from a real-world case. The provision combines language of release, assumption of risk, and waiver.

> You acknowledge that your attendance or use of Company's facility including without limitation your participation in any of Company's programs or activities and that your use of Company's equipment and facilities and transportation provided by Company could cause injury to you. In consideration of your membership in Company, you hereby **assume all risks of injury** which may result from or arise out of your attendance at or use of Company or its equipment, activities, facilities, or transportation.

You agree, on behalf of yourself and your heirs, executors, administrators, and assigns to fully and forever **release** and discharge Company and affiliates and their respective officers, directors, employees, agents, successors and assigns, and each of them (collectively the "Releasees") from any and all claims, damages, rights of action or causes of action, whether present or future, known or unknown, anticipated or unanticipated, resulting from or arising out of your attendance at or use of Company or its equipment, activities, facilities or transportation, including without limitation any claims, damages, demands, rights of action or causes of action resulting from or arising out of the negligence of the Releasees.

Further, you hereby agree to **waive** any and all such claims, damages, demands, rights of action or causes of action. Further you hereby agree to release and discharge the Releasees from any and all liability for any loss or theft of, or damage to, personal property. You acknowledge that you have carefully read this waiver and release and fully understand that it is a waiver and release of liability.[15]

These types of clauses may be incorporated in various types of contracts (e.g., a contract for performance of services or a contract providing a license to use someone's facilities or land). If the client is in the business of providing recreational opportunities that involve risk (e.g., skydiving, horseback riding, or skiing), the client's contract may consist primarily of an exculpatory agreement given in exchange for the opportunity to participate in the activity. To draft an exculpatory clause, we recommend that you apply the principles set out in Subsection C.

B.　Limits on Enforceability

Before drafting an exculpatory clause, know where your state's courts stand on enforcement. Though most states will enforce an exculpatory clause that exempts a party from ordinary negligence if enforcement would not violate public policy, many states strictly construe[16] or *very* strictly construe[17] such clauses. Some states are more lenient.[18]

In general, courts do not enforce exculpatory clauses that exempt a party from liability for intentional, willful, or wanton wrongdoing[19] or that protect a party from liability for violating a statute.[20] Many state courts will not enforce an exculpatory clause that protects a party from liability for the party's gross negligence.[21] In some states, a party may be precluded from limiting its future liability for causing physical injury.[22]

The nature of the contract may preclude enforcement of an exculpatory clause if the transaction affects the public interest. For example, courts have refused on public policy grounds to enforce exculpatory clauses that would exempt medical and legal practitioners from liability.[23]

In some states, legislation bars enforcement of an exculpatory clause regarding a particular type of transaction. For example, New York prohibits enforcement of a provision exempting the owner in charge of "any pool, gymnasium, place of amusement or recreation, or similar establishment" from liability to the user for negligence if the owner receives a fee for use of the facility.[24]

Exculpatory clauses that limit liability for ordinary negligence have often been challenged on public policy grounds. Be aware when you draft such a clause of the presence of factors that may cause a court to determine that the clause violates public policy. In general, courts are most likely to invalidate exculpatory provisions on public policy grounds in cases in which (1) there was a great disparity in bargaining power and (2) the party seeking exemption from negligence was providing a service or other benefit (e.g., electricity) that significantly affects the public interest and that was essential to the other party. In determining whether an exculpatory clause violates public policy, many courts are guided by the so-called *Tunkl* factors[25] (after a much-cited 1963 California case[26]), though different courts may give greater weight to different factors.[27] Other state courts have developed their own tests. If you draft an exculpatory clause that has public policy implications, check the law that applies in your state.[28]

Unconscionability may also invalidate an exculpatory clause. A court may find an exculpatory clause unconscionable if it appears in a contract that is otherwise harshly one-sided, if there is a great disparity in bargaining power, and if other elements of procedural unconscionability are present. A West Virginia court stated that an exculpatory clause in a contract of adhesion is presumptively invalid if it would prevent a person from enforcing rights protected by state law and public policy.[29] Chapter 6 discusses unconscionability and contracts of adhesion.

C. Drafting an Exculpatory Clause

1. Use Language That Is "Clear and Unequivocal"

The requirements for drafting an enforceable exculpatory clause vary from state to state, but clarity is crucial in every state. For the provision to exempt a party from liability for negligence, most courts require that the language *unequivocally* extend to a claim alleging negligence. A Florida case states a useful standard, requiring an exculpatory clause to be "so clear and understandable that an ordinary and knowledgeable party will know what he is contracting away."[30]

In some states, it may be necessary to include the word "negligence" in an exculpatory clause.[31] Courts in other states have said that there are no "magic words" necessary to create an exemption from liability for negligence, but "words conveying a similar import must appear."[32] The safest approach is to specify that the clause applies to negligence.[33]

If an exculpatory clause exempts a party from liability for negligence, make sure that language elsewhere in the contract is not inconsistent with the exemption. In a case in which a camp had promised to take "reasonable precautions ... to assure the safety and good health" of the campers, a Florida court found it inconsistent on the part of the camp to seek to be released from liability for negligence (i.e., failure to use reasonable care).[34]

2.   Identify Persons to Whom the Exculpatory Clause Applies

In setting out the scope of an exculpatory clause, make it clear to whom the exemption from liability extends by precisely identifying (1) the person who is assuming the risk, releasing the other from liability, or waiving its claim; and (2) the person protected by the exculpatory clause. If the clause extends to a range of persons, make sure that you have adequately identified all to whom you intend for the exculpatory clause to apply. Typically, it is not necessary for the exculpatory clause to identify by name the persons to whom it applies; instead, the drafter may identify those persons by identifying the class to which they belong (e.g., owner, tenant, or customer).[35] Some courts may adopt a stricter approach,[36] so check state law.

In any contract, you may need to decide whether the exculpatory clause extends to the party's successors or assigns. If one of the parties is a corporation or other legal entity, you must consider whether the provision extends to officers, directors, other agents, shareholders, subsidiaries or other related entities. If one of the parties is an individual, you may need to consider whether the exculpatory clause should extend to the party's representatives, heirs, beneficiaries, or other persons.

3.   Articulate the Scope of an Exculpatory Clause

(a) Specify Items Released or Waived or Risks Assumed

In articulating the types of items to which a release or waiver applies, some drafters include a long list of released or waived items, many of which overlap other items in the list. For example, the release or waiver may refer to "all claims, rights, liabilities, actions, causes of action, damages, lawsuits, and demands."

We prefer to frame a release so that it broadly extends to "all liability, including liability for negligence" and a waiver to "all claims, including a cause of action for negligence." However, when expressing risks assumed, we prefer to be specific as to those we can anticipate and to use general language to capture those we cannot.

Reasonable minds differ as to the best way of drafting exculpatory clauses. Chapter 26 discusses choosing between broad and specific language, including considerations relating to rules of construction that a court might apply.

(b) Articulate Circumstances to which Clause Applies

How specific must a drafter be in setting out the circumstances in which an exculpatory clause applies? To know the level of specificity that your state's courts require, examine cases in which courts have construed exculpatory clauses.

Some courts require that you specify the types of situations to which the exculpatory clause applies. For example, Illinois courts require that any exculpatory clause contain "clear, explicit, and unequivocal language referencing the type of activity, circumstance, or situation that it encompasses."[37]

However, even in Illinois, the drafter does not have to list every possible circumstance, so long as the actual injury on which the case is based falls within the scope of possible dangers ordinarily accompanying the activity.[38]

For example, an Illinois court enforced a release signed by a man who was ultimately killed in a plane crash during flight-formation training for an air show. The release recited that he recognized the danger of flight training and formation flying, that he understood that there was a possibility of death, and that he released the defendant and other persons from "any and all claims" sustained as a result of "instruction, training, attending, participating in, practicing for, and traveling to and *from activities involving formation flights*."[39] Though the exact occurrence was not listed, the court held that the release applied to all claims that resulted from activities involving formation flying.[40] Some courts may adopt a stricter approach, so check state law.

Regarding releases and waivers, we recommend that the drafter err on the side of stipulating the circumstances that the drafter anticipates are likely to give rise to liability. Regarding assumption of risk provisions, we recommend that the drafter specify any risk that needs to be covered and include catchall language to cover additional risks that the drafter cannot anticipate. Regarding catchall language, remember that some courts might apply a rule of construction such as *ejusdem generis* (as discussed in Chapter 26).

4. Conspicuousness of Provision

Some states may require that an exculpatory clause be conspicuous. A conspicuous clause is one that would attract an ordinary reader's attention.[41] Look to state law for guidance.

IV.　Clauses Used to Limit Damages or Remedies

A.　Limitation-of-Damages Clauses

1.　Characteristics of a Limitation-of-Damages Clause

In addition to or instead of an exculpatory clause, a drafter might include in a contract a provision for limitation of damages. Whereas an exculpatory clause exempts a party from liability, a limitation-of-damages clause limits the maximum amount of a party's potential recovery to a stipulated amount.[42]

If a limitation-of-damages clause applies, the damages must still be proved: the limitation merely caps the recovery. Such provisions differ from a liquidated-damages clause, which provides a party with the right, following a breach, to an agreed-upon sum of money *without* the need to prove damages.[43] Liquidated damages are discussed in Chapter 9.

Limitation-of-damages clauses are useful in situations in which the damages for breach or negligence would far exceed the value of the contract. For example, a burglar alarm company might agree to maintain and monitor a jewelry store's alarm system. What happens if the jewelry store is robbed? The store's loss could easily far exceed the alarm company's service fees (and thus the value to the company of the contract). Clauses that limit damages are frequently used in alarm companies' contracts and are frequently enforced.[44]

The following is a typical (but not well drafted) limitation-of-damages clause from a contract between an alarm company and a client.

> It is further agreed that [Alarm Provider] is not an insurer of the Customer's property and that all charges and fees herein provided for are based solely on the cost of installation, service of the System and scope of liability hereinafter set forth and are unrelated to the value of the Customer's property or the property of others located on the Customer's premises.

> The parties agree that if loss or damage should result from the failure of performance or operation or from defective performance or operation or from improper installation or servicing of the System, that [Alarm Provider's] liability, if any, for the loss or damage thus sustained shall be limited to a sum equal to ten (10%) per cent of one year's service charge or $250.00, whichever sum is the greater, and that the provisions of this paragraph shall apply if loss or damage, irrespective of cause or origin, results, directly or indirectly to persons or property from performance or nonperformance of obligations imposed by this Agreement or from negligence, active or otherwise, of [Alarm Provider], its agents or employees.[45] [Emphasis added]

Note the use in the example of initial recitals explaining the justification for the clause. We recommend that you include such recitals because courts have sometimes considered them in deciding whether to enforce limitation-of-damages clauses. In drafting a limitation-of-damages clause, apply the drafting principles discussed in Chapter 6 and in Part VI.

2. Enforceability of a Limitation-of-Damages Clause

In some states, limitation-of-damages clauses are strictly construed; in others, they might not be.[46] In some states, the court may be reluctant to extend them to non-commercial transactions (i.e., between a service provider and a consumer).[47] Check your state's law.

A court is not likely to enforce a limitation-of-damages clause if the clause diminishes remedies provided by statute[48] or otherwise violates the state's public policy. A court might not enforce a limitation-of-damages clause if the court finds gross negligence,[49] bad faith,[50] reckless conduct[51] or intentional conduct.[52] Limitation-of-damages clauses that limit damages for negligence or gross negligence have sometimes been challenged on public policy grounds.[53] In resolving the question, courts might look to factors similar to those considered in challenges to exculpatory provisions.[54] To determine whether a limitation-of-damages clause can protect a party against gross negligence, check state law.[55]

We recommend that you apply the same principles in drafting a limitation-of-damages clause that you would apply in drafting an exculpatory clause (discussed in Section III of this chapter).

Enforcement of a limitation-of-damages clause in a contract for delivery of professional services may depend on the nature of the service, whether the other party is a consumer or business entity, or whether the limitation on damages is *reasonable*.[56]

B. Limitation-of-Remedies Clauses

1. Characteristics of a Limitation-of-Remedies Clause

While a limitation-of-damages clause caps the amount of damages, a limitation-of-remedies clause limits the party's remedies by excluding remedies that would otherwise be available.

Many limitation-of-remedies clauses bar a party from recovering consequential damages, which are damages that flow from the consequences of a breach.[57] In an action for breach of contract, consequential damages might encompass certain types of lost profits,[58] loss of goodwill,[59] or business-interruption losses. Thus, a party's potential liability for consequential damages may greatly exceed what the party can afford to lose.

In addition to limiting consequential damages, a limitation-of-remedies clause could also extend to other types of damages, such as incidental[60] or special damages.[61] As the next subsection explains, the clause may limit the party's remedy not only by excluding certain remedies but also by limiting the party to a specified remedy.

Such clauses are useful in situations in which the damages for breach or negligence would significantly exceed the value of the contract or would be difficult for the parties to predict in advance.[62] For example, suppose that you were selling tomato seeds to farmers. What is your potential liability if all the seeds sold to all the farmers yield unmarketable tomatoes?

In an Alabama case involving similar facts, the court determined that the following limitation-of-remedies clause *would* prevent the farmers from recovering consequential damages:[63]

> Buyer's and user's exclusive remedy and [Seller's] sole liability for loss or damage arising from purchase or use of [Seller's] Seeds shall be an amount equal to the price paid for the seeds used.... Buyer or user <u>may not recover any amount for incidental or consequential damages</u>, including loss of profit, loss of yield and amounts expended in using or growing such seeds, or for harvesting the produce of such seeds. This limitation ... shall be applicable to any claim presented to [Seller] whether the legal theory forming the basis of such claim involves contract, tort, negligence, strict liability or otherwise. Buyer and user agree that if [Seller] refunds an amount equal to the price buyer or user paid for [Seller's] ... Seeds, this limitation ... will not have failed in its essential purpose.[64]

Not all courts have agreed with that analysis.[65] The drafter must check applicable law.

We recommend that you apply the drafting principles discussed in Chapter 6 when you draft a limitation-of-remedies clause. To reduce the possibility of dispute, we also recommend that you specify any items of recovery that you intend to exclude so that it is clear to a court and to the other party what the party is giving up.

2.   Enforceability of a Limitation-of-Remedies Clause

(a) Sales Contracts Under the UCC

Limitation-of-remedies clauses often appear in sales contracts.[66] Section 2–719 of the Uniform Commercial Code (UCC) authorizes limitation or exclusion of consequential damages, except with respect to consumer goods.[67] An exclusion with respect to consequential damages is prima facie unconscionable.

Limitation-of-remedies clauses that exclude consequential damages often specify an exclusive remedy to which the purchaser is limited (e.g., recovery of the purchase price of the goods). In specifying an exclusive remedy, the drafter must provide enough of a remedy for the court to find it reasonable in the circumstances.[68] If the remedy is inadequate or unfair, the court can strike the limitation, entitling the other party to the full range of UCC remedies.

(b) Non–UCC Contracts

Drafters designing contracts that are not governed by the UCC may include a limitation-of-remedies clause. A court should enforce such a clause—absent circumstances indicating fraud, contravention of public policy, or unconscionability.[69]

Some courts might treat these clauses as equivalent to exculpatory clauses and might apply strict construction. For example, according to a Georgia court, a limitation-of-remedies clause operates as an exculpatory clause and should be "explicit, prominent, clear and unambiguous."[70] Check to see how courts construe such clauses in your state.

Public policy considerations might limit enforcement. For example, a clause purporting to exclude or limit a remedy that is provided by a statute probably is not enforceable if the statute is designed to protect a significant public interest.[71]

If no public interest is implicated, how far may a contract go in excluding or limiting remedies that the law otherwise provides? According to a Georgia decision, parties "are free to waive numerous and substantial rights."[72] Some states might follow the UCC policy of requiring that the provision not deprive the party of at least some minimum reasonable remedy.[73] Check your state's law.

V. Limiting or Excluding Warranties Under the UCC

A. Express Warranties

The UCC applies both to the sale and to the lease of goods.[74] Article 2 (sales) and Article 2A (leases) contain many parallel provisions, though we focus on Article 2. Whether your client is selling or leasing goods, make sure that you understand the relevant provisions of the UCC.

A warranty is a guarantee or assurance relating to the nature, characteristics, or quality of goods or services. Under the UCC's Article 2, a drafter can create an express warranty relating to the goods that are the subject-matter of the contract by making a statement of fact or a promise regarding the goods[75] or by incorporating in the contract a description of them.[76]

If your client is providing goods to the other party, make sure that you understand how far the client is willing to go in specifying the nature of the goods, their characteristics, or their quality. When describing the contract's subject-matter, make sure that you do not *unintentionally* create an express warranty. If you include language in a contract that amounts to an express warranty, a provision purporting to exclude "all express warranties" is unlikely to be enforced.[77]

B.   Implied Warranties

1.   Types of Implied Warranties

Two types of UCC warranty that will always be of interest to a drafter are **the implied warranty of merchantability** and the **implied warranty of fitness for a particular purpose**. (For treatment of other types of implied warranties, consult the applicable law.) Unlike express warranties, implied warranties are not based on any express assurance or description. Instead, they arise by operation of law.[78]

Absent an exclusion of the warranty, a seller *impliedly* warrants to the other party that the goods are merchantable[79] if a seller qualifies under the UCC as a "merchant" with respect to the goods being sold (i.e., if the seller is a dealer in goods of that type).[80] Among other criteria, goods are "merchantable" only if they are in a fit condition to be used for the purposes for which goods of that kind ordinarily are used.[81]

The implied warranty of fitness for a particular purpose arises if the seller knows or has reason to know (a) of the particular purpose for which the buyer needs the goods and (b) that the buyer is relying on the seller to exercise its judgment or expertise by choosing or providing goods that are suitable.[82]

2.   Exclusion of Implied Warranties

If you intend to exclude implied warranties in a contract for the sale of goods, choose your words carefully and make sure that you follow the guidance in UCC section 2–316(2). That section provides the exact language needed to exclude or limit both the implied warranty of merchantability and the implied warranty of fitness for a particular purpose.

Section 2–316(3) of the UCC provides that all implied warranties are excluded by expressions such as "as is" or "with all faults" unless the circumstances indicate otherwise.[83] Even if you use as-is-type language to exclude all warranties, a cautious drafter might also use the language that we recommend for excluding the warranties of merchantability and fitness for a particular purpose.

When drafting an exclusion of warranty, use recitals of fact as necessary. Section 2–316(c) of the UCC indicates circumstances in which such recitals might be useful. For example, if the buyer had a chance before signing the contract to inspect the goods as extensively as the buyer wished *and* either accepted or declined the opportunity, no implied warranty arises as to a defect that the inspection should have disclosed.[84] If these circumstances apply, we recommend that you include recitals of fact stating that the buyer had an opportunity to make an examination and either did so or refused to do so.

Subsection 2–316(3)(c) indicates that the parties' prior course of dealing or a usage of trade might exclude or limit an implied warranty.[85] If facts concerning their prior dealings or concerning trade usage would be helpful, such recitals are appropriate.

3. The Requirement of Conspicuousness

According to the UCC, a warranty exclusion must be conspicuous.[86] UCC section 2–103(10) indicates that a drafter can meet the conspicuousness requirement through devices that would reasonably be expected to call attention to the exclusion. Whether a provision is conspicuous is a decision for the court;[87] thus, case law can be useful in identifying ways to make a provision conspicuous.[88]

A drafter should be careful about adopting any method of heightening conspicuousness that involves building in an extra step (such as having the other party sign or initial the provision). In a New Mexico case, for example, a car dealership included a signature line under the exclusion of implied warranty, but the buyer failed to sign it.[89] The court pointed out that the UCC does not require such a step but merely identifies the minimum requirements for preventing unfair surprise.[90] Because the seller opted for the additional step, the court stated that it would uphold the effort by treating the unsigned exclusion as failing to exclude the implied warranty.[91]

VI. Agreements to Indemnify

A. Purpose of Indemnity Agreements

"Indemnify" means to reimburse someone for loss or harm. An indemnity agreement requires the indemnifying party to compensate the other party (the indemnitee) for losses. Typically, the indemnifying party reimburses damages that the indemnitee becomes obligated to pay to a third party,[92] though some courts have found that indemnity agreements can apply to claims between the parties.[93] Basically, indemnity agreements shift financial risks and burdens from one party to another.

An indemnity agreement can protect the indemnitee against liability for claims that arise due to the indemnifying party's fault. The following is a real-world provision that was litigated in an Illinois case:

> [Indemnifying Party] agrees to hold harmless and indemnify [Indemnitee] against any losses, damages, judgments, claims, expenses, costs and liabilities imposed upon or incurred by or asserted against [Indemnitee], including reasonable attorney's fees and expenses, <u>arising out of [Indemnifying Party's] activities</u>

or the activities of its officers, agents, students, faculty or employees, under this Agreement.[94]

In some states and under some circumstances, an indemnity agreement can also protect the indemnitee from liability that is due to the indemnitee's own fault. The following is a provision that protects the indemnitee against the indemnitee's own neglience, a real-world indemnity agreement that was litigated in a Florida case:

> Lessee agrees to indemnify, defend and hold harmless Lessor, its employees, operators and agents from any and all claims ... for bodily injury ... resulting from the use, operation or possession of the crane and operator whether or not it be claimed or found that such damage or injury resulted in whole or in part from Lessor's negligence.[95]

Courts are more reluctant to enforce indemnity provisions that protect the indemnitee against its own negligence. Some states have made such agreements unenforceable with respect to certain transactions in the construction industry.[96]

To minimize the probability of litigation, we recommend that you (1) check state law, and (2) draft your provision with extreme care.

B. Construction and Enforceability of Indemnity Agreements

Courts in some states might strictly construe any type of indemnity agreement, meaning that an indemnity agreement of any kind must be set out in clear and unequivocal terms to ensure enforceability.[97] However, strict construction is not the general rule for all types of indemnity clauses.[98] Within a single state, construction may vary depending on the circumstances in which the agreement arises.

For example, courts generally state that agreements indemnifying the indemnitee for the indemnitee's own negligence are disfavored, closely scrutinized, and strictly construed against the indemnitee.[99] Some courts require the word "negligence" to appear in such an indemnity agreement.[100] Other courts do not, so long as the meaning is not in any doubt.[101]

In some states, the drafter may be able to provide for indemnification against liability or loss resulting from the indemnitee's *gross* negligence.[102] State public policy concerns are likely to prevent shifting the party's risk of liability that arises from the indemnitee's willful, reckless, or intentional actions.[103] Similarly, an agreement to indemnify a party against liability for punitive damages may violate public policy: to allow indemnification would defeat the purpose of punitive damages (i.e., punishing and deterring misconduct).[104] Consult applicable law.

In commercial settings, courts are usually willing to treat an indemnity agreement as a realistic method for the parties to allocate the risk of loss.[105] In other settings, some courts may hold the parties to a stricter standard.[106]

C. Some Crucial Considerations Regarding Drafting

An indemnitee's losses can be huge, and litigation is expensive. For that reason, indemnity agreements can have severe consequences for either party to a contract. Thus, an attorney must make sure—before the client signs the agreement—that the agreement is precisely framed in a way that will lead to the outcome that the attorney and client want.

We recommend that you resist the urge to blindly borrow boilerplate language from other contracts. Instead, a drafter should (1) precisely set forth the intended outcome of any indemnity agreement and (2) make sure that the outcome is feasible under applicable law.

In most circumstances, the following issues and contingencies are crucial for a drafter to address when drafting an indemnity agreement:

- To whom it applies.

- In what circumstances it applies.

- When the right to indemnification arises (e.g., after the indemnitee pays the third party or after the indemnitee is found liable).

- Whether indemnification is available if a claim is settled or dismissed.

A drafter must be aware of the consequences of word choice when drafting an indemnity clause. It is crucial in some states to pay attention to the language that explains the agreement's nature because the clause operates differently depending on whether it protects against "liability" as opposed to "loss" or "damages" (or "loss and damages").

States that make this distinction typically allow the indemnitee to bring an action for indemnity against "liability" as soon as liability is legally imposed. In contrast, if the indemnity is against "loss" or "damages," the indemnitee may be required to pay the third party before the indemnitor pays the indemnitee.[107] For example, a California statute provides that an indemnity agreement against "claims," "damages, "costs," or "demands" means that the indemnitee cannot recover indemnification without *first* paying the third party.[108]

To decide how to frame such a clause, you must think through how it affects the client's right to recover in various possible contexts: e.g., if the claim is dismissed or settled or if judgment is imposed. We recommend that *you express* exactly what you want the outcome to be instead of relying on words such as "loss" or "liability" to decide this issue.

A drafter must also consider whether the indemnity agreement covers attorney's fees and other losses. Some courts require that the indemnity clause specify that attorney's fees are covered in order for the indemnitee to recover them;[109] some courts apparently do not.[110] Unless you have clear authority to the contrary, we recommend that you specifically provide for attorney's fees in the indemnity clause.

There are other issues and contingencies that a drafter must consider when drafting an indemnity agreement, but they are beyond the scope of this book. The drafter must thoroughly understand what is permitted under applicable law and must consider numerous issues and contingencies. Good research-related resources include statutes, case law, journal articles, and CLE materials.

VII.   Agreement to Defend

A contract can assign to one party responsibility for the other party's legal defense.[111] Parties have great freedom to allocate such responsibilities as they see fit.[112] Agreements to defend are often paired with indemnity agreements.

In an agreement to defend, the duty usually arises when a claim is made against the other party and continues until the claims are resolved.[113] Whether the duty to defend is triggered depends on the precise language of the contract and the factual allegations in the pleadings.[114]

An agreement to defend involves more than an agreement to indemnify a party for its defense costs. For example, one major issue relating to an agreement to defend is how much influence the defended party has over how the defense is conducted (e.g., who chooses the attorney and who decides whether to accept a settlement offer).

Agreements to defend can have serious consequences. Thus, a drafter must thoroughly consider the ramifications. The safest way for a drafter to protect a client with respect to an agreement to defend is to (1) anticipate and address contingencies and (2) precisely state the intended outcome.

CHAPTER 9

CONTRACT COMPONENTS: TERMINATION, BREACH, AND REMEDIES

■ ■ ■

I. Termination of Contractual Obligations

A. Purpose and Effect of Termination Provision

In this text, we use the Uniform Commercial Code's (UCC) terminology regarding cancellation and termination, even when we discuss contracts that are not governed by the UCC. According to the UCC, "termination" is an ending that is not based on breach[1]; "cancellation" is an ending following a party's breach.[2] Many lawyers and courts use the terms interchangeably or reverse their meaning.

A termination provision gives a party the right to end certain obligations under the contract usually before the anticipated ending of the contractual relationship.[3] After termination, any right of either party that arises based on the other party's prior breach[4] or prior performance[5] survives.[6] Thus, provisions of the contract that govern disputes that arose before the contract ended survive (e.g., a right to arbitration,[7] to enforcement of a forum-selection clause,[8] or to enforcement of an indemnity agreement[9]).

The common expression "termination of a contract" may not convey to a layperson an accurate picture of the effects of termination. Laypersons may view "termination" as terminating *all* the parties' contractual agreements. One way to avoid confusion is to identify in the provision which unperformed obligations are terminated and which ones survive. Below are two examples.

**Examples: Termination Provisions that Specify
the Provisions Terminated**

- Either party may, by giving notice of termination to the other party, put an end to the parties' unperformed obligations under Sections 3 through 8 and Section 10 of this contract. <u>All other provisions survive termination.</u>

- Either party may, by giving notice of termination to the other party, put an end to the parties' unperformed obligations under Sections 3 through 8 and Section 10 of this contract. The following provisions do not survive termination: Sections 3 through 8 and Section 10.

Caveat: if you specify the provisions that survive, make sure to cover *all* the provisions that survive.[10] An unintentional omission of a surviving provision could lead to litigation, and the court might refuse to enforce the provision.[11] It might be safer to stipulate the provisions that *do not* survive.

B.   When a Termination Right May Be Necessary

If the contract calls for recurring or ongoing performance by the parties without providing any limit on the duration of performance, you may need to provide the parties with a way out. Typically, the parties could terminate performance by giving reasonable notice, but drafting an open-ended contract with no termination provision invites litigation.

Even if the contract stipulates a period of performance, you should still draft a termination provision. For example, your client might be willing to lease property to another party for three years *so long as* the other party agrees that the client may terminate the arrangement earlier if the client finds a buyer for the property. Similarly, if your client hires an independent contractor to sell micro-gadgets for three years, your client may want the right to end the arrangement if the client decides to stop manufacturing micro-gadgets. In such cases, you should draft a provision setting out how to terminate performance.

C.   Enforcement of Termination Provision

1.   Unilateral Right of Termination

Courts have enforced unilateral termination provisions. As the Nebraska Supreme Court said, courts have held that the existence of the right does not make the contract illusory if the party to whom the right is granted is "irrevocably bound for any appreciable period of time."[12] Thus, even a slight restriction on the exercise of the termination right (e.g., a requirement that advance notice be given) may be sufficient to prevent a unilateral right of termination from being regarded as illusory."[13] Check state law.

2. Termination-for-Convenience Clause

A provision that permits a party to terminate a contract regardless of cause is sometimes called a "termination-for-convenience" clause.[14] A termination-for-convenience clause bars a claim for wrongful termination.[15] Such a clause permits a party to exercise its right of termination without becoming liable for benefit-of-the-bargain damages.[16]

3. Termination Clause in a Contract With a Fixed Duration

If a contractual performance period is of a fixed duration and if the parties want the right to terminate early, then the drafter should include a termination provision.[17] If a contract contains a provision setting out a fixed duration for the parties' performance *and* a provision permitting one of the parties to terminate that performance before the period ends, you will need to draft those provisions so as to minimize any apparent conflict that might lead to confusion or dispute.

Example: Non–Conflicting Duration and Termination Provisions

Section 4.   Period of Performance

The leasing period is for a maximum of three years. It begins on _____ and continues for a minimum one-year period ending on _____. After the minimum period ends, the leasing period continues in effect for an additional two-year period ending on _____, unless Kwok Properties exercises its right of termination under Section 11.

Section 11.   Termination of Performance

After the end of the first year of the three-year leasing period, Kwok Properties may terminate the leasing period and the obligations set forth in Sections 3–9 if Kwok Properties finds a purchaser for the property. Kwok Properties may terminate the leasing period by sending notice of termination to Tenant by registered mail. The leasing period ends on the 30th day after the date that Kwok Properties sends the termination notice.

Cases exist in which one party has argued that enforcement of a "without cause" termination clause would render the duration clause meaningless.[18] However, courts have enforced termination clauses that permit a party to cut off the period stipulated in a duration clause, even if the duration clause makes no reference to the termination clause.[19]

D.   Procedural Requirements for Termination

Termination clauses typically condition effective termination on the terminating party's compliance with certain procedural requirements. If, for example, a termination clause requires notice in a certain form (e.g., written), a party seeking to terminate must comply with that requirement for the termination to become effective.[20]

During the notice period (i.e., the period between the sending of the termination notice and the termination's effective date), the parties must continue to perform. Their obligations do not end until the date on which termination becomes effective.[21] After that date, other obligations may become effective, such as obligations regarding the winding up of the transaction or relationship.

When drafting a termination clause, give careful thought to any requirements that you impose. If the clause is strictly for the benefit of the client, consider minimizing the hoops that the party has to jump through to end the contractual arrangement.

In some circumstances, it might be in your client's best interest to allow the other party to end the contractual arrangement if the other party is unhappy. If that is the case, you may need to provide for each party to refund money for benefits not received as of the time of termination and to restore any property that belongs to the other party.

In some cases, your client may be willing to allow a termination so long as the other party is willing to pay a fee to cover some of the client's resulting losses. Below is an example, based on a provision that was litigated in Texas.[22]

Example: Termination Clause Requiring a Termination Fee

Operator shall have the right to terminate the Contract at any time after the date of execution of the Contract by both parties and prior to the expiration of the first 1,095 calendar days thereafter (the "Early Termination") by giving thirty (30) days' prior written notice to the Contractor, conditional upon Operator paying Contractor the Early Termination amount and other amounts specified below. In the event of Early Termination, Operator shall pay to the Contractor an Early Termination Amount equal to the number of days remaining in the 1,095 calendar day term multiplied by $14,000. Operator shall pay in one payment (within thirty (30) calendar days of the date of Contractor's invoice) such Early Termination amount. The Early Termination amount is in addition to all other amounts due and owing under the Contract prior to the date of such Early Termination, including without limitation the mobilization and demobilization payments.

Check with the client. In an appropriate case a reasonable termination fee can prevent the client from being placed in a seriously disadvantageous position while the client is looking for another customer, lessee, supplier, buyer, service provider, or patron.

II. Breach of Contract

A. Elements of Breach Action

The elements of a breach of contract claim are as follows: (1) the existence of a valid contract, (2) the non-breaching party's performance or tender of performance, (3) the breaching party's failure to provide the promised performance, and (4) resulting damages suffered by the non-breaching party.[23]

B. Party's Recovery for Breach

1. Remedies Provided by Law

(a) Remedies Generally

In some circumstances, the drafter may be satisfied to allow the law of contracts to govern available remedies for breach. The drafter would need to understand what sort of recovery is possible under general contract law. Remedies for breach typically include expectation or benefit-of-the-bargain or reliance damages, specific performance, and restitution.[24]

(b) Damages

A party who sues for breach essentially affirms the contract by asking the court to enforce it.[25] The usual remedy for breach is recovery of compensatory damages.[26] Typically, the non-breaching party recovers *expectation* or *benefit-of-the-bargain* damages.

The purpose of **benefit-of-the-bargain damages** is to put the non-breaching party in as good a position as that party would have been in if the other party had not breached.[27] Thus, the party recovers the benefit, including certain profits, that the party would have received from the other party's full performance.[28] To be entitled to recover such damages, the party must show that the losses are not speculative or uncertain and that the court can estimate with reasonable accuracy the amount necessary to compensate the other party.[29]

Reliance damages are awarded to compensate a party for expenses that the party would not have incurred but for reliance on the contractual obligation that was not performed.[30] The purpose of reliance damages is to put the non-breaching party in the position that it was in before entering the contract. The court might allow the party to recover reliance damages if the non-breaching party cannot prove the amount of *expectation* or *benefit-of-the-bargain* damages with reasonable certainty. As a Texas Court of Appeals explained, reliance damages are measured by the *out-of-pocket* expenditures made by one party in reliance on the actions of another party, not by the amount of lost profits and sales.[31]

(c) Specific Performance

Specific performance is court-ordered performance of a party's contractual obligations. Typically, specific performance is granted only if the non-breaching party is clearly entitled to it, if there is no adequate remedy at law, and if the court believes that justice requires it.[32] This remedy is appropriate if the subject-matter of the contract is unique in its nature, characteristics, or associations.[33] Even if the subject-matter of the contract is unique, the court considers whether suitable substitutes are unobtainable or unreasonably difficult to procure.[34]

If you are considering making specific performance an automatic or exclusive remedy for a breach, be sure to check state law. There are some obligations (e.g., personal services) that courts generally *will not* order a party to specifically perform.[35] State law might impose other limits.[36] For example, a California statute lists circumstances in which specific performance is unavailable.[37]

(d) Rescission and Restitution

In some cases, a party injured by a breach has the choice to rescind the contract and receive restitution instead of continuing it and recovering damages for breach.[38] Rescission "unmakes" the contract through disaffirming it—in contrast to affirming it and suing for breach.[39] A party cannot recover both (1) restitution resulting from rescission and (2) damages for breach; restitution and damages are alternative and mutually exclusive remedies.

The right to rescind a contract does not arise from every breach: the breach must be material, and the failure to perform must be substantial enough to defeat the party's object in making the contract.[40] If a breach is not material and damages would be an adequate remedy, the party is limited to a claim for damages and cannot rescind the contract. The test for materiality is whether a breach is of such nature and importance, if anticipated in advance, that the party would have not made the contract.[41]

If a court permits a party to rescind a contract and if the party has conferred a benefit on the other, the party might be entitled to recover restitution.[42] The idea of rescinding a contract implies that each party should receive back what the party gave up.[43] Thus, the goal of rescission and restitution is to place the parties in the same position they were in just before the execution of the contract.[44]

In an action for breach, restitution is typically available if the non-breaching party has conferred a benefit on the breaching party.[45] The breaching party may have to return the subject-matter of the contract or to pay compensation for any performance that the breaching party received from the non-breaching party.[46]

2. Remedies Provided by the Contract

(a) Right of Parties to Fashion Their Own Remedies

As the Iowa Supreme Court stated, contracting parties have "wide latitude to fashion their own remedies" for a breach, and a court usually should not deny full effect to such provisions because by doing so that court would effectively reconstruct the contract contrary to the parties' intent.[47] It may be useful to the parties and the courts if the contract directly addresses the parties' intended remedies for breach.

The law of contracts requires mutuality of obligation, meaning that both parties are bound to perform.[48] As a Maryland court pointed out, the law of contracts does *not* require an even exchange of identical rights and obligations for a contract to be deemed valid. Thus, the law does not generally require "mutuality of remedies" in the sense that both parties must have the same remedies for breach in order for the contract to be enforceable,[49] and a valid contract may provide certain remedies to one party but not the other party. Note that a serious imbalance, particularly in a contract of adhesion, may raise concerns about unconscionability (discussed in Chapter 6).

(b) Non-breaching Party's Suspension or Cancellation of Performance

Typically, courts allow rescission as a remedy for breach only if the breach is material and goes to the basis of the contractual relationship. If getting the other party's performance of certain obligations is important to your client, you might want to deal with this issue in the contract by stipulating that a breach of those obligations *is material* and permits your client to suspend or cancel performance.[50] Doing so is a good idea if a court might not view the provisions as material. If you want your client to be able to end the parties' primary ongoing obligations, you can provide for cancellation. If your client is amenable, you might allow the other party an opportunity to cure the breach and might provide for your client to suspend performance until the other party cures the breach.

Suppose, however, that the client wants to be able to get out of the contract if the other party breaches *any* provision of the contract. In some contexts, such a desire might be reasonable.[51] Check state law.

The parties to a contract may specify certain procedures that the non-breaching party must follow if a breach occurs[52]: e.g., providing that the non-breaching party must give written notice to the other party before the breach becomes effective. (Email is a good way to ensure that a notice is in writing and includes the date and time.)

Building in provisions for giving notice of a breach and a period of time to cure it is sometimes helpful (particularly to allow *your client* to cure the breach). Think through the timing of the notice. When drafting a cancellation clause, consider what "reasonable notice" means if an ongoing breach could cause injury or loss to your client or your client's associates.

We recommend that you apply the same principles discussed in Section I–A of this chapter when you draft a cancellation clause.

**Examples: Cancellation Clauses that Specify
the Provisions Cancelled**

- Either party may, by giving notice of cancellation to the other party, put an end to the parties' unperformed obligations under Sections 3 through 8 and Section 10 of this contract. <u>All other provisions survive cancellation.</u>

- Either party may, by giving notice of cancellation to the other party, put an end to the parties' unperformed obligations under Sections 3 through 8 and Section 10 of this contract. <u>The following provisions do not survive cancellation</u>: Sections 3 through 8 and Section 10.

(c) Liquidated–Damages Clause

A liquidated-damages clause is an agreement to pay a predetermined sum of money to compensate a non-breaching party in the event of breach.[53] These clauses permit the parties to agree in advance on the amount of damages for breach, thereby avoiding the difficulty, uncertainty and expense of litigation if a breach occurs.[54] A liquidated-damages clause is appropriate in situations in which actual damages are uncertain, difficult to ascertain, or of a purely speculative nature.[55]

For a liquidated-damages clause to be enforceable, the amount of the liquidated damages must be a *reasonable estimate* of the actual amount that would be needed to compensate the party for the losses resulting from the breach (taking into account the difficulty of proving the loss).[56] Courts differ as to whether reasonableness should be determined as of the time the parties entered the contract or the time the damages actually were incurred.

A liquidated-damages clause must not be designed to punish the breaching party.[57] If the amount of liquidated damages is unreasonably large, it is a penalty, and the court will not enforce the provision. Whether the amount is a penalty depends on the case's underlying circumstances and is a question of law for the court.[58]

A liquidated-damages clause that might pass muster in one state might be deemed a penalty in another. To understand the factors involved in enforcement, you must look to state law. The following is a liquidated-damages clause that was discussed by the Kansas Supreme Court, which concluded that the clause did *not* constitute a penalty:

OWNER and CONTRACTOR ... recognize the delays, expense and difficulties involved in proving the actual loss suffered by OWNER if the Work is not completed on time. Accordingly, instead of requiring any such proof, OWNER and CONTRACTOR agree that as liquidated damages for delay (but not as a penalty) CONTRACTOR shall pay OWNER Six Hundred Dollars ($600.00) for each day that expires after the time specified in paragraph 3.1 for the work to start, and Eight Hundred Fifty Dollars ($850.00) for each day that expires after the time specified in paragraph 3.2 for Substantial Completion until the Work is substantially complete....[59]

If the contract gives a party a right to liquidated damages, the party does not have the right to reject the liquidated damages in order to pursue a greater amount of damages.[60] If the party has the option to select the "liquidated damages," the court might refuse to enforce the clause, since the party seeking damages could choose the clause as a penalty if it happened to exceed the actual damages.[61]

Drafting a liquidated-damages clause is a context-specific task. To understand how to predict what would be "just compensation" in a particular type of case, the drafter must investigate the applicable law. We also recommend that you refer to resources such as bar journal articles and CLE materials.

(d) Limitation of Damages or Remedies and Exclusion of Warranties

A drafter may limit a client's liability for breach by including in the contract certain provisions that are discussed in Chapter 8: limitation of damages, limitation of remedies, and exclusion of warranties.

CHAPTER 10

CONTRACT COMPONENTS: WINDING–UP, NON–COMPETE, SEVERANCE, INTEGRATION, AND DISPUTE–RESOLUTION PROVISIONS

■ ■ ■

I. Winding up the Contractual Relationship

At some point, the contractual relationship comes to an end. Regardless of how the relationship ends (e.g., expiration, termination, or cancellation), the contract should address any arrangements that the parties have made for winding things up.

The arrangements may depend on the way that the performance ends. In an employment contract, for example, the winding-up arrangements may differ depending on whether the contract ends because the employment period expires or because one of the parties breaches the contract. In other instances, winding-up arrangements will be the same, regardless of how the contract ends. In some types of transactions, such as the setting up of a business, the parties' arrangements for ending the contractual relationship can become very complex.

If the contract requires an exchange of property, the drafter must address the method by which the owner gets the property back. Which party makes the arrangements to return the property? When must the return occur? Who bears costs for disassembly, packing, or transport? What happens if the party in possession fails to timely return the property? What happens if the party loses or damages the property?

Similarly, the drafter may need to consider the arrangements for the return of refundable deposits or of advance payments for services or benefits that the party did not receive due to the relationship's ending.

II. Covenants that Protect Business Interests after Relationship Ends

A. Types of Activities Restricted

Despite statutes prohibiting restraint on trade,[1] most states make a limited exception for certain restrictive covenants if the covenants are reasonable and do not violate public policy.[2] These covenants typically appear in contracts involving contracts for employment or the transfer of a business (e.g., the sale of a business and its goodwill or the breaking up of a partnership). Courts generally require that a covenant restraining trade be supported by consideration, ancillary to a lawful contract, and not inconsistent with public policy.[3]

To be enforceable, such a covenant typically must be designed to protect a *legitimate business interest*,[4] such as protection of a business's customer base or goodwill,[5] its relationship with its employees, or its confidential information or trade secrets.[6] Another (generally more controversial interest) is a business's interest in preventing *unfair* competition by the other party.[7]

The following are among the types of actions that such a covenant might restrict:

- Competition with the other party by carrying on the same trade, occupation, or business.

- Solicitation of the other party's customers or actions that would affect "goodwill."

- Luring away of the other party's employees or agents.[8]

- Disclosure of the other party's confidential information or trade secrets.

A drafter can include in a contract any of these covenants that the relevant state's law permits, if the covenant meets the state's requirements for enforceability.

B. Enforcement of Covenants

One of the most litigated types of covenant is a non-compete covenant (i.e., one that restricts a party from engaging in the same trade, occupation, or profession as the party seeking enforcement). Courts that enforce non-compete covenants will typically do so to protect against unfair competition, not ordinary competition.[9] Know your state's policy regarding such covenants.

In many states, non-compete covenants between an employer and employee are strictly construed.[10] Since non-compete covenants prevent a party from competing by using "general knowledge, skill, and experience gained from his or her work,"[11] courts are often loath to enforce them.[12] Furthermore, these clauses are often the product of unequal bargaining power, and the employer may not give sufficient attention to the hardship the employee may suffer through loss of his or her livelihood.[13] In determining enforceability, some courts take into account whether the covenant causes undue hardship to the employee.

Some courts deal differently with non-compete covenants that arise in other contexts. If the covenant is part of a contract for the sale of a business or an arrangement between partners in a business, the restriction on competition may be an essential component of the consideration (e.g., protection of the goodwill purchased pursuant to the sale). Some courts are fairly lenient in enforcing non-compete covenants in these contexts. For example, the Idaho Supreme Court said, "Non-compete covenants are only disfavored in the employment context."[14]

Courts in some states may treat non-compete covenants between members of certain professions (e.g., lawyers[15] or doctors[16]) as violating public policy or may construe them more strictly than other covenants. In other states, statutes may limit such covenants or make them unenforceable.

Courts may be more lenient in enforcing other types of covenants that do not prevent a party from engaging in the party's profession, occupation, or trade.[17] Thus, enforcement of a non-compete covenant may depend on the nature of the covenant if the covenant has a more limited effect, such as preventing the employee from soliciting former customers or disclosing confidential information. Some courts, such as the Idaho Supreme Court, do not apply more lenient standards in determining enforceability but focus on whether a covenant (regardless of the type) is broader than it needs to be.[18] Know your own state's approach.

C. Factors to Consider When Drafting

1. Factors That May Affect Enforceability

A state will not enforce a covenant that it finds to be overly broad. To be enforceable, such a covenant must not limit competition more than is necessary to protect the legitimate business interest.[19] The standard applied may vary depending on the nature of the covenant; if the court applies strict scrutiny, the court is more likely to find the covenant reasonable and therefore enforceable if it is drafted narrowly. Courts may consider the reasonableness of the following:

- Duration (whether the covenant is in force longer than necessary).[20]

- Geographic territory in which the covenant applies.[21]

- Persons to whom the covenant restricts the party's access (e.g., former clients).[22]

- Type of activities that the covenant restricts.[23]

In determining what is "reasonable," courts may consider the nature of the covenant. For example, a court is likely to find a restriction for a longer period reasonable in a non-disclosure covenant than in a covenant preventing an employee from competing with an employer.

2. Reformation of Overbroad Covenant

A drafter should be aware of whether the enforcing court would be willing to reform an overbroad covenant. Courts in some states may allow a limited type of reformation through "blue-penciling," which permits a court to delete overbroad language if a grammatically meaningful, reasonable restriction remains after the words rendering the restriction unreasonable are stricken.[24] Courts that permit "blue-penciling" usually will not apply the "blue pencil" if doing so would require the court to redraft the agreement by adding new provisions or conditions instead of merely removing the overbroad language (i.e., the overbroad covenant would fail).[25]

In some states, the nature of the covenant may affect the availability of reformation. For example, Georgia courts will use blue-penciling to reform an overbroad non-compete covenant that is ancillary to the sale of a business[26] but will not use blue-penciling to save an over-broad non-compete covenant between an employer and employee.[27]

Courts in some states apply a different principle in reforming covenants: those that apply a "reasonableness" test will refashion an overbroad covenant so that it is reasonable as between the parties.[28] In some states, statutes provide that the court must reform a covenant that is unreasonable so that it is reasonable.[29]

Some states will not reform an overbroad covenant.[30] In South Carolina, for example, an overbroad covenant cannot be enforced unless the invalid parts can be severed. In those states, drafters must use care to ensure that the covenant is only as broad as the existing law allows; otherwise, the covenant might not be enforced at all.

III. Severance of an Unenforceable Provision

As discussed in Chapter 6, a contract provision is invalid if it is illegal or unconscionable or if it violates public policy. However, the invalidity of a single provision does not necessarily invalidate the entire contract.[31] Courts favor enforcement of contracts and usually prefer, if possible, to sever the invalid provision and enforce the remainder.

For an invalid provision to be severed and the remainder of the contract enforced, the invalid provision must not be central to the parties' contract[32] or inextricable from its essentials. If a court determines that the entire contract is "tainted"[33] or "permeated"[34] by invalidating defects (such as illegality), the court typically will refuse to sever the invalid provision and will treat the contract as unenforceable.

In a California case, the Court of Appeals said that the trial court had discretion to refuse to sever an unconscionable arbitration provision from a contract because the contract overall was so one-sided that unconscionability "permeated" the contract.[35] In some jurisdictions, courts may refuse to sever an otherwise severable provision if the party seeking enforcement is guilty of moral turpitude.[36]

A drafter can include in a contract a severance clause expressing the parties' intention that invalid clauses be severed from the contract and that the remainder of the contract be enforced. Courts have given weight to such provisions.[37] As the Texas Court of Appeals remarked, the inclusion in the contract of such provisions indicates that severance of invalid provisions is the policy choice of the parties.[38] However, a court can decide to sever a provision regardless of whether a contract contains a severance clause.

Examples: Severance Clauses

- The parties intend for any invalid provision of this contract to be severable from the remainder. If a court or other competent tribunal determines that any provision of this contract is invalid and unenforceable for any reason, the invalid and unenforceable provision is to be severed from the contract and the remaining provisions are to continue in effect.

- The parties intend for any invalid provision of this contract to be severable. If any provision is invalid, the remaining provisions continue in effect.

IV. Integration (or Merger) Clauses

An integration clause (also known as a "merger clause") states that the written contract is the complete and final expression of the parties' agreements and that the written contract supersedes any understandings or agreements that do not appear in the written contract.[39] If the contract is fully integrated, the parol evidence rule prevents a party from later altering the contract by introducing inconsistent extrinsic evidence of prior oral agreements and negotiations.[40]

The parol evidence rule thus protects a fully integrated contract from a "verbal assault" that might contradict, add to, or subtract from the contract's unambiguous provisions.[41] The parol evidence rule does not apply if the written contract is not fully integrated.[42] Courts can admit parol evidence to clarify contract terms if the meaning is uncertain or to assist the court in determining the parties' intent.[43]

In some states, courts presume that a written contract is integrated if, on its face, it is fully executed, is unconditional, and contains all the elements of a contract.[44] Nevertheless, inclusion of an integration clause is the most reliable way to signify to the court that the parties have adopted the contract as the complete and final expression of their agreement.

Examples: Integration (or Merger) Clauses

Section 10.   Integration of the Contract

This contract is the complete and final agreement of the parties regarding the lease of the Property. All agreements of the parties made prior to this contract's execution are merged into this contract.

Section F.   Merger of All Agreements

By signing this contract, the Parties affirm that this contract contains all of the parties' agreements in final form and that the Parties are not relying on any agreement that is not contained in this written contract. All of the Parties' prior and contemporaneous agreements—including any warranty, all conditions, and all negotiations—are merged into this final and complete contract.

Some states may treat an integration clause as conclusively establishing that the contract is fully integrated.[45] In many states, inclusion of an integration clause is not conclusive,[46] but courts have held that its inclusion strongly supports[47] or is highly persuasive[48] as to the integration of the contract.

In other states, inclusion of an integration clause may have less impact. For example, the courts may consider it as only one factor to take into account when determining whether the contract is fully integrated.[49] Context matters. A Washington court refused to give effect to a "boilerplate" integration clause in a dispute over a standardized form contract.[50]

If you intend for the written contract to be integrated, include an integration clause in your contract.

V. Dispute Resolution

A. Forum–Selection Clause

1. Purpose and Effect of Forum–Selection Clause

The parties to a contract can agree to a forum for resolving disputes that arise between them. If the parties select a *mandatory* and *exclusive* forum, this clause typically trumps any privilege that the law might give the plaintiff to make the venue selection.

Forum-selection clauses can have a substantial impact on the parties' interests because the location of the forum has a bearing on litigation costs and on the convenience of defending an action. In Florida, for example, the distance between a state court in Gainesville and one in Miami is over 300 miles. A Gainesville party required to litigate in Miami could spend a great deal of time and money travelling to the forum and transporting lawyers, witnesses, and evidence.

For this reason, forum-selection clauses are often hotly negotiated. In form contracts, they typically favor the drafter of the form. The following is an example of a mandatory forum-selection clause:

> The parties have selected Templeton, Texifornia as the <u>exclusive</u> and <u>mandatory</u> forum for the resolution of any dispute that arises out of this contract. A party wishing to resolve a dispute through litigation or any other means shall do so in the selected forum and in no other forum.

2.   Enforceability of Forum–Selection Clause

Federal policy strongly favors enforcement of forum-selection clauses. According to the U.S. Supreme Court in *The Bremen v. Zapata Off–Shore Co.*,[51] a forum-selection clause should be given full force and effect.[52] Both federal and state courts have recognized the utility of forum-selection clauses.[53]

A forum-selection clause is presumptively valid if the clause (1) applies to the claims and to the parties involved in the dispute, (2) has *mandatory* force, and (3) was *communicated* to the party against whom it is enforced.[54] To prevent enforcement, a party must make a strong showing that enforcement would be unfair, unjust, or unreasonable.[55] The party would have to establish one of the following:

1)   that the clause is the product of fraud, overweening bargaining power, or undue influence[56];

2)   that enforcement of the clause would effectively deprive a party of the party's day in court because traveling to the forum would be gravely difficult and inconvenient; or

3)   that enforcement of the clause would contravene an important public policy of the forum in which the action is filed.

This burden is typically heavy, and the party attempting to challenge enforcement is not very likely to prevail.

3.   Drafting a Presumptively Valid Forum–Selection Clause

(a) *Drafting a* Mandatory *Forum–Selection Clause*

Typically, a forum-selection clause must be mandatory to be presumptively valid. To be mandatory, it must clearly state that the selected forum is the *only* forum for the resolution of disputes. If the clause authorizes dispute resolution in the selected forum *but does not preclude* all other forums, it is permissive rather than mandatory.[57] If it is permissive, it is not considered dispositive as to the forum: a permissive clause might be merely one factor that a court considers in analyzing a party's objection to the forum on the basis of forum non conveniens.[58]

The safest way to draft a mandatory forum-selection clause is to state unequivocally that the forum selected is the only (i.e., exclusive) forum for resolution of any disputes relating to the contract.

Pay attention to the language you use. In determining whether the provision is mandatory or permissive, courts tend to find clauses framed using "may" and "should" permissive,[59] and to find clauses using "shall," "must" and sometimes "will" mandatory.[60] The effect of these words depends on the context.[61] Florida courts provide useful guidance: they require that a mandatory forum selection clause contain "words of exclusivity,"[62] such as "forsaking any other jurisdiction," "only" and "exclusively."[63]

If your client decides to sign a contract containing a mandatory forum-selection clause, make sure that the client understands the consequences. For example, if the clause restricts the parties to a specific state forum where no federal courts sit or to a non-federal jurisdiction, the forum-selection clause might override the client's statutory right to remove the action to federal court.[64] Federal courts are split regarding whether a forum-selection clause precludes federal jurisdiction if the clause restricts the parties' venue choice to a municipality or county in which a federal court does not sit.[65]

(b) Reasonably Communicating the Clause to the Party

If a party does not receive reasonable notice of the clause, a court might not enforce it.[66] To ensure that the clause is reasonably communicated, consider using devices to make it conspicuous, particularly if it is likely that the other party will not notice the forum-selection clause (e.g., if the clause is included in a digital contract or in a document that might not appear to be a contract, such as an invoice).

(c) Delineating the Scope of the Clause

If a party invokes a forum-selection clause in a dispute, the threshold question for the court is whether the dispute falls within the scope of the clause.[67] An action for breach of the contract would fall within a forum-selection clause, but what about a cause of action based on tort or on a statute if the cause of action is based on circumstances related to the contract? The exact scope of a forum-selection clause depends on its language.[68]

We recommend that you state exactly what you intend for the scope to be. Otherwise, enforcement may turn on the construction that the court gives to the words you use. Cases have turned on the meaning that a court ascribes to phrases such as "arising out of the contract,"[69] "arising in relation to the contract,"[70] "in connection with the contract,"[71] "relating to" the contract,"[72] "arising under" the contract.[73] We recommend that you state in the contract whether a forum-selection clause extends to non-contractual claims that require interpretation of the contract or that otherwise involve the contract.

B. Choice-of-Law Clauses

1. Purpose and Enforceability of Choice-of-Law Clause

A choice-of-law clause enables the parties to choose which state's law will govern the resolution of a dispute. Typically, a drafter chooses the law of the state stipulated as the selected forum, though that is not always the case.

Courts usually favor enforcement of choice-of-law clauses, but limitations apply. For example, the UCC permits the parties to choose as the governing law for a contract the law of any state *if* the contract has some reasonable relationship to that state.[74]

In non-UCC cases, many states base their rules regarding choice of law on section 187 of Restatement (Second) of Conflicts of Law, which reflects a strong policy in favor of enforcing choice-of-law clauses.[75] Typically, courts that base their rules on the Restatement will apply a choice-of-law clause to any dispute regarding an issue that the parties could have addressed in the contract.[76] If the dispute does not involve such an issue, the court must decide whether to enforce the choice-of-law clause. In such circumstances, a court might decide not to enforce it (1) if the court cannot discern a sufficient connection between the chosen law and the contract or (2) if enforcing the clause would violate the public policy of a state whose law would have applied to the contract if the parties had not made a different choice.[77]

Not all states follow the Restatement approach. Oregon, for example, has statutes governing the interpretation of choice-of-law clauses.[78]

2. Construction of Choice-of-Law Clause

(a) Determining Whether the Clause Is Valid

The following is an example of a standard choice-of-law clause:

> The law of Calivada governs any dispute <u>arising under or out of</u> this contract.

In deciding whether the choice-of-law clause is valid and enforceable, the court of the forum state where the dispute is being litigated typically applies its own law.[79] Assume that two parties, one residing in Calivada and one in Texabama, enter a contract containing the clause shown above. Suppose that the contract does *not* contain any clause selecting a forum for dispute resolution and that the plaintiff files an action in Texabama.

In deciding whether the choice-of-law clause is valid, the Texabama court will most likely apply its own law, not Calivada law.[80] As noted above, the policy in most jurisdictions favors a determination that a choice-of-law clause is valid.

(b) Determining Whether the Clause Applies to the Dispute

In some instances, a cavalier approach to drafting a choice-of-law clause is not likely to create a problem. For example, if both parties are residents of the state whose law is selected and if the contract is to be executed and performed in that state, the question of governing law might never arise.

Drafting a choice-of-law clause that actually protects your client can involve complex questions. For example, do you want it to apply if the dispute is not based on breach of contract: e.g., if it relates to the contract but is based on a tort or statutory cause of action? The question is much more complicated than it sounds.

First, you must understand whether the forum court (presumably stipulated in a mandatory forum-selection clause) will resolve the question of the choice-of-law clause's scope based on its own law or based on the law stated in the choice-of-law clause. As the U.S. Second Circuit Court of Appeals explained, different states approach this question in different ways.[81]

Second, you must know how the forum state resolves these issues. Even if you pick the same forum (Calivada) and the same law (Calivada), the answer might not come out the way you intend if you fall back on boilerplate choice-of-law language without checking to see how Calivada interprets choice-of-law clauses.

Finally, you must understand what the selected state's position is regarding the scope of a choice-of-law clause.[82] For example, does Calivada law cover tort claims related to the contract? If not, how would the court determine what law applies to related tort claims?

The best way to learn about choice-of-law clauses is to read cases involving choice-of-law clauses. The safest way to draft a choice-of-law clause is to stipulate in the forum-selection clause exactly what outcome you want.

**Examples: Choice of Law Clauses that Stipulate
Outcome**

• This choice of law clause applies to any dispute arising out of or relating to this contract or its construction, including but not limited to any claim based on a tort or statute. The parties stipulate that Calivada law governs any dispute arising out of or relating to this contract or the parties' contractual relationship, including a dispute based on tort or a statute. If any such dispute arises, no other state's law governs the dispute, including the law of the forum state relating to the scope of the choice-of-law clause.

• The law of Calivada governs any dispute for breach of contract. No other state's law applies to such a dispute. Calivada law does not govern a dispute that does not directly arise from a breach of a specific provision of this contract. In such a case, the tribunal shall apply the law of the forum state to determine the law governing the dispute.

Caveat: no matter how well you draft a choice-of-law clause, it is possible that a judge might refuse to enforce the provision on public policy grounds.

C. Provisions Allowing Attorney's Fees

In most states, the so-called "American rule" precludes the prevailing party in a lawsuit from recouping legal fees from the losing party unless attorney's fees are authorized by statute, agreement, or court rule."[83] Ordinarily, each party must bear the burden of his or her own attorney's fees. Though most states follow this rule, some states do not.[84]

Courts typically enforce unambiguous contractual provisions that allow recovery of attorney's fees,[85] though the court may review and determine the reasonableness of the fees.[86] Check state law as to the availability of attorney's fees covered by the contract and the standard that a court applies in making the determination.

If you want a party to be able to recover attorney's fees in an action arising out of the contract, we recommend that you use the phrase "attorney's fees" instead of relying on more general language such as "all expenses of litigation." The Tennessee Supreme Court, for example, said that the term "expenses," without more, does not cover attorney's fees.[87] It is generally safest to state your intent unequivocally.

In most states, the failure to provide for recovery of attorney's fees means that neither party will recover them. If a drafter wishes to make it clear that attorney's fees are unavailable, the drafter can express that intention in plain English: e.g., "Each party bears the expense of the party's own attorney's fees."

Disputes sometimes arise over the circumstances in which a party is entitled to contractual attorney's fees. In a Nebraska case, for example, a contract stated that the drafting party would be entitled to attorney's fees if the drafting party were forced to sue to enforce the contract.[88] Because *the other party* had sued, the Nebraska Supreme Court concluded that the drafting party was not entitled to attorney's fees.[89]

Another issue to address is whether attorney's fees are available if the parties settle. Be sure that both you and your client understand the scope of the provision.

Will a court enforce an attorney's fees provision that allows only one party to recover attorney's fees? Some courts do not require that a fee-shifting provision be mutual to be enforceable.[90] Some states have statutes that allow or require a court to construe a one-sided attorney's fees provision as creating an equal right for the other party to receive attorney's fees if the other party prevails in an action covered by the attorney's fees provision.[91]

If you authorize attorney's fees for the "prevailing" or "successful" party, you must understand how the courts determine whether a party to litigation has prevailed or succeeded.[92] What does it mean to say that a party must "prevail"? To know the answer, you must consult state law. The Montana Supreme Court, for example, stated that neither party prevails if both "gain a victory but also suffer a loss."[93] A drafter who is concerned about the issue could state in the contract how the court is to determine which party has prevailed or whether either has prevailed.

D. Arbitration Agreements

1. Purpose and Effect of Arbitration

Arbitration is an alternative to litigation—usually a simpler, less formal, and less expensive alternative.[94] According to the U.S. Supreme Court, an arbitration clause provides a means of resolving disputes between parties "by molding a system of private law" to deal with them.[95] The key elements of an arbitration are (a) a third-party decision maker selected by the parties, (b) a mechanism for ensuring neutrality with respect to the rendering of the decision, (c) an opportunity for both parties to be heard, and (d) the resolution of the dispute by the arbitrator.[96]

2. Federal Arbitration Act

In 1925, Congress enacted the Federal Arbitration Act.[97] The Act requires courts to enforce privately negotiated arbitration agreements in accordance with their terms.[98]

The Act is very broad. The U.S. Supreme Court said that the language of the Act signals the broadest permissible exercise of Congress's power under the Commerce clause;[99] in enacting this section, Congress declared a nationwide policy in favor of arbitration and withdrew the states' power to require a judicial forum to resolve claims that contracting parties have agreed to resolve through arbitration.[100] The Act provides that a written provision in a contract to settle by arbitration a controversy that arises out of the contract or a written agreement to submit to arbitration an existing controversy arising out of the contract is *valid, irrevocable, and enforceable.*[101]

The Federal Arbitration Act applies in state courts as well as federal.[102] Though the federal act preempts certain state laws, it does *not* prevent the enforcement of agreements to arbitrate under different rules from those set out in the act.[103] The U.S. Supreme Court said that if the parties to an arbitration agreement decide that state rules of arbitration should apply, the rules that they select should be enforced.[104] Thus, the states can enact legislation governing arbitration. Many states have adopted a version of the Uniform Arbitration Act.[105]

3.   Drafting Arbitration Agreements

Under the Federal Arbitration Act, arbitration is "a matter of consent, not coercion"; thus, parties may structure their agreement as they wish.[106] The parties can limit the "arbitrable" issues and can also specify the rules under which arbitration is conducted.[107] A typical arbitration agreement might address the following:

- The parties' mutual agreement to submit to arbitration.

- The method for selecting and compensating the arbitrator.

- Whether arbitration is mandatory or whether it becomes mandatory if a party exercises the option to arbitrate.

- Whether the arbitration is binding and, if so, whether the party waives the right to appeal the outcome.

- The arbitration procedure (i.e., the steps), including the alternative dispute resolution rules that the parties want the arbitrator to apply[108] and guidelines concerning discovery.

- Choice of law and forum selection.

- Availability of attorney's fees.

Under the Federal Arbitration Act, arbitration clauses are very liberally construed,[109] with doubts or ambiguities resolved in favor of arbitration.[110] Nevertheless, a court can compel arbitration only to the extent that a dispute falls within the clause's scope.[111]

The drafter must therefore think carefully about the intended scope of the clause. A "broad" arbitration clause is one that covers all disputes arising out of a contract. A "narrow" arbitration clause limits arbitration to specific types of disputes. The U.S. Second Circuit Court of Appeals has directed courts to compel arbitration whenever a party has asserted a claim that on its face is governed by a broad arbitration clause, even if the claim appears frivolous on its face.[112]

A drafter intending to draft a narrow arbitration clause should bear in mind that courts tend to construe such a clause to ensure that the clause extends to as many claims as it reasonably can.[113] If the drafter intends to limit the scope of an arbitration clause, the drafter needs to be extremely clear about this intention.

The drafter should take note of applicable state law regarding arbitration provisions. For example, a Missouri court stated that the public policy favoring arbitration is not enough to justify the court in applying an arbitration clause "far beyond its intended scope."[114] A New Jersey court determined that despite the liberal policy favoring arbitration, an arbitration clause that applied to a fee-related dispute arising under a contract for professional services did not extend to a claim for damages based on improper performance or lack of good-faith dealing.[115]

4. "Clear and Unequivocal" Language

If a drafter intends for arbitration to be the exclusive remedy for a dispute covered by the arbitration clause, the drafter should set out the clause in clear and unequivocal language.[116] If the agreement provides for binding arbitration, the arbitrator's decision is generally final and is not subject to judicial review absent a mistake or fraud so substantial as to indicate bad faith or a failure to make an honest judgment.[117]

Can a provision for binding arbitration waive the party's right to appeal the decision? There is some authority that a party can do so under the Federal Arbitration Act,[118] but if the drafter intends this outcome, the provision should state this intention clearly and unequivocally. The drafter should check existing law regarding the effect of such language.

If you intend for a party to be able to compel arbitration, express this intention unequivocally. For example, the following clause was litigated in a Maryland case, with one party contending that it was intended to make arbitration *optional*:

> "However, if you and we are not able to resolve our differences informally, you and we agree that any dispute, regardless of when it arose, shall be resolved, at your option or ours, by arbitration."

The court determined that the clause gave either party the option to compel arbitration.[119] The bottom line: whatever your intention is, state it clearly and unequivocally.

Chapter 11

Contract Components: Modification, Execution, and Effective Date

■ ■ ■

I. Modification Provisions

Parties are free to modify a contract so long as all the parties assent to the modification.[1] In most instances, a party cannot unilaterally modify a contractual provision.[2] An effective modification requires a supplemental agreement.[3] The agreement to modify a contract must contain all the elements of a valid contract, including a meeting of the minds.[4] If the modification is inconsistent with one or more provisions of the existing contract, the modification rescinds the portion of the contract with which it is inconsistent.[5]

Though oral modifications are possible, it is safer for the parties to insist on a written modification. Disputes can arise relating not only to the scope of an oral modification, but also to whether the oral modification occurred at all.[6]

We recommend that you routinely include in your contracts a provision addressing the parties' right to modify the contract and include in the provision procedures that result in all of the following:

- A written record of the modification agreement signed by all parties.

- A clear stipulation as to the nature of the modification.

- A clear identification of the provisions to which the modification applies.

In some contexts, you may wish to carve out an exception to your modification provision. For example, you might authorize a different procedure for modifying certain sections of the contract.

Examples: Modification Provisions

Section 11.   Modification of Lease

To modify any part of this lease other than the Apartment Complex Rules that are set out in Section E, the parties must set out the modification in a signed writing. In the writing, the parties must clearly identify any provision to which the modification applies. To modify the Apartment Complex Rules, the Landlord must follow the modification procedure that is set out in Section E.

Section 14.   Modification of Contract

The parties may modify this contract by executing a valid written agreement setting forth the intended modification. For the modification to be effective, the parties must sign the modification agreement.

Prohibiting the parties from orally modifying the contract might not actually prevent them from doing so.[7] If the elements of a valid contract are present and the Statute of Frauds does not require a writing, a court might determine that an oral modification was effective, even if the original contract prohibits oral modification.[8] The parties' consent to the modification might be inferred from their subsequent actions. Check the applicable law.

II.   Execution of the Contract

A.   Signatures of the Parties

A contract drafter should impress upon the client how important it is for the parties to sign the contract. By signing the contract, the parties show mutuality of assent.[9] If both parties sign a contract, the parties generally are bound by the contract.[10] Courts generally presume that parties who sign a legal document mean what they say and should be bound by the agreements they have made.[11]

A drafter must use the same care in drafting a signature clause as in drafting any other part of the contract. Otherwise, a drafter could inadvertently incorporate language in a signature clause that suggests that the parties intend to impose conditions on the execution of the contract. In a Maryland case, for example, a party to an unsigned arbitration agreement was seeking enforcement.[12] Because the contract stated "this agreement is effective and binding ... **when** both parties sign it," the court concluded that *no* enforceable agreement existed in the absence of one of the parties' signatures.[13]

If you want to make signing (by one or all parties) a condition precedent to the contract's becoming effective or if you want to require additional formalities, choose language that clearly reflects that intention. Be wary of requiring additional formalities that are not required by any rule or statute (such as initialing certain provisions or requiring the signatures to be witnessed). Unless you have a good reason for doing so, it is usually best *not* to build in extra hoops for the parties to jump through.

Before designing the signature section of the contract, review any conventions that apply in your state. For general use, we recommend the following conventions:

1) At the end of the contract, provide a place for each party to sign.

2) Include the client's name below the client's signature line and, if the signatory is an agent or representative, the agent's or representative's name and title.

3) Place the client's contact information after the line for the client's signature (unless you put it somewhere else).

4) If you know the other party's identity, do steps 1–3 for the other party.

5) If you do not know the other party's identity, place under the signature line, the name by which you have referred to the party (e.g., "Lessee") and leave space below for the other party's name and other information to be filled in.

Below are examples of signature lines in a lease.

Example: Signature Line (known party)

_____   _____
Kwok Commercial Properties, Inc.   (date)
By Nicholas Temple, Chief Executive Officer
2601 Industrial Plaza, Suite A
Gainesville, Florida 32601
555–555–5555
KCP@kwokprop.com

Example: Signature Line (unknown party)

_____   _____
Lessee   (date)
Name of Signatory:
Business Name:
Business Address:
Telephone:
Email Address:

Though courts generally presume that a party who signs a contract understands its contents, you may want to include in the signature clause a recital affirming that the other party has read the contract, understands it, and assents to all its provisions. If you wish to ensure that the other party has read a particular provision (such as a provision protecting your client from liability), you can include a statement drawing the party's attention to that provision and reciting that the party is aware of and assents to it.

Nowadays, many parties to contracts use electronic media. If you intend to use electronic documents, be aware of both the Uniform Electronic Transactions Act[14] and The Electronic Signatures in Global and National Commerce Act.[15] Section 2–211 of the 2003 version of the Uniform Commercial Code also recognizes electronic contracts, records, and signatures. In other words, consult the applicable state law regarding electronic signatures.

B. Effective Date of Contract

Many people assume that the date on which a contract becomes binding (i.e., effective) is the date on which the last party to sign did the signing. In many cases that conclusion is correct, but the parties can select a different date for the contract to become effective. A court might even hold that a contract can set an effective date that *precedes* the date of signing.[16]

Substantial rights and obligations may depend on a court's determination of when a contract became effective.[17] Courts have sometimes determined that an act of the parties other than the party's signing made the contract binding and effective.

Similarly, language in the contract or in a governing rule or regulation can make the contract's validity contingent on some event that occurs *after* both parties have signed the contract. For example, a statute might make the effectiveness of a contract contingent on the subsequent approval of a governmental entity.

To prevent disputes between the parties, make sure that the effective date is clear and is set out in only one place. If needed, consider setting out a rule for determining the contract's effective date. What if the parties sign on different dates? What if a party fails to promptly sign and return the contract—and in the meantime your client receives an offer from another potential party? Below are examples of rules for determining a contract's effective date.

Examples: Provisions Relating to Effective Date

- This contract becomes effective beginning on the day that Cupples signs and dates the contract. Her signature is a condition precedent to effectiveness.

Examples: Provisions Relating to Effective Date (cont.)

- This contract is effective on the date that the last party to sign the contract has signed the contract.

- This contract becomes effective on the date on which the Department issues its notice of approval (determined by the date on the notice). The Department's signature is a condition precedent to the contract's becoming effective.

- For this contract to become effective, Thomason must return the signed document by mail not later than March 12, 2012; otherwise, the offer is withdrawn. If Thomason timely returns the signed contract, it becomes effective on March 19, 2012.

If you make signing (or some other event) a condition precedent to effectiveness, the court will treat it as such. Make sure that your client understands the importance of ensuring that the condition is met.[18]

CHAPTER 12

HOW COURTS READ AND CONSTRUE CONTRACTS

■ ■ ■

I. Why a Drafter Needs to Know How Courts Construe

If the parties dispute the meaning of a contract provision and litigate over the dispute, the court must construe (determine the meaning of) the provision. To draft a provision that a court would construe in a way that reflects the drafter's intended meaning, the drafter must understand how courts read and construe contracts.

Understanding some of the widely used "canons" (rules) that courts apply when construing a disputed provision can help you understand the importance of the principles set out in Part IV of this book. Understanding how the courts in *your* jurisdiction read and construe contracts can help you know which of these principles is of greatest importance.

II. Questions for Which a Drafter Needs Answers

If the parties dispute a contract's meaning, how does the court decide which meaning is correct? The following is a list of key questions for a drafter regarding a court's construction of a document:

1) How does the court determine that a provision is ambiguous?

- How does the court define "ambiguity"?

- How does the court determine that a disputed contract is ambiguous? Will the court admit extrinsic evidence to assist it in determining whether an ambiguity exists or only if the court finds an ambiguity?

2) Which "canons of construction" do the courts typically apply?

3)   What types of provisions do courts strictly construe? What biases appear in the court's decisions? For example, does the court tend to be more lenient regarding transactions between commercial entities than in consumer transactions?

4)   What resources does the court typically use in determining meaning? Does it often turn to the dictionary?

5)   In identifying or resolving ambiguity, how much weight does the court give to recitals of fact?

Courts apply rules of construction to a range of documents, including some that you might not think of as contracts. Such documents include but are not limited to (1) a deed;[1] (2) a promissory note,[2] a mortgage contract,[3] or deed of trust;[4] (3) an assignment;[5] (4) an insurance policy,[6] a guaranty or suretyship contract;[7] (5) a license[8] or a lease[9] (including an oil and gas lease or lease of mineral rights[10]); (6) a power of attorney;[11] (7) a declaration of covenants and restrictions;[12] (9) an arbitration agreement;[13] (9) corporate by-laws,[14] articles of incorporation,[15] or a corporate charter;[16] (10) a pre-or post-nuptial agreement[17] or a separation agreement;[18] (11) a divorce settlement[19] or divorce decree;[20] and (12) a letter of intent.[21]

III.   Goal of Construction

If the meaning of a contract provision is disputed in court, the court will *construe* the contract to determine its meaning. Virtually all courts say that the cardinal rule of construction is to give effect to what the parties intended. Courts often speak of this intention as their polestar,[22] touchstone,[23] or cornerstone.[24] Though effectuating the parties' intent is the goal, the intent that ends up being effectuated is typically the intent that a court finds *expressed in the contract*.[25] Thus, the starting point for courts is the contract's language.

IV.   Approaches to Construction

A.   Basics About Approaches to Construction

Different courts may take different approaches when construing a contract. A breakdown of the various approaches is beyond this book's scope, but the following discussion focuses on some of the issues that a drafter needs to understand.

Usually, a court's first task in construing a disputed provision is to determine whether the document is ambiguous. Courts tend to agree on the definition of "ambiguity" in a contract. Most courts (including federal courts applying federal common law[26]) generally will not find that a document is ambiguous unless (1) *in context* there is more than one *plausible* or *reasonable* interpretation[27] or (2) the language is of doubtful or uncertain meaning.[28] That the parties disagree about a contract's meaning[29] or that a party subjectively perceives the contract as ambiguous[30] does not necessarily mean that *a court* will find the contract ambiguous.

For many courts, an initial determination that a disputed provision is unambiguous puts an end to any inquiry regarding the provision's meaning.[31] If the meaning is clear, the court enforces the provision as written.[32]

If a court finds ambiguity in a contract, the court might apply rules of construction, consider extrinsic evidence, or do both. Some differences between courts' approaches to contract construction include the courts' practices regarding the use of extrinsic evidence and use of canons of construction.

According to a Florida court, for example, the court must look for intent first from "the whole of the contract" and should not resort to rules of construction and extrinsic evidence to determine intent unless the contract is ambiguous.[33] Mississippi courts describe their process as a "three-tiered approach:" (1) the court seeks the legal purpose and intent in "an objective reading" of the contract without reference to extrinsic evidence; (2) if the court cannot determine the parties' intent from the contract's four corners, the court may apply the canons of construction;[34] and (3) if the court *still* cannot determine the meaning, the court can consider extrinsic evidence.[35]

B. Use of Extrinsic Evidence

Extrinsic evidence relates to the contract but does not appear within the contract's "four corners." Under what circumstances will a court look outside a contract's "four corners" to extrinsic evidence? If the parties have adopted a contract as the complete and final agreement,[36] the parol evidence rule prevents a party from introducing evidence of pre-signing oral agreements and negotiations[37] to *change* or *contradict*[38] the agreed-upon final terms. The parol evidence rule does *not* require the courts to exclude such evidence if the evidence is introduced to clarify an ambiguity.[39]

While some courts will admit extrinsic evidence only to resolve an existing ambiguity,[40] other courts will look beyond the document's four corners to determine whether an ambiguity exists.[41] For example, under Washington law, a court can consider the following (among other things) regardless of whether the court finds a provision ambiguous: the circumstances surrounding the making of the contract, the subsequent conduct of the parties, statements made by the parties in preliminary negotiations, usages of trade, and the parties' course of dealing.[42] However, the extrinsic evidence is admitted only to illuminate the meaning of the writing, not to show a party's subjective intention concerning the meaning of a term or to vary or contradict any written term.[43]

The New Mexico Supreme Court said that ambiguity (or lack of ambiguity) cannot be discerned without "a full examination of the circumstances surrounding the making of the agreement."[44] Thus, even if the contract's language *appears* clear and unambiguous, a New Mexico court may admit evidence of the context to determine whether a provision is in fact ambiguous.[45]

Obviously, a drafter cannot draft recitals relating to the parties' future course of performing,[46] but the drafter can incorporate recitals concerning the background of the transaction or use definitions to nail down the meaning of key terminology. Courts typically do not permit recitals to create or extend rights or duties; however, courts often look to recitals in determining intent, though courts may differ as to the weight that they give to recitals.[47] Chapters 6 and 7 discuss the use of recitals. Chapter 27 discusses definitions.

C. Use of Canons of Construction

1. Role of the Canons in Promoting Fair Dealing

The canons (or rules) of construction are principles that reflect a court's assumption about how a court should read a contract. One of the assumptions underlying the canons is that the parties intended for a written contract to work and to bring about a rational outcome. Cumulatively, the canons of construction reduce the likelihood of success of a drafter who manipulates language to trick the other party or to build in ambiguities and loopholes. The courts' reading of a contract tends to undercut the effectiveness of deliberate obfuscation.

2. Canons That Guide the Court in Reading the Contract

(a) Reading to Give the Contract Validity

Courts generally assume that the parties intend for a written contract to be valid. Thus, if one reading would make a contract illusory and unenforceable and if the other reading would make it valid, the court typically will favor the reading that gives it validity.[48]

(b) Reading to Give Effect to the Whole

Courts generally assume that the parties intend for all provisions of the contract to be meaningful and for the document *as a whole* to make sense. Thus, courts read each part of the contract in relation to its other parts, instead of interpreting words in isolation.[49] In other words, courts read the provisions in context.

Moreover, courts generally emphasize the importance of reading the contract to give effect (if possible) to the contract's *every word and phrase*.[50] As the U.S. Eighth Circuit Court of Appeals said, a basic tenet of contract law is that "each word in the agreement should be interpreted to have a meaning, rather than to be redundant and superfluous."[51]

To use a word that repeatedly appears in the case law, courts "harmonize" the contract's provisions in order to give effect to the whole.[52] Courts typically apply this canon when deciding at the outset whether a disputed provision is ambiguous or when determining whether two apparently conflicting provisions can be reconciled. As a Utah court explained, seeming ambiguities may disappear if the court properly "harmonizes" the contract's provisions by reading them so that they *do not* conflict.[53]

Thus, if one of the parties argues for a reading that requires the court to enforce one provision and treat the other as surplusage, the court will reject that party's interpretation and attempt to resolve the ambiguity through application of another rule of construction.

(c) *Reading as a Reasonable Average Person Would*

Unless a contract indicates a contrary intent, courts will read language in its ordinary and usual sense.[54] To direct the court to read language in a specialized, technical, or legal sense, the drafter must build in definitions or use some other device indicating this intention. Applying this canon, courts typically reject a party's contention that language that otherwise seems plain has a meaning that departs from normal usage or that requires a strained or forced reading. Thus courts refuse to "torture words to import ambiguity"[55] or to resort to "subtle and forced construction" that is contrary to the natural and obvious meaning of the language.[56]

This canon makes it clear that the drafter should (as we recommend in Chapter 26) choose words that mean precisely what the drafter intends to say and to use them in their proper sense.

(d) *Reading Consistent Terms Consistently*

Unless there is reason for the court to do otherwise, a court will usually interpret the same word or phrase consistently throughout a contract.[57] However, as the Arizona Court of Appeals stated, giving words a reasonable interpretation in one context does not necessarily compel that identical meaning in another context.[58] The D.C. Court of Appeals concurred.[59]

(e) *Reading to Produce a Rational Outcome*

If provisions in a contract conflict (or appear to conflict), courts will choose a reading that produces an outcome that is rational from the standpoint of both parties, not an outcome that is implausible, arbitrary, or nonsensical. Thus, if the contract is fairly susceptible to two constructions—one that is rational and probable and one that is not—the court will choose the meaning that is rational and probable.[60]

3. Canons Used to Resolve Uncertain Meaning

(a) *Words Take Meaning From Associated Words*

Courts frequently apply the canons of construction *noscitur a sociis* and *ejusdem generis* (discussed in Chapter 27) when determining the meaning of words that are grouped together. Though some courts state that they resort to these canons only if language is ambiguous, some courts will apply them without first finding that the language is ambiguous.

(b) Modifier Placement: Doctrine of Last Antecedent

When construing an ambiguity in a contract that results from modifier placement, courts sometimes apply the "doctrine of the last antecedent."[61] According to that doctrine, a court applies modifying language to the words or phrases that *immediately precede* the modifying language, unless such an application seems contrary to the sentence's intended meaning.[62] Courts that apply this doctrine tend to do so when the drafter provides no other guidance.

(c) Omissions May Be Regarded as Intentional

Be aware of the implications of addressing an issue in one provision of the document that you do not address elsewhere. This problem is easily created. If, for example, you state in the rent provision of a lease that failure to pay for two consecutive months is a material breach automatically entitling your client to cancel the leasing arrangement, what inference might arise concerning your failure to stipulate that breach of other provisions is similarly material?

4.   Canons for Choosing Between Conflicting Provisions

As previously stated, courts will try to read a contract in a way that harmonizes conflicts so that the court can give effect to all of the contract's provisions. What if the court cannot harmonize a conflict, and the result is that enforcing one provision would make the other meaningless?

In such a case, courts might apply "fall-back" rules reflecting certain assumptions about the way parties tend to prioritize information in contracts. Consider the following:

- Many courts will give priority to a specific provision over a more general provision.[63]

- A few courts have sometimes given preference to provisions stated earlier in the contract over the later provisions.[64]

- A few courts have given preference to provisions deemed to be "principal" (more important) provisions over those of minor importance[65]; some courts have stated that a subsidiary provision should not be interpreted in a way that would conflict with the "dominant purpose" of the contract.[66]

5. Ambiguity Construed Against Drafter

Courts assume that a drafting party will draft a contract in the way that best promotes the party's own interests.[67] If a court cannot otherwise resolve an ambiguity, the court may give up trying to enforce the parties' intent and may fall back on the rule that the ambiguous provision should be construed against the drafter (i.e., *Contra Proferentum*). Addressing this canon, the U.S. Supreme Court pointed out that as between "two reasonable and practical" constructions of an ambiguous contractual provision, a court should construe the ambiguity against the person who selected the ambiguous language.[68]

Once the court applies the rule, it is no longer looking to ascertain the parties' intent:[69] the purpose of applying the rule is to choose between reasonable interpretations of disputed language. *Contra proferentem* serves policies that courts want to promote, such as encouraging drafters to create reasonable form contracts and protecting non-drafting parties "from hidden traps not of their own making."[70]

In many courts (though not all), this canon is generally used as a last resort when there is no other way to determine the meaning of doubtful language, even after applying rules of construction[71] and considering extrinsic evidence.[72] For example, Michigan and Texas courts describe the rule as a "tie-breaker."[73]

Contra proferentem applies against a *drafting* party, so a court will typically refuse to apply it if the parties participated equally in the drafting process. If the parties bargained at arm's length and did not have disparate bargaining power—particularly if they were equally represented and equally sophisticated—a court may refuse to construe the contract against the nominal drafter.[74] If these circumstances apply, a drafter should consider including recitals of facts that would indicate to the court that *contra proferentem* should not apply.

6. Types of Provisions That Tend to Be Strictly Construed

Certain types of contractual provisions are generally strictly construed against the benefited party (typically, the drafting party). If strict construction applies to a provision, the drafter must ensure that the language is clear and unequivocal so that the parties' intent is unmistakable.[75] The following are examples of provisions that are usually strictly construed:

- A covenant restricting the use of land in a lease, declaration, or other document is strictly construed with all doubts resolved in favor of the free use or alienability of the land.[76]

- An insurance policy is strictly construed against the insurer with doubts resolved in favor of broader coverage for the insured.[77]

- A power of attorney is strictly construed against granting broader power to the agent than the language warrants.[78]

- A guaranty or suretyship contract is strictly construed against extending the liability of the guarantor or surety by implication or interpretation.[79]

- A release of a party from liability or a party's obligation to indemnify the other against liability is strictly construed.

- A restriction on competition is strictly construed.

As a practical matter, strict construction means that the court is likely to do very little construction of any kind: if the literal meaning is not clear on the face of the document, the court will probably not enforce the provision.

CHAPTER 13

EXERCISES FOR PART 2: CONTRACT DRAFTING

■ ■ ■

Project 1. Service Contract: Tree Removal and Care

Your clients are Erik Hervaux and Kelsey Clay, partners in Hervaux & Clay, who have just started up a tree removal and tree care service in Hanna Falls, Alaskabama. The clients want you to draft a contract.

The fact pattern and sample contract are in Chapter 22 (Project 1). The following materials will help you draft the contract:

- Chapter 6 (statements used in contracts)

- Chapter 7 (background and duration)

- Chapter 8 (release and indemnity clause)

- Chapter 10 (forum-selection and choice-of-law clauses)

- Chapter 11 (modification provision, execution)

- Chapters 26, 28, 29 (word choice, ambiguity, and time clauses)

- Chapter 31–33 (grammar, punctuation, style)

Project 2. Residential Lease Assignments

You are revising a contract for your new client, Rhonda Siler, CEO of Siler Properties. The contract is the lease that her company uses for its three apartment complexes.

The fact pattern and sample contract are in Chapter 22 (Project 2). The following materials will help you draft the lease:

- Chapter 6 (statements used in contracts).

- Chapter 7 (background, duration, prepayment).

- Chapter 8 (release and indemnity clause).

- Chapter 10 (refund, forum-selection, choice-of-law).

- Chapter 11 (modification provision, execution).

- Chapters 26, 28, 29 (word choice, ambiguity, time clauses).

- Chapter 31–33 (grammar, punctuation, style).

Project 3.   Pre–Incident Release and Express Assumption of Risk

Fact Pattern

Before beginning this assignment, read the material in Chapter 8 on drafting exculpatory clauses.

Your clients, Don and Iola Lee, are starting up a company known as "Lee Boat Rentals." They plan to rent boats for use on Blue Lake in Thomason County, Nebrada. They also rent other gear, including paddles, seat cushions, life preservers, and coolers.

The lake is large and has a lot of boat traffic. The Lees would like you to draft a pre-incident release form that will protect them from liability for injury and property damage suffered by any minor, even if the injury is due to the Lees' or their staff's negligence.

Assignment

Draft a release for your clients, using the two sample releases set out below. The releases were found in Nebrada cases: despite drafting problems that should be corrected, the two releases were enforced.

You might wish to begin with a bulleted list of all points covered in the sample releases, as suggested in Chapter 20. The following materials may be helpful:

- Chapter 8 (release, assumption of risk clause)

- Chapter 11 (execution of contract)

- Chapters 26, 28, 29 (word choice)

- Chapter 31–33 (grammar, punctuation, style)

Releases from Nebrada Case Law

(1)

In addition to my payment of $35 stated above, I expressly affirm that I intend in consideration of the opportunity to participate in this experience to exonerate Caillebotte Riding Stables, Gerry and Sheldon Caillebotte, and their staff from any liability to me or to the minor child on whose behalf I now assent to the following: I consent to the renting of a horse from Caillebotte Riding Stables by Megan Alcott, a minor, and to her assumption of the risks inherent in horse-back riding. I agree, personally and on her behalf, to waive any claims or causes of action that she or I may now or hereafter have against Caillebotte Riding Stables, Gerry and Sheldon Caillebotte, or any of their staff arising out of any injuries of any kind (including serious personal injury such as death) that she may sustain as a result of her participation in this experience. I understand that this applies even if the aforesaid persons fail to exercise reasonable care with respect to the minor child. I affirm by signing this contract that I have read the list of horseback riding risks attached to this document. I am the minor child's <u>sister</u>, I am over 21 years old, and I affirm I have authority to act on her behalf.

(2)

In consideration for the opportunity to participate in the adventure of a lifetime, I will pay to Mountain Adventures the sum of $495. I affirm that in participating in this adventure I assume all risks inherent in rock-climbing and outdoor trail hiking, including the risk of death, serious physical injury, and property damage. I understand that specific risks include but are not limited to the following: falling, equipment failure, wild animals, falling rocks, drowning, dehydration, hypothermia, disorientation, panic attacks, illness or injury, without immediate access to emergency personnel, forest fires, broken bones, and getting lost.

Project 4.   Settlement and Release

Fact Pattern

Your client is Brown Investment Properties, Inc. (94 Eldon Road, Old Town, New Mexas). Brown is settling a case with Ron Bates, a customer of a company that leases property (a storefront in a mall) from Brown. The customer fell in the entrance way to the mall, in an area in the control of both Brown and the tenant. Brown stated in an email that he wants the release to be broad enough to preclude Bates from suing on any related claim of *any* kind. Brown will be paying a lump sum of $18,000.

Assignment

Using the memo and the two sample agreements set out below, draft a release for your clients. (You might wish to begin with a list of bulleted points covered in the sample releases, as suggested in Chapter 19.) The following materials may be helpful:

- Chapter 8 (release).

- Chapter 11 (execution of contract).

- Chapters 26–27 (word choice & definitions).

- Chapter 31–33 (grammar, punctuation, style).

Memorandum

To: You
From: Rimba Srigala
Re: Brown Properties, Inc.

In New Mexas, courts will enforce a valid release from liability included within a settlement agreement. The New Mexas Supreme Court stated that absent fraud or duress, a ***clear and unequivocal*** release, supported by valuable consideration, will be given effect according to the intention of the parties from what appears in the four corners of the document itself. Parol evidence is not admissible to vary its terms.

New Mexas courts strictly construe such releases. The language delineating a release's "scope" must be "clear and unequivocal so that the party is fairly apprised of what is being given up." The rationale for this requirement is to "improve the quality of form settlement contracts" and to ensure that those who waive substantial rights are clearly apprised of the effect of their actions.

The Court of Appeals held that language stating that the release applied to all "personal injury caused by the said incident" *did not* apply to a wrongful death action by the releasor's estate following his death three years after he signed the release—even though his death was allegedly due to injuries resulting from the incident. The court said that the language did not put the releaser on notice that the release would extend to death from injuries of which the releaser was unaware at the time of signing.

Both of **the releases below need a great deal of tweaking to meet the "clear and unequivocal" standard**. I found the first one in our files and the second on the internet. Most of the release and settlement agreements I have seen are designed to be witnessed as well as signed.

(1) Settlement & Release of All Claims

IN CONSIDERATION of the payment to me of $28,000, I, Herman Molenaer, being of lawful age, release and discharge for myself, my heirs, executors, administrators, and assigns, release, acquit, and forever discharge East Theatres Corporation (East) and any and all of their successors and assigns from any and all liability for actions, causes of actions, claims, demands for damages, costs, or any other thing in any way growing out of any unknown and known personal injuries, property damage, or other loss resulting from the occurrence or incident that happened on their property on May 25, 2009.

This release applies to ALL consequences of any personal injury or property damage. I assume all risk that the injuries or damage may become permanent or more extensive.

In executing this release I do not rely upon any statement made to me by East, its agents, managers, operatives, attorneys, or other representatives other than as herein included concerning their liability, the nature of any claim I might have against East, or the damages I might otherwise be entitled to.

I understand that this settlement is the compromise of a disputed claim. The payment is not an admission of liability on the part of East or any person connected with East.

This release contains our ENTIRE AGREEMENT.

I have read the foregoing and know the contents. I sign of my own free will, knowingly and voluntarily.

Herman Molenaer   _July 9, 2009_
Herman Molenaer   (Date)
14 Selden Avenue
Oldtown, Ohiowa

We were present at the time that the person named hereinabove executed this release, at which time he stated that it was in complete settlement of his claims against East Theatres.

Tracy Delacroix   _July 9, 2009_
Tracy Delacroix   (Date)
456 Daria Street
Oldtown, Ohiowa

Oren Petrov   _July 9, 2009_
Oren Petrov   (Date)
3900 Unaka Drive
Oldtown, Ohiowa

(2) Settlement Agreement and Release

On or about _____, 20___, Releasor was allegedly injured while present at _____, property allegedly under the control of Releasee. The parties desire to enter into this settlement agreement in order to provide for certain payments in full settlement of all claims relating to the occurrence.

In exchange for the payment stated below, Releasor releases Releasee from liability of any kind, present or future, relating to the incident and releasing Releasee's officers, directors, stockholders, employees, and successors in interest. This release applies to all claims, demands, and rights involving the incident. Releasee has paid Releasor the sum of $_____. This shall be a complete and final discharge of any liability of Releasee for the incident. Releasor understands that Releasee does not admit liability.

I am ___ years of age.

The following statements are to be initialed by Releasor prior to signing:

_____ (1) By signing this document, I affirm that I understand that I am giving up EVERY RIGHT I have to sue the parties who are listed in the document for anything relating to the incident.

_____ (2) I understand that this is a binding contract.

Name and Address of Releasor   Date

Project 5.   Requirements Contract for Sale of Gravel

You represent Grafton Gravel, Inc. of St. Grafton Beach, John County, Floregon. Grafton owns gravel pits in John, Sandiston, and Victorina Counties.

Grafton's CEO, Frank Hals, wants you to draft a form contract for Grafton to use with buyers in the three counties listed who want to buy all their gravel requirements from Grafton.

The type of gravel that Grafton supplies is crushed limestone. It is widely used in John County for pipe bed draining, septic systems, drainage bedding, retaining walls, driveways, rural county roads, and concrete manufacture. Grafton sells it by the ton. The price depends on the size of the individual pebbles and the amount that Buyer orders. In general, the wholesale price in John County ranges from $35 to $45 per ton. A typical order would be around 30–40 tons. Grafton charges an additional $35 for loading and delivery.

You have an interview with Hals scheduled for next week. To prepare for the interview, you need to do some preliminary research regarding Floregon's version of the Uniform Commercial Code and to prepare a preliminary issue list and outline. You also need to prepare some client questions.

Assignment

Using the two contracts below (which are **_not well drafted_**), draft a contract that meets your client's needs. You might begin with a bulleted list of all points covered in the two contracts and develop an outline using the template discussed in Chapters 20 and 21. The following materials may also be helpful:

- Chapter 6 (statements used in contracts).
- Chapter 7 (background and duration).
- Chapter 8 (release and indemnity clause).
- Chapter 9 (breach and termination).

- Chapter 10 (forum selection, choice-of-law).

- Chapter 11 (modification provision, execution of contract).

- Chapters 26–29 (word choice, definitions, ambiguity, time clauses).

- Chapter 31–33 (grammar, punctuation, style).

Before you begin drafting, look up the following in a law dictionary or your state's version of the UCC: "requirements contract" and "output contract." Is either of the contracts below a requirements contract? Is either one an output contract?

Contracts

(1) CONTRACT TO SUPPLY DECORATIVE GRAVEL

Made and entered on August 22, 2012, Outdoor Décor Inc., a Floregon corporation with its offices at 2201 N.W. 23rd Boulevard, Saunders, Floregon 34000 (Outdoor Décor), and K-scapes, a Floregon corporation with its offices at 457 Commerce Plaza, Saunders, Floregon 34000 (herein referred to as "K-scapes") enter this contract for the sale of decorative gravel:

WHEREAS, Outdoor Décor is in the business of selling decorative gravel; and

WHEREAS, K-scapes wishes to find a supplier capable of meeting its ongoing requirements for gravel for use in its nationwide landscaping business;

NOW THEREFORE, the parties agree as follows:

A. GRAVEL SUPPLIED

Polished pebbles suitable for use in landscaping in the following mixes sold exclusively by Outdoor Décor: "Tiger Mix," "Zebra Mix," "Sea Grey," "Sunlight," and "Firelight."

B. AGREEMENT FOR SALE OF REQUIREMENTS

K-scapes will purchase from Outdoor Décor and Outdoor Décor will sell to K-scapes all of K-scapes' requirements for the gravel described.

C. ESTIMATED AMOUNT

K-scapes has estimated the amount of each type of gravel listed above that it requires on a monthly basis from Seller. The amounts are set out in attachment.

D. WARRANTIES

Outdoor Décor makes no warranty to K-scapes beyond that stated in paragraph A and expressly disclaims, excludes, and waives any other warranty, express or implied.

E. TERM AND TERMINATION OF TERM

1. Initial Term

The contract term shall begin on the date of signing and runs for 3 years, unless terminated pursuant to subsection 3. This term renews automatically on August 22, 2015, unless either party shall give notice that the party intends to not renew this contract by February 22, 2015.

2. Automatic Renewal of Term

Term shall be deemed to renew automatically without action of either party unless either party shall give the aforesaid notice of intent to not renew. Notice shall be given by email. Following such notice, all current provisions of the contract remain in effect.

3. Termination

Outdoor Décor may terminate this agreement by giving notice to Buyer for any good faith reason if Outdoor Décor's circumstances undergo a substantial change or if Buyer refuses to negotiate in good faith for a price adjustment as required by the following section or for the reason stated in subsection 4 herein. Either party shall have the right to cancel upon the aforesaid notice with cancellation becoming effective on day following notice if either shall become a debtor in bankruptcy or insolvent. If contract is terminated, obligations pursuant to the following provisions survive termination: A–E and J–K.

4. Cancellation for Breach

Either party may cancel this contract for a material breach, including but not limited to the following: K-scapes' failure to pay Outdoor Décor within the time limit stated in section G and K-scapes presenting more than three orders for gravel during any year that shall be deemed by Outdoor Décor be unreasonably disproportionate to amount estimated.

F. PRICING AND PAYMENT

1. K-scapes agrees to pay the price per cubic yard for each variety of gravel that is stated in the attachment. On January 1 of each year in period/term, K-scapes agrees to negotiate in good faith with Outdoor Décor for a price adjustment. Parties to negotiate according to commercially reasonable standards and adjustment to any price of variety of gravel shall not exceed by more than 3% the stated prices on attachment. If parties are unable to agree following negotiation, the prices hereinabove stated remain in effect and Outdoor Décor may at its option terminate as provided above.

2. Payment for each order is due within 7 days of delivery date. Outdoor Décor gives a 5% discount (excluding delivery costs) for any order that is paid within 3 days. If paid after the deadline, K-scapes owes to Outdoor Décor a charge of 3% of the order price (excluding delivery charges) as a late fee.

G. DELIVERY DUE DATE

The delivery due date is 3 full business days from the date that Outdoor Décor RECEIVES such order.

H. ORDERING/DELIVERY

K-scapes must order gravel through Outdoor Décor's website portal for customers at outdoordecor.web. An order is deemed submitted if submitted before 5 p.m. on a business day (M–F excluding holidays); otherwise, on the next business day. Due date for delivery: 3 full days from date that order received, at K-scapes's Saunders, Floregon warehouse. K-scapes will pay $20 per delivery. Payment is not made in full for purpose of discount if delivery costs are not paid at time of paying for order.

I. UNREASONABLY DISPROPORTIONATE ORDER

It is specifically understood, represented, and agreed by parties that K-scapes may not in any month order gravel in an amount unreasonably disproportionate to the estimate in Section C.

J. INDEMNITY

K-scapes shall indemnify Outdoor Décor from any and all claims that arise out of Outdoor Décor's delivery of an order to K-scapes's warehouse, including injury or damage to third parties or K-scapes even if such claims arise out of negligence or gross negligence of Outdoor Décor's operatives in making delivery, and including such injuries or damage that arise out of negligence, gross negligence, or other fault or misconduct to K-scapes. K-scapes is likewise to indemnify Outdoor Décor for any property damage or related loss Outdoor Décor suffers as a result of a delivery of order to K-scapes's warehouse if damage or other loss arises out of negligence, gross negligence, or other fault or misconduct to K-scapes.

K. IMPRACTICABILITY

A party shall not perform or be required to perform if performance becomes impracticable under Floregon Commercial Code 153–2–28.

L. NOTICES

All notices required or permitted under this contract or Floregon Commercial Code shall be by email to Outdoor Décor through its customer web portal and to K-scapes at the address set out under the signature line, which must be updated if changed.

M. AMENDING OR MODIFYING

Such amendment requires a supplemental writing signed by the party against whom the amendment is sought to be enforced.

(Signatures)

(2) CONTRACT TO SELL ROCK SALT

FLOREGON ROCK SALT, INC. SALES AGREEMENT
Industrial Square, Building 4–A, Hanna, Floregon
florock@florock.co.flo

Effective on January 30, 2013, Seller, Floregon Rock Salt, Inc., a Floregon corporation, and Buyer _____ (NAME/BUSINESS ADDRESS/EMAIL/PHONE) enter this contract for Seller to sell to Buyer and Buyer to purchase from Seller for rock salt.

I. *Definitions*

Rock salt shall mean the rock salt described in section II. The rock salt sold is suitable to be used melting ice and snow on walkways, roads, parking lots, and other thoroughfares and is stored on Seller's premises using a system designed to keep the rock salt dry. Beyond this, Seller makes no other warranties.

Estimate shall mean Buyer's estimated requirements per month of ____ 50–pound bags or ___ tons of rock per order. Buyer understands that Seller has no obligation to fulfill an order that unreasonably exceeds this stated amount, though Seller does not waive its right to refuse a subsequent unreasonably excessive order by fulfilling one that unreasonably exceeds such estimate.

Unreasonably exceeds shall mean that the order is unreasonably disproportionate to the estimate. Parties agree that order is unreasonably disproportionate if it exceeds the estimate by more than ___ bags or ___ tons.

II. *Party Background*

Seller is a wholesale supplier and distributor supplying rock salt in bulk to commercial property owners, hospitals, retirement centers, schools, and colleges with all their rock-salt needs at wholesale prices. Buyer is one of the foregoing, located within Hanna County. Buyer intends for the period set out in III to buy all its rock salt needs from Seller.

III. *Description*

The rock salt is rock salt of the following type: _____, to be delivered in bulk in an amount of ___ tons | in ___ 50–pound bags.

IV. *Requirements Period*

The requirements term is for ___ months. It begins on _____, 20___ and ends on _____, 20___.

V. *Inspection of Buyer*

Buyer has 3 business days to inspect the rock salt and notify Seller of any defect in condition or breach of warranty. If Buyer returns the full order in 5 days in condition in which it was received (excluding any damage to packaging necessitated by inspection), Seller shall refund the full purchase price.

VI. *Order for Rock Salt*

Buyer shall order rock salt from Seller by logging in to Buyer's account at Seller's website and posting the order online.

VII. *Risk of Loss*

Risk of loss passes to Buyer at time of delivery/time of collection. Beginning as of that time, Buyer is responsible for taking steps to prevent deterioration or damage to the order.

VIII. *Delivery*

(a) Delivery to Buyer. Seller does not charge for delivery to Buyer's location unless Seller is required to reschedule delivery after having made the attempt below, in which case, delivery charge shall be set at $35. Delivery date is a date not less than 1 business day after Seller receives order. Within that time frame, Buyer and Seller shall determine a date, time, and place for delivery. Buyer shall ensure that Seller has access to the stipulated location.

(b) No Damages for Delay Beyond Seller's Control. If Seller is unable to provide delivery or complete delivery at the appointed place, time, and location due to circumstances beyond Seller's control, Seller is excused and no liability for an damages due to delay shall apply. Such circumstances include, but are not limited to, any force majeure, equipment failure, or inability of Seller to gain access.

(c) Definition

"Business day" means M–F, 8 AM–5:30 PM and shall not include a legal holiday.

IX. *Payment*

For each order, Buyer is responsible for paying ___ per ton or ___ per 50–pound bag. Buyer pays at the time of ordering by credit card or other method provided through Seller's website.

X. *Signatures and Effective Date*

The contract is effective upon the signature of both parties, determined by the date that the last party to sign the contract signs the contract.

(Signatures)

PART 3

LEGISLATIVE DRAFTING: PUBLIC AND PRIVATE RULE–MAKING DOCUMENTS

■ ■ ■

- Chapter 14. Introduction to Legislative Drafting: Public and Private Rule-Making Documents
- Chapter 15. Drafting Private Rule-Making Documents
- Chapter 16. Drafting Public Legislation
- Chapter 17. How Courts Construe Statutes and Other Public Rule-Making Documents
- Chapter 18. Exercises for Part 3

187

CHAPTER 14

INTRODUCTION TO LEGISLATIVE DRAFTING: PUBLIC AND PRIVATE RULE–MAKING DOCUMENTS

■ ■ ■

I. Public and Private Rule–Making Documents

Legislative documents regulate the conduct of persons. We view legislative documents as falling into two categories: public versus private rule-making documents.

As we use the phrase, "public rule-making documents" are those that are generated by a governmental entity. Examples include constitutions, statutes, ordinances, regulations, regulatory agency opinions, executive orders, rules of civil procedure, rules of court, judicial directives, and state bar disciplinary rules.

"Private rule-making documents" are generated by non-governmental entities. Examples include corporate bylaws, an employer's code of conduct for employees, rules regulating members of a private club, a university's honor code, and declarations of covenants and restrictions for a condominium or subdivision.

II. Organization of a Rule–Making Document

Many governmental legislative bodies have drafting manuals that contain guidelines and requirements for a legislative document's format, style, and language. Many states' legislative drafting manuals are available online, and many links are available through the National Conference of State Legislatures' website (NCSL.org). We recommend that you check there to see if your state's guidelines are linked. If not, you might find them through your state government's website.

If you are drafting for a client who wants you to follow a particular manual, then follow that manual. If you do not have a drafting manual to follow, the principles and template in Chapter 20 will be useful.

III. Articulating Legislative Statements

A. Recommended Verbs

If you do not have a statute or legislative-drafting manual to follow, then we recommend that you use the following verbs to articulate various types of legislative statements.

Recommended Verbs for Rule-Making Documents	
• Duty to act	Shall + verb
• Prohibition of action	Shall not + verb
• Right to act	May + verb
• Requirement for exercising a right	Must + verb
• Condition precedent	Must + verb
• Legislative policy	Present tense
• Statement of fact	Present or Past tense

B. Stating a Duty or Prohibition

Significant case law and widespread agreement confirm that "shall" is usually interpreted as mandatory.[1] If you are imposing a duty to act on a person to whom a rule-making document applies, we recommend that you use "shall."

Examples: Use of "Shall" to Impose a Duty to Act
1. A student <u>shall comply</u> with the university's code of conduct.
2. If a homeowner leases the home site to a third party, the homeowner <u>shall notify</u> the association.

If you are prohibiting a person from acting (i.e., creating a duty to refrain from acting in a specified way), we recommend that you use "shall not."

Examples: Use of "Shall Not" to Express a Prohibition
1. A member <u>shall not remove</u> a golf cart from the club's property.
2. An officer of the corporation <u>shall not lend</u> company funds to a third party.

In some circumstances, some courts have treated "shall" as merely *directory* (i.e., as a guideline for what is advisable). For example, an Illinois appellate court stated that it presumes that language issuing a procedural command to a government official indicates an intention for the statute to be directory.[2]

Similarly, the Rhode Island Supreme Court stated that statutes imposing apparently mandatory time restrictions on public officials are often directory in nature.[3] In making this determination, that Court looked to a variety of factors, including (1) whether the provision imposes a sanction, (2) whether the provision expresses the essence of the statute, and (3) whether the provision is directed to public officers.[4] Other courts may apply different standards. Check state law.

C. Stating a Right

Significant case law and widespread agreement confirm this interpretation: that "may" is permissive.[5] We recommend that you use "may" to confer a right, privilege, permission, or option. Many decisions by courts make it clear that "may" is the auxiliary verb of choice for this purpose.

Examples: Use of "May" to Confer a Right or Privilege

- A member <u>may bring</u> a guest to the club.

- A student <u>may live</u> in off-campus housing.

D. Stating a Right–Related Requirement or Condition Precedent

We recommend that you use "must" (1) to state a requirement for exercising a right or (2) to state a condition precedent.

Examples: Use of "Must"

1. **Requirement for Exercising a Right:**
   - To obtain a refund, the member <u>must give</u> notice of cancellation to the club.

   - To build an addition, the homeowner <u>must get</u> approval of the association.

2. **Condition Precedent:**
   - To buy alcoholic beverages, a person <u>must be</u> 21 years old or older.

   - To receive health care benefits, an employee <u>must be</u> a full-time employee.

E. Stating a Legislative Policy

A policy becomes effective at the moment that the document does—no further action is required. Thus, we recommend that you use a present-tense verb to state a legislative policy.

Examples: Use of Present Tense to Express a Policy

- This declaration <u>applies</u> to any person who owns a home site in the development.

- This provision <u>becomes</u> effective on March 31, 2013.

F. Stating a Fact

Statements of fact pertain to either facts that exist at the time that a rule-making document becomes effective or facts that existed before that time. For that reason, we recommend that you use present tense or past tense verbs to articulate statements of fact.

Examples: Statements of Fact

- The legislature <u>found</u> that the use of cell phones by drivers while driving a motor vehicle <u>presents</u> a danger to citizens of the state.

- To preserve the beauty and the value of property in Old Florida Acres, the Developer <u>declares</u> the following covenants and restrictions to be applicable to all homeowners and all property within the development.

IV. Drafting Style for Rule–Making Documents

A. Verb Tense

Verb tense has an impact on meaning. When interpreting statutes, courts have commented on the importance of verb tense.[6] For example, a California appellate court said "In construing statutes, the use of verb tense by the Legislature is considered significant."[7] Similarly, the Oregon Supreme Court said, "we do not lightly disregard the legislature's choice of verb tense, because we assume that the legislature's choice is purposeful."[8] Verb tense is further discussed in Chapter 31.

B. Concise Language

A "concise" sentence is one that contains no more words than are needed for clarity. Conciseness does not mean merely deleting words; it means deleting *unnecessary* words. Chapter 33 discusses conciseness.

All state legislative drafting manuals that we have consulted emphasize the importance of conciseness. For example, the Texas legislative drafting manual urges the drafter to try not to use longer words and phrases than are needed.[9]

Example: Wordy versus Concise Sentences

Wordy:

It has been found by the legislature that the use of cellular telephones by drivers while operating trucks, cars, or motorcycles on public roads poses a danger, threat, risk, or hazard to the public safety. [36 words]

Concise:

The legislature finds that drivers who use cellular telephones while operating vehicles endanger the public. [16 words]

C. Positive Versus Negative Statements

Some states' legislative drafting manuals express a preference for positive rather than negative statements.[10]

Examples: Negative versus Positive Statements

Negative:

<u>Unless</u> the owner has obtained a permit for construction of the fence, the owner <u>shall not</u> begin construction of the fence.

Positive:

<u>If</u> the owner has obtained a permit for construction of a fence, the owner <u>may</u> begin construction of the fence.

The negatively framed sentence does not do a good job of *authorizing* the owner to begin construction. The positively framed sentence does not carry the same prohibitive tone as the negatively framed one. Changing the sentence changes the impact, which is part of the meaning. The language of a rule-making provision should reflect what the client is trying to achieve (e.g., permitting versus prohibiting an action).

The words "no" and "not" negate whatever they apply to. We recommend that you negate the action—*not* the actor.

Examples: Negation of Action versus Actor

Action:

A person <u>shall not</u> use a cellular telephone while driving a vehicle.

Actor:

<u>No person</u> shall use a cellular telephone while driving a vehicle.

Negating the action is more precise because the purpose of a prohibition is to prohibit *an action*—not to negate an actor.

D. Active Versus Passive Voice

We recommend that you avoid using passive voice unless you have a strategic reason for using it. Chapters 31 and 33 discuss active and passive voice.

E. Singular Versus Plural Nouns

Plural nouns can create ambiguity.

Example: Ambiguous Plural Noun

A homeowner shall not park recreational <u>vehicles</u> (RVs) in the street.

That statement prohibits the homeowner from parking more than one RV in the street—but it does not literally prohibit an owner from parking *one* RV in the street. If every homeowner parked one RV in the street, the subdivision's streets would become cluttered by RVs.

If the drafter's goal is to prohibit the owner from parking even one RV in the street, then the more precise way to express that prohibition is to use a singular noun.

Example: Unambiguous Use of Singular Noun

A homeowner shall not park a recreational <u>vehicle</u> (RV) in the street.

By prohibiting an owner from parking a single RV in the street, that rule also prohibits the owner from parking multiple RVs in the street (the owner cannot park two RVs without first parking one). We recommend that you use singular nouns unless you have a good reason for using plural nouns.

F.   Needless Synonyms

We recommend that you avoid stringing together needless synonyms.

> **Example: String of Needless Synonyms**
>
> The legislature finds that drivers who use cellular telephones while operating a vehicle pose a <u>danger</u>, <u>threat</u>, <u>risk</u>, or <u>hazard</u> to the public safety.

In this context, "danger," "threat," "risk," and "hazard" each mean roughly the same thing. Neither word adds significant content or clarity to the sentence. Why not pick the one that you find most suitable and delete the rest?

G.   Needless Legal Jargon

Often, legal jargon complicates a document and confuses readers. If you have a good reason to use a legal term, then do so. We recommend that you avoid using needless legal jargon. Below are examples of the types of words that qualify as needless legal jargon.

> **Examples: Needless Legal Jargon**
>
> | | | |
> |---|---|---|
> | aforementioned | heretofore | theretofore |
> | aforesaid | notwithstanding | to wit |
> | forthwith | said | unto |
> | hereinabove | saith | whereas |
> | hereinafter | thenceforth | witnesseth |

We are not alone in our aversion to needless legal jargon. Many state legislative drafting manuals direct drafters to avoid using legalese—some manuals even list specific words and phrases that drafters should avoid.[11]

H.   Using "And," "Or," and "And/Or"

The words "and" and "or" have had to be construed in a number of cases. Chapter 28 discusses problems relating to "and," "or," and "and/or." The term "and/or" can be ambiguous, as some courts have noted.[12] Some states' drafting manuals specifically direct drafters to avoid using "and/or."[13]

Chapter 15

Drafting Private Rule–Making Documents

■ ■ ■

I. Drafting Process for Private Rule–Making Documents

Many lawyers draft private rule-making documents such as corporate by-laws, declarations of restrictive covenants for developments or condominiums, and various rules and regulations for clients who need them. Courts typically construe these documents as they would construe contracts (discussed in Chapter 12), but the process for drafting private rule-making documents is more closely akin to that used in drafting legislation.

For that reason, we recommend that you use the template for rule-making documents (Chapter 20)—unless your client has different preferences regarding the organization of those documents. The rest of this chapter discusses a few types of private rule-making documents.

II. Documents for Property Owner Associations

A. Declaration of Covenants

1. Purpose of Declaration

A real estate developer who creates a development (e.g., a subdivision, condominium complex, or cooperative) usually has a vision for the property. A developer realizes that vision through covenants. A "covenant" is a promise to do or not do something.

Through covenants, a developer might legislate the homeowners' land use or other conduct. For example, a covenant might prohibit the owners from placing a disused automobile on blocks in the front yard or might require that all residences be painted in coordinating colors.

As the Vermont Supreme Court wrote, covenants are "characterized by the type of burden they impose: an affirmative covenant calls for the covenanter to perform an act, while a negative covenant requires the covenanter to refrain from performing one."[1] Negative covenants are often called "restrictive covenants."[2]

A "declaration of covenants" is a document that contains all the covenants that apply to a specific development. The document might also be called a "Declaration of Covenants and Restrictions" or "Declaration of Covenants, Conditions and Restrictions." For brevity's sake, we refer to it simply as a "declaration of covenants."

A development's property owners form a governing association. As a California appellate court explained, the declaration is the primary governing document of the association.[3]

An important aspect of covenants is that they may "run with the land": i.e., they are binding on the original owner's successors. To know the criteria for determining whether covenants run with the land, consult your state's law.

Typically, courts strictly construe covenants that restrict the owner's free use of the land. For example, an Indiana appellate court said that restrictive covenants are generally disfavored and courts resolve all doubts "in favor of the free use of property and against restrictions."[4] Other courts concur.[5]

Courts in different jurisdictions may treat declarations of covenants differently. For example, a South Carolina appellate court stated that a party wishing to enforce a restrictive covenant must either point to express language or show "a plain unmistakable implication."[6] An Ohio appellate court said that the court will enforce a covenant if the language is clear but will not enforce it if the language is "indefinite, doubtful, and capable of contradictory interpretations."[7]

In a North Carolina case, homeowners in a subdivision took the Homeowners' Association to court seeking a declaratory judgment and injunctive relief, hoping to stop the association from enforcing a restrictive covenant that required the owners to keep "campers" in their garages or in a screened area.[8] The homeowners argued that their recreational vehicle was not strictly a "camper" because the homeowners also used it for trips to the grocery store.

Because the restriction was written in 1985, the court consulted a 1985 version of Merriam–Webster's Dictionary for the definition of "camper."[9] Based partly on that definition, the court concluded that the vehicle *was* a camper and that the parking requirement applied.[10]

Because courts are reluctant to extend a restrictive covenant to a use that it does not clearly encompass, it is crucial to draft covenants clearly and precisely. Chapter 26 discusses the delineation of a provision's scope.

2. Drafting the Declaration

Generally, state law controls the establishment and administration of developments such as condominiums and cooperatives. An attorney must become familiar with applicable law before drafting a declaration. For those who are not familiar with such declarations, state statutes and the Uniform Common Interest Ownership Act are good places to start. The Act is available at the website of the National Conference of Commissioners on Uniform State Laws (NCCUSL.org).

A declaration of covenants typically addresses issues such as the following:

- Statement of the name and type of common interest community.

- Description of the real estate included in the common interest community.

- Statement authorizing the Association.

- Restrictions on use and maintenance of property.

- Restrictions on appearance of property.

- Restrictions on owners' conduct.

- Creation of a governing body.

- Enforcement of the declaration.

If you draft a declaration for a client, make sure that the client understands the requirements for effective execution. For example, Colorado's Common Interest Community Act requires that a declaration be executed in the same manner as a deed.[11] In a case in which the declarant failed to sign the declaration, a Colorado appellate court said that the unsigned declaration was invalid.[12]

B. By–Laws for Property Owners Association

The bylaws under which an owners association operates are another major type of private rule-making document. Typically, the owners association has the power and duty to adopt bylaws. Thus, owners associations create their own legislation. Often, bylaws provide for an executive board to act for the association. Board members and officers have a fiduciary duty to the association.

State law may specify issues that the bylaws must address and may address. Consult applicable law. Examples of issues that bylaws typically cover include the following:

- Number of and titles for members of the executive board.

- Qualifications for and duties of officers and board members.

- Procedures for electing the board.

- Procedures for filling board member or officer vacancies.

- Method for amending bylaws.

- Statement of which duties are delegable.

- Provisions concerning meetings, quorums and votes.

III. Documents Relating to Corporations

A. Articles of Incorporation

The U.S. Supreme Court described a corporation as an artificial being that is invisible and intangible and that exists only in the law.[13] Incorporation creates a legal entity that the law treats as a person, that is distinct from the shareholders, and that can sue and be sued.

To form a corporation, the incorporator must file appropriate documentation (typically, the "articles of incorporation") with the state (typically, the Secretary of State). Different states may have different requirements regarding the articles of incorporation. Below are some issues that articles of incorporation might address:

- Name and address of incorporator.

- Name of the corporation.

- Corporation's principal place of business and mailing address.

- Purpose of corporation.

- Number of shares (sometimes class) that the corporation may have.

- Names and contact information for directors and officers.

- Name and contact information for registered agent.

- Effective date.

The articles of incorporation determine the corporation's nature and delineate the scope of its power to act. The *statement of purpose* contained in the articles of incorporation may be seen as determining the corporation's true nature.[14]

A corporation must act within the scope of authority as stated in the purpose clause. Thus, if you are drafting articles of incorporation, be careful not to draft the purpose clause so narrowly that it creates obstacles for the client.

In many states, incorporators can file articles of incorporation online by filling out a form. Many courts treat the articles of incorporation as a contract.[15]

B.　Corporate By–Laws

A corporation is governed not only by its articles of incorporation and the state's statutory scheme, but also by its by-laws.[16] Corporate bylaws are self-imposed rules for conducting the corporation's business in a particular way. For example, a Delaware statute states the following regarding bylaws:

> The bylaws may contain any provision, not inconsistent with law or with the certificate of incorporation, relating to the business of the corporation, the conduct of its affairs, and its rights or powers or the rights or powers of its stockholders, directors, officers or employees.[17]

Different states may have different restrictions or requirements regarding corporate bylaws. Below are some issues that bylaws could address:

- Directors: qualifications, powers, tenure, and removal.

- Officers: duties, elections, tenure and removal.

- Compensation for directors and officers.

- Meetings of shareholders and directors.

- Voting procedures.

- Issuing and transferring of shares.

- Procedure for amending bylaws.

Though bylaws are rule-making documents, some courts construe them using the rules of construction that apply to contracts.[18] Some courts apply rules of statutory construction instead. For example, a New York court stated that a court may apply rules of statutory construction to corporate bylaws.[19]

Many incorporators do not hire attorneys to draft corporate bylaws from scratch. Instead, they rely on forms or templates—for better or worse.

IV. Documents Relating to Limited–Liability Companies

A. Articles of Organization

A limited-liability company (LLC) is a business structure (similar to a corporation) that limits the owners' personal liability for debts or actions of the LLC. In an LLC, owners are typically called "members." LLCs are governed by state statute.

To form an LLC, one typically has to file articles of organization with the state. Articles of organization are analogous to articles of incorporation (discussed in Section III–A of this chapter), though requirements may differ. In many states, members can file articles of organization online by filling out a form. Attorneys working with LLCs must become familiar with applicable state law.

B. Members Operating Agreement

Analogous to bylaws for a corporation (which are discussed in Section III–B of this chapter), an "Operating Agreement" for an LLC sets out provisions for the regulation and management of the LLC's affairs. Different states might have rules regarding what an operating agreement must or may address.

In Florida, for example, LLC members do not necessarily have to have an operating agreement—and if they do, it does not necessarily have to be in writing.[20] Similarly, Connecticut does not seem to require that operating agreements be in writing.[21]

Even if state law allows oral operating agreements, we recommend that you put them in writing so that the parties have a document to refer to as a guide. An attorney working with LLCs will have to become familiar with applicable state law.

V. Other Documents That Regulate Conduct

Any type of entity or organization might have rules and might call upon an attorney to draft or amend those rules. Examples include a university's honor code, an extra-curricular organization's rules, an employer's code of conduct, or a professional association's bylaws.

If your client wants you to draft a set of rules from scratch, we recommend that you use the template for rulemaking documents, which is in Chapter 20. If you are merely amending a set of rules, then you would likely have to follow the format of the existing document. The principles for clearly articulating rules are the same for all rulemaking documents and are discussed in Chapter 14.

CHAPTER 16

DRAFTING PUBLIC LEGISLATION

■ ■ ■

I. Preparing to Draft Public Legislation

A. Understanding the Legislative Process

Statutes start out their lives as bills. What happens from there? What are the steps between the initial draft of a bill an its enactment into law? To understand how a bill becomes a statute, you must thoroughly understand the legislative process in the jurisdiction in which you are drafting.

B. Consulting State Legislative Drafting Manuals

State legislative drafters usually have for guidance an official legislative drafting manual. Some state legislative drafting manuals are available online. The website of the National Conference of State Legislators has links to some states' legislative drafting manuals [http://www.ncsl.org].

C. Checking Legal and Factual Background

Typically, after a legislator or other authorized person requests a bill, the legislative drafter has to research relevant law. Researching relevant law might include the following: reviewing related statutes that the proposed legislation might affect, reviewing other jurisdictions' statutes that are similar to the proposed legislation, and reviewing model acts. Legislative drafting manuals that we examined make it clear that legislative drafters should familiarize themselves with constitutional and statutory limitations on legislation—including any preemption issues.[1] The drafter must review the law and facts underlying the bill.[2] The drafter must also develop a full understanding of relevant case law.

A legislative drafter does not begin work in a vacuum. The Oregon legislative drafting manual suggests that a drafter *not* start from scratch if there is an existing statute or bill on which the drafter's bill could be patterned, though the drafter might need to check other sources to determine possible issues with any bill that the drafter uses as a starting point.[3]

These concerns also apply to the drafting of ordinances (discussed in Section III). Though city and county ordinances have the force of law, they cannot contradict state or federal law and cannot intrude into an area that is preempted by state or federal law.

II.   Basics About Bills

A.   Single Subject Rule

A single-subject rule requires a law to relate to only one subject. In South Carolina's constitution, for example, the single-subject rule is expressed as follows:

> Every Act or resolution having the force of law shall relate to but one subject, and that shall be expressed in the title.[4]

Many states have single-subject rules.[5] The single-subject rule prevents legislative log-rolling.[6] An Illinois court described "log-rolling" as "the practice of bundling less popular legislation with more palatable bills so that the well received bills would carry the unpopular ones to passage."[7] Essentially, the single-subject rule prevents the adoption of policies through stealth or fraud.[8]

Though most courts liberally construe statutes in favor of constitutionality,[9] legislation that violates a state's constitutionally based single-subject rule is unconstitutional. One court testily wrote:

> Over the last two decades we have addressed the single subject rule at least seven times.... We are growing weary of admonishing the Legislature for so flagrantly violating the terms of the ... Constitution. It is a waste of time for the Legislature and the Court, and a waste of the taxpayer's money. The Legislature ignored our earlier opinions, especially in [one case].... when it apparently consolidated five separate multi-subject bills into Senate Bill 1878 which facially, patently, and obviously contained multiple subjects.... [W]e again restate: THE CLEAR LANGUAGE OF THE ... CONSTITUTION REQUIRES THAT ALL LEGISLATIVE ACTS SHALL EMBRACE BUT ONE SUBJECT.[10]

Courts in other states, such as Illinois and Delaware, have found unconstitutional legislation that violates the single-subject rule.[11] State courts that have single-subject rules differ in how they determine compliance.[12] To know what the rule requires in a particular jurisdiction, you must consult state law.

B. Typical Components of a Bill

1. Identifying Information and Title

Depending on the state's practices, a bill might include identifying information such as the bill number,[13] the session number,[14] and the bill's sponsor.[15] Check your state's legislative drafting guidelines.

Choosing a title for a state statute is a serious drafting issue. The title's function is to put legislators and the public on notice of the general subject covered by proposed legislation.

Typically, states require a bill's single subject to be expressed in the title. According to the Kentucky Supreme Court, the purpose of the title requirement is "to prevent surprise or fraud upon the Legislature by means of provisions in bills, of which the titles gave no intimation, and which might, therefore, be overlooked and carelessly or unintentionally adopted."[16]

In some states, violation of a state's title rule might render the bill unconstitutional.[17] In general, courts liberally construe their constitution's title rules in favor of the legislation's constitutionality.[18] However, a legislative drafter needs to know where the state courts draw the line.

According to the Missouri Supreme Court, for example, there are two ways in which a title may be constitutionally unclear: "the subject may be too broad and amorphous, *or* so restrictive and underinclusive that some provisions fall outside it."[19]

The New Mexico legislative drafting manual discusses two schools of thought relating to titles: one school advocates a tightly written title, which limits amendments to a bill; the other school advocates more general titles that merely include sufficient detail to notify the reader of the bill's content.[20] Courts have articulated various standards for determining whether a title is sufficient.[21]

The full titles of bills may be lengthy, giving not only their subject and purpose, but also listing the statutes to be amended or repealed. The following is a lengthy and complex title that contains all the elements necessary for the title of a North Dakota bill:

> A BILL for an Act to create and enact sections 13–05–04.1, 13–05–04.2, 13–05–05.1, and 13–05–06.3 of the North Dakota Century Code, relating to surety bonds, minimum net worth, notice regarding change of name and address, and prohibited acts and practices of licensed collection agencies; to amend and reenact subsection 2 of section 6–08–16, subsection 4 of section 13–05–01.1, and sections 13–05–02.1, 13–05–02.3, 13–05–03, 13–05–04, 13–05–06, 13–05–06.1, 13–05–06.2, 13–05–07, and 13–05–08 of the North Dakota Century Code, relating to definition of creditor, branch offices, entities exempt from licensing,

forms for application for licensing, powers of the department of financial institutions, suspension and removal of agency officers and employees, investigations and subpoenas, agency record-keeping, and revocation of licenses for collection agencies.[22]

Some states' requirements may not result in such complex titles. For example, the New Mexico manual cautions drafters that an overly detailed title might omit a reference to part of the bill or might fail to cover later amendments to the bill.[23]

The Florida's Senate's legislative drafting manual recommends that a drafter never draft a title until the bill is fully drafted.[24] That makes sense because a drafter cannot draft an adequate title without understanding all components of the bill. Florida's manual also recommends that the drafter look at the actual bill while creating the title, instead of trying to remember the content.[25]

2. The Enacting Clause

In most states, a bill must open with a constitutionally-mandated enacting clause. Below are two examples:

- Be it enacted by the general assembly of the State of Arkansas ...[26]

- The people of the State of California do enact as follows....[27]

The exact language of enacting clauses for congressional bills is prescribed by 1 U.S.C. § 101. State constitutions prescribe the language in many states, though a few states prescribe the language by statute.

3. Preamble Section

Some bills contain a preamble that precedes the enacting clause, though some states discourage preambles. A preamble generally does not become a part of the enacted legislation, though courts may resort to the preamble in interpreting the legislation.[28] Some state drafting manuals (e.g., Arkansas' and Oregon's) direct the drafter to begin preamble statements with "whereas,"[29] though both manuals suggest that a drafter rarely needs to include them.[30] In some states, the clauses must be numbered.[31]

The following is an excerpt from the preamble to a Florida bill drafted in response to a court decision:

> WHEREAS, the Legislature recognizes and agrees with the limitations on the applicability of the doctrine of implied warranty of fitness and merchantability or habitability for a new home as established in.... seminal cases ..., and does not wish to expand any prospective

rights, responsibilities, or liabilities resulting from these decisions, and ...

WHEREAS, it is the intent of the Legislature to reject the decision ... insofar as it expands the doctrine of implied warranty of fitness and merchantability or habitability ..., NOW THEREFORE,

Be It Enacted by the Legislature of the State of Florida: ...[32]

4. Purpose or Intent Section

In contrast to a preamble, a purpose or intent statement is an actual section of a bill that follows the enacting clause and has the force of law. Such provisions serve the same purpose as background recitals in a contract (i.e., they may aid a court in construing the document).

Some states' legislative drafting manuals prohibit inclusion of a purpose section. For example, purpose sections are prohibited in North Dakota;[33] the drafting manual states that *the bill* should make its purpose clear.[34]

Some states permit but discourage use of purpose or intent sections. For example, the Florida Senate's drafting manual suggests that a drafter who finds that an intent section is needed to clarify the bill needs to redraft the bill.[35] Oregon's legislative drafting manual suggests that a drafter include such a section only if the drafter is asked to do so,[36] because a purpose section can create more problems than it resolves (e.g., if the purpose statement is broader than the related statute).[37]

The following is an excerpt from a Georgia bill:

(a) It is the purpose of this article to establish in the state a system of personnel administration which will attract, select, and retain the best employees based on merit, free from coercive political influences, with incentives in the form of equal opportunities for all; which will provide technically competent and loyal personnel ...; and which will remove unnecessary and inefficient employees. It is specifically the intent of the General Assembly to promote this purpose by allowing agencies greater flexibility in personnel management so as to promote the overall effectiveness and efficiency of state government....[38]

5. Legislative Findings Section

In some states, a legislative drafter may have the option to include a findings section in a bill. Such sections recite the legislating body's findings concerning facts that gave rise to the need for legislation. Different state legislatures may have different views on the utility of the findings section. The following is an example of a findings section from a California bill:

> SECTION 1. The Legislature finds and declares that reducing barriers to employment for people who have previously offended, and decreasing unemployment in communities with concentrated numbers of people who have previously offended, is a matter of statewide concern ... The Legislature further finds and declares that, consistent with [the Act] ..., increasing employment opportunities for people who have previously offended will reduce recidivism and improve economic stability in our communities.[39]

Are findings clauses needed? An Oregon court commented as follows:

> These findings are only a recital of premises for legislation.... But lawmakers do not need to find or declare the factual predicates for legislation, unless some special statute requires it, and such a recital gains nothing for the validity of the legislation, though it can sometimes help toward its purposeful interpretation. It is the operative text of the legislation, not prefatory findings, that people must obey and that ... judges enforce.[40]

None of the legislative-drafting manuals that we reviewed were enthusiastic about including legislative findings in a bill. A findings clause cannot fix a poorly drafted bill. However, in states that permit them, most of the manuals we looked at conceded that a drafter should include a findings clause if a requester or sponsor asks for it.

Hawaii's legislative drafting manual advises drafters to draft the document first *without* a findings section to see if it is needed because a well-drafted bill may not need a findings section.[41]

6. Short Title Section

The first numbered section in some federal and state bills sets forth a short title by which to cite the legislation after it is enacted. The following are examples of short titles:

> Short title. This chapter may be known and cited as "the Service Contracts Act."[42] (Maine)

> Short title. This article may be cited as the "Small Business Development Incentive Program for Internal Growth Act."[43] (West Virginia)

One drafting manual indicates that short titles are appropriate if the bill is lengthy, deals comprehensively with new material, and does not amend any existing legislation.[44] Another encourages the use of a short title but advises the drafter to keep short titles short.[45] Another discourages the use of short titles unless the requester or sponsor asks for it or unless the drafter determines that it would be useful.[46]

7. Definitions Section

A drafter should not ordinarily set out in the definitions section the ordinary or dictionary meaning of words. Chapter 27 further discusses the drafting of definitions.

8. Body of the Bill

The body of the bill contains the legislation's core provisions: i.e., the rules that the legislation is intended to implement. The New Mexico legislative drafting manual advises legislative drafters *not* to draft a bill so as to address all potential exceptions or to preempt all possible legal arguments against it.[47]

9. Some Technical Provisions

(a) Purpose of Technical Provisions

As well as the substantive provisions that form the bill's core, a bill may include technical provisions. These provisions are typically placed at the end of the main body of the bill. A full discussion of all types of technical provisions is beyond the scope of this book, but the following discussion will familiarize you with the types of matters that they typically address.

(b) Saving Clause

A saving clause is intended to (1) keep in effect some aspect of a law that would otherwise have been abrogated by passage of other legislation or (2) keep in effect some right or status that the law would otherwise alter. The following is an example:

> (a) The change in law made by this article applies only to an offense committed on or after the effective date of this article. For purposes of this section, an offense is committed before the effective date of this article if any element of the offense occurs before the effective date.
>
> (b) An offense committed before the effective date of this article is covered by law in effect when the offense was committed, and the former law is continued in effect for that purpose.[48]

A saving clause may allow for persons who meet stated criteria to be "grandfathered in" under a statute that would otherwise have altered their status (e.g., a licensing act).[49] The following is an example of a saving clause from a Pennsylvania bill:

(1) Any athletic trainer who holds a valid certificate issued by the board or the State Board of Osteopathic Medicine, relating to the practice of athletic training, prior to the effective date of this subsection shall, on or after the effective date of this subsection, be deemed to be licensed by the board or the State Board of Osteopathic Medicine as provided in this act.[50]

(c) Sunset Clause

A sunset clause puts an end to something created by a statute, such as an agency or program (unless the legislature extends the agency or program for a further period). Below is an example of a sunset clause in a Texas bill relating to "the office of public insurance counsel":

Sec. 501.003. SUNSET PROVISION. The office is subject to Chapter 325, Government Code (Texas Sunset Act). Unless continued in existence as provided by that chapter, the office is abolished September 1, 2023.[51]

(d) Severability and Non–Severability Clauses

A severability clause states that an invalid provision may be severed from the legislation and that the remaining provisions continue in effect. The following severability provision was included in a Florida bill:

Section 16. Severability.—If any section, subsection, sentence, clause, or phrase of this act is held to be unconstitutional, such holding shall not affect the validity of the remaining portions of the act, the Legislature hereby declaring that it would have passed this act and each section, subsection, sentence, clause, and phrase thereof, irrespective of any separate section, subsection, sentence, clause, or phrase thereof, and irrespective of the fact that any one or more other sections, subsections, sentences, clauses, or phrases thereof may be declared unconstitutional.[52]

Such provisions may not be necessary in states whose courts typically attempt to sever invalid provisions from a statute so that the remainder continues in effect. Some states' legislative drafting manuals prohibit or discourage their inclusion in a bill.[53]

A *non-severability* clause states that the bill (or a specific section) is not severable: if a provision is held invalid, the remaining provisions *do not* continue in effect. For example, an Arkansas bill states the following:

SECTION 4. The provisions of this act are not severable, and if any provision of this act is declared invalid for any reason, then all provisions of this act shall also be invalid.[54]

To understand how your state views severability and non-severability clauses, check relevant law and drafting guidelines.

(e) Effective Date Clause and Emergency Clause

An effective date clause states the date on which (a) legislation becomes effective or (b) individual sections become effective. The following are examples of effective date clauses:

> 5. This act shall take effect immediately, except that section 1 of this act shall take effect on the 90th day after the date of enactment and section 3 of this act shall take effect January 1 next following the date of enactment.[55] [New Jersey]
>
> SECTION 2. This act shall take effect upon passage.[56] [Rhode Island]

Effective date clauses are not always necessary; state law may govern the effective date of legislation absent a provision stipulating otherwise. Some states have laws imposing an effective date that cannot be altered absent an emergency. For example, the Oregon constitution provides the following:

> No act shall take effect until ninety days from the end of the [legislative] session at which the same shall have been passed, except in case of emergency; which emergency shall be declared in the preamble, or in the body of the law.[57]

If a legislative drafter in Oregon intends for a bill to take effect on some other date, the drafter must include an emergency clause. Below is an example of an emergency clause from an Oregon bill:

> SECTION 3. This 2011 Act being necessary for the immediate preservation of the public peace, health and safety, an emergency is declared to exist, and this 2011 Act takes effect on its passage.[58]

The Arkansas legislative drafting manual indicates that drafters of emergency clauses should consider describing the background conditions that brought about the need for the bill and the reasons why it must become immediately effective.[59] In some states, detailed findings showing an emergency may appear in the bill's preamble. In a Maine bill that we looked at, the emergency clause simply referred to the preamble:

> Emergency clause. In view of the emergency cited in the preamble, this legislation takes effect when approved.[60]

(f) Retroactivity of Part or All of an Act

If retroactivity will not produce an ex post facto law or otherwise be unconstitutional, a bill can usually be made retroactive. The following are two examples of retroactivity clauses:

> Sec. 2. Retroactivity. This Act is retroactive to January 1, 2012.[61]

> Sec. 34. Retroactivity. That section of this Act that repeals and replaces the Maine Revised Statutes, Title 36, section 2531 applies retroactively to taxes on all premiums received on or after July 1, 2011 ... Those sections of this Act that amend Title 36, section 5122, subsection 2, paragraph II; section 5142, subsection 8–B, paragraph C; and section 5200–A, subsection 2, paragraph V apply retroactively to tax years beginning on or after January 1, 2011....[62]

III.   Drafting Local Ordinances

A.   Authority of City or County to Legislate

Cities and counties have only the powers that the state delegates to them.[63] A state may grant to cities and counties the power to regulate certain matters of local concern. An ordinance is a law enacted by a local governmental body, such as a county commission or city council.[64] If an ordinance is created in compliance with state law,[65] it has the force and effect of law.

A state may limit the areas in which local government can act. For example, the Florida legislature has limited the power of any entity of local government to do the following: (a) impose price controls on lawful business activities that are not owned, franchised, or under contract with a governmental agency; and (b) impose rent controls unless certain conditions are met.[66]

If you examine the matters addressed by local ordinances, you will find a wide range of topics. For example, our local code of ordinances (Gainesville, Florida) includes provisions that deal with (among other things) alcoholic beverages; cemeteries; animal control; art in public places; discrimination; fire prevention; streets, sidewalks, and other public places; and land development.

Because an ordinance operates like a statute, states normally require the enacting body to comply with procedures, such as a record vote, a public hearing, and published notice.[67] Courts generally presume that a legislative body that has enacted an ordinance acted within its authority so that the burden rests on those challenging validity.[68]

Under certain circumstances, an ordinance might be invalid. An ordinance cannot contradict state or federal law and cannot address a matter that is preempted by state or federal law.[69]

In what circumstances would a state court determine that an ordinance is invalid under state law? To answer that question, you must check state law.

B.   Preparing to Draft an Ordinance

1.   Researching Existing Law

Before drafting an ordinance, a drafter must go through the same process as the drafter of a statute would (as discussed in Section I of this chapter):

- Learning about the local legislative process.

- Researching the factual background of the proposed ordinance.

- Researching relevant law.

- Consulting local drafting guidelines.

Again, a drafter should be reluctant to re-invent the wheel. If other cities or counties have enacted similar ordinances, review as many versions as you can find and tweak them until they meet your exacting standards.

2.   Consulting a Drafting Manual

Some cities and counties set out in drafting manuals guidelines for ordinance drafters. Some manuals are available online. Among other things, these manuals typically set out the desired format for chapter and section numbering.

For drafters who do not have local drafting manuals, we recommend the template for drafting rule-making documents (set out in Chapter 20).

CHAPTER 17

HOW COURTS CONSTRUE STATUTES AND OTHER PUBLIC RULE-MAKING DOCUMENTS

■ ■ ■

I. Introduction to Statutory Construction

This chapter introduces certain aspects of statutory construction that are useful for a drafter of statutes or other public rule-making documents to know. The discussion that follows is limited to those aspects. Categorization of the various processes used in different courts is beyond the scope of this book.

As well as to statutes, courts typically apply principles of statutory construction to other types of public rule-making documents, including the following:

- Administrative regulations promulgated by a state, federal, city, or county agency.[1]

- Rules promulgated or adopted pursuant to some state or federal authority, such as a rules of procedure or evidence for a court[2] or local court rules of court or the state bar.[3]

- Local (city or county) ordinances.[4]

- Government resolutions.[5]

To get an overview of how statutory construction works, we recommend that you review the Uniform Statute and Rule Construction Act. To understand a particular jurisdiction's or a particular court's approach to statutory construction, the drafter will usually need to delve into the case law.

II. Goal of Courts in Construing a Statute

Statutory construction is a process guided by both established rules and a court's sense—gleaned from the disputed text—of how the legislative body intended for the statute to function as a whole. The D.C. Court of Appeals described statutory interpretation as "a holistic endeavor" that "must account for a statute's full text, language as well as punctuation, structure, and subject matter."[6]

Courts generally agree that the ultimate goal of statutory construction is the effectuation of legislative intent.[7] Thus, courts may refer to legislative intent as the "polestar"[8] or "touchstone"[9] that guides statutory construction. In construing a statute or constitutional provision, courts typically presume the following:

- That the legislature was aware of the laws in existence at the time of an enactment and of their effect and implication.[10]

- That the legislature intended to create (1) policies that were practical and not unjust, indefensible, or capricious;[11] and (2) enactments that would serve the public interest and promote public welfare.[12]

- That the legislature intended the provision to be constitutional and valid.[13]

III. Process of Statutory Construction

A. Circumstances in Which Construction is Required

Courts generally agree that an ambiguous statute requires construction to clarify its meaning. They also generally agree on the definition of "ambiguous." Courts typically state that a provision is ambiguous (1) if it is *reasonably* susceptible to more than one reasonable interpretation[14] or (2) if a provision is of such doubtful or obscure meaning that *reasonable* minds might be uncertain or might disagree as to its meaning.[15]

Thus, a court usually must find at least two *plausible* readings of the same text to determine that the text is ambiguous. That parties to a lawsuit disagree about the meaning of a provision[16] or that different interpretations are technically conceivable[17] does not necessarily cause a court to find a provision ambiguous.

B. Varying Approaches to Statutory Construction

A court's determination that a provision is ambiguous has certain consequences. First, the determination implies that the text has more than one meaning that the court considers plausible. Second, the determination means that the court is willing to use resources in addition to the bare text to determine the meaning that reflects the legislature's true intent.

Courts' discussion of how they decide that a statute is *unambiguous* is often confusing. How does a court get to that conclusion?

According to the U.S. Supreme Court, the first step is for the court to examine the text using the "cardinal canon of construction" that applies before all others:

> We have stated time and again that courts must presume that a legislature says in a statute what it means and means in a statute what it says there. When the words of a statute are unambiguous, then, this first canon is also the last: "judicial inquiry is complete."[18]

That is the theory, and many state courts' decisions include similar language.[19] Not all courts follow the Supreme Court's approach regarding the initial determination of meaning; in fact, many appear to be engaging in construction at that initial stage.

Courts do generally agree that if the language is ambiguous, they must apply a process of construction to try to resolve the ambiguity. In doing so, they may apply judicially-adopted or statutorily-imposed guidelines ("canons of construction") for reading a statute whose meaning is uncertain. At some point, a court that cannot resolve an ambiguity turns to extrinsic aids—though the point at which courts turn to turn to extrinsic aids varies. In the following sections, we discuss some of the canons of construction and extrinsic aids that courts tend to use.

IV. Use of Canons of Construction

A. Nature and Purpose of Canons

Virtually all courts begin their construction process by reciting the canon that their primary goal is to effectuate legislative intent as gleaned from the statute's language. If courts cannot do so, they will apply the canons of construction to justify their reading of the disputed statute. How they apply the canons is often unpredictable.

The U.S. Supreme Court explained the rationale for using canons of construction:

> "Those who write statutes seek to solve human problems. Fidelity to their aims requires us to approach an interpretive problem not as if it were a purely logical game, like a Rubik's Cube, but as an effort to divine the human intent that underlies the statute."[20]

How well do the canons of construction serve this purpose? On this point, reasonable minds may differ. In a famous article, Professor Karl Llewellyn set out an extensive series of dueling canons of construction (each leading to an opposite result), thus illustrating that widely used canons may be limited by other canons that contradict or that recognize exceptions to the rule expressed in the canon.[21]

To what extent are courts bound by canons of construction? Recently, the U.S. Supreme Court characterized the canons of construction as "no more than rules of thumb."[22] The "rule of thumb" approach to canons might not apply if a state's legislature has codified the canons, thereby presumably mandating the canons' application.[23] For example, Connecticut law requires a court to apply the following principle to determine whether a statute is ambiguous:

> The meaning of a statute shall, in the first instance, be ascertained from **the text of the statute itself and its relationship to other statutes**. If, after examining such text and considering such relationship, the meaning of such text is plain and unambiguous..., extratextual evidence of the meaning of the statute shall not be considered.[24]

Understanding the canons can provide insight into how courts view statutory language. For example, a drafter whose state courts apply a rule such as the one stated in the Connecticut statute quoted above would want to use extra care in ensuring that the drafted provision is consistent with any related statutes.

A drafter of statutes or other public rule-making documents should *not* rely on a canon of construction to plug a loophole or to resolve an ambiguity. Instead, the drafter should precisely draft the text to minimize the possibility that the document would be disputed.

B.   Certain Canons of Interest to the Drafter

1.   Canons Favoring One Reading Over Another

(a) *Characteristics of These Canons*

Certain canons favor one reading of a disputed statute over another reading that a party might be contending for, even if both meanings are *superficially* plausible based on the text. Applying such rules of construction could permit a court to find—in the first phase of analysis—that a provision is not ambiguous and does not require further construction. Such canons could also be used (at a later phase in the analysis) to resolve ambiguity.

(b) *Canons Favoring Validity and Constitutionality*

Legislative enactments are presumed to be constitutional.[25] A party challenging such an enactment typically bears a heavy burden to establish unconstitutionality.[26] In order to effectuate the legislature's intentions, Courts must interpret a statute in a way that makes it constitutional if there is a reasonable construction that would allow the court to avoid unconstitutionality.[27]

(c) *Canons Favoring Enforcement to Achieve Rational Purpose*

Courts assume that the legislature intended to create policies that are practical rather than absurd[28] and that are based on common sense[29] and logic.[30] As one California court said, it is reasonable for courts to infer that "the legislators intended an interpretation producing practical and workable results rather than one resulting in mischief or absurdity."[31]

Courts also assume that the legislature designs provisions to serve the public's best interests, to promote public welfare,[32] and to operate rationally to fulfill the legislation's general purpose.[33]

Thus, in construing a statute, a court will avoid adopting a contended-for meaning that would lead to an absurd, unreasonable, or unjust result[34] or that would undermine the statute's general purpose.

(d) Canons Favoring Enforcement of the Entire Statute

Courts seek to give effect to the *entire* statute. Courts generally attempt to harmonize conflicting provisions in order to give effect to *all* of a statute's parts.[35] Thus, a court will typically reject a reading of an allegedly ambiguous statute that would make any word, phrase, or clause meaningless.[36]

What if the court is unable to harmonize a conflict between related provisions? In that case, a court might fall back on a rule for prioritizing the conflicting language. For example, if one conflicting provision governs the specific circumstance at issue and the other is more general in application,[37] the court might conclude that the more specific provision trumps the more general one.[38] If the conflicting provisions were enacted at different times, a later enactment might trump the earlier one.[39]

(e) Canons Favoring Consistency with Related Enactments

If necessary to determine a provision's meaning, a court might extend its analysis to the related enactments—or even to the *entire statutory scheme* of which the enactment is a part.[40]

According to the *in pari materia* doctrine, a court can read together statutes that relate to the same subject-matter so that one clarifies an uncertainty in the other. This doctrine has the greatest force if the provisions were part of the same enactment[41] or passed during the same legislative session.[42] If provisions are *in pari materia*, courts will do their best to harmonize them to ensure that each provision is given effect.[43] If statutes passed during the same session cannot be reconciled, a court might conclude that the later modifies the earlier.[44]

2. Use of a Statute's Components

A statute's title and section headings are generally not considered to be part of a statute, though some courts use the title[45] and headings[46] as an aid to construction. A North Carolina court noted that if the meaning of a statute is doubtful, the title serves as a legislative declaration of the tenor and object of the Act.[47] A California court stated that section headings of an ambiguous statute are entitled to considerable weight.[48]

Some courts might consider a statute's purpose clause[49] or findings[50] or a bill's preamble.[51] For example, a Pennsylvania statute permits a court to consider a statute's preamble in construing the statute.[52] Such clauses do not trump the plain language of the statute. Courts typically disregard statements of purpose, intent or fact if those statements contradict operative provisions.[53]

3. Determination of a Term's Meaning or Application

(a) Preference for Ordinary Meaning of a Term

In construing statutory language, courts tend to assume that the legislature (1) used words in a normal and ordinary sense and (2) did not intend a narrow or strained construction."[54] In construing statutes, courts typically give the ordinary or dictionary meaning to words and phrases chosen by the legislature unless the statute indicates a contrary intent.[55]

Thus, the U.S. Supreme Court recently said that if Congress uses a phrase with a common-law meaning (e.g., stating that a patent is "presumed valid"), the Court assumes that the phrase has its common-law meaning—absent anything pointing another way.[56] If a term has a well-defined legal meaning, the court will assume that the legal meaning applies.[57] For instance, an Oregon court stated that it would interpret the word "must" according to its connotation when used in Oregon law.[58]

A court typically will give a term its technical meaning if the legislature indicates, through a definition or in some other way, that the term has a technical meaning.[59]

If the legislature defines a term in a statute, the court will apply the stipulated definition.[60] A state statute may stipulate generally for all state statutes the meaning of certain words or phrases.

(b) Effect of Consistent and Inconsistent Language

Absent some indication that the legislature intended otherwise, courts generally assume that if the same term appears in different parts of a statute, the term means the same thing throughout.[61] A court might extend that principle to a term that appears in different statutes, particularly if the statutes were enacted at the same time or are in pari materia.[62]

On the other hand, if a legislature uses a different word or phrase in the same statute, courts generally assume that the legislature intended—by changing the language—to indicate a different meaning.[63]

(c) Effect of Associated Terms

Grouping a term with other terms affects a court's interpretation of the term's meaning. Chapter 26 discusses the canons noscitur a sociis and ejusdem generis. These canons are important for the drafter to know, because a court's application of them can limit text in a way that the drafter did not intend. Some courts might apply these canons even without first determining that a provision is ambiguous.[64]

(d) Effect of Omission or Express Exclusion

According to the canon *expressio unius est exclusio alterius,* the expression of some things in a statute necessarily implies the intention to omit things that are not expressed.[65] This canon and its drafting implications are discussed in Chapter 26.

V.   Extrinsic Aids to Construction

A.   Use of Extrinsic Aids to Determine Meaning

As discussed in Section II, a court typically will allow extrinsic aids to clarify legislative intent if the court has determined that a statute is ambiguous. Many courts refrain from resorting to extrinsic aids unless the text is in fact ambiguous.[66]

The circumstances in which a court resorts to extrinsic aid depends on the jurisdiction. To determine when courts in your jurisdiction resort to extrinsic aids, check applicable law.

B.   Types of Extrinsic Aids

The following is a list of some extrinsic aids that courts have consulted when construing statutes:

a)   The legislative history, including the following:

- Prior versions of the same legislation and amendments made as it passed through the legislature.[67]

- The report of a commission that proposes a statute.[68]

- Remarks made on the floor of the legislative body.[69]

- Testimony before a legislative committee,[70] the minutes of a legislative committee hearing,[71] or committee reports.[72]

- The opinion of legislative counsel.[73]

b)   Prior legislation that the provision accepted or changed.[74]

c)   The general historical context of the legislation, including the circumstances that existed at the time it was passed.[75]

d)   Relevant prior case law on the same subject as the statute[76] (e.g., another jurisdiction's construction of a statute on which the disputed provision was modeled).[77]

e) The official comments to Uniform Acts or Model Laws from which the statute is derived and case law from jurisdictions that have adopted the same Uniform Act or Model Law.[78]

f) A reasonable construction of a statute by an agency charged with enforcing the statute.[79]

Courts differ regarding the weight that they give to the various extrinsic aids. To know how they are valued in your jurisdiction, consult applicable law.

VI. Strict Versus Liberal Construction

If a court strictly construes a statute or other legislative provision, the court will not extend it beyond its plain meaning or to cases that are not clearly within its scope.[80] Thus, such provisions must be drafted with care in order to ensure that they operate as intended and are found valid.

For example, courts typically will strictly construe ambiguous penal statutes based on the policy that a statute should give the public fair warning of what conduct is criminal.[81] The "rule of lenity" requires construction in the defendant's favor of ambiguous penal statutes.[82]

Other statutes are liberally construed: i.e., the courts tend to read them leniently in order to ensure that they achieve their purpose. For example, courts typically will liberally construe remedial statutes.[83] Remedial statutes resolve or redress an existing problem or grievance,[84] create a new remedy to enforce an existing right,[85] or otherwise address themselves to the public good.

Some statutes contain provisions stating that courts are to apply liberal construction. For example, Florida's Consumer Pricing Unit Act states that the act "shall be liberally construed" to promote certain purposes.[86]

To determine which types of statutes are strictly or liberally construed, refer to the case law and to legislative drafting manuals.

CHAPTER 18

EXERCISES FOR PART 3:
RULE–MAKING DOCUMENTS

■ ■ ■

Project 1.   Declaration of Covenants and Restrictions

Your client is Sarah M. Proust of Trouville, Clovis County, Tennsylvania. Proust's company, "Proust Properties" owns land in Trouville that Proust intends to develop. She intends to subdivide it into 75 lots, each about 4 acres.

The development will be called "Forest of Arcadia." In addition to the homesites, the subdivision will include two parks (common areas). The parks will include playground equipment, picnic grills, and tables.

Proust intended to use a document she found online for the declarations and restrictions, but she decided that the document she generated from the online sample was confusing. Though **poorly drafted**, the document shown below does reflect her intentions as to the content of the declaration.

Client's Attempt at Drafting Covenants & Restrictions

WHEREAS, the firm of Proust Properties, LL.C., hereinafter called "Declarant," intends to impose certain restrictions on the use of the subdivision hereinafter known as The Forest Of Arcadia (Arcadia) for the benefit of the development, consisting of 75 subdivided tracts of land; and

WHEREAS, the purpose of the aforesaid restrictions is to preserve the property's natural beauty, protect property values by promoting its desirability, and create an appealing environment for owners of homesites,

THEREFORE,

Declarant, on behalf of its successor and assigns, declares the subsequent covenants and restrictions on the hereinbefore-mentioned property:

Article I. Covenants Run with Land

1. These covenants are to run with the land until January 1, 2020, at which time said covenants are to extend automatically for successive periods of ten years (absent a vote otherwise by a majority of the owners of the lots who must at that time agree to change said covenants in whole or in part).

Article 2. Architectural Review Board

2. An Architectural Control Committee (ACC) is established. The board is composed of Jacob Joyce, an architect, and Sarah M. Proust, but ACC may designate a representative to act on its behalf. Its purpose is to approve plans for construction or installation to determine harmony with subdivision in accordance with the goals expressed in this document.

3. The ACC shall approve a submitted plan within 21 days of the date of submission of these plans. Approval shall be in writing. In the writing, the ACC shall state the reason and changes, if any, that would result in approval. In the event that the ACC or its designated representative fails to approve or disapprove within the stated time, approval is deemed granted and related covenants shall be deemed to have been fully complied with by owner.

4. Upon occurrence of death or resignation of either member, the remaining member shall designate a successor member. If at any time the membership of such committee is changed, notice shall be recorded in the Office of the Clerk of the Court of Marcel County, Tennsylvania.

Article 3. Homesites

5. The land is to be subdivided into 75 homesites. Each homesite is to be solely and only used for residential purposes. No other free-standing residential dwelling, whether permanent or temporary, shall be constructed upon any lot other than one detached, single-family dwelling.

6. No building is to be constructed or altered upon any premises until construction plans and specifications and a plot plan reflecting the location of such building have been approved. The Architectural Control Committee shall approve such plans only if in conformity and harmony of external design with existing buildings in the development.

7. No such building shall exceed 3 stories in height.

8. Provided that the homeowner has received the ACC's permission to construct a swimming pool, the owner or a successor may construct a pool cabana that is constructed in proximity to a swimming pool providing that the homeowner submits the plans for approval to

the ACC and that the cabana is otherwise harmonized with the development.

9. Every dwelling or other building shall be constructed within the setback lines indicated on the recorded plat: said structures are to be at least 35 feet from the front of said property line and at least 35 feet from the back of the property line.

Article 4. Common Areas

10. Parks are common areas for all homeowners' benefit within the development. All owners are responsible for making sure that their families and guests refrain from damaging any playground or other equipment installed for the use of others and that they leave such areas clean and free of trash or other debris. They shall not permit dogs to enter parks.

Article 5. Easements

11. As indicated on the recorded plat, easements for utility installation and maintenance are reserved. The owner shall construct no structures of any kind upon the area within the easements indicated. Owner shall not place anything within the area of the drainage easements indicated on the recorded plat if it would impede or alter flow of water within such drainage easements.

Article 6. Prohibitions on Homesites

12. No out-building including a tent or shack shall be placed or constructed upon a homesite except for an approved pool cabana that is constructed for use with an approved swimming pool.

13. No out-building shall at any time be used for human habitation, temporarily or permanently. No structure of a temporary character, such as a tent or motor home, shall be used for human habitation.

14. No building shall be constructed on any building site covered by these covenants the habitable floor area of which exclusive of basements porches and garages is less than 3000 square feet (not applicable to pool cabana). No pool or fence shall be placed upon the homesite unless first approved by the ACC.

15. No mobile home, either with or without wheels, shall be placed on the homesite. Self propelled motor homes (unless in a garage) and prefabricated homes shall not be kept.

16. At no time shall there be any repairing, dismantling, or other mechanical work done on any automobiles or other vehicles, except in a closed carport or garage.

17. On each building site, there shall be garages, carports, or paved area for the parking of at least four vehicles. No car shall be parked, stored, or otherwise left on any unpaved area. All garages and

carports shall have side entrances with the design of the front portion being of the same type and design as the remainder of the dwelling house. A carport or garage shall not face the front of the property.

18.　Only if contained completely within a structure that has been architecturally approved shall any motor boat, house boat, boat trailer, or similar water-borne vehicle be maintained, stored, or kept on a homesite.

19.　A driveway or parking area must be paved. A driveway must be paved to the curb line.

20.　No fence, wall, or hedge shall extend beyond the minimum building set back lines.

21.　House pets shall be confined within the dwelling or an approved fence or pen. They shall not be left free to roam the subdivision. Poultry, animals, or pigs of any kind other than house pets shall not be maintained on any part of said homesite.

22.　No noxious activity shall be carried on upon any homesite. No trade shall be carried on. Anything that may be or become an annoyance or nuisance to the neighborhood is prohibited.

Article 7. Signs

23.　When any building is for sale, only one "For Sale" sign will be permitted for each lot. Such sign is not to exceed 6 square feet, with the exception of a sign used by a builder or real estate broker to advertise a new property for sale if the sale takes place during the time when not all lots have yet been built upon. In such instance, a builder can use a sign up to 30 square feet. Under no circumstances shall any other commercial sign be permitted.

Article 8. Violations

24.　If the parties or their heirs, successors, or assigns shall violate any of the covenants herein or attempt to violate them, any other person owning any real property situated in said subdivision has the right to prosecute any proceedings in law or equity against such person and to seek injunction to prevent such person from so doing or, if damages would be a more suitable remedy, to recover damages for such violation.

Article 9. Severability of Invalid Covenant

25.　If any covenant or part thereof shall be held invalid by judgment or court order, such invalidity does not affect other provisions, which shall remain in full force and effect.

IN WITNESS WHEREOF, the DECLARANT has affixed its signature this _____ day of _____ A.D. 20_____.

[Signature block and notary block omitted]

Assignment A. Prepare a Detailed Issue List and Outline

Review Chapters 19–21. Prepare a detailed issue list and outline based on the clients' version of the covenants (above).

Assignment B. Prepare a Client Letter

Prepare a formal letter to the clients, including at least three questions that meet the requirements of Chapter 19.

Assignment C. Draft the Document

Draft the covenants and restrictions for your clients, using your issue list (Assignment A) and the drafting principles set out in Chapters 15 and 26–33.

Project 2.   School Dress Code

As a member of the school board for Jeffcoates County, Wyowa, you have been asked to draft a dress code for county schools. After reading the materials below, draft an effective provision.

An ad hoc committee that was assigned to conduct a study of dress codes currently in force in Jeffcoates County has compiled a rough list of the rules that they would like to implement. They have also listed their findings, purposes and thoughts about enforcement of the dress code (which they want incorporated in the code).

Committee's Informal Issue List Regarding Dress Code

Goals and Findings:

1.   safe learning environment, all students perform well.

2.   personal appearance: key component of learning environment.

3.   teach respect for community and importance of adapting appearance to situation; teach good judgment about appropriateness.

4.   students to adhere to standards of dress to promote goals.

5.   sent home from school or in-school suspension if no one available at home to pick up.

7.   provide copy of dress code for first offense and dress code mailed to parent.

8.   second offense, suspension can result.

9.   applies on school property or any property under jurisdiction of Board of Education.

10.   on school trips or school-sponsored event, on buses.

11.   does not apply to school-approved uniforms such as for dance teams or gymnastic team.

<u>Rules</u>

1. Clothing: not revealing or provocative

2. No extremely baggy or tight clothing

3. No shoes with cleats or metal toe-caps, sandals without back strap (slip-ons)

4. No underwear worn as clothing, clothing revealing underwear

5. No strapless top, halter top, spaghetti straps, stiletto heels,

6. No see-through (lace or mesh)

7. No garment shorter than mid-thigh (skirt, shorts, kilt)

8. No trousers/shorts pulled below natural waist level, flip-flops

9. No sunglasses inside building. platform soles

10. No head covering, sweat band, bandanna or head gear except when worn for religious reasons

11. No jewelry bookbags or other articles or components of dress that depict profanity, vulgarity, violence, drug use, criminal acts, associated with violent groups, intimidation, violence

12. No negative stereotypes or negative messages re: any group re: race, creed, national origin, religious beliefs, patriotism, political validity or importance, gender identity, sexual preference, gender, age, or other demeaning message

13. No items promoting use of drugs, tobacco, alcohol

14. No items likely to be upsetting or provocative to other students

15. No items disruptive to educational processes or operation of school

16. leave discretion to make allowances for medical condition or religious beliefs

Formatting Guidance

The title of the policy should be "County-wide Dress Code for Public Schools of Jeffcoates County, Wyowa." It should be numbered JCSB 310–4G. Use the formatting guidelines in Chapter 20 for headings and text.

Assignment A. *Prepare an Outline*

Based on the committee's issue list (above) and on the principles in Chapters 20 and 21, prepare an outline of the dress code.

Assignment B. *Prepare a List of Questions for the Committee*

Using the principles in Chapter 19, make a list of questions and advice for the committee regarding any procedural or policy matter that is unclear to you. Include at least three questions.

Assignment C. Draft the Code

Can you come up with a way of boiling down the Committee's detailed list of goals and rules to state a coherent policy? Can you distill from these lists of specifics some general principles? To do this assignment, review the following materials:

- Chapter 14 (language appropriate to rule-making documents)
- Chapter 26 (choosing words)
- Chapter 31–33 (grammar, punctuation, and style)

Project 3. Frazier County Ordinance (Curfew)

You are the county attorney for Frazier, Minnezona. In the last few years, the county has seen an enormous increase in juvenile crime and crimes against juveniles, not only in the large city of Toulouse but also in the smaller towns. A recent study by an independent organization (Citizens Against Juvenile Crime) showed that by far the greatest number of these crimes take place between 10 PM and 6 AM. There has been enormous pressure to enact a county-wide ordinance imposing a curfew on minors in Frazier County.

A poorly drafted ordinance from nearby Currier County appears to address most of the issues that your county wants its policy to address— though the organization, writing, and language used in the sample ordinance leave much to be desired. Review the materials below, then do the assignments.

Concerns About the Currier Ordinance

The Currier County ordinance has survived one constitutional challenge on grounds of over-breadth. However, your county has the following concerns:

> The study regarding juvenile crime found that the crimes take place between 10 PM and 6 PM; however, the staggered curfew times for juveniles of different ages imposes an earlier curfew on children under the age of 12 (and the study did not address whether younger children should have an earlier curfew).

> You feel that the Currier ordinance does not do a good job of putting citizens and enforcing agents on notice of the conduct that it is regulating because of defects in the writing and organization.

Sample Ordinance from Currier County

ORDINANCE NUMBER 2010–16
Currier County, Minnezona

An Ordinance Providing for Prohibition of Violation by
Juveniles or Adults of County–Wide Curfew

The County Commissioners of Currier County, Minnezona do hereby ordain:

SECTION 2011–16A.   Definitions of Words and Phrases

(1) "Public place" is any place to which members of the public are invited or have the right to be and remain, including but not limited to public streets, public buildings (including schools and school property), public grounds (including but not limited to parks, hospital, and school grounds), and private property onto which the public is invited to be and remain pursuant to some invitation such as shopping malls, apartment complexes, and bus stations.

(2) "Emergency" means that the situation requires the juvenile to act immediately to prevent serious bodily injury (involving substantial risk of long-term physical consequences or death) or property damage.

(3) "Custodial adult" means birth parent, adoptive parent, stepparent, an adult appointed pursuant to Minnezona. Stat. § 46.302(a) or (b), or a responsible adult in whose care such adult has entrusted the juvenile.

(4) "Juvenile" refers to a minor child (under the age of eighteen). It does not include a married juvenile or one legally emancipated.

SECTION 2011–16B.   Findings and Purpose of Currier County Commissioners

It is found that a recent increase in juvenile crime and crimes against juveniles has occurred in the preceding years. It is found likewise that maturity, judgment, and experience are lacking in juveniles, particularly younger juveniles the county has an interest in protecting. The substantial interests of the County require that (a) juvenile crime and crime against juveniles be prevented and (b) that a curfew be implemented, promoted, and required, that the welfare of the community be thereby safeguarded. It shall be the purpose of this ordinance hereby and forthwith to protect these substantial interests.

SECTION 2011–16C.   Prohibited acts; Curfew Hours

A curfew is hereby imposed on juveniles based on the age of the juvenile. It is hereby declared to be unlawful in Currier County that a juvenile be in violation of the curfew imposed on juveniles of that age. A juvenile shall violate the curfew if he is, appears, or remains present in a public place in the County of Currier during the hours of curfew, as follows:

(a) For a juvenile between 16 and 17, between 11 PM Sunday–Thursday and 5 AM of the following day and between midnight on Friday or Saturday and 5 AM on the following day.

(b) For a juvenile age 15 or16, between 10 PM Sunday–Thursday and 5 AM of the following day and between 11 PM on Friday or

Saturday and 5 AM on the following day.

(c) For a juvenile age 12, 13, or 14, between 9 PM Sunday–Thursday and 5 AM of the following day and between 10 PM on Friday or Saturday and 5 AM on the following day.

(d) For a juvenile aged under 12, between 8 PM Sunday–Thursday and 5 AM of the following day and between 8:30 PM on Friday or Saturday and 5 AM on the following day.

It is intended that the following shall be an exception to the preceding and this section shall therefore not be applied if the juvenile was: accompanied by the custodial adult; standing, sitting, or otherwise present on an area adjacent to the property on which is located the residence of the juvenile or the next door property, structure, or residence; responding or involved in responding to an emergency not brought about by the intentional or criminal act of said juvenile; going to, attending, traveling to, going home from an official school, church or recreational event or activity that was sponsored and/or supervised by said school, church, or other public or civic entity and/or organization; by a direct route performing an errand at the direction of the custodial adult at a time and said adult is present at home; engaged in interstate travel; or exercising First Amendment rights that are protected by law.

2011–16D.   Law Enforcement Action

A law enforcement official may issue a citation, detain, or take into custody a juvenile based on violating section 2011–16C except that the law enforcement official shall not issue, detain, or take him into custody unless the law enforcement official has spoken to the juvenile and fully considered the facts and circumstances and reasonably has concluded that he is in violation of section 2011–16C and considers that no exception in that section applies to the circumstances and that his interests shall be best served by issuing a citation, detaining or taking into custody the juvenile. If a juvenile refuses to be returned to a custodial adult, the law enforcement official shall contact Child Protective Services and shall place the juvenile in its custody.

2011–16E.   Penalty

Appropriate penalties may be imposed under the criminal law. A juvenile may be adjudged delinquent and the aforesaid penalties shall be imposed if determined to be appropriate, as well as a penalty provided in the state Juvenile Code.

2011–16F.   EFFECTIVE DATE

Effective date shall be September 1, 2010.

Formatting Considerations

In Minnezona, all counties use the same format in their legislative documents. Thus, the format used in the Currier County ordinance is the format you should follow, except that the ordinance number should reflect the current year (e.g., 2013–1 or 2014–1).

Assignment A.   *Prepare a Detailed Issue List and Outline*

Review Chapter 19. Prepare a detailed list of all the issues that appear in the sample ordinance (above). Using the principles set out in Chapters 20 and 21 (and the template for a rule-making document), prepare a detailed outline for a revised version of the sample ordinance.

Assignment B.   *Prepare a List of Questions for the Currier Attorney*

The Currier County attorney is just as busy as you are but is also your good friend from law school. Prepare a list (not a letter) of questions that could easily be answered by one of the County attorney's assistants or interns. Include at least four questions concerning the ordinance and its application.

Assignment C.   *Draft the Ordinance*

After reviewing the following materials, draft the ordinance:

- Chapter 14 (focus on legislative language).

- Chapter 16 (focus on ordinance drafting).

- Chapter 26 (word choice).

- Chapter 27 (definitions).

- Chapter 28 (ambiguity).

- Chapters 31–33 (grammar, punctuation, style).

Project 4.   Bill (Enforcement of Non–Compete Covenants)

You are a legislative drafter for the state of Arkansington. You have been assigned to draft a bill establishing criteria for enforcement of covenants not to compete. The legislators proposing the bill have given you their rough draft of the criteria. Read the following materials and do the assignments.

Arkansington Senate Bill No. 42, 112th Legislative Session

Be it enacted by the people of Arkansington:

Section 1.   Short Title.

This Act shall be cited as the "Arkansington Covenants Not to Compete Act."

Section 2. Definition.

"Trade secret" means that the information is defined as a "trade secret" under Arkansington law, common and/or statutory.

"Former Employee" shall mean and include a former employee or independent contractor who has entered a non-compete covenant.

"Former Employer" shall mean and include a former employer (either of an employee or independent contractor) who has entered a restrictive convent that prevents a former employee or independent contractor from providing to a person or entity that competes with the promise.

"Non-compete covenant" shall mean and include a restrictive convent that prevents a promisor from providing services or entering into an employment contract with a former employer's business competitors.

Section 3. Establishes the Criteria for Enforceability of Non–Compete Covenant

Such a covenant shall not be enforced by an Arkansington court and shall be void as an illegal restraint on trade, except that it meets the criteria set out hereinbelow:

A. <u>Protection of Legitimate Business Interest</u>

A non-compete covenant to be enforceable must protect a legitimate business interest. Such interest includes, and is limited to, the following: [1] the Former Employer's interest in protecting its business goodwill; [2] the Former Employer's trade secrets and/or other proprietary information if the Convenantor was subject to and in fact received access to such trade secrets and/or proprietary information on a regular basis and/or in a manner that gave to the Former Employee substantial opportunity to become apprised thereof; [3] the Former Employer's existing substantial business relationships, meaning business relationships with customers, clients, patrons, or patients which a reasonable person would consider to be ongoing at the time at which the non-compete covenant went into effect.

B. <u>Covenant Shall be No Broader than Necessary</u>

A non-compete covenant shall be no broader in its scope than is necessary to protect a legitimate business interest stated in subsection (A). If a court shall find that the Former Employer drafted the covenant with knowledge and intent that its scope would be broader than necessary in order to have a chilling effect on fair competition, then a court shall refuse to enforce it and shall not adjust its scope to cause it to become valid as authorized in section 4.

C. Non-compete Covenant Applicable to Certain Circumstances

A non-compete covenant to be enforceable shall apply only to a management representative who entered the covenant knowingly and in exchange for good and substantial consideration

[1] Persons qualifying as "Management Representative"

A former employee or independent contractor shall be a management representative if he is either an executive, manager, or supervisor with substantial oversight responsibilities or is significantly involved in assistance to an executive or manager and has significant involvement in management activities; or has in the course of his duties had substantial opportunity to gain knowledge concerning trade secrets or proprietary information; and/or has been paid in the 6–month period prior to the time his employment was terminated compensation (including stock options, bonuses, and commissions) such that he was among the Former Employer's highest paid (top 5%) personnel (including employees or independent contractors).

[2] Persons Entering into Covenant Knowingly and for Good and Substantial Consideration

A former employee or independent contractor shall have entered into a non-compete covenant knowingly if the Former Employer can establish by written evidence that the former employee or independent contractor knew or should have known of the covenant at the time of entering because the Former Employer informed him via letter within 14 days in advance of signing date that the hiring would be conditional on such covenant, OR the contract or other writing contains clear and conspicuous language giving notice of such covenant; AND in exchange for acceptance, there was receipt of good and substantial consideration in the form of the employment or engagement, or some other significant benefit, such as a promotion, compensation increase, or bonus.

Section 4. Modification of Unenforceable Covenant

Except as otherwise stated above, a court shall in its discretion make such modifications to a covenant that violates the criteria of section 3(B) but that meets the criteria of sections 3(A) and 3(C) as shall be necessary for the protection of the legitimate business interest, providing that in such case the court does not in addition award damages to the former employer incurred prior to the modification.

Section 5. Void Covenant

(A) Presumption

A non-compete covenant shall be void and shall not meet the foregoing criteria if the covenant is designed to be in effect for a period exceeding one year from the time of the termination of employ-ment, AND its geographic scope extends beyond the area where the former employee or independent contractor was in fact employed in performing actual services; OR the covenant is designed to prevent the former employee or independent contractor from performing or engaging activities or services of a type beyond the scope of his actual duties in the one-year period from the date of termination. Moreover, it shall not be drafted so as to prevent the former employee or inde-pendent contractor from performing services or selling products that do not in fact compete with the former employer's.

(B) Rebuttability

The former employer is entitled to introduce evidence that the circumstances justify the more extensive restrictions and if the court so finds, the covenant shall not be void even if it would otherwise be void under (A).

Section 6. Fformer Employer has Right to Enforce Valid Covenant

A former employer has the right to enforce a valid non-compete covenant, including by request for declaratory judgment pursu-ant to Ark. Code § 68.122.

Section 7. Expenses of Enforcement

If the contract or covenant provides for attorney's fees to be awarded to the former employer to cover expense of enforcement, the prevailing party shall have the right to recover attorney's fees or costs notwithstanding such other language.

Section 8. Effective Date

This Act shall take effect January 1, 2012 and shall apply to any non-compete covenant that is executed after that date.

Formatting Considerations

The format used by the proposers is correct.

Assignment A. Prepare a Detailed Issue List and Outline

For useful background on non-compete covenants, refer to Chapter 10. Prepare a detailed list of all the issues that appear in this document. Using the principles set out in Chapters 19–21 and the template for a rule-making document, prepare a detailed outline for a revised version of this ordinance.

Assignment B. Prepare a List of Questions for the Bill's Proposers

Using the principles in Chapter 19, prepare a list of questions for the bill's proposers, who have made it clear that they would like for you to con-sult them if you have any questions. You do not need to draft a formal letter.

Assignment C.   Draft the Bill

Review the following chapters: 14 (rule-making documents, legislative language), 16 (ordinance drafting) 26 (word choice), 27 (definitions), and 28 (ambiguity), and 31–33 (grammar, punctuation, style).

Draft the bill. While there are additional materials (such as a bill summary and the identity of the proposers) that you will eventually need to include, the draft to be submitted to your supervisor should include only the following elements in the following order:

- Bill number (fill in current year) title.

- Enacting clause (correctly stated in draft).

- Short title and definitions.

- Findings.

- Rules.

- Administrative Procedures.

- Savings clause (included in draft).

- Effective Date.

PART 4

GENERATING AND ORGANIZING CONTENT OF A CONTRACT OR RULE–MAKING DOCUMENT

■ ■ ■

- Chapter 19.   Generating Your Document's Content
- Chapter 20.   Creating an Outline
- Chapter 21.   Refining the Draft's Organizational Scheme
- Chapter 22.   Exercises for Part 4

CHAPTER 19

GENERATING YOUR DOCUMENT'S CONTENT

■ ■ ■

I. Researching the Document's Legal Background

Before drafting a document, you must inform yourself about the applicable law, including the enforceability of certain types of provisions. For a contract of a particular type, avail yourself of CLE materials or journal articles written by practitioners. Many useful resources are available online and through Westlaw.

Also, you should review any form or similar real-world contracts that you can find—not to copy or to blindly rely on, but to give you ideas about the types of issues a particular type of contract could address. Some specifics about contract-drafting are covered in Part II of this book.

You should do a similar review for rule-making documents such as corporate bylaws, homeowners' association covenants, or rule-making documents for a particular type of client (such as a school system or club). Issues relating to such documents are addressed in Part III of this book.

If you are drafting legislation or regulations for a government entity, you will need to review the client's drafting guidelines and any manual that provides guidance. You will also need to review rules of construction (i.e., rules that courts sometimes apply when construing documents) and laws that affect a provision's enforceability, along with any cases in which similar provisions were construed.

II. Researching the Document's
Factual Background

A. For Contracts and Private Rule–Making Documents

Every document operates against a particular factual background and for a particular purpose. When drafting contracts and private rule-making documents, you may need to educate yourself concerning industry or trade usage, local practices regarding similar transactions, and your client's customs and objectives. CLE and other practitioner-oriented materials can help you to understand some of the background issues. Your client is likely the best resource regarding the client's own practices and objectives.

B. Impact of the Negotiating Context

If you are negotiating and drafting a contract between your client and another party, you will have *at least* a dual role: first, as your client's advocate; and second, as the person charged with expressing the parties' arrangements. If the other side's counsel proposes language for inclusion in the document, you must also act as your client's advisor. You must understand the operation of each provision both as drafted and as it would be interpreted by courts.

III. Assessing the Client's Needs

A. Regarding Contracts and Private Rule–Making Documents

A sophisticated client may already know exactly what is needed in a document, while an unsophisticated client may look to you to explain what is needed. If you are in-house counsel, the client is likely to have similar documents on hand that indicate the client's preferences regarding the document's content, scope, organization, and style.

If you are a private practitioner, the client might present you with a "term sheet" (i.e., a list of things that the client wants the contract or rule-making document to cover) or a document that the client previously used but wants you to revise. If so, you will start with a good idea of what the client wants included in the document regarding issues that the client has already thought about. You might need to advise the client regarding the legality of the requested terms and regarding issues that the client has not addressed.

During the initial client interview, get any necessary background information. The following is a partial list of typical background questions for a client who is starting a business.

Background Questions For Contract or Private–Law Document

1. What is the nature of the client's business?

2. If the client is a business organization, what type (e.g., corporation or LLC)?

3. Is the client doing business under a fictitious name?

4. What is the nature of the document (e.g., lease or corporate by-laws)?

5. Does your client want you to create a document or revise an existing one?

Background Questions For Contract or Private–Law Document
(cont'd)

6.   If the client has an existing document, has the client dealt with disputes, lawsuits, and so on?

7.   If the document is to be negotiated with another party, what is your role in the process (e.g., will you draft provisions or simply negotiate for changes)?

8.   If it is not a negotiated contract, are you designing a form contract for the client to use with multiple, unknown parties (e.g., a software-licensing agreement)?

B. Regarding Public Legislation

Drafting public legislation (such as a statute, ordinance, or regulation) is different from drafting a contract or private rule-making document. To create public legislation requires a broader background in the applicable law. If you are preparing to draft public legislation, the following checklist might be useful.

Background Questions for Legislative Document

1.   Who is your client?

2.   Who proposed the legislation and why?

3.   If you are revising current legislation, what problems made the revision necessary?

4.   Are there issues concerning the legislation's constitutionality?

5.   What categories of persons does it regulate or protect?

6.   How will it relate to existing legislation?

7.   If it is based on similar legislation from other jurisdictions, how has that legislation been applied?

IV. Generating a Master Term Sheet and Client Questionnaire

A. What a "Master Term Sheet" Is

A **master term sheet** is a list of the potential content points of the document you are creating. Create a master term sheet based on materials that you collect on your own and that the client provides.

B. Steps for Preparing a Master Term Sheet

Step 1: Prepare a Bulleted List of Topics

You can create a "master term sheet" for contracts or private rule-making documents by working from forms or existing documents drafted by other attorneys. You may also want to consult CLE materials or other practitioner-geared guidance. If you are drafting legislation, you can use similar statutes, ordinances, or regulations. If the client has provided you with a term sheet or documents, incorporate the materials that your client has given you.

After gathering your materials, compile a list of topics common to all the forms or documents you consulted. If you find unique topics, add them to the list if they appear useful. For example, a partial list for a lease of commercial property might look like this:

> **Example: Partial List for Lease of Commercial Property**
>
> * Security deposit due on day of signing
> * Refund of security deposit not later than 30th day after period ends
> * Monthly rent (amount, time, method of payment)
> * Proof of insurance due at signing

Generating a master term sheet is a time-consuming process, but once you have created a master term sheet for a particular type of document (e.g., lease of real property), you should be able to adapt the term sheet for future documents of the same kind. This process represents part of the learning curve for drafting a particular type of document. Consider whether it is appropriate to bill the client for the hours you put into preparing a master term sheet.

Step 2: Sequence the Topics per Template

If you are drafting a contract, use the contracts template in Chapter 20 to put your bulleted list of issues in order. If you are drafting a public or private rule-making document and do not have a drafting manual, use the template for rule-making documents (also found in Chapter 20). As you sequence your topics, jot down any questions that you might have for your client.

Below is an example of a term sheet for an equipment lease (the example is organized based on the contract template).

Example 1: Partial Master Term Sheet for Contract
(lease of farm equipment)

Information for exordium clause and signatures

Client = Kwok of Gatorboro, LLC
Client's representative: Hanna Kwok, CEO
Business name = Same as company (?)
Address = 2601 NW Boulevard, Gatorboro, Florida 32001
Email address for notices = (?)
Business telephone for facility = (?)

Preliminary Information

Conditions Precedent to Effectiveness of Contract

- Prepayment of Security Deposit
- Proof of Insurance

Description of Subject–Matter

- Describe in attachment: recite that Lessee inspected equipment, accepts "as is"
- Exclude all UCC warranties?

Background Recitals

- Recital that Kwok fully disclosed all information required by statute

Duration of Performance

- Minimum period for lease
- Period renews automatically unless party gives notice?
- Effect of automatic renewal (if Client wants it)

While setting up a term sheet like the one above, an attorney might come up with questions or notes such as the following:

1) Does Client want a security deposit?

2) Does Client want proof of insurance in advance?

3) Is it one kind of equipment or several kinds?

4) Does Client want to exclude UCC implied warranties?

5) Be sure to inform Client of statutory disclosure requirement.

6) Check whether Client wants automatically-renewing period.

Below is an example of a term sheet for an ordinance requiring fencing around swimming pools.

Example 2: Partial Master Term Sheet for City Ordinance
(fence requirement for swimming pools)

Initial Recitals: Findings and Purpose

- Findings: unprotected swimming pools are a hazard to trespassing children
- Purpose: to protect children from injury

Application of Ordinance

- Applicable only to property owners who build a pool after effective date?

Operative Provisions

Provision Identifying the Enforcing Authority

- Enforced by Department of Zoning and Code Enforcement

Major or Fundamental Rules

- Fence must be non-climbable and non-penetrable
- Materials to be fixed in place, not easily dislodged
- Fence must surround pool on all sides, unless access is blocked by house

---

While setting up a term sheet like the one above, an attorney might come up with notes or questions such as the following:

1) Height of fence depends on age of protected class.

2) Fence should be designed to protect children of what age?

3) Does it apply only to in-ground pools or also to above-ground?

4) Does it apply to small, pre-fab, portable pools?

5) Does it apply to ornamental ponds or lakes?

6) Are exact specifications required (e.g., size of links in fence)?

7) Do screened-in pools meet the requirements?

C.   Creating a Client Questionnaire From the Master Term Sheet

Once you have generated your master term sheet and list of questions, you are ready to draft a client questionnaire. You could give the questionnaire to the client or use it as an interview guide. Once you have developed a client questionnaire for a particular type of document, you can use it when drafting similar documents in the future.

Useful client questions have the following characteristics:

1) They explain the issue to the client so that the client must think through the problem.

2) They notify the client of any legal limitations on the client's options.

3) They sometimes make specific recommendations.

4) They are narrowly focused so that the client can answer briefly.

Below are examples of questions for one type of provision in a lease, followed by examples of questions relating to an ordinance.

Partial Questionnaire for a Lease

Preliminary Information

Conditions Precedent to Effectiveness of Contract

1.   Are you going to require Lessee to pay a security deposit? I recommend that you do so. The statute allows a maximum of 10% of the total lease payment for the leasing period.

2.   Will the security deposit be due at signing? I recommend that you make it due no later than that date.

3.   If you collect a security deposit, the statute requires that you keep it in either a non-interest-bearing escrow account or in an interest-bearing escrow account if you pay all interest to Lessee. I recommend that you keep it in a non-interest bearing account. Is that your intention?

4.   The statute requires that you give notice to Lessee of the bank and account number. You can do so in the lease or in a separate document to be attached to the lease. Do you know the bank you would be using?

5.   What happens if Lessee wants to sign the contract but is not prepared to pay the deposit at signing? Would you sign anyway? If so, and if Lessee failed to pay the deposit, would you want the right to end the arrangement? Would you want to delay Lessee's right to take possession until Lessee *has* paid?

Partial Questionnaire for an Ordinance Requiring Pool Fences
(for City of Smithville)

Initial Recitals: Findings and Purpose

1. Is the ordinance intended to protect only trespassing children—and not, for example, straying pets?

Application of Ordinance

2. Does it apply to city-owned pools? If so, we need to check for conflicts with existing ordinances.

3. Does it apply to owners who construct a swimming pool after the ordinance's effective date? The City of Gatorboro's ordinance applies to all pools, regardless of when they were built.

4. Does it apply to any type of swimming pool? I suggest that it apply to all pools except above-ground pools over a certain height if the pools have removable ladders. Ordinances for the Cities of Gatorboro and Micanopia do not apply to such pools.

CHAPTER 20

CREATING AN OUTLINE FOR YOUR DOCUMENT

■ ■ ■

I. Overview of Document Organization

A document consists of sentences organized into sections. Each section should deal with one major topic, and that topic should be named in the heading. By quickly scanning the main headings, the reader should understand what topics are addressed in the document.

If the topic contains discrete subtopics, the section should be subdivided into subsections, each dealing with one mutually exclusive subtopic of the topic identified in the major section's heading. If a subsection is further divided, each of the sub-subsections should deal with only one subtopic of the subtopic identified in the subsection's heading.

Section II of this chapter deals with dividing a document's text into sections and subsections. Section III deals with naming the topics that your sections and subsections address. Section IV deals with sequencing sections and subsections. Section V deals with eliminating overlaps.

II. Generating an Outline

A. Dividing the Master Term Sheet into Major Sections

After you have drafted a master term sheet (discussed in Chapter 19), related information should already be grouped together according to the applicable template in Section III of this chapter. Within each grouping, identify the topics that will become the major sections of your document.

For the document to work, each section should deal with a single topic, and all aspects of that single topic should be addressed in that section only. In other words, do not scatter information about a single topic among multiple sections of a document. Topic scattering forces the reader to wade through the document to find all information relevant to a single topic.

For example, after you have gathered into sections all related information items in a lease, the section addressing rent might look like this:

Rent–Related Information:

- Lessee to pay $1000 per month

- Rent due on first day of month

- Late fee of $100

- Total for one-year lease = $12,000

- Rent to be paid by check

- If check bounces, Lessee reimburses for bank's fee

Each section should be labeled by a heading that identifies the topic. Creation of headings is addressed in the next subsection of this chapter.

B.   Creating Headings

1.   Purpose of Headings

Headings should make the document easy for the reader to navigate, like road signs on a highway. Major headings should name each major topic addressed in the text, so that a person scanning the document is on notice of each major topic. A number or letter should precede each heading to make headings easy to reference.

An effective heading allows the reader to predict the section's content. To achieve this effect, the heading should be both broad enough to encompass everything included in the section and narrow enough to exclude topics that are not covered in the section.

Example: Heading that is Narrower than Section's Content

Section 5. Payment of Rent

Before signing the contract, Tenant must pay a security deposit equal to one month's rent together with advance rent for the first calendar month of the rental period. For subsequent calendar months, Tenant will pay rent in the amount of $ _____ on or before the first day of the calendar month to which it applies. Landlord will hold the security deposit in a non-interest-bearing escrow account at Midlothian Bank of Gatorboro until the date on which Landlord sends notice to Tenant of Landlord's deduction plus any refund due to Tenant.

The paragraph in the example addresses both rent and the security deposit, but the heading indicates that only rent is addressed. A reader scanning the document's headings for information about the security deposit would likely skip past the "Payment of Rent" section. One way to solve the problem would be to create two sections: one dealing with security deposit and one dealing with rent.

A heading can also be too broad to enable the reader to predict the section's content.

Example: Heading Too Broad to Reflect Section's Content

F.   Uses of Storage Unit

Lessee shall not store in the storage unit any flammable or toxic material or any material that could present a danger to persons or property.

The text in the example names one very narrow, prohibited use; it does not deal with all uses. To solve the problem, the drafter could easily narrow the heading's scope: "Prohibition on Storage of Dangerous Materials."

2.   Using a Template to Generate Headings

For legal documents, we recommend that every heading consist of a **minimum of three words**—with a few exceptions, such as "Signatures." We recommend that you use the following template to generate headings for contracts and rule-making documents.

Template for Heading Based on Action or Subject Matter

- <u>Name</u> of the type of action or the subject-matter **plus**

- <u>Preposition</u> (e.g., *of, for, to, from, with, by, for*) **plus**

- <u>Explanatory information</u> describing the provision's context.

Below are examples of headings generated through use of this template.

Examples: Headings for a Contract

Based on type of action	Based on subject-matter
Installation of Alarm System	Cost of Project
Compensation for Employee's Services	Total Rent for Period
Exclusion of Implied Warranties	Insurance Coverage for Building
Delivery of Equipment	Billing Procedures of Company
Planting of Crop	Specifications for Materials

Examples: Headings for a Rule–Making Document

Based on type of action	**Based on subject-matter**
Application for Variance	Procedure for Obtaining Consent
Placement of Notice–Board	Notice of Violation
Disclosures to Department	Costs to City of Removing Debris
Allocation of Costs	Privacy Protections for Applicant

Do not feel constrained to the format prescribed by the template if you can generate an acceptable variant. For example, while we recommend using a preposition in a heading, omitting the preposition might be grammatically necessary or stylistically preferable in some cases. We consider headings such as the following to be acceptable variants.

Examples: Clear Headings without Prepositions

- Garbage Collection Procedure
- Employment Application Process
- Shipping the Harvested Crop
- Installing the Alarm System

The reason that we recommend a three-word minimum for headings is that one- and two-word headings tend to be less clear. Reasonable minds may differ on this point, and there are exceptions: for example, using the one-word heading "Definitions" to label a section that defines words is unlikely to cause confusion. Below are examples of unclear one- and two-word headings.

Examples: Unclear One- and Two–Word Headings

- **Payment**
  [Payment of Rent? Security Deposit? Purchase price? Shipping costs?]

- **Fees**
  [Fees for a service? Late fees?]

- **Contractor Reimbursement**
  [Is the contractor being reimbursed or doing the reimbursing?]

- **Architect Certification**
  [Is the architect being certified or certifying something?]

---

3.   Some Heading Formats to Avoid

We recommend that you avoid the following types of headings in a legal document:

- Full-sentence headings.

- Question or command headings.

- Catch-all headings (e.g., "Miscellaneous" or "General Provisions").

One problem with full-sentence headings is that they can make redundant the text that they label. Another problem is that some courts may not treat a heading as part of the text; thus, if you put crucial information in a heading but not in the text, the section's text will be missing information.

Headings in the form of a question or command may be suitable for a consumer contract, but (in the authors' opinion) they are too informal for many other types of contracts and for most rule-making documents.

Catch-all headings fail to name the specific actions or topics addressed in the sections that those headings label. Thus, catch-all headings do not help the reader easily navigate the document or find specific information.

C.   Subdividing Major Sections and Subsections

To determine whether subdivision is necessary, evaluate the information items listed in the section. If a section or subsection contains no more than two or three sentences of manageable length, you might choose not to subdivide.

If it appears that a section will contain more than two or three manageable sentences, subdivision might be necessary. To subdivide, you must be able to identify within a section at least two distinct subtopics. If you do not have at least two distinct subtopics, *do not* subdivide. Below is an example of a major section that should be divided.

Section 3. Payment of Rent

- Lessee to pay $1000 per month
- Rent due on first day of month
- Late fee of $100
- Total for one-year lease = $12,000
- Rent to be paid by check
- If check bounces, Lessee reimburses for bank's fee

In the example, there are three distinct subtopics: (1) amount, (2) due date, and (3) payment method. Each subtopic should become a subsection. Below is an example of how the section would look if divided into subsections.

Section 3. Payment of Rent

a.   Amount of Rent
- Total for one-year lease = $12,000
- Lessee to pay $1000 per month

b.   Due Date of Rent
- Rent due on first day of month
- Late fee of $100

Section 3. Payment of Rent (cont.)

c.   Method of Payment
    • Rent to be paid by check
    • If check bounces, Lessee reimburses for bank's fee

If any of a major section's subsections contain at least two distinct sub-subtopics, then subdivide that subsection into sub-subsections. You could do the same with any sub-subsection that contains at least two distinct subtopics.

Example: Subdividing Subsections

Section 5. Payment of Rent

A.   Total Rent Due Per Rental Period
B.   Monthly Payment of Rent
    1.   Amount of Monthly Rent Payment
    2.   Time for Payment of Monthly Rent
       (a)   Due Date for Payment
       (b)   Failure to Timely Pay Rent
          (1)   Payment of Late Fee
          (2)   Non-payment of Rent
    3.   Procedure for Payment of Monthly Rent
       (a)   Location for Payment
       (b)   Form of Payment

Reasonable minds differ regarding how many levels of subdivision are manageable for the reader. For example, one co-author of this textbook limits her subdivision to three levels; another co-author does not mind going to five. As long as you produce a coherent and reader-friendly organizational scheme, you can decide for yourself how much subdivision is too much.

D.   Common Errors in Subdivision Schemes

1.   The Single–Subsection Error

If you subdivide a major section, you should have *at least two* subsections. If you have only one subsection, you have not subdivided. You cannot "divide" a whole apple pie into one portion: the whole pie already is one portion.

Make sure that your document does not have a lone subsection within a major section.

Error: Single–Subsection

Section 3. Payment of Rent

    A.   Amount of Rent

---

2. The Organization-by-Party Error

Avoid using headings such as "Party A's Duties" and "Party B's Rights." First, such headings do not name distinct topics; thus, they are too broad to be useful. Generally, a reader who refers to a contract or rule-making document is looking for information about *a particular topic*.

Second, organizing a document based on the parties' duties or rights means that some topics will be covered under two different headings. If you address one topic in multiple sections, the reader will have to go back and forth through the document to understand a single topic.

Error: Lease Sections Organized by Party

A. **Duties of Landlord**
   1. Holding and Disposition of Security Deposit
   2. Pro Rating of Rent
   3. Payment for Water
   4. Maintenance of Apartment Complex
      a. Maintenance of Common Areas
      b. Maintenance of Apartment Interior

B. **Duties of Tenant**
   1. Payment of Advance Rent and Security Deposit at Signing
   2. Payment of Pro–Rated Rent and Monthly Rent
   3. Payment for Remaining Utilities
   4. Maintenance of Apartment
      a. Maintenance of Apartment Interior
      b. Duty to Reimburse Certain Repair Costs

In the example above, the reader would have to go back and forth within the contract to get a clear picture of who has which duties regarding any single topic (i.e., maintenance, rent, security deposit, or utilities). Below is an example of how the headings could instead be organized by topic.

Lease Sections Re-organized by Topic (Error Corrected)

A. **Security Deposit for Apartment**
   1. Payment of Security Deposit
   2. Holding of Security Deposit in Escrow
   3. Disposition of Security Deposit

B. **Payment of Rent**
   1. Payment of Advance Rent
   2. Payment of Monthly Rent and Prorated Rent

C. **Payment for Utilities**
   1. Payment for Water
   2. Payment for Electricity and other Third–Party Services

D. **Maintenance of Apartment Complex**
   1. Maintenance of Common Areas
   2. Maintenance of Apartment Interior
   3. Reimbursement for Costs of Certain Repairs ...

Because the sections in the example are organized by topic, the reader would have to consult only one section of the lease to determine both parties' duties or rights regarding any single topic. Thus, the reader's task would be easier—which is one purpose of using headings.

3.   The Overlapping–Headings Error

After you have subdivided a section, examine the main heading and its subheadings. All of the topics named in your subheadings should be distinct. Below is an example of non-distinct (i.e., overlapping) subheadings.

Example: Overlapping Subsections (error)

Section D.   Payment of Monthly Rent
    1.   Amount of Monthly Payment
    2.   Time for Monthly Payment
    3.   Form of Payment
    4.   Late Fee and Returned Check Fee

In the example, subheadings 1, 2, and 3 name distinct aspects of "Payment of Rent." Subheading 4 is different, in that it combines two enforcing mechanisms: one ensuring that rent is paid on time (which relates to subheading 2), and one ensuring that the landlord is reimbursed if rent is paid by a check that bounces (which relates to subheading 3). Thus, subheading 4 overlaps subheadings 2 and 3.

The following example shows how the section could be re-subdivided to eliminate overlaps.

Overlaps Eliminated (Error Corrected)

Section D.   Payment of Monthly Rent
    1.   Amount of Monthly Payment
    2.   Time for Monthly Payment
       [should address obligation to timely pay and late fees]
    3.   Form of Monthly Payment
       [should address right to pay by check and returned-check fees]

III.   Sequencing Sections and Subsections of Your Outline

A.   Templates for Creating an Initial Sequencing Scheme

1.   Template for Contracts

The template printed below may be a useful starting point for your initial sequencing scheme for a contract.

Basic Template for a Contract

1. **Title** (Contract for…)

2. **Caption** (optional): blocks of text that identify the parties and set out their contact information.

3. **Exordium Clause**: an introductory paragraph that sets out the date that the parties enter the contract; the parties' names and addresses (unless you put that information in a caption); and a statement of mutual assent (e.g., "The parties mutually agree as follows").

4. **Definition of Terms** (if needed)

5. **Preliminary Information:** facts related to the basis of the bargain (e.g., conditions precedent to document's effectiveness, description of contract's subject matter, background recitals, information about the performance period, other understandings of the parties).

6. **Duration of Core Obligations**: period for performance, if applicable (i.e., fixed period, renewable period, or automatically renewing period).

7. **Core Obligations:** sections that address issues such as the following:
    - The main performance that the parties bargained for: the promise to provide a thing of value, followed by the promise to pay (amount, time, method).
    - Any additional promises that implement the exchange (e.g., delivery arrangements or installation guidelines).

8. **Subsidiary Agreements:** sections (if needed) that address the following:
    - Maintenance of the contract's subject-matter (e.g., routine care, repairs).
    - Use of subject-matter.
    - Insurance relating to subject-matter.
    - Restrictions on the parties' conduct.

9. **Limitation on Liability:** e.g., waiver, indemnification, express assumption of risk, limitation on damages.

10. **Termination of Certain Obligations**: provisions relating to ending performance in situations <u>not</u> involving breach (e.g., grounds, procedure, and consequences).

11. **Breach of Contract:** procedures and remedies (e.g., cancellation, liquidated damages, excuse, limitation of remedies).

Basic Template for a Contract (cont.)

12. **Dispute resolution:** e.g., arbitration, mediation, provision for attorney's fees.

13. **Controlling Law:** e.g., choice of law and forum selection.

14. **Provisions that apply <u>after</u> main transaction ends:** e.g., return of property to owner, refund of security deposit, non-compete covenant, anti-piracy agreement.

15. **Rules of Construction:** e.g., merger and severability clauses.

16. **Modification of the Contract:** right and procedure.

17. **Signatures**

---

2.   Template for Rule–Making Documents

If you have official guidance for drafting a rule-making document (e.g., a city's or state's legislative drafting manual), then follow it. If you do not have such guidance, you might use the template below as a starting point.

Template for Rule-making Document

1. **Initial clause**

   - For a City or County Ordinance
     Use the required form for an ordaining clause (e.g., "The Board of County Commissioners for the city of Gatortown, Florida ordains…,").

   - For a Statute
     Do not include an initial clause unless required to.

   - For a Private Rule–Making Document
     Draft an appropriate introductory clause if needed (e.g., "For the benefit of the Homeowners of Sundown Hills, Thomason Properties declares the following covenants and restrictions . . .").

2. **Findings and Purpose (Recitals)**: sections setting out the relevant findings of fact and the purpose (if needed).

3. **Definition of Terms** (if needed)

4. **Application of the Rule-making Document**: section addressing the persons, things, or circumstances to which the rules apply; exemptions from rules.

Template for Rule-making Document (cont.)

5. **The Rules**: sections setting out duties, directives, prohibitions, and restrictions; sections setting out procedures for permitting and variances.

6. **Enforcement Procedures**: e.g., determination of violation, notice, rights of enforcing authority.

7. **Creation of Governing Agency or Administering Body** (if needed): sections setting out members, duties, selection procedure, vacancies.

8. **Technical Provisions**: e.g., amendment procedure, severability, effective date.

B. Tweaking the Initial Sequencing Scheme

A fundamental goal of sequencing sections and subsections is this: to give the reader the information that the reader needs in the order in which the reader needs it. Use the following principles to tweak (if necessary) your initial sequencing of sections and subsections:

- Deal first with the earliest event in time, and set out subsequent events chronologically;

- Place the most closely-related provisions next to each other;

- Deal with ordinary or routine circumstances before extraordinary, exceptional, or emergency circumstances;

- Give sequencing priority to topics of greatest concern to your client.

These principles are not mutually exclusive. You might use different ones for different sections of the document.

IV. Basic Format Design for the Document

A. Traits of an Informative and Reader–Friendly Format

An informative and reader-friendly format has the following characteristics:

- Headings and subheadings stand out conspicuously from the text.

- Information is easy for the reader to locate.

- Different levels of headings look different (e.g., size, formatting).

B.　Designing an Informative and Reader–Friendly Format

1.　Form of Headings

Headings in a document should stand out visually from the text to which those headings apply. To create headings that stand out, use any or a combination of the following devices: underlining, bolding, italics, or enlarged fonts.

Some drafters may prefer to vary the appearance of headings at different levels. Make sure that all headings and subheadings stand out clearly at each level of subdivision. Below are a few tips:

- Use all-caps sparingly, if at all (they are difficult to read).

- Underline the heading's words, not the letter or number (it looks sloppy).

- Do not use more than two or three heading-emphasis techniques in a single document (it looks busy and is difficult to read).

- Avoid putting a heading or subheading on the same line as the related text (this makes the heading harder to see).

2.　Lettering and Numbering of Headings

Letter or number every heading and subheading so that you can easily cross-reference or cite to a specific section or subsection. We recommend a system that alternates letters and numbers (or vice-versa).

If you are drafting legislation, the relevant drafting guidelines may provide a notation system for headings and subheadings. If not, feel free to develop your own.

In general, avoid Roman numerals except for the highest level of headings, as they are difficult to read.

3.　Spacing Between Provisions

A well-designed format leaves ample "clear space" between separate sections and between the end of a subsection and the heading of the next provision. Reasonable opinions differ as to whether you should leave space between a heading and the text to which it applies—use your judgment.

4.　Indenting Certain Text

One way to indicate that certain sections of your document are subsections is to "block indent" subsections within a major section. The drawback of indenting is that if you subdivide all the way to the fourth level, your subsections will likely end up in the middle of your page. Some drafters dislike that, but others do not mind. Among other things, indenting of subsections increases the number of pages in the document.

Variations are possible. For example, you do not have to begin indenting your provisions at the first or even the second level of subdivision. Instead, you could begin block indenting at the third or fourth level. If you need to conserve space, you could adjust the indent function so that it moves only three spaces instead of five.

5.   Page Numbering

Every page in a document should be numbered. Unless you are instructed otherwise, the preferred form for page numbering identifies the number of the page and the total number of pages in the document: e.g., "Page 3 of 9." We recommend that you put page numbers at the bottom of each page.

6.   Examples of Formats

Below are two sample formats.

Format Example 1

1.   First Major Heading

Text text text text text text text text text text text text text text text text text text text.

2.   Second Major Heading

    A.   First Subsection
    Text text text text text text text text text text text text text text text text text text text.

    B.   Second Subsection

        1.   First Sub-subsection
        Text text text text text text text text text text text text text text text text text.

        2.   Second Sub-subsection

            (a) First Sub-sub-subsection
            Text text text text text text text text text text text text text text text text text text.

            (b) Second Sub-sub-subsection
            Text text text text text text text text text text text.

Format Example 2

1. First Major Heading

Text text text text text text text text text text text text text text text text text text text text text text.

2. Second Major Heading

A. First Subsection

Text Text text text text text text text text text text text text text text text text text text text text text text text.

B. Second Subsection

    1. First Sub-subsection

    Text text text text text text text text text text text text text text text text text text text text text text text.

    2. Second Sub-subsection

        (a) First Sub-sub-subsection
        Text text text text text text text text text text text text text text text text text text text text text.

        (b) Second Sub-sub-subsection
        Text text text text text text text text text text text text text text text text text text text text text.

CHAPTER 21

REFINING THE DRAFT'S ORGANIZATIONAL SCHEME

■ ■ ■

I. Reassessing the Drafted Document's Organization

This chapter addresses organizational problems that tend to emerge after the drafter has written text. After you have written the first draft of a document, reassess the organization to determine whether adjustments are needed.

II. Common Problems

A. The Wall of Text

When reviewing your draft, you might find a paragraph that is so long that it appears to be a "wall of text" that the reader has to wade through to find specific information. We recommend that you consider subdividing such paragraphs. Check for multiple sub-topics if a paragraph has the following characteristics:

- More than three sentences; or

- Three or fewer sentences, one of which is very long or complex.

Usually, a paragraph that has the characteristics listed directly above will contain at least two sub-topics—in which case, you should subdivide that paragraph. Below is an example of a city ordinance's major section that addresses multiple sub-topics and looks like a "wall of text."

Example: Wall of Text
(large, un-subdivided paragraph)

2012–8.   Construction of Wooden Fence for Pool

A pool owner may use wooden slats in constructing a fence around the pool. The pool owner shall use only slats made from solid wood that are at least 1 1/2 inches thick and that have been treated to prevent damage to the wood from insects or natural deterioration. The pool owner shall construct the wooden fence to prevent entry into the pool by trespassing children. To ensure that a trespassing child cannot easily climb the fence, the pool owner shall ensure that the fence is constructed so that each slat is spaced no more than 1 inch from the adjacent slat. The pool owner shall ensure that the slats are placed and secured so that a trespassing child attempting to climb the fence could not dislodge them. The pool owner shall ensure that the wooden fence meets the minimum height requirement for a swimming pool barrier set out in section 2012–7. To ensure that a trespassing child cannot gain access to the pool through a gate, the pool owner shall ensure that the gate complies with the construction requirements set out in (b)(1) and that the gate is secured by a spring lock or other child-proof device.

The one-paragraph section in the example above is dense, making it difficult for the reader to find a specific piece of information. By subdividing that paragraph, we make information easier for the reader to find. If, after subdivision at the first level, one of the resulting paragraphs still contains dense text, you could further subdivide by identifying sub-subtopics within that paragraph.

Example: Subdivided Wall of Text

2012–8.   Construction of Wooden Fence for Pool

A.   Specifications for Materials

A pool owner may use wooden slats in constructing a fence around the pool. The pool owner shall use only slats made from solid wood that are at least 1 1/2 inches thick and that have been treated to prevent damage to the wood from insects or natural deterioration.

B.   Specifications for Construction to Prevent Access by Children

Example: Subdivided Wall of Text (cont.)

(1) **Construction of Fence to Prevent Climbing by Children**

    (a) **Placement of Slats**

    To ensure that a trespassing child cannot easily climb the fence, the pool owner shall ensure that the fence is constructed so that each slat is spaced no more than 1 inch from the adjacent slat. The pool owner shall ensure that the slats are placed and secured so that a trespassing child attempting to climb the fence could not dislodge them.

    (b) **Height of Fence**

    To ensure that a trespassing child cannot easily climb the fence, the pool owner shall ensure that the wooden fence meets the minimum height requirement for a swimming pool barrier set out in section 2012–7.

(2) **Construction of Gate to Prevent Access by Children**

To ensure that a trespassing child cannot gain access to the pool through a gate, the pool owner shall ensure that the gate meets the construction specifications set out in (b)(1) above and that the gate is secured by a spring lock or other child-proof device.

B. The "Displaced Text" Error

If a section is subdivided, then each sentence should be placed under one of the subsections. Text should not appear between a major heading and its first subheading.

Example: Displaced Text Error

Section 1. Kennel's Requirements for Kibble

Kennel will buy all of its requirements for kibble from Pet Pleasers, and Pet Pleasers will supply Kibble to meet all of Kennel's requirements. **[displaced text]**

    a. <u>Minimum Order for Kibble</u>

    During each requirements period, Kennel will order a minimum of 50 pounds of dog kibble and 40 pounds of cat kibble.

Example: Displaced Text Error (cont.)

b.   Placement of Order

To order kibble from Pet Pleasers, Kennel must submit the order through the Pet Pleasers website....

How could you accurately cross-reference that displaced text? You could not simply state that it is "in Section 1," because Section 1 contains multiple sentences. If you end up with displaced text, rethink your subdivision scheme. The error in the previous example could be resolved as follows:

Displaced Text Eliminated (Error Corrected)

Section 1.   Kibble to be Purchased by Kennel

    a.   Kennel's Requirements for Kibble

    During each requirements period, Kennel will purchase from Pet Pleasers all of the kibble that Kennel requires. During each requirements period, Kennel will order from Pet Pleasers a minimum of 50 pounds of dog kibble and 40 pounds of cat kibble.

    b.   Pet Pleasers' Fulfillment of Kennel's Orders

    During each requirements period, Pet Pleasers will fulfill all Kennel's orders for kibble. To order kibble from Pet Pleasers, Kennel must submit the order through the Pet Pleasers customer website.

C.   The Heading–Replacing–Content Error

If you have drafted headings that meet Chapter 20's guidelines, check to make sure that you have not omitted necessary text and relied on your headings to supply information. A court might not treat a heading or subheading as part of the text.

In the following provision, the drafter identifies "prevention of access through gate" as the purpose of the provision but does not articulate the purpose in the related text.

Example: Heading–Replacing–Content Error

Section B.   Fee for Rescheduled Inspection

If Client fails to make the premises available on the date scheduled for Alarm Company's monthly inspection, Client will schedule another date for the inspection and will pay to Alarm Company an additional fee of $100.

In the example above, the drafter fails to state that the payment is for an additional inspection. Below is an example of how one might correct that error.

Example: Heading–Replacing–Content Error Corrected

Section B.   Fee for Rescheduled Inspection

If Client fails to make the premises available on the date scheduled for Alarm Company's monthly inspection, Client will schedule another date for the inspection and will pay to Alarm Company an additional fee of $100 <u>for the rescheduled inspection</u>.

D.   Overlapping Sentences

1.   Redundant Sentences

The same sentence should not appear more than once in a document. This principle applies to sentences that are identical in substance, even if the phrasing differs.

Redundant sentences can confuse the reader, who cannot be sure whether a sentence merely states the same rule in multiple places or whether the sentence has different ramifications in the different sections.

Instead of repeating a sentence, determine where it fits *best.* If a sentence is relevant to multiple sections, use unambiguous cross-referencing to point the reader to those other sections. Cross-referencing is discussed in Section III of this Chapter.

2.   Conflicting Sentences

Every sentence in a contract should be true as it stands and therefore should not have terms that conflict with another sentence. Conflict between sentences can occur if the drafter fails to reconcile related sentences that create conflicting results. Sometimes, a qualifier is necessary to make all sentences true. The following is an example of conflicting sentences.

> **Error: Conflicting Sentences**
>
> Before entering the rental premises, Lessor shall give to Tenant advance notice. In an emergency, Lessor may enter the rental premises without giving advance notice to Tenant.

If analyzed literally, both sentences in the example *cannot* be true. The first sentence states—without exception—that Lessor has to give notice to Tenant before entering the premises. The second sentence states an exception to that rule: sometimes Lessor can enter the premises without first giving notice to Tenant. Through the use of qualifiers, this type of conflict is easy to resolve, as shown by the example below.

> **Conflict Resolved**
>
> <u>In an emergency</u>, Landlord may enter the rental premises without giving Tenant advance notice. <u>In any other circumstance</u>, Landlord shall give Tenant advance notice before Landlord enters the rental premises.

If any sentence in your document literally negates the truth of another sentence, add appropriate qualifying language to each sentence.

As well as occurring in the same paragraph, conflicting sentences could occur in different sections or subsections.

> **Example: Conflicting Sentences in Different Subsections**
>
> 3.   **Time for Payment**
>
>   (a)   **Due Date for Installment Payment**
>   Purchaser will pay the installments on the following dates: January 15, 2013; April 15, 2013; June 15, 2013; and September 15, 2013.
>
>   (b)   **Extension of Time for Payment**
>   If on or before the due date Purchaser requests an extension of time to pay, Seller may in its discretion allow extension. An extension period begins on …

Subsection (b) contradicts the unqualified statement in subsection (a) that Purchaser *will pay* the installments on the specified dates. Below is an example of how to eliminate the conflict using a qualifying statement and cross-reference (cross-referencing is discussed in Section III of this chapter).

Example: Conflict Resolved

3.   **Time for Payment**

    (a)   **Due Date for Installment Payment**
        Unless Purchaser requests an extension of time for pay-
        ment pursuant to subsection (1)(b), Purchaser will pay
        the installments on the following dates: January 15,
        2013; April 15, 2013; June 15, 2013; and September 15,
        2013.

    (b)   **Extension of Time for Payment**
        If on or before the due date Purchaser requests an
        extension of time to pay, Seller may in its discretion
        allow extension. An extension period begins on …

III. Using Cross–Referencing (if needed)

A. When to Use Cross–Referencing

The main principle for cross-referencing is to *avoid cross-referencing* unless it is necessary. Unnecessary cross-referencing is not reader-friendly, as it bounces the reader back and forth throughout the document to understand one topic.

Generally, people consult documents to find specific information, and they expect all the relevant discussion of that information to appear in one place. If the drafter has effectively consolidated related topics, only minimal cross-referencing should be necessary.

B. How to Write Useful Cross–References

To be informative and reader-friendly, a cross-reference must do the following: (1) tell the reader exactly how the referenced material fits into the section or subsection that references it, and (2) send the reader to the *exact* section or subsection where the referenced information is found.

Examples: Useful Cross–References:

- Purchaser shall provide to Seller proof that Purchaser has procured all forms of insurance that section 10(B) requires Purchaser to procure and in the amounts set forth in that provision.

- If by 5 PM of the 25th day after the due date for the payment Buyer has not paid the full amount due to Seller, Seller may cancel the installment contract by proceeding pursuant to section 8.

When drafting cross-references, avoid the following:

- Avoid stating "See section 10(A)": either tell the reader *why* the reader should see the section or omit the cross-reference.

- Avoid conflating the referenced thing with the referenced provision: e.g., "Buyer will procure the insurance in section 10(B)": that statement is not accurate if you mean "the insurance *that is described in* section 10(B)."

Watch for ambiguity when you cross-reference. Misplacement of the typical referencing phrases ("pursuant to," "as set forth in," "as provided in") can create ambiguity, as shown in the example below.

Example: Ambiguous Cross–Reference
(caused by misplacement)

If Buyer discovers that the items in the shipment do not conform to the description, City shall give notice to Seller of the defect and allow Seller a minimum of 10 days to cure it, <u>pursuant to section 12</u>.

In the example, to *what part of the sentence* does the cross-referenced section apply? To the 10–day minimum? To the obligation to give notice *and* to allow 10 days to cure? To the entire sentence? Below is an example of how one could eliminate the ambiguity.

Example: Unambiguous Cross–Reference

If Buyer discovers that the items in the shipment do not conform to the description, City shall give notice to Seller of the defect and shall—<u>pursuant to section 12</u>—allow Seller a minimum of 10 days to cure the defect.

As shown in the example directly above, the key to removing the ambiguity is to place the referencing phrase in such a way that the phrase can modify only one element of the sentence. Chapter 31 discusses modifier placement.

CHAPTER 22

EXERCISES FOR PART 4: GENERATING CONTENT AND CREATING AN ORGANIZATIONAL SCHEME

■ ■ ■

Project 1.   Service Contract: Tree Removal and Care

Fact Pattern

Your clients are Erik Hervaux and Kelsey Clay, partners in Hervaux & Clay, who have just started up a tree removal and tree care service in Hanna Falls, Alaskabama. Both are certified arborists under Alaskabama law. They would like you to draft them a form contract. They have emailed to your office a list of the terms that they want you to incorporate in the document. The term sheet follows:

<u>Term Sheet for Hervaux & Clay</u>

Both of us are arborists; both have been state certified.

We perform services specified (see below) for price agreed to in professional manner by certified and experienced staff (just us right now)

Customer has to own trees or must have the tree owner's written permission for us to work; by signing document, they authorize us to do the agreed-on work at agreed on time

PROVIDED: necessary tools and equipment to do the agreed on job.

PROVIDED: tree removal and tree care (including treatment for disease and removal of branches), stump-grinding; for particular job, we would have to write out description of the service and the agreed-on price and attach to the contract (e.g., "Removal of two lower limbs of liveoak tree extending over apartment building 7-A: $1200)

TO BE COVERED: scheduled date should be in contract. We will make "best" efforts to work on scheduled date/finish at completion date (ESTIMATED). BUT do NOT want to have to compensate for any damage (such as branch breaking off or tree coming down) that is due to our being unable to start on the scheduled start date or finish or completion date.

Removal of wood and brush debris is included in price.

If we get sued by property's owners because customer does not get permission, they have to protect us from liability; however: we are bonded <u>and</u> insured for liability for personal injury, either to owners or third parties; we have property damage insurance; and all employees (if we hire any) will be covered by Worker's Compensation insurance. (We don't want to put all this in the contract.)

We are paid when we present our invoice after completing the job. We don't do payment plans unless previously arranged.

Assignment A.   Issue List, Initial Outline, Client Questions

Study the materials in Chapters 19 and 20. Prepare a detailed list of the issues addressed in the document. Using the template, create an initial outline scheme. Jot down a *list* of questions for the client. (Do not draft a formal client letter at this time).

Assignment B.   Revised Outline and Formal Client Letter

After receiving feedback on your outline, revise it so that it complies with the principles set out in Chapters 20 and 21.

Using the guidance set out in Chapter 19, draft a business letter addressed to the clients letter. Organize your questions and set them out so that the client understands the issues.

Project 2.   Residential Lease Assignments

Assignment A.   Evaluation of Organizational Scheme

Your new client, Rhonda Siler, CEO of Siler Properties, Inc., has asked you to revise the lease that her company uses for its three apartment complexes. The main headings are as follows:

1. Payments.
2. Grant of Right to Use and Possession of Premises.
3. Duration of Leasing Period.
4. Duty of Landlord to Maintain Premises.
5. Maintenance Obligations of Tenant.
6. Maintenance of Grounds, Parking Lot, and Walkways.
7. Liability.
8. Utilities and Other Third–Party Services; Insurance.
9. Providing of Pest Control.
10. Prohibition on Keeping Pets; Pet Deposit.

11. Occupancy Rules and Regulations.

12. Use of Amenities.

13. Damage to Premises.

14. Right of Landlord to Enter Premises.

15. Security Deposit—Refund.

16. Breach of Contract.

17. Selection of Forum.

18. Choice of Law.

19. Integration of Contract.

20. Modification and Amendment.

21. Background of Contract.

22. Signature and Effective Date.

After reading Chapter 20, answer the following questions regarding the major headings set out above:

1) Which section headings are not in proper form?

2) Which section headings appear to overlap (i.e., deal with parts of the same topic)?

3) Rearrange the sequence to reflect the template in Chapter 20.

Assignment B.

Identifying Serious Subdivision Errors

Below are a few section headings and subheadings that appear in your client's current contract:

4. Duty of Landlord to Maintain Premises

     (a) Landlord's Maintenance Obligations

     (b) Repairs to Premises

9. Providing of Pest Control

     (a) Expenses for Pest Control

11. Occupancy Rules

     (a) Disturbance of Other Tenants

     (b) Violation of Swimming Pool Rules

     (c) Misuse of Other Amenities

14. Right of Landlord to Enter Premises

     (a) L can enter premises for stipulated purposes: (consult state law).

     (b) L must give ___ days' notice (consult state law)

     (c) L can enter at any time w/o notice in emergency situation

Review Chapter 20 regarding subdivision. Critique each section above, identifying as many problems as you can.

Assignment C.   Creating Issue List and Outline From a Form

Your paralegal created a complete "as is" outline of your client's current contract. It is set out below. Using the Chapter 20's principles, do the following:

1) Make a <u>list</u> (no headings) of all the issues in the document.

2) Arrange the list items in order, using the template in Chapter 20.

3) Create sections and subsections with headings that meet Chapter 20's requirements.

Residential Lease and Rental Agreement

[In exordium clause]

Party names, date of signature; apartment #_____ at _____ complex; total rent during term = _____

1. <u>Payment</u>

(a) <u>Monthly rent</u>

monthly rent in the amount of _____ on or before the due date; pro rated amount if T takes possession before 1st of month: ___ per day

(b) <u>Time for Payment</u>

due date = 1st day of month to which rent applies (i.e., payment in advance)

(c) <u>Method of Payment</u>

by personal check; by delivering to office; if received after 5 pm on first business day after due date rent is LATE; if returned for insufficient funds, T reimburses L for any fee L incurs

(d) <u>Late rent</u>

Late rent (paid after due date) → $ _____ late fee

2. <u>Transfer of Premises to Tenant</u>

first day of period, L to transfer possession of apartment to T by making it available to T; T retains right to possession and use for as long as leasing arrangement remains in effect

3. <u>Duration of Leasing Period</u>

Period: one year; begins _____ and ends on _____.

4. <u>Duty of Landlord to Maintain Premises</u>

(a) <u>Landlord's Maintenance Obligations</u>

L to provide routine maintenance throughout leasing period as needed to keep apartment and premises (incl. grounds) in good condition and repair; maintenance performed by L or by contractor hired by L

(b) Repairs to Premises

L to repair or make arrangements for performance of repairs to apartment (incl. fixtures and appliances belonging to L) as needed during leasing period; L defrays costs for repairs

5.   Maintenance Obligations of Tenant

(a) Tenant to report immediately any damage to or malfunctioning of L's property (incl. fixtures and appliances belonging to L).

(b) T cannot make repairs to L's property (incl. fixtures and appliances belonging to L)

(c) T obligated to reimburse L for cost of repairing damage in excess of ordinary wear and tear or any malfunction if damage or malfunction arises out of negligence of T or person using property with T's consent

(d) T not to prevent L or contractor hired by L from entering for maintenance if L complies with 14

6.   Maintenance of Grounds, Parking Lot, and Walkways/Paths

(a) Grounds

L performs or arranges for performance of all maintenance to grounds (incl. parking lot)

(b) Responsibility of T

T has to remove of ordure deposited by pets from trails or walkways.

7.   Liability

(a) T releases L to full extent permitted by state law

(b) T indemnifies L against liability for injuries to third parties caused by negligence or neglect of T

8.   Utilities and Other Third–Party Services; Insurance

(a) Expenses for Utilities

T to procure in T's name utilities (electricity, water, sewage) and to pay all bills on time to ensure continued service; T to procure and pay for other utilities such as internet, cable, telephone as desired

(b) Insurance of Tenant's Property Against Loss

T understands L does not insure T's property against loss, incl. loss arising out of act of God, fire, theft, negligence of fellow tenant, or damage to premises, incl. damage attributable to defect in fixtures, appliances, or other part of premise; L recommends (doesn't require) T obtain renter's insurance sufficient to protect T's property

9. Providing of Pest Control

(a) Expenses for Pest Control

L pays expenses for pest control; T may not deny access to PRO-VIDER on scheduled service date

10. Occupancy

During the entire occupancy period, Tenant will comply with the following rules and regulations:

(a) Disturbance of Other Tenants

T shall not disturb other Tenants in quiet enjoyment of premises; Disturbance includes making excessive noise (incl. barking or other pet noises), emitting fireworks of any kind at any time, behaving in manner that reasonable person would recognize as disruptive to other's quiet enjoyment

(b) Violation of Swimming Pool Rules

T to comply with rules posted at pool re: diving, guests, hygiene, safety.

(c) Misuse of Other Amenities

T shall not violate section 12.

11. Use of Amenities

Tenant must comply with posted rules for use of amenities such as the club-house, playgrounds, laundry, gymnasium, tennis courts, and walkways and trails.

12. Damage to Premises

(a) Prepayment of Security Deposit

At or before signing, T must pay security deposit (one month's rent)

(b) Use of Security Deposit

defrays cost of repairing damage to premises in excess of ordinary wear and tear at the end of the leasing period

(c) Refund of Security Deposit

will be refunded ___ days after the leasing term ends; if L determines that there is damage in excess of ordinary wear and tear, L will retain amount sufficient to cover repair costs

13. Right of Landlord to Enter Premises

(a) L can enter premises for stipulated purposes: repairs & maintenance, to show apartment to prospective tenant; to inspect the premises

(b) L must give 24 hours' notice

(c) L can enter at any time w/o notice in emergency situation

14. Security Deposit—Refund

Security deposit is refunded as provided in section 13(c).

15. Breach of Contract

If Tenant breaches, Landlord may pursue remedies permitted by state law.

16. Selection of Forum

Disputes to be resolved in Southerland County, New Mexas

17. Choice of Law

New Mexas law applies.

18. Integration of Contract

This is the complete and final agreement of the parties.

19. Modification and Amendment

The parties cannot modify except by a writing signed by both parties.

20. Background of Contract

The parties intend for this contract to be effect and to be bound thereby.

21. Signatures and Effective Date

Assignment D.   Getting Information From the Client

After reading the following information and reviewing your outline, prepare a formal letter to the client.

Your paralegal interviewed the client and got the following background information:

Client's Contract Information

SILER PROPERTIES, INC.,

249 S. Main Street, Sawgrass, New Mexas

Tel. 000–111–1111

SPI@premier.web

Apartment Description

The amount of rent depends on the apartment model leased. The contract should permit the Manager to fill in the unit number and model when the lease is signed. A description can be attached (we have them pre-printed).

Insurance

The provision relating to insurance is extremely important, as we have been sued in the past by tenants whose property suffered damage as a result of flooding or whose property was stolen.

Liability

We would like the broadest protection against liability that state law permits and would like to ensure that Tenant indemnifies us against liability to a third party that arises from Tenant's negligence.

After consulting applicable law, you found the following statutes, which relate to residential leases:

§ 200.39 Obligations of Landlord to Maintain Premises

A landlord shall make any repair or perform maintenance that is necessary to keep the leased premises in a habitable condition and to keep the leased premises in compliance with local or state law that applies to such premises and shall keep such areas as are in common use in clean and good condition. The landlord has the duty to maintain the structural components of the leased premises, including all systems such as wiring, ventilation, air-conditioning, heating, plumbing, and toilets in good and safe condition and to maintain any appliance or fixture that is leased with the leased premises. If the premises consist of a single-family dwelling, the landlord may provide in the lease that the tenant perform the foregoing duties regarding maintenance of structural components; but not otherwise.

§ 200.41 Prohibited Provisions

A landlord shall not provide in the lease contract for exemption or limitation of landlord's liability for personal injury or property damage to Tenant, or other related loss, if the injury, damage, or less arises from any negligence, gross negligence, or other misfeasance or malfeasance of Landlord in performing a duty imposed by this Act on Landlord. If such an agreement is included in a lease contract it shall be void and unenforceable on grounds of public policy.

§ 200.50 Security Deposits

(1) Any landlord who requires a security deposit in advance of Tenant's occupancy must hold the deposit in an escrow account in a bank that is subject to regulation by the State of New Mexas or by any agency of the United States Government. The landlord must provide the tenant with account information, including the account number and whether the account is interest-bearing or non-interest bearing. If the landlord does not place the deposit in an escrow account, the landlord is not entitled to retain any portion of the security deposit.

(2) Before accepting payment of a security deposit, the landlord shall provide the tenant with an itemized list of any damage to the leased premises that exists at the time of signing that would be of a nature to warrant retention of the deposit. The landlord shall provide the tenant with the opportunity to inspect the premises to determine whether

the list reflects all existing damage. If the tenant signs the detailed list, tenant's signature is conclusive evidence that the tenant had the opportunity to inspect the leased premises and either assented to the accuracy of the itemized list or waived the right to inspection; however, a tenant may state in writing on the itemized list any additional damage that the tenant has discovered during the inspection. If the landlord does not comply with this provision, the landlord is not entitled to retain any portion of the deposit.

(3) At the termination of the lease arrangement the landlord shall conduct an inspection to determine any damage that the landlord intends to charge against the deposit and shall create an itemized list of each item of damage and the cost to repair the damage. The landlord may retain from the security deposit a sufficient amount of rent to cover the items of damage that did not appear on the list reflecting the damage at the time of signing. If the landlord withholds any part of the security deposit to pay repair costs, the landlord shall provide to the tenant by certified mail a copy of this itemized list together with the itemized list of the damage that existed at the time of signing together with a notice to the tenant of the landlord's intent to withhold a portion of the deposit. If the landlord does not comply with this provision, the landlord is not entitled to retain any portion of the deposit.

(4) Not later than the 30th day after the lease period has ended, the landlord shall refund to the tenant the security deposit, or any amount remaining after the landlord has withheld from the security deposit the amount that is reflected on the itemized rent.

Make sure your lease does not contain any provision that is inconsistent with applicable law.

PART 5

WILLS

■ ■ ■

- Chapter 23. Background for Drafting a Will
- Chapter 24. Drafting and Executing the Will
- Chapter 25. Exercises for Part 5

CHAPTER 23

BACKGROUND FOR DRAFTING A WILL

■ ■ ■

I. Preparation for Drafting a Will: An Overview

A. Limited Scope of This Discussion

Will-drafting is merely *one aspect* of estate planning, as a will is generally only one component of an estate plan. An estate planner who drafts a will does so as part of an overall plan for the disposition of an estate. While a will may be the centerpiece of some estate plans, the drafter of a real-world will takes account of a host of factors.

Even the basic issues involved in will-drafting are complex. Before attempting to draft a will for a client, be sure that you educate yourself. The following is a partial list of areas of law that an attorney must understand in order to advise a client effectively about estate planning:

- Laws governing wills, probate of a will, and administration of the estate.

- Laws governing insurance, joint tenancies, revocable trusts, and all types of transfers that do not pass through probate.

- Laws governing trusts generally (testamentary and inter vivos) and inter vivos gifts.

- Family protection statutes that may affect the overall estate plan, such as laws governing the right of a surviving spouse to take against the will,[1] to receive certain exempt property,[2] or to receive maintenance during administration; and the rights of after-born children.

- The law governing access of creditors to assets in the estate and the priority of claims against the estate.

- Estate tax law (federal and possibly state).

- State inheritance tax laws.

- Federal and state income tax law (e.g., if the primary asset in the estate is income-producing property).

- The law regulating partnerships (e.g., if the decedent's primary asset is a partnership interest in an ongoing business).

Merely knowing the law is not enough. An attorney advising a client concerning the disposition of the client's estate must be prepared to offer *practical* guidance so as to minimize the adverse impact of the law on the estate. Furthermore, the attorney must be able to draft appropriate documents to effectuate the plan.

There was a time when a general practitioner without significant training in the field of estate planning would draft a will for a client. Should a non-specialist ever do so now? Many general practitioners draft wills, but one who does so must be knowledgeable about the field of estate planning in order to advise the client and to draft a will that protects the client's interests.

Even if the client has few assets, a transfer by will can raise complex issues. Suppose that a client's only asset is an ongoing business and that the person she wants to benefit is not involved in the business and does not want to be? If such a client existed (i.e., one without other assets), would you know how to advise that client?

We do not address estate planning in this book. Instead, we address only some of the basic issues involved in drafting and executing a will. Learning how to draft a will can help prepare an attorney to deal with wills in other contexts (e.g., as a litigator representing a client in a dispute over a will).

B.   The Basics

1.   What Is the Purpose of a Will?

A formal, attested will is a writing in which a person (the testator) declares his or her intentions regarding the disposition of property after the testator's death. Via a will, a testator may also appoint (1) a personal representative to administer the estate, (2) a trustee for a testamentary trust, (3) a guardian for minor children, and (4) a conservator for any minor children's property.

Making a will is generally not regarded as a natural right but instead as a statutory privilege that the legislature grants.[3] As a result, the drafter of a will must comply with the requirements of the state's wills act.

A will does not take effect until after the testator's death.[4] During the testator's lifetime, the will is "ambulatory," meaning that the testator has the right to revise or revoke it. It thus differs from an inter vivos gift (e.g., a transfer of an interest by deed), which conveys a present interest in the estate. For a will to be enforced, the testamentary disposition must meet the requirements for a valid will.

2. What Property Can Pass by Will?

A testator can pass by will property or an interest in property that the testator has at the date of death. State wills acts sometimes say little more than that.[5]

3. Who Can Make a Will?

A testator must be of lawful age and have capacity to make a will. State wills acts vary as to the minimum age of a testator: for example, the minimum age in New Hampshire[6] and West Virginia[7] is 18. In Georgia, a person 14 years old or older who has testamentary capacity can make a will.[8]

To make a valid will, a person must have testamentary capacity. State wills acts generally describe the criteria, but you must consult the specific requirements in your state and the relevant case law. Though specifics may differ, testamentary capacity *generally* requires that the testator meet the following requirements: (1) that the testator understands the nature of the act (i.e., that the testator is providing for the disposition of his or her property at death); (2) that the testator understands the nature, extent, and situation of his or her property; and (3) that the testator remembers and understands his or her relationship to persons considered the natural objects of the testator's bounty (i.e., living descendants, parents, and spouses).[9] Some states may add to this typical list of requirements.

4. Who Can Be Beneficiaries of a Will?

Some states' wills acts identify persons who can be beneficiaries. For example, the California Probate Code states that a will can dispose of property to *any person*, including but not limited to the following: (a) an individual; (b) a corporation; (c) an unincorporated association, society, lodge, or a branch of the association, society, or lodge; (d) a county, city, or any municipal corporation; (e) any state; (f) the U.S. government or any of its instrumentalities; or (g) a foreign country or a governmental entity in a foreign country.[10]

Some states restrict, on public policy grounds, the persons who can benefit under a will. For example, a Texas statute voids dispositions to an attorney who is unrelated to the testator and who supervises the will's preparation.[11]

II. Nomination and Duties of an Executor

In addition to disposing of the testator's estate, another function of a will is to nominate an executor and to delineate the executor's powers (typically by giving the executor the same powers over the testator's property that the testator would have had). The will also should provide a means for determining a successor to the executor.

The executor carries out all lawful provisions of the will. The executor stands in the decedent's shoes with respect to the decedent's rights and obligations. Among other tasks, the executor probates the will, collects and distributes the assets in the estate, keeps and maintains records, protects the assets, notifies creditors of the estate, pays debts, pays funeral expenses, distributes the property, and closes the estate. The executor is expected to do these things on or before statutory deadlines.[12]

If there are many assets or complex issues, the executor's task can be extremely time-consuming. It can also be a thankless job. Thus, the client should give serious thought to choosing an executor, and the attorney must be prepared to offer guidance. The more complex the estate, the more thought the testator needs to give to selecting an executor—and to potential successors, in case the named executor predeceases the testator or is unwilling to act.

The executor's primary duty may be to the estate,[13] but the person serving as an executor is an officer of the court[14] and has a fiduciary duty to *all* the parties who have an interest in the estate.[15] This is a complex relationship because carrying out the duty to the estate sometimes puts the executor in conflict with beneficiaries or creditors.[16] Courts hold an executor to a high standard of care: executors are required to exercise the same degree of judgment, skill, care, and diligence that a reasonable or prudent person would ordinarily exercise in the management of his or her own affairs.[17]

In return for these services, the executor is generally entitled to compensation and to reimbursement of reasonable expenses that he or she incurs in good faith for the estate's benefit. The will may provide for compensation—yet another matter that an attorney must discuss with the testator.

III. Requisites for a Valid Will

A. Requirement of Testamentary Intent

Testamentary intent is the intent to make a revocable disposition that will take effect at death.[18] The first question for a court to which a will is presented is *not* how to effectuate the relevant intent but whether the necessary intent exists at all.[19] If the will's language does not reflect testamentary intent, the instrument is not a will and the dispositions cannot be enforced. Some documents offered to probate were never intended by the testator to become the testator's will (e.g., mere drafts, letters or notes setting out possible dispositions that were never finally reduced to a valid writing). Though testamentary intent alone is not enough to make a will valid, it is essential to validity.

The requirement of testamentary intent exists in part because of the inability of a court to confirm the decedent's intentions. Whereas an inter vivos gift is demonstrated by delivery of the gift to the recipient, a testamentary gift turns on the construction of a piece of paper. Thus, though no particular words are necessary to establish testamentary intent,[20] the court must be convinced that the testator intended the document presented for probate to *be* a will.

The Georgia Supreme Court provides valuable guidance for a drafter of wills: "It is not the writing that makes the will legal and binding, but the testamentary intent crystallized and expressed in the writing."[21] The best way to ensure that this intent is reflected is to identify the document as a will and to make it clear that the dispositions are intended to take effect at death.

B.   Compliance with the Wills Act Formalities

1.   Purpose of Wills Act Formalities

How does a court know that a paper reflecting testamentary intent was a final document instead of a draft? Testamentary intent is not enough to make a valid will. For the same reasons that courts insist on a will's expressing testamentary intent, courts accept for probate only wills that comply with the formalities essential to a valid will under state law.[22]

A number of commentators have discussed the function of formality in ensuring (1) that the document presented for probate was intended by the testator to be a will and (2) that the document is the testator's authentic will.[23] Courts have acknowledged that the wills formalities serve a useful function. According to the Mississippi Court of Appeals, for example, the formalities make the testator aware of the significance of the interests that the testator is creating.[24] The Vermont Supreme Court said that the formalities' obvious purpose is to supply ample evidence of testamentary intent and capacity and to prevent fraud.[25]

2.   Formalities for Attested Wills

Though some states recognize informal (e.g., holographic or handwritten) wills as valid if they meet the statutory standards for such wills, an attorney should consider drafting a client's will with the maximum level of formality to ensure that the will is deemed valid.

We have therefore focused here on the requirements for executing an attested will. What level of formality is required? The minimum level of formality necessary differs from state to state. Thus, you must consult your own state's wills act. Some of the issues that you must consider are discussed below.

Attested wills must be in writing.[26] The testator must sign or have the will signed on the testator's behalf. At least two individuals must sign as witnesses[27] to indicate that they either saw the signing or (where the statute permits) heard the testator acknowledge the signature or the will. Typically, anyone who is competent to be a witness is competent to be a witness to a will, though a witness to a will may forfeit an interest under that will in certain circumstances (discussed in Chapter 24).[28] Some wills act provisions state that the witnesses must be "credible."[29] Texas's provision states that the witness must be over 14 years old.[30]

Additional formal requirements vary significantly. Just looking at the statute is not enough: some case law, in "clarifying" the statutory formalities, may actually impose additional formalities that the statute does not address. The following is a sampling of formalities-related questions, the answers to which an attorney would have to know before drafting an attested will:

> **Means of signing**: If the testator is unable to sign the will, what requirements apply to having *someone else sign* on the testator's behalf (besides the typical requirements that the person do so in the testator's presence and at the testator's direction[31])? Must the person sign in the testator's *conscious* presence?[32] Must the person do so at the testator's express direction?[33] Must the person signing on the testator's behalf include a statement that the person is signing on the testator's behalf and sign the will?[34]

> **Placement of signature:** Must the testator sign the will at its end? Alternatively, must the signing occur in a way that shows that the signed name is intended as a signature?[35]

> **Witnessing of signature:** If the testator has already signed the will at the time of witnessing, can the testator meet the requirement of signing in the witness's presence by acknowledging the signature to the witness[36] or acknowledging that the document is the testator's will?[37]

> **Attestation by witnesses:** Must witnesses sign "at the request of the testator"?[38] Must they sign in the testator's presence?[39] Must they sign in the testator's *conscious* presence?[40] Must witnesses sign the will within a certain time after witnessing the signature or acknowledgment?[41] Must the witnesses sign in each other's presence?[42]

To understand the extent to which different states impose different levels of formality, compare the approaches of Arkansas and Alabama, as set out below.

Arkansas (very formal)

To be valid as an attested will, a writing must be executed with all of the following formalities:

(1) at least two attesting witnesses;

(2) as part of the signing, a declaration by the testator to the witnesses that the document is the testator's will;

(3) signature by one of the means stipulated in (4) at the end of the will;

(4) signature in the presence of at least two attesting witnesses;

(5) signature completed as follows: (i) by the testator's signing, (ii) by the testator's mark witnessed by a person who writes his or her own name as witness, (iii) signature by someone in the testator's presence who signs for the testator and writes his or her own name with a statement explaining that he or she signed the testator's name at the testator's request, or (iv) acknowledgment by the testator that a previous signature is the testator's signature;

(6) a request by the testator that the attesting witnesses sign;

(7) signature by the witnesses in the testator's presence.[43]

Alabama (less formal)

To be valid as an attested will, a writing must be executed with the following formalities:

(1) signature by the testator or by someone else who signs for the testator in the testator's presence and by the testator's direction,

(2) signatures by at least two persons who witness the testator's signing of the will, the testator's acknowledgment of a previous signature, or the testator's acknowledgment of the will.[44]

As shown by the examples above, the requirements for a valid will can differ drastically among states. Which requirements apply in your state?

3. Degree of Compliance with the Wills Act Formalities

Twenty years ago, the rule in virtually all American courts was to require strict compliance with the formalities required to execute a valid will. If a testator failed to tick all the boxes, the will would not be enforced. Many states still retain a standard of strict compliance. Consider the following hypothetical:

- You are practicing law in a state that requires that a will be signed by two or more witnesses "who shall, at the request of the testator and in the testator's presence, attest to the testator's signature."[45]

- You drafted a will for a gravely ill client.

- The caregiver asks you to come to the house and arranges for two neighbors to come over to witness the will.

- You arrive and find the testator in bed: she is clear-headed, knows what she is doing, and is determined to execute the will.

- The caregiver and a hospice worker are in the room with her.

- The witnesses are sitting on a sofa directly across from the testator's bed, where she can plainly see them.

- The testator signs the will and states that it is her last will and testament.

- She then requests that the witnesses sign the will.

- One witness tries, but the pen isn't working.

- Both witnesses follow the caregiver into the testator's office down the hall, where both witnesses sign the will.

- They bring the will back to you.

If your state requires *strict* compliance with the wills act formalities, you have a problem because the witnesses were not actually in the testator's presence when signing.

In some states, the rule of strict compliance no longer applies. Some states apply a doctrine of "substantial compliance."[46] This doctrine allows a court to excuse "slight or trifling departures from technical requirements."[47]

Other states have adopted rules that allow or require the court to treat a will as valid if the proponent of the will can produce evidence that the testator intended the document to be a will. For example, a California statute provides the following:

If a will was not executed in compliance with [the formalities], the will shall be treated as if it was executed in compliance with that paragraph if the proponent of the will establishes by clear and convincing evidence that, at the time the testator signed the will, the testator intended the will to constitute the testator's will.[48]

Colorado has a similar provision, which applies to wills, revocations, additions, alterations, and revivals.[49] Other states have adopted similar legislation.

That state law may be less inflexible toward a testator whose will does not meet the state's execution requirements is of little relevance to the attorney, since a failure to do the job correctly is still a failure even if the mistake is ultimately not fatal to the will.

An attorney who oversees the execution of a will must make sure that he or she understands the minimum level of formality that the state requires. Most attorneys, using an abundance of caution, will ensure that the will is executed with *more* formality than the law requires.

IV. Changes to the Will

1. Codicils

A testator can alter a will by means of a codicil. Our recommendations to attorneys for drafting a codicil are exactly the same as our recommendations for a will: make sure that the document reflects testamentary intent[50] and that the codicil is executed with exactly the requisite formalities (which in many states is the same degree of formality required to execute a will).[51]

Before drafting a codicil, the drafter should carefully review the existing will (especially if someone else drafted it).

The codicil should state that it is a codicil to the will, so that it is clear that it is not a replacement will. A codicil may include recitals, such as the following, regarding the reasons for it:

- "During the last year, I have acquired additional property in the form of two office buildings located in downtown Asheville...."

- "Three months ago, my primary beneficiary, Marianne Jones, died and therefore ..."

The codicil should identify the provisions that it affects and the dispositions that are affected. Disputes can arise if it is unclear whether the codicil revokes a provision or simply modifies it. If the codicil replaces an existing provision or set of provisions, it should so state. If it merely modifies one aspect, that too should be explained so that it is clear exactly how it changes the provision.

It may be better to redraft the entire provision than to make a surgical tweak that creates a question concerning the viability of the previous language, unless you are certain that no one could misunderstand your meaning.

2. Replacement Wills

State law governing revocation permits a testator to revoke a will by executing a subsequent will.[52] In some states, statutes address how courts resolve disputes over whether a document is a will or a codicil.[53] Your goal is to eliminate the possibility of any such dispute. If you are drafting a replacement will, make this clear. The first thing that a replacement will should do is to revoke any prior wills. The use of such recitals is discussed in Chapter 24.

3. Effect of Changed Circumstances

Some changes to the testator's circumstances will obviously have an effect on the estate: e.g., the death of a beneficiary or the testator's selling of the property in the estate after making the will. As Chapter 24 explains, such changes are dealt with by state law if the testator does not update the will.

Changes in the testator's personal relationships might also cause changes in the will. For example, state law may provide that the entry of a final divorce decree acts as a revocation of any provision in the will for the (former) spouse's benefit unless the will was made in contemplation of the divorce.[54]

What happens if the testator dies following a legal separation but before a divorce is finalized? The disposition to the spouse might remain in effect. In Maine, for example, a decree of separation does not terminate the status of husband and wife and would not revoke dispositions in the will for the (separated) spouse.[55]

What about marriage or the birth of a child? A testator's marriage may result in the spouse's acquiring rights in the testator's property whether or not the testator changes the will. State law may also deal with after-born children.

If the testator's circumstances at the time of executing a will suggest the need, be prepared to advise the testator concerning the effect of such changes.

Chapter 24

Drafting and Executing the Will

■ ■ ■

I. Organizing the Components of a Simple Will

A. Organizational Issues Specific to Wills

There are different ways to organize a will. The organization depends largely on the complexity of the estate and expectations as to the persons who will be administering the will.

In general, we recommend that a will be drafted using the same organizational principles discussed in Chapters 20 and 21. It is conventional for wills to be organized into "Articles." As explained in Subsection I–B, certain provisions should appear at the beginning or at the end. Otherwise, the sequence of the provisions depends on the drafter's and testator's priorities. Because there is so much variation in drafters' and testators' priorities, we cannot provide a template for wills.

B. Components of the Will

1. Components Conventionally Set Out at the Beginning

(a) Preamble with Initial Recitals

The will should start out by naming the testator. Many wills begin with certain recitals that are intended to prevent a dispute over the will. Some are included based on convention; others may be required by state law. The point of such recitals is to show evidence of testamentary intent. Below are examples of declarations that are typically included:

- Declaration that the document is the testator's last will and testament, intended to take effect after the testator's death.

- Declaration that the will revokes all prior wills.

- Declaration that the testator is of sound mind.

Other declarations may be included if the drafter considers them useful. The recital that the testator is of sound mind may be backed up by statements intended to demonstrate the testator's capacity—e.g., a statement identifying the persons who are the natural objects of the testator's bounty or describing generally the nature and extent of the testator's property. Whether such a provision would have any practical use is a matter you would need to determine by researching applicable law.

Some states might *require* that the will include certain recitals (or declarations) in order to be valid.[1] If this is so, you must include those recitals.

Sometimes, it may be important to include declarations explaining dispositions that are contrary to what the court generally expects. (Alternatively, such declarations can be included in the provisions to which they relate.)

(b) Definitions Article

If you include definitions, set them out in a section at the beginning of the will. You might want to place them before the recitals if any defined terms appear in the recitals. Chapter 27 discusses how to set up a definitions section.

2.   Components Set Out at the End

(a) Rules Regulating Dispositions

One job of the attorney is to anticipate and deal with certain circumstances (discussed in Section IV) that could affect the testamentary scheme: e.g., anti-lapse rules or rules governing transfers to an incapacitated beneficiary. The drafter might incorporate (either literally or by reference) the state's rules or might create a different rule.

(b) Signatures of Testator and Witnesses With Supporting Recitals

The last element of the will should be the signature of the testator and the attesting witnesses. Chapter 23 discusses the procedures that we recommend for actually executing the will. The will *itself* should be designed to minimize the chances of any challenge to its validity based on failure of the testator to comply with the requisite formalities.

Drafters often include in the will a testimonium clause setting out information that is included to avoid certain types of disputes. The testimonium clause recites certain facts included to avoid a will contest. The following is an example:

> I am signing this writing, which is my last will and testament, on _____, 20___. I am signing immediately this clause in the presence of the three persons who at

my request are witnessing the will and my signing of the will. I have declared to them that this writing is my last will and testament. The final writing consists of ___ printed pages.

Harold Weiss

Be sure that the signature line is conspicuous. If the will includes an affidavit to make it "self-proving" (discussed in Section V), be sure that it is clear to the testator that he or she must sign the will itself as well as the affidavit. If the testator is unable to sign the will, the signature clause should state the name of the person (someone other than a witness) who signed on the testator's behalf and should state that the person did so at the testator's express request and in the testator's conscious presence. The person who signed on the testator's behalf should sign his or her own name.

Though state law may not require it in order for the will to be effective, we highly recommend that you include an attestation clause. Without an attestation clause, a court has less basis for certainty that the writing is the testator's final will. Most attestation clauses recite the formalities used to execute the will. An example of an attestation clause follows:

> By affixing our signatures, we the undersigned certify that on _____, 20___, in our presence Harold Weiss declared that this writing is his last will and testament and requested that we subscribe the will as his witnesses. We have subscribed our names below in order to attest that in our presence, Harold Weiss signed the writing. We attest that we have subscribed our names below in the presence of Harold Weiss and of each other.

Carolyn Wingate, 2300 Arlington Road, Caraway, Delasota

Frederick M. Finch, 89 Bethany Lane, Caraway, Delasota

3. Other Components (Sequence Varies)

(a) Dispositive Provisions

Dispositive provisions express an intended transfer of property from the testator to the recipient. Though dispositive provisions are often set out before other types of provisions, they need not be. You should create a sequencing scheme that reflects your client's priorities.

The dispositive provisions should be set out so that the residuary clause that deals with all property not otherwise accounted for is the last dispositive provision. Otherwise, organize the will in the manner that seems most coherent based on the testamentary scheme. Many simple wills are organized based on the type of property to which each disposition relates (e.g., gifts of real property, gifts of items of personal property, gifts of money or stock). Others are organized based on the type of disposition (discussed in Section IV): e.g., specific legacies, general legacies, demonstrative legacies, residuary clause.

(b) Nomination of the Personal Representative or Appointment of a Guardian

The provision appointing the personal representative (discussed in Section III) might precede the dispositive provisions in some circumstances. Provisions for the appointment of a guardian for the testator's minor children typically precede the dispositive provisions.

II. Choosing Your Language

A. Types of Statements

1. Expressing a Disposition

The will "speaks" from the date of the testator's death. Most statements in a will should be in present tense and should be in active voice (e.g., "I leave my gold watch to....").

Key verbs for drafting a will include "bequeath" and "devise." Traditionally "devise" has been applied to gifts of real property and "bequeath" to gifts of personal property. In most states, this distinction means little nowadays. The more general terms "give" or "leave" are just as effective. We *do not* recommend the redundant synonym-strings found in some wills: e.g., "bequeath, devise, leave, and give."

Other words that are useful for wills are "nominate," "appoint," "direct," "grant," and "assign." If you are not sure of their meaning, we recommend that you look them up.

We recommend that you *do not* use language expressing an intention ("I intend to leave my gold watch to ...") or a *future* disposition ("I will leave my gold watch to...."). Such statements do not clearly indicate testamentary intent.

2. Expressing a Right or Power

The will typically includes some provisions empowering the executor to act. It might also include other provisions conferring a right on one of the will's beneficiaries.

The auxiliary verb "may" coupled with a verb expressing the appropriate action is generally treated by courts as granting the right or power of the executor to act or refrain from acting; however, there are other ways to express a right or power. Check local practice regarding the formulation of statements granting rights and powers. Below are examples of differently phrased grants of power:

- My executor <u>may exercise</u> any power granted to an executor under state law.

- I <u>authorize</u> my executor to exercise any power granted to an executor under state law.

3. Imposing a Duty

The will might also impose duties on the executor or others. When imposing a duty on any person to perform (or refrain from performing) any kind of action, we recommend that you use "shall" and "shall not."

> My executor <u>shall not</u> treat a gift I make to any of my children during my lifetime as an advancement to be deducted from their shares under Articles I through III.

4. Stating Facts (Declarations)

Section I–B discusses certain "declarations" that a will may contain. Declarations are recitals of fact in past or present tense. The following are examples:

- I declare that this document is my last will and testament and that it revokes all prior wills and codicils executed prior to this date.

- I am making this disposition to the non-profit organization known as St. Caroline Emanuel Cat Rescue Foundation in recognition of its assistance in bringing me together with my best and most loyal friend, Mr. Purrkins.

B. Word Choice

1. Importance of Understanding the Scope of Words and Phrases

Drafting a will requires extraordinary clarity. Due to the different requirements for making different types of dispositions (discussed in Section IV), the drafter must be keenly aware of when to use more specific versus more general language.

An attorney must adjust the language to the type of disposition that the testator intends to make. In identifying classes of beneficiaries and types of property, an attorney must understand the scope of the testator's property or scope of any class of persons to whom a gift is made.

2. Checking the Meaning of Words

(a) Ordinary Versus Technical Language

The case law on wills suggests that courts give terms used in wills their "ordinary" meaning.[2] Some cases state that the testator (whom you represent) is presumed to know and intend the legal effect of the language used in the will.[3] A Texas case, for example, states that the court "ascertains intent from the normal, usual, *and legal* meaning of the terms."[4]

Before plugging into your document a term of art that you *think* you know or a phrase that you *think* is a legal term of art,[5] you must ensure that you really do know. Even when you think you are being precise, you must question the meaning of the words that you choose.

As discussed in Chapter 26, courts tend to read technical terms in their technical sense. The law of wills provides a number of useful shorthand phrases (e.g., "share and share alike," "per stirpes," "per capita"). Do you know the meaning of those phrases? Do you understand what happens when a court applies them? While technical language can be helpful, an attorney must understand not only its facial meaning, but also its practical ramifications.

(b) Checking Statutory Terminology Against Your Usage

Governing statutes often contain definitions. These definitions may serve as "gap fillers" if you fail to make your meaning clear. However, you need to know what the statutorily defined terms mean before you rely on them. You also need to make sure that you have not used statutorily-defined terms inadvertently.

Suppose that you are drafting a will. The testator says that she wants to make a disposition to her children. Since this seems natural and logical, you fail to question her and therefore do not find out that the testator always refers to her son and step-son as her "children." If you make the gift to the testator's "children," will the step-son be left out in the cold? Some states may define "children" to exclude persons who are not blood relatives.[6]

(c) Checking Assumptions About the Client's Terminology

When interviewing the client, the drafter must be systematic and detailed in collecting information concerning the nature and extent of the client's assets and the identities of the persons whom the client wishes to benefit.

Do not rely on vague characterizations. Get the full names and current addresses of all relatives that the client intends to benefit (and the names of *their* relatives, when possible or germane). If the testator speaks of a class of persons such as "children" or "grandchildren," make sure that you understand whether any individual in the class is not related to the testator by blood (e.g., is adopted or is a step-child) or was born out of wedlock. That way, you can ensure that the language you use covers those children.

Sometimes it might not occur to the testator to mention a relative who fits into a benefited class whom the testator never thinks about and does *not* want to benefit (for example, her estranged brother whom no one in the family has heard from in 20 years).

Regarding the client's property, get as much detailed information as you can get the client to give you regarding the nature, extent, and current value of the property. Check your assumptions (and the client's). If the client wishes to leave specific property to a legatee, make sure that you can describe the property in enough detail to enable the executor to distinguish it from any similar property.

Suppose the testator tells you that she wants to leave a memento to the woman in her book group who was so helpful after the testator fell and broke her hip. The testator wants to give the woman something from what the testator calls her "ceramic collection" but is not sure what the woman would like best. The testator instructs you to state that "Lillian" may choose from the collection "any item" she would like as "a keepsake."

First, what is this "ceramic collection"? You might be picturing a row of bunny figurines that you saw at a yard sale, a set of "collectible" plates that your aunt displays in a cabinet, or the Roman potsherds that you saw at the British Museum. What *exactly* is the testator intending to give away? What can go wrong if you do not delve into this question?

Once you understand what types of items the phrase encompasses, think about how to frame the legacy. Suppose that some pieces are antique and valuable. What happens if you just state that Lillian can choose "any item"? Suppose that Lillian picks a 24–piece set of antique Limoges valued at $5,000? What is the ordinary meaning of "item"? Might a court's interpretation of "item" turn, in part, on whether the value of the set depends upon its being kept together as a set?

You can look to case law for guidance, but it is unlikely to tell you how a particular word in a particular context is going to be applied. You have to look ahead and provide the context.

3.   Creating Definitions

One way to avoid potential conflict with statutorily-defined words *and* to make the will more concise is to create your own definitions. Use the principles discussed in Chapter 27. Below are examples of how a drafter might set out certain types of definitions:

Defining Categories of Persons

- "Children" means my daughter, Margaret Hinton Lee of 12–A 10th Street Holly Hills, Gainestown, Florindiana and my stepdaughter, Deborah Frazier of 350 K Street, Oberon, Calohio.

- "Charitable Beneficiaries" means the Temple–Smith Cat Rescue Foundation, a non-profit corporation whose office is located at 23 4th Street, Cupplestown, Delasota; and the Wenger Life–Transitioning Work Group, a nonprofit corporation whose office is located at 425 Tower Woods, Cupplestown, Delasota.

Defining Categories of Property

- "Item" means any individual piece of china in my collection, including components generally considered part of a single item (such as a cup and saucer), but does not include an item that is part of a set of items of the same kind (such as a tea set) and does not include a set of items, even though they are of the same kind.

- "NG stock" means the 1000 shares of Nicholas–Grafton stock that I received from my father on my 18th birthday and includes any additional shares resulting from stock splits.

Clarifying Terms of Art

- "Legacy" means any gift made by this will, regardless of whether the gift would technically be classed as a "bequest" or "devise."

III. Nomination and Powers of Executor and Related Issues

Chapter 23 discusses some of the considerations involved in drafting a provision selecting a personal representative. Some of the issues that it should cover include the following:

- Identification of the person nominated as personal representative.

- Identification of successors in case the primary nominee does not survive the testator, fails to qualify under state law, does not wish to act, or ceases to act.

- The powers of the personal representative.

- Provisions regarding the executor's compensation and expenses.

- Waiver of state-imposed bonds (if applicable).

State statutes address specific powers and limitations on the executor's general powers and duties. To understand these issues, check state law. The following are examples of typical provisions:

Nomination of Executor and Successors

I nominate my wife, Jolene Green, as executor to serve as personal representative of my estate. If Jolene does not survive me, fails to qualify as executor, or declines or ceases to serve for any reason, then I nominate my daughter, Frances Green Winslow, to serve as my executor. If Frances does not survive me, fails to qualify as executor, or declines or ceases to serve for any reason, then I nominate my son, Jonathan Green, to serve as my executor.

Executor's Powers

To my executor I give full power over all assets in my state to the full extent permitted by law, with the right to do anything that I could do if I were living, including the right to invest, sell, mortgage, lease, dispose of, and distribute in kind all property, both real and personal, when and on whatever terms my executor deems appropriate.

IV. Basics for Drafting Simple Dispositive Provisions

A. Types of Provisions Addressed

First, a caveat: a will drafted by an estate planner may include a number of devices designed to minimize taxes and ensure that the beneficiaries will receive the maximum benefit possible under the law. Such sophisticated devices are the proper subject of an estate-planning course. This section provides guidance for drafting a *very simple* will involving the four basic types of dispositions discussed below.

Though there are other words for referring to these testamentary gifts (e.g., "devise" or "bequest") we use the word "legacy" throughout. You might wish to do otherwise if your state or local practice maintains the traditional distinction between "devises" of real property and "bequests" of personal property. Courts generally recognize the following types of provisions:

- **Specific legacy**: a gift of property that can be satisfied only by the legatee's receiving that exact item (as opposed to a similar item or cash equivalent).

- **General legacy**: a gift of property or money that can be satisfied in cash or in kind from the estate's general assets.[7]

- **Demonstrative legacy**: a gift of money or property (such as stock) found in a specified fund or account; if the amount in the fund or account is not sufficient, the legacy can be satisfied from the estate's general assets.[8]

- **Residuary legacy**: a gift of all the property, real and personal, that remains in the estate after all other legacies have been satisfied.

Thus, the language chosen by the drafter tells the executor and the court what the source of the gift is to be—whether it is a specified piece of property or fund or whether it can be satisfied out of the estate's general assets.

B. Certain Consequences of a Legacy's Characterization

1. Ademption of Specific Legacies

What happens if property or a fund that the will refers to is missing in the estate when the testator dies?

The answer depends on the character of the legacy. If the language reflects that the gift was a specific legacy (as explained in Section A), the gift is "adeemed" (extinguished), unless the will or state law specifies that the legatee should receive a replacement gift or cash equivalent.[9] In a Pennsylvania case, for example, an intended gift of the testator's "large, multi-diamond dinner ring" was adeemed when the executor could not find a ring matching the description; the intended recipient did not get anything at all.[10]

Suppose your 47–year–old client specifies that he wants his son Greg to receive his "2012 Inamasu Q–3000 Bedivere convertible." How do you know whether a provision should be framed as a specific legacy? Ask questions to find out what the gift is intended to accomplish.

Is the value of the gift sentimental or symbolic? If so, it is possible that the value can be represented *only* by the particular item. Is the asset unique (e.g., the car was built from a kit by the testator)? In that case, the testator might intend for the son to receive *that particular car*—a specific legacy that can be satisfied only by the transfer of that car.

On the other hand, it is possible that the testator just wants the son to receive whatever car the testator has at death or a cash equivalent if the testator does not have a car. In that case, you might draft a general legacy (to which ademption does not apply).

In some states, anti-ademption statutes may prevent ademption in certain circumstances.[11] If your state has such a statute in place, you need to know how it would operate. As the will's drafter, you can create your own ademption rule or rules.

2. Abatement of Legacies

Even the best-laid testamentary plans can fail if the estate does not have sufficient assets for the executor to carry them out. If the estate is insufficient to cover all the testator's legacies, the gifts abate: i.e., are reduced ratably (to the extent that some assets remain) or eliminated (if no assets remain).

Before any legacies get paid, the executor must comply with state statutes that prioritize claims of creditors. Many claims take priority over the legacies. For example, if the estate's assets are not sufficient, New Mexico provides that the claims are paid in the following order: (1) the expenses of estate administration; (2) reasonable funeral expenses; (3) taxes and debts that receive preference under federal law; (4) reasonable expenses for hospitalization and medical care resulting from the decedent's final illness; (5) debts and taxes that receive preference under state law; and (6) any remaining claims.[12] In some cases, the estate's assets might be exhausted before all these claims are paid.

What if some amount remains, but that amount is not sufficient to cover all the testator's intended gifts? The order in which they abate is generally covered by statute and typically depends on the type of legacy. Though there are some differences in how state statutes operate,[13] the following reflects a typical scheme for prioritizing the legatee's interests:

1) Specific legacies are distributed first (with the specified fund from which a demonstrative legacy is paid typically treated as specific to the extent of the fund).

2) After the specific legacies are distributed, the general legacies are distributed.

3) After the general legacies are distributed, the residue is distributed.

Suppose that after paying off all creditors' claims, the executor finds that the estate is not sufficient to pay all the legacies but is sufficient to cover specific legacies. In that case, the executor must first satisfy the specific legacies. If some remains over, then the executor would satisfy the general legacies. If there is not enough for the general legacies to be satisfied in full, the gifts to the general legatees are ratably reduced. The residuary legatees would take nothing because no assets remain.

If the testator wants a different order of abatement, the drafter is free to draft abatement rules that reflect that intent. The statutory scheme typically applies only to the extent that the will does not change it.

3. Other Consequences

The characterization of a legacy can have other consequences, depending on the applicable law. For example, the Arkansas Probate Code provides that beginning 15 months after administration of the estate begins, general legacies bear interest at the rate of 6% per annum or the then-prevailing legal rate (unless the will states otherwise),[14] but the courts have determined that gifts characterized as specific legacies do not bear interest.[15] On the other hand, a specific legacy, unlike a general legacy, may include income that accrues while the property remains in the executor's hands.[16]

If the legacy is a gift of stock, whether the legatee is entitled to stock splits can depend on whether the gift is characterized as a general or specific legacy. For example, a South Carolina statute provides that if the testator intended a *specific* legacy of certain securities (instead of the equivalent value of the shares), then the legatee is entitled to any shares that resulted from the company's merger, consolidation, or similar action initiated by the company.[17]

A full discussion of all possible consequences (including tax consequences) of a legacy's characterization is beyond the scope of this book. Consult applicable law and practice manuals.

C. Drafting Legacies

1. Specific Legacy

To design a specific legacy, you must *identify* and *describe* the specific item with sufficient particularity to distinguish it from all of the testator's other property. If the legacy is unambiguously set out so that it is obviously a specific legacy, you do not have to mention ademption if the testator's intention is that the gift be adeemed; the doctrine should apply. However, you may deal with the issue yourself.

Our philosophy is that the drafter should state the outcome that the drafter intends. Characterizing a legacy as a "specific legacy" at least notifies the court that the legacy is intended to operate as such. The following is an example of stating outcomes:

> I leave to my son Henry, as a specific legacy as a reminder of our shared hobby, my custom-built Inamasu Q–3000 Bedivere convertible sports car. If I do not own that car at the date of my death, I leave to him instead any convertible sports car that I do own. If I do not own any convertible sports car, this gift is adeemed.

A gift of money (a pecuniary legacy) can be a specific legacy if it is not payable out of the estate's general assets but out of a particular source that is specified in the will and if the legacy can be satisfied *only* out of that fund.[18] An example follows:

> To my daughter Jane, I leave as a specific legacy any money remaining in the cardboard box found on the top shelf of my closet. If no money remains, the legacy is adeemed.

2. General Legacy

A general legacy should be drafted to make it clear that it is *not* limited to any specific property (if it is a gift of property) or any specific fund (if it is a gift of cash). To avoid disputes over the testator's intentions, make the nature of the legacy clear in your description. An example follows:

> To my daughter, Emma, I leave as a general legacy a cash gift of $5000. This legacy is not limited to any specific fund but is payable from the general assets belonging to the estate that are not otherwise disposed of in this will.

3. Demonstrative Legacy

Reminder: a demonstrative legacy has some characteristics of a specific legacy in that it identifies a specific fund out of which the legacy is to be paid *if* the fund is sufficient to cover it. If the fund is not sufficient, then the executor can pay the legacy from the estate's general assets.[19] Thus, to the extent that the fund is not sufficient, the executor can treat the gift as a general legacy.[20]

To ensure that a demonstrative legacy is not construed as a specific legacy, we recommend that you make clear that the fund is specified as the preferred source for payment but *not the only* source. An example follows:

> To Caroline Moss, I leave $25,000 in cash as a demonstrative legacy to be paid as follows:
>
> > (1) to the extent that the funds in my bank account numbered 124345 at First Bank of Palmettoville are sufficient to cover the legacy, out of those funds; and
> >
> > (2) to the extent that this fund is not sufficient to pay the legacy, out of the estate's general funds if the estate contains sufficient funds not otherwise disposed of out of which it can be satisfied.

4. Residuary Legacy

To ensure that all property in the estate passes under the will, rather than by intestacy, be sure to include a residuary clause. In the residuary clause, the testator disposes of all of the testator's remaining estate (i.e., whatever remains after all the other legacies). The following is an example of a residuary legacy:

> I leave in equal shares to my children the entire residue of my estate wherever situated, including real property and personal property.

In some instances, a testator may prefer to deal with the bulk of the estates through specific, demonstrative, or general legacies—leaving the residue to address property that the testator did not consider sufficiently important to dispose of otherwise. In other instances, the residue contains most of the estate's value, with the testator making only token gifts through legacies to a few people and leaving all the remainder to the persons that the testator primarily wishes to benefit.

In setting up the testamentary scheme, bear in mind that if the estate's assets are insufficient, the first type of legacy to abate is the residuary legacy.

D.   Preventing Lapse of Legacies

If a legatee predeceases the testator, the gift may lapse (i.e., fail) unless the will or state law prevents this outcome. To understand what happens when a gift lapses, you must consult state law. For example, Texas law provides that if a legacy other than a residuary legacy lapses, the legacy falls into the residuary estate.[21] If the residue is left to two or more persons and the residuary legacy lapses, the surviving residuary legatees take in proportion to their shares in the residue.[22] If no one survives the testator, the property passes by intestacy.[23] This arrangement seems fairly common.

In many instances, state anti-lapse statutes prevent legacies from lapsing. How well do anti-lapse statutes actually implement a testator's intent? In some cases, not at all: the anti-lapse statutes reflect the legislature's assumptions about how property should pass if the will's provision would otherwise fail. These assumptions vary.

When does your state's anti-lapse statute kick a gift to a deceased legatee's children or grandchildren?

- If the legatee is the testator's child or a child's descendant?[24]

- If the legatee is the testator's parent or is a parent's lineal descendant (e.g., testator's niece)?[25]

- If the legatee is the testator's grandparent or is a grandparent's lineal descendant (e.g., testator's first cousin)?[26]

- If the legatee is related to the testator in *any* degree of kinship (e.g., testator's third cousin)?[27]

- If the legatee is any legatee who does not survive the testator (e.g., testator's friend)?[28]

Depending on the statute, the outcome could be very different from what the testator would have wanted. For example, if the testator leaves property to a cousin who predeceases the testator, would the testator want the cousin's children or grandchildren to receive the gift or would the testator rather it pass to some person that the testator selects?

The drafter of a will can find out what the testator wants by asking. Since the anti-lapse statute is a rule of construction that applies only if the will does not deal with the issue, the drafter can draft the will to implement the testator's *actual* intent.

In deciding how to draft a legacy to prevent lapse, be sure that you understand state law relating to class gifts (e.g., a gift to all the testator's aunts). If one of the aunts does not survive the testator, what happens? Does the gift lapse and go into the residue? Does the anti-lapse statute kick in so that the aunt's share goes to her descendants? Do the other members of the class get her share? Check state law.[29]

The following are examples of dispositions that particular testators wished to make:

- **Individual Anti–Lapse Provision**

I leave all my jewelry to my friend, Jane Heath of 123 Blalock Way, Merrymount, Georginia. If Jane predeceases me, I leave my jewelry to my stepdaughter, Susan Browning of 33 Altamont Lane, Entwistle, Connorado. If Susan predeceases me, I leave my jewelry to Susan's daughter, Roxanne Browning.

- **General Anti–Lapse Provision**

If any legatee named in Articles III through V predeceases me, I direct that the gift (whether it be property, an interest in property, or money) should pass to the Sempernel County Homeless Fund, a not-for-profit corporation located at 212 Main Street, Sempernel, Arkansington.

- **Lapse of the Residue**

I leave the residue of my estate to my children, Sarah and Nicholas, with each taking 50%. If either child predeceases me, that child's 50% share passes to his or her children to be shared equally among those children.

E. Dealing With Simultaneous Death

What happens if the testator and a legatee die at the same time? Suppose that your clients are a husband and wife. The husband provides in his will that all of his property goes to his wife. The wife provides that all of hers goes to the husband. If both die in the same car accident, does the husband's property go to the wife to be disposed of by her will, or does it remain in his estate to be disposed of by his will as if he had survived her?

State statutes typically deal with the outcome of simultaneous death. In Vermont, for example, if the devolution of property depends on order of death and if there is not sufficient evidence that the testators died other than at the same time, each testator's property is disposed of as if he or she had been the survivor.[30] State laws are not uniform.[31] Check state law so that you can decide whether you need to draft a provision that is tailored to the testator's needs. The following is an example of such a provision:

> If apparent simultaneous death leaves it uncertain whether a legatee or I was the first to die, I am to be treated as the survivor of the two without regard to any period required under state law to establish my survivorship.

V.   Setting Up an Execution Ceremony

Chapter 23 addresses the execution requirements of state wills acts and how non-compliance might affect the validity of the will. What steps should an attorney take to ensure that a will is validly executed?

First, an attorney must understand the state's minimum requirements for execution. As Chapter 23 explains, these requirements vary significantly from state to state. Out of an abundance of caution, attorneys often set up a formal execution ceremony to ensure that the boxes are all ticked. Consider the utility of the following:

- Ensuring that there are at least three disinterested witnesses (i.e., witnesses who are not entitled under the will to any share of the estate) even if the statute requires only two.

- Ensuring that the testator and witnesses are gathered in the same room at the same time and that they all remain there until the will is fully executed and that each can both see and hear the others.

- Having the testator announce that the document is his or her will and having the testator expressly request that the witnesses attest the signing.

- Ensuring that the signatures appear at the will's end.

State law may provide the option of making the will "self-proving." If a will is self-proving, it can be admitted to probate without testimony of the subscribing witness, thereby avoiding the problems raised by a witness's imperfect recollection of the execution procedure. Check state law.[32]

If the testator later wants to execute a codicil to an attested will, remember that the wills act formalities apply to the codicil (as discussed in Chapter 23).

VI. How Courts Read Wills

The principles that govern construction of a will are not extremely different from those that govern construction of contracts and statutes. However, disputes over wills are likely to involve emotionally laden questions of fairness, need, and just deserts—issues that typically do not arise in a dispute over the meaning of a contract or statute.

The actual probate of the will may not take place until years after its drafting, and the person whose intent is in question is not around to shed any light. In the time between the drafting of the will and the executor's presenting it for probate, many changes may have occurred. The following general discussion is intended only to call your attention to typical approaches to will construction, but you must check your own state's law.

In construing a will, the law that the court applies is the law in effect on the date of the testator's death.[33] Courts generally agree that a court's primary duty in construing a will is to determine the testator's intent and to give effect to it, so long as it does not contradict law or public policy.[34] As is the case for contracts and rule-making documents, the intent under consideration is the intent expressed in the writing's four corners.[35]

If the language of a will is unambiguous, courts give effect to it as written.[36] In such a case, the court typically will not resort to rules of construction[37] or extrinsic evidence to contradict or add to the will[38] or to create an ambiguity where none is apparent.[39]

When is a will ambiguous? The definition of ambiguity is the same for wills as for contracts and statutes. Courts typically find a will ambiguous if its meaning is obscure due to indefiniteness of expression or if it is susceptible to two or more reasonable interpretations.[40]

In construing a will, the court determines the testator's intent based on the entire document. For example, a Nebraska court said that to give effect to a testator's intent, a court must examine the entire will, consider each provision and liberally interpret it using the generally accepted literal and grammatical meaning of the words.[41]

Since the law favors testacy over intestacy, courts generally are reluctant to adopt a reading that would make the entire will or any part of the will meaningless (which would force part or all of the estate to pass by intestacy).[42] For the same reason, if one construction would make a legacy unlawful but another would make it valid, courts generally favor the construction favoring validity.[43]

How does the court determine the meaning of the language? Courts read the words in their ordinary grammatical sense, unless doing so is clearly contrary to their meaning.[44] As discussed in Chapter 23, courts tend to presume that the testator or the drafter knew the law that was in effect when making the will—including the meaning of legal terminology.[45] Courts may presume that the testator knew that the law could change at any time[46] and that changed circumstances could affect the testator's dispositions.[47] Some states may distinguish between the knowledge attributed to a layperson and knowledge attributed to an attorney.[48]

If the will is ambiguous, courts may admit extrinsic evidence to clarify the meaning of the ambiguity.[49] Courts typically state that extrinsic evidence is to be used *only* to show what the testator meant by the will's language—not to introduce other terms not covered in the will[50] or to contradict the words used in the will.[51] In this case, a court may admit extrinsic evidence of the testator's life and circumstances to clear up the question.[52]

To prevent litigation, the drafter should be aware of presumptions that courts may apply in construing an ambiguous will or provision. If the testator's intention runs counter to the usual presumptions concerning meaning, the drafter should take care to make the intention crystal clear so that there is no room for dispute or misunderstanding.

CHAPTER 25

EXERCISES FOR PART 5: WILLS

■ ■ ■

Project: Draft a Will

You are a first-year associate at the high-powered Siler City, Uvada law firm of Thomason and Kwok. Your client is Arthur Jones, who has asked you to draft a will for him based on the format and fact pattern that are set out below.

Before beginning, review Chapters 23 and 24. Keep Chapter 24 open as you draft: you will need it for guidance.

1. Typical Format

Wills are commonly divided into "Articles." The following is an example of a typical format.

Example: Typical Format of a Will

WILL OF _____

Preamble (often incorporating recitals)

ARTICLE ONE
Definitions

ARTICLE TWO
Legacies of Real Property

Section A. Subheading

Section B. Subheading

    (1) Sub-subheading

    (2) Sub-subheading

ARTICLE THREE
Legacies of Personal Property

ARTICLE FOUR
Legacies of Cash or Securities

Example: Typical Format of a Will (cont.)

ARTICLE FIVE
Residue

[Refer to Chapter 24 for additional sections]

---

2. Fact Pattern

A. Facts About Client and Beneficiaries

1. Arthur Jones's Current address: 58 Benjamin Place, Siler City, Occitan County, Uvada.

2. Age: 49.

3. Marital status: Single (never married).

4. Information about intended beneficiaries (name, age, relationship, current address)

- Maybelle Jones Albrecht, age 79, mother, widow, 2 children, 1 grandchild: 58 Schmid Parkway, Siler City, Uvada.

- Alison Jones Temple, age 49, sister, married, 2 children, 1 grandchild: 689 Norton Lane, Lake Merovee, Uvada.

- Brandon Temple, age 24, nephew, married, no children: 45 Grayson Street, Lake Merovee, Uvada.

- John Arkin, age 45, long-time friend and pastor, widowed, 1 child: 49–A Clovis Place, Siler City, Uvada.

- Scout Arkin, age 20, friend's daughter, single: 2411 College Street, St.Germain, Idaware.

- Jane Crawford, age 33, first cousin, single, 3 children: 4590 Tweedle Road, Siler City, Uvada.

- The Siler City Poverty Law Foundation: 10 Main Street, Siler City, Uvada.

- Siler City Community Church: 123 Phoenix Boulevard, Siler City, Uvada.

- The Merovee County Pet Rescue Foundation: 505 Front Street, Lake Merovee, Occitan County, Uvada.

B. Executor

Mr. Jones would like John Arkin to serve as his executor. As successor in case Arkin does not survive or does not serve, Jones has named his sister, Alison Temple; Brandon Temple (nephew) would be successor to Alison. Mr. Jones agreed that the executor should have all the powers available to the executor under Uvada law.

He would like to direct that the executor be permitted to serve without any bond or security being required.

C. Dispositions of Property

Mr. Jones would like to dispose of his real estate as follows: his beach house at 239 North Shore Drive, Port Lochloosa, Floregon is to be sold and the proceeds divided equally between the Poverty Law Foundation, the Siler City Community Church, and the Merovee Pet Rescue Foundation.

Mr. Jones would like you to draft provisions making the following specific dispositions of property. In each case, he intends for the person to receive *the particular* property. When we asked what should happen if it is no longer in his estate at death, he said, "I guess they won't get it." He would like you to *include any quoted language* in the provisions:

- To his twin sister, Alison: his Swinburne teak china cabinet and dining room table ("from our grandmother's house").

- To Jane Crawford: his collection of Jean Albion "World of Dickens" figurines ("to remind her of our trip to London").

- To Scout Arkin: his collection of 28 Mirkwell crystal Christmas tree ornaments ("in memory of so many happy Christmases").

- To John Arkin: his Harley–Davidson 2012 Sportster 1200 Custom Motorcycle ("two words: Occitan Beach!").

- To John Arkin: two paintings by Frans Schalken: "Ice Fair" and "A Game of Chance."

- To Jane Crawford: all the stock in his Nicholas–Grafton account.

- To the Poverty Law Foundation Thrift Shop: all his clothing owned at his death.

- To Jane Crawford: his car.

Mr. Jones would like to make the following gifts of cash or securities:

- To his mother: a cash gift of $50,000 and 5,000 shares of stock; if she does not survive him, the gift to go to his sister, Alison; if Alison does not survive him, the gift to go to his nephew, Brandon Temple; if Brandon does not survive him, to Jane Crawford.

- To his sister Alison: a cash gift of $100,000; if she does not survive him, the gift to go to his nephew, Brandon

Temple; if Brandon does not survive him, to Jane Crawford.

- To John Arkin: a cash gift of $100,000 and 10,000 shares of stock; if John does not survive him, the gift to go to Scout Arkin; if neither Scout nor John survives him, the gift to go to the Siler City Community Church for its benefit and general purposes.

- To Jane Crawford: a cash gift of $50,000 and 2,000 shares of stock; if Jane does not survive him, the gift to go to Jane's children or grandchildren.

- To the Merovee County Pet Rescue Foundation: an unrestricted cash gift of $50,000 for its benefit and general purposes.

- To the Poverty Law Foundation: a cash gift of $25,000, to be used for litigation on behalf of homeless persons, but if at any time in the judgment of the Foundation's trustees it is impracticable to carry out this purpose, Jones wishes them to select an alternative purpose that reflects the spirit of the stated purpose.

- To the Siler City Community Church: an unrestricted cash gift of $30,000 for its general purposes.

Mr. Jones would like to leave the residue of his estate, including all cash, securities, and other personal property in equal shares to John Arkin; if John does not survive him, the residue goes in equal shares to the Merovee County Pet Rescue Foundation, the Poverty Law Foundation, and the Siler City Community Church.

D. Other Issues

1. After questioning Mr. Jones, we concluded that the will should stipulate that a lapsed gift passes into the residue unless the will states otherwise. In other words, he does *not* wish the Uvada anti-lapse statute to apply. (Review Chapter 24 on lapse.)

2. He would like the will to provide that if the order of death determines an interest in property in the case of simultaneous death, he should be deemed the survivor, unless the Legatee survives him by 100 hours. (Review Chapter 24 on simultaneous death).

E. Execution

Under Uvada law, a will must be in writing, signed or acknowledged by the testator in the presence of at least three competent witnesses; witnesses sign in the presence of the testator or each other.

Mr. Jones would like to execute the will at your offices. He will bring three witnesses, who are friends of his from his church:

- Steven Eldon (62–B South End Place, Siler City, Uvada).

- Kevin Heath (210 Lake Street, Lake Merovee, Uvada).

- Jacqueline McLaughlin (128 Donald Street, Siler City, Uvada).

PART 6

ARTICULATING CONTENT

■ ■ ■

- Chapter 26. Choosing Language
- Chapter 27. Drafting Definitions
- Chapter 28. Eliminating Ambiguity
- Chapter 29. Time Clauses and Conditional Statements
- Chapter 30. Exercises for Part 6

CHAPTER 26

CHOOSING LANGUAGE

■ ■ ■

I. Precise Drafting as Preventive Law

Drafting contracts, wills, and rule-making documents is about protecting the client and fulfilling the client's intent. It is about *preventing* disputes—or at least enabling the parties to resolve disputes without the inconvenience, uncertainty, and expense of litigating the text's meaning.

A client hires an attorney to draft a contract for three primary reasons: to help the parties understand their rights and obligations; to provide the parties a written document that will ensure that the transaction runs smoothly; and to enable the parties to resolve disputes by referring to the contract. If the parties get into a dispute and the contract does not resolve the issue, the contract has failed to serve one of its primary functions.

II. Choosing Your Words

A. Know the Meaning of the Words You Choose

1. When Choosing Key Words, Reach for the Dictionary

Courts use dictionaries, and you should too.[1] A Westlaw search will reveal numerous cases in which courts have used dictionaries when construing legal documents. Some courts have looked to more than one dictionary when construing one word or phrase.[2]

Courts read words in a document in their "ordinary" sense unless the document or context indicates that a word is being used in a technical sense or as a term of art. To use a word in its ordinary sense, a drafter must know the ordinary meaning of the word. Where does one find a word's ordinary meaning? As one court suggested, the ordinary meaning of a word "is often best determined through standard, non-legal dictionaries."[3]

Using a dictionary while you draft will reduce the risk of dispute regarding the meaning of a word in your document. If the meaning of a word *is* disputed in court, the dictionary will provide authority for your usage.

When you select a key word to use in a document, make sure that you understand the full range of potential meanings—that you can distinguish between words that seem similar but are not the same. Consider the following groups of words:

- Pay, reimburse, compensate, remit, refund, is liable for.

- Claim, interest, right, demand, liability, cause of action.

- Ensure, assure, insure.

- Fee, compensation, reimbursement, cost, expense, price.

- Insurer, surety, guarantor.

- Contract, agreement, promise, covenant, undertaking.

- Damage, injury, loss, harm, damages, liability.

- Limiting, restricting, prohibiting.

Do you know *all* of the meanings of the words and phrases listed above? Do you know which ones have exactly the same meanings? As between any two, do you know whether one includes the meaning of the other plus additional meanings? Do you know which words have a broad range of meanings and which have a narrow range?

Words are an attorney's primary tool. To draft with precision, you must understand the full range of meanings of key words in your document. A familiar word's full range of meanings might include a meaning that you do not intend to incorporate into your document.

2.   Technical Language or Terms of Art

If you are using a word or phrase in a technical or specialist sense, your usage should be consistent with the word's technical meaning.[4] If you are drafting a contract in a specific field of law (such as insurance law) or if you are drafting a license for a patent, you will not get very far if you do not consult sources that define the technical meaning of the terms of art that apply. Numerous resources are available for drafters entering a new field, such as treatises, journal articles, and CLE presentations.

Courts often adopt or create definitions for words used in legislation or in a particular type of contract. Sometimes, a definition adopted in one type of case is applied in a different type of case. For example, the U.S. Supreme Court, in considering the meaning of a drug trafficking statute, wrote that the word "any" has an expansive meaning: "one or some... of whatever kind."[5] The U.S. Eighth Circuit Court of Appeals later used that definition of "any" when deciding two cases involving insurance policies.[6]

Sometimes, you need to consult case law rather than a dictionary to determine how courts will interpret a word. The same word or phrase may have different meanings in different jurisdictions. Small variations in language may substantially change meaning. Consider the following hypothetical.

Assume that your client, a farmer, has a contract to sell a crop of tomatoes to a manufacturer. When the manufacturer's trucks come to the client's farm to take delivery, one of the trucks runs over the farmer. The contract that your client signed contains a forum-selection clause requiring the parties to litigate in a forum that is 400 miles away all actions "arising out of the contract."

The client does not want to litigate 400 miles away from his farm but would have to do so if a court finds that the negligence action "arises out of the contract." Does it? Would your answer change if you substituted for "arising out of the contract" any of the following phrases?

- Arising under the contract.

- Originating incident to the contract.

- Flowing from the contract.

- Relating to the contract.

- In connection with the contract.

- Resulting from the contract.

As a drafter, you should know whether a judicially interpreted phrase has a settled meaning when used in a particular type of document. To know how such phrases would be interpreted, you must consult case law in your jurisdiction.

Another example: suppose that your client, a musician, retained noted promoter Nicholas Kwok to promote the band. Which type of effort would you prefer him to promise to use:

- Best efforts?

- Reasonable efforts?

- Good faith effort?

- Due diligence?

Again, you would have to consult case law to know how courts in your jurisdiction interpret each phrase and which one would work best for your client.

B. Choose the Right Word

As Mark Twain advised, "Use the right word, not its second cousin." The English language offers a wealth of synonyms. Instead of seizing upon the first word that comes to mind, consult a thesaurus. After you know your options, look up those words in a dictionary to be sure that you choose the ones that have the meaning *that you intend.*

Rather than take the necessary steps to make good choices, many attorneys adopt the "kitchen sink" approach: they throw in every word that could possibly apply—and then some. Insecure or lazy drafters often create a maze of words that leave their readers lost. Given the resources available to drafters (including excellent online dictionaries and thesauruses), no one should substitute excess verbiage for simplicity and clarity.

True, some clients may wish to use a poorly written document to lure gullible parties into a disadvantageous agreement. As Chapter 6 explains, the law has its own ways of dealing with harsh and one-sided agreements that are deliberately designed to entrap the unsuspecting party.

Try working your way through the following real-world settlement agreement (assume that it does not violate any applicable law):

> For the sole consideration of $65,000 to me in hand paid, the receipt of which is hereby acknowledged, I, Releasor, being over 18 years of age, do hereby release and forever discharge Kwok Industries (Releasee) and all other persons, firms, corporations, subsidiaries, successors, parents, officers, directors, and other agents of Releasee from any and all actions, causes of action, claims, rights, lawsuits, liabilities, or demands for damages, costs, loss of use, loss of services, expenses, compensation, consequential damages, or any other thing whatsoever on account of, originating from, arising out of, or in any way growing out of any and all personal injuries (and consequences thereof, including death, and specifically including also any injuries which may exist, but which at this time are unknown and unanticipated and which may develop at some time in the future, and all unforeseen developments arising from known injuries) and any and all property damage resulting from or to result from the occurrence that happened on or about September 30, 2012 at or near 2601 NW Commercial Blvd., Gatortown, Florida.

How far did you get before you lost the plot and started scanning ahead to the end of the sentence, trying to understand what *specifically* the person known as "I" was agreeing to do?

Compare the following, which is the same type of agreement after the drafter eliminated redundant language. Is it easier to understand?

In exchange for payment of $65,000 by Kwok Industries, I release Releasees from any liability to me for personal injury, property damage, or loss of any kind that I suffered as a result of the occurrence on September 30, 2012 at or near 2601 Commercial Blvd., Gatortown, Florida (Occurrence). "Releasees" means Kwok Industries and any of its agents, successors, shareholders, related corporations, related LLCs, or other related entities. I understand that by signing this release, I am giving up all of my future rights to file against Releasees a lawsuit relating to the Occurrence or to any harm resulting from the Occurrence. I am over 18 years old.

III. Delineating the Scope of a Provision

A. Determining the Scope of a Provision

When attorneys negotiate over a provision in a contract or when legislators negotiate over a provision in a law, much of what they are arguing about is the scope of the provision: the extent to which the provision applies to circumstances or persons. One of a drafter's primary tasks is to draft provisions that will apply to all persons to whom and all circumstances in which the client intends the provisions to apply.

A drafter's goal is to delineate precisely the scope of each burden imposed and each right conferred by the document. To determine the scope of a provision, you must first ascertain your client's intentions regarding each of the following:

- Persons or parties to whom the client intends for the provision to apply (including successors in interest, legal representatives, assigns, and agents).

- Rights or interests the client intends for the provision to confer or protect.

- Rights or interests the client intends for the provision to limit or qualify.

- Circumstances or events the client intends to trigger the application of the provision.

- Length of time the client intends for the provision to remain effective.

If the drafter is an effective advocate for a position, the scope of the provision should reflect the client's priorities. Which party was the drafting party in the following examples?

Example 1: Provision Allowing Landlord's Entry

In an emergency, Landlord or its authorized agents may enter the building without giving notice to Tenant. "Emergency" means a situation in which

    (1)   the building or grounds are in immediate danger of serious damage;

    (2)   entry is immediately necessary to prevent serious bodily injury to a person in the building.

Example 2: Provision Allowing Landlord's Entry

In an emergency, Landlord or its authorized agents may enter the building without giving notice to Tenant. "Emergency" means a situation in which entering the building may be necessary

    (1)   to protect landlord's property from damage, or

    (2)   to prevent harm to a person.

The first example is more Tenant friendly: the definition of "emergency" is narrower. The second example is more Landlord friendly, as the definition is broader.

The following examples are statutory provisions that regulate a type of business designated in the statute as a "repair facility." Which provision reflects greater trust by the legislature in the repair facility's good faith? Which shows a greater concern for protecting the consumer?

Example 1: Statutory Provision Regarding "Repair Facility"

Prior to initiating any repair work, the repair facility shall present the customer with a written estimate of the cost of each repair. The repair facility shall provide space for the customer to sign a written authorization for the repairs. The repair facility shall not charge the customer for work performed prior to the customer's written authorization.

Example 2: Statutory Provision Regarding "Repair Facility"

Prior to initiating any repair work, the repair facility shall first present the customer with a written estimate, including an itemized list of the components needing to be repaired or replaced and a firm estimate of the cost of each listed repair. The repair facility shall provide space for

> **Example 2: Statutory Provision Regarding "Repair Facility"** (cont.)
>
> the customer to sign a statement authorizing each repair and to fill in both the date and time of the authorization. The repair facility shall not charge the customer for any work that the repair facility performs prior to the time of the authorization. Unless the repair facility receives the customer's written authorization, the repair facility shall not charge the customer for any authorized repair if the charge exceeds the cost of the repair set out in the itemized statement.

Both provisions build in some consumer protections, but the second example creates more hoops for the repair facility to jump through. The second example reflects greater distrust for the repair facility and greater concern for protecting the consumer.

B. Choosing Language to Delineate the Scope of a Provision

1. Creating Flexible Provisions

(a) Role of Vague Language in Drafting

Vague language plays an important role in the law. Many principles that lawyers take for granted are vague. Where *exactly* does the seller's conduct in making a sale under the UCC cross the line from "good faith" (a vague standard) into "bad faith" (another vague standard)? Under what circumstances is it fair to say that a party has "substantially complied" with a contractual obligation? What does it mean to say that a party has not exercised "due diligence" in complying with a court order or performing a contractual obligation?

A drafter does not always need to specify every circumstance to which a provision applies. When drafting, the drafter might know that a provision needs to extend to a certain *type of circumstance* without being able to specify each specific circumstance that would fit the category—either because the various circumstances would be too numerous or because the precise way that they might come about cannot be predicted. To draft a provision that extends to such circumstances, a drafter needs to use vague language.

Vague language can be *un*ambiguous. Technically, a term is ambiguous if it has two or more inconsistent meanings; legally, it is ambiguous if it is reasonably susceptible to two or more interpretations. In contrast, vague language does not have conflicting meanings; instead, some of the circumstances that could apply are not *clearly* within its scope. While a drafter may intentionally use vague language, a competent drafter would probably not intentionally choose ambiguous language. Compare the following:

Example: Vagueness vs. Ambiguity

Vague:
Landlord shall give Tenant <u>reasonable notice</u> before entering the premises.

Ambiguous:
Buyer may cancel the sale <u>within 3 days</u> after signing the contract.

The phrase "within 3 days" has two possible meanings that conflict: either (1) that the three-day period begins on the date of signing, or (2) that the day of signing is excluded and the period begins on the day after signing. The phrase "reasonable notice" has only one meaning: notice that is "reasonable." However, the language does not define "reasonable," and different readers might not agree as to where the line between "reasonable" and "unreasonable" lies.

A vague standard can work well for the client if the standard is sufficiently definite so that its application and meaning are clear in *most* circumstances in which it is expected to apply. If a circumstance arises that falls within a "gray area," the client may be willing to take the chance that the party or person to whom it applies will argue for a more restrictive application. On the other hand, it is possible for a provision to be overly vague. Subsection III–B–1–(d) discusses the consequences of language that is overly vague.

(b) Using Vague Language to Create Flexible Tests and Standards

A test or standard states a general rule for determining whether a provision applies. Learning to draft tests and standards is essential for a drafter. By using vague language, a drafter can articulate a flexible test or standard instead of having to list every circumstance to which the test or standard applies.

Sometimes it is in the client's interest to draft a narrow test or standard. Sometimes the client may need broader and more flexible language to allow the client greater discretion. Of the following, which test would you prefer if you were the publisher? Which would you prefer if you were the illustrator?

Examples: Tests of Varying Scope

(1)   Unless Author is prevented from timely submitting the illustrations by <u>events not within his control</u>, he will submit the first set of illustrations to Publisher not later than March 31, 2013.

Examples: Tests of Varying Scope (cont.)

(2) Unless Author has obtained an extension of the deadline from Publisher, he will submit the first set of illustrations to Publisher not later than March 31, 2013.

In the first sentence, "not in his control" is a vague standard that gives Health an excuse for missing his deadline. This provision takes away some of the publisher's control over when the manuscript gets submitted and allows the author a degree of flexibility. In the second sentence, the only way that the author can obtain an extension is with the publisher's permission. This provision gives the publisher more control over when the manuscript is submitted, which would be better for the publisher.

Suppose that the City of Gatorboro has asked you to draft a "Code of Professional Conduct" for its employees. Among other things, the city's representatives want a provision that will apply to all employees regarding appropriate dress. One way to accomplish this would be to prepare a detailed dress code for each type of job. Another way would be to draft a standard incorporating vague but limiting language.

Example: Standard Incorporating Vague but Limiting Language

Any person employed by the city at any location shall at all times dress in attire that is conservative, clean, in good condition, appropriate to the nature of the job, and otherwise suitable for a person who represents the city.

Because of vague language, this standard is flexible enough to work for persons doing different jobs: maintenance personnel, lifeguards at the city pool, and all office workers. As framed, the standard provides guidance as to the city's expectations: people are to dress conservatively according to the nature of the job (i.e., the people who maintain the parks should not show up for work in a bathing suit, but a lifeguard can if the swimsuit is also "conservative" and "suitable for a person who represents the city)."

Even so, some gray areas remain. Can the manager of Gatorboro Park (which consists of a swimming pool, clubhouse, playground, and tennis courts) wear a swimsuit to work? In choosing a flexible standard, the city must take for granted that employees would make reasoned decisions about what the standards require.

The downside of a vague and flexible standard is that it can leave room for dispute. When the standard can be enforced by disciplinary action, the drafter must give careful thought to the potential for disagreement between those who enforce the standard and those who have to follow it. When imposing rules that are backed up by the power to impose punishments, those drafting legislation might best protect the public from unintentional infringement by drafting narrowly. Below are more examples of flexible tests or standards.

Examples: Flexible Tests or Standards

- In selecting members of the Litigation Screening Committee, the Board shall ensure that <u>at least two-thirds</u> of the members are environmental attorneys or <u>experts in environmental issues</u>.

- For a student to fulfill the Legal Skills certification requirement, the student must submit to the professor work that is of <u>good professional quality for an attorney</u>.

- The property owner shall <u>regularly</u> inspect the pool fence. If at any time the fence <u>is damaged</u>, the property owner shall <u>promptly</u> repair the fence.

Vague standards are also useful when your client is interested in ensuring a particular outcome without wishing to control how the person to whom the document applies gets to that result. For example, suppose that the City of Gatorboro wants to stop private property owners from allowing lawn sprinklers to spray over city sidewalks. The city does not care how the property owner achieves this result, whether by relocating or removing the sprinklers. Rather than attempting to specify exactly what each owner must do to carry out the ordinance's purpose, the ordinance can focus on the desired outcome (e.g., "An owner of property shall not place a sprinkler in a way that ...").

One flexible standard that is sometimes used in contract drafting is the promise of a party to use "best efforts." Different courts interpret this standard differently.[7] In fact, the U.S. Supreme Court stated that the standard "cannot be defined in terms of a fixed formula; it varies with the facts and the field of law involved."[8]

One federal appellate court determined that "best efforts" means efforts that are reasonable in relation to a party's ability, the means available to the party for carrying out its obligations, and the other party's expectations.[9] A state appellate court found that "best efforts" is primarily a subjective standard under which a party agrees to do the best that it can regardless of the capabilities of others. That court added that "neither success nor the single-minded pursuit of the objective is required."[10]

If you decide to use a vague and flexible standard such as "best efforts," you can reduce the potential for dispute by balancing the vague standard with specific guidelines.

Example: Flexible Standard with Specific Guidelines

Heath will use his <u>best efforts</u> to sell at least 50% of the available seats in the auditorium. To maximize sales, Heath will do the following:

    (1)   Place advertisements for the concert in The Gator Herald,

    (2)   Arrange for ticket sales through all available local outlets, and

    (3)   Post announcements on University bulletin boards.

(c) Consequences of Over–Vagueness

(i) In Public Legislation

In some circumstances, a provision in public legislation can be so uncertain in its application that a court will find that the legislation, if challenged, is void for vagueness. According to the U.S. Supreme Court, it is a basic principle of due process that a statute is void for vagueness if its prohibitions are not clearly defined.[11] Public legislation must therefore be drafted so that a person of ordinary intelligence has a reasonable opportunity to know what is prohibited and to "steer between lawful and unlawful conduct."[12]

Overly vague legislation "impermissibly delegates basic policy matters to policemen, judges, and juries for resolution on an ad hoc and subjective basis, with the attendant dangers of arbitrary and discriminatory application."[13] Thus, the void for vagueness doctrine is concerned both with providing notice to individuals and with establishing minimal guidelines for law enforcement.[14] To determine how courts in your state apply this doctrine, consult the applicable law.

(ii) In a Contract or Private Rule–Making Document

Vague language in a contract or private rule-making document should not be so indefinite that a court cannot determine how the provision is intended to operate. Some courts have said that a provision of a contract is ambiguous if its indefiniteness obscures the parties' intentions.[15] Excessive vagueness can create sufficient uncertainty about meaning and scope to qualify as ambiguity.[16] Thus, while vague language has its uses in contract drafting, a provision must be sufficiently definite to give notice as to what the provision requires.

2.   Drafting to Achieve Definiteness

(a) Using Specific Language

Whereas vague language creates flexibility, specific language creates certainty. Suppose that you draft a rule that is intended to apply to all students at a university. You could *conceivably* draft the provision so that it lists every student who is enrolled at the university—though the provision might contain thousands of names. Also, any unintentional omission of a name would defeat the purpose of the provision. Furthermore, such a provision would be inflexible, as it would apply to only the students whose names are listed. If a new student arrives, the list would have to be updated in order for the provision to remain current.

(b) Using General Categories

A drafter can use general categories for stating a test or standard that applies to all members of a category, even members that do not exist when the provision is drafted. Consider the following example:

> This Conduct Code applies to <u>all students who are registered at this university</u>.

The following is a list of general categories. They are not vague because each contains a finite number of members at any one time (though counting them might not be feasible):

- All of your surviving first and second cousins.

- All of the buildings owned by the university.

- All of the buildings located on campus.

- All of the students attending this university.

- All Texas residents.

C. Canons of Construction Relating to Word Choice

1. Relevance of Canons

The canons of construction are rules to which a court may resort when interpreting a legal document. Typically, a court applies the canons of construction if the plain meaning of the document is not apparent or if the document is open to conflicting interpretations that the court cannot reconcile. Canons of construction are discussed in Chapters 12 and 17.

A drafter who is familiar with the canons can avoid creating the types of problems that require a court to impose its own assumptions about the meaning of language onto the document. A drafter who is unfamiliar with the canons might inadvertently create exactly the type of problem that the canons were designed to resolve. If a court imposes its assumptions onto a document, the outcome might be very different from that intended by the drafter.

2. Common Canons of Construction

(a) Noscitur a Sociis

The canon *noscitur a sociis* ("a word is known by the company it keeps") has been applied in a variety of contexts.[17] A drafter who incorporates a list of related words or phrases in a document must pay attention to how they relate to one another. One court explained, "Terms in a list are interpreted in light of the common characteristics of other terms in the same list."[18]

A court applying *noscitur a sociis* may adopt a narrow meaning of a listed item if (a) giving it a broader meaning would make other listed words or phrases redundant or unnecessary or (b) a broader meaning would make the word or phrase "markedly dissimilar" to the other listed items.[19]

A drafter who includes a list in a document should therefore be attentive to the overall theme that emerges from a list of specifics.[20] The drafter should also be attentive to the placement of the items in a list, because associated words "take color" from each other.[21] Consider the following provision from a contract between a country club and a management company:

> Management Company will regularly inspect and maintain the parking lot, playground, swimming pool, <u>any fence or barrier</u>, the area surrounding the swimming pool, and the swimming pool equipment (such as the diving boards).

Does the management company have to maintain and inspect *all* fences or barriers on the property or only those surrounding the pool? Applying the canon *noscitur a sociis*, a court might conclude that the management company's duties extend only to a fence or barrier that surrounds the pool.

If your goal is to have the provision apply to all the fences and barriers on the property, you might redraft the provision as follows:

> Management Company will regularly inspect and maintain the following: <u>any fence or barrier</u>, the parking lot, the playground, the area surrounding the swimming pool, and the swimming pool equipment (such as the diving boards).

By moving "any fence or barrier" to the beginning of the list, we ensure that it is no longer between two items relating to the pool; thus, it is no longer colored by the swimming-pool theme.

The application of this canon to contracts is discussed in Chapter 12. Its application to statutes and other public rule-making documents is discussed in Chapter 17.

(b) Ejusdem Generis

The canon known as *ejusdem generis* ("of the same kind") is similar in its effects to *noscitur a sociis*.[22] Drafters often include in provisions lists of specifics followed by a general catch-all that the drafter intends to encompass circumstances that were not specifically listed. If a list of specific items is followed by a more general item, a court applying *ejusdem generis* typically will construe the general item as referring to things of the same kind as those specifically listed.[23]

Ejusdem generis is easily illustrated. If a contract excuses a party's performance if the performance is prevented by "tornado, hurricane, flood, or other act of God," would you expect the excuse to apply if the party did not perform due to persistent but moderate rain? By listing "tornado," "hurricane," and "flood" before the general category "act of God," the drafter seems to be signaling that the three specifics are offered as *examples* of what he or she means by "act of God." The three specific examples, taken together, suggest that the theme of the list is sudden and catastrophic events: a lightning strike that causes extensive property damage might qualify, whereas persistent but moderate rains might not. Because of *ejusdem generis*, catch-all language such as "and other similar conditions" might not greatly expand the scope of a list.

In some jurisdictions you can prevent or at least limit application of the canon by using the words "including but not limited to."[24] The U.S. Ninth Circuit Court of Appeals stated that the phrase mitigates "the sometimes unfortunate results of rigid application of the ejusdem generis rule."[25] Other federal court decisions (including decisions from the Tenth and Third Circuits) state that including this language may make *ejusdem generis* inapplicable,[26] but there is contrary authority.[27] Decisions in state courts also vary.[28] Consult the applicable case law.

The application of *ejusdem generis* to contracts is discussed in Chapter 12. Its application to statutes and other public rule-making documents is discussed in Chapter 17.

(c) Expressio Unius est Exclusio Alterius

The canon *expressio unius est exclusio alterius* ("to express one thing is to exclude the others") has been applied in a broad range of situations.[29] One court explained that *expressio unius* is often applied when the drafter lists items in an associated group or series, justifying the inference that items not mentioned were excluded by deliberate choice, not by inadvertence.[30]

If a drafter inadvertently omits a circumstance to which a provision is intended to apply but includes other related circumstances, a court might conclude that the omission was intentional. For example, if one of two related provisions states that it applies to "a trade, business or profession" and the other provision states that it applies to "a trade or business," a court might conclude that the omission of "profession" from the second provision was intentional.

The application of *expressio unius* to contracts is discussed in Chapter 12. Its application to statutes and other public rule-making documents is discussed in Chapter 17.

CHAPTER 27

DRAFTING DEFINITIONS

■ ■ ■

I. When to Use Definitions

It is best to treat definitions as a necessary evil and to keep usage of definitions to a minimum. A reader cannot remember more than a few definitions, and a reader who must constantly refer to a list of definitions will be distracted from the substance of your text.

Deciding which terms to define should not occur until *after* you have completed at least one draft of the document. Only then would you know which terms warrant definition.

When you have decided which definitions you need, these definitions can be placed in a definitions section. Section IV discusses some options for creating definitions sections.

As Chapter 26 discusses, terms in a document are assumed to have their ordinary (dictionary) meaning unless the drafter stipulates otherwise. When selecting your drafting terminology, try to select terms that do not require definition. If you choose terms that accurately reflect your intended meaning and that are used in their usual sense, you may not need to define them.

If you truly need to define a term, make sure that your usage is consistent throughout the document. Avoid defining a term that you then do not actually use in your text.

II. Stipulated Definitions

A. When to Stipulate a Definition

1. In Contracts and Statutes

As numerous cases indicate, courts construing documents read terms in their ordinary and customary sense, unless such a reading would not make sense or unless the drafter stipulates through a definition that the drafter intends for the court to read terms in a broader or more restrictive sense. This principle applies to contracts[1] and to statutes.[2] The U.S.

Supreme Court identified it as a basic principle for statutory construction.[3] It holds as true in the U.S. Tax Court as in any state court. In a 2012 case, for example, the Tax Court, interpreting a provision from the tax code, consulted a Webster's dictionary to ascertain the meanings of terms such as "drill" and "commence."[4]

Consequently, in drafting a contract or statute, you need not stipulate through definition the meaning of even your document's key terms if your usage is consistent with the terms' ordinary meaning. (As discussed in Chapter 26, you might want to cross-check a key term's ordinary meaning in two or three standard dictionaries).

In document drafting, you *should* define a term in the following circumstances:

1) When you use a **term** that has a well-established meaning in a way that narrows or broadens its ordinary scope.

2) When you have invented a **short-hand term** to cover circumstances that would otherwise have to be repeatedly described in the text.

3) When you use a **technical term or legal term of art** that is likely to be unfamiliar to any of the document's users.

4) When the existing case law suggests that including a definition of a particular **term** might prevent litigation.

In what instances is a definition clearly unnecessary? A definition is unnecessary if it merely sets out the ordinary meaning of an ordinary term or defines a technical term if context suggests that the term must be familiar to all parties.

Example: Unnecessary Definition

"Sign" means a display of characters, letters, graphics, or ornamentation that is designed or used for advertising, providing directions or instructions, or making an announcement.

The definition above merely provides the ordinary meaning of the term "sign" as understood by any person with reasonable English-speaking skills. Therefore, there is no need to include the definition in the document.

2. In Wills

As stated in Chapter 23, wills are governed by statute, and the meaning of certain common terms that are likely to be used in a will may be stipulated by statutory definition. In drafting wills, the drafter needs to be aware of the legal meaning of certain terms and to stipulate a definition if the drafter's usage varies. While courts typically do give terms used in a will their plain and ordinary meaning[5] if the terms have no legal meaning, a court may assume that technical language is used in the technical sense.[6] (Some courts are more likely to give language its technical meaning when drafted by a lawyer and more likely to be open to other meanings if drafted by the testator.[7]) Chapter 24 deals with selecting terms for use in a will.

B. Framing a Definition

1. Redefining a Term

To alert a reader to a term used in a specialized sense, you must *stipulate* the definition. The most common type of stipulated definition redefines an ordinary term using the word "means." The word "means" signifies that a complete definition of the term (within the context of the document) is forthcoming. You can use "means" both to change the ordinary scope of a term and to define a shorthand term created to cover certain circumstances.

To alter the ordinary scope of a term, stipulate the term you are defining and set out your definition. For example, *"Document" means a printed document.* The drafter has limited the scope of the term "document" to mean *only* printed material. Such a stipulated definition would be useful if the drafter had reason to expect that some readers might argue that a "document" also includes an electronic document or audio recording. A properly framed definition using "means" effectively redefines the term.

Draft definitions in present tense to reflect that they become effective at the moment the document becomes effective. Below is an example of a term that has been defined three different ways through alteration of the term's scope.

Example: Redefined Term

- "Property" <u>means</u> only tangible personal property.

- "Property" <u>means</u> only privately owned real estate within the city limits.

- "Property" <u>means</u> the building, all fixtures and appurtenances, and the parking lot.

Redefinition of a term using "means" can be useful if you need to expand the meaning to include *future forms* of a person, place, or thing as it changes over time.

Examples: Definitions that Deal with Future Changes

- "Board" means the Board of Directors for Haile Greenery Homeowners' Association <u>and any successor to that Board</u>.

- "Doll" means Dyna–Toy's model 3XZ–001 interactive doll <u>and any future models of that doll</u>.

Another circumstance in which you might stipulate a definition is when you create a shorthand term to substitute for a longer explanation.

Example: Creation of a Short–Hand Term

- "Project K-ban" means the construction project approved by the United States government and described in the attached plans and specifications.

- "Riding animal" means a horse, donkey, mule, camel, ostrich or any other animal that has been trained to carry a rider for a recreational purpose or as a featured show-piece in an attraction.

- "Recreational area" means the main swimming pool and all adjacent areas, including the snack kiosk, changing rooms, and adjoining water-slide pool.

---

2. Narrowing the Ordinary Meaning of a Term

If your intention is to alert a reader that *part* of the ordinary meaning of a term is excluded, you may achieve this by using the phrase "does not include."

Examples: Use of "Does Not Include"

- "Land" <u>does not include</u> land that is owned or under lease to the county, city, state, or federal government.

- "Student" <u>does not include</u> a graduate student.

Using "does not include" subtracts part of the ordinary meaning of the term. It assumes that the reader will understand the meaning that remains. Be sure that readers would understand the ordinary meaning of a term before using "does not include" to narrow the scope of the ordinary meaning.

In general, we recommend that you use both "means" and "does not include" unless you are certain that the reader will understand the meaning that remains when the "not included" meaning is subtracted.

> **Examples: Use of "Means" and "Does Not Include"**
>
> - "Property" <u>means</u> tangible personal property <u>but does not include</u> property used strictly for family or household use.
>
> - "Public way" <u>means</u> a city-owned road, street, or other public way <u>but does not include</u> a sidewalk.

3.   Broadening the Ordinary Meaning of a Term

If your intention is to alert a reader that you are broadening the scope of a term, you may achieve this by using the word "includes." For example, *"Document" includes a video file in AVI or Mpeg format.*

An "includes" definition might also signal that you are using the term in a sense that in context is unexpected:

- "Land" includes <u>land under lease to the county, city, state, or federal government</u>.

- "Student" includes <u>a part-time student or an exchange student visiting from another University</u>.

When you use "includes" to define a term, do not list all the possible meanings; instead, list only those that are added to the ordinary meaning.

Used with a "means" definition that redefines a term, "includes" can serve a useful function in delineating the scope of a defined term:

> **Examples: Use of "Means" and "Includes"**
>
> - "Doll house" <u>means</u> a doll house constructed by Katie T. or her apprentice and <u>includes</u> a floor model of the doll house.
>
> - "Thoroughfare" <u>means</u> any county-owned street, road, or access way and <u>includes</u> a sidewalk, bicycle path, trail, or bridge.

III.   Setting Out Definitions in the Document

A.   Placement and Format

Definitions should be placed in alphabetical order within a definitions section. You should use some sort of device (e.g., quotation marks, italicizing, or bolding) to distinguish the defined term from its definition.

**Examples: Device for Distinguishing
Term from Definition**

- "Property" <u>means</u> only tangible personal property.

- *Property* <u>means</u> only privately owned real estate within the city limits.

- **Property** <u>means</u> the building, all fixtures and appurtenances, and the parking lot.

Choose the option that you think best or that your teacher prefers.

B.   Definitions Sections

1.   Single Definitions Section for Entire Document

A drafter could set up a single definitions section for the entire document. A definitions section is adequately identified by the heading "Definitions," lettered or numbered like any other section of the document. Usually legislative documents and wills that contain definitions will put all defined terms within a single section at or near the beginning of the document.

Example: "Definitions" Section

Section 44–11. Definitions

   (1) "At large" means off-leash and unconstrained by a restraining device or a pen.

   (2) "City" means the City of Micanopia, Florida.

   (3) "Dog custodian" means a person who owns, has custody of, or is otherwise in control of a dog.

   (4) "Pen" means an enclosure that meets the requirements of section 4–15(c) of this ordinance.

   (5) "Under restraint" means under the dog custodian's physical control by means of a leash, halter, or similar restraining device.

---

2.   Placement of Definition of Term That Appears Only Once

If a term appears only once in a document, a drafter may choose not to place it in a definitions section but to define it "in place" (i.e., near the text where the term appears). A drafter who defines a term in the text should place the definition immediately *after* the sentence in which the defined term appears, as in the following example:

A dog custodian shall not permit a dog to wander at large within the city limits. "At large" means off-leash and unconstrained by a restraining device or a pen.

3.   Creation of Multiple Definitions Section

In a contract, the drafter has a great deal of flexibility regarding placement of definitions. In a lengthy or complex contract or in any contract containing numerous definitions, the drafter could create multiple definitions sections. The value of this approach is that the definitions appear where the defined terms are used. Thus, the reader does not have to keep looking back at one definitions section to check the meanings of terms. Below are some guidelines for creating multiple definitions sections:

- If the term appears under more than one main heading, then the term should be defined in the definitions section at the beginning of the document.

- If the term appears under more than one subsection of a main heading, then the term should be defined in a definitions section under that main heading.

- If the term appears under more than one sub-subsection of a subsection, then the term should be defined in a definitions section at the beginning of that subsection.

**Example: Definitions in Multiple Sections
of an Ordinance**

Section 44–1. Definitions

  (1) "City" means the city of Micanopia, Florida.

  (2) "Dog custodian" means a person who owns, or who has custody or is otherwise in control of, a dog.

  (3) "Under restraint" means under the dog custodian's physical control, by means of a leash, halter, or similar restraining device.

Section 44–2. Restraint of Dogs within City …

Section 44–3. Enforcement of Ordinance

   (A)   Definition

   "At large" means off-leash and unconstrained by another restraining device or pen and therefore free to wander about at will.

   (B)   Notice to Dog Custodian of Violation

**Example: Definitions in Multiple Sections
of an Ordinance** (cont.)

(C)   **Restraint of Dangerous Dog**

   (1) **Confinement of Dangerous Dog within a
   Pen**

   Unless the dog is muzzled according to the
   requirements of subsection (2) below, the dog
   custodian shall keep the dangerous dog confined
   within a pen. "Pen" means an enclosure made
   from ... that is enclosed on four sides and over
   its top.

   (2) **Muzzling of Dangerous Dog** ...

IV.   Common Errors

A.   Check the Grammar of Your Definition

The defined term and its definition must be grammatically parallel to one another. Parallel structure is discussed in Chapter 31. Can you see the problem with the following?

Examples: Grammatically Un-parallel Definitions

1.   "Under restraint" means that the dog's owner has placed the dog on a leash or other restraining device.

2.   "Approved course" means that the course is a seminar, externship, clinical course, or independent study that the committee has approved for inclusion in the program.

If the defined term and the definition are grammatically parallel, you can substitute the definition for the defined term at any point in your text. Try that with the first definition in the example above. If you substitute the definition for the defined term in the sentence, the sentence would not work:

> The dog's owner shall keep the dog ~~under restraint~~ the dog's owner has placed the dog on a leash or other restraining device.

Suppose that you rephrase the definition as follows:

> "Under restraint" means on a leash or other restraining device.

The defined term and the definition are now grammatically parallel. You *can* substitute the definition for the defined phrase:

> The dog owner shall keep the dog ~~under restraint~~ on a leash or other restraining device.

B.   Avoid Burying Rules in Definitions

Do not bury substantive rules in definitions because the reader might not look at the definition to find the rule. As a result, buried rules may seldom be seen or followed.

A definition is not really part of the *operative provisions* of a document because a definition simply notifies the reader of the scope of a term. If, in setting out a term's definition, you find yourself articulating a rule, obligation, requirement, or right, then you have buried a rule in a definition. The best way to avoid burying rules in definitions is to write your text first and decide afterward whether it is necessary to create definitions.

**Example: Rules Buried in Definition and
Way to Solve Problem**

Definition:

"Notice" means written notice of a breach which, <u>no later than the 3rd day after the non-breaching party becomes aware of the breach</u>, is delivered to the breaching party.

Problem:

The drafter improperly framed as a definition of "notice" a rule for giving notice.

Solution:

- Restate the definition as a rule: "To give notice of a breach, the non-breaching party must deliver written notice of the breach to the breaching party no later than the 3rd day after the non-breaching party becomes aware of the breach"; and

- Place the rule in the part of the text where it belongs instead of in the Definitions Section.

C.   Strained Definitions

A definition is strained when the definition distorts the ordinary meaning of the defined term. Drafters are likely to encounter this problem when drafting very broad definitions or when broadening the meaning of a redefined term to include unusual meanings. Consider the following examples:

Examples: Strained Definitions

1. "Pool" means the swimming pool, the diving area, all areas or platforms surrounding the pool, and <u>the refreshment kiosk</u>.

> **Solution:** pick a broader term to apply to the area, such as "pool area."

2. "Car" includes a pick-up truck, <u>motorcycle</u>, or other non-commercial gasoline-propelled vehicle.

> **Solution:** pick a broader term to apply to these vehicles, such as "vehicle."

If a stipulated definition departs too far from the ordinary meaning of a term, it strains the reader's willingness to accept the stipulation. For that reason, we recommend that you avoid creating strained definitions.

CHAPTER 28

ELIMINATING AMBIGUITY

■ ■ ■

I. Recognizing Ambiguity

A word or phrase is ambiguous if it is susceptible to more than one reasonable meaning. Detecting ambiguity is difficult for the drafter: as the person who drafted the document, you know what you meant. As the person who selected the language, you will usually be too close to it to spot problems unless you step away from it for a bit. For that reason, you should leave time in your drafting process to step away from a document so that you can come back to it with fresh eyes.

Below are six common causes of ambiguity:

1) Modifier placement.

2) Pronoun usage.

3) Plural usage.

4) Words or phrases with more than one meaning in a context.

5) Inconsistent sentences or provisions.

6) Punctuation (or lack thereof).

II. Ambiguity Caused by Modifier Placement Problems

A. Importance of Modifier Placement

A modifier is a word or phrase that limits or qualifies another word or phrase in a sentence. In English, it is very easy to write an *apparently* clear and grammatical sentence that is ambiguous due to the misplacement of a modifier. This form of ambiguity occurs whenever a modifier—or even a modifying symbol, such as a percentage sign—falls in a position that makes unclear to which part of the sentence the modifier applies.

Courts sometimes resolve modifier-placement issues by applying the doctrine of the last antecedent, a rule of construction (discussed in

Chapters 12 and 17). Do not rely on rules of construction, and do not count on them being applied in your favor if your document ends up being litigated.

Instead, prevent ambiguity by precisely placing all modifiers in your document. The key to precise modifier placement is to place the modifier:

- As close as possible to the word or phrase that it is supposed to modify.

- In a position that prevents the modifier from potentially modifying a different word or phrase.

Chapter 31 discusses modifier-placement problems and how to resolve them.

B. Examples: Common Modifier–Placement Problems

1. Imprecise Use of Percentages

A percentage in an awkwardly worded sentence might seem to apply where it is not intended to apply.

Example: Ambiguous Placement of Percentage Symbol

K–Marketing will reimburse <u>50%</u> of Employee's per diem expenses for meals and all expenses for hotel accommodations.

Does the 50% apply only to "per diem expenses for meals" or also to "all expenses for hotel accommodations"? Or will K–Marketing reimburse the employee 50% of per diem expenses for meals and 100% of expenses for hotel accommodations?

Examples: Clear Placement of Percentage Symbol

- K–Marketing will reimburse Employee for <u>50%</u> of Employee's per diem expenses for meals and <u>50%</u> of Employee's expenses for hotel accommodations.

- K–Marketing will reimburse Employee for <u>50%</u> of Employee's per diem expenses for meals. K–Marketing will reimburse <u>100%</u> of Employee's expenses for hotel accommodations.

A related problem does not result from modifier misplacement but from the failure of the drafter to state *to what* a percentage applies.

Example: Unstated Application of Percentage

If the owner does not timely reimburse the city for the city's expenses for removing the debris from the owner's property, the owner shall pay the city a <u>10% penalty</u>.

The owner shall pay 10% *of what*? Of the market value of the owner's property? Of the owner's property-tax assessment? The drafter likely meant 10% of the city's cost of removing the debris, but that is not what the text actually says.

Do not rely on the reader to make assumptions about your text. Instead, devote a few keystrokes to clearly stating what the percentage applies to.

Example: Clearly Stated Application of Percentage

If the owner does not timely reimburse the city for its expenses for removing the debris from the owner's property, the owner shall pay the city a penalty equal to <u>10% of the city's total costs for removing debris from the owner's property</u>.

---

2. Ambiguous Maximum (or Cap)

Payment provisions may involve a maximum or cap. If you are not careful about sentence structure, it is easy to draft such provisions so that they are ambiguous.

Example: Cap with Unclear Application

K–Marketing will reimburse 80% of Employee's per diem expenses for hotel accommodations, <u>not to exceed a maximum of $200 a day</u>.

What cannot exceed $200 a day: the total per-night-hotel expenses or 80% of those expenses? If Employee spent $400 for one night in a hotel, the reimbursement would work out as follows:

1) If the cap applies to the per-night-hotel expenses, then Employee would get <u>$160</u> (i.e., 80% of $200).

2) If the cap applies to the total reimbursement (80% of per-night-hotel expenses), then Employee would get <u>$200</u> (the cap).

That $40–per–day difference could become significant to K–Marketing if the employee travels regularly.

Again, all it would take to remove the ambiguity is some thought and a few keystrokes.

Example: Cap with Clearly Stated Application

Section 6. For Employee's per diem expenses for hotel accommodations, K–Marketing will reimburse to Employee a maximum amount that is the lesser of the following:

(A) $200 per day for accommodations, or

(B) 80% of the amount that Employee expends per day for accommodations.

---

3. Ambiguous Price and Quantity Provisions

Yet another common problem is ambiguity relating to the price or number of items. Below are two examples.

Examples: Ambiguous Payment Amount and Number of Items

1. In return for this valuable memento, Buyer will pay to Sports Museum $1,000 in four monthly installments.

2. Thomason Industries will ship to Buyer 9,000 decorative plates in three shipments.

The examples directly above leave important questions open:

1) Will Sports Museum pay $1,000 total (i.e., four installments of $250 each) or $4,000 (i.e., four installments of $1,000 each)?

2) Will Thomason Industries ship a total of 9,000 plates (three shipments of 3,000 plates each) or 27,000 plates (three shipments of 9,000 each)?

Minor revisions could prevent those ambiguities.

Examples: Clearly Stated Payment Amount and Number of Items

1(a) In return for this valuable memento, Buyer will pay to Sports Museum a total of $1,000 by paying four monthly installments of $250 each.

1(b) In return for this valuable memento, Buyer will pay to Sports Museum a total of $4,000. Buyer will make the payment in four monthly installments of $1,000 each.

Examples: Clearly Stated Payment Amount and Number of Items (cont.)

2(a)   Thomason Industries will ship to Buyer <u>a total of 9,000</u> decorative plates in <u>three shipments of 3,000 plates each</u>.

2(b)   Thomason Industries will ship to Buyer a <u>total of 27,000</u> decorative plates. Thomason Industries will ship the plates in three <u>shipments of 9,000 plates each</u>.

---

4.   Ambiguity Arising From "Squinting Modifier"

A "squinting modifier" is one that is placed between two words or phrases and could apply to either one.

Example: Squinting Modifier

If Edeback Imports gives notice of a defect, <u>on or before the 15th day after the day that Edeback Imports receives the shipment</u>, Seller shall refund to Edeback Imports the purchase price of the shipment.

To which part of the sentence does the underlined language apply: when Edeback gives notice or when Seller gives the refund? One way to revise this sentence is to break it into two separate sentences.

Example: Squinting Modifier Eliminated

• <u>Modifier Applies to Notice</u>

For Edeback Imports to be entitled to a refund of the purchase price, Edeback Imports must give notice to Seller on or before the 15th day after the day that Temples Imports receives the shipment. If Edeback Imports timely gives notice of the defect, Seller shall refund to Edeback Imports the purchase price of the shipment.

• <u>Modifier Applies to Refund</u>

If Edeback Imports gives Seller notice of the defect, Seller shall refund to Edeback Imports the purchase price of the shipment. Seller shall refund the purchase price no later than the 15th day after Edeback Imports receives the shipment.

Watch out for "only," "exclusively," and "solely," as they are particularly likely to squint in two directions. Chapter 31 further discusses modifier-related ambiguity.

III. Ambiguity Caused by Pronouns

Pronoun usage can cause ambiguity that context might resolve—or might not. Even if you can rely on context, you should get rid of ambiguous pronouns wherever you see them. Creating clarity is a good habit to develop.

Ambiguity caused by pronoun usage commonly arises in documents that apply to human beings of the same sex or to legal entities.

**Examples: Ambiguous Pronoun Usage: Humans
and Legal Entities**

1. For <u>her</u> actual expenses in putting on the event, Deb will reimburse Maggie either $10,500 or <u>her</u> total actual expenditures in putting on the event, whichever is less.

2. Plaza, LLC will reimburse Kwokscaping, Inc. for any difference in expense for any landscaping material that <u>it</u> determines is a reasonable substitute.

Which "her" is intended: Deb or Maggie? Which party gets to decide what qualifies as a "reasonable substitute": Plaza, LLC or Kwokscaping, Inc? Those ambiguities are disputes waiting to happen.

Even if the parties could figure out the answers, fix the problematic pronoun usage anyway by omitting the pronouns and using the parties' names instead.

Examples: Clear Provisions (i.e., no pronouns)

1(a) For <u>Maggie's</u> actual expenses in putting on the event, <u>Deb</u> will pay <u>Maggie</u> either $10,500 or <u>Maggie's</u> total actual expenditures in putting on the event, whichever is less.

1(b) For <u>Deb's</u> actual expenses in putting on the event, <u>Maggie</u> will pay <u>Deb</u> either $10,500 or <u>Deb's</u> total actual expenditures in putting on the event, whichever is less.

2(a) Plaza, LLC will reimburse Kwokscaping, Inc. for any difference in expense for any landscaping material that <u>Kwokscaping, Inc.</u> determines is a reasonable substitute.

2(b) Plaza will reimburse Kwokscaping for any difference in expense for any landscaping material that <u>Plaza, LLC</u> determines is a reasonable substitute.

As the examples in this section show, it is easy to eliminate ambiguity resulting from pronouns. All you have to do is remove the pronouns altogether. A pronoun-free writing style may be more cumbersome, but it will be clearer and less likely to create a costly dispute.

If you are drafting a form contract, it is easy to unintentionally create pronoun ambiguity since you cannot know in advance whether the other party will be a male, female, or corporation. If you are drafting a form contract, it is best to avoid pronouns altogether. Use the principles discussed in Chapter 33 for drafting gender-neutral documents.

IV. Ambiguity Caused by Plurals

When possible, avoid plurals in document drafting. Though plurals will not necessarily create two meanings that are *reasonably* susceptible to different interpretations, they can be pointlessly confusing.

Example: Ambiguous Plurals

Students with disabilities shall file medical reports in support of their applications for accommodations.

How many disabilities does the student have to have to qualify for an accommodation? How many medical reports and applications need to be filed per accommodation? If you want the person reading the provision to understand what he or she is actually supposed to do, use singular nouns. Below is the revised provision.

Example: Clear Use of Singular Nouns

A Student with a disability shall file a medical report in support of the student's application for an accommodation.

V. Ambiguity Caused by Word Choice

A. Words and Phrases With More Than One Meaning

If a word or phrase in a document has more than one meaning within the context, ambiguity can result. Chapters 26 and 27 discuss some techniques for clarifying meaning.

B. Common Examples

1. "Subject to"

The phrase "subject to" often appears in legal documents. Its exact meaning is rarely apparent from its use. Below are two examples.

Examples: Ambiguous Usage of "Subject to"

1. A Lessee who fails to timely pay rent is <u>subject to</u> a late fee.

2. An employee who either threatens or verbally abuses another employee is <u>subject to</u> dismissal by the employer.

The two provisions directly above leave important questions unanswered:

1) Would the lessee automatically have to pay a late fee, or would the lessor have the option of charging a late fee?

2) Would the threatening or abusive employee automatically be fired, or would the employer have the option of firing that employee?

Instead of using "subject to," write language that precisely expresses your meaning.

Examples: Clearer Provisions (without "Subject to")

1(a) If Lessee pays the rent after the due date, Lessee <u>shall pay</u> Lessor a late fee.

1(b) If Lessee pays the rent after the due date, Lessor <u>may charge</u> Lessee a late fee.

2(a) The employer <u>shall dismiss</u> an employee who either threatens or verbally abuses another employee.

2(b) The employer <u>may dismiss</u> an employee who either threatens or verbally abuses another employee.

---

2. "Term"

In a document, "term" could refer to any of the following:

- The time period during which the parties' must perform.
- Any provision of the document.
- A particular right, obligation, duty, requirement, or policy.
- A word or phrase.

Below are examples of "term" used in various ways and some substitutes.

"Term or Terms"	Substitute word or phrase
For the entire lease <u>term</u>, Tenant will comply with the Landlord's rules and regulations.	For the entire lease <u>period</u>, Tenant will comply with Landlord's rules and regulations.

"Term or Terms"	Substitute word or phrase
The parties may modify a lease term if they set forth the modification in a writing that is signed by both parties.	The parties may modify a lease provision if they set forth the modification in a writing that is signed by both parties.
In this lease, the following terms have the following meanings:	In this lease, the following words and phrases have the following meanings:

Instead of the word "term," consider other options. If you use the word "term" in a document, choose *one* of its possible meanings. For example, do not use it in the same document to refer both to time periods and to provisions.

3. "And" and "Or"

The words "and" and "or" can create ambiguity. As courts have pointed out, the conjunctions 'and' and 'or' are frequently used interchangeably.[1] The words "and" and "or" have an overlapping as well as a distinct meaning.

Issues that require a court to muse upon the meaning of "and" and "or" arise when the context does not make it absolutely clear which meaning of "and" or "or" is intended.[2]

Example: Ambiguous "Or"

In determining whether to admit an applicant to the program, a committee member may consider the applicant's response to the essay question, score on the aptitude test, or videotaped interview.

May the committee member consider *all* of those items in making the determination or should the member consider only one of them? To clarify the meaning, the drafter should tweak the language to more precisely reflect the drafter's intent.

Examples: Clarified "Or"

- In determining whether to admit an applicant to the program, a committee member may consider any one of the following: the applicant's response to the essay question, score on the aptitude test, or videotaped interview.

- In determining whether to admit an applicant to the program, a committee member may consider all of the following: the applicant's response to the essay question, score on the aptitude test, or videotaped interview.

Because the meaning of "and" and "or" are so context driven, a drafter can easily miss an ambiguity that may cause problems.

Example: Ambiguous "And"

The manager shall dismiss the employee for threatening <u>and</u> verbally abusing another employee.

Is the manager required to fire an employee only if the employee *both* threatens and verbally abuses another employee? If so, does that mean that if the employee merely threatens another employee that the manager *does not* have to fire the threatening employee? Or was the provision intended to require the manager to fire any employee who *either* threatens or verbally abuses another employee?

The way to clarify the provision is to redraft it. Below are three examples of ways to redraft that provision.

Examples: Clarified "And"

1. The manager shall dismiss an employee if the employee <u>both</u> threatens <u>and</u> verbally abuses another employee.

2. The manager shall dismiss an employee <u>if</u> the employee threatens another employee <u>or if</u> the employee verbally abuses another employee.

3. The manager shall dismiss an employee who <u>either</u> threatens <u>or</u> verbally abuses another employee.

Example 1 requires the manager to fire an employee only if the employee engages in *both* forms of misconduct. Examples 2 and 3 require the manager to fire an employee who engages in *only one* form of misconduct.

As we have shown, there are multiple ways to reframe a sentence to eliminate an ambiguity regarding "and" or "or." Below are some clarifying words and phrases:

- Either … or.
- Both … and.
- All of the following.
- Each of the following.
- Any of the following.
- Any one of the following.
- Any combination of the following.

Some drafters use "and/or" when trying to eliminate ambiguity, though "and/or" can create logical flaws if it is misused. Below are two examples.

Examples: Illogical "And/or"

1. Cupples Imports will pay the amount due in installments <u>and/or</u> in a one-time payment.

2. The penalty for first degree murder is the death penalty <u>and/or</u> life imprisonment.

Once a person is executed, how can that person also serve a life sentence? If a party pays the amount due as a one-time payment, why would that party also pay multiple installments?

We do not recommend "and/or." Cases in which courts have analyzed the meaning of "and/or" indicate that "and/or" can actually create ambiguity.[3]

4. "Is Responsible ..." and "Has the Responsibility ..."

Chapter 6 discusses why "is responsible ..." and "has the responsibility ..." are ambiguous and how to reframe a sentence to remove the ambiguity.

VI. Ambiguity Caused by Inconsistency

Consistency is crucial to clarity. Inconsistent words, phrases, sentences, or provisions can produce internal conflict within the document. If the text conflicts, it may be susceptible to two or more reasonable interpretations: i.e., an ambiguity may arise. In that case, a dispute may follow, and judicial construction may ensue. What follows are a few ways that drafters commonly create inconsistency:

*   By using different words or phrases to refer to one thing.

*   By addressing part of an issue in one sentence or section and another part in another sentence or section without making clear how the related sentences or sections affect each other.

*   By addressing the same issue in two different sections without inserting a cross-reference or without making clear how the provisions affect each other.

To eliminate ambiguity, check for the following:

*   Inconsistency in the use of words or phrases.

*   Overlapping sentences.

*   Overlapping sections (i.e., multiple sections covering the same issue).

- Sentences or sections that could be triggered by the same action or event but that would produce different outcomes.

Chapter 21 addresses how to resolve ambiguity caused by conflicting sentences, provisions or sections.

VII. Ambiguity Caused by Punctuation Usage

Punctuation errors can lead to disputes that end up in litigation. While courts are typically loath to allow punctuation to override the plain meaning that is otherwise discernible from a document's language,[4] courts do rely on punctuation to illuminate a document's plain meaning.[5] To understand courts' attitudes toward ambiguous punctuation, you must read and reconcile relevant cases.

Punctuation and grammar can play a significant role in determining meaning, and punctuation can actually mandate a particular reading of a text.[6] In a U.S. Ninth Circuit Court of Appeals case, lack of proper punctuation had expensive consequences for the drafter.[7] An often-quoted Texas case said, "While punctuation may be resorted to in order to solve an ambiguity which it has not created, punctuation or the absence of punctuation will not of itself create ambiguity."[8] A Delaware court said something similar.[9]

In an Indiana case involving a badly punctuated statute regarding the illegal sale of fireworks, the defendants relied partly on a semicolon when arguing that the defendants had not violated that statute.[10] The case went up to the Indiana Supreme Court, which examined the statute's language and found that legislative intent trumped the legislature's bad punctuation.[11] That court said, "We are not obligated to engage in a debate on the significance of semicolons and disjunctives when doing so renders the statute absurd or produces a result repugnant to the apparent intent of the legislature."[12]

In short, a drafter cannot rely solely on punctuation to set forth intent but cannot afford to get punctuation wrong. Chapter 32 further discusses punctuation.

CHAPTER 29

TIME CLAUSES AND CONDITIONAL STATEMENTS

■ ■ ■

I. Drafting Time Clauses

A. The Importance of Ambiguity–Free Time Clauses

Time clauses are crucial to contracts and rule-making documents. Some courts might find a contract unenforceable if there is uncertainty concerning the time for performance of material obligations.[1] Uncertainty regarding a time period in a statute might create, in the words of the California Supreme Court, "the gravest considerations of public order and security."[2]

Many jurisdictions have guidelines dictating how courts should interpret time clauses in statutes, which suggests that ambiguity in time clauses has historically been a problem for drafters.[3] By drafting a time clause without ambiguity, you eliminate the need for intervention by a court—which can be costly, time-consuming, and aggravating.

B. Types of Time Clauses

There are four basic types of time clauses:

1) A **due date**, which establishes a single date for an action.

2) A **deadline**, which requires action on or before a certain date.

3) A **cut-off date**, which precludes a person from receiving a benefit or exercising a right after a certain date.

4) A **duration period**, which sets a time frame.

Time clauses are easy to draft when the drafter knows in advance any relevant dates. For example, a local government could decide that the deadline for paying property taxes is October 31, or a landlord could decide that rent is due on the third of each month. Even if you do not know the dates when drafting a contract, your client and the other party might be able to fill in the dates during negotiations or at signing.

In some cases, neither the drafter nor the parties can know in advance the exact dates of relevant events. For example, a drafter might draft a city ordinance that imposes a fine on any person who fails to remedy a violation before a certain number of days after receiving notice of the violation. In that case, the drafter cannot know on what date any person will violate the ordinance or receive notice.

Similar problems can occur regarding contracts. For example, a drafter might draft a contract for an orange grower who wants to sell her entire crop to a juice manufacturer, and the parties might want to enter the contract *before* the oranges are even buds on the trees. In that case, the parties would not know in advance the exact date that the crop would be ready for harvest or delivery. Situations in which the parties cannot determine relevant dates in advance require the drafter to draft a formula for determining the date.

As discussed in the remainder of Section I, we recommend that you use certain precise phrases in drafting time clauses. If you choose another way to articulate time-related terminology, make sure that the other way is completely ambiguity-free.

C. Drafting Time Clauses Stating a Due Date, Deadline or Cut-off

1. Due Dates, Deadlines and Cut-offs with Specified Dates

If you are stating a due date, deadline or cut-off and know the date in advance, the following template should work:

Basic Template for Time Clause with Specified Date

Time-clause-signifying word or phrase + Date

(On or before May 2, 2013)

Unless you intend to stipulate the time of day, we recommend that you use one of the following words or phrases as a time-clause signifier:

Examples: Precise Time–Clause Signifiers

For Due Dates:

"On"

For Deadlines and Cut-offs:

- On or before …

- No (or not) later than …

- On a date that is no (or not) later than …

Examples: Precise Time–Clause Signifiers (cont.)

- On or after …

- No (or not) earlier than …

- On a date that is no (or not) earlier than …

Below are a few examples of due dates, deadlines and cut-offs.

**Examples: Due Dates, Deadlines and Cut-offs
with Specified Dates**

- <u>On or before the first day of each calendar month</u>, Tenant shall pay rent to Landlord.

- <u>No later than February 18, 2012</u>, the student may apply to the committee for reconsideration of the application.

- <u>On a date that is not later than January 15 of each year of membership</u>, Member shall pay dues to Club.

- <u>No earlier than 8:00 a.m. on September 9, 2013 and no later than 5:00 p.m. on September 30, 2013</u>, a contractor may submit a bid to The City.

---

2. Due Dates, Deadlines, and Cut-offs with Unspecified Dates

For a time clause to be unambiguous, (1) the exact date of a due date, deadline or cut-off must be determinable; and (2) the formula for determining the date must be such that it *cannot* yield more than one result. Below are the steps for stating a precise time clause that has an unspecified date.

Steps for Stating Time Clause with Unspecified Date

Step 1. Set out the time-clause signifier:
    e.g., "No later than"

Step 2. State the exact day of the due date, deadline or cut-off:
    e.g., "the 30th day"

Step 3. Exclude the day on which the countdown begins:
    e.g., "after"

Step 4. Tie the countdown-triggering event to *one* day:
    e.g., "the date that"

Step 5. Describe in present tense the event that triggers the countdown:
    e.g., "Buyer takes delivery of the goods"

Below is a time clause that we created by using the steps and sample language listed above.

Example: Unambiguous Deadline

<u>No later than the 30th day after the date that Buyer takes delivery of the goods</u>, Buyer will pay Seller for the goods.

One common problem with time statements is the ambiguously phrased countdown-triggering event.

Example: Ambiguous Countdown–Triggering Event

On or before the 20th day after <u>the notice date</u>, the occupant shall complete any maintenance that the City has specified in the notice.

What does "notice date" mean? The date that the City sent the notice? The date that appears on the notice? If the occupant cannot determine what "notice date" means, how can she figure out the deadline for compliance?

To avoid ambiguity, precisely describe the event that triggers the countdown. Use present tense, and eliminate *only* those words that perform no function in the sentence.

Examples: Clear Countdown–Triggering Event

• On or before the 20th day after <u>the date that appears on the notice</u> …

• On or before the 20th day after <u>the date that the City sends the notice</u> …

Another common problem is the *omission* of a triggering event, which creates an ambiguity that could result in a dispute about the provision's meaning.

Examples: Missing Triggering Events

1. Buyer must send notice to Seller <u>within three days</u>.

2. Lessee <u>has five days</u> to cure the breach.

3. The City shall give <u>60 days' notice</u> to the property owner.

The examples above leave open some important questions:

1) Within three days *of what*, and is that before or after some event?

2)   Is the deadline five days after Lessee commits a breach or five days after Landlord makes some sort of demand?

3)   Sixty days counted from *when?*

In each example, the ambiguity could have been removed through a few minutes of thought and a few keystrokes.

Below are a few more examples of clear, unambiguous time clauses.

Examples: Unambiguous Time Clauses with Unspecified Dates

- To prevent renewal of the lease period, the non-renewing party must notify the other party no later than the 30th day before the date that the lease expires.

- On or before the 20th day after the date that appears on the notice, the occupant shall complete performance of any maintenance that the City has required in the notice.

- At or before 1:00 p.m. on the 15th day following the day on which Farmer Kwok tenders the crop for delivery at his warehouse, FlaJuice will pay Farmer Kwok the full amount due for the crop.

- At least three days before entering the premises, Landlord shall provide written notice to Tenant.

D.   Drafting Time Clauses That State a Duration Period

1.   Duration Periods With Specified Dates

Drafting a duration period is easy if you know the beginning and ending dates in advance or if your client can determine them at some point before signing a contract or adopting a rule-making document. If you know the dates, write them into the contract or legislation. If you do not know the dates but will know them before the document becomes effective, leave blanks to be filled in.

Even if you know the dates in advance, we recommend that you use at least two sentences when establishing a duration period:

1)   a sentence that states the intended length of the period.

2)   a sentence that sets forth the dates (or provides blanks).

**Examples: Duration Periods with Specified
Dates (or Blanks)**

• The consulting period is for six months. The consulting period begins on January 1, 2012 and ends on June 30, 2012.

• The lease period is for one year. The lease period begins on _____ and ends on _____.

---

2. Duration Periods With Unspecified Dates

When drafting a duration period that has unspecified dates, clearly state the formula for figuring out both the beginning and ending date. To reduce the formula's complexity and the chances of creating ambiguity, we recommend that you use at least three sentences.

**Template for Drafting Duration Periods Containing
Unspecified Dates**

1. A sentence stating the period's intended length.

2. A sentence stating the formula for figuring out the beginning date.

3. A sentence stating the formula for figuring out the ending date.

Below are a few examples of unambiguous duration periods with unspecified beginning and ending dates. These duration periods are based on the number of days between the beginning date and the ending date.

**Examples: Unambiguous Duration Periods with
Unspecified Dates**

• The winding-up period lasts for 30 consecutive days. The winding-up period begins on the date that Thomason Consulting sends notice to Restaurant that Thomason Consulting is terminating all further contractual obligations of the parties. The winding-up period ends on the 29th day after the date that Thomason Consulting sends the notice.

• The consignment period for each work of art lasts for 90 consecutive days. The consignment period begins on the day on which Gallery receives the work of art from Consignor. The consignment period ends on the 89th day after the beginning date of the consignment period.

> **Examples: Unambiguous Duration Periods with Unspecified Dates** (cont.)
>
> - Kwok may have a mechanic of his choice evaluate the classic motorcycle. The evaluation period lasts for 7 days. The evaluation period begins on the date that Kwok pays Owner the deposit. The evaluation period ends on the 7th day after the date that Kwok pays the deposit.

Drafting a duration period that is based on a number of months or years is trickier than drafting a duration period based on a number of days. You could convert a month-based or year-based duration period to a day-based period (e.g., 180 days, 365 days, or 730 days), but it is not easy for the parties to count hundreds of days on a calendar to determine when a duration period ends. Month-based periods can be confusing because a month could have 28, 29, 30, or 31 days.

If you know the beginning date of a period before the parties sign the contract, then simply leave blanks to be filled in. If the parties will not know in advance the beginning and ending dates, state the formula for determining the beginning and end dates.

> **Examples: Month–Based and Year–Based Duration Periods**
>
> - Each consignment period lasts <u>four months</u>. The consignment period begins on the date that Gallery notifies Artist that Gallery has accepted the artworks. The consignment period ends <u>on the same day of the month but in the fourth month after</u> the date that Gallery accepted the artworks.
>
> - Each consignment period lasts <u>two years</u>. The consignment period begins on the date that Gallery notifies Artist that Gallery has accepted the artworks. The consignment period ends <u>on the same day and month but in the second year after</u> the date that Gallery accepted the artworks.
>
> - Each consignment period lasts <u>two years</u>. The consignment period begins on the date that Gallery notifies Artist that Gallery has accepted the artworks. The consignment period ends <u>on the second anniversary of</u> the day on which Gallery notified Artist.

3. Drafting a Renewable or Extendable Performance Period

(a) Extension by Giving Notice

A performance period does not have to end on a fixed date. Your client might need a performance period that is extendable. One way to achieve this is to allow a party to extend a performance period by giving notice to the other party.

If a party is entitled to extend the period for performance, the drafter must clearly articulate the following:

- The beginning and ending dates of the minimum period.
- The procedure for extension (notice, other requirements).
- The effect of the extension.
- The duration of the extension period.
- The number of allowable extensions.

If it is possible for the parties to work out the extension periods at the time of signing, leave space for the parties to do so.

Example: Articulating an Extension Period
(Equipment Lease)

The lease period lasts for a minimum of 15 days, beginning on _____ and ending on _____. Lessee may extend the lease period for no more than three extension periods, each lasting 15 days. Each extension period begins on the day after the last day of the previous period; each extension period ends on the 15th day after its beginning date. The three allowable 15–day extension periods begin and end on the following dates:

(1) The first allowable extension period begins on _____ and ends on_____ .

(2) The second allowable extension period begins on _____ and ends on _____.

(3) The third allowable extension period begins on _____ and ends on _____.

To exercise the right to extend the lease period, Lessee must give notice to Edeback Properties no later than 5 PM of the day preceding the last day of the current period. If the parties extend the lease period, all provisions of the contract remain in effect.

(b) Extension by Automatic Renewal

Automatic-renewal provisions (a.k.a. "evergreen" provisions) cause the performance period to renew automatically if a party fails to timely give notice to prevent the renewal. They allow the parties to continue an arrangement—without renegotiating—for as long as the parties permit.

State law might affect the use of these provisions. For example, New York has a law designed to protect persons who sign certain types of contracts if the contract contains an automatic-renewal provision.[4] Illinois has a statute designed to protect consumers who enter contracts that contain an automatic-renewal feature if the contract relates to the sale of products or services.[5]

Automatic-renewal clauses must address the following:

- The beginning and ending dates of the minimum period.

- The automatic renewal of the period for a stipulated time.

- The method of determining the beginning and ending dates of renewal periods.

- The procedure for preventing automatic renewal.

- The effect of automatic renewal.

Non-renewal is different from *cancellation* or *termination* of the performance obligations. If a party prevents the renewal of an automatically renewing period, the contractual obligations continue until the end of the current period. If a party terminates or cancels current obligations, the party can put an end to performance before it would otherwise come to an end. Cancellation and Termination are discussed in Chapter 9.

Language in a contract that does not clearly distinguish between a procedure for preventing renewal and a procedure for terminating the contract may cause a dispute that results in litigation.[6] To indicate that a procedure is for non-renewal, use phrases such as "notice of non-renewal" or "prevention of renewal."

E.   Placement of Time Clauses Within a Sentence

A time clause is a type of modifier. Misplacement of modifiers is a common cause of ambiguity, as discussed in Chapters 28 and 31. The key to avoiding modifier misplacement is to place the modifier where it cannot modify any element of the sentence other than the element that the modifier is intended to modify.

If a time clause is intended to modify a sentence's main verb, we recommend that you set out the time clause at the beginning of the sentence (as an introductory clause followed by a comma).

> **Example: Time Clause as Introductory Clause**
>
> <u>No later than the third day of each month</u>, Subscriber shall pay Company for that month's services.

If you put the time clause at the beginning of the sentence, the time clause will always modify the main verb of the main clause ("shall pay" in the example above). If a sentence contains only one actor and one verb, you can put the time statement at the end without creating ambiguity: for example, "Tenant shall pay rent to Landlord *no later than the third day of each month.*"

If you intend for a time clause to apply to an element of the sentence other than the main verb, make sure that the placement does not create ambiguity.

Examples: Ambiguity Caused by Placement of Time Clause

1. Buyer will pay full market price for each delivery of gribble <u>after the 10th day after the date that Buyer orders the gribble</u>.

2. For each ton of gribble, Buyer will pay the market price posted at CMGGX1.org <u>on the day that Buyer orders the gribble from Worldwide Gribble</u>.

3. If Buyer returns a shipment of gribble to Seller, <u>no later than May 7</u>, Seller will send to Buyer a refund of the purchase price.

In sentence (1), does the time clause apply to the date of delivery or the date of payment? In sentence (2), does the time clause apply to the date that the price for gribble is posted or to the date that Buyer is intended to pay for the gribble? In sentence (3), does the time clause apply to the date that Buyer returns the gribble or to the date that Seller would send a refund?

F. Avoid Potentially Ambiguous Phrasing

1. Avoid "Upon," "When," and "Once"

The words "upon," "when," and "once" can create ambiguity with respect to timing.

Example: Ambiguous Usage of Upon, When, and Once

* <u>Upon</u> Architect's certification of the plans, Owner will pay Contractor the remaining balance.

> **Example: Ambiguous Usage of Upon, When,
> and Once** (cont.)
>
> • <u>When</u> Architect certifies the plans, Owner will pay Contractor the remaining balance.
>
> • <u>Once</u> Architect has certified the plans, Owner will pay Contractor the remaining balance.

When *exactly* is the remaining balance due? At the moment that Architect issues the certificate? Any time that day? A day or two later?

Even if the drafter intended to set the deadline on the date of the countdown-triggering event (which might be unrealistic in terms of performance), a layperson or a court might construe "upon" to mean "*if* Architect certifies the plans" as opposed to "on the day that Architect certifies the plans."

2. Avoid "Between" When Setting a Date Range

The word "between" means the space separating two objects or markers—and that space does not include the markers themselves. For example, the meat in a sandwich is between the two pieces of bread, but those pieces of bread cannot be between themselves. Still, some people might interpret "between" as including the two markers. Thus, when used to establish a date range, "between" can create ambiguity.

> **Example: Potentially Ambiguous use of "Between"**
>
> Lessee may pick up the equipment from Kwok Farms <u>between</u> June 16 and June 30.

What are the earliest and latest dates on which Lessee may pick up the equipment? There are two possible interpretations:

> 1) Lessee cannot pick up the equipment before 12:00 a.m. on June 17 and must pick it up no later than 11:59 p.m. on June 29.
>
> 2) Lessee can pick up the equipment no earlier than the beginning of June 16 and no later than the end of June 30.

3. Avoid "Within" When Drafting a Due Date, Deadline, or Cut-off

The word "within" implies something surrounded by some external boundary. We could say that a pie's filling is within the crust, but the crust is not within the crust.

Example: Potentially Ambiguous use of "Within"

Buyer must send the notice to Seller <u>within</u> three days from the signature date.

Is the signature date included in the three days or outside them? What about the third day of the three days? If something is "within" three days, would the day of the triggering event and the final day *both* be outside the stipulated time? Different courts in different jurisdictions might construe "within three days" differently.

4.   Avoid "To," "Until," and "By" to Signify an End Date

As the example below shows, the use of the prepositions "to," "until," and "by" to signify an end date can cause ambiguity.

Examples: Ambiguous Use of "To," "Until," and "By"

• To avoid a fine, the festival host must dispose of all the trash during the period from July 4 <u>to</u> July 7.

• To avoid a fine, the festival host has <u>until</u> July 7 to dispose of all trash.

• To avoid a fine, the festival host must dispose of all trash <u>by</u> July 7.

In the examples above, all three prepositions leave questions open:

· Must the festival host pick up all trash before 12:00 a.m. on July 7?

· Or would the festival host avoid a fine as long as the trash is gone no later than 11:59 p.m. on July 7?

That's a nearly 24–hour difference, which could be significant to the festival host.

To rectify such an ambiguity, insert the date *and* the time of day: "By 5:00 p.m. on the 3rd day of each month, Tenant shall pay rent to Landlord." Yes, there is still an ambiguity: does "by 5:00 p.m." mean before the clock strikes 5:00 or until the clock strikes 5:01? If that one-minute difference matters to your client, then do not use "by"; instead, use "at or before 5:00 pm."

5.   Avoid "Month" to Stipulate a Range of Days

As discussed in Section I–D–2, basing a time period on months requires very careful drafting because not all months consist of the same number of days. Thus, the use of "month" in a time clause can create ambiguity.

> **Example: Ambiguous Use of "Month"**
>
> If Buyer is dissatisfied with a business opportunity kit, then Buyer has <u>one month</u> to mail it back to Seller for a full refund, counting from and including the day that Buyer takes delivery of the kit.

Suppose that Buyer receives the kit on January 31. If Buyer wants a refund, does Buyer have to return the kit no later than February 28 (or February 29 if it is a leap year)?

6. Avoid "Week" to Stipulate a Range of Days

In a time clause, the word "week" can be ambiguous. Some people interpret "week" as signifying seven days, while others interpret it as signifying the same day of the week (e.g., Monday or Friday) but during the following week.

> **Example: Potentially Ambiguous Use of "Week"**
>
> If Buyer is dissatisfied with a beer-brewing kit, then Buyer has <u>one week</u> to mail it back to Seller for a full refund, counting from and including the day that Buyer takes delivery of the kit.

If Buyer receives the kit on Friday, April 22, what is the last day that Buyer can return the kit? The day that Buyer takes delivery is included in the count, so the last day in a seven–day count is Thursday, April 28. If the provision had allowed the return of the kit on the next Friday, Buyer would actually have eight days (which is longer than a week).

7. Avoid "Midnight" to Express a Deadline

Technically, "midnight" is *not* ambiguous. It means 12:00 a.m., which occurs once at the beginning of each day. That aside, "midnight" may confuse some readers because it contains the word "night" but refers to morning. Some people might erroneously interpret "midnight of January 1" as the end of January 1; others may interpret it as the beginning of January 1 (which would be correct).

Why leave any room for argument? Why not simply specify another time of day, such as 11:59 p.m. or 12:01 a.m.?

G. Drafting Time Clauses in Your Jurisdiction

As discussed in Chapters 12 and 17, different jurisdictions may follow different rules of construction when interpreting contractual or legislative provisions. We recommend that you become familiar with how courts in your jurisdiction interpret time clauses.

II. Conditional Statements

A. Articulating Conditional Statements

In a legal document, a conditional statement makes a right or undertaking conditional on a future circumstance, act or event.

Examples: Conditional Statements

- Unless you complete the course, you will not graduate.
        (qualifier)   (main clause)

- If you pay me $150, I will detail your car.
        (qualifier)   (main clause)

The words "if," "unless," and "except" are commonly used to signify conditional statements. These words send a powerful signal about the relationship between the conditional statement and the main clause.

We recommend that you avoid using cumbersome substitutes such as "in the event that," "on condition that," "subject to," or "provided that." Also, avoid ambiguous substitutes for "if," such as "upon," "when," "where," or "once": a reader might initially mistake clauses beginning with these words as time clauses, rather than conditional statements.

We recommend also that you *not* use qualifying signals (e.g., "notwithstanding," "however," or "nonetheless") that take back what you just said in a preceding sentence, as doing so creates an avoidable conflict within the text.

A conditional statement may need to be paired with a parallel conditional statement that explains what happens if the first condition is not met or does not apply. Unless X occurs, what happens? If X occurs, what then?

Examples: Pairs of Conditional Statements

(1) Unless Buyer, no later than the 5th day of the month in which the shipment is due, notifies Seller that Buyer intends to cancel the order, Seller will ship the oranges on the 15th day of the month. If Buyer gives timely notice of cancellation, Seller will not ship the oranges that month.

> **Examples: Pairs of Conditional Statements** (cont.)
>
> (2) To cancel the order, Buyer must notify Seller on or before the 5th day of the month in which the shipment is due. If Seller does not receive notice of cancellation, Seller will ship the oranges on the 15th day of that month.
>
> (3) Before beginning construction of the pool, the owner shall install a pool fence. After the owner has installed the pool fence, the owner may construct the pool.

Do not leave the alternative scenario unaddressed (i.e., to be inferred by the reader) unless you are certain that the alternative scenario is self-evident. Typically, you should err on the side of fully articulating the parties' intentions.

B.   Placement of Conditional Statement in Sentence

In most instances, a conditional statement modifies the main verb in the sentence. It therefore belongs at the beginning of the sentence.

Sometimes, a sentence contains both a conditional statement and a time clause. If the time clause modifies the condition, the time clause must be incorporated within the conditional statement:

> **Examples: Time Clause Modifying Conditional Statement**
>
> •   If—during the period beginning on October 1, 2012 and ending on December 31, 2012—Employee meets all monthly sales targets set by the Regional Manager, Employer will pay to Employee a bonus equal to 10% of Employee's total commissions for the period.
>
> •   If—on or before the 30th day after the date that the Architectural Control Committee issues its decision—the property owner appeals the decision, the Review Board shall hold a hearing.

Suppose (1) that a sentence contains a time clause and a conditional statement and (2) that both are intended to modify the sentence's main verb. In that case, careful placement of the time clause is required in order to avoid creating ambiguity.

> **Example: Ambiguity Caused by Placement of Conditional Statement and Time Clause**
>
> If Lessor *is satisfied* with the condition of the premises, <u>on or before the 30th day after the last day of the lease period</u>, Lessor *will refund* the security deposit to Tenant.

The example above is ambiguous because the time clause is between two verbs that it could modify: "is satisfied" and "will refund."

> **Examples: Two Ways to Remove the Ambiguity**
>
> **Solution 1: Use Two Sentences**
>
> If Lessor is satisfied with the condition of the premises, Lessor will refund the security deposit. <u>On or before the 30th day after the last day of the lease period</u>, Lessor will refund the security deposit.
>
> **Solution 2: Place Time Clause at End of Sentence**
>
> If Lessor is satisfied with the condition of the premises, Lessor will refund the security deposit <u>on or before the 30th day after the last day of the lease period</u>.

In the examples, the key to removing the ambiguity is to place the conditional statement and time clause so that neither one is between two verbs within the sentence. Solution (1) accomplishes this by placing the conditional statement and time clause in different sentences, though this solution requires repetition of the main clause ("Lessor will refund the security deposit").

Solution (2) works because the time clause is no longer between two verbs. The verb that is nearer to the time clause ("will refund") is the one that the time clause modifies. Solution (2) might not work so well in a sentence whose main clause has multiple verbs: in that case, multiple sentences might be better.

As shown in the two solutions above, one way to avoid ambiguity is to place the time clause so that it is near the verb that it is intended to modify and *not* near any other verb. Another way is to carefully embed the time clause within the conditional statement, as shown in the examples below.

> **Examples: Time Clause Embedded within Conditional Statement**
>
> **Time Clause Placed Before the Verb:**
>
> To renew the lease period, Lessee, <u>on or before the 15th day of the last calendar month in the current lease period</u>,

---

**Examples: Time Clause Embedded within
Conditional Statement** (cont.)

must notify Landlord of Lessee's intention to renew the
lease period.

**Time Clause Embedded within Main Verb Using
Dashes:**

To renew the lease period, Lessee *must*—on or before the
15th day of the last calendar month in the current lease
period—*notify* Landlord of Lessee's intention to renew the
lease period.

Though embedding a time clause within a conditional statement can preclude ambiguity, this placement can also result in a convoluted sentence
structure. It might be easier on the reader if you try one of the other ways
that are discussed earlier in this section of the chapter.

CHAPTER 30

EXERCISES FOR PART 6: WORD CHOICE, AMBIGUITY, AND TIME CLAUSES

■ ■ ■

Project 1.   Word Choice

Assignment A.   *How Does the Word Change the Meaning?*

Each of the following sentences contains a pair or series of words or phrases in parentheses. Explain how a court's interpretation of the sentence's meaning might change depending on which one you pick. Consult the dictionary where necessary.

1. Employer (will pay) (will reimburse) (is liable for) Employee's out-of-pocket travel expenses.

2. Sidda may (assign) (waive) her right to compensation.

3. Plaintiff agreed to settle (the lawsuit) (any claim) that resulted from the incident.

4. Branwell had no legal (claim to) (interest in) the disputed property.

5. This provision applies to any dispute that (arises out of) (arises under) the contract.

6. Lessee (understands) (affirms) that Lessor has the right to enter the property for this purpose.

7. Defendant was ordered to pay Plaintiff's (fees) (expenses) (costs).

8. Contractor will make (best efforts) (reasonable efforts) to timely complete the project.

9. Greengage shall not (assign its interest in) (sublease) the property.

10. The excavator shall indemnify the city for any (damage) (damages) resulting from the excavation.

Assignment B.   *Who Wins the Dispute?*

Hypothetical 1

A local ordinance restricts "signage" in the "Historic Downtown District" in the city of McIntosh, Colohio, an area restricted to businesses that qualify under the city's definition of "small business." The city is embroiled in a bitter dispute with Harold Morissey, owner of an antique store. The sign in Morissey's storefront window is 24 inches tall and 36 inches wide: it takes up about twenty percent of the storefront window.

The city claims that the sign is too large. Morissey contends that he purchased his custom-designed sign in good faith based on the exact language of the ordinance. Here's what the ordinance says:

> "The business owner may place a small business sign in the storefront window."

Make an argument that Morissey is right. How should the city redraft the language of the ordinance to avoid the same misunderstanding arising in the future?

Hypothetical 2

G.D. Kwok is the author of the bestselling book, *Swimming to Success.* Through his corporation—Master Kwok's "Swimming to Success" Workshop, Inc. (MKW)—Kwok holds conferences nationwide addressing the principles espoused in his book. The following **questionably drafted** language appears in the contract between the Gainestown Royal Hotel and the:

(7) Return of Deposit or Advance Payment to Conference Attendee

> If any of the following circumstances occurs within the 48 hours prior to the scheduled workshop date, MKW may cancel the conference and Hotel will refund to GKW and to any registered conference attendee the full amount of any deposit or other advance payment for the conference:
>
>> (a) A labor dispute or other circumstance that results in a significant curtailment in food services, guest services, or amenities;
>>
>> (b) A transportation crisis, regardless of cause, that results in significant curtailment nationally of individuals' access to any one of the following modes of transportation: air, rail, or automobile;
>>
>> (c) Any serious local or national health crisis or epidemic of any kind;
>>
>> (d) Any civil unrest, act of terrorism, or act of a public enemy if a reasonable person using ordinary caution would be deterred from travelling to or staying in Hotel's facility;
>>
>> (e) Severe illness of or severe injury to "Master K" or other personal bereavement (such as loss of a loved one) that would be likely to impair the quality of his presentation; or
>>
>> (f) Any cause similar in effect to those listed above if the cause is beyond KWG's and "Master K's" control.

During the two days before the first day of the conference, the city of Gainestown was hit by a succession of freak thunderstorms that caused a six-hour city-wide power outage and paralyzed transportation by air and train. Based on the above provision, KWG cancelled the conference.

The hotel maintains that KWG had no right to do so and is threatening a lawsuit. It has refused to refund KWG's $25,000 deposit.

Who wins the dispute? Explain your answer.

Hypothetical 3

Quantum Physiques Health Studio (QP) is a large health club that charges members monthly or annual fees depending on the type of membership. In QP's contact with its members, the following **poorly drafted** clause appears:

> By signing the contract, Member consents to assume certain risks, **including the risk of negligence** on the part of Gym, its personnel, or its independent contractors. Member consents to assume the risk of physical injury caused by any of the following:
>
> > (a) Use of Gym's equipment, including injury caused by equipment malfunction, design defects, or the negligence of Gym, its personnel, or its independent contractors in maintaining, inspecting, or supervising the equipment's use;
> >
> > (b) Use of Gym's facilities (including the pool, showers, or hot tubs), including injuries due to swimming, diving, slipping, misuse or negligent use of facilities, or by the negligence of Gym, its personnel, or its independent contractors in repairing or inspecting the equipment or supervising its use;
> >
> > (c) Any risk inherent in the use of Gym's facilities or equipment; or
> >
> > (d) The risk that the negligence of Gym, its personnel, or independent contractors might increase the risks inherent in Member's use of the gym, its facilities, or equipment.

A member sues QP for serious injuries that she sustained when a maintenance company used the wrong mixture of chemical while cleaning the showers and restrooms. When QP pointed to this provision, the trial court said that the provision did not cover the circumstance and found in favor of the member. The appellate court affirmed, stating that the circumstance was "obviously" not covered.

Where did the drafter of QP's contract go wrong? Was the drafter too specific not specific enough? How would you fix the problem if QP were to hire you to redraft that provision?

Project 2.   Definitions

Review Chapter 27. What is wrong with the following definitions? How could you correct them?

1.   "Staff" includes employees, management personnel, independent contractors performing services on the premises, and any other service personnel.

2. *Notice* means notice given by email no later than the 3rd day before the date of Landlord's entry.

3. "Former Employee" includes an independent contractor.

4. "Emergency" means that the situation requires immediate action in circumstances involving imminent danger to person or property.

5. "Equine recreational activity" is any recreational activity involving a horse or other animal of the equine class, including but not limited to a pony ride, a petting zoo, a gymkhana, or horse show.

Project 3. Increasing Your Ambiguity–Awareness

Each of the following sentences contains an ambiguity. Explain the ambiguity.

1. Seller will package 1000 units of Miracular–B in four properly insulated containers.

2. Lessee will keep in good condition and repair all components of the tractor.

3. Promoter fully understands that Venue Owner may refuse to admit anyone to the concert.

4. After the ambulance company's negligence got Med–Assist sued, Med–Assist's H.R. Director discussed making arrangements to replace the ambulance company with Med–Assist's senior management.

5. If Consultant is unable to perform in an emergency maintenance staff may be assigned by Company.

6. The senior partner wrote, "Bob could not have performed better than he did on this project."

7. Pursuant to section 3B of its contract, Defendant agreed to hire Plaintiff, the event planners, Fresh Ideas, an equipment rental company, Gervais, a caterer, and PAR–TAY Unlimited.

8. If Employee appeals to the Regional Manager, the Regional Manager shall immediately send Employee to the Deputy Director.

9. If a corporation files a notice of a violation with the Department, it must provide a full account of the grounds for forwarding the matter to the state attorney's office.

10. Tenant will close the storefront to the public at or before 7:00 PM Monday through Sunday and will not open before 2:00 PM on Sunday.

11. Seller will provide Buyer with an invoice stating the market price of the sand on the delivery date.

12. Lessor only may enter the storage shed.

13. Defendant gave notice to Plaintiff that she would be unable to supply two menu items only three days prior to the wedding.

14. The contractor charged the city a total of $20,000 for project costs and her fee.

15. Condominium Owners shall remove excrement deposited by pets on walkways or grass.

16. The party may file an action for damages exclusively in the county court.

17. To qualify for the exemption, applicants must file proofs of qualifying disabilities.

18. When a dispute arose that the parties could not resolve without recourse to arbitration the parties agreed to terminate their relationship.

19. Defendant misrepresented the nature of its services in violation of the Act.

20. No member of the public was permitted to enter the area that was roped off without clearance from the district attorney.

Project 4.　Time Clauses and Conditional Statements

The following sentences are ambiguous. Make the changes necessary to bring them into compliance with Chapter 29.

1. A party who signs a consumer contract (as defined by section 23.01(a)) has the right to cancel within three days.

2. Tenant will allow Landlord to enter the premises to show the premises to a prospective tenant and for maintenance if Landlord provides the requisite notice.

3. If the property owner objects to the council's determination, within 5 days of receiving the notice, the property owner may request a hearing.

4. The price for the shipment of ore is determined based on the market price per ton posted at the Mineral Resources Board's website on the order date.

5. If Buyer pays for the shipment between the shipment date and the third day following the shipment date, Buyer may pay a discounted price of 90% of the invoice price.

PART 7

GRAMMAR, PUNCTUATION, AND STYLE

■ ■ ■

- Chapter 31. Some Basics About Grammar
- Chapter 32. Some Basics About Punctuation
- Chapter 33. Style
- Chapter 34. Exercises for Part 7

371

CHAPTER 31

SOME BASICS ABOUT GRAMMAR

■ ■ ■

I. The Importance of Grammar Handbooks

Courts have consulted grammar handbooks when discerning the meaning of text in a legal document.[1] A reputable grammar handbook can authoritatively support an attorney's assertion about the meaning of text.

We recommend that you get at least one standard grammar handbook that addresses punctuation rules, as well as grammar, and that you develop the habit of referring to the handbook when you have questions concerning grammar or punctuation. The following are among the most reputable handbooks: *The Hodges Harbrace Handbook* (a.k.a., *The Harbrace*); *The Bedford Handbook*; and *The McGraw–Hill Handbook of English Grammar and Usage*.

II. Refresher: Some Key Grammatical Terms

A. The Eight Parts of Speech

There are eight parts of speech in modern English.

Eight Parts of Speech		
• Noun	• Verb	• Conjunction
• Pronoun	• Adverb	• Interjection
• Adjective	• Preposition	

Below are basic descriptions of the parts of speech. Anything beyond basic descriptions is beyond the scope of this book—another reason that we recommend that you buy a grammar handbook.

A **noun** names a person or other life form, place, thing, or idea. Nouns have case (subjective, objective, possessive). Nouns express number (singular or plural).

Examples: Nouns		
courts	Wyoming	clause
Smith	jurisprudence	merger
judge	venue	warranty

A **pronoun** substitutes for a noun. Pronouns have case and express number.

Examples: Pronouns		
I	you	it
she	he	them
our	they	their

The noun to which a pronoun refers is called the **antecedent**.

An **adjective** modifies or describes a noun or pronoun. **Articles** (e.g., *a, an, the*) are a subclass of adjectives.

Examples: Adjectives Paired with Nouns	
• Effective lawyer	• Vague statute
• Subject-matter jurisdiction	• Complex pleading

A **verb** signifies action or state of being. A verb can consist of one or more words. Verbs show timing (e.g., past, present, future). Verbs have moods and *can* have voice (mood and voice are discussed in Section III).

Examples: Verbs		
is	have	is reading
was	defend	was overruled
will be	affirmed	has been analyzed

An **adverb** modifies or describes a verb, an adjective or another adverb. Many adverbs end in *-ly* but not all of them.

Examples: Adverbs
• He drafts well. [Adverb *well* modifies the verb *drafts*.]
• The contract was fairly complete. [Adverb *fairly* modifies the adjective *complete*.]

Examples: Adverbs (cont.)

• The buyer inspected the goods <u>very</u> <u>thoroughly</u>.
  [Adverb *very* modifies the adverb *thoroughly*, which modifies the verb *inspected*.]

A **preposition** shows the relationship between words, phrases, or clauses. Often, prepositions show the position of one thing with respect to another.

Examples: Prepositions

• The defendant was <u>at</u> the crime scene.

• The buyer gave notice <u>to</u> the seller.

• The plaintiff was driving <u>on</u> a public road.

• The dispute was <u>about</u> the license.

A **conjunction** connects (or conjoins) words, phrases, or clauses.

Examples: Conjunctions

• Lessors <u>or</u> lessees
  [conjoining two words]

• The buyer inspected the silica sand <u>and</u> the loose gravel.
  [conjoining two phrases]

• Plaintiff prepared to receive the shipment, <u>but</u> it was late.
  [conjoining two clauses]

An **interjection** expresses emotion and can consist of one or more words. We do not see many appropriate uses for interjections in legal documents.

Note that some words can be used as different parts of speech, depending on the context. The word "that" is a good example.

Example: "That" Used as Different Parts of Speech

• Adjective: The tenant failed to comply with <u>that</u> provision.

• Adverb: The court has not applied the statute <u>that</u> often.

• Conjunction: Defendant was aware <u>that</u> the fence was damaged.

• Pronoun: <u>That</u> is the testator's signature.

B. Other Key Grammatical Terms

Courts use grammatical terms when construing legal text.[2] Whether drafting legal text or litigating the meaning of a contract or statute, an attorney who is unfamiliar with grammar is at a disadvantage. Below are basic descriptions of some key grammatical terms.

A **sentence** is a set of words that expresses a complete thought. A sentence must contain at least a subject and a predicate. A **subject** is a noun, noun phrase, or pronoun about which a sentence says (or asks) something. In a sentence that has only one subject and one verb, the sentence's subject is also the verb's subject.

The **predicate** is what is said (or asked) about a sentence's subject. A predicate must include at least one verb.

Examples: Subjects and Predicates

- Defendant <u>had actual knowledge of the condition.</u>
     S   P

- Landlord <u>shall maintain the pool and adjacent areas.</u>
     S   P

- The lessor <u>may enter the property to perform repairs.</u>
     S   P

A **clause** is a group of related words that contains a subject and a predicate. An **independent clause** can stand alone as a complete sentence, while a **dependent clause** cannot:

- **Independent clause**:   Tenant will vacate the premises.

- **Dependent clause**:   If Landlord cancels the lease period,

- **Combined**:   If Landlord cancels the lease period, Tenant will vacate the premises.

A **phrase** is a group of related words that acts as a grammatical unit. In the following sentences, the phrases are underlined:

- **Noun phrase**:   <u>Two non-conforming shipments</u> arrived.

- **Verb Phrase**:   Plaintiff <u>had been injured</u> by Defendant.

- **Prepositional Phrase**:   Plaintiff went <u>to Defendant's store.</u>

An **object** is a noun or noun substitute that relates to a preposition or verb. An object relating to a preposition is called an "object of the preposition." Some verbs also take objects (discussed in Section III–A). There are two types of objects relating to verbs: direct and indirect. A **direct object** receives the action of a transitive verb (the verb's action is directly transferred to the object). In the following examples, the verb is bolded, and the direct object is underlined.

Examples: Direct Objects of a Verb

- Defendant **threw** <u>the rock</u>.
- The negligent driver **hit** <u>a pedestrian</u>.

An **indirect object** is a noun or noun substitute showing to whom or for whom an action is done. A preposition often precedes an indirect object. In the following examples, prepositions are bolded, and indirect objects are underlined.

Example: Indirect Objects of a Verb

- Buyer received goods **from** <u>Seller</u>.   [with the preposition "from"]
- Seller sent the goods **to** <u>Buyer</u>.   [with the preposition "to"]
- Seller sent <u>Buyer</u> the goods.   [without a preposition: "to" is implied]

Understanding objects is crucial to understanding verb voice (discussed in Section III–A).

A **modifier** is a word, phrase or clause that describes another word, phrase or clause. Adjectives and adverbs are types of modifiers.

Examples: Modifiers

- The release was <u>invalid</u>.   [adjective]
- The seller <u>promptly</u> sent goods to the buyer.   [adverb]
- The employee complained <u>to the grievance officer</u>.   [phrase]
- <u>Because the contract is illegal</u>, it is unenforceable.   [clause modifying clause]
- <u>Admittedly</u>, the testator did not date the codicil.   [adverb modifying clause]

A **gerund** is a word consisting of a verb + *ing*. A gerund functions as a noun.

Examples: Gerunds

- <u>Entering</u> the premises requires notice to the tenant.
- <u>Keeping</u> a pet on the premises is a breach of section 9(b) of the lease.

A **participle** can be a verb + *ing* (present participle) <u>or</u> a past-tense verb (past participle) except in the case of some irregular verbs. A participle can function (1) as part of a verb phrase or (2) as a modifier.

Examples: Participles

- The attorney is withdrawing from the case.   (verb phrase)
- The court was reviewing the record.   (verb phrase)
- The reviewing court discussed the record.   (modifier)
- The injured party had no remedy under state law. (modifier)

III.   A Bit About Verbs

A.   Voice of Verbs

1.   Determining Whether Verbs Have Voice

A verb can be either transitive or intransitive, and only transitive verbs have voice. A **transitive verb** expresses an action that requires a direct object to *receive* the action in order for the action (and the sentence) to be complete. In the following examples, the transitive verb is bolded, and the direct object is underlined.

Examples: Transitive Verbs

1. The buyer **has inspected** the shipment.
2. Defendant **threw** an explosive device.
3. Lessor **will notify** Lessee.

In the first example above, you could not end the sentence with "inspected" and still have a complete sentence because the verb "inspect" requires a direct object for the action. In other words, the buyer had to have inspected *something*. The same is true of the second and third examples: the verbs "threw" and "will notify" are not complete without a direct object.

An **intransitive verb**, by definition, does not take a direct object. Intransitive verbs can express status or condition.

Examples: Intransitive verbs (status or condition)

- The release **is** invalid.
- One party **seemed** ready to sign the contract.
- The other party **will be** ready soon.

Intransitive verbs can also express certain types of actions that are complete in themselves (without a direct object).

Examples: Intransitive verbs (Actions)

- The defendant **ran**
- The plaintiff **slipped** and **fell**
- The trial **will begin** tomorrow.

Some verbs can be transitive *or* intransitive, depending on how they are used in a sentence.

> **Examples: Verbs that Can be Intransitive or Transitive**
>
> - Intransitive: Plaintiff's windshield **cracked**.
> - Transitive: The impact **cracked** the windshield.
>
> - Intransitive: The lease period **had ended**.
> - Transitive: Lessor **had ended** the lease period.

2. The Voices: Active and Passive

Only transitive verbs have "voice." A sentence containing a transitive verb can tell its story from the point of view of the actor *or* the recipient of the action.

In **active voice**, the actor is the subject of the sentence and actively carries out the action expressed by the verb. The usual sequence is *Actor → Action → Recipient of action*.

> **Examples: Active Voice**
>
> - **The defendant** <u>punched</u> the victim.
>   Subj.   verb   obj.
>
> - **The seller** <u>will ship</u> the goods.
>   Subj.   verb   obj.
>
> - The **court** <u>rejected</u> that defense.
>   Subj.   verb   obj.

Passive voice reverses the story: the *thing being acted upon* is the subject of the sentence, and the subject passively sits there being acted upon by the verb. The usual sequence (if the actor is named) is *Recipient → Action → Actor*.

To express the idea of a recipient that is *acted upon,* passive voice requires both a verb that expresses the action and a form of "be":

is acted upon	will be acted upon	is being acted upon
was acted upon	may be acted upon	has been acted upon.

If named in a passive-voice sentence, the actor usually follows the word "by." In the following examples, the passive verb is underlined, and the subject is bolded.

> **Examples: Passive Voice with Actor Named**
>
> - **The victim** <u>was punched</u> by the defendant.
> - **The goods** <u>will be shipped</u> by the seller.
> - **That defense** <u>was rejected</u> by the court.

In passive voice, the actor does not even need to be mentioned, yet the sentence is complete.

> **Examples: Passive Voice without Actor**
>
> - **The victim** <u>was punched</u>.
> - **The goods** <u>will be shipped</u>.
> - **That defense** <u>was rejected</u>.

Passive voice is *not* grammatically incorrect. If used strategically, passive voice can be effective because it allows the writer to state the consequence of an action while de-emphasizing the actor—or omitting the actor altogether. Compare the following pairs of examples:

> **Examples: Using Passive Voice to De–Emphasize the Actor**
>
> 1(a)　Honey, your car was totaled.　(passive)
> 1(b)　Honey, I totaled your car.　(active)
>
> 2(a)　Bribes were taken.　(passive)
> 2(b)　The client took bribes.　(active)

In other words, passive voice allows the writer to de-emphasize an actor's responsibility for bringing about an action.

In legal documents, the responsibility of the actor is usually a central concern. Thus, we recommend that you avoid using passive voice unless the identity of the actor is irrelevant or better left unexpressed.

B.　Verb Tense

Verb *tense* addresses timing. There are three or four tenses (depending on whether you consider the progressive to be a "form" or a "tense"):

1) Simple.

2) Perfect.

3) Progressive.

4) Perfect progressive.

In drafting, choose the correct tense to express your exact meaning. Case law shows that verb tense can make a difference in how a court construes text.[3]

Examples of the verb tenses are below, followed by an explanation of each tense's meaning. Pay special attention to the difference between the simple and perfect tenses.

Verb Tenses in Active Voice

	Present	Past	Future
Simple	draft (or drafts)	drafted	will draft
Progressive	is drafting	was drafting	will be drafting
Perfect	has drafted	had drafted	will have drafted
Perfect Progressive	has been drafting	had been drafting	will have been drafting

Verb Tenses in Passive Voice

	Present	Past	Future
Simple	is drafted	was drafted	will be drafted
Progressive	is being drafted	was being drafted	[questionable, omitted]
Perfect	has been drafted	had been drafted	will have been drafted

The **simple tense** indicates that something is, was, or will be.

Examples: Simple Tense		
Simple Present	He <u>works</u>.	(presently, in general—maybe this minute, maybe not)
Simple Past	He <u>worked</u>.	(he worked in the past, but we do not know about the present or future)
Simple Future	He <u>will work</u>.	(he will work in the future, but we do not know about the present or past)

The **perfect tense** indicates that something is, was, or will be *complete* as of a certain point in time.

Examples: Perfect Tense		
Present Perfect:	She <u>has worked</u> before now.	(act is complete as of the present)
Past Perfect:	She <u>had worked</u> before yesterday.	(act was complete as of some past point)
Future Perfect:	She <u>will have worked</u> by tonight.	(act will be complete as of some future point)

The **progressive tense** (or form) shows that something is, was, or will be *in progress* (i.e., continuous).

Examples: Simple Progressive

Present Progressive: I <u>am working</u>. (now)

Past Progressive: I <u>was working</u>. (in the past, nothing about present or future)

Future Progressive: I <u>will be working</u>. (in the future, nothing about present or past)

The **perfect progressive** tense combines elements of completion with elements of progression. The perfect progressive can relate to the present, past, or future.

The **present perfect progressive** indicates that an action originated in the past and is still in progress at present.

Examples: Present Perfect Progressive:

• She <u>has been working</u> on the project for one month.

• They <u>have been working</u> at the job site for six months.

The **past perfect progressive** indicates that an action was in progress but no longer is.

Examples: Past Perfect Progressive

• She <u>had been working</u> on the project for one month when they fired her.

• They <u>had been working</u> at the job site for six months when the dispute began.

The **future perfect progressive** indicates that at some point in the future, an action will have been in progress for a while.

Examples: Future Perfect Progressive

• By June 15, she <u>will have been working</u> on the project for one month.

• By January 2014, they <u>will have been working</u> at the job site for six months.

Note: the mere presence of a form of the verb "to be" does *not* signify passive voice. The verb "to be" is used in the progressive tense (as shown in examples above) and on its own as an intransitive verb. Progressive verbs can be intransitive (no voice) or transitive (either active or passive voice).

Examples: Form of "Be" but <u>Not</u> Passive Voice

- The Plaintiff <u>is responding</u>.   Present progressive, intransitive

- The release <u>is</u> valid.   Present tense, intransitive

- The judge <u>will be reviewing</u> the case.   Future progressive, active voice

---

C.   Verb Mood

The **mood** of a verb expresses the drafter's attitude toward what is being expressed. Three moods concern the authors.

Three Moods of a Verb

- **Indicative mood**:   expresses a statement or question
- **Imperative mood**:   expresses a command or request (in second person)
- **Subjunctive mood**:   expresses a hypothetical or contrary-to-fact statement

---

In some cases, courts construing a legal text have discussed a verb's mood.[4]

Examples: Verb Moods

Indicative: Plaintiff **released** Defendant from liability for further claims.

            Did Plaintiff **release** Defendant from liability for further claims?

Imperative: **Release** Defendant from liability for further claims.

Subjunctive: Defendant wished that he **<u>be released</u>** from further claims.

            Defendant asked that Plaintiff **<u>release</u>** him from further claims.

Drafters sometimes have trouble knowing when to use the subjunctive. Verbs in subjunctive mood appear in certain clauses that express the idea of an action or status that is hypothetical, proposed, wished for, or contrary to fact.

One type of clause that frequently occurs in legal documents expresses a demand, request, or requirement. The clause containing the subjunctive-mood action is typically introduced by the word "that":

Examples: Use of "That" with Subjunctive

ask (that)	demand (that)	insist (that)
order (that)	prefer (that)	propose (that)
recommend (that)	request (that)	suggest (that)

Subjunctive mood makes a difference (1) if the clause contains a verb in **third person singular** (i.e., the form that you use with "he," "she," or "it") or (2) if the main verb contains or is a form of "be." The rules are easier to illustrate than to explain.

Examples: Subjunctive Mood (active, passive, to be)

Active Voice, Third-person Singular:

- Plaintiff *asked that* this court <u>award</u> damages to Plaintiff.

- The court *may require that* the family member <u>repay</u> the outstanding debt.

Verb Contains or is a form of "be":

- We *suggested that* the debt <u>be</u> <u>disclosed</u> to the buyer.

- You *urged that* the restriction not <u>be</u> <u>enforced</u>.

The two rules are as follows:

1) if the verb is third-person singular active voice, drop the -s or -es from the verb;

2) if the main verb contains or is a form of "be" (regardless of voice), replace the form of "be" with the word "be."

If the main clause contains *could, would, might,* or *should*, then the if-clause is in the subjunctive.

Examples: Subjunctive in Present Hypothetical

Correct:	If Buyer <u>were</u> to notify Seller, Seller could cure the breach.
Incorrect:	If Buyer <u>was</u> to notify Seller, Seller could cure the breach.
Correct:	If Seller <u>were</u> to be notified, Seller would cure the breach.
Incorrect:	If Seller <u>was</u> to be notified, Seller would cure the breach.

Examples: Subjunctive in Present Hypothetical (cont.)

Correct: If Lessor <u>were</u> willing to refund the rent, Lessee would vacate.

Incorrect: If Lessee <u>was</u> willing to refund the rent, Lessee would vacate.

As the examples show, an if-clause is in subjunctive mood if the if-clause presents a hypothetical set of facts.

In a sentence addressing a past event, an if-clause must be framed in past perfect tense.

Examples: Subjunctive in "If" Clause in Past Hypothetical

Correct: If Plaintiff <u>had notified</u> Defendant of the defect, Defendant would have cured it.

Incorrect: If Plaintiff <u>notified</u> Defendant of the defect, Defendant would have cured it.

Correct: If Defendant <u>had been notified</u> of the defect, Defendant would have cured it.

Incorrect: If Defendant <u>was notified</u> of the defect, Defendant would have cured it.

Correct: If we <u>had known</u> the deadline, we could have timely vacated.

Incorrect: If we <u>knew</u> the deadline, we could have timely vacated.

IV. A Bit About Pronouns

A. Overview of Pronouns

As discussed in Section II–A, a pronoun substitutes for a noun. The noun for which the pronoun substitutes is called the "antecedent."

Examples: Pronouns and Antecedents
(Pronouns are underlined, and antecedents are bolded)

• **The lawyer** was good at research, and <u>he</u> enjoyed doing it.

• **The defendants** asked for a recess, and the judge gave it to <u>them</u>.

• Though <u>it</u> was new, the **alarm system** at the courthouse was malfunctioning.

There are seven types of pronouns: personal, relative, reflexive, intensive, interrogative, demonstrative, and indefinite. This section addresses only the personal, relative, reflexive, and intensive because those are the pronouns that tend to cause people trouble.

B. Pronoun Case

1. The Three Cases

Pronouns (words that substitute for an antecedent noun) have "case." The case used depends on how the pronoun is used.

	Subjective Case		Objective Case		Possessive Case	
	Singular	Plural	Singular	Plural	Singular	Plural
1st person	I	We	Me	Us	My/Mine	Our/Ours
2nd person	You	You	You	You	Your/Yours	Your/Yours
3rd person	He/She/it	They	Him/Her/It	Them	His/Hers/Its	Their/Theirs

The **subjective case** is proper if the pronoun is the subject of a verb. The **objective** case is proper if the pronoun is the object of a verb (e.g., "called me" or "inspected them") or the object of a preposition (e.g., "from her," "by me," or "to us"). The **possessive** case is proper to express possession.

2. Choosing Between Subjective and Objective Case

The choice between subjective and objective case is fertile ground for error. Many drafters get it right when a sentence involves one pronoun after the preposition or verb, but many get confused when multiple objects appear after the preposition or verb.

The following examples show how to test whether a pronoun's case is correct:

Examples: Objective versus Subjective Case

a. Defendant **contacted** Plaintiff, the credit card company, and I/me.
   - Is it correct to say "Plaintiff contacted I"?
   - No: the transitive verb "contacted" takes an object ("me").

b. The executor distributed the assets **to** the son, a cousin, and she/her.
   - Is it correct to say "The executor distributed the assets to she"?
   - No: the preposition "to" takes an object ("her").

The question of "who" versus "whom" is a question of case. "Who" and "whom" are relative pronouns: they link a relative clause to a main clause by relating back to an antecedent within the main clause.

To determine whether to use "who" or "whom," determine how the relative pronoun is functioning within the relative clause:

(1)   as the verb's subject,

(2)   as the verb's direct object, or

(3)   as a preposition's object.

If the relative pronoun functions as a verb's subject, use the subjective case ("who"). If it functions as an object, use the objective case ("whom").

One shortcut is to substitute "he" and "him" for the relative pronoun: if "he" is correct, then "who" is the correct relative pronoun; if "him" is correct, then "whom" is correct. It is easy to associate "whom" with "him" because they both end in "m."

Examples: Applying Shortcut Regarding "Who" and "Whom"

a.   Plaintiff paid the creditors who/whom had violated the order.
- Is it correct to say "him had violated the order"?
- No: the verb "had violated" needs a subject ("he"); thus, "who" is correct.

b.   The creditor who/whom the judge chastised had to pay Plaintiff's fees.
- Is it correct to say "the judge chastised he"?
- No: the verb "chastised" requires an object ("him"); thus, "whom" is correct.

c.   The judge chastised the lawyers who/whom represented the creditors.
- Is it correct to say "him represented the creditors"?
- No: the verb "represented" needs a subject ("he"); thus, "who" is correct.

d.   The judge sanctioned the partners with who/whom each creditor was associated.
- Is it correct to say "Each creditor was associated with he"?
- No: the preposition "with" requires an object ("him"); thus, "whom" is correct.

---

3.   Possessive Case

The possessive case indicates that the pronoun possesses something (e.g., *my* schedule or *your* book). One common error is to add an apostrophe to a possessive pronoun. Many people confuse "its" with "it's," though they are different words:

- **Its**   (possessive pronoun)   The firm pays <u>its</u> lawyers well.

- **It's**   (contraction of "it is")   <u>It's</u> the firm's policy to pay well.

Possessive pronouns do not have an apostrophe, as the possession is part of the specific pronoun's definition:

- The car was <u>hers</u>, not Defendant's.   (not her's)

- The land was <u>ours</u>, not Plaintiff's.   (not our's)

C.   Pronoun Number and Gender

A pronoun must agree in number (singular v. plural) with its antecedent.

Examples: Pronoun Number Disagreement and Agreement

Incorrect: If Builder breaches this section, <u>they</u> will pay damages.
Correct: If Builder breaches this section, <u>he</u> or <u>she</u> will pay damages.

["Builder" is a singular antecedent; thus, the pronoun must be singular.]

When making a general statement, some writers prevent the number-disagreement problem by using "he or she." Other writers find "he or she" cumbersome. The best way to prevent this problem (and retain gender neutrality) is to repeat the antecedent.

**Preventing Number–Disagreement: Omit the Pronoun
and Repeat the Antecedent**

- If an employee files a grievance, the <u>employee</u> will notify the Manager.
- If the builder violates this section, the <u>builder</u> will pay liquidated damages.

In document drafting, repetition of the antecedent is preferable to writing in the plural because plurals cause imprecision and sometimes ambiguity (as discussed in Chapter 28).

Another problem relating to pronoun number is the handling of groups or of entities comprised of multiple people. An entity or a group is singular; thus, any pronoun referring to an entity or group should also be singular.

Examples: Singular Nature of an Entity or Group

- The **court** reconsidered <u>its</u> order.

- The **group** of protesters filed <u>its</u> complaint as a single association.

- The **law firm** appealed the sanctions imposed on <u>its</u> partners.

- The **council** shall provide <u>its</u> members with regular updates.

As well as agreeing in number, pronouns and their antecedents must agree in gender. The rules are simple.

Gender–Agreement Rules

- If the antecedent is feminine, the pronoun should be feminine.
- If the antecedent is masculine, the pronoun should be masculine.
- If the antecedent is neutral, the pronoun should be neutral.

In some contexts, violation of the gender-agreement rule has become a tradition (e.g., sailors refer to a boat as "she"). When you are drafting legal documents, we recommend that you draft gender neutrally. Gender-neutral drafting is discussed in Chapter 33.

D. Avoiding Ambiguous Pronoun Usage

To avoid creating ambiguity, make sure that a pronoun's antecedent is clear.

Examples: Unclear Antecedents

- Defendant notified Plaintiff that <u>he</u> had breached the provision.
- The attorney plans to contact the client when <u>she</u> returns from a trip.
- When Defendant slammed the vase onto the glass table, <u>it</u> broke.

Who breached the provision: Defendant or Plaintiff? When *who* returns from a vacation: the attorney or the client? *What* broke: the vase or the glass table? The easiest way to prevent antecedent-related ambiguity is to omit the pronoun and instead use the antecedent.

Examples: Ambiguity Removed

- Defendant notified Plaintiff that <u>Plaintiff</u> had breached the provision.

- The attorney plans to contact the client when <u>the attorney</u> returns from a trip.

- When the defendant slammed the vase onto the glass table, the <u>table</u> broke.

Repetition of the antecedent may seem inelegant, and elegance might be a consideration for the writer of a brief, academic article, or work of fiction. In document drafting, however, precision and clarity trump elegance.

V. Parallel Structure

A list (or series) has **parallel structure** if each list item is grammatically similar. For example, if the first list item is a noun, then each of the other list items should be a noun. If the first item is a prepositional phrase, then each of the other list items should be a prepositional phrase.

Thus, being familiar with the parts of speech (which are discussed in Section II) will help you create parallel structure.

Examples: Non-parallel and Parallel structure

1a. Non-parallel:

Lawyers often encounter <u>anger</u>, <u>those who are anxious</u>, and <u>resentment</u>.
                              (noun)   (clause)   (noun)

1b. Parallel:

Lawyers often encounter <u>anger</u>, <u>anxiety</u> and <u>resentment</u>.
                              (noun)   (noun)   (noun)

2a. Non–Parallel:

Defendant failed to <u>fix the stairs</u>, <u>light the staircase</u>, and <u>there was no rail</u>.
                          (vb./adj/n)   (vb./adj/n)   (ind. clause)

2b. Parallel:

- Defendant <u>failed to light the staircase</u>, <u>failed to fix the stairs</u>, and <u>failed to provide a rail</u>.

- Defendant failed to <u>fix the stairs</u>, <u>light the staircase</u>, and <u>provide a rail</u>.

Not all sentences lend themselves to parallel structure, especially if parts of the sentence address different concepts. Consider the following example:

> Plaintiff suffered a <u>concussion</u>, <u>pain</u>, <u>anguish</u>, and <u>he will lose income</u>.

"Concussion," "pain," and "anguish" are nouns and are direct objects of "suffered." The "and" suggests that what follows is also a noun and direct object, but "he will lose income" is *not* a noun or noun substitute and cannot be a direct object. One way to resolve the non-parallelism is to use two sentences:

> Plaintiff suffered a <u>concussion</u>, <u>pain</u>, and <u>anguish</u>. Plaintiff will lose income.

If you find yourself struggling to make a sentence's list items parallel, consider addressing the material in two or more sentences.

Parallel structure makes a sentence easy to read and understand, while non-parallel structure forces the reader to stop and figure out what the writer intended to convey. Beyond an issue of mere style, parallelism can have an impact on a sentence's meaning—which is why courts have analyzed the parallel (or non-parallel) structure of provisions in legal documents.[5]

Avoid "bungled parallelisms," a term used by a California appellate-court judge analyzing the following poorly drafted sentence from a county ordinance:

> No person shall <u>set up</u>, <u>use</u>, <u>operate</u> or <u>maintain</u> an <u>amplified sound system</u>, <u>music</u> and <u>live music</u> within any park, beach or recreational area except in those areas specifically designated, nor shall any person set up, use, operate or maintain an amplified sound system, music and live music without first obtaining a written permit.[6]

That sentence is problematic partly because it includes a list of verbs ("set up," "use," "operate," "maintain") that must be parallel to each other while also applying sensibly to each item in the list of nouns ("amplified sound system," "music," "live music"). What follows is part of the California judge's analysis of that sentence's flaws:

> Grammatically, the parallel series must begin after "maintain." But, so read, the series consists of, literally: (1) an amplified sound system; (2) music; and (3) live music. And if that's the series, the ordinance is clearly overbroad because, literally, it would require a permit to "maintain ... music" in the park. You would need a permit to hum a tune under that reading.
>
> Of course, this raises the collateral question, how exactly does one "set up, use, operate or maintain ... music?" A singer might "maintain" a high c for a period of time, a rock band might "maintain a beat," but "maintain ... music" is awkwardness bordering on unintelligibility.[7]

Parallel structure can require more words than non-parallel structure, but the benefits outweigh the costs.

VI. Avoiding Problems With Modifiers

A. Placement of Modifiers

A modifier is a word or phrase that describes, qualifies, or explains some other word or phrase in the sentence. Modifiers may attach to more than one element of a sentence, and the result might be a sentence with more than one meaning.

Modifiers should be placed so that it is clear to the reader which element of the sentence the modifier is describing, qualifying, or explaining. Consider the following example:

Buyer will purchase computer equipment <u>exclusively</u> from Seller.

Is Buyer prohibited from buying the equipment from anyone but Seller or prohibited from buying anything but computer equipment from Seller?

Modifiers such as "exclusively" and "only" can be tricky because they can be correctly placed *after or before* the term that they modify. Also, such modifiers can correctly modify different types of terms (e.g., other modifiers, nouns, or verbs). Thus, the mere placement of such modifiers can change a sentence's meaning.

Examples: Moving "Only" Changes the Meaning

1. **Only** she litigated criminal cases in Smithville.

2. She **only** litigated criminal cases in Smithville.

3. She litigated criminal cases **only** in Smithville.

4. She litigated criminal cases in Smithville **only**.

The first and fourth sentences in the example each have one possible meaning: (1) that she—and nobody else—litigated criminal cases in Smithville and (4) that Smithville was the only place where she litigated criminal cases. The reason that neither sentence has additional possible meanings is that "only" is in a position where it can modify *nothing but one* term in each sentence.

The second sentence has two possible meanings: (1) nobody else in town litigated criminal cases or (2) she did nothing but litigate (e.g., she did no research). That is because "only" is between two words that it could modify: "she" and "litigated."

In the third sentence, the "only" is similarly between two terms that it could modify: "criminal cases" and "in Smithville." Thus, the third sentence has two possible meanings: (1) criminal cases were the only ones she litigated or (2) she litigated criminal cases nowhere but in Smithville.

What is true of "only" is true of other modifiers: poor placement can create ambiguity or confusion. For that reason, we recommend that you make a habit of following the tips below:

> **Tips for Preventing or Solving Modifier–Placement Problems**
>
> 1. Place a modifier so that it can modify one term only, <u>or</u>
>
> 2. Rephrase a sentence to clarify to which term a modifier applies.

Consider this example again: "She litigated criminal cases **only** in Smithville." If you want the sentence to mean that she litigated the cases nowhere but in Smithville, you could either move the modifier (so that it can modify one term only) or rephrase the sentence:

- She litigated criminal cases in Smithville <u>only</u>.

- She litigated criminal cases nowhere but in Smithville.

If instead you want the sentence to mean that she litigated nothing but criminal cases, merely moving the modifier would not solve the problem, as you would end up with this:

She litigated <u>only</u> criminal cases in Smithville.

In that sentence, "only" could modify one of two terms: either "litigated" or "criminal cases." Thus, the sentence still has two possible meanings. To place the modifier so that it can modify one term only, you would have to restructure or rephrase the sentence. Examples follow:

- In Smithville, she litigated criminal cases <u>only</u>.

- She litigated nothing but criminal cases in Smithville.

Misplaced modifiers can create momentary confusion, though context might enable the reader to figure out the intended meaning. Consider the following example:

A car was reported stolen <u>by the Gatortown Police</u>.

"By the Gatortown Police" is placed in such a way that it can modify nothing but "stolen" (meaning that the police stole the car). The more likely intended meaning is that the police reported the car stolen. There are at least two ways to rephrase the sentence to precisely convey the likely intended meaning:

1) A car was reported by the Gatortown Police to have been stolen.

2) The Gatortown Police reported that a car was stolen.

Some misplaced modifiers can cause serious ambiguity if nothing in the context resolves the question of intended meaning. Consider the following example:

If Buyer returns the goods, <u>no later than June 10</u>, Seller will send a refund to Buyer.

Is June 10 the deadline for Buyer's returning the goods or for Seller's sending a refund? Below are examples of how to fix the sentence so that the modifier applies (1) to Seller's sending of the refund and (2) to Buyer's returning of the goods:

1)   If Buyer returns the goods, Seller will send a refund to Buyer <u>no later than June 10</u>.

2)   If Buyer, <u>no later than June 10</u>, returns the goods, Seller will send a refund to Buyer.

In the first sentence, the modifier is placed so that it can modify one thing only: "will send." In the second sentence, the modifier is placed so that it can logically modify "returns" but nothing else (the deadline cannot logically apply to "Buyer").

We recommend that you carefully place modifiers to prevent any question as to which term a modifier is intended to modify. Chapter 28 discusses examples of modifier-related ambiguity that commonly occurs in contracts and rule-making documents.

B.   Phrasing of Modifiers

One of the most common problems caused by the mis-phrasing of modifiers is the **dangling modifier.** A dangling modifier does not attach grammatically (or otherwise) to the word or phrase that it is intended to describe, qualify, or explain.

Examples: Dangling Modifiers

1.   <u>After considering the application</u>, the permit shall be issued.

2.   Landlord will maintain the grounds, <u>including mowing the lawn, sweeping the sidewalks, and removing trash from the property</u>.

3.   The defendant's car collided with the plaintiff's car <u>to avoid hitting a dog</u>.

The first sentence's structure signals that "after considering the application" modifies the main clause's subject: "the permit." However, the permit is *not capable* of considering anything. Context suggests that an unnamed person must consider the application before issuing the permit, but the sentence's phrasing prevents the modifier from logically applying to anything in the sentence.

The second sentence's structure and phrasing lead the reader to expect that the examples following "including" relate to the contents of "the grounds." Instead, "mowing," "sweeping," and "removing" are examples of ways that the landlord must maintain the grounds. The modifier does not connect grammatically with the phrase "will maintain" due to lack of parallel structure (parallel structure is discussed in Section V). Thus, the modifier is left "dangling."

In the third sentence, "to avoid hitting a dog" modifies "defendant's car." The literal meaning is nonsensical because the defendant's car is *not capable* of forming motive or intent. Obviously, "to avoid hitting a dog" is intended to modify "the defendant" but cannot do so because "the defendant" is not the subject of the sentence ("the defendant's car" is the subject).

Examples: Dangling Modifiers Corrected

1. <u>After considering the application</u>, the Department shall issue the permit.

2. Landlord will maintain the grounds by performing upkeep-related tasks, <u>including mowing the lawn, sweeping the sidewalks, and removing trash from the property</u>.

3. <u>To avoid hitting a dog</u>, Defendant swerved, and Defendant's car collided with Plaintiff's.

We recommend that you carefully phrase modifiers so that (1) they are grammatically correct, (2) they make sense, and (3) it is obvious to which term the modifier applies.

VII. Deal–Breaking Grammatical Errors

Not all grammatical problems are created equal. There are some errors that even people who have not studied grammar will recognize. A list of deal-breaking grammatical errors follows (errors are underlined).

Examples: Deal–Breaking Grammatical Errors

<u>Type of Error</u>	<u>Examples</u>
• Subject-verb disagreement:	The case <u>do</u> not apply.
• Verb-tense error:	He had <u>gave</u> it to me.
• Pronoun-case error:	The judge rebuked my partner and <u>I</u>.
• Pronoun-number error:	One defendant consulted <u>their</u> lawyer.
• Sentence fragment:	<u>To quote the court of appeals</u>.
• Comma splice:	The trial ended, Plaintiff appealed.
• Apostrophe errors:	e.g., *her's* or *our's*; misusing *it's*

CHAPTER 32

SOME BASICS ABOUT PUNCTUATION

■ ■ ■

I. The Importance of Punctuation

Incorrect punctuation can affect the meaning of legal text, can cause ambiguity or confusion, and can make a writer seem illiterate. Though punctuation is not always dispositive, courts consider punctuation when construing legal text.[1]

As stated in Chapter 31, we recommend that you get an authoritative grammar handbook that also explains punctuation, such as *The Hodges Harbrace Handbook* or *The Chicago Style Manual*. This chapter addresses some rules and guidelines regarding some punctuation marks that tend to cause problems.

II. Commas

A. The Comma's Impact on Meaning

Commas cause problems for a drafter because comma placement can affect the meaning of a sentence. Consider the following examples.

Examples: Comma's Effect on Meaning
1. When Defendant's car struck, Plaintiff James lost consciousness.
2. When Defendant's car struck Plaintiff, James lost consciousness.

The first sentence mentions one victim (Plaintiff James), who lost consciousness. The second sentence mentions two victims (Plaintiff and James), and James is the one who lost consciousness.

Comma misplacement is not the only cause of problems. Under-use and over-use can cause reader confusion or even ambiguity. For example, a Florida appellate court found ambiguous a key provision in an insurance policy, in part due to the "plethora of commas."[2] Similarly, a comma in a building-construction contract led to litigation that had to be resolved by the South Carolina Supreme Court.[3]

The comma is sometimes misunderstood. Some people place a comma wherever they feel that a reader should pause. Others place or omit a comma based on their recollection of an English teacher's instructions from years earlier. One result is that some drafters unintentionally create confusion or ambiguity in legal text by comma misplacement, under-use, or over-use.

We recommend that you habitually consult at least one reputable grammar guide for comma usage, instead of relying on feelings or memories. We have included some rules of comma usage in the following subsection.

B.   Some Basic Comma–Usage Rules

1.   Commas in a Series

A **series** contains three items or more. Commas should separate items in a series unless at least one of the items contains a comma (in which case, as discussed in Section III, a semicolon should separate the items).

Examples: Use of Commas in a Series

- Defendant refused to return Plaintiff's computer, iPod, and DVDs.

- Plaintiff suffered a broken arm, a broken leg, and a concussion.

- Seller shall harvest the crop, package the crop, and deliver the crop to Buyer.

  Note: whether a comma should precede the "and" in a series is still debated. Some writers habitually insert it; other writers omit the comma if its absence does not cause confusion.

---

2.   When to Use and Not Use Commas With Conjunctions

A comma should precede a coordinating conjunction that links two independent clauses (i.e., clauses that can stand alone as a sentence, as discussed in Chapter 31). Coordinating conjunctions include *and, but, or, for, nor, so* and *yet*. Other types of conjunctions are beyond the scope of this book.

In the following examples, the independent clauses are underlined, and the commas are correctly placed before the coordinating conjunction.

> **Examples: Comma + Conjunction Separating Independent Clauses**
>
> • Seller timely shipped the order, but it arrived after the deadline.
>
> • The school needed a new roof, yet the school board denied the funding.

If a coordinating conjunction separates the sentence's subject from one of its *two verbs*, **do not** place a comma before the conjunction. The subjects in the following examples are bold, and the verbs are underlined:

• No comma: **The court** imposed sanctions and rebuked the lawyer.

• No comma: **Builder** will provide labor and procure insurance.

Note: for emphasis, some writers insert a comma before the conjunction even if the comma would separate the subject from its second verb. If you choose to use a comma that way, do it *sparingly* because regularity diminishes emphasis.

If a subject has *three or more verbs* (i.e., a series of verbs), use commas to separate the verbs—the same way that you would use commas to separate a series of nouns, adjectives, phrases, or clauses.

> **Examples: Commas in a Series of Verbs**
>
> • Farmer will harvest, package, and deliver the corn to Manufacturer.
>
> • Defendant selected Plaintiff's horse, saddled the horse, placed Plaintiff on the horse, and led the trail ride.

3.   Commas and Restrictive vs. Non–Restrictive Modifiers

When analyzing legal text, courts have considered the functions of restrictive and non-restrictive modifiers.[4] A **restrictive modifier** restricts the meaning of what it modifies and is necessary to distinguish the particular person or thing from other similar persons or things. A **non-restrictive modifier** is *not* essential for identification; one could delete the modifier without changing the sentence's essential meaning because the non-restrictive modifier is merely additional information.

**Examples: Commas and Restrictive vs.
Non-Restrictive Modifiers**

1. **Restrictive**: no comma

    Context: several lawyers, one in a gray suit, are outside
    the courtroom

    Example: The plaintiff approached the lawyer <u>who was
    wearing the gray suit</u>.

2. **Non–Restrictive**: comma

    Context: only one lawyer stands outside the courtroom

    Example: The plaintiff approached the lawyer**,** <u>who was
    wearing a gray suit</u>.

In the first example, the modifier describing suit color is essential to distinguish one lawyer from the others. In the second example, it is not because there is only one lawyer outside the courtroom.

Restrictive and non-restrictive modifiers do not have to be placed at the end of a sentence. If a non-restrictive modifier is somewhere other than the end of a sentence, enclose the modifier within a pair of commas.

Examples: Modifiers not at the End of the Sentence

•   **Non-restrictive**: commas

The lawyer**,** <u>who had represented the defendant in a previous case</u>**,** requested that the judge impose sanctions.

> [The pair of commas tells us that the detail is not included to distinguish the lawyer from other lawyers; it is mere back-story.]

•   **Restrictive**: no commas

The lawyer <u>who had represented the defendant in a previous case</u> requested that the judge impose sanctions.

> [The absence of commas tells us that the modifier is necessary to distinguish one lawyer from others: perhaps the defendant has more than one lawyer.]

The traditional rule[5] regarding "that" versus "which" is this: use "that" to signify a restrictive modifier, and use "which" to signify a non-restrictive modifier. When you are drafting legal documents, we recommend that you follow the traditional rule.

**Examples: Modifiers Beginning with "Which"
or "That"**

- **Non-restrictive (which)**

The fence**,** <u>which Defendant had recently replaced</u>, had a gap in it.

> [The "which" phrase enclosed within commas tells us that the modifier is not included to distinguish this fence from another fence; the previous repair is this fence's back-story.]

- **Restrictive (that)**

The fence <u>that Defendant had recently replaced</u> had a gap in it.

> [The "that" phrase is included to distinguish this fence from other fences that Defendant had not recently replaced.]

---

4. Commas and Introductory Elements

Traditionally, a comma follows an introductory element that begins a sentence. In the following examples, the introductory elements are underlined:

- <u>On or about May 13</u>**,** Defendant's car struck Plaintiff.

- <u>If Tenant fails to timely pay rent</u>**,** Tenant will pay Landlord a late fee.

III.   Semicolons

A.   Semicolons in a Series

Use semicolons to separate items in a series if at least one item contains a comma:

Examples: Semicolons vs. Commas in a Series

1. The jury heard the testimony of the following witnesses: Daniels**,** a subcontractor**;** Paulson**;** and Roberts.

2. The jury heard the testimony of the following witnesses: Daniels**,** a subcontractor**,** Paulson**,** and Roberts.

In the first sentence, the jury heard testimony from *three* witnesses: Daniels, Paulson, and Roberts. The semicolons mark the separation of each series item from another: one item ("Daniels, a subcontractor") contains descriptive information about Daniels that is set off by a comma.

In the second sentence, the jury heard testimony from *four* witnesses: three are named, and one is not. The commas signify the separation of each series item; thus, "a subcontractor" is a distinct item in the series (instead of a mere description of an item).

B.   Semicolons Separating Independent Clauses

You can separate independent clauses with a semicolon by inserting the semicolon between the two clauses—but do not add a coordinating conjunction (such as *and* or *but*).

Examples: Semicolon Joining Independent Clauses

- The plaintiff sent notice to the Defendant; the defendant ignored it.

- After the buyer received non-conforming goods, the buyer wanted to cancel the contract; the seller wanted to cure the defects.

If you prefer to separate independent clauses with a coordinating conjunction such as *and* or *but*, use a **comma** instead of a semicolon (as discussed in Section II–B–2):

> Plaintiff sent notice to Defendant, and Defendant ignored the notice.

It is incorrect to separate independent clauses by using a comma without a conjunction. That usage results in a "comma splice."

Example: Comma Splice

Plaintiff sent notice to Defendant, Defendant ignored the notice.

Examples: Ways to Fix the Comma Splice

- Plaintiff sent notice to Defendant; Defendant ignored the notice.

- Plaintiff sent notice to Defendant, **and** Defendant ignored the notice.

- Plaintiff sent notice to Defendant. Defendant ignored the notice.

IV.   Colons

Use a colon to introduce a series of items, a list that contains at least two items, a quotation, or an explanation.

Examples: Colon Usage

- The complaint contained three counts: negligence, strict liability, and breach of warranty.

- The provision is one that the company vigorously negotiated to delete: a forum-selection clause that made Gator County the exclusive forum for dispute resolution.

- The ambiguous statute stated the following: "The seller shall provide for a right to cancel upon three days' notice."

Notice that an independent clause precedes the colon in each example sentence. There is debate as to whether an independent clause must precede a colon that is introducing a series, list, quotation, or explanation: some grammar and style guides indicate that it must.[6] Based on this rule, the following sentence would be *incorrect*:

> The Buyer may choose either: (1) a discount or (2) a rebate.

However, many writers introduce lists with colons that are *not* preceded by independent clauses, and the practice has gained acceptance.

When you draft a legal document, we recommend that you play it safe by placing an independent clause before a colon that introduces a series, list, quotation, or explanation.

V.　Apostrophes

A.　Showing Possession of Nouns

Whether to use apostrophes to express possession is *not* a matter of preference: there are rules. Use an apostrophe to show the possessive case of a noun (but *not* of a personal pronoun). As the following examples indicate, apostrophe placement varies based on the last letter of the word and whether the word is singular or plural.

Examples: Apostrophe Placement

<u>Singular Nouns</u>:

- If the singular noun does not end in *s*, add apostrophe + *s*:

　　Plaintiff's Motion　　　　(one plaintiff)
　　Defendant's Answer.　　　(one defendant)

Examples: Apostrophe Placement (cont.)

- If the singular noun ends in *s*, you have a choice:

Cupples' car	or	Cupples's car
Socrates' writings	or	Socrates's writings

Plural Nouns:

- If a noun is plural and ends in *s*, add only an apostrophe:

  Plaintiffs' Motion to Strike
  Defendants' negligence

- If a noun is plural and does not end in s, add apostrophe + s:

  The people's rights
  The brethren's duties

To show joint possession, use the possessive case for the last noun only. To show individual possession, use the possessive case for each noun.

Examples: Joint versus Individual Possession

Joint: Defendant entered Davis and Mitchell's office building.

[Davis and Mitchell co-own one office building.]

Individual: Buyer's and Seller's drafts both contained a liquidated damages clause.

[Buyer and Seller each have different drafts.]

B. Plurals of Numerals, Letters, and Words

Some writers use an apostrophe to form the plural of a numeral, a letter referred to as letter, and a word referred to as word:

- Omission of two **5's** from the statute's section number created ambiguity.

- Company will ship to Seller the timber marked with three **A's**.

- The sentence contained two ***provided's*** used in different senses.

- Fry began doing business in Florida in the early **2000's**.

C. Signifying a Contraction or Omission

A **contraction** is a shortened version of a word or word group. A contraction is created through the omission of letters, syllables, or words—and an apostrophe signifies the omission. Examples of common contractions follow, though these contractions are generally inappropriate in a legal document:

- Don't   (a contraction of "do not").

- Would've   (a contraction of "would have").

- It's   (a contraction of "it is").

Apostrophes are also used in abbreviations to show the omission of at least one letter or number. Occasionally, it might be appropriate to use such a contraction in a formal legal document.

- Gov't   (meaning "government").
- The '20's   (meaning the "1920's").

VI. Dashes

A. Typing the Dash

To form a dash, type two hyphens (--), and leave *no space* between the dash and the word on either side of the dash. Some word-processing programs can be set to automatically change the two hyphens into a single line of sufficient length to qualify as a dash. If your word-processing program does not automatically convert two hyphens into a dash, then use the two hyphens.

B. Creating Emphasis

Use a single dash or a pair of dashes to set off words that you wish to emphasize. If the emphasized words are at the end of the sentence, use a single dash. If the words are not at the end of the sentence, use a pair of dashes.

Examples: Single Dash versus Pair of Dashes

- Plaintiff breached several provisions of the contract—starting with the obligation to provide proof of insurance.

- If Lessee does not cure the breach, Lessor—following the lapse of the stipulated time period—may take possession of the equipment.

C. Inserting a Series of Modifying Words or Phrases

A drafter might need to use modifying language that consists of a series of words or phrases that are separated from each other by commas. In that case, the drafter should use punctuation that clearly separates the series from the main clause, but a pair of commas cannot effectively do that work.

Examples: Pair of Dashes versus Pair of Commas

Clear (dashes)

Three counts of the complaint—negligence, misrepresentations, and breach of warranty—survived the motion.

Confusing (commas)

Three counts of the complaint, negligence, misrepresentations, and breach of warranty, survived the motion.

Another option is to use parentheses (instead of a pair of dashes), but parentheses tend to de-emphasize the importance of the inserted language by suggesting that it is of secondary interest (i.e., "parenthetical").

D. Introducing or Explaining a List

Though a dash is less conventional than a colon, a drafter could use a dash to introduce a list:

> The judge dismissed two counts for failure to state a claim—negligent infliction of emotional distress and breach of contract.

VII. Hyphens

A. Typing the Hyphen

A hyphen requires a single stroke of the hyphen key (-). There should be no blank space before or after a hyphen.

B. Usage With Some Prefixes and Compound Words

When attached to a word, some prefixes must be followed by a hyphen. Similarly, some compound words require a hyphen between the words. Examples follow:

• Testator leaves to Anne Jones, his <u>ex-wife</u>, his entire estate.

• The attorney <u>cross-examined</u> Plaintiff's business partners.

There is no simple rule for determining whether a prefix or compound word requires hyphenation. The best way to make the determination is to consult a dictionary.

C. Usage With Compound Adjective

A **compound adjective** is two or more words that function together as one adjective. If a compound adjective comes *before* the noun that it modifies, use a hyphen (or hyphens) to join the words that form the compound adjective.

Examples: Hyphenation of Compound Adjectives		
1(a)	The contract included a <u>liquidated-damages</u> **clause**.	(hyphen)
1(b)	The **clause** addressed liquidated damages.	(no hyphen)
2(a)	A <u>well-drafted</u> **provision** might be found unconscionable.	(hyphen)
2(b)	The **provision** is unconscionable, though it is well drafted.	(no hyphen)

Examples 1(b) and 2(b) do not contain compound adjectives: "liquidated" is an adjective modifying "damages," and "well" is an adverb modifying "drafted." Thus, hyphenation would be incorrect.

Do not place a hyphen between an adverb that ends in *–ly* and the adjective that the adverb modifies:

- Correct: The **intensely aggrieved** plaintiff chose to testify.

- Incorrect: The intensely-aggrieved plaintiff chose to testify

VIII.   Punctuating Quoted Language

A. Periods and Commas

In American English, a period or comma at the end of a quotation usually goes **inside** the quotation mark:

- "We attempt to discern the text's plain meaning," the court said.

- The court said, "We attempt to discern the text's plain meaning."

B. Colons and Semicolons

In American English, a colon or semicolon at the end of a quotation usually goes **outside** the quotation marks:

- The trial judge wrote, "Failure to comply with the order was inexcusable"; the Court of Appeals said, "We endorse this view."

- Defendant repeatedly emphasized one phrase in the proposal entitled "Specifications for Mural": "community-appropriate art."

C. Question Marks

Place a question mark **inside** the quotation marks if the quotation is the question. Place a question mark **outside** the quotation marks if the quoted material is not a question. Examples follow:

- The client asked, "Should we obligate the lessee to obtain insurance?" [quoted material *is* the question]

- On what date did the buyer write "The goods are non-conforming"? [quoted material is merely part of a question]

IX. Parentheses: Does the Period Go Inside or Outside?

If a stand-alone sentence is enclosed within parentheses, then put the period **inside** the parentheses:

- The goods were sold as-is. (There was no warranty.)

- The court construed Section I. (It found that Section II did not apply.)

If the material within parentheses is part of and ends a sentence, then put the period **outside** the parentheses:

- The goods were sold as-is (with no warranty).

- The court severed the provision (because it was invalid).

CHAPTER 33

STYLE

■ ■ ■

I. Style Handbooks

We recommend that you obtain and read a reputable style handbook, such as *The Redbook* by Garner, *The Elements of Style* by Strunk and White, or *The Chicago Manual of Style*.

Writing style is not correct or incorrect: it is a matter of preference. Some styles are more effective than others for certain purposes. This chapter sets forth writing-style tips that are useful for the drafter of legal documents.

II. Write Concisely

Most people read legal documents because they need to find information, and those people tend to be busy. Wordy writing increases the reader's burden, while concise writing makes information easier for the reader to find and grasp.

A concise sentence contains no *unnecessary* words. Conciseness is not about deleting words to save space: it is about deleting words that do not serve a worthwhile purpose. In the following examples, the deletion of unnecessary words increases conciseness.

Examples: Deletion of Unnecessary Words	
1(a) The pleading was a long one.	(6 words)
1(b) The pleading was long.	(4 words)
2(a) The fact is that Defendant negligently failed to remove liquid from the store's floor.	(14 words)
2(b) Defendant negligently failed to remove liquid from the store's floor.	(10 words)

Words and phrases are the building blocks of a sentence. One way to achieve conciseness is to choose shorter words or phrases that say the same thing as their longer counterparts. Below are examples:

Needlessly long	More concise
any and all	any (or all)
subsequent to	after
utilize	use
utilization	usage (or use)
on account of the fact that	because
the reason why is because	because
in spite of the fact that	though (or although)
at the present time	now (or presently)
the State of Pennsylvania	Pennsylvania
in the month of June	in June
on the fifth day of June	on June 5
yellow in color	yellow
seven in number	seven
a distance of ten miles	ten miles

The possessive form of a noun is usually more concise than a noun preceded by the word "of."

Examples: Possessive Form vs. Of-Phrasing

1(a)	The allegations of the plaintiff …	(5 words)
1(b)	The plaintiff's allegations …	(3 words)
2(a)	The judge read the notes of a committee of the legislature of the state of Iowa.	(16 words)
2(b)	The judge read an Iowa legislative committee's notes.	(8 words)

An active-voice sentence is usually more concise than a passive-voice sentence that names the agent. The reason: passive voice requires extra words (a form of "be" and a preposition). In the following examples, the extra words are underlined:

Examples: Possessive Form vs. Of-Phrasing

1(a)   **Passive:** The plaintiff <u>was</u> attacked <u>by</u> the Defendant.   (6 words)

1(b)   **Active:** The Defendant attacked the plaintiff.   (4 words)

2(a)   **Passive:** The case will <u>be</u> reviewed <u>by</u> the judge.   (8 words)

2(b)   **Active:** The judge will review the case.   (6 words)

Another way to achieve conciseness is to omit extraneous details. Consider the following example, which is an allegation in a complaint. The context: Plaintiff is suing a grocery-store owner after Plaintiff slipped in a puddle of water in the breakfast-cereal aisle, fell to the floor, and suffered a broken leg:

> On or about May 3, 2012, Plaintiff was shopping in Defendant's grocery store, <u>which also contained a pharmacy and a section where lawn furniture was sold</u>.

Plaintiff slipped in the *cereal* aisle: it is probably irrelevant to the law suit that Defendant's store happened to sell prescription drugs and lawn furniture in different areas of the store. By removing the unnecessary details, we reduce that sentence from 26 words to 13 words.

Do not remove necessary content merely for the sake of reducing sentence length. Some sentences need to cover more content than others; thus, some sentences require more words. Again, conciseness is about removing *unnecessary* words or content.

III.   Avoid Passive Voice Unless You Need It

As discussed in Chapter 31, passive voice can be useful—especially if a drafter strategically intends to omit the actor or agent from a sentence. We recommend that you avoid using passive voice unless you have a good reason for using it. Many states' legislative drafting manuals similarly advise against the needless use of passive voice.[1]

One reason for choosing active over passive voice in legal documents is that active voice emphasizes the actor, while passive voice de-emphasizes the actor. As noted in Chapter 31, an actor's responsibility for an action is often relevant in legal documents.

Another reason for choosing active voice is that active-voice sentences are more concise than passive-voice sentences that identify the actor (as discussed in Section II).

IV. Refrain From Overloading Sentences

An overloaded sentence is needlessly packed with information, some of which could easily go into a separate sentence or sentences. Generally, a sentence that expresses a single thought is easier to grasp than a sentence that expresses many thoughts.

The contents of a sentence should be digestible in a single reading. Forcing an overloaded sentence on a reader is like trying to cram a whole pizza into a person's mouth: it is overwhelming and hard to digest. Courts have criticized overloaded sentences in documents.[2]

Example: Overloaded Sentence

Landlord <u>shall maintain</u> in good and usable condition all of the apartment complex's common areas, including the pool, gym, grounds, and parking lot and in addition, <u>shall keep</u> the outside of the buildings in good condition, including the roof and exterior walls, and any appliance that Landlord furnished <u>shall be timely repaired or replaced</u> if that appliance fails to properly function and if Tenant notifies Landlord of the failure.

The sentence in the example contains only one subject ("Landlord") but three separate actions, each relating to a different issue: common areas, exterior of buildings, and appliances. The issues are complex; for example, the "repair or replace" action includes not only the rule but also the procedure for notifying Landlord. No individual component of the sentence is difficult to understand, but placing all components in a single sentence makes them difficult to digest in a single reading.

An easy way to resolve the sentence-overload is to devote one sentence to each of the landlord's actions and the relevant details (i.e., to cut the pizza into manageable slices).

Example: Sentence–Overload Resolved

1. Landlord <u>shall maintain</u> in good and usable condition all of the apartment complex's common areas, including the pool, gym, grounds, and parking lot.

2. Landlord <u>shall keep</u> the outside of the buildings in good condition, including the roof and exterior walls.

3. Landlord <u>shall timely repair</u> or replace any appliance that Landlord furnished if that appliance fails to properly function and if Tenant notifies Landlord of the Failure.

True, we had to add a few extra words, but there is a payoff: the reader can easily read and digest each sentence.

As discussed in Section II, some sentences must be long because they convey complex or detailed information. Other sentences are long for no reason other than that the drafter chose to not break them up.

One goal in drafting legal documents is to draft sentences that a reader can understand after reading them only once. Thus, drafters should strive to draft sentences that are of a manageable length. One guideline—though not a firm rule—is to limit sentences to the following:

- Only one major actor.

- Only one major verb.

- Only a manageable number of details.

If a series of sentences contains a substantial amount of repeated material, an indented list might be appropriate. (Indented lists are discussed in Section VII.)

V.　Strive for Simplicity

Simplicity often leads to clarity. The indiscriminate use of convoluted sentences or "hundred-dollar" words does not make a drafter's text seem more sophisticated or legal: it makes the text harder to follow.

It is with good cause that courts have criticized needlessly complex language in legal documents[3] and that states' legislative drafting manuals generally recommend simplicity.[4] Unnecessarily complex phrasing or sentence structure (1) increases the reader's burden and (2) can create confusion and ambiguity.

A drafter's goal should be to simplify complex matters, not to complicate them.

Tips for Achieving Simplicity

- Choose ordinary terms over *needlessly* esoteric or technical terms.

- Choose simpler sentence structure over a *needlessly* complex structure.

- Break a *needlessly* lengthy sentence into multiple shorter ones (as discussed in Section IV).

We do not recommend that you choose simplicity over accuracy. Some concepts expressed in a legal document require technical or esoteric terms. Some concepts require longer or more complex sentences than other concepts do. As emphasized in the tips listed above, the key for the drafter is to choose simplicity over *needless* complexity.

While complexity can create ambiguity, complex or technical language is not always ambiguous. That a layperson would find language in legal text complex would not necessarily cause courts to find that text ambiguous.[5]

VI. Omit Needless Legal Jargon

As noted in Section V, legal and technical terms may be necessary in a legal document.[6] However, some of the esoteric modifiers and prepositions to which some lawyers seem addicted are usually not necessary. Even worse, those words and phrases tend to overburden readers and can reduce clarity.[7]

Needless legal jargon does not make a drafter seem sophisticated—at least not to readers who understand legal jargon. Instead, needless legal jargon can create the appearance that the drafter is engaging in puffery or is lazy about editing.

We recommend that you omit needless legal jargon from documents. We are in good company: many states' legislative drafting manuals give similar advice, and some even contain lists of terms to avoid.[8] Furthermore, a recent study suggests that many judges (both federal and state) prefer documents written in plain English.[9]

Examples: (Usually) Needless Legal Jargon	
Aforementioned	Hereinafter
And/or	Hereinbefore
Any and all	Moneys (it's all "money")
By and through	Notwithstanding
Foregoing	Said (when you mean "the")
Forthwith	Such (when you mean "the")
Herein	Subsequent to

A good rule of thumb is this: if you do not have a good reason for using a legal term, then omit it from your document.

Some busy attorneys blindly copy language from sample documents without fully considering the meaning. If you see legal jargon in a sample document, do not assume that the sample's drafter included those terms for good reasons. When reviewing sample documents, look up any terms of questionable meaning and try to phrase your provisions without legal jargon.

VII. Indented Lists

As long as you do not over-use the device, an indented list is an excellent way to highlight the components of a sentence that contains a pair or series of items.

The list items should be united by a strong common theme. The sentence should generally include the words "the following." A well-drafted, indented list (such as the one below) has the following characteristics:

(1) Items in the list are set out in an indented format.

(2) Items are grammatically parallel with each other.

(3) Items work grammatically if read together with the introductory clause.

(4) Items are lettered or numbered (in a formal legal document) or bulleted (in less formal writing).

(5) Items are properly punctuated.

(6) Each item can be a component of the sentence or a complete sentence.

(7) Ideally, items are introduced by an <u>independent clause</u> ending with a colon.

To punctuate an indented list, choose one of the following options:

(1) begin each list item with a capital letter and end it with a period (as shown above); <u>or</u>

(2) begin each item with a lower-case letter and end it with a comma (where appropriate) or semicolon (where needed) and place "and" or "or" after the next-to-last item in the list, as shown here.

Both of the indented lists shown above are properly drafted. However, as you can see, having one right after another makes them both less effective.

VIII. Use Gender–Neutral Nouns and Pronouns

It is widely agreed[10] that legal documents should be drafted gender-neutrally (1) when gender is not relevant and (2) when the drafter does not know the subject's gender.

Provisions in laws, contracts, and other legal documents can apply to women, to men, or to genderless entities. Thus, accuracy is one reason for drafting gender-neutrally. Another reason is that some readers, including some clients, might take exception to gender-specific language. Why risk offending anyone when it is so easy to eliminate the potential problem?

Gender-neutrality is easy to achieve: all the drafter must do is choose gender-neutral nouns and pronouns. Below are examples of gender-specific nouns and their gender-neutral substitutes:

Gender–Specific Nouns	Gender–Neutral Nouns
Businessman	Businessperson
Chairman	Chairperson, Chair
Fireman	Firefighter
Foreman	Supervisor
Mailman	Mail carrier
Policeman, policewoman	Police officer
Salesman, saleswoman	Salesperson
Waiter, Waitress	Server
Workman	Worker

The easiest way to achieve gender-neutrality with respect to pronouns is to omit pronouns altogether and to repeat the antecedent instead (as discussed in Chapter 31). Additionally, the omission of pronouns benefits the drafter by eliminating the potential for two types of errors: (1) pronoun-related ambiguity and (2) pronoun-case errors.

If you insist on using pronouns in legal documents, you can achieve gender-neutrality by using phrases such as "he or she"; "him, her, or it"; and "his, hers, or its." Many readers may consider such phrasing cumbersome, but the choice is yours.

If you use pronouns, use them correctly. As discussed in Chapter 31, pronouns must agree in number (singular vs. plural) with their antecedents. Thus—while "they," "them," and "their" are gender-neutral—you cannot correctly use a plural pronoun to refer to a singular antecedent.

CHAPTER 34

EXERCISES FOR GRAMMAR, STYLE, AND PUNCTUATION

■ ■ ■

Assignment 1. Key Grammatical Terms

Answer the questions about each of the following sentences.

Sentence 1: Judge Jones reduced the fees of the lawyer.

1) What is the main verb?

2) What is the main verb's subject?

3) What is the sentence's subject?

4) What is the sentence's predicate?

5) Which part of speech is the word "of"?

6) Which type of phrase is "of the lawyer"?

7) What is the direct object of the verb "reduced"?

Sentence 2: After the lawyer filed the brief, she requested a hearing.

1) What is the sentence's subject?

2) Which type of clause is "after the lawyer filed the brief"?

3) Which type of clause is "she requested a hearing"?

4) What is the direct object of the verb "filed"?

5) What is the direct object of the verb "requested"?

Sentence 3: The appellant's lawyer presented two arguments on appeal.

1) What is the main verb?

2) What is the main verb's subject?

3) What is the sentence's subject?

4) What type of phrase is "the appellant's lawyer"?

5) What type of phrase is "on appeal"?

Sentence 4: Defendant selected the horse, saddled the horse, and placed Plaintiff on the horse.

1) What are the three verbs?

2) What is the direct object of "selected"?

3) What is the direct object of "saddled"?

4) What is the direct object of "placed"?

5) The word "the" is an article: what part of speech is it?

6) What part of speech is the word "and"?

Sentence 5: Persuading the court will be difficult.

1) What is the verb?

2) What is the verb's subject? (Gerunds function as nouns)

3) Which part of speech is "difficult"?

Assignment 2.   Voice of Verbs

For each underlined verb or verb phrase, answer the following questions:

Questions:

1.   Is it transitive or intransitive?

2.   Is it active voice, passive voice, or no voice?

---

1. The judgment <u>was</u> final.

2. The judgment <u>was filed</u>.

3. The client <u>had purchased</u> the goods.

4. The goods <u>had been bought</u> by the client

5. The duty <u>was delegated</u> to a third party.

6. Payments <u>will be</u> timely.

7. The attorney <u>was objecting</u>.

8. The evidence <u>was</u> inadmissible.

9. The evidence <u>will be admitted</u>.

10. That lawyer <u>will be hired</u>.

11. The lawyer <u>is being</u> obstructive.

12. The judge <u>may impose</u> the sanction.

13. The decision <u>was made</u>.

14. The decision <u>would have been</u> wrong.

15. The court <u>made</u> the decision.

16. The panel <u>reviewed</u> the findings.

17. The Tenant <u>will pay</u> on time.

18. Rent <u>will be paid</u> on time.

19. Rent <u>might have been paid</u> on time.

20. The client <u>was</u> undecided.

Assignment 3.   Pronouns

a. *Number*

If an underlined pronoun is incorrect, replace it with the correct one. Assume that gender is correct in sentence (1). In the other sentences, "person" or "buyer" could refer to a human being or a corporation.

1.   If Plaintiff changes <u>his</u> address, <u>he</u> will notify buyer.

2.   If any person changes <u>their</u> address, <u>they</u> will notify the city.

3.   If a buyer wants to terminate the sale, <u>they</u> will notify Seller.

4.   If a buyer wants <u>their</u> money back, <u>he or she</u> should notify Seller.

b. *Ambiguous Usage*

Please (1) choose one party as the ambiguously used pronoun's antecedent and (2) re-write each sentence so that the meaning is clear (i.e., re-use the antecedent). Assume that gender is correct.

1.   The lawyer told her client that <u>she</u> was right.

2.   The judge told the client's lawyer that <u>he</u> was mistaken.

3.   Plaintiff informed Defendant that <u>it</u> needed to make certain necessary repairs.

4.   The department heads told their managers that <u>they</u> needed to provide information to the CEO regarding budget shortfalls.

5.   If a corporation files a formal notice with the Agency to process the exemption request, <u>it</u> must include all the information that the regulation requires.

c. *Case*

If an underlined pronoun is incorrect, replace it with the correct one. Assume that gender is correct.

1.   The judge rebuked <u>him.</u>

2.   The judge rebuked the defendant's attorney and <u>I</u>.

3.   We sent the notice to <u>yours</u> and <u>their</u> attorneys.

4.   The Board of Directors copied the letter to <u>you</u> and <u>I</u>.

5.   <u>Who</u> was it besides <u>I</u> that <u>she</u> spoke to regarding the attorney on <u>who</u> the judge imposed the sanctions after that incident involving <u>she</u> and <u>him</u>?

6.   <u>Who</u> besides <u>he</u> did the seller notify?

7.   If <u>we</u> do not get involved, will the problems that <u>we</u> have with <u>she</u> and <u>him</u> continue to escalate?

8. <u>Whom</u> was the person <u>who</u> had custody of the dog after Animal Control notified <u>you</u> and <u>I</u> that <u>he</u> did not qualify as a dangerous dog?

9. Did the warning apply to <u>whomever</u> else was involved in the altercation? Did it mention <u>she</u> or <u>I</u>?

10. The city attorney consulted with <u>you</u>, <u>she</u>, <u>they</u> and a commissioner <u>who</u> <u>we</u> and <u>her</u> did not recognize.

Assignment 4.   Punctuation

a.   Spotting Punctuation Errors

Circle any comma, semi-colon, colon, or apostrophe that is <u>incorrectly used</u> in the following sentences.

1. The argument seemed spurious to me, but the judge did not agree.

2. We provided oversight, and acted as a liaison with the client.

3. The court affirmed the decision below; but criticized the trial court for allowing that line of questioning to continue.

4. By failing to take action after her dogs' escape from it's pen on her company's premise's, she violated the statute.

5. The board consisted of three directors: Karswell, a trademark lawyer, Smith, the owner of the company, and Cullen, the current Chief Financial Officer.

b.   Adding Punctuation

Where appropriate, add a comma, semicolon, apostrophe or period. If a sentence requires no additional punctuation, write NPR.

1. After notifying the seller of its dissatisfaction with the goods that the seller had shipped to buyers warehouse the buyer demanded a refund.

2. On or about August 19 Plaintiff Harris attorney notified Defendant James attorney that the testators will reflected that he wanted to reward Plaintiffs services; as Plaintiff contended, the money was rightfully hers under the wills plain terms.

3. We selected three attorneys to oversee the drafting: Richard Brydan an attorney from the firm of Caillebotte Yuon and Hokusai William Moran a European-law expert from the firm of Frye Turner and Dennis and Katerina Valadon an attorney who is an expert on international business law.

4. The Grants parents left them the house but left the bulk of the estate to charities named in the will.

5. The doctors covenant with the clinic applied to three counties Victorina which was the site of the clinics main offices Micano-

pia which was where the clinic planned to open a new office and Putnam where the clinic had already established an office.

Assignment 5. Parallel Structure

Re-write each of the following sentences so that it has parallel structure.

1. Plaintiff suffered injuries, emotional distress and humiliation resulted, he developed a seizure disorder, wages were lost, and other injuries occurred that are at this time still unascertainable.

2. Defendant owned the building, was leasing it to Plaintiff for use as a grocery store, and the grocery business was operated by Plaintiff.

3. In performing the project, the student shall refrain from consulting another student, not create interference with another student's access to research materials, and unauthorized resources shall not be used.

4. The lessee promised that the lessee would ensure the following: its vehicles would be driven only on mapped roads; the lessee would collect and dispose of debris resulting from its cutting operations; at no time would any fires be set; and the lessee would not leave cut timber on the roads.

5. If an owner installs a sign on the premises, the sign shall not extend more than 5 feet over a public right of way; the sign shall not exceed an area of 12 square feet; it must be securely attached to the building; vehicular sight-lines shall not be impeded by the sign; the sign should not be in day-glow or neon-type colors; and no flashing illumination shall be used.

Assignment 6. Conciseness

a. Words and Phrases

Write a more concise substitute for each of the following words and phrases.

- In the event that   _____

- On account of the fact that   _____

- Prior to   _____

- Subsequent to   _____

- Utilize   _____

- Utilization   _____

- In the month of July   _____

- On the 5th day of July   _____

- At the present time   _____

- Red in color   _____

- Ten in number   _____

- A distance of 10 miles   _____

b. Sentences

Make the following sentences as concise as you can without changing the essence. Try to reduce each sentence to no more than 2 or 3 lines.

1. Notwithstanding the fact that substantial losses were reported by Defendant Corporation and that the company had made an announcement that in consequence of those losses it had become necessary in the circumstances for a significant number of individuals who were then employed by the company at non-management levels to be laid off in order to conserve reduced financial resources, huge bonuses were nevertheless paid out by the company to employees at the executive level in addition to other compensation that the top 10% of management had already previously received for their work.

2. In actual fact, Alcott is a judge who has expressed a strong preference for concise writing and who has in consequence insisted on the submission by attorneys of pleadings and motions that are written with a high level of clarity and precision and that do not under any circumstances contain more words than are actually necessary for the attorney to express his or her meaning and intention with the requisite clarity and precision.

3. Engineering is a subject that is a necessary prerequisite as a field of study for a person who has an aspiration to become a member of the legal profession dealing primarily or solely with issues involving or relating to the matter of patents as addressed in the law.

4. It is demonstrably the case that notice that was both in writing and sent by certified mail as the statute requires was in fact provided to the lessee by an agent who was at that time acting on behalf of our client, our client being then as now the person having the actual ownership interest in the property to which the lease applied.

5. It has been brought to the Board's attention that a request for information concerning the best way of making a gift in the form

of a significant monetary contribution to the general fund of this organization has been submitted by an individual who has recently been granted membership privileges in the organization.

ENDNOTES

■ ■ ■

We have provided these endnotes in order to share with interested readers the research that provides the background of many of our thoughts, conclusions, and recommendations and to provide a starting point for those wishing to delve more deeply into the issues. In the interest of reducing page count, we have not included parallel state cites or (for most cases) a full case history.

Endnotes for Chapter 1: General Introduction to Litigation–Related Documents

1. Iowa R. Civ. P. 1.401 (West 2011).

2. La. Code Civ. Proc. Ann. art. 891 (West 2011).

3. Mo. Sup. Ct. R. 55.01 (West 2011).

4. Tex. R. Civ. P. 45 (West 2011).

5. Fla. R. Civ. P. 1.100 (West 2012).

6. *See, e.g.*, Erickson v. Pardus, 551 U.S. 89, 93 (2007) (Federal Rule 8(a)(2) requires "short and plain statement of claim" showing that the pleader is entitled to relief; specific facts not necessary).

E.g., regarding the purpose of the pleadings: Kovacs Constr. Corp. v. Water Pollution & Control Auth. of City of New Haven, 992 A.2d 1157, 1165 (Conn. App. Ct. 2010) (pleading apprises court and opposing counsel of issues to be tried); Dalley v. Dykema Gossett, 788 N.W.2d 679, 686 (Mich. Ct. App. 2010) (pleading's primary function is to give sufficient notice of nature of claim or defense for opposite party "to take a responsive position"); Echols v. City of Riverside, 332 S.W.3d 207, 211 (Mo. Ct. App. 2010), *transfer denied* (Mar. 29, 2011), *reh'g and/or transfer denied* (Feb. 1, 2011) (pleadings present, define, and isolate the issues to give notice to trial court and all parties); James v. Commission for Lawyer Discipline, 310 S.W.3d 598, 608 (Tex. App. 2010) (pleading gives fair notice of party's claims and relief sought).

7. Cal. Civ. Proc. Code § 428.80 (West 2012).

8. *See* Fed R. Civ. P. 7(a) (West 2011). The Rule states that an *answer* to a counter-claim is one of the types of pleadings allowed. Other jurisdictions likewise refer to the responsive pleading as an "answer," including but not limited to the following: California (Cal. Civ. Proc. Code § 422.10 (West 2011)); Florida (Fla. R. Civ. P. 1.100 (West 2012)).

9. *E.g.,* states that refer to the responsive pleading as a "reply" include but are not limited to the following: Alabama (Ala. R. Civ. P. 7(a) (West 2011)); Arizona (Ariz. R. Civ. P. 7(a) (West 2012)); Georgia (Ga. Code Ann. § 9–11–7 (West 2011)); Iowa (Iowa R. Civ. P. 1.401 (West 2011)); Maine (Me. R. Civ. P. 7(a) (West 2012)); Nevada (Nev. R. Civ. P. 7(a) (West 2012)); and Oregon (Or. R. Civ. P. 13 (West 2012)).

10. Fed. R. Civ. P. 10(a) (West 2011).

11. *Id.*

12. *See, e.g.*, the rules on captions for Florida (Fla. R. Civ. P. 1.100 (West 2012)); Louisiana (La. Code Civ. Proc. Ann. art. 891 (West 2011)) (made specifically applicable to motions as well as pleadings by La. Prac. Civ. Proc. art. 962 (West 2010)); New Mexico (N.M. R. Civ. P. 1–008.1 (West 2011).

13. 28 U.S.C. § 2071 (West 2012) states that "all courts established by Act of Congress may from time to time prescribe rules for the conduct of their business. Such rules shall be consistent

with Acts of Congress and rules of practice and procedure prescribed under section 2072 of this title."

Federal Rule 83 provides that each district "acting by a majority of its district judges," may adopt and amend rules governing its practice, so long as the rules are consistent with, but not duplicative of, statutes and rules adopted under 28 U.S.C. §§ 2072 and 2075. FED R. CIV. P. 83(a) (West 2012).

14. U.S. Dist. Ct. M.D. Fla.L.Rule 1.05(a) (West 2012) (to search in Westlaw: FL R USDCTMD Rule 1.05); U.S. Dist. Ct. N.D. Fla. L. Rule 5.1. (West 2012) (to search in Westlaw: FL R USDCTND Loc. R. 5.1(B)(3)); U.S. Dist. Ct. S.D. Fla. Gen. R. 5.1(a)(4) (West 2012) (to search: FL R USDCTSD Gen. Rule 5.1).

15. CONN. PRACTICE BOOK 1998, § 4–1 (West 2011) (stipulating that all documents printed on paper must be 8 ½ × 11, with 2–inch blank space at bottom of first page for notations or receipt of filing time by clerk, with 2 inch blank space at top of each page, with 2 holes punched and with exact specifications regarding centering and placement of holes).

16. COLO. R. CIV. P. 10(d) (West 2012) (stating that paper documents must be printed on plain white 8 ½ by 11 paper, preferably recycled, that all documents must be legible and printed on one side only, that all must follow margins specifications, that all documents other than caption must use a left-justified margin, and that all must use no less than a 12–point font).

17. UTAH R. CIV. P. 10(d) (West 2012) (stating that all pleadings and other papers other than exhibits and court-approved forms must be 8 ½ × 11 on white background and setting out margin specifications; requiring double-spacing "except for matters customarily single-spaced," and requiring font not smaller than 12–point size).

18. FLA. R. JUD. ADMIN. 2.520(a) (West 2012).

19. FLA. R. JUD. ADMIN. 2.520(e) (West 2012).

20. U.S. Dist. Ct. W.D.N.C., LCvR 7.1 (West 2012) (to search in Westlaw: NC R USDCTWD LCvR 7.1).

21. *E.g.*, treating exhibit as incorporated in a pleading for all purposes: Arizona (ARIZ. R. CIV. P. 10(C) (West 2012)); Minnesota (MINN. R. CIV. P. 10.03 (West 2012)); North Carolina (N.C. R. CIV. P. § 1A–1, 1A–110).

22. Second Judicial District Local Rules, LR2–119 (New Mexico) (West 2012) (to search in Westlaw: NM R 2 DIST LR2–119).

23. FED. R. CIV. P. 11(a) (West 2011).

24. *E.g.*, stating that unless a rule or statute specifically provides otherwise, a pleading need not be verified or accompanied by an affidavit: ALASKA R. CIV. P. 11(a) (West 2012); FLA. R. CIV. P. 1.030 (West 2012); IOWA R. CIV. PRO. 1.413 (West 2012); KAN. STAT. ANN. § 60–211(a) (West 2011); KY. R. CIV. P. 11 (West 2012); ME. R. CIV. P. 11(a) (West 2012); MASS. R. CIV. P. 11(a) (West 2012); MICH. CT. R. 2.114(B)(1) (West 2012); MISS. R. CIV. P. 11(a) (West 2011); NEV. R. CIV. P. 11(a) (West 2012); N.C. GEN. STAT. § 1A–1, Rule 11(a) (2011); N.D. R. CIV. P. 11(a) (West 2012); S.C. R. CIV. P. 11(a) (West 2012); S.D. CODIFIED LAWS § 15–6–11(a) (West 2011); VT. R. CIV. P. 11(a) (West 2012).

25. *See* FLA. R. CIV. P. 1.110(b) (West 2012).

North Carolina's rule spells out the procedure for verification by affidavit when verification is required, explaining that a verification must state in substance that the contents of the pleading are true to the knowledge of the person verifying it, except as to matters stated on information and belief, and that as to those matters the person believes them to be true. N.C. R. Civ. P. § 1A–1,1A–111(b) (West 2012).

26. *Cf.* U.S. Dist. Ct. N.D. Fla. L. Rule 5.1 (West 2012) (to search in Westlaw: FL R USDCTND Loc. R. 5.1) (stating that all documents in civil and criminal cases to be filed by electronic means, except for documents filed pro se and documents identified by Administrative Order and except for those to whom a judicial officer grants exception for good cause); U.S. Dist. Ct. M.D. Fla. ECF Procedures (West 2012) (to search in Westlaw: FL R USDCTMD ECF Procedures) (stating that electronic filing mandatory, unless otherwise permitted by these administrative procedures, by general order of the court, or by authorization of judge); U.S. Dist. Ct. S.D. Fla. CM/ECF (West 2012) amended by 2012 FLORIDA COURT ORDER 1611 (C.O. 1611) (to search in Westlaw: FL R USDCTSD CM/ECF) (stating that electronic filing mandatory for all attorneys admitted to practice in that district).

27. U.S. Dist. Ct. N.J. Order 05–1 (West 2011) (to search in Westlaw: NJ R USDCT Order 05–1) (stating that electronic case filing is mandatory for all civil and criminal cases other than pro se cases and requests for exemption by attorneys permitted for good cause hardship only and reviewed in individual basis by court).

28. U.S. Dist. Ct. N.M. CM/ECF Procedure (West 2011) amended by 2011 NEW MEXICO COURT ORDER 4003 (C.O. 4003)) (to search in Westlaw: NM R USDCT CM/ECF Proc) (unless otherwise excepted, electronic filing mandatory).

29. U.S. Dist. Ct. W.D. OK ECF Policies (West 2011) amended by 2012 OKLAHOMA COURT ORDER 4701 (C.O. 4701) (to search in Westlaw: OK R USDCTWD ECF Policies) (stating that attorneys and other permitted registrants are required to file papers electronically, with limited exceptions, in civil and criminal cases).

30. U.S. Dist. Ct. W.D. Wa. ECF Procedures (West 2012) amended by 2012 WASHINGTON COURT ORDER 6001 (C.O. 6001) (to search in Westlaw: WA R USDCTWD ECF Procedures) (requiring electronic filing).

31. *See, e.g.*, FED. R. CIV. P. 4 (West 2011) (summons) and 4.1 (other process) (West 2011); FLA. R. CIV. P. 1.070 (process) (West 2012).

32. FED. R. CIV. P. 4(a) (West 2011).

33. FED. R. CIV. P. 5(a)(1) (West 2011).

34. *See* Cobell v. Norton, 211 F.R.D. 7, 10 (D.D.C. 2002).

35. *See* FED R. CIV. P. 11(b) and (c) (West 2011).

36. *Id.*

37. FED R. CIV. P. 11(b) (West 2011).

38. FED. R. CIV. P. 11(c)(1) (West 2011).

39. *E.g.*, U.S. Dist. Ct. M.D.N.C., LR 7.1 (West 2012) (to search in Westlaw: NC R USDCTMD LR7.1) (Attorneys signing papers submitted for filing must state their telephone numbers, mailing addresses and e-mail addresses. Attorneys admitted to practice before this Court must also include their state bar number).

40. *See, e.g., id.* and U.S. Dist. Ct. S.D.Ill., ECF Rule 8 (West 2012) (to search in Westlaw: IL R USDCTSD ECF Rule 8), the local rule for the Southern District of Illinois, which deals with the effect of an electronic signature. The rule states that when "filing users" register, they automatically endorse their electronic signature for purposes of Federal Rule 11 specifically, the Federal Rules of Procedure (civil and criminal) generally, and the local rules. The electronic signature is a valid signature for purposes of unsworn declarations pursuant to 28 U.S.C. § 1746, service and filing pursuant to Federal Rule of Civil Procedure 5, and establishing perjury pursuant to 18 U.S.C. §§ 1621–1623.

41. CAL. CIV. PROC. CODE § 128.7 (West 2011).

42. HAW. R. CIV. P. 11 (West 2012).

43. S.D. CODIFIED LAWS § 15–6–11(a)–(d) (West 2011).

44. UTAH R. CIV. P. 11 (West 2012).

45. W. VA. R. CIV. P. 11 (West 2011).

46. Regarding state rules that retain language from previous versions of Rule 11, *see, e.g.*, IDAHO R. CIV. P. 11 (West 2011) as amended by 2011 IDAHO COURT ORDER 0031 (C.O. 0031); KY. R. CIV. P. 11 (West 2012); ME. R. CIV. P. 11(a) (West 2012); N.C. R. CIV. P. 1A–1, 1A–111(a) (West 2012).

47. FLA. R. JUD. ADMIN. 2.515 (West 2012).

48. FLA. STAT. ANN. § 57.105(a) (West 2012).

Endnotes for Chapter 2: The Initial Pleading

1. *E.g.*, stating the purpose of pleading rules: Dauti Constr., LLC v. Water & Sewer Auth. of Town of Newtown, 10 A.3d 84, 89 (Conn. App. Ct. 2010), *appeal denied*, 15 A.3d 629 (2011); Estate of Kuhns v. Marco, 620 N.W.2d 488, 491 (Iowa 2000); LaSalle Bank, N.A. v. Reeves, 919 A.2d 738, 749 (Md. Ct. Spec. App. 2007); Echols v. City of Riverside, 332 S.W.3d 207, 211 (Mo. Ct. App. 2010), *transfer denied* (Mar. 29, 2011), *reh'g and/or transfer denied* (Feb. 1, 2011); Casaday v. All-state Ins. Co., 232 P.3d 1075, 1079 (Utah Ct. App. 2010), *cert. denied*, 238 P.3d 443 (Utah 2010).

2. *E.g.*, stating that the purpose of providing notice is to allow the defendant to prepare for trial: Dalley v. Dykema Gossett, 788 N.W.2d 679, 686 (Mich. Ct. App. 2010); Sanford v. Waugh & Co., Inc., 328 S.W.3d 836, 848 (Tenn. 2010); Fadness v. Fadness, 667 S.E.2d 857, 863 (Va. Ct. App. 2008).

3. *E.g.*, discussing elements of a negligence cause of action or theory: Stein v. Ryan, 662 F.3d 1114, 1117 (9th Cir. 2011) (Arizona law); Swearingen v. Momentive Specialty Chemicals, Inc., 662 F.3d 969, 972 (7th Cir. 2011) (Illinois law); Estate of Cummings v. Davie, 40 A.3d 971 (Me. 2012);

Newman v. Lichfield, 272 P.3d 625, 631 (Mt. 2012); Davenport v. D.M. Rental Properties, Inc., 718 S.E.2d 188, 189 (N.C. Ct. App. 2011); Klasch v. Walgreen Co., 264 P.3d 1155, 1158 (Nev. 2011); Pyeritz v. Commonwealth, 32 A.3d 687, 692 (Pa. 2011); Hymas v. UAP Distribution, Inc., 272 P.3d 889, 895 (Wash. 2012).

4. Fed. Rule Civ. P. 8(a) (West 2011).

5. 355 U.S. 41 (1957).

6. *Id.* at 45–46.

7. 550 U.S. 544, 557, 127 S.Ct. 1955, 1966 (2007) (*abrogating* Conley v. Gibson, 355 U.S. 41, 78 S.Ct. 99 (1957)).

8. *Id.*

9. 556 U.S. 662, 129 S.Ct. 1937, 1950 (2009).

10. *Twombly*, 550 U.S. at 547.

11. *Iqbal*, 556 U.S. at 684.

12. *Iqbal*, 556 U.S. at 664.

13. *Id.*

14. *Twombly*, 550 U.S. at 555 (internal citations omitted).

15. *Iqbal*, 556 U.S. 662, 679 (stating that if the well-pleaded facts do not permit the court to infer "more than the mere possibility of misconduct," the complaint has alleged, but has not shown, that the pleader is entitled to relief).

16. Trimble v. District of Columbia, 779 F. Supp. 2d 54, 57 (D.D.C. 2011) (quoting *Twombly*, 550 U.S. at 557 (2007)).

17. *See, e.g.*, Arthur R. Miller, *From Conley to Twombly to Iqbal: A Double Play on the Federal Rules of Civil Procedure*, 60 Duke L.J. 1, 2 (2010). In *In re Travel Agent Comm'n Antitrust Litig.*, 583 F.3d 896, 914 (6th Cir. 2009), the dissenting opinion notes that district judges across the country "have dismissed a large majority of Sherman Act claims on the pleadings misinterpreting the standards from *Twombly* and *Iqbal,* thereby slowly eviscerating antitrust enforcement under the Sherman Act." The judge further noted that under the new pleading rule, "it is possible to do away with price fixing cases based on reasonable inferences from strong circumstantial evidence.... But this direction is unlikely to be changed unless the Supreme Court steps in to make it clear that *Twombly* may not be used, as my colleagues propose, as a cover for repealing regulation of the marketplace through private antitrust enforcement." *Id.* at 915–16 (Merrit, J., dissenting).

18. *See* Khalik v. United Air Lines, 671 F.3d 1188, 1191 (10th Cir. 2012).

19. Travel Agent Comm'n, 583 F.3d at 915–16 (6th Cir. 2009) (Merrit, J., dissenting).

20. *See, e.g.,* Ramzi Kassem, *Implausible Realities: Iqbal's Retrenchment of Majority Group Skepticism Towards Discrimination Claims*, 114 Penn St. L. Rev. 1443, 1446 (2010).

21. *See* Travel Agent Comm'n, 583 F.3d at 911–12 (6th Cir. 2009) (Merritt, J., dissenting). The dissent in that case stated, "[T]he Supreme Court has started to modify somewhat, but not drastically, the notice pleading rules that have reigned under *Conley v. Gibson*.... Here my colleagues have seriously misapplied the new standard by requiring not simple 'plausibility,' but by requiring the plaintiff to present at the pleading stage a strong probability of winning the case...."

22. Khalik v. United Air Lines, 671 F.3d 1188, 1191 (10th Cir. 2012).

23. Tamayo v. Blagojevich, 526 F.3d 1074, 1084 (7th Cir. 2008).

24. *E.g.,* regarding states with provisions mirroring Federal Rule 8 rule requiring a short and plain statement showing that the pleader is entitled to relief: Ala. R. Civ. P. 8(a) (West 2012); Alaska R. Civ. P. 8(a) (West 2012); Colo. R. Civ. P. 8(a) (West 2012); Ga. Code Ann. § 9–11–8(a)(2) (West 2011); Haw. R. Civ. P. 8(a) (West 2012); Ind. R. Trial P. 8(A) (West 2012); Iowa R. Civ. P. 1.403(1) (West 2012); Kan. Stat. Ann. § 60–208(a) (West 2011); Ky. R. Civ. P. 8.01(1) (West 2012); Mass. R. Civ. P. 8(a) (West 2012); Minn. R. Civ. P. 8.01 (West 2012); Mont. R. Civ. P. 8(a) (West 2012); Nev. R. Civ. P. 8(a) (West 2012); N.M. Dist. Ct. R. 1–008(A) (West 2011); R.I. R. Civ. P. 8(a) (West 2010); S.D. Codified Laws § 15–6–8(a) (West 2012); Tenn. R. Civ. P. 8.01 (West 2011); Utah R. Civ. P. 8(a) (West 2012); Vt. R. Civ. P. 8(a) (West 2012); W. Va. R. Civ. P. 8(a) (West 2011); Wyo. R. Civ. P. 8(a) (West 2012).

25. *E.g.,* these opinions emphasize the notice function of the initial pleading: Story v. Bly, 217 P.3d 872, 876 (Colo. Ct. App. 2008) *aff'd*, 241 P.3d 529 (Colo. 2010); Bolin v. Davis, 283 S.W.3d 752, 756 (Ky. Ct. App. 2008); Peterson v. Volkswagen of Am., Inc., 679 N.W.2d 840, 850 (Wis. Ct. App. 2004) *aff'd*, 697 N.W.2d 61 (Wis. 2005).

26. Colby v. Umbrella, Inc., 955 A.2d 1082, 1090 (Vt. 2008) (Vermont rules strike a fair balance by encouraging valid but undeveloped causes of action and discouraging baseless or legally insufficient ones).

27. McCurry v. Chevy Chase Bank, FSB, 233 P.3d 861, 863 (Wash. 2010); *see* Webb v. Nashville Area Habitat for Humanity, Inc., 346 S.W.3d 422, 430 (Tenn. 2011).

The Alabama Court of Appeals refused to adopt the plausibility standard on the ground that it was bound to apply the Alabama Supreme Court's interpretation of the rules of civil procedure until the Alabama Supreme Court alters or abrogates that standard. McKelvin v. Smith, 85 So.3d 386, 390–391 (Ala. Civ. App. 2010), *cert. denied* (Dec. 9, 2011).

28. McCurry v. Chevy Chase Bank, FSB, 233 P.3d 861, 863 (Wash. 2010) (stating that plausibility standard adds a determination of the likelihood of success on the merits, allowing a trial judge to dismiss a claim if the judge does not consider it plausible that the claim will ultimately succeed even if the law would provide a remedy).

29. Webb v. Nashville Area Habitat for Humanity, Inc., 346 S.W.3d 422, 430 (Tenn. 2011).

30. *Id.* at 431–32.

31. *See, e.g.*, Doe v. Board of Regents of Univ. of Nebraska, 788 N.W.2d 264 (Neb. 2010).

32. *See, e.g.,* WIS. STAT. ANN. § 802.02 (West 2011) (stating that a pleading setting forth a claim for relief shall contain a statement of a claim identifying "the transaction or occurrence or series of transactions or occurrences out of which the claim arises and showing that the pleader is entitled to relief"). The Wisconsin Supreme Court characterized the rule as a "notice pleading standard," Doe v. Archdiocese of Milwaukee, 700 N.W.2d 180, 190–91 (Wis. 2005), though the Court stated that the rule nevertheless requires the plaintiff to state circumstances, occurrences, and events in support of the claim presented).

North Carolina has a similar rule. N.C. R. Civ. P. § 1A–1,1A–18 (West 2012) (stating that pleading must give court and parties notice of "the transactions, occurrences, or series of transactions or occurrences, intended to be proved showing that the pleader is entitled to relief"). In *Sutton v. Duke*, 176 S.E.2d 161, 167 (N.C. 1970), the North Carolina Supreme Court said, "Under the 'notice theory' of pleading contemplated by Rule 8(a)(1), detailed fact-pleading is no longer required. A pleading complies with the rule if it gives sufficient notice of the events or transactions which produced the claim to enable the adverse party to understand the nature of it and the basis for it."

33. ARK. R. CIV. P. 8(a) (West 2012) (stating that pleading must include a statement in ordinary and concise language of *facts* showing entitlement to relief); CAL. CIV. PROC. CODE § 425.10(a) (West 2012) (stating that complaint must contain a statement of *the facts* constituting the cause of action in ordinary and concise language); CONN. PRACTICE BOOK § 10–1 (West 2011) (stating that pleading must contain a plain and concise statement of the *material facts* on which the pleader relies); FLA. R. CIV. P. 1.110(b) (West 2012) (stating that pleading shall contain a short and plain statement of the ultimate *facts*); IL ST CH 735 § 5/2–603 (West 2012) (stating that pleadings shall contain a plain and concise statement of the pleader's *cause of action*); LA. CODE CIV. PROC. ANN. art. 854 (West 2011) (editor's note) (article preserves the Louisiana system of pleading *facts* as preferable to notice pleading); MD. R. CIV. P. 2–303(b) (West 2012) (stating that pleading to contain only such statements of *fact* as are necessary to show entitlement to relief); MICH. CT. R. 2.111 (West 2012) (stating that complaint must contain a *statement of the facts* on which the pleader relies in *stating the cause of action*); MO. SUP. CT. R. 55.05 (West 2012) (stating that a pleading setting forth a claim for relief shall contain a short and plain statement of *facts* showing that the pleader is entitled to relief); N.J. R. 4:5–2 (West 2012) (stating that the complaint must contain statement of the *facts* on which the claim is based); PA. R. CIV. P. 1019 (West 2012) (stating that complaint shall state the material *facts* on which a cause of action is based); S.C. R. CIV. P. 8(a) (West 2011) (stating that a pleading shall set forth a cause of action containing the *facts* showing that the pleader is entitled to relief); TEX. R. CIV. P. 47 (West 2011) (stating that a claim for relief must contain a short statement of the *cause of action* sufficient to give fair notice of the claim).

34. *E.g.,* CAL. CIV. PROC. CODE § 425.10(a) (West 2012) (complaint must state the facts constituting the *cause of action*); FLA. R. CIV. P. 1.110(b) (West 2012) (stating that pleading must *state a cause of action*); IL ST CH 735 § 5/2–603 (West 2012) (pleadings shall state the pleader's *cause of action*); LA. CODE CIV. PROC. ANN. art. 854 (West 2011) (editor's note) (stating that it is necessary in Louisiana to state the *cause of action*); MICH. CT. R. 2.111 (West 2012) (stating that complaint must state the *cause of action*, "with any specific allegations reasonably necessary to inform other party of the nature of the claims"); TEX. R. CIV. P. 47 (West 2011) (stating that claim for relief must contain a short statement of the *cause of action* sufficient to give fair notice of the claim).

35. MD. R. CIV. P. 2–303(b) (West 2012) (stating that pleading is to contain only such statements of *fact* as are necessary to show entitlement to relief).

36. Tavakoli–Nouri v. State, 779 A.2d 992, 1001 (Md. Ct. Spec. App. 2001) (*quoted in* 1000 Friends of Maryland v. Ehrlich, 907 A.2d 865, 870 n.8 (Md. Ct. Spec. App. 2006)).

37. RoTec Services, Inc. v. Encompass Services, Inc., 597 S.E.2d 881, 884 (S.C. Ct. App. 2004).

38. *Id.*

39. *E.g.,* regarding importance of alleging facts that if presumed true provide basis for subject-matter jurisdiction: Heffernan v. Brothers, 2012 WL 777505 at *2 (E.D. Va. 2012); Wohletz v. United States, 2012 WL 628830 at *1 (E.D. Wash. 2012); Guzman v. Higa, 2012 WL 488096 at *1 (D. Haw. 2012); Righthaven LLC v. Newman, 838 F.Supp.2d 1071, 1074 (D. Nev. 2011); Ching Yee Wong v. Napolitano, 654 F. Supp. 2d 1184, 1187 (D. Or. 2009); Huff v. U.S. Dept. of Army, 508 F. Supp. 2d 459, 462 (D. Md. 2007), *aff'd*, 390 F.Appx. 208 (4th Cir. 2010); Sheridan v. Reidell, 465 F. Supp. 2d 528, 533 (D.S.C. 2006).

40. 28 U.S.C.A. § 1332 (West 2012).

41. 28 U.S.C.A. § 1331 (West 2012).

42. 28 U.S.C.A. § 1332(a) (West 2012).

43. 28 U.S.C.A. § 1331 (West 2012).

44. ARIZ. R. CIV. P. 8(a)(1) (West 2012).

45. COLO. R. CIV. P. 8(a)(1) (West 2012).

46. FLA. R. CIV. P. 1.110(b)(1) (West 2012).

47. IDAHO R. CIV. P. 8(a)(1) (West 2011).

48. S.C. R. CIV. P. 8(a)(1) (West 2011).

49. WYO. R. CIV. P. 8(a)(1) (West 2012).

50. E.g., Tamburo v. Dworkin, 601 F.3d 693, 700 (7th Cir. 2010) *cert. denied,* 131 S. Ct. 567, 178 L. Ed. 2d 413 (U.S. 2010).

51. Goodyear Dunlop Tires Operations, S.A. v. Brown, 131 S. Ct. 2846, 2853–54, 180 L. Ed. 2d 796 (U.S.N.C. 2011).

52. Touchcom, Inc. v. Bereskin & Parr, 574 F.3d 1403, 1411 (Fed. Cir. 2009).

53. International Shoe Co. v. Washington, 326 U.S. 310, 66 S.Ct. 154 (1945); Hanson v. Denckla, 357 U.S. 235, 78 S.Ct. 1228 (1958); Goodyear Dunlop Tires Operations, S.A. v. Brown, 131 S. Ct. 2846, 2853 (U.S.N.C. 2011).

54. FLA. STAT. § 48.19 (West 2012).

55. CAL. CIV. PROC. CODE § 410.10 (West 2012).

56. *See, e.g.,* Monster Cable Products, Inc. v. Euroflex S.R.L., 642 F. Supp. 2d 1001, 1007 (N.D. Cal. 2009).

57. *See* Burger King Corp. v. Rudzewicz, 471 U.S. 462, 105 S. Ct. 2174, 2184 (1985); Hanson v. Denckla, 357 U.S. 235, 78 S. Ct. 1228, 1240 (1958).

58. *See, e.g.*, Goodyear Dunlop Tires Operations, S.A. v. Brown, 131 S. Ct. 2846, 2857 (U.S.N.C. 2011) (addressing exercise of general versus specific jurisdiction).

59. Touchcom, Inc. v. Bereskin & Parr, 574 F.3d 1403, 1411 (Fed. Cir. 2009).

60. *See* Goodyear Dunlop Tires Operations, F.A. v. Brown, 131 S. Ct. 2846, 2853 (U.S.N.C. 2011).

61. IND. R. TRIAL P. 8(A)(2) (West 2012).

62. N.M. DIST. CT. R. CIV. P. 1–008 (West 2011).

63. *E.g.,* regarding treatment of attorney's fees as special damages: Perry v. Serenity Behavioral Health Sys., 2009 WL 1259367 at *2 (S.D. Ga. 2009) (citing United Indus., Inc. v. Simon Hartley, Ltd., 91 F.3d 762, 764–65 (5th Cir. 1996)); In re Am. Cas. Co., 851 F.2d 794, 802 (6th Cir. 1988); Maidmore Realty Co. v. Maidmore Realty Co., 474 F.2d 840, 843 (3d Cir. 1973); Western Cas. & Sur. Co. v. Southwestern Bell Tel. Co., 396 F.2d 351, 356 (8th Cir. 1968) (stating that all but one of the circuits to have considered the issue held that attorney's fees are special damages that must be specifically pleaded under Federal Rule 9(g)).

64. *E.g.,* Stockman v. Downs, 573 So.2d 835, 838 (Fla. 1991) (stating that a party cannot recover attorney's fees if the claim was not pleaded or the objection to the failure to plead waived, *including* attorney's fees authorized by contract or statute).

65. *E.g.,* stating that if the exhibit contradicts allegations in the complaint, the exhibit trumps the allegations: Northern Indiana Gun & Outdoor Shows, Inc. v. City of S. Bend, 163 F.3d 449, 454 (7th Cir. 1998); Schatz v. Republican State Leadership Comm., 777 F. Supp. 2d 181, 189 (D. Me. 2011), *aff'd*, 669 F.3d 50 (1st Cir. 2012); Degirmenci v. Sapphire–Fort Lauderdale, LLLP, 693 F. Supp. 2d 1325, 1341 (S.D. Fla. 2010), *reconsideration denied* (Apr. 20, 2010); Venezia v. 12th & Div. Properties, LLC, 685 F. Supp. 2d 752, 759 (M.D. Tenn. 2010).

66. *E.g.,* regarding state rules relating to exhibits (including effect of attachment *or* of incorporation by reference): ALA. R. CIV. P. 10(c) (West 2011); COLO. R. CIV. P. 10(c) (West 2012); FLA. R. CIV. P. 1.130 (West 2012); GA. CODE ANN. § 9–11–10(c) (West 2011); KAN. STAT. ANN. § 60–210(c) (West 2011); KY. R. CIV. P. 10.03 (West 2012); ME. R. CIV. P. 10(c) (West 2012); MASS. R. CIV. P. 10(c) (West 2012); MICH. CT. R. 2.113(F) (West 2012); MISS. R. CIV. P. 10 (c) (West 2011); MONT. R. CIV. P. 10(c) (West 2012); NEV. R. CIV. P. 10 (c) (West 2012); N.D. R. CIV. P. 10(c) (West 2012); R.I. R. CIV. P. 10(c) (West 2010); WASH. R. SUPER. CT. CIV. C.R. 10(c) (West 2011); W. VA. R. CIV. P. 10(c) (West 2011); WYO. R. CIV. P. 10(c) (West 2012).

67. ARK. R. CIV. P. 10(d) (West 2012).

68. IL ST CH 735 § 5/2–606 (West 2012); MISS. R. CIV. P. 10 (d) (West 2011).

69. MICH. CT. R. 2.113(F) (West 2012).

70. TENN. R. CIV. P. 10.03 (West 2011).

71. *E.g.,* COLO. R. CIV. P. 8 (West 2012); FLA. R. CIV. P. 1.100(c)(2) (West 2012).

72. *See* Pastva v. Naegele Outdoor Adver., Inc., 468 S.E.2d 491, 493 (N.C. Ct. App. 1996), *review denied*, 471 S.E.2d 74 (1996).

73. Khalik v. United Air Lines, 671 F.3d 1188, 1192 (10th Cir. 2012).

74. *E.g.,* stating that in determining whether a pleading states a cause of action, court is free to disregard conclusions not supported by facts: Ford Motor Credit Co. v. Updegraff, 218 S.W.3d 617, 621 (Mo. Ct. App. 2007); Tyler v. Nebraska Dept. of Corr. Services, 701 N.W.2d 847, 851 (Neb. Ct. App. 2005); J & M Lumber & Constr. Co., Inc. v. Smyjunas, 20 A.3d 947 (N.H. 2011); Crozer Chester Med. Ctr. v. Department of Labor & Indus., Bureau of Workers' Comp., Health Care Services Review Div., 22 A.3d 189, 194 (Pa. 2011).

75. *Iqbal*, supra note 9, 566 U.S at 679, 129 S. Ct. at 1950.

76. *Id.*

77. Chatham Surgicore, Ltd. v. Health Care Serv. Corp., 826 N.E.2d 970, 974 (Ill. App. Ct. 2005).

78. *See, e.g.*, Doe v. Board of Regents of Univ. of Nebraska, 788 N.W.2d 264 (Neb. 2010).

79. *E.g.,* indicating that the plaintiff need not include evidentiary facts to support allegations of ultimate fact: Birke v. Oakwood Worldwide, 87 Cal.Rptr.3d 602, 609 (Ct. App. 2009), *reh'g denied* (Jan. 26, 2009), *review denied* (Apr. 15, 2009); Pickel v. Springfield Stallions, Inc., 926 N.E.2d 877, 882 (Ill. App. Ct. 2010); Whipple v. Allen, 324 S.W.3d 447, 449 (Mo. Ct. App. 2010); State ex rel. Children, Youth and Families Dept. v. Cosme V., 215 P.3d 747, 751 (N.M. Ct. App. 2009) *cert. denied*, 223 P.3d 359 (N.M.2009), *cert. denied*, 223 P.3d 359 (N.M. 2009).

80. Apollo Real Estate Inv. Fund, IV, L.P. v. Gelber, 935 N.E.2d 963, 976 (Ill. App. Ct. 2010), *reh'g denied* (Aug. 17, 2010), *appeal denied*, 942 N.E.2d 452 (2010).

81. Brown & Brown, Inc. v. Blumenthal, 1 A.3d 21 (Conn.2010); *see.* CONN. PRACTICE BOOK § 10–1 (stating that a pleading shall contain a plain and concise statement of the material facts, but not the evidence by which they are to be proved).

82. *See, e.g.,* LA. CODE CIV. PROC. ANN. art. 854 (2011) (editor's note) (Louisiana requires party to state cause of action and allege material facts, but not evidence).

83. Snierson v. Scruton, 761 A.2d 1046, 1048 (N.H. 2000).

84. *E.g.,* regarding materiality of allegations of time and place: ALASKA R. CIV. P. 9(g) (West 2012); ARIZ. R. CIV. P. 9(f) (West 2012); COLO. R. CIV. P. 9(f) (West 2012); IDAHO R. CIV. P. 9(f) (West 2011); IND. R. TRIAL P. 9(f) (West 2012); MASS. R. CIV. P. 9(f) (West 2012); MONT. R. CIV. P. 9(f) (West 2012); N.J. CT. R. 4:5–8 (West 2012); R.I. R. CIV. P. 9(f) (West 2010); S.C. R. CIV. P. 9(f) (West 2011); S.D. CODIFIED LAWS § 15–6–9(f) (West 2012); TENN. R. CIV. P. 9.06 (West 2011); W. VA. R. CIV. P. 9(f) (West 2011); WYO. R. CIV. P. 9(f) (West 2012).

85. FED. R. CIV. P. 8(d)(2)–(3) (West 2011).

86. *E.g.,* regarding state rules for pleading alternatively, inconsistently, or hypothetically: ALA. R. CIV. P. 8(e)(2) (West 2011); ALASKA R. CIV. P. 8(e)(2) (West 2012); COLO. R. CIV. P. 8(e)(2) (West 2012); HAW. R. CIV. P. 8(e)(2) (West 2012); IL ST CH 735 § 5/2–613(a)–(b) (West 2012); ME. R. CIV.

P. 8(e)(2) (West 2012); Mich. Ct. R. 2.111(A)(2) (West 2012); Minn. R. Civ. P. 8.05(b) (West 2012); N.J. R. Civ. P. 4:5–6 (West 2012); N.M. R. Civ. P. 1–008(e)(2) (West 2011); N.C. R. Civ. P. § 1A–1, 1A–18(e)(2) (West 2012); Or. R. Civ. P. 16(C); R.I. R. Civ. P. 8(e)(2) (West 2010); Vt. R. Civ. P. 8(e)(2) (West 2012); Wash. Super. Ct. Civ. CR 8(e)(2) (West 2011); W. Va. R. Civ. P. 8(e)(2) (West 2011); Wyo. R. Civ. P. 8(e)(2) (West 2012).

87. Mendoza v. Rast Produce Co., Inc., 45 Cal.Rptr.3d 525, 531 (Ct. App. 2006).

E.g., regarding pleading in alternative: Anzalone v. Administrative Office of Trial Court, 932 N.E.2d 774, 779 (Mass. 2010); Mays–Maune & Associates, Inc. v. Werner Bros., Inc., 139 S.W.3d 201, 205 (Mo. Ct. App. 2004); James River Equip., Inc. v. Mecklenburg Utilities, Inc., 634 S.E.2d 557, 560 (N.C. Ct. App. 2006).

88. Anzalone v. Administrative Office of Trial Court, 932 N.E.2d 774, 779 (Mass. 2010).

89. *E.g.,* stating that the plaintiff can allege alternative theories regarding the facts: Nalen v. Jenkins, 741 P.2d 366, 368 (Idaho Ct. App. 1987); City of Glenn Heights v. Sheffield Dev. Co., Inc., 55 S.W.3d 158, 165 (Tex. App. 2001), *review denied* (Feb. 28, 2002); *see* Fed. R. Civ. P. 8(d)(2)–(3) (West 2011).

90. *E.g.,* regarding limitations on paragraph content: Ala. R. Civ. P. 10(b) (West 2011); Ark. R. Civ. P. 10(b) (West 2012); Fla. R. Civ. P. 1.110(f) (West 2012); Ga. Code Ann. § 9–11–10(b) (West 2011); Ind. R. Trial P. 10(B) (West 2012); Me. R. Civ. P. 10(b) (West 2012); Mich. Ct. R. 2.113(E) (West 2012); Minn. R. Civ. P. 10.02 (West 2012); N.D. R. Civ. P. 10(b) (West 2012); Or. R. Civ. P. 16B (West 2012); Pa. R. Civ. P. 1022 (West 2012); R.I. R. Civ. P. 10(b) (West 2010); Wash. R. Super. Ct. Civ. C.R. 10(b) (West 2011); Wis. Stat. Ann. § 802.04(2) (West 2011); Wyo. R. Civ. P. 10(b) (West 2012).

91. IL ST CH 735 § 5/2–603(b) (West 2012).

92. Conn. Practice Book § 10–26 (West 2011).

93. *E.g.*, regarding separation of allegations into counts: Alaska R. Civ. P. 10(b) (West 2012); Fla. R. Civ. P. 1.110(f) (West 2012); Ga. Code Ann. § 9–11–10(b) (West 2011); Ind. R. Trial P. 10(B) (West 2012); Ky. R. Civ. P. 10.02 (West 2012); Mass. R. Civ. P. 10(b) (West 2012); N.D. R. Civ. P. 10(b) (West 2012); Nev. St. R. Civ. P. 10(b) (West 2012); R.I. R. Civ. P. 10(b) (West 2010); S.C. R. Civ. P. 10(b) (West 2011); S.D. Codified Laws § 15–6–10(b) (West 2012); Wash. R. Super. Ct. Civ. C.R. 10(b) (West 2011); W. Va. R. Civ. P. 10(b) (West 2011); Wis. Stat. Ann. § 802.04(2) (West 2011); Wyo. R. Civ. P. 10(b) (West 2012).

94. Or. R. Civ. P. 16B (West 2012); *cf.* Pa. R. Civ. P. 1020(a) (West 2012) (requiring separate cause of action to be set forth in a separate count); *accord* Md. R. Civ. P. Cir. Ct. 2–303 (West 2012).

95. *E.g.,* regarding adoption or incorporation by reference: Ala. R. Civ. P. 10(c) (West 2011); Ark. R. Civ. P. 10(c) (West 2011); Colo. R. Civ. P. 10(c) (West 2012); Ga. Code Ann. § 9–11–10(c) (West 2011); Ky. R. Civ. P. 10.02 (West 2012); Mass. R. Civ. P. 10(c) (West 2012); Me. R. Civ. P. 10 (West 2012); Md. Civ. P. Cir. Ct. R. 2–303(d) (West 2012); Mont. R. Civ. P. 10(c) (West 2012); Nev. R. Civ. P. 10(c) (West 2012); N.D. R. Civ. P. 10(c) (West 2012); Or. R. Civ. P. 16D (West 2012); R.I. R. Civ. P. 10(c) (West 2010); Tex. R. Civ. P. 58 (West 2011); Vt. R. Civ. P. 10(c) (West 2012); Wyo. R. Civ. P. 10(c) (West 2012).

96. *E.g.,* Byrne v. Nezhat, 261 F.3d 1075, 1133 (11th Cir. 2001), *abrogated on other grounds in* Douglas Asphalt Co. v. QORE, Inc., 657 F.3d 1146 (11th Cir. 2011). The court said if a defendant faced with a shotgun complaint does not move the district court to require a more definite statement, the court must intervene sua sponte and order a repleader. *Id.* "Implicit in such instruction is the notion that if the plaintiff fails to comply with the court's order … the court should strike his pleading or, depending on the circumstances, dismiss his case and consider the imposition of monetary sanctions."

97. Degirmenci v. Sapphire–Fort Lauderdale, LLLP, 693 F. Supp. 2d 1325, 1336 (S.D. Fla. 2010), *reconsideration denied* (Apr. 20, 2010).

Endnotes for Chapter 3: Answers (Defensive Pleadings)

1. *E.g.,* regarding time for presenting defenses and objections: Ark. R. Civ. P. 12(a) (West 2012); Cal. Civ. Proc. Code § 430.40 (West 2012); Conn. Practice Book § 10–8 (West 2011); Fla. R. Civ. P. 1.140 (West 2012); Mass. R. Civ. P. 12(a) (West 2012); Mo. Sup. Ct. R. 55.25 (West 2012); S.D. Codified Laws § 15–6–12(a) (West 2011); Va. Sup. Ct. R. 3:8 (West 2011); Wash. R. Super. Ct. Civ. C.R. 12(a) (West 2011).

2. Fed. R. Civ. P. 55(a) (West 2011).

3. FED. R. CIV. P. 55(b)(1) (West 2011). "If the plaintiff's claim is for a sum certain or a sum that can be made certain by computation, the clerk—on the plaintiff's request, with an affidavit showing the amount due—must enter judgment for that amount and costs against a defendant who has been defaulted for not appearing and who is neither a minor nor an incompetent person."

4. *Id.*

5. CommScope, Inc. of N. Carolina v. Commscope (U.S.A.) Int'l Group Co., Ltd., 809 F. Supp. 2d 33, 37 (N.D.N.Y. 2011).

6. *E.g.,* In re Suprema Specialties, Inc., 330 B.R. 40, 44–45 (S.D.N.Y. 2005) (court shares general judicial distaste for disposing of cases by defaults rather than on the merits); In re Reilly, 213 B.R. 50, 52 (Bankr. D. Conn. 1997) (defaults generally disfavored, "reserved for rare occasions," and good cause "should be construed generously); Eastern Elec. Corp. of New Jersey v. Shoemaker Constr. Co., 652 F. Supp. 2d 599, 604 (E.D. Pa. 2009) (finding that entry of default judgment generally disfavored because it prevents a decision on the merits); TIP Sys., LLC v. SBC Operations, Inc., 536 F. Supp. 2d 745, 767 (S.D. Tex. 2008), *appeal dismissed*, 275 F.Appx 959 (Fed. Cir. 2008) (stating that default judgments generally disfavored and should not be granted on a claim that a party has failed to meet a procedural time requirement without more).

7. United States v. Signed Pers. Check No. 730 of Yubran S. Mesle, 615 F.3d 1085, 1091–92 (9th Cir. 2010) (quoting Falk v. Allen, 739 F.2d 461, 463 (9th Cir. 1984)).

8. Enron Oil Corp. v. Diakuhara, 10 F.3d 90, 96 (2d Cir. 1993) *cited in* State St. Bank & Trust Co. v. Inversiones Errazuriz Limitada, 374 F.3d 158, 168 (2d Cir. 2004).

9. State St. Bank & Trust Co. v. Inversiones Errazuriz Limitada, 374 F.3d 158, 168 (2d Cir. 2004), *cert. denied*, 543 U.S. 1177 (2005).

10. Stafford v. Mesnik, 63 F.3d 1445, 1450 (7th Cir. 1995).

11. *E.g.,* Southeast Land Developers, Inc. v. All Florida Site & Utilities, Inc., 28 So.3d 166, 167 (Fla. Dist. Ct. App. 2010) (stating a strong preference for lawsuits to be decided on merits rather than by default judgment); In re TW, 248 P.3d 234, 238 (Haw. Ct. App. 2011), *as corrected* (Mar. 2, 2011) (stating that the sanction is a harsh one and default judgments are not favored because they do not afford parties the opportunity to litigate on the merits); Sears Roebuck & Co. v. Soja, 932 N.E.2d 245, 248–49 (Ind. Ct. App. 2010), *transfer denied* (Jan. 21, 2011) (stating that default judgments are held in disfavor and trial court should resolve in favor of the defaulting party, since "there is a marked judicial deference for deciding disputes on their merits and for giving parties their day in court"); Hutcherson v. Hicks, 320 S.W.3d 102, 104 (Ky. Ct. App. 2010) (stating that default judgments are disfavored and trial court has broad discretion to set them aside); Agnello v. Walker, 306 S.W.3d 666, 673 (Mo. Ct. App. 2010), *as modified* (Apr. 27, 2010) (stating that Missouri courts disfavor default judgments and prefer that cases be decided on their merits); Khanal v. Sheldon, 904 N.Y.S.2d 453, 454 (App. Div. 2010) (stating that court may vacate a default if moving party demonstrates reasonable excuse and existence of potentially meritorious cause of action or defense; public policy favors determination of controversies on their merits).

12. Thomas v. Brown, 707 S.E.2d 900, 903 (Ga. Ct. App. 2011).

13. East Winds Properties, LLC v. Jahnke, 772 N.W.2d 738, 742 (Wis. Ct. App. 2009).

14. *E.g.,* regarding rules governing responses to allegations in complaint ("form of denials"): GA. CODE ANN. § 9–11–8(b) (West 2011); IND. R. TRIAL P. 8(B) (West 2012); KAN. STAT. ANN. § 60–208(b)(2)–(5) (West 2011); KY. R. CIV. P. 8.02 (West 2012); MO. SUP. CT. R. 55.07 (WEST 2012); MONT. R. CIV. P. 8(b) (West 2012); NEV. R. CIV. P. 8(b) (West 2012); N.M. DIST. CT. R. CIV. P. 1–008(B) (West 2011); N.C. R. CIV. P. § 1A–1, 1A–18(b) (West 2012); N.D. R. CIV. P. 8(b)(2)–(5) (West 2012); OR. R. CIV. P. 19(A) (West 2012); PA. R. CIV. P. 1029(a)–(c) (West 2012); R.I. R. CIV. P. 8(b) (West 2010); S.C. R. CIV. P. 8(b) (West 2011); S.D. CODIFIED LAWS § 15–6–8(b) (West 2012); WYO. R. CIV. P. 8(b) (West 2012).

15. *See* FED. R. CIV. P. 11(b)(4) (West 2011) (in presenting a litigation document to the court, an attorney certifies to the best of his or her knowledge, information, and belief, formed after a reasonable inquiry, that responses asserting insufficient information are reasonably based on lack of information).

16. Djourabchi v. Self, 571 F. Supp. 2d 41, 50 (D.D.C. 2008). The court said that the defendant's argument that he believed he operated under a licensed contractor's supervision (though without specifying the licensed contractor's identity) only lent support to the inference that the defendant knew that he had no license. Furthermore, if he in fact believed he operated under the supervision of a licensed contractor hired by the plaintiffs, that belief would not shield him from liability. The court concluded that defendant knew he was not licensed in the District of Columbia as a home improvement contractor.

17. *Id.*

18. *Id.*

19. *See* PA. R. CIV. P. 1029 (West 2012).

20. *E.g.,* regarding rule that allegations are admitted if not denied: Pedroza v. Lomas Auto Mall, Inc., 716 F. Supp. 2d 1031, 1044 (D.N.M. 2010); Kozak v. Hillsborough Pub. Transp. Comm'n, 695 F. Supp. 2d 1285, 1303 (M.D. Fla. 2010), *aff'd sub nom.* Kozak v. Hillsborough County, Fla., 644 F.3d 1347 (11th Cir. 2011); Lauter v. Anoufrieva, 642 F. Supp. 2d 1060, 1110 (C.D. Cal. 2009).

21. FED. R. CIV. P. 8(b)(3) (West 2011).

22. N.J. CT. R. 4:5–3 (West 2012).

23. MO. SUP. CT. R. 55.07 (West 2012).

24. PA. R. CIV. P. 1029 (West 2012).

25. State Farm Mut. Auto. Ins. Co. v. Riley, 199 F.R.D. 276, 278 (N.D. Ill. 2001).

26. PA. R. CIV. P. No. 1029 (West 2012).

27. Controlled Env't Sys. v. Sun Process Co., Inc., 173 F.R.D. 509, 510 (N.D. Ill. 1997).

28. *E.g.,* Lane v. Page, 272 F.R.D. 581, 603 (D.N.M. 2011).

29. *See* Farrell v. Pike, 342 F. Supp. 2d 433, 441 (M.D.N.C. 2004).

30. Rohrer v. Pope, 918 A.2d 122, 129 (Pa. Super. Ct. 2007) (quoting Mellon Bank, N.A. v. National Union Ins. Co. of Pittsburgh, PA, 768 A.2d 865, 869 n.1 (Pa. Super. Ct. 2001)).

31. Azza Int'l Corp. v. Gas Research Inst., 204 F.R.D. 109, 110 (N.D. Ill. 2001).

32. Lane v. Page, 272 F.R.D. 581, 598 (D.N.M. 2011).

33. Pujals ex rel. El Rey De Los Habanos, Inc. v. Garcia, 777 F. Supp. 2d 1322, 1327 (S.D. Fla. 2011).

34. *E.g.,* Lane v. Page, 272 F.R.D. 581, 598 (D.N.M. 2011) (stating that burden for establishing affirmative defenses generally lies on defendant).

35. Florida Health Sciences Ctr., Inc. v. Humana Med. Plan, Inc., 190 F. Supp. 2d 1297, 1304 (M.D. Fla. 2001) (failure to plead affirmative defense generally results in waiver of defense; affirmative defense must be pleaded in answer to give opposing party sufficient notice and ability to gather evidence and develop arguments to refute defense).

36. Failing to raise the defense in the answer might not automatically waive it if the court determines that the plaintiff had timely notice. *E.g.,* Gilbert v. Ferry, 413 F.3d 578, 579–80 (6th Cir. 2005) (that although the defendants did not raise the defense of collateral estoppel, the failure to raise an affirmative defense in the answer does not always result in waiver); Senn v. Carolina E., Inc., 111 F. Supp. 2d 1218, 1223 (M.D. Ala. 2000) *aff'd sub nom.* Senn v. Carolina E., 245 F.3d 796 (11th Cir. 2000) (holding that the purpose of Rule 8(c) is to ensure that the opposing party has notice of an issue that may be raised at trial; if plaintiff has notice, noncompliance with Rule 8(c) results in no prejudice and trial court does not err by hearing evidence on issue).

37. *E.g.,* FED. R. CIV. P. 8(b)(6) (West 2011).

38. *E.g.,* setting out certain affirmative defenses recognized under state law: ARK. R. CIV. P. 8(c) (West 2012); COLO. R. CIV. P. 8(c) (West 2012); FLA. R. CIV. P. 1.110(d) (West 2012); GA. CODE ANN. § 9–11–8(c) (West 2011); IDAHO R. CIV. P. 8(c) (West 2011); IND. R. TRIAL P. 8(c) (West 2012); ME. R. CIV. P. 8(c) (West 2012); MASS. R. CIV. P. 8(c) (West 2012); MICH. CT. R. 2.111(F)(3) (West 2012); MINN. R. CIV. P. 8.03 (West 2012); MONT. R. CIV. P. 8(c) (West 2012); N.J. CT. R. 4:5–4 (West 2012); N.M. DIST. CT. R. CIV. P. 1–008(C) (West 2011); OR. R. CIV. P. 19(B) (West 2012); R.I. R. CIV. P. 8(c) (West 2010); TEX. R. CIV. P. 94 (WEST 2011); WIS. STAT. ANN. § 802.02 (West 2011).

39. COLO. R. CIV. P. 8(c) (West 2012).

40. *Id.*

41. 5A R. Lloyd, C. Wright & A. Miller, FEDERAL PRACTICE AND PROCEDURE § 1294 (3d ed. 2010).

42. *E.g.,* F.D.I.C. v. Cheng, 832 F.Supp. 181, 188 (N.D. Tex. 1993).

43. *E.g.,* Smeed v. Carpenter, 274 F.2d 414, 418 (9th Cir. 1960) (though Defendant attempted to raise the defense that complaint failed to state a claim for which relief could be granted, the alleged defect was not apparent and Defendant should have supported the defense with "sufficient particularity to apprise the court of the defect.")

44. Woodfield v. Bowman, 193 F.3d 354, 362 (5th Cir.1999).

45. Lawrence v. Chabot, 182 F. App'x. 442, 456–57 (6th Cir. 2006) (discussing Davis v. Sun Oil Co., 148 F.3d 606, 612 (6th Cir.1998)).

46. *See, e.g.*, Memory Control Enter., LLC v. Edmunds.com, Inc., 2012 WL 681765 at *4 (C.D. Cal. 2012) (unreported case) (stating that no Court of Appeals, including the Ninth Circuit, had as of that date ruled on whether the *Twombly* and *Iqbal* "plausibility" standard applies to affirmative defenses).

47. *See, e.g.*, Bradshaw v. Hilco Receivables, LLC, 725 F. Supp. 2d 532, 536 (D. Md. 2010) (unreported) (pointing out that Supreme Court in *Twombly* and *Iqbal* did not address pleading requirements for affirmative defenses and Courts of Appeal have not resolved the question, though majority of district courts that have addressed the issue have answered in the affirmative; and in fact Rule 8 uses similar language to describe requirements for pleading claims and defenses); Barnes v. AT & T Pension Benefit Plan–Nonbargained Program, 718 F. Supp. 2d 1167, 1171–72 (N.D. Cal. 2010) (stating that the majority of courts presented with the issue have extended *Twombly's* heightened pleading standard to affirmative defenses and only a few have reached the contrary conclusion; and reasoning in favor of extending the heightened pleading standard is persuasive).

48. *E.g.*, regarding some of the courts that have determined that plausibility standard applies to affirmative defenses: Barnes v. AT&T Pension Benefit Plan—Nonbargained Program, 718 F. Supp. 2d 1167, 1171 (N.D. Cal. 2010) (stating that requirements of Rule 8 applicable to pleading defenses parallels requirements for pleading claims; heightened pleading standard should apply to affirmative defenses); Racick v. Dominion Law Associates, 270 F.R.D. 228, 232 (E.D.N.C. 2010) (stating that Rule 8 uses similar language regarding requirements for pleading claims and for pleading defenses); Hayne v. Green Ford Sales, Inc., 263 F.R.D. 647, 650 (D. Kan. 2009) (stating that it makes no sense to apply heightened pleading standard to claims but not defenses); United States v. Quadrini, 69 Fed. R. Serv. 3d 953 (E.D. Mich. 2007) (stating that plausibility standard applies to defenses; like the plaintiff, defendant must plead sufficient facts to demonstrate a plausible affirmative defense or one with "reasonably founded hope" of success).

See Topline Solutions, Inc. v. Sandler Sys., Inc., 2010 WL 2998836 at *1 (D. Md. 2010) (stating that at a minimum, facts asserted in affirmative defenses and reasonable inferences to be drawn from them must plausibly suggest a cognizable defense); Castillo v. Roche Laboratories Inc., 2010 WL 3027726 (S.D. Fla. 2010); Palmer v. Oakland Farms, Inc., 2010 WL 2605179 at *3–5 (W.D. Va. 2010).

49. *See, e.g.*, J & J Sports Productions, Inc. v. Franco, 2011 WL 794826 at *2 (E.D. Cal. 2011) (out of 29 boilerplate defenses alleged in an answer, many were inapplicable to the pleading).

50. Safeco Ins. Co. of Am. v. O'Hara Corp., 2008 WL 2558015 at *1 (E.D. Mich. 2008) (plausibility standard rules out boilerplate defenses; those submitted were not "presently sustainable"). *See* Ulyssix Technologies, Inc. v. Orbital Network Eng'g, Inc., 2011 WL 631145 at *15–16 (D. Md. 2011) (striking defenses that assert bare legal conclusions); Castillo v. Roche Laboratories Inc., 2010 WL 3027726 at *3 (S.D. Fla. 2010) (stating that purpose of the defense is to give notice of some plausible factual basis for it, which boilerplate does not).

51. Safeco Ins. Co. of Am. v. O'Hara Corp., 2008 WL 2558015 at *1 (E.D. Mich. 2008).

52. *E.g.*, regarding refusal of some courts to apply the plausibility standard to affirmative defenses: Lane v. Page, 272 F.R.D. 581, 591 (D.N.M. 2011); Tyco Fire Products LP v. Victaulic Co., 777 F. Supp. 2d 893, 900 (E.D. Pa. 2011).

See Memory Control Enter., LLC v. Edmunds.com, Inc., 2012 WL 681765 at *4–5 (C.D. Cal. 2012); Cottle v. Falcon Holdings Mgmt., LLC, 2012 WL 266968 at *2–3 (N.D. Ind. 2012); Bennett v. Sprint Nextl Corp., 2011 WL 4553055 at *1–2 (D. Kan. 2011); Bank of Beaver City v. Southwest Feeders, LLC, 2011 WL 4632887 at *6 (D. Neb. 2011) (stating that applying plausibility to affirmative defenses seems incompatible with law in 8th Circuit and district court is not free to extend the rule absent guidance); Chiancone v. City of Akron, 2011 WL 4436587 at *3–4 (N.D. Ohio 2011); Lopez v. Asmar's Mediterranean Food, Inc., 2011 WL 98573 at *2–3 (E.D. Va. 2011); McLemore v. Regions Bank, 2010 WL 1010092 at *13 (M.D. Tenn. 2010), *aff'd*, 682 F.3d 414 (6th Cir. 2012) (stating that *Twombly* and *Iqbal* did not change standard for affirmative defenses).

53. Lane v. Page, 272 F.R.D. 581, 591 (D.N.M. 2011) ("The Court declines to extend the heightened pleading standard the Supreme Court established in *Bell Atlantic v. Twombly* and *Ashcroft v. Iqbal* to affirmative defenses.") Accord: Tyco Fire Products LP v. Victaulic Co., 777 F. Supp. 2d 893, 900 (E.D. Pa. 2011); Lopez v. Asmar's Mediterranean Food, Inc., 2011 WL 98573 at *2–3 (E.D. Va. 2011).

54. FED. R. CIV. P. 9(a)(1) (West 2011).

55. *See, e.g.*, Kiernan v. Zurich Companies, 150 F.3d 1120, 1123–24 (9th Cir. 1998) (stating that Rule 9(g) applies a loose standard for averring satisfaction of conditions precedent); Campos v. Las Cruces Nursing Ctr., 828 F.Supp.2d 1256 (D.N.M. 2011) (holding that plaintiff can allege generally occurrence of conditions precedent, but defendant must deny occurrence with particularity); El–Ad Residences At Miramar Condo. Ass'n, Inc. v. Mt. Hawley Ins. Co., 2009 WL 3019786 at *2 (S.D. Fla. 2009) (Rule 9(c) provides that it is sufficient to aver generally that all conditions precedent have been performed or have occurred; though denial of performance must be made specifically and with particularity).

56. Arbor Acres Farm, Inc. v. GRE Ins. Group, 2002 WL 32107944 at *4 (E.D. Cal. 2002) (emphasis in original).

57. *E.g.,* Fort Howard Paper Co. v. Standard Havens, Inc., 119 F.R.D. 397, 405 (E.D. Wis. 1988) *aff'd*, 901 F.2d 1373 (7th Cir. 1990) (if a denial of a condition precedent is not made specifically and with particularity, Rule 9(c) requires it to be stricken).

58. E.E.O.C. v. Service Temps, Inc., 2010 WL 1644909 at *4 (N.D. Tex. 2010) *reconsideration denied*, 2010 WL 2381499 (N.D. Tex. 2010), *aff'd sub nom.*, EEOC v. Serv. Temps Inc., 679 F.3d 323 (5th Cir. 2012).

59. *E.g.,* Server Tech., Inc. v. American Power Conversion Corp., 2011 WL 1743872 at *1 (D. Nev. 2011) (stating that because affirmative defense of inequitable conduct sounds in fraud, must be pleaded with particularity under Rule 9(b)); Novartis Pharmaceuticals Corp. v. Roxane Laboratories, Inc., 2011 WL 1322271 at *7 (D.N.J. 2011) (stating that though inequitable conduct is broader concept than fraud, it must be pleaded with particularity under rule 9(b)); KeyBank Nat'l Ass'n v. Perkins Rowe Associates, Inc., 2010 WL 4942206 at *3 (M.D. La. 2010) (holding that plaintiff did not plead affirmative defense of fraud with sufficient particularity); Operating Engineers' Pension Trust Fund v. Fife Rock Products Co., 2010 WL 2635782 at *4 (N.D. Cal. 2010) (court granted motion to strike affirmative defense of fraud not stated with particularity and granted defendants leave to amend).

60. Schutz Container Sys., Inc. v. Mauser Corp., 2010 WL 2408983 at *1 (N.D. Ga. 2010) (finding the allegations in the defense sufficient, though simple).

61. Barnes v. AT & T Pension Benefit Plan–Nonbargained Program, 718 F. Supp. 2d 1167, 1170 (N.D. Cal. 2010).

Endnotes for Chapter 4: Motions

1. U.S. Dist. Ct. Rules D. S.C. Civ R, 7.02 (West 2011) (to search in Westlaw: SC R USDCT Civ Rule 7.02).

2. U.S. Dist. Ct. Rules D. R.I., LR Civ. 7(a) (West 2012) (to search in Westlaw: RI R USDCT LR Cv 7).

3. U. S. Dist. Ct. Rules D. Vt., LR Civ. 7 (West 2012) (to search in Westlaw: VT R USDCT LR 7).

4. Fed. R. Civ. P. 11 (2011).

5. U.S. Dist. Ct. Rules D. S.C. Civ Rule 7.09 (West 2011) (to search in Westlaw: SC R USDCT Civ Rule 7.09).

6. U.S. Dist. Ct. Rules W.D. Mo., LR Civ. P. 7.0 (c)–(f) (West 2012) (to search in Westlaw: MO R USDCTWD Rule 7.0).

7. U.S. Dist. Ct. Rules D. Neb. Civ. R 7.0.1(a)(2) (West 2012) (to search in Westlaw: NECivR 7.0.1); *cf.* U.S. Dist. Ct. Rules M.D.N.C., LR7.3(c) (West 2012) (to search: NC R USDCTMD LR7.3).

8. Joint U.S. Dist. Ct. Rules D. Ky., LR 7.1(a) (West 2012) (to search in Westlaw: KY R USDCT LR 7.1).

9. U.S. Dist. Ct. Rules N.D. Fla. Loc. R. 7.1(A) (West 2012) (to search in Westlaw: FL R USDCTND Loc. R. 7.1).

10. U.S. Dist. Ct. Rules S.D. W.Va., LR Civ. P. 7.1(a)(2) (West 2011) (to search in Westlaw: WV R USDCTSD LR Civ P 7.1).

11. U.S. Dist. Ct. Rules S.D. Cal. Civ. LR 7.1(f)(2) (West 2011) (to search in Westlaw: CA R USDCTSD CivLR 7.1).

12. *E.g.,* Joint U.S. Dist. Ct. Rules D. Ky., LR 7.1(e) (West 2012) (to search in Westlaw: KY R USDCT LR 7.1).

13. U.S. Dist. Ct. Rules S.D. Cal. Civ. LR 7.1(d)(1) (West 2011) (to search in Westlaw: CA R USDCTSD CivLR 7.1).

14. U.S. Dist. Ct. Rules Neb. Civ. R 7.01(d) (West 2012) (to search in Westlaw: NECivR 7.0.1).

15. U.S. Dist. Ct. Rules Neb. Civ. R 7.01(d) (West 2012) (to search in Westlaw: NECivR 7.0.1).

16. U.S. Dist. Ct. Rules M.D.N.C., LR7 7.3(c) (West 2012) (to search in Westlaw: NC R USDCTMD LR7.3).

17. U.S. Dist. Ct. Rules S.D. Cal. Civ. LR 7.1(d)(2) (West 2011) (to search in Westlaw: CA R USDCTSD CivLR 7.1).

18. *E.g.,* U.S. Dist. Ct. Rules M.D.N.C., LR7 7.3(h) (West 2012) (to search in Westlaw: NC R USDCTMD LR7.3); U.S. Dist. Ct. Rules D. Neb. Civ. R. 7.0.1(c) (West 2012) (to search in Westlaw: NECivR 7.0.1).

19. FED. R. CIV. P. 12(b) (West 2011); *e.g.,* ALASKA R. CIV. P. 12(b) (West 2012); ARIZ. R. CIV. P. 12(b) (West 2012); ARK. R. CIV. P. 12(b) (West 2012); FLA. R. CIV. P. 1.140(b) (West 2012); IDAHO R. CIV. P. 12(b) (West 2011); KAN. STAT. ANN. § 60–212(b) (West 2011); ME. R. CIV. P. 12(b) (West 2012); N.D. R. CIV. P. 12(b) (West 2012); N.M. R. CIV. P. 1–012 (b) (West 2011); S.C. R. CIV. P. 12(b) (West 2011); UTAH R. CIV. P. 12(b) (West 2012); VT. R. CIV. P. 12(b) (West 2012).

20. *E.g.,* WIS. STAT. ANN. § 802.06(2) (West 2011).

21. CAL. CIV. PROC. CODE § 430.10 (West 2012); MO. R. CIV. P. 55.27(a) (West 2012); WIS. STAT. ANN. § 802.06(2) (West 2011).

22. MO. R. CIV. P. 55.27(a) (West 2012).

23. MD. R. CIV. P. 2–322(a) (West 2012).

24. FED. R. CIV. P. 12(g)(2)–(h) (West 2011).

25. FED. R. CIV. P. 12(h)(3) (West 2011).

26. FED. R. CIV. P. 12(h)(2) (West 2011).

27. Advanced Cardiovascular Sys., Inc. v. Scimed Life Sys., Inc., 988 F.2d 1157, 1160 (Fed. Cir. 1993).

28. *E.g.,* Scheuer v. Rhodes, 416 U.S. 232, 236, 94 S.Ct. 1683, 1686 (1974) *abrogated on other grounds in* Harlow v. Fitzgerald, 457 U.S. 800, 102 S.Ct. 2727 (1982), *cited in* Bell Atl. Corp. v. Twombly, 550 U.S. 544, 555, 127 S.Ct. 1955, 1964–65 (2007) (Souter, J., writing for the majority) and at 550 U.S. 544, 583, 127 S.Ct. 1955, 1981 (2007) (Stevens, J., dissenting).

29. *E.g.,* Eastern Shore Markets, Inc. v. J.D. Associates Ltd. P'ship, 213 F.3d 175, 185 (4th Cir. 2000) (stating that rule 12(b)(6) motion does not invite analysis of potential defenses to the claims asserted in the complaint and a court may consider defenses only when the face of the complaint "clearly reveals the existence of a meritorious affirmative defense").

30. County of Hudson v. Janiszewski, 520 F. Supp. 2d 631, 649 (D.N.J. 2007), *aff'd,* 351 F.Appx 662 (3d Cir. 2009) (stating that although statute of limitations defense usually unavailable in a motion to dismiss, exception arises where complaint "facially shows noncompliance with the limitations period and the affirmative defense clearly appears on the face of the pleading").

31. *E.g.,* Tregenza v. Great Am. Communications Co., 12 F.3d 717, 718 (7th Cir. 1993) (a plaintiff might plead himself right out of court if he pleads facts showing that the claim is time-barred or without merit); Theuerkauf v. United Vaccines Div. of Harlan Sprague Dawley, Inc., 821 F.Supp. 1238, 1240 (W.D. Mich. 1993) (dismissal of complaint necessary if an affirmative defense appears on its face).

32. Advanced Cardiovascular Sys., Inc. v. Scimed Life Sys., Inc., 988 F.2d 1157, 1160 (Fed. Cir. 1993).

33. *E.g.,* Landy v. Heller, White & Co., 783 F.Supp. 125, 133 (S.D.N.Y. 1991) (though under Rule 15(a), leave to amend must be given when justice requires, dismissal with prejudice proper if dismissal based on valid ground).

34. Foman v. Davis, 371 U.S. 178, 182, 83 S.Ct. 227, 230 (1962); *e.g.,* regarding limits of amendment rule: Ward Electronics Serv., Inc. v. First Commercial Bank, 819 F.2d 496, 497 (4th Cir. 1987); Lemieux v. City of Holyoke, 641 F. Supp. 2d 60, 62 (D. Mass. 2009); Fletcher v. Tidewater Builders Ass'n Inc., 216 F.R.D. 584, 587 (E.D. Va. 2003).

35. Foman v. Davis, 371 U.S. 178, 182 S.Ct. 227, 230.

36. *E.g.,* Cortec Indus., Inc. v. Sum Holding L.P., 949 F.2d 42, 48 (2d Cir. 1991), *cert. denied,* 503 U.S. 960, 112 S.Ct. 1561 (1992).

37. *E.g.,* regarding the court's obligation to stay within the "four corners" of the complaint: Ryder Energy Distribution Corp. v. Merrill Lynch Commodities Inc., 748 F.2d 774, 779 (2d Cir. 1984); Ventrassist Pty Ltd. v. Heartware, Inc., 377 F. Supp. 2d 1278, 1285 (S.D. Fla. 2005); In re Catfish Antitrust Litig., 826 F.Supp. 1019, 1025 (N.D. Miss. 1993).

38. *E.g.,* Corrigan v. Methodist Hosp., 853 F.Supp. 832, 834 (E.D. Pa. 1994); D.P. Tech. Corp. v. Sherwood Tool, Inc., 751 F.Supp. 1038, 1039 (D. Conn. 1990).

39. *E.g.,* Poling v. K. Hovnanian Enterprises, 99 F. Supp. 2d 502, 507 (D.N.J. 2000), *appeal dismissed*, 32 F.Appx 32 (3d Cir. 2002); Leach v. Quality Health Services, Inc., 869 F.Supp. 315, 316 (E.D. Pa. 1994).

40. *E.g.,* regarding matters of which court can take judicial notice: In re Colonial Mortgage Bankers Corp., 324 F.3d 12, 15–16 (1st Cir. 2003); Farley v. Shaw's Supermarkets, Inc., 497 F. Supp. 2d 23, 25–26 (D. Mass. 2007); Lauria v. Donahue, 438 F. Supp. 2d 131, 143 (E.D.N.Y. 2006).

41. *E.g.,* regarding consideration of documents that are *not* attached to the complaint: Roginsky v. County of Suffolk, N.Y., 729 F. Supp. 2d 561, 565 (E.D.N.Y. 2010); International Audiotext Network, Inc. v. American Tel. & Tel. Co., 62 F.3d 69, 72 (2d Cir. 1995); Wiles v. Department of Educ., 555 F. Supp. 2d 1143, 1150 (D. Haw. 2008) (stating that court may consider documents whose contents are alleged in a complaint and whose authenticity are not questioned by any party).

42. *E.g.,* remarking on state's liberal amendment policy: Swanstrom v. Teledyne Cont'l Motors, Inc., 43 So.3d 564, 582 (Ala. 2009), *reh'g denied* (Mar. 5, 2010); Bauman v. Day, 942 P.2d 1130, 1132 (Alaska 1997); Board of Trustees of Leland Stanford Jr. Univ. v. Superior Court, 57 Cal.Rptr.3d 755, 762 (Ct. App. 2007); Gulko v. Gen. Motors Corp., 710 A.2d 213, 214 (Del. Super. Ct. 1997); ABC Liquors, Inc. v. Centimark Corp., 967 So.2d 1053, 1057 (Fla. Dist. Ct. App. 2007); Carl H. Christensen Family Trust v. Christensen, 993 P.2d 1197, 1202 (Idaho 1999); Coan v. New Hampshire Dept. of Envtl. Services, 8 A.3d 109, 117 (N.H. 2010); Notte v. Merchants Mut. Ins. Co., 888 A.2d 464, 470 (N.J. 2006); Bresnick v. Baskin, 650 A.2d 915, 916 (R.I. 1994); Hunters, Anglers & Trappers Ass'n of Vermont, Inc. v. Winooski Valley Park Dist., 913 A.2d 391, 399 (Vt. 2006).

43. Cullen v. Auto–Owners Ins. Co., 189 P.3d 344, 346 (Ariz. 2008) (citing Mackey v. Spangler, 301 P.2d 1026, 1027–28 (Ariz. 1956)).

44. Cullen v. Auto-Owners Ins. Co., 189 P.3d 344, 346 (Ariz. 2008).

45. *Id.*

46. Mohave Disposal, Inc. v. City of Kingman, 922 P.2d 308, 311 (Ariz. 1996).

47. Davio v. Nebraska Dept. of Health & Human Services, 786 N.W.2d 655, 661–62 (Neb. 2010).

48. Moats v. Republican Party of Nebraska, 796 N.W.2d 584, 591 (Neb. 2011), *cert. denied*, 132 S.Ct. 251 (U.S. 2011).

49. *Id.*

50. *Id.*

51. *Id.*

52. *Id.*

53. Md. R. Civ. P. 2–303(b) (West 2012).

54. Md. R. Civ. P. 2–305 discussed in Parks v. Alpharma, Inc., 421 Md. 59, 72 (2011) (citing RRC Ne., LLC v. BAA Maryland, Inc., 994 A.2d 430, 433 (Md. 2010).

55. *See, e.g.,* Tavakoli–Nouri v. State, 779 A.2d 992, 1001 (Md. Ct. Spec. App. 2001).

56. RRC Ne., LLC v. BAA Maryland, Inc., 994 A.2d 480, 440 (Md. 2010).

57. *See* Resolution Trust Corp. v. Dean, 854 F.Supp. 626, 648–49 (D. Ariz. 1994) (stating that Rule 12(e) strikes at unintelligibility rather than want of detail and should not be used to test an opponent's case).

58. *See* Woods v. Reno Commodities, Inc., 600 F.Supp. 574, 580 (D. Nev. 1984) (stating that complaint was not so ambiguous that defendant could not reasonably respond).

59. Regarding federal courts' line-drawing: Holmes v. Fischer, 764 F. Supp. 2d 523, 531 (W.D.N.Y. 2011); Greater New York Auto. Dealers Ass'n v. Environmental Sys. Testing, Inc., 211 F.R.D. 71, 76 (E.D.N.Y. 2002).

60. *E.g.,* regarding availability in many states (list is not exhaustive) of motion for more definite statement or equivalent: Alaska R. Civ. P. 12(e) (West 2012); Ariz. R. Civ. P. 12(e) (West 2012); Ark. R. Civ. P. 12(e) (West 2012); Cal. Civ. Proc. Code § 430.10(f) (West 2012); Fla. R. Civ. P. 1.140(e) (West 2012); Ga. Code Ann. § 9–11–12(e) (West 2011); Idaho R. Civ. P. 12(e) (West 2012); Ind. R. Trial P. 12(E) (West 2012); Iowa R. Civ. P. 1.433 (West 2012) (motion for more specific statement); Kan. Stat. Ann. § 60–212(e) (West 2011); Ky. R. Civ. P. 12.05 (West 2012); Me. R. Civ. P. 12(e) (West 2012); Mass. R. Civ. P. 12(e) (West 2012); Md. R. Civ. P. 2–322(d) (West 2012); Mich. Ct. R. 2.115(A) (West 2012); Minn. R. Civ. P. 12.05 (West 2012); Mo. R. Civ. P. 55.27(d) (West 2012);

MONT. R. CIV. P. 12(e) (West 2012); NEV. R. CIV. P. 12(e) (West 2012); N.M. R. CIV. P. 1–012(E) (West 2011); S.C. R. CIV. P. 12(e) (West 2011); S.D. CODIFIED LAWS § 15–6–12(e) (2011); TENN. R. CIV. P. 12.05 (West 2011); UTAH R. CIV. P. 12(c) (West 2012); VT. R. CIV. P. 12(e) (West 2012); WASH. SUPER. CT. R. CIV. P. 12(e) (West 2011); W. VA. R. CIV. P. 12(e) (West 2011); WIS. STAT. ANN. § 802.06(5) (West 2011); WYO. R. CIV. P. 12(e) (West 2012).

61.   *E.g.,* Wilkerson v. Butler, 229 F.R.D. 166, 170 (E.D. Cal. 2005).

62.   *See, e.g.*, McGlauflin v. RCC Atlantic, 269 F.R.D. 56, 57–58 (2010).

63.   *E.g.*, Mag Instrument, Inc. v. JS Products, Inc., 595 F. Supp. 2d 1102, 1106 (C.D. Cal. 2008).

64.   *See, e.g.*, Schramm v. Krischell, 84 F.R.D. 294, 299 (D. Conn. 1979).

65.   *E.g.,* regarding the need to show prejudice to the movant: Holmes v. Fischer, 764 F. Supp. 2d 523, 532 (W.D.N.Y. 2011); Uzlyan v. Solis, 706 F. Supp. 2d 44, 51–52 (D.D.C. 2010); Frisby v. Keith D. Weiner & Associates Co., LPA, 669 F. Supp. 2d 863, 865 (N.D. Ohio 2009); E.E.O.C. v. FPM Group, Ltd., 657 F. Supp. 2d 957, 966 (E.D. Tenn. 2009); American S. Ins. Co. v. Buckley, 748 F. Supp. 2d 610, 626 (E.D. Tex. 2010).

66.   Wilkerson v. Butler, 229 F.R.D. 166, 170 (E.D.Cal. 2005).

67.   *E.g.,* Mullaney v. Hilton Hotels Corp., 634 F. Supp. 2d 1130, 1147 (D. Haw. 2009).

68.   Marseglia v. JP Morgan Chase Bank, 750 F. Supp. 2d 1171, 1175 (S.D. Cal. 2010).

69.   Kelley v. Corrections Corp. of Am., 750 F. Supp. 2d 1132, 1137 (E.D. Cal. 2010).

70.   *E.g.,* regarding determination of immateriality: Kent v. AVCO Corp., 849 F.Supp. 833, 835 (D. Conn. 1994); Federated Dept. Stores, Inc. v. Grinnell Corp., 287 F.Supp. 744, 747 (S.D.N.Y. 1968).

71.   Federated Dept. Stores, Inc. v. Grinnell Corp., 287 F.Supp. 744, 747 (S.D.N.Y. 1968).

72.   Marseglia v. JP Morgan Chase Bank, 750 F. Supp. 2d 1171, 1175 (S.D. Cal. Nov. 12, 2010); *see* Kelley, 750 F. Supp. 2d at 1137–38.

73.   *See* Holmes v. Fischer, 764 F. Supp. 2d 523, 532 (W.D.N.Y. 2011).

74.   *See* In re Food Mgmt. Group, LLC, 359 B.R. 543, 557 (Bankr. S.D.N.Y. 2007).

75.   *See id.*

76.   In re Gitto Global Corp., 422 F.3d 1, 12 (1st Cir. 2005) (quoting 5 Charles Alan Wright & Arthur R. Miller, FEDERAL PRACTICE AND PROCEDURE § 1382 (3d ed. 2004)).

77.   *E.g.,* some state rules authorizing motion to strike (list is not exhaustive): ALASKA R. CIV. P. 12(f) (West 2012); ARIZ. R. CIV. P. 12(f) (West 2012); FLA. R. CIV. P. 1.140(f) (West 2012); GA. CODE ANN. § 9–11–12(f) (West 2011); HAW. R. CIV. P. 12(f); IDAHO R. CIV. P. 12(f) (West 2012); IND. R. TRIAL P. 12(F) (West 2012); KAN. STAT. ANN. § 60–212(f) (West 2011); KY. R. CIV. P. 12.06 (West 2012); ME. R. CIV. P. 12(f) (West 2012); MASS. R. CIV. P. 12(f) (West 2012); MD. R. CIV. P. 2–322(e) (West 2012); MICH. CT. R. 2.115(B) (West 2012); MO. RULE. CIV. P. 55.27(e) (West 2012); MONT. R. CIV. P. 12(f) (West 2012); NEV. R. CIV. P. 12(f) (West 2012); N.M. R. CIV. P. 1–012(F) (West 2011); S.C. R. CIV. P. 12(f) (West 2011); S.D. CODIFIED LAWS § 15–6–12(f) (2011); TENN. R. CIV. P. 12.06(West 2011); UTAH R. CIV. P. 12(f) (West 2012); VT. R. CIV. P. 12(West 2012); WASH. SUPER. CIV. R. 12(f) (West 2011); W. VA. R. CIV. P. 12(f) (West 2011); WIS. STAT. ANN. § 802.06(6) (West 2011); WYO. R. CIV. P. 12(f) (West 2012).

78.   OR. R. CIV. P. 21(E) (West 2012).

79.   Anderson v. Liberty Lobby, Inc., 477 U.S. 242, 250, 106 S.Ct. 2505, 2511 (1986).

80.   Celotex Corp. v. Catrett, 477 U.S. 317, 323–24, 106 S.Ct. 2548, 2553 (1986).

81.   Quinn v. Syracuse Model Neighborhood Corp., 613 F.2d 438, 445 (2d Cir. 1980).

82.   *See* Shaw v. Santa Monica Bank, 920 F.Supp. 1080, 1083 (D. Haw. 1996).

83.   Beaumont v. J.P. Morgan Chase Bank, N.A., 782 F. Supp. 2d 656, 663 (N.D. Ill. 2011).

84.   *E.g.,* Williams v. Johnson, 794 F. Supp. 2d 22, 26–27 (D.D.C. 2011).

85.   Anderson v. Liberty Lobby, Inc., 477 U.S. 242, 252, 106 S.Ct. 2505, 2512 (1986); Gallo v. Prudential Residential Services, Ltd. P'ship, 22 F.3d 1219, 1224 (2d Cir. 1994).

E.g., regarding this standard: Westport Ins. Corp. v. Gionfriddo, 524 F. Supp. 2d 167, 173 (D. Conn. 2007); Ramirez v. New York City Bd. of Educ., 481 F. Supp. 2d 209, 216 (E.D.N.Y. 2007); Dargento v. Bally's Holiday Fitness Centers, 990 F.Supp. 186, 189 (W.D.N.Y. 1997); Rubin v. Smith, 919 F.Supp. 534, 537 (D.N.H. 1996); Stella Stylianou v. St. Luke's/Roosevelt Hosp. Ctr., 902 F.Supp. 54, 55 (S.D.N.Y. 1995).

86.   Anderson v. Liberty Lobby, Inc. 477 U.S. 242, 248, 106 S.Ct. 2505, 2510 (1986).

87.   Walder v. White Plains Bd. of Educ., 738 F. Supp. 2d 483, 492 (S.D.N.Y. 2010). *E.g.,* regarding presumption that non-movant's evidence is true: Knopick v. Connelly, 639 F.3d 600, 606 (3d Cir. 2011), *cert. denied,* 132 S.Ct. 1094 (U.S. 2012); United States v. Storey, 640 F.3d 739, 743 (6th Cir. 2011), *reh'g denied,* (June 30, 2011); Williams v. Johnson, 2011 WL 2519663 (D.D.C. 2011); Iannuzzi v. American Mortg. Network, Inc., 727 F. Supp. 2d 125, 133 (E.D.N.Y. 2010); Sussman v. Rabobank Int'l, 739 F. Supp. 2d 624, 627 (S.D.N.Y. 2010).

88.   M & M Med. Supplies & Serv., Inc. v. Pleasant Valley Hosp., Inc., 981 F.2d 160, 163 (4th Cir. 1992), *cert. denied,* 508 U.S. 972 (1993).

89.   *E.g.,* Andrews Farms v. Calcot, Ltd., 693 F. Supp. 2d 1154, 1163 (E.D. Cal. 2010).

90.   FED. R. CIV. P. 56(b) (West 2011).

91.   U.S. Dist. Ct. Rules N.D. Ill., LR 56.1(a) (West 2012) (to search in Westlaw: IL R USDCTND LR 56.1).

92.   *Id.*

93.   *E.g.,* Meridian Fin. Advisors, Ltd. v. Pence, 763 F. Supp. 2d 1046, 1055 (S.D. Ind. 2011), *reconsideration denied* (Mar. 15, 2011); Tirado v. Johnson & Johnson D.O.C., Inc., 240 F. Supp. 2d 144, 148–49 (D.P.R. 2003).

94.   Wyatt Tech. Corp. v. Smithson, 345 F. App'x. 236, 239 (9th Cir. 2009).

95.   United States v. Dunkel, 927 F.2d 955, 956 (7th Cir.1991) *quoted with approval in* Meridian Fin. Advisors, Ltd. v. Pence, 763 F. Supp. 2d 1046, 1055 (S.D. Ind. 2011).

96.   *E.g.,* Kempski v. Toll Bros., Inc., 582 F. Supp. 2d 636, 640 (D. Del. 2008) (stating that burden on the moving party can be discharged by "showing'—that is, pointing out to the district court—that there is an absence of evidence supporting the nonmoving party's case).

97.   Clark v. County of Tulare, 755 F. Supp. 2d 1075, 1083 (E.D. Cal. 2010), *reconsideration denied* (Dec. 21, 2010).

98.   28 U.S.C.A. § 1746 (West 2012).

99.   *E.g.,* Lane v. Department of Interior, 523 F.3d 1128, 1134 (9th Cir. 2008).

100.   Resolution Trust Corp. v. North Bridge Associates, Inc., 22 F.3d 1198, 1203 (1st Cir. 1994).

101.   *E.g.,* regarding "fishing expeditions": Davis v. G.N. Mortg. Corp., 396 F.3d 869, 885 (7th Cir. 2005); Pony Computer, Inc. v. Equus Computer Sys. of Missouri, Inc., 162 F.3d 991, 996–97 (8th Cir. 1998).

102.   Wells v. City of Bowling Green, 344 S.W.3d 141, 144–45 (Ky. Ct. App. 2011), *review denied* (Aug. 17, 2011).

103.   Adkins v. Vigilant Ins. Co., 927 N.E.2d 385, 388 (Ind. Ct. App. 2010) *transfer denied,* 940 N.E.2d 828 (Ind. 2010), a *transfer denied,* 940 N.E.2d 828 (2d 2010).

104.   *See* Jackson v. Olam West Coast, 2012 WL 4863797 at *6, quoting 3550 Stevens Creek Associates v. Barclays Bank of California, 915 F.2d 1355, 1356 (9th Cir. 1990), *cert. denied,* 500 U.S. 917 (1991) (slip op.).

105.   Hamilton v. Cunningham, 880 F.Supp. 1407, 1410 (D. Colo. 1995).

106.   *E.g.,* regarding circumstances in which a court will grant judgment on the pleadings (no material issue of fact remains to be resolved and movant is entitled to judgment as a matter of law): Minch Family LLLP v. Buffalo–Red River Watershed Dist., 628 F.3d 960, 965 (8th Cir. 2010); Waldron v. Boeing Co., 388 F.3d 591, 593 (8th Cir. 2004); Henry Hous. Ltd. P'ship v. United States, 95 Fed. Cl. 250, 254 (2010); Old Republic Sur. Co. v. Quad City Bank & Trust Co., 681 F. Supp. 2d 970, 972 (C.D. Ill. 2009); Butler v. Resurgence Fin., LLC, 521 F. Supp. 2d 1093, 1095 (C.D. Cal. 2007).

107.   Johnson v. Dodson Pub. Sch., Dist. No. 2–A(C), 463 F. Supp. 2d 1151, 1156 (D. Mont. 2006).

108.   *Id.*

109.   *E.g.,* Doe v. United States, 419 F.3d 1058, 1061 (9th Cir. 2005); McGuigan v. Conte, 629 F. Supp. 2d 76, 80 (D. Mass. 2009).

110.   *E.g.,* Norcal Gold, Inc. v. Laubly, 543 F. Supp. 2d 1132, 1135 (E.D. Cal. 2008); Progressive Cas. Ins. Co. v. Estate of Crone, 894 F.Supp. 383, 385 (D. Kan. 1995).

111.   *E.g.,* regarding opposing party's allegations and their construction: Waldron v. Boeing Co., 388 F.3d 591, 593 (8th Cir. 2004); Friedman v. Fidelity Serv. Corp., 888 F.Supp. 110, 111 (D. Neb. 1994) *aff'd sub nom.,* Friedman v. Fidelity Brokerage Services, Inc., 56 F.3d 866 (8th Cir. 1995); Minch Family LLLP v. Buffalo–Red River Watershed Dist., 628 F.3d 960, 965 (8th Cir.

2010); Ramirez v. Arlequin, 491 F. Supp. 2d 202, 203 (D.P.R. 2006).

112. Creighton v. City of Livingston, 628 F. Supp. 2d 1199, 1207 (E.D. Cal. 2009).

113. *E.g.*, regarding cases that discuss treating a Rule 12(c) motion for judgment on the pleadings as functionally equivalent to a Rule 12(b)(6) motion to dismiss for failure to state a claim: Turbe v. Government of Virgin Islands, 938 F.2d 427, 428 (3d Cir. 1991); Westcott v. City of Omaha, 901 F.2d 1486, 1488 (8th Cir. 1990); Rivera v. City of Camden Bd. of Educ., 634 F. Supp. 2d 486, 488 (D.N.J. 2009); Butler v. Resurgence Fin., LLC, 521 F. Supp. 2d 1093, 1095 (C.D. Cal. 2007).

114. *E.g.,* Westcott v. City of Omaha, 901 F.2d 1486, 1488 (8th Cir. 1990); Webster Indus., Inc. v. Northwood Doors, Inc., 234 F. Supp. 2d 981, 989 (N.D. Iowa 2002).

115. In re McMillen, 440 B.R. 907, 910 (Bankr. N.D. Ga. 2010).

116. *See, e.g.*, regarding the application of the "plausibility" standard to Rule 12(c) motions: Sensations, Inc. v. City of Grand Rapids, 526 F.3d 291, 295–96 (6th Cir. 2008); Albergottie v. New York City, 2011 WL 519296 at *3 (S.D.N.Y. 2011); S. Star Cent. Gas Pipeline, Inc. v. Cline, 754 F. Supp. 2d 1257, 1259 (D. Kan. 2010), *reconsideration denied* (Jan. 23, 2011); Vieira v. Honeoye Cent. Sch. Dist., 756 F. Supp. 2d 302, 304 (W.D.N.Y. 2010); Williams v. United States, 754 F. Supp. 2d 942, 946–47 (W.D. Tenn. 2010); Loud Records LLC v. Minervini, 621 F. Supp. 2d 672, 676–77 (W.D. Wis. 2009).

117. Fed. R. Civ. P. 12(d) (West 2011). *E.g.,* Tolbert–Smith v. Chu, 714 F. Supp. 2d 37, 40 (D.D.C. 2010).

118. *E.g.,* regarding matters incorporated in or integral to the pleadings: Curran v. Cousins, 509 F.3d 36, 44 (1st Cir. 2007); Henke v. Allina Health Sys., 698 F. Supp. 2d 1115, 1121 (D. Minn. 2010); Atiyeh v. National Fire Ins. Co. of Hartford, 742 F. Supp. 2d 591, 595 (E.D. Pa. 2010); Rebaudo v. AT & T, 562 F. Supp. 2d 345, 349 (D. Conn. 2008).

119. Curran v. Cousins, 509 F.3d 36, 44 (1st Cir. 2007); Atiyeh v. National Fire Ins. Co. of Hartford, 742 F. Supp. 2d 591, 595 (E.D. Pa. 2010).

120. *E.g.,* regarding public records: Sensations, Inc. v. City of Grand Rapids, 526 F.3d 291, 296 (6th Cir. 2008); Baumann v. District of Columbia, 744 F. Supp. 2d 216, 222 (D.D.C. 2010); Atiyeh v. National Fire Ins. Co. of Hartford, 742 F. Supp. 2d 591, 595 (E.D. Pa. 2010); Henke v. Allina Health Sys., 698 F. Supp. 2d 1115, 1121 (D. Minn. 2010); Loud Records LLC v. Minervini, 621 F. Supp. 2d 672, 675 (W.D. Wis. 2009).

121. *E.g.,* Yang v. Dar Al–Handash Consultants, 250 F. App'x. 771, 772 (9th Cir. 2007); Fisher v. Rite Aid Corp., 764 F.Supp.2d 700, 702 (M.D. Pa. 2011); Baumann v. District of Columbia, 744 F. Supp. 2d 216, 222 (D.D.C. 2010).

122. Regarding courts' discretion to decline to treat the motion as one for summary judgment: Henke v. Allina Health Sys., 698 F. Supp. 2d 1115, 1121 (D. Minn. 2010); McGuigan v. Conte, 629 F. Supp. 2d 76, 81 (D. Mass. 2009); Lijoi v. Continental Cas. Co., 414 F. Supp. 2d 228, 237 (E.D.N.Y. 2006).

123. Regarding state rules that are similar to Federal Rule 12(c) (list not exhaustive): Alaska R. Civ. P. 12(c) (West 2012); Ariz. R. Civ. P. 12(c) (West 2012); Fla. R. Civ. P. 1.140(c) (West 2012); Ga. Code Ann. § 9–11–12(c) (West 2011); Idaho R. Civ. P. 12(c) (West 2012); Ind. R. Trial P. 12(c) (West 2012); Kan. Stat. Ann. § 60–212(c) and (d) (West 2011); Ky. R. Civ. P. 12.03 (West 2012); Me. R. Civ. P. 12(c) (West 2012); Mass. R. Civ. P. 12(c) (West 2012); Mo. Sup. Ct. R. 55.27(c) (West 2012); Mont. R. Civ. P. 12(c) (West 2012); Nev. R. Civ. P. 12(c) (West 2012); NMRA, Rule 1–012(c) (West 2011); S.D. Codified Laws § 15–6–12(c) (2011); Tenn. R. Civ. P. 12.05(West 2011); Utah R. Civ. P. 12(c) (West 2012); Vt. R. Civ. P. 12(c) (West 2012); Wash. Sup. Ct. R. 12(West 2011); W. Va. R. Civ. P. 12(c) (West 2011); Wis. Stat. Ann. § 802.06(3) (West 2011); Wyo. R. Civ. P. 12(c) (West 2012).

124. Riverwood Commercial Park, LLC v. Standard Oil Co., Inc., 729 N.W.2d 101, 105 (N.D. 2007) (quoting Tibert v. Minto Grain, LLC, 682 N.W.2d 294, 296 (N.D. 2004)).

125. Bennett v. Spaight, 277 S.W.3d 182, 187 (Ark. 2008).

126. Universal Underwriters Ins. Co. v. Thompson, 776 So.2d 81, 83 (Ala. 2000).

127. Hannon Law Firm, LLC v. Melat, Pressman & Higbie, LLP, 2011 WL 724742 at *3 (Colo. Ct. App. 2011), *cert. granted in part*, 2011 WL 3855738 (Colo. 2011).

128. Fla. R. Civ. P. 1.140(c) (West 2012).

129. Castner v. Ziemer, 113 So.2d 263, 266 (Fla. Dist. Ct. App. 1959) (Florida rule on judgment on the pleadings omits language found in federal rule allowing the motion to be treated as one for summary judgment; since Florida rules were patterned on federal, "it must be concluded that the omission of this permissive provision of the rule was intentional by the draftsmen of our rules;" and trial court was not authorized to consider matters outside the pleadings on motion for judgment on the pleadings); Reinhard v. Bliss, 85 So.2d 131, 133 (Fla. 1956).

See, e.g., regarding non-existence in Florida of conversion option and restriction of court to pleadings and attachments: Brewster v. Castano, 937 So.2d 1268, 1269 (Fla. Dist. Ct. App. 2006) (stating that trial court erred in granting judgment on pleadings when it considered matters outside the pleadings; case remanded so parties could raise same issue on a motion for summary judgment); Britt v. State Farm Mut. Auto. Ins. Co., 935 So.2d 97, 98 (Fla. Dist. Ct. App. 2006) (stating that in considering motion, trial court precluded from relying on matters outside pleadings such as requests for admissions, interrogatories, answers to interrogatories, depositions, affidavits, stipulations, and any other documents permitted to be considered under Florida [summary judgment rule]); Martinez v. Lieberman, 920 So.2d 128, 129 (Fla. Dist. Ct. App. 2006) (stating that motion for judgment on the pleadings is decided only based on the pleadings).

130. Ohio Civ. R. 12(C) (West 2012).

Endnotes for Chapter 6: Introduction to Contract Drafting

1. Applied Equip. Corp. v. Litton Saudi Arabia Ltd., 869 P.2d 454, 461 (Cal. Sup. Ct. 1994) (quoting the appellant's brief).

2. For discussion of contracts as "relational" documents, see *The Many Futures of Contracts,* 47 So. Cal. L. Rev. 691 (1974); Restatement (Second) of Contracts and Presentation, 60 Va. L. Rev. 589 (1974).

3. *E.g.,* that the law operates in the background: Cypress on Sunland Homeowners Ass'n v. Orlandini, 257 P.3d 1168, 1178–79 (Ariz. Ct. App. 2011), *review denied* (Oct. 25, 2011); State v. Two Jinn, Inc., 264 P.3d 66, 69 (Idaho 2011); Connolly v. Connolly, 952 N.E.2d 203, 207 (Ind. Ct. App. 2011); Rios v. Jennie–O Turkey Store, Inc., 793 N.W.2d 309, 316 (Minn. Ct. App. 2011); Lake Colony Const., Inc. v. Boyd, 711 S.E.2d 742, 747–48 (N.C. Ct. App. 2011); Doe v. Ronan, 937 N.E.2d 556, 562 (Ohio 2010); City of Houston v. Williams, 353 S.W.3d 128, 141 (Tex. 2011); Cornish Coll. of the Arts v. 1000 Virginia Ltd. P'ship, 242 P.3d 1, 12 (Wash. App. 2010) *review denied,* 171 Wash.2d 1014, 249 P.3d 1029 (2011).

4. *E.g.,* regarding decisions relating to this covenant: Vetromile v. JPI Partners, LLC, 706 F. Supp. 2d 442, 454 (S.D.N.Y. 2010) quoting Travellers Int'l A.G. v. Trans World Airlines, Inc., 41 F.3d 1570, 1575 (2d Cir.1994); CNL Hotels & Resorts, Inc. v. Maricopa County, 244 P.3d 592, 598 (Ariz. Ct. App. 2010); Hill v. Medlantic Health Care Group, 933 A.2d 314, 333 (D.C. 2007); Airborne Health, Inc. v. Squid Soap, LP, 984 A.2d 126, 145–46 (Del. Ch. 2009); Schipporeit v. Khan, 775 N.W.2d 503, 505, *reh'g denied* (Dec. 22, 2009); Oakwood Vill. LLC v. Albertsons, Inc., 104 P.3d 1226, 1239 (Utah 2004).

5. Embry v. Innovative Aftermarket Sys. L.P., 247 P.3d 1158, 1161 (Okla. 2010) *reh'g denied* (Feb. 28, 2011).

6. Paul v. Howard Univ., 754 A.2d 297, 310 (D.C. 2000).

7. Perez v. Citicorp Mortg., Inc., 703 N.E.2d 518, 525 (Ill. App. Ct. 1998).

8. *E.g.,* stating that "shall" generally expresses a mandatory action: General Elec. Co. v. G. Siempelkamp GmbH & Co., 29 F.3d 1095, 1099 (6th Cir. 1994); In re Vidal, 234 B.R. 114, 120 (Bankr. D.N.M. 1999); Ex parte Bad Toys Holdings, Inc., 958 So.2d 852, 856 (Ala. 2006); In re Marriage of Ackerley, 775 N.E.2d 1045, 1060 (Ill. App. Ct. 2002); Town of Homer v. United Healthcare of Louisiana, Inc., 948 So.2d 1163, 1167 (La. App. 2007); Travertine Corp. v. Lexington–Silverwood, 683 N.W.2d 267, 272 (Minn. 2004); Glick v. Chocorua Forestlands Ltd. P'ship, 949 A.2d 693, 701 (N.H. 2008); Stephenson v. Oneok Res. Co., 99 P.3d 717, 721 (Okla. Ct. Civ. App. 2004); Lesikar v. Moon, 237 S.W.3d 361, 367 (Tex. App. 2007); Caperton v. A.T. Massey Coal Co., Inc., 690 S.E.2d 322, 339 (W. Va. 2009); Christensen v. Christensen, 176 P.3d 626, 631 (Wyo. 2008).

9. *E.g.,* regarding courts' interpretation of "may" as generally expressing permissive action: PCH Mut. Ins. Co., Inc. v. Casualty & Sur., Inc., 750 F. Supp. 2d 125, 144 (D.D.C. 2010); In re Oneida, Ltd., 400 B.R. 384, 391 (Bankr. S.D.N.Y. 2009) *aff'd sub nom* Peter J. Solomon Co., L.P. v. Oneida Ltd., 2010 WL 234827 (S.D.N.Y. 2010); In re Ionosphere Clubs, Inc., 111 B.R. 436, 441 (Bankr. S.D.N.Y. 1990); Prof'l Executive Ctr. v. LaSalle Nat. Bank, 570 N.E.2d 366, 373 (Ill. App. Ct. 1991); Nalle v. Taco Bell Corp., 914 S.W.2d 685, 687 (Tex. App. 1996).

10. *E.g.,* regarding fact that in the right context, "may" can have a mandatory meaning similar to "must" or "shall": RLS Associates, LLC v. United Bank of Kuwait PLC, 380 F.3d 704, 710 (2d Cir. 2004); Burgess Mining & Const. Corp. v. City of Bessemer, 312 So.2d 24, 26 (Ala. 1975).

11. *E.g.,* regarding principle that "freedom of contract" is an important policy and that courts should not blithely void contracts on public policy grounds: Kaufman v. Goldman, 124 Cal.Rptr.3d 555 (Ct. App. 2011), *reh'g denied* (May 18, 2011); Garfinkel v. Mager, 57 So.3d 221, 224 (Fla. Dist.

Ct. App. 2010), *reh'g denied* (Mar. 11, 2011); Jordan v. Knafel, 823 N.E.2d 1113, 1118 (Ill. App. Ct. 2005); City of New Albany v. Cotner, 919 N.E.2d 125, 134 (Ind. Ct. App. 2009), *reh'g denied* (Mar. 5, 2010), *transfer denied*, 940 N.E.2d 821 (Ind. 2010); Nelson v. Nelson, 985 So.2d 1285, 1293 (La. Ct. App. 2008); Baugh v. Novak, 340 S.W.3d 372, 383 (Tenn. 2011); Wellington Power Corp. v. CNA Sur. Corp., 614 S.E.2d 680, 685 (W. Va. 2005).

12. *E.g.,* regarding preference for enforcing contracts rather than setting them aside: 1800 Ocotillo, LLC v. WLB Group, Inc., 196 P.3d 222, 224 (Ariz. 2008); Kaufman v. Goldman, 124 Cal.Rptr.3d 555 (Ct. App. 2011), *reh'g denied* (May 18, 2011); Garfinkel v. Mager, 57 So.3d 221, 224 (Fla. Dist. Ct. App. 2010), *reh'g denied* (Mar. 11, 2011); Bruzas v. Richardson, 945 N.E.2d 1208, 1213 (Ill. App. Ct. 2011); Baugh v. Novak, 340 S.W.3d 372, 384 (Tenn. 2011); Jezeski v. Jezeski, 763 N.W.2d 176, 180 (Wis. Ct. App. 2008).

13. Rivero v. Rivero, 216 P.3d 213, 226 (Nev. 2009).

14. *E.g.,* In re Marriage of Newton, 955 N.E.2d 572 (Ill. App. Ct. 2011).

15. *E.g.,* Taylor v. AIA Services Corp., 261 P.3d 829, 841 (Idaho 2011) (illegal contract is one that rests on illegal consideration, consisting of any act or forbearance that is contrary to law or public policy; such a contract is illegal and unenforceable).

16. *E.g.,* Snyder v. Snyder, 865 N.E.2d 944, 949 (Ohio Ct. App. 2007) (illegal contract is a promise that is prohibited because performance, formation, or object of the agreement is against the law).

17. *E.g.,* Universal Structures, Ltd. v. Buchman, 937 N.E.2d 668, 676 (Ill. App.), *appeal denied* 238 Ill.2d 676 (2010) (contract unenforceable if the subject matter of the contract or the purpose of the contract violated the law); Snyder v. Snyder, 865 N.E.2d 944, 949 (Ohio Ct. App. 2007) (illegal contract is a promise prohibited because the performance, formation, or object of the agreement is against the law).

18. Academy of Skills & Knowledge, Inc. v. Charter Sch., USA, Inc., 260 S.W.3d 529, 545 (Tex. App. 2008) (contract to do a thing that cannot be performed without violation of the law is void).

19. *E.g.,* regarding the illegality of a contract: Baccouche v. Blankenship, 65 Cal.Rptr.3d 659, 664 (Ct. App. 2007) (contract whose object is violation of law is itself against the policy of law and renders bargain unenforceable); In re Marriage of Newton, 955 N.E.2d 572, 584–85 (Ill. App. Ct. 2011) (if subject matter of a contract is that illegal, contract is void *ab initio*); Scheeler v. Sartell Water Controls, Inc., 730 N.W.2d 285, 288 (Minn. Ct. App. 2007) (contract violating law or public policy is void); Mayfly Group, Inc. v. Ruiz, 144 P.3d 1025, 1026 (Or. Ct. App. 2006) (general rule is illegal contract cannot be enforced); SCI Texas Funeral Services, Inc. v. Hijar, 214 S.W.3d 148, 156 (Tex. App. 2007) (contract is illegal if parties undertake to do act forbidden by the law of place where it is to be done).

20. Bryant v. PMC Capital, Inc., 535 S.E.2d 319, 320 (Ga. Ct. App. 2000). *See* FCI Group, Inc. v. City of New York, 862 N.Y.S.2d 352, 356 (App. Div. 2008) (to constitute valid defense to action on contract, alleged illegality must be central to or dominant part of plaintiff's whole course of conduct in performance).

21. Baugh v. Novak, 340 S.W.3d 372, 385 (Tenn. 2011) (general rule is that contract expressly prohibited by statute is most clearly unenforceable when statute specifically condemns contract or term as illegal or void or where the statute expressly disentitles party to civil remedy on transaction); Coursey v. Fairchild, 436 P.2d 35, 40 (Okla. 1967) (where statute expressly declares that certain contracts shall be void, agreement is unlawful).

E.g., regarding invalidity of contracts that violate statutes: 1800 Ocotillo, LLC v. WLB Group, Inc., 196 P.3d 222, 224 (Ariz. 2008) (contract provisions unenforceable if they violate legislation (including constitutions, ordinances, and applicable regulations); Amedeus Corp. v. McAllister, 232 P.3d 107, 109 (Colo. Ct. App. 2009), *cert. denied* (June 22, 2009); Balagtas v. Bishop, 910 N.E.2d 789, 796 (Ind. Ct. App. 2009) *transfer denied*, 919 N.E.2d 556 (Ind. 2009); Bolt v. Giordano, 310 S.W.3d 237, 245 (Mo. Ct. App. 2010); Gramby v. Cobb, 422 A.2d 889, 892 (Pa. Super. Ct. 1980); Thiles v. County Bd. of Sarpy County, 200 N.W.2d 13, 19 (Neb. 1972); Cole v. Wellmark of S. Dakota, Inc., 776 N.W.2d 240, 249 (S.D. 2009).

22. Peterson v. Sunrider Corp., 48 P.3d 918, 930 (Utah 2002). *E.g.,* regarding possible validity of contracts despite statutory violation: Yank v. Juhrend, 729 P.2d 941, 944 (Ariz. Ct. App. 1986); Estate of Welch, 797 S.W.2d 742, 745 (Mo. Ct. App. 1990); LeClair v. Town of Norwell, 719 N.E.2d 464, 472 (Mass. 1999); Jackson Nat. Life Ins. Co. v. Receconi, 827 P.2d 118, 131 (N.M. 1992); Mountain Fir Lumber Co., Inc. v. Employee Benefits Ins. Co., 679 P.2d 296, 299 (Or. 1984).

23. *E.g.,* regarding court leaving parties to illegal contract "where it finds them": Wernecke v. St. Maries Joint Sch. Dist. No. 401, 207 P.3d 1008, 1018 (Idaho 2009); O'Conner v. Follman, 747 S.W.2d 216, 222 (Mo. Ct. App. 1988); Ussery v. Hollebeke, 391 S.W.2d 497, 503 (Tex. Civ. App.

1965); Evans v. Luster, 928 P.2d 455, 457 (Wash. Ct. App. 1996); Abbott v. Marker, 722 N.W.2d 162, 165 (Wis. App. 2006).

24. Jezeski v. Jezeski, 763 N.W.2d 176, 178 (Wis. Ct. App. 2008).

25. Kedzie & 103rd Currency Exch., Inc. v. Hodge, 619 N.E.2d 732, 738 (Ill. 1993).

26. *E.g.*, Jezeski v. Jezeski, 763 N.W.2d 176, 181 (Wis. Ct. App. 2009) (general rule is that both at law and in equity court will not aid either party to an illegal agreement but leaves parties where it finds them; exceptions apply if parties are not *in pari delicto* or if there is slight illegality, in which case recovery of anything transferred is permitted if necessary to prevent a harsh forfeiture.).

27. *E.g.*, regarding unenforceability of contracts that violate public policy: Fisher v. DCH Temecula Imports LLC, 114 Cal.Rptr.3d 24, 34 (Ct. App. 2010), *review denied* (Dec. 1, 2010); Fleissner v. Fitzgerald, 937 N.E.2d 1152, 1163 (Ill. App. Ct. 2010); In re Paternity of N.L.P., 926 N.E.2d 20, 24 (Ind. 2010); Family Care Services, Inc. v. Owens, 46 So.3d 234, 241–42 (La. Ct. App. 2010); State Farm Mut. Auto. Ins. Co. v. Koshy, 995 A.2d 651, 665 (Me. 2010); Frishman v. Maginn, 912 N.E.2d 468, 478 (Mass. App. Ct. 2009); Bamford v. Bamford, Inc., 777 N.W.2d 573, 580 (Neb. 2010); Alpert, Goldberg, Butler, Norton & Weiss, P.C. v. Quinn, 983 A.2d 604, 619 (N.J. Super. Ct. App. Div. 2009); Hackett v. Moore, 939 N.E.2d 1321, 1326 (Ohio Ct. Com. Pl. 2010).

28. Baugh v. Novak, 340 S.W.3d 372, 383 (Tenn. 2011).

29. *E.g.*, regarding source of public policy in state law (*e.g.*, constitutions, statutes, and courts' decisions): Dow–Westbrook, Inc. v. Candlewood Equine Practice, LLC, 989 A.2d 1075 (Conn. App. Ct. 2010) *quoting* Hanks v. Powder Ridge Restaurant Corp., 885 A.2d 734 (Conn. 2005); RSN Properties, Inc. v. Engineering Consulting Services, Ltd., 686 S.E.2d 853, 854 (Ga. Ct. App. 2009), *cert. denied* (Mar. 15, 2010); Hill v. American Family Mut. Ins. Co., 249 P.3d 812, 816 (Idaho 2011), *reh'g denied* (Apr. 29, 2011); Fleissner v. Fitzgerald, 937 N.E.2d 1152, 1163 (Ill. App. Ct. 2010); Marcinczyk v. State of New Jersey Police Training Comm'n, 5 A.3d 785, 789–90 (N.J. 2010); Lubov v. Horing & Welikson, P.C., 898 N.Y.S.2d 244, 245 (App. Div. 2010); Bowman v. Sunoco, Inc., 986 A.2d 883, 886 (Pa. Super. Ct. 2009) *appeal granted*, 610 Pa. 7 (2011).

30. State Farm Mut. Auto. Ins. Co. v. Koshy, 995 A.2d 651, 665 (Me. 2010).

31. *E.g.*, regarding the reluctance of a court to determine that the entire contract is unenforceable except sparingly and when case is free from doubt: RSN Properties, Inc. v. Engineering Consulting Services, Ltd., 686 S.E.2d 853, 854 (Ga. Ct. App. 2009), *cert. denied* (Mar. 15, 2010); Precision Planning, Inc. v. Richmark Communities, Inc., 679 S.E.2d 43, 45 (Ga. Ct. App. 2009), *reconsideration denied* (May 21, 2009), *cert. denied* (Nov. 2, 2009); Phoenix Ins. Co. v. Rosen, 949 N.E.2d 639, 645 (Ill. 2011); In re Marriage of Witten, 672 N.W.2d 768, 779–80 (Iowa 2003); Clark v. O'Malley, 973 A.2d 821, 838 (Md. Ct. Spec. App. 2009) *cert. granted*, 979 A.2d 707 (Md. 2009); Hearst–Argyle Properties, Inc. v. Entrex Commc'n Services, Inc., 778 N.W.2d 465, 472 (Neb. 2010).

32. Baugh v. Novak, 340 S.W.3d 372, 384 (Tenn. 2011).

33. Motsinger v. Lithia Rose–FT, Inc., 156 P.3d 156, 160 (Or. Ct. App. 2007); *see* Deutsche Bank Natl. Trust Co. v. Pevarski, 932 N.E.2d 887, 896 (Ohio App. 2010); The Cantamar, L.L.C. v. Champagne, 142 P.3d 140, 152 (Utah Ct. App. 2006).

34. Deutsche Bank Natl. Trust Co. v. Pevarski, 932 N.E.2d 887, 895–96 (Ohio App. 2010). *See* In re Marriage of Shanks, 758 N.W.2d 506, 515 (Iowa 2008).

35. *E.g.*, regarding distinction between procedural unconscionability (manner of entering contract) and substantive unconscionability (harsh, unreasonable, and unfair): Fonte v. AT & T Wireless Services, Inc., 903 So.2d 1019, 1025 (Fla. Dist. Ct. App. 2005); Motsinger v. Lithia Rose–FT, Inc., 156 P.3d 156, 160 (Or. Ct. App. 2007); Philpot v. Tennessee Health Mgmt., Inc., 279 S.W.3d 573, 579 (Tenn. Ct. App. 2007); Sec. Serv. Fed. Credit Union v. Sanders, 264 S.W.3d 292, 297 (Tex. App. 2008); Drake v. West Virginia Self–Storage, Inc., 509 S.E.2d 21, 24 (W.Va. 1998).

36. See Wattenbarger v. A.G. Edwards & Sons, Inc., 246 P.3d 961, 974 (Idaho 2010), *reh'g denied* (Dec. 23, 2010).

37. Vann v. Vann, 767 N.W.2d 855, 861 (N.D. 2009) (involvement of only one attorney "troubling," but did not alone conclusively establish unconscionability).

38. For example, courts have considered the following in determining substantive unconscionability.

(1) The contract reflects a bargain no reasonable person would make. *E.g.*, Wattenbarger v. A.G. Edwards & Sons, Inc., 246 P.3d 961, 974 (Idaho 2010), *reh'g denied* (Dec. 23, 2010); Sanford v. Castleton Health Care Ctr., LLC, 813 N.E.2d 411, 417 (Ind. Ct. App. 2004); In re Marriage of Shanks, 758 N.W.2d 506, 514 (Iowa 2008); Kauffman Stewart, Inc. v. Weinbrenner Shoe

Co., Inc., 589 N.W.2d 499, 502 (Minn. Ct. App. 1999); Vann v. Vann, 767 N.W.2d 855, 861 (N.D. 2009).

(2) The contract is unreasonably favorable to the stronger party. *E.g.,* Emigrant Mortg. Co., Inc. v. Fitzpatrick, 2012 WL 1860670 (N.Y. App. Div. 2012); Philpot v. Tennessee Health Mgmt., Inc., 279 S.W.3d 573, 579 (Tenn. Ct. App. 2007); Cottonwood Fin., LTD v. Estes, 784 N.W.2d 726, 730 (Wis. Ct. App. 2010).

(3) The contract is harshly and unfairly one-sided or "oppressive." *E.g.,* In re Marriage of Pownall, 5 P.3d 911, 914 (Ariz. Ct. App. 2000); Wattenbarger v. A.G. Edwards & Sons, Inc., 246 P.3d 961, 974 (Idaho 2010), *reh'g denied* (Dec. 23, 2010); In re Marriage of Shanks, 758 N.W.2d 506, 515 (Iowa 2008); In re Gibson–Terry & Terry, 758 N.E.2d 459, 467 (Ill. App. Ct. 2001). Markwed Excavating, Inc. v. City of Mandan, 791 N.W.2d 22, 31 (N.D. 2010); Satomi Owners Ass'n v. Satomi, LLC, 225 P.3d 213, 232 (Wash. 2009).

39. *E.g.,* regarding the requirement (probably the prevailing view) that the contract be both procedurally and substantively unconscionable: Arguelles–Romero v. Superior Court, 109 Cal.Rptr.3d 289, 299 (Ct. App. 2010), *as modified* (May 20, 2010); Romano ex rel. Romano v. Manor Care, Inc., 861 So.2d 59, 62 (Fla. Dist. Ct. App. 2003); Wattenbarger v. A.G. Edwards & Sons, Inc., 246 P.3d 961, 974 (Idaho 2010), *reh'g denied* (Dec. 23, 2010); Doyle v. Finance Am., LLC, 918 A.2d 1266, 1274 (Md. Ct. Spec. App. 2007); Shaffer v. Royal Gate Dodge, Inc., 300 S.W.3d 556, 559 (Mo. Ct. App. 2009); Markwed Excavating, Inc. v. City of Mandan, 791 N.W.2d 22, 31 (N.D. 2010).

40. Keefe v. Allied Home Mortg. Corp., 912 N.E.2d 310, 315 (Ill. App. Ct. 2009) (finding of unconscionability in Illinois can be based on *either* procedural unconscionability or substantive unconscionability *or* on combination of both).

41. Vasquez–Lopez v. Beneficial Oregon, Inc., 152 P.3d 940, 949 (Or. Ct. App. 2007).

42. *E.g.,* regarding characteristics of a contract of adhesion: Sanford v. Castleton Health Care Ctr., LLC, 813 N.E.2d 411, 417 (Ind. Ct. App. 2004) (though adhesion contract is standardized contract drafted by party with superior bargaining strength that relegates to the other party only opportunity to adhere to the contract or reject it, adhesion contract is *not* per se unconscionable); *see* Mattingly v. Palmer Ridge Homes LLC, 238 P.3d 505, 510–11 (Wash. Ct. App. 2010).

Endnotes for Chapter 7: Contract Components: Preliminary Matters, Core Transaction, and Subsidiary Agreements

1. *See, e.g.,* Susan M. Chesler, *Drafting Effective Contracts How to Revise, Edit, and Use Form Agreements*, Bus. L. Today, November/December 2009, at 35, 36–37; M. H. Sam Jacobson, *A Checklist for Drafting Good Contract*s, 5 J. Ass'n Legal Writing Directors 79 (2008); Munoz, *Writing Tips for the Transactional Attorney*, 21 No. 3 Prac. Real Est. Law. 33 (May 2005); Maureen Collins, *Drafting Transaction Documents: The Pieces of the Puzzle*, 88 Ill. B.J. 110 (Feb. 2000); James P. Nehf, *Writing Contracts in the Client's Interest*, 51 S.C. L. Rev. 153, 157–58 (1999); George H. Hathaway, *Plain English in Contract Recitals and Boilerplate*, Mich. B.J., NOVEMBER 1998, at 1226; James P. Nehf, *Writing Contracts in the Client's Interest*, 51 S.C. L. Rev. 153, 157–58 (1999).

2. *E.g.,* discussing fact that conditions precedent are disfavored: Cajun Constructors, Inc. v. Velasco Drainage Dist., 2012 WL 1513698 at *5 (Tex. App. 2012) (courts will not construe a contract provision as a condition precedent unless compelled to do so by language that may be construed no other way); Edelman Arts, Inc. v. Art Int'l (UK) Ltd., 841 F.Supp.2d 810, 825 (S.D.N.Y. 2012).

3. *E.g.,* regarding language expressing condition precedent: Gay v. Brencorp, Inc., 2012 WL 162354 at *8–9 (M.D. Fla. 2012); Edelman Arts, Inc. v. Art Int'l (UK) Ltd., 841 F.Supp.2d 810, 825 (S.D.N.Y. 2012); Gunderson v. School Dist. of Hillsborough County, 937 So.2d 777, 779 (Fla. Dist. Ct. App. 2006); Catholic Charities of Archdiocese of Chicago v. Thorpe, 741 N.E.2d 651, 654 (Ill. App. Ct. 2000).

4. *E.g.,* regarding language expressing condition precedent: Gay v. Brencorp, Inc., 2012 WL 162354 *8–9 (M.D. Fla. 2012) (law well-settled in Florida and elsewhere that conditions precedent must be explicit and unambiguous and express wording must reflect intention).

5. *E.g.,* regarding waiver of conditions precedent: Downs v. Rosenthal Collins Group, L.L.C., 963 N.E.2d 282, 290–91 (Ill. App. Ct. 2011), *reh'g denied* (Jan. 30, 2012); Catholic Charities of Archdiocese of Chicago v. Thorpe, 741 N.E.2d 651, 654–55 (Ill. App. Ct. 2000).

6. E.g., regarding disfavor in which courts hold perpetual duration provisions; *e.g.,* A.T.N., Inc. v. McAirlaid's Vliesstoffe GmbH & Co. KG, 557 F.3d 483, 486 (7th Cir. 2009); Roger Edwards, LLC. v. Fiddes & Son, Ltd., 245 F. Supp. 2d 251, 262 (D. Me. 2003*) aff'd in part, dismissed in part* *sub nom.* Roger Edwards, LLC v. Fiddes & Sons, Ltd., 387 F.3d 90 (1st Cir. 2004); Western Taney County Fire Prot. Dist. v. City of Branson, MO, 334 S.W.3d 627, 631 (Mo. Ct. App. 2011), *reh'g and/or transfer denied* (Mar. 4, 2011), *transfer denied* (Apr. 26, 2011).

7. Western Taney County Fire Prot. Dist. v. City of Branson, MO, 334 S.W.3d 627, 631 (Mo. Ct. App. 2011), *reh'g and/or transfer denied* (Mar. 4, 2011), *transfer denied* (Apr. 26, 2011).

8. *E.g.,* regarding courts treating indefinite contracts as terminable-at-will by reasonable notice: Williams v. Classic Locksmith, L.L.C., 405 F. App'x. 884 (5th Cir. 2010); Minnesota Deli Provisions, Inc. v. Boar's Head Provisions Co., Inc., 606 F.3d 544, 549 (8th Cir. 2010); Andrade v. Jamestown Hous. Auth., 82 F.3d 1179, 1186 (1st Cir. 1996); W. Reserve Life Assur. Co. of Ohio v. Bratton, 464 F. Supp. 2d 814, 837 (N.D. Iowa 2006); United States v. Hardy, 916 F.Supp. 1373, 1381 (W.D. Ky. 1995); Varni Bros. Corp. v. Wine World, Inc., 41 Cal.Rptr.2d 740, 746 (Ct. App. 1995); Voyles v. Sasser, 472 S.E.2d 80, 81 (Ga. Ct. App. 1996); Rogier v. American Testing & Eng'g Corp., 734 N.E.2d 606, 616 (Ind. Ct. App. 2000); City of Starkville v. 4–County Elec. Power Ass'n, 819 So.2d 1216, 1232 (Miss. 2002); Better Living Now, Inc. v. Image Too, Inc., 889 N.Y.S.2d 653, 655 (N.Y. App. Div. 2009); Klamath Off–Project Water Users, Inc. v. Pacificorp, 240 P.3d 94, 99–100 (Or. Ct. App. 2010) *review denied,* 249 P.3d 123 (2011); City of Corpus Christi v. Taylor, 126 S.W.3d 712, 722 (Tex. App. 2004).

9. *E.g.,* regarding courts treating a contract containing a period for indefinite duration as terminable after a *reasonable* period of time: Italian & French Wine Co. of Buffalo, Inc. v. Negociants U.S.A., Inc., 842 F.Supp. 693, 699 (W.D.N.Y. 1993); Varni Bros. Corp. v. Wine World, Inc., 41 Cal.Rptr.2d 740, 746 (Ct. App. 1995); J.M. Smith Corp. v. Matthews, 474 S.E.2d 798, 800 (N.C. Ct. App. 1996); City of Corpus Christi v. Taylor, 126 S.W.3d 712, 722 (Tex. App. 2004).

10. Lafarge N. Am., Inc. v. K.E.C.I. Colorado, Inc., 250 P.3d 682, 689 (Colo. Ct. App. 2010) *cert. denied,* 10SC242, 2011 WL 85780 (Colo. Jan. 10, 2011).

11. Ford Motor Credit Co. v. Ryan, 939 N.E.2d 891, 920 (Ohio Ct. App. 2010) *appeal not allowed,* 941 N.E.2d 804 (Ohio 2011). *E.g.,* regarding the definition of "assignment" as the voluntary transfer of a right or interest to another person—*i.e.,* a transfer vesting in the assignee all the assignor's rights in property that is the subject of the assignment: State Farm Fire & Cas. Co. v. Weiss, 194 P.3d 1063, 1067 (Colo. Ct. App. 2008); YPI 180 N. LaSalle Owner, LLC v. 180 N. LaSalle II, LLC, 933 N.E.2d 860, 864 (Ill. App. Ct. 2010); Sherman v. Sherman, 751 N.W.2d 168, 175 (Neb. Ct. App. 2008); Shipley v. Unifund CCR Partners, 331 S.W.3d 27, 28 (Tex. App. 2010), *reh'g overruled* (Dec. 21, 2010).

12. *E.g.,* regarding assignment as one party's stepping into shoes of the other: YPI 180 N. LaSalle Owner, LLC v. 180 N. LaSalle II, LLC, 933 N.E.2d 860, 864 (Ill. App. Ct. 2010); Ford Motor Credit Co. v. Ryan, 939 N.E.2d 891, 920 (Ohio Ct. App. 2010) *appeal not allowed,* 941 N.E.2d 804 (Ohio 2011); In re Liquidation of Home Ins. Co., 953 A.2d 443, 449 (N.H. 2008); Shipley v. Unifund CCR Partners, 331 S.W.3d 27, 28–29 (Tex. App. 2010), *reh'g overruled* (Dec. 21, 2010).

13. *E.g.,* Pope v. Winter Park Healthcare Group, Ltd., 939 So.2d 185, 188–89 (Fla. Dist. Ct. App. 2006).

14. Jenkins v. Eckerd Corp., 913 So.2d 43, 50 (Fla. Dist. Ct. App. 2005) (contracts are assignable unless assignment is specifically prohibited, the contract involves obligations of personal nature, or public policy prohibits assignment); *see* Restatement (Second) of Contracts § 317(2)(b) and (c) (1981).

15. Mountain Peaks Fin. Services, Inc. v. Roth–Steffen, 778 N.W.2d 380, 385 (Minn. Ct. App. 2010), *review denied* (Apr. 28, 2010).

16. Regency Realty Investors, LLC v. Cleary Fire Prot., Inc., 260 P.3d 1, 5 (Colo. Ct. App. 2009) (while the law favors assignability of rights generally, it does not allow assignments for matters of personal trust or confidence or personal services).

17. Kim v. Moffett, 234 P.3d 279, 287 (Wash. Ct. App. 2010). *E.g.,* regarding the non-assignability of personal services: North Country Villas Homeowners Ass'n v. Kokenge, 163 P.3d 1247, 1253 (Kan. Ct. App. 2007) (exception to general rule for assignments is assignment of rights arising out of contracts involving personal and confidential relations to which liabilities are attached); Burnison v. Johnston, 764 N.W.2d 96, 99 (Neb. 2009) (a contractual right cannot be assigned if obligor reasonably intended only the person with whom it contracted to exercise the right, a rule that usually applies when the contract involves relationship of personal trust or confidence); HD Supply Facilities Maint., Ltd. v. Bymoen, 210 P.3d 183, 186 (Nev. 2009) (personal services contracts are not assignable absent consent).

18. Kim v. Moffett, 234 P.3d 279, 287 (Wash. Ct. App. 2010).

19. *E.g.,* Ellington v. Sony/ATV Music Publ'g LLC, 925 N.Y.S.2d 20, 21–22 (App. Div. 2011) (overall tenor of agreement contradicted plaintiff's attempt to characterize the contract as a personal services contract involving management of plaintiff's artistic career or assets).

20. *E.g.*, Kenneth D. Corwin, Ltd. v. Missouri Med. Serv., 684 S.W.2d 598, 600 (Mo. Ct. App. 1985) (in a contract for personal services, which involves special knowledge, skill or a relation of personal confidence, the duty to perform is not assignable without consent of both parties).

21. *E.g.*, Reserves Dev. LLC v. Crystal Properties, LLC, 986 A.2d 362, 370 (Del. 2009), *reargument denied* (Jan. 6, 2010). *See* UAW–GM Human Res. Ctr. v. KSL Recreation Corp., 579 N.W.2d 411, 422 (Mich. Ct. App. 1998) (an obligor can properly delegate the performance of his or her duty to another unless delegation contrary to public policy; main exceptions relate to contracts for personal services or exercise of personal discretion or skill).

22. *E.g.*, Reserves Dev. LLC v. Crystal Properties, LLC, 986 A.2d 362, 370 (Del. 2009), *reargument denied* (Jan. 6, 2010). Regarding unenforceability based on public policy and contractual prohibitions: UAW–GM Human Res. Ctr. v. KSL Recreation Corp., 579 N.W.2d 411, 422 (Mich. Ct. App. 1998) (an obligor can delegate performance of party's duty to another unless delegation is contrary to terms of party's promise).

23. *See* Restatement (Second) of Contracts § 318(2) (1981). *E.g.*, regarding delegation of duties: BDI Laguna Holdings, Inc. v. Marsh, 689 S.E.2d 39, 43 (Ga. Ct. App. 2009), *reconsideration denied* (Dec. 16, 2009), *cert. denied* (June 28, 2010) (although a duty is not delegable where performance by delegate would vary materially from performance by original obligor, the parties may agree to such an assignment or delegation); Brooks v. Hayes, 395 N.W.2d 167, 173 (Wis. 1986) (rule for delegation of performance of contractual obligation is that obligor may delegate a contractual duty without obligee's consent unless duty is personal).

24. *See* Pope v. Winter Park Healthcare Group, Ltd., 939 So.2d 185, 188–89 (Fla. Dist. Ct. App. 2006). *E.g.*, regarding fact that delegating party remains liable for performance of the delegated duties: Norton v. First Fed. Sav., 624 P.2d 854, 860 (Ariz. 1981) (delegation neither extinguishes the duty to perform nor prevents damages for failure to perform); Club Telluride Owners Ass'n, Inc. v. Mitchell, 70 P.3d 502, 504 (Colo. Ct. App. 2002) (obligor may effectively delegate performance to another who is willing to perform the delegated duty, but obligor remains liable as surety unless obligee consents to delegation); Bashir v. Moayedi, 627 A.2d 997, 1000 (D.C. 1993) (delegating party cannot free herself from liability by delegating her duties of performance to another); Gilmore v. SCI Texas Funeral Services, Inc., 234 S.W.3d 251, 259 (Tex. App. 2007) (unless obligee agrees otherwise, neither delegation of performance nor a contract to assume duty made with obligor by person delegated discharges any duty or liability of delegating obligor).

Endnotes for Chapter 8: Limitation or Exclusion of Liability

1. Hampton Island, LLC v. HAOP, LLC, 702 S.E.2d 770, 775 (Ga. Ct. App. 2010), *cert. denied* (Mar. 7, 2011).

2. The party relying on the third party to perform has a duty to ensure that the party does perform and to prod along a third party who is delinquent. *E.g.*, regarding delay or nonperformance by a third party: S. Leo Harmonay, Inc. v. Binks Mfg. Co., 597 F.Supp. 1014, 1028 (S.D.N.Y. 1984) *aff'd sub nom.* Harmonay Inc. v. Binks Mfg. Co., 762 F.2d 990 (2d Cir. 1985); Warner v. Denis, 933 P.2d 1372, 1381 (Haw. Ct. App. 1997); Missouri Dept. of Transp. ex rel. PR Developers, Inc. v. Safeco Ins. Co. of Am., 97 S.W.3d 21, 35 (Mo. Ct. App. 2002).

3. Typically, the impossibility doctrine applies in circumstances in which performance becomes objectively impossible (e.g., because subject-matter or means of performance is destroyed or by operation of law) in circumstances that the parties could not have anticipated and addressed in the contract.

E.g., regarding requirement that performance be objectively impossible: East Capitol View Cmty. Dev. Corp., Inc. v. Robinson, 941 A.2d 1036, 1040 (D.C. 2008); Innovative Modular Solutions v. Hazel Crest Sch. Dist. 152.5, 965 N.E.2d 414, 421 (Ill. 2012), *as modified on denial of reh'g* (Mar. 26, 2012); Comprehensive Bldg. Contractors Inc. v. Pollard Excavating Inc., 251 A.D.2d 951, 952, 674 N.Y.S.2d 869, 871 (1998).

E.g., regarding unavailability of defense if event making performance impossible could have been foreseen and addressed in the contract: Specialty Beverages, L.L.C. v. Pabst Brewing Co., 537 F.3d 1165, 1176 (10th Cir. 2008); East Capitol View Cmty. Dev. Corp., Inc. v. Robinson, 941 A.2d 1036, 1040 (D.C. 2008); Walter T. Embry, Inc. v. LaSalle Nat. Bank, 792 So.2d 567, 570 (Fla. Dist. Ct. App. 2001); Warner v. Denis, 933 P.2d 1372, 1381 (Haw. Ct. App. 1997); Lagarenne v. Ingber, 710 N.Y.S.2d 425, 428 (App. Div. 2000); Silsbe v. Houston Levee Indus. Park, LLC, 165 S.W.3d 260, 265 (Tenn. Ct. App. 2004).

4. Typically, the impracticability doctrine applies if the party is prevented from performing by an event the non-occurrence of which was a fundamental assumption on which the contract was based. For the doctrine to apply, the party asserting it must not have been at fault. *See* Uniform

Commercial Code § 2–615(a). *E.g.,* regarding impracticability of performance: O'Hara v. State, 590 A.2d 948, 953 (Conn. 1991); Summit Properties, Inc. v. Pub. Serv. Co. of New Mexico, 118 P.3d 716, 727 (N.M. Ct. App. 2005); M.J. Paquet, Inc. v. New Jersey Dept. of Transp., 794 A.2d 141, 148 (N.J. 2002); Luber v. Luber, 614 A.2d 771, 774 (Pa. Super. Ct. 1992); Frederick Mgmt. Co., L.L.C. v. City Nat. Bank of W. Virginia, 723 S.E.2d 277, 286–87 (W. Va. 2010).

5. Typically, frustration of purpose occurs if a change in circumstances whose non-occurrence was a fundamental assumption on which the contract was based has effectively frustrated the party's main purpose for entering the contract by destroying the value of the other party's performance. *See* Restatement (Second) of Contracts § 265 (1981). *E.g.,* regarding frustration of purpose: State v. Jones, 271 P.3d 1277, 1281 (Kan. Ct. App. 2012); America's Floor Source, L.L.C. v. Joshua Homes, 946 N.E.2d 799, 808 (Ohio Ct. App. 2010); Silbernagel v. Silbernagel, 800 N.W.2d 320, 329 (N.D. 2011); City of Flint v. Chrisdom Properties, Ltd., 770 N.W.2d 888, 891 (Mich. App. 2009); In re Estate of Sheppard, 789 N.W.2d 616, 619 (Wis. Ct. App. 2010) *review denied*, 791 N.W.2d 382 (Wis. 2010).

6. *E.g.,* regarding excuse of performance that was prevented by the other party: Doucot v. IDS Scheer, Inc., 734 F. Supp. 2d 172, 188 (D. Mass. 2010); Narvaez v. Wilshire Credit Corp., 757 F. Supp. 2d 621 (N.D. Tex. 2010); Paul Morrell, Inc. v. Kellogg Brown & Root, Inc., 682 F. Supp. 2d 606, 631 (E.D. Va. 2010); Hale v. Sharp Healthcare, 108 Cal.Rptr.3d 669, 680 (Ct. App. 2010).

7. *E.g.,* URI Cogeneration Partners, L.P. v. Board of Governors for Higher Educ., 915 F.Supp. 1267, 1276 (D.R.I. 1996).

8. *E.g.,* Northern Indiana Pub. Serv. Co. v. Carbon County Coal Co., 799 F.2d 265, 275 (7th Cir. 1986) (force majeure clause does not buffer a party against normal risks of a contract); Pillsbury Co., Inc. v. Wells Dairy, Inc., 752 N.W.2d 430, 440 (Iowa 2008) (force majeure clause allocates risk if performance is impossible or impracticable due to an event that parties could not anticipate or control).

9. Route 6 Outparcels, LLC v. Ruby Tuesday, Inc., 931 N.Y.S.2d 436, 438 (N.Y. App. Div. 2011).

10. *E.g.,* regarding typical "catchall" language: Kentucky Natural Gas Corp. v. City of Leitchfield ex rel. Its Util. Comm'n, 2011 WL 4501976 at *6 (Ky. Ct. App. 2011) (provision applied to "other causes, whether the kind herein enumerated or otherwise, not within the control of the party claiming suspension and which by the exercise of due diligence such party is unable to prevent or overcome"); Allegiance Hillview, L.P. v. Range Texas Prod., LLC, 347 S.W.3d 855, 867 (Tex. App. 2011) (provision operates only "so long as such event is beyond the reasonable control of the Party claiming the benefit of such Force Majeure and only in the event such Party is taking all reasonable action to remedy such Force Majeure").

11. *E.g.,* regarding restrictive interpretation of language relating to what events outside the party's control: Langham–Hill Petroleum Inc. v. Southern Fuels Co., 813 F.2d 1327, 1329–30 (4th Cir. 1987); Kel Kim Corp. v. Cent. Markets, Inc., 519 N.E.2d 295, 296 (N.Y.1987).

12. *E.g.,* Kel Kim Corp. v. Cent. Markets, Inc., 519 N.E.2d 295, 296–97 (N.Y. 1987) (principle of interpretation applicable to such clauses is that the general words are not to be given expansive meaning; they are confined to things of the same kind or nature as the particular matters mentioned).

13. Kel Kim Corp. v. Cent. Markets, Inc., 519 N.E.2d 295, 296–97 (N.Y. 1987)

14. Kel Kim Corp. v. Cent. Markets, Inc., 519 N.E.2d 295, 296–97 (N.Y. 1987).

15. Palmer v. Lakeside Wellness Ctr., 798 N.W.2d 845, 848–49 (Neb. 2011).

16. *E.g.,* regarding strict construction and disfavoring of exculpatory clauses: Wycoff v. Grace Cmty. Church of Assemblies of God, 251 P.3d 1260, 1265 (Colo. Ct. App. 2010); Harris v. State, ex rel. Kempthorne, 210 P.3d 86, 90 (Idaho 2009); Hamer v. City Segway Tours of Chicago, LLC, 930 N.E.2d 578, 581 (Ill. App. Ct. 2010); Easley v. Gray Wolf Investments, LLC, 340 S.W.3d 269, 272–73 (Mo. Ct. App. 2011); Stelluti v. Casapenn Enterprises, LLC, 1 A.3d 678, 688 (N.J. 2010); Provoncha v. Vermont Motocross Ass'n, Inc., 974 A.2d 1261, 1264 (Vt. 2009).

17. Wisconsin courts apparently do not readily enforce exculpatory clauses, though they do not treat exculpatory clauses as invalid per se. *See* Alexander T. Pendleton, *Enforceable Exculpatory Agreements: Do They Still Exist?*, Wis. Law., August 2005, at 16, 17–18; Mettler ex rel. Burnett v. Nellis, 695 N.W.2d 861, 865 (Wis. Ct. App. 2005).

Oklahoma views exculpatory clauses that exempt a party from liability for negligence as "distasteful to the law" and therefore requires that an exculpatory clause satisfy "a gauntlet of judicially-crafted hurdles." Schmidt v. United States, 912 P.2d 871, 874 (Okla. 1996).

18. In Indiana, courts presume that exculpatory clauses represent the "freely bargained agreement of the parties" and that no public policy bars enforcement of an exculpatory clause, unless the provision is prohibited by statute, injures an important public policy, or is unconscionable. *See* Indiana Dept. Of Transp. v. Shelly & Sands, Inc., 756 N.E.2d 1063, 1072 (Ind. Ct. App. 2001); Fresh Cut, Inc. v. Fazli, 650 N.E.2d 1126, 1130 (Ind. 1995).

19. *E.g.,* regarding public policy as a bar to contract protecting party against liability for willful, wanton, or intentional wrongdoing: Dargis v. Paradise Park, Inc., 819 N.E.2d 1220, 1232 (Ill. App. Ct. 2004); Kalisch–Jarcho, Inc. v. City of New York, 448 N.E.2d 413, 416 (N.Y. 1983).

20. *E.g.,* JM Family Enterprises, Inc. v. Winter Park Imports, Inc., 10 So.3d 1133 (Fla. Dist. Ct. App. 2009).

21. *See* City of Santa Barbara v. Superior Court, 161 P.3d 1095, 1115 (Cal. 2007). In a 2007 case involving the drowning of a developmentally disabled child at a city-sponsored summer camp, the California Supreme Court determined that a pre-injury release that purported to release the city from liability for gross negligence was void. The California Supreme Court said that its decision would discourage, or at least not facilitate, aggravated wrongs. Other courts that agree in refusing to allow a party to exempt itself from liability for gross negligence include, *e.g.,* Wheelock v. Sport Kites, Inc., 839 F.Supp. 730, 736 (D. Haw. 1993); Wolf v. Ford, 644 A.2d 522, 525 (Md. 1994); Xu v. Gay, 668 N.W.2d 166, 170 (Mich. Ct. App. 2003); Yang v. Voyagaire Houseboats, Inc., 701 N.W.2d 783, 789 (Minn. 2005); New Light Co., Inc. v. Wells Fargo Alarm Services, Div. of Baker Protective Services, Inc., 525 N.W.2d 25, 30 (Neb. 1994);); Stelluti v. Casapenn Enterprises, LLC, 1 A.3d 678, 694 (N.J. 2010); Sommer v. Federal Signal Corp., 593 N.E.2d 1365, 1371 (N.Y. 1992).

22. *See* Hiett v. Lake Barcroft Cmty. Ass'n, Inc., 418 S.E.2d 894, 896 (Va. 1992) (Virginia decisions have limited the right to contracting for release of liability for property damage); La. Civ. Code Ann. art. 2004 (West 2011) (declares "null" an exculpatory clause that limits a party's future liability for causing physical injury to the other party).

23. *See, e.g.,* regarding refusal of courts to enforce exculpatory clauses between clinic and patient relating to medical malpractice or other negligence in providing medical treatment): Cudnik v. William Beaumont Hosp., 525 N.W.2d 891, 897 (Mich. Ct. App. 1994) (court joined "overwhelming majority of jurisdictions holding that an exculpatory agreement executed by a patient before treatment is not enforceable to absolve a medical care provider from liability relating to medical care); Ash v. New York Univ. Dental Ctr., 564 N.Y.S.2d 308, 309 (App. Div. 1990) (court refused on public policy grounds to enforce a release of a University dental clinic from liability for negligence of doctors, employees, or students that stated it was given "in consideration of reduced rates"); Eelbode v. Chec Med. Centers, Inc., 984 P.2d 436, 441 (Wash. Ct. App. 1999) (release that medical clinic required patient to sign before clinic's physical therapist administered a pre-placement physical violated public policy).

24. N.Y. Gen. Oblig. Law § 5–326 (McKinney) (2012).

25. *See* Dow–Westbrook, Inc. v. Candlewood Equine Practice, LLC, 989 A.2d 1075, 1084–85 (Conn. App. Ct. 2010) quoting Tunkl v. Regents of the University of California, 32 Cal.Rptr. 33, 383 P.2d 441 (1963).

The Connecticut case provides a useful summary of the *Tunkl* factors. Briefly, the factors are as follows: (1) whether the contract involves a business that is "generally thought suitable for public regulation;" (2) whether the party whom the exculpatory clause protects has contracted to provide a service of great public importance or that is essential to some members of the public; (3) whether the party whom the exculpatory clause protects holds itself out as available to perform that service for all members of the public (or for members of the public who meet certain established criteria); (4) whether because its services are essential, the party protected by the exculpatory clause has "a decisive advantage of bargaining strength;" (5) whether the exculpatory clause is part of a standardized contract of adhesion that does not offer the other party the option to obtain protection against negligence in exchange for additional reasonable fees; (6) whether as a result of the transaction, the person who is releasing the other from liability or waiving its right to file a claim is thereby placed under the control of the person who is protected by the release or waiver, and therefore subject to the risk of the other party's negligence. Dow-Westbrook, Inc., *supra*, at 1084–85.

26. Tunkl v. Regents of the University of California, 32 Cal.Rptr. 33, 383 P.2d 441 (Cal. 1963).

27. *See, e.g.,* Storm v. NSL Rockland Place, LLC, 898 A.2d 874, 886–87 (Del. Super. Ct. 2005); Hinely v. Florida Motorcycle Training, Inc., 70 So.3d 620, 624–25 (Fla. Dist. Ct. App. 2011); Banfield v. Louis, 589 So.2d 441, 446 (Fla. Dist. Ct. App. 1991); Berlangieri v. Running Elk Corp, 76 P.3d 1098, 1104 (N.M. 2003); Crawford v. Buckner, 839 S.W.2d 754, 757 (Tenn. 1992); Berry v. Greater Park City Co., 171 P.3d 442, 446–47 (Utah 2007); Kyriazis v. University of W. Va., 450 S.E.2d 649, 654–55 (W.Va. 1994).

28. *E.g.,* regarding tests applied by court in determining whether exculpatory clause violates public policy: Jones v. Dressel, 623 P.2d 370, 376 (Colo. 1981); Schlobohm v. Spa Petite, Inc., 326

N.W.2d 920, 924 (Minn. 1982) (post–*Tunkl* cases generally consider disparity of bargaining power and whether service being offered is public or essential service); Hamer v. City Segway Tours of Chicago, LLC, 930 N.E.2d 578, 581 (Ill. App. Ct. 2010); Ransburg v. Richards, 770 N.E.2d 393, 402 (Ind. Ct. App. 2002); Wolf v. Ford, 644 A.2d 522, 527 (Md. 1994); Stelluti v. Casapenn Enterprises, LLC, 975 A.2d 494, 505 (N.J. Super. Ct. App. Div. 2009) *aff'd*, 203 N.J. 286 (N.J. 2010); Eelbode v. Chec Med. Centers, Inc., 984 P.2d 436, 440 (Wash. Ct. App. 1999).

29.   State ex rel. Dunlap v. Berger, 567 S.E.2d 265, 275–76 (2002) (court stated that absent exceptional circumstances, exculpatory clause in a contract of adhesion unconscionable if application "would prohibit or substantially limit a person from enforcing and vindicating rights and protections or from seeking and obtaining statutory or common-law relief and remedies that are afforded by or arise under state law that exists for the benefit and protection of the public").

30.   Hinely v. Florida Motorcycle Training, Inc., 70 So.3d 620, 624 (Fla. Dist. Ct. App. 2011).

31.   *E.g.,* some Florida appellate courts have indicated that exculpatory clauses must contain the word negligence: Bender v. CareGivers of Am., Inc., 42 So.3d 893, 894 (Fla. Dist. Ct. App. 2010), *reh'g denied* (Sept. 23, 2010); Witt v. Dolphin Research Ctr., Inc., 582 So.2d 27, 28 (Fla. Dist. Ct. App. 1991); Van Tuyn v. Zurich Am. Ins. Co., 447 So.2d 318, 320 (Fla. Dist. Ct. App. 1984) (release); O'Connell v. Walt Disney World Co., 413 So.2d 444, 447 (Fla. Dist. Ct. App. 1982).

But see Cain v. Banka, 932 So.2d 575, 578 (Fla. Dist. Ct. App. 2006) (5th D.C.A.) (no need for express language referring to "negligence" or "negligent acts" for release to be effective).

32.   Gross v. Sweet, 400 N.E.2d 306, 309–10 (N.Y. 1979). *E.g.,* stating a release need not contain "magic words" to be valid: City of Hammond v. Plys, 893 N.E.2d 1, 3 (Ind. Ct. App. 2008); Wycoff v. Grace Cmty. Church of Assemblies of God, 251 P.3d 1260, 1265 (Colo. Ct. App. 2010); Seigneur v. National Fitness Inst., Inc., 752 A.2d 631, 636 (Md. Ct. Spec. App. 2000); Colgan v. Agway, Inc., 553 A.2d 143, 146 (Vt. 1988).

33.   *See* Colgan v. Agway, Inc., 553 A.2d 143, 146 (Vt. 1988).

34.   Goyings v. Jack & Ruth Eckerd Found., 403 So.2d 1144, 1145–46 (Fla. Dist. Ct. App. 1981). A Florida court reached a similar conclusion in Murphy v. Young Men's Christian Ass'n of Lake Wales, Inc., 974 So.2d 565, 568–69 (Fla. Dist. Ct. App. 2008).

35.   *E.g.,* Banfield v. Louis, 589 So.2d 441, 445 (Fla. Dist. Ct. App. 1991) (a waiver that identifies parties by capacity is sufficient to absolve those parties from liability as a matter of law).

36.   *See, e.g.,* Burd v. KL Shangri–La Owners, L.P., 67 P.3d 927, 929–30 (Okla. Civ. App. 2002) (applying Schmidt v. United States, 912 P.2d 871, 874 (Okla. 1996) in which the court said that a contractual provision which one party claims excuses it from liability for future tortious acts or omissions must clearly and cogently (1) demonstrate an intent to relieve *that* particular person from fault and (2) describe the nature and extent of damages from which that party seeks to be relieved). In *Burd,* the court said that a waiver that released "any facility" that was a venue for tennis tournaments was not sufficient to release a particular facility that was not known to the plaintiff at the time she signed the waiver. Burd, *supra,* at 929–30. The court said that "Patron could not contract away Shangri–La's liability," because (1) Patron did not know she would be playing at Shangri–La; (2) the identity of the tortfeasor was not known to her at the time of the contract; (3) there was no intent, and thus no meeting of the minds, to exculpate Shangri–La, and (4) the language of the exculpatory contract was vague and ambiguous. Id.

37.   Hamer v. City Segway Tours of Chicago, LLC, 930 N.E.2d 578, 581 (Ill. App. Ct. 2010).

38.   Evans v. Lima Lima Flight Team, Inc., 869 N.E.2d 195, 200 (Ill. App. Ct. 2007).

39.   *Id.*

40.   *Id.* at 203–04. *But see* Larsen v. Vic Tanny Int'l, 474 N.E.2d 729, 731 (1984) in which an Illinois court concluded that an assumption of risk clause in a contract between a gymnasium and a member did not encompass the risk that the member would suffer injury from inhaling cleaning fumes, even though the provision stated all of the following (1) the gymnasium would not be liable for personal injury resulting from use of the facilities and equipment, (2) the member assumed "full responsibility" for injuries that occurred on the premises, (3) the member released the gymnasium from any claim resulting from or arising out of the member's use. The court said that inhaling vapors from cleaning fumes was not a risk that the party would have contemplated or could have mitigated by using extra care. Id.

41.   Scott By & Through Scott v. Pacific W. Mountain Resort, 834 P.2d 6, 10 (Wash. 1992).

42.   General Bargain Ctr. v. American Alarm Co., Inc., 430 N.E.2d 407, 411 (Ind. Ct. App. 1982).

43.   *See* General Bargain Ctr. v. American Alarm Co., Inc., 430 N.E.2d 407, 411 (Ind. Ct. App. 1982). *See* Berggren v. Hill, 928 N.E.2d 1225, 1229 (Ill. App. Ct. 2010) (liquidated-damages clause does not limit a non-defaulting party's remedies but instead provides an agreed-upon measure of damages).

44. *E.g.,* regarding enforcement of limitation-of-damages clause relating to alarm services: Omni Corp. v. Sonitrol Corp., 303 F. App'x. 908, 910 (2d Cir. 2008); Fox Alarm Co., Inc. v. Wadsworth, 913 So.2d 1070, 1080 (Ala. 2005); North River Ins. Co. v. Jones, 655 N.E.2d 987, 992 (Ill. App. Ct. 1995).

45. Rollins, Inc. v. Heller, 454 So.2d 580, 583 (Fla. Dist. Ct. App. 1984).

46. Applying Pennsylvania law, the U.S. Third Circuit Court of Appeals said that limitation-of-damages clauses are not tested by the same stringent standard as exculpatory clauses in Valhal Corp. v. Sullivan Associates, Inc., 44 F.3d 195, 202–03 (3d Cir. 1995). On the other hand, an Illinois court concluded that limitation-of-damages clauses are strictly construed in Jewelers Mut. Ins. Co. v. Firstar Bank Illinois, 792 N.E.2d 1, 5 (Ill. App. 2003) *aff'd*, 820 N.E.2d 411 (Ill. 2004).

47. For example, the Tennessee Court of Appeals has determined that it is against public policy to enforce a contractual limitation of damages for negligence in a contract between a would-be home purchaser and the home inspector. Russell v. Bray, 116 S.W.3d 1, 8 (Tenn. Ct. App. 2003) In an unreported case, the Kentucky Court of Appeals followed Tennessee. Mullins v. Northern Kentucky Inspections, Inc., 2010 WL 3447630 at *5 (Ky. Ct. App. 2010), *review denied* (Apr. 13, 2011). The Illinois Court of Appeals, however, concluded that a clause limiting damages for a home inspector is enforceable, "absent a violation of a settled public policy of the state." The court in that case found no such violation. Zerjal v. Daech & Bauer Const., Inc., 939 N.E.2d 1067, 1072 (Ill. App. Ct. 2010) appeal denied, 949 N.E.2d 665 (Ill. 2011).

48. *See, e.g.,* Gessa v. Manor Care of Florida, Inc., 86 So.3d 484, 493 (Fla. 2011) (limitation provision in an arbitration agreement between a nursing home and a patient that placed a $250,000 cap on noneconomic damages and waived punitive damages violated the public policy of the State of Florida and were unenforceable.)

49. *E.g.,* Lousiana Rest. Ass'n Self Insurer's Fund v. The Semarca Corp., 2011 WL 652002 at *3 (E.D. La. 2011) (damages limitation clause in contract between purchaser and seller of a software system would not be enforceable if court found gross negligence or bad faith); Honeywell, Inc. v. Ruby Tuesday, Inc., 43 F. Supp. 2d 1074, 1079 (D. Minn. 1999) (party could not limit by contract its liability for intentional or grossly negligent acts).

50. *See* Lousiana Rest. Ass'n Self Insurer's Fund v. The Semarca Corp., 2011 WL 652002 at *3 (E.D. La. 2011); Onconome, Inc. v. University of Pittsburgh, 2010 WL 1133425 at *3 (W.D. Pa. 2010) (unreported case).

51. *See* Abacus Fed. Sav. Bank v. ADT Sec. Services, Inc., 967 N.E.2d 666 (N.Y. 2012). The Court of Appeals said that under New York public policy, a party cannot "insulate itself from damages caused by grossly negligent conduct," so a limitation-of-damages clause is not enforceable in circumstances involving gross negligence; however, when invoked "to pierce an agreed-upon limitation of liability in a commercial contract, the gross negligence "must smack of intentional wrongdoing," i.e., conduct evincing a reckless indifference to the rights of others. *Id.* quoting Kalisch–Jarcho, Inc. v. City of New York, 448 N.E.2d 413 (1983).

52. *E.g.,* Onconome, Inc. v. University of Pittsburgh, 2010 WL 1133425 at 3 (W.D. Pa. 2010) (unreported case) (though limitation-of-damages clauses negotiated between parties at arms' length are *generally* enforceable, they cannot limit damages for breaches that are "intentional, willful, wanton, reckless or otherwise in bad faith").

53. *E.g.,* Omni Corp. v. Sonitrol Corp., 303 F. App'x 908, 909–10 (2d Cir. 2008) (provision in contract between company that monitored for flooding and customer did not violate public policy); Valhal Corp. v. Sullivan Associates, Inc., 44 F.3d 195, 204–07 (3d Cir. 1995) (provision in contract with a firm of architects did not violate public policy); Lanier At McEver, L.P. v. Planners And Engineers Collaborative, Inc., 663 S.E.2d 240, 241–42 (Ga. 2008) (provision limiting liability of a civil engineering firm did not violate public policy); Blaylock Grading Co., LLP v. Smith, 658 S.E.2d 680, 683 (N.C. Ct. App. 2008) (provision in contract with land surveyor did not violate public policy); Synnex Corp. v. ADT Sec. Services, Inc., 928 A.2d 37, 45–47 (N.J. Super. Ct. App. Div. 2007) (provision in contract for burglar alarm services did not violate public policy).

54. For example, factors that a New Jersey court considered included the contract's subject matter, whether the contract implicates public health or safety, the parties' relative bargaining positions, and the extent to which necessity compelled the person against whom the clause operates to contract for the service or other consideration. Synnex Corp. v. ADT Sec. Services, Inc., 928 A.2d 37, 45 (N.J. Super. Ct. App. Div. 2007).

55. *See, e.g.,* Synnex Corp. v. ADT Sec. Services, Inc., 928 A.2d 37, 44 (N.J. Super. Ct. App. Div. 2007) (clause can insulate an alarm company from liability even for "very negligent or grossly negligent performance"); Rollins, Inc. v. Heller, 454 So.2d 580, 584 (Fla. Dist. Ct. App. 1984) (regarding a burglar alarm services contract, trial court erred in (1) not limiting liability for gross negligence and in (2) finding that limitation provision did not apply).

56. In enforcing a limitation-of-damages clause in favor of a firm of architects, the U.S. Third Circuit Court of Appeals pointed out that the limitation was reasonable and not so drastic as to remove the incentive to perform with reasonable care. Valhal Corp. v. Sullivan Associates, Inc., 44 F.3d 195, 204 (3d Cir. 1995). Likewise, in a case involving land surveying services, the North Carolina Court of Appeals determined that a limitation-of-damages clause that limited the liability of the land surveyors to $50,000 was enforceable. Blaylock Grading Co., LLP v. Smith, 658 S.E.2d 680, 683 (N.C. Ct. App. 2008). Addressing the public policy aspects of the case, the court said that while North Carolina requires engineers and land surveyors to be licensed, those facts alone do not "automatically convert a profession into a public service." Furthermore, "when a breach of contract between two parties involves only economic loss, as in the present case, the health and safety of the public are not implicated." Id.

57. *See* Harris Moran Seed Co., Inc. v. Phillips, 949 So.2d 916, 930 (Ala. Civ. App. 2006) quoting Southland Farms, Inc. v. Ciba–Geigy Corp., 575 So.2d 1077, 1081 (Ala. 1991); Reynolds Health Care Services, Inc. v. HMNH, Inc., 217 S.W.3d 797, 803 (Ark. 2005).

58. *See* Imaging Sys. Int'l, Inc. v. Magnetic Resonance Plus, Inc., 490 S.E.2d 124, 128 (Ga. App. 1997) (lost profits in a breach of contract action could mean either direct damages that represent the benefit of the bargain if the phrase refers to profits that are inherent in the arrangement or consequential damages if the phrase "lost profits" applies to "profits which might accrue collaterally as a result of the contract's performance").

59. *See* Baeza v. Superior Court, 135 Cal.Rptr.3d 557, 568 (Ct. App. 2011), *reh'g denied* (Jan. 9, 2012), *review denied* (Mar. 28, 2012).

60. *See* Uniform Commercial Code 2–719 (2003 amendments).

61. *See* Imaging Sys. Int'l, Inc. v. Magnetic Resonance Plus, Inc., 490 S.E.2d 124, 128 (1997).

62. *See* Uniform Commercial Code § 2–719 (2003 amendments) (comment).

63. *See* Harris Moran Seed Co., Inc. v. Phillips, 949 So.2d 916, 930–31 (Ala. Civ. App. 2006).

64. *See id.* at 924.

65. In a federal case in Arizona, the court reached the opposite conclusion: Nomo Agroindustrial Sa De CV v. Enza Zaden N. Am., Inc., 492 F. Supp. 2d 1175, 1181 (D. Ariz. 2007) (true value of seeds only comes from crop yielded after considerable time and cost expended by the farmer; lost growing season and accompanying loss of expected profits due to defective seeds not compensated by simply replacing or refunding the price of the defective seeds; in consequence, numerous courts have found that such limitation of damages provisions fail of their essential purpose and are unconscionable).

66. Harris Moran Seed Co., Inc. v. Phillips, 949 So.2d 916, 924 (Ala. Civ. App. 2006).

67. Uniform Commercial Code § 2–719(3) (2003 amendments).

68. *See* Uniform Commercial Code § 2–719 (2003 amendments) (comment).

69. *See* Gessa v. Manor Care of Florida, Inc., 86 So.3d 484, 493 (Fla. 2011) (circumstances in which provision violated public policy).

70. Imaging Sys. Int'l, Inc. v. Magnetic Resonance Plus, Inc., 490 S.E.2d 124, 128 (Ga. App. 1997).

71. *See e.g.,* In re TFT–LCD (Flat Panel) Antitrust Litig., 2011 WL 4017961 at 6 (N.D. Cal. 2011) (An arbitration clause contained a limitation on treble damages that was unenforceable under the applicable law; the court therefore severed the treble damages limitation from the agreement); Gessa v. Manor Care of Florida, Inc., 86 So.3d 484, 493 (Fla. 2011) (Florida nursing home statute provided for an award of punitive damages for gross or flagrant conduct or conscious indifference to residence rights and did not place a cap on pain and suffering; provision that excluded punitive damages and capped pain and suffering directly frustrated the statutory remedies).

72. Imaging Sys. Int'l, Inc. v. Magnetic Resonance Plus, Inc., 490 S.E.2d 124, 127 (Ga. Ct. App. 1997).

73. Several different courts that considered the same pest-control contract's limitation-of-remedies clause determined that the exclusive remedy (re-treatment for termite infestation) set out in that clause was enforceable. *See, e.g.,* Roossinck v. Orkin Exterminating Co., Inc., 1998 WL 34385273 at *4–5 (W.D. Mich. 1998); Groth v. Orkin Exterminating Co., Inc., 909 F.Supp. 1150, 1152 (C.D.Ill.1995); Palmer v. Orkin Exterminating Co., 871 F.Supp. 912, 913 (S.D.Miss.1994); Harmon v. Orkin Exterminating Co., 794 F.Supp. 589, 590–91 (W.D.Va.1992).

74. Uniform Commercial Code Art. 2 and Art. 2A, respectively.

75. *See* Uniform Commercial Code § 2–313.

76. *See* Uniform Commercial Code § 2–313.

77. *See* Uniform Commercial Code § 2–316(1) (cmt 1).

78. *E.g.,* Salazar v. D.W.B.H., Inc., 192 P.3d 1205, 1209 (N.M. 2008).

79. Uniform Commercial Code § 2–314; *see* § 2A–212.

80. *See* Uniform Commercial Code § 2–104(1) (2003 amendments) (defining "merchant").

81. *See* Uniform Commercial Code § 2–314.

82. *See* Uniform Commercial Code § 2–315.

83. *See* Uniform Commercial Code § 2–316 (2003 amendments); Uniform Commercial Code § 2A–214(3) (2003 amendments).

84. *E.g.,* regarding effect on implied warranty of the buyer's failure to examine the goods: Ladner v. Jordan, 848 So.2d 870, 872–73 (Miss. Ct. App. 2002) (the buyers of a horse were experienced with horses, present at the time of sale, chose not to have a veterinarian examine the horse, and did not ride the horse, but discovered after the sale that it was lame; under UCC, buyer who fails to examine goods prior to use when defect complained of would have been revealed by examination cannot rely on implied warranty of fitness for a particular purpose).

85. *E.g.,* regarding exclusion by course of dealing or usage of trade: R.O.W. Window Co. v. Allmetal, Inc., 856 N.E.2d 55, 60 (Ill. App. Ct. 2006) (record showed that plaintiff was defendant's customer for several years, the parties had business dealings during that period, and during that period all invoices that defendant sent to plaintiff contained conspicuous disclaimer of implied warranties printed on them in center of page; in addition, yearly product catalogue contained conspicuous disclaimer; their course of dealing supplemented terms of the parties' agreement and established that exclusion of implied warranties was part of the bargain).

86. Uniform Commercial Code § 2–316(2) (2003 amendments); *see* § 2A–214(2) (2003 amendments).

87. *See* Uniform Commercial Code § 1–201(10) (2003 amendments).

88. *E.g.,* regarding the requirement of "conspicuousness": Tague v. Autobarn Motors, Ltd., 914 N.E.2d 710, 718 (Ill. App. Ct. 2009) *appeal denied*, 920 N.E.2d 1082 (Ill. 2009) (discussing means used by party to make warranty conspicuous—*e.g.,* title in bold capital letters, underlining of contents, and crucial paragraph appeared directly above the other party's signature); Brown Sprinkler Corp. v. Plumbers Supply Co., 265 S.W.3d 237, 240 (Ky. Ct. App. 2007) (discussing formatting devices that met statutory definition of conspicuous—*e.g.,* location of language on front of invoice in "readable size print," type size contrasting with remaining printed information, segregation of paragraph from other printed information, plain language stating that it excluded all implied warranties).

89. Salazar v. D.W.B.H., Inc., 192 P.3d 1205, 1210–11 (N.M. 2008).

90. *Id.*

91. *See id.*

92. *E.g.,* Zalkind v. Ceradyne, Inc., 124 Cal.Rptr.3d 105, 113 (Ct. App. 2011); Indianapolis City Mkt. Corp. v. MAV, Inc., 915 N.E.2d 1013, 1023 (Ind. Ct. App. 2009); Michael v. Huffman Oil Co., Inc., 661 S.E.2d 1, 10 (N.C. Ct. App. 2008).

93. *See, e.g.,* Water Tower Realty Co. v. Fordham 25 E. Superior, L.L.C., 936 N.E.2d 1127, 1133 (Ill. App. 2010) *appeal denied*, 943 N.E.2d 1110 (Ill. 2011).

94. Smith v. West Suburban Med. Ctr., 922 N.E.2d 549, 553 (Ill. App. Ct. 2010).

95. Zeiger Crane Rentals, Inc. v. Double A Indus., Inc., 16 So.3d 907, 913 (Fla. Dist. Ct. App. 2009).

96. *E.g.,* regarding statutes making certain indemnity clauses that shift liability for a party's negligence void as against public policy: Alaska Stat. § 45.45.900 (West 2012); Cal. Civ. Code § 2782 (West 2012); Conn. Gen. Stat. Ann. § 52–572k (West 2012); Del. Code Ann. tit. 6, § 2704 (West 2012); Ga. Code Ann. § 13–8–2(b) (West 2011); Ind. Code Ann. § 26–2–5–1 (West 2012); Illinois Stat. Ch. 740 § 35/1 (West 2012); Neb. Rev. Stat. § 25–21,187(1) (West 2011); Ohio Rev.

Code Ann. § 2305.31 (West 2011); Or. Rev. Stat. Ann. § 30.140 (West 2012); R.I. Gen. Laws § 6–34–1 (West 2012).

97. *E.g.,* regarding strict construction of indemnity agreement: Downs v. Rosenthal Collins Group, LLC, 895 N.E.2d 1057, 1058 (Ill. App. 2008); England v. Alicea, 827 N.E.2d 555, 559 (Ind. Ct. App. 2005); George L. Brown Ins. v. Star Ins. Co., 237 P.3d 92, 97 (Nev. 2010); Sansone v. Morton Mach. Works, Inc., 957 A.2d 386, 393 (R.I. 2008); MEMC Elec. Materials, Inc. v. Albemarle Corp., 241 S.W.3d 67, 71 (Tex. App. 2007).

98. *See, e.g.,* DeWitt v. Western Pac. R. Co., 719 F.2d 1448, 1452 (9th Cir. 1983) (in California indemnity contract need not be strictly construed against indemnification if the indemnitee is not negligent); One Beacon Ins., LLC v. M & M Pizza, Inc., 8 A.3d 18, 21 (N.H. 2010) (court construes "express indemnity agreements" narrowly, particularly when they purport to shift responsibility of an entity's negligence to another); Ryan v. Gina Marie, L.L.C., 20 A.3d 442, 450 (N.J. Super. App. Div. 2011) (contract purporting to indemnify an indemnitee against its own fault or negligence must so state in "unequivocal" terms and should be "strictly construed against the indemnitee" if its meaning is ambiguous"); 2632 Realty Dev. Corp. v. 299 Main St., LLC, 941 N.Y.S.2d 252, 255 (App. Div. 2012) (in absence of a *legal duty to indemnify*, a contract for indemnification should be strictly construed to avoid imputing any duties which the parties did not intend to assume).

99. *E.g.,* regarding tendency of courts to disfavor agreements to indemnify the indemnitee against the indemnitee's own negligence: Otis Elevator Co. v. Midland Red Oak Realty, Inc., 483 F.3d 1095, 1101 (10th Cir. 2007) (applying Oklahoma law); Potlatch Corp. v. Missouri Pac. R. Co., 902 S.W.2d 217, 222 (Ark. 1995); Lafarge N. Am., Inc. v. K.E.C.I. Colorado, Inc., 250 P.3d 682 (Colo. Ct. App. 2010) *cert. denied*, 2011 WL 85780 (Colo. 2011); Zeiger Crane Rentals, Inc. v. Double A Indus., Inc., 16 So.3d 907, 914 (Fla. Dist. Ct. App. 2009); McGill v. Cochran–Sysco Foods, 818 So.2d 301, 306 (La. Ct. App. 2002) *writ denied*, 825 So.2d 1196 (La. 2002); One Beacon Ins., LLC v. M & M Pizza, Inc., 8 A.3d 18, 21 (N.H. 2010); Ryan v. Gina Marie, L.L.C., 20 A.3d 442, 450 (N.J. Super. App. Div. 2011); Cortes v. Town of Brookhaven, 910 N.Y.S.2d 171, 173 (N.Y. App. Div. 2010); Estate of King v. Wagoner County Bd. of County Com'rs, 146 P.3d 833, 844 (Okla. Civ. App. 2006); Union Pac. R. Co. v. Caballo Coal Co., 246 P.3d 867, 872 (Wyo. 2011).

100. *E.g.,* regarding requirement that the word "negligence" appear in the provision: Englert v. The Home Depot, 911 A.2d 72, 77 (N.J. Super. Ct. App. Div. 2006); Ivey Plants, Inc. v. FMC Corp., 282 So.2d 205, 209 (Fla. Dist. Ct. App. 1973).

101. *E.g.,* Cortes v. Town of Brookhaven, 910 N.Y.S.2d 171, 173 (N.Y. App. Div. 2010) (otherwise enforceable indemnity clause need not contain express language referring to negligence of indemnitee, but intention to indemnify must be clearly implied from language and purposes of entire agreement and surrounding facts and circumstances).

102. *See e.g.,* regarding enforcement of promise to indemnify a party for the party's own gross negligence: Zeiger Crane Rentals, Inc. v. Double A Indus., Inc., 16 So.3d 907, 914 (Fla. Dist. Ct. App. 2009); Valero Energy Corp. v. M.W. Kellogg Const. Co., 866 S.W.2d 252, 257 (Tex. App. 1993).

But see CSX Transp., Inc. v. Massachusetts Bay Transp. Auth., 697 F. Supp. 2d 213, 226 (D. Mass. 2010); Energy XXI, GoM, LLC v. New Tech Eng'g, L.P., 787 F. Supp. 2d 590, 611 (S.D. Tex. 2011) (more support under maritime law for position that indemnity clause that protects a party from liability for its own gross negligence is invalid than for appropriateness of such a clause).

103. *See, e.g.,* regarding public policy limitation on indemnity against a party's own willful, reckless, or intentional misconduct: Equitex, Inc. v. Ungar, 60 P.3d 746, 750 (Colo. Ct. App. 2002); Lincoln Logan Mut. Ins. Co. v. Fornshell, 722 N.E.2d 239, 242 (Ill. App. Ct. 1999); Lake Cable Partners v. Interstate Power Co., 563 N.W.2d 81, 87 (Minn. Ct. App. 1997); Purk v. Purk, 817 S.W.2d 915, 917 (Mo. Ct. App. 1991).

But see Remote Solution Co., Ltd. v. FGH Liquidating Corp, 568 F. Supp. 2d 534, 542–43 (D. Del. 2008) *aff'd sub nom.* Remote Solution Co., Ltd. v. FGH Liquidating Corp., 349 F. App'x 696 (3d Cir. 2009) (New York law does not permit indemnification for one's own intentional, reckless or grossly negligent conduct *absent express indemnification language*).

104. *See, e.g.,* Biondi v. Beekman Hill House Apartment Corp., 692 N.Y.S.2d 304, 308 (App. Div. 1999) *aff'd,* 731 N.E.2d 577 (N.Y. 2000).

105. Dow–Westbrook, Inc. v. Candlewood Equine Practice, LLC, 989 A.2d 1075, 1082 (Conn. App. Ct. 2010) quoting Laudano v. General Motors Corp., 388 A.2d 842 (1977).

106. *See e.g.,* Potlatch Corp. v. Missouri Pac. R. Co., 902 S.W.2d 217, 222 (Ark. 1995) (strict construction need not be applied in interpretation of indemnity agreement entered into by business entities "in the context of free and understanding negotiation").

107. *E.g.* regarding point at which cause of action for indemnity arises under an agreement for indemnity "against liability" (as soon as liability is established and becomes fixed) versus an agreement for indemnity against "loss" or "damages" (not until the loss is actually paid): Hausler v. Felton, 739 F. Supp. 2d 1327, 1331 (N.D. Okla. 2010); MT Builders, L.L.C. v. Fisher Roofing, Inc., 197 P.3d 758, 763 (Ariz. Ct. App. 2008); Amoco Oil Co. v. Liberty Auto & Elec. Co., 810 A.2d 259, 264 (Conn. 2002); Henthorne v. Legacy Healthcare, Inc., 764 N.E.2d 751, 757–58 (Ind. Ct. App. 2002); Pulte Home Corp. v. Parex, Inc., 942 A.2d 722, 730 (Md. 2008); Rouge Steel Co. v. Suli & Sons Cartage Inc., 2004 WL 1621191 at *2 (Mich. Ct. App. 2004) (unreported case).

108. Cal. Civ. Code § 2778 (West 2012) (rules of construction relating to indemnity): "In interpreting a contract for indemnity, the following rules are to be applied, unless a contrary intention appears: (1) Upon an indemnity against liability, expressly, or in other equivalent terms, the person indemnified is entitled to recover upon becoming liable; (2) Upon an indemnity against claims, or demands, or damages, or costs, expressly, or in other equivalent terms, the person indemnified is not entitled to recover without payment thereof."

109. *E.g.,* Riley Acquisitions, Inc. v. Drexler, 946 N.E.2d 957, 967 (Ill. App. 2011), *as modified on denial of reh'g* (Apr. 5, 2011) (Illinois law makes it clear that a party cannot recover attorney's fees absent a statute or a contractual agreement and principle applies even to indemnity clause); Montana Rail Link v. CUSA PRTS., LLC., 222 P.3d 1021, 1029–30 (Mont. 2009) (precedent establishes that attorney fees are not available in the absence of a specific contractual provision or statutory basis providing for attorney fees and indemnity provision did not specifically provide for them; therefore it did not provide a basis for an award); Kessler v. Gleich, 13 A.3d 109, 114–15 (N.H. 2010).

110. *See, e.g.,* regarding circumstances in which attorney's fees were recoverable under an indemnity clause even though the indemnity agreement did not so specify: Dent v. Beazer Materials & Services, 993 F.Supp. 923, 939 (D.S.C.1995) (lessor could recover "attorneys' fees, settlement costs, and all other allowable costs" pursuant to lease indemnity provision requiring lessee to "hold the lessor harmless for any claim made against the lessor arising out of the use of the leased premises"); DeWitt v. Western Pac. R. Co., 719 F.2d 1448, 1452–53 (9th Cir. 1983) (Cal.Civ.Code § 2778(3) states that unless contrary intention appears, indemnity against claims, or demands, or liability, expressly, or in other equivalent terms, embraces costs of defense incurred in good faith and in exercise of a reasonable discretion; costs, expenses and attorney's fees paid in defense the claim are included within amount that must be indemnified); English v. BGP Int'l, Inc., 174 S.W.3d 366, 370 (Tex. App. 2005) (if parties include an indemnity provision contract, duty to indemnify generally includes duty to pay for all costs and expenses associated with defending suits against the indemnitee).

111. Crawford v. Weather Shield Mfg. Inc., 187 P.3d 424, 430 (Cal. 2008).

112. *Id.*

113. *E.g., id.* at 131–32.

114. English v. BGP Int'l, Inc., 174 S.W.3d 366, 372 (Tex. App. 2005).

Endnotes for Chapter 9: Contract Components: Termination, Breach, and Remedies

1. *See* U.C.C. § 2–106(2) (2003 amendment) (sale of goods). According to the definition, a party who *terminates* a sales contract ends the contractual arrangement for a reason *other than breach*, discharging all obligations on both sides that are still executory; however, a right that arises from a breach or from a prior performance survives the termination. *Compare* U.C.C. § 2A–103(b) (2003 amendment) (lease of goods). According to the definition, a party who *terminates* lease puts an end to it for a reason other than breach, i.e., based on a right created in the contract or based on law.

2. *See* U.C.C. § 2–106(4) (sale of goods) (2003 amendment). According to the definition, a party who *cancels* a sales contract ends the contractual arrangement based on a *breach* by the other party, discharging all obligations on both sides that are still executory; however, a right that arises from a breach or from a prior performance survives the cancellation and cancelling party remedies for breach of the contract. *Compare* U.C.C. § 2A–103 (2003 amendment) (lease of goods) (according to definition, a party who *cancels* a lease ends leasing arrangement due to a breach by the other party); U.C.C. § 2A–505(2) (2003 amendment) (lease of goods). According to that definition, the cancellation will end obligations that are still executory on either side, but the parties retain any rights resulting from prior breach or performance.

3. Johnson Lakes Dev., Inc. v. Central Nebraska Pub. Power & Irrigation Dist., 568 N.W.2d 573, 582 (Neb. Ct. App. 1997) *aff'd sub nom,* Johnson Lakes Dev., Inc. v. Cent. Nebraska Pub. Power & Irrigation Dist., 576 N.W.2d 806 (Neb.1998).

4. *E.g.*, White v. Longley, 244 P.3d 753, 758 (Mont. 2010) (termination or cancellation entitles a party to look to the contract to determine what compensation the party is entitled to for the breach that gave the party the "right of abandonment").

5. *See, e.g.*, Mitchell v. Frederich, 431 So.2d 727, 728 (Fla. Dist. Ct. App. 1983) (right of salesman under an agreement giving him an exclusive right of sale survived termination of employment); Arbeeny v. Kennedy Executive Search, Inc., 893 N.Y.S.2d 39, 44 (App. Div. 2010) (right to commissions earned during period of employment survived termination).

6. *See* U.C.C. § 2–106(3) (2003 amendment).

7. *E.g.*, Shams v. Howard, 165 P.3d 876, 879 (Colo. App. 2007) (contractual arbitration right survived contract's end); Auchter Co. v. Zagloul, 949 So.2d 1189, 1194 (Fla. Dist. Ct. App. 2007) (obligation to arbitrate under construction agreement survived its end); Doctors Associates, Inc. v. Thomas, 898 So.2d 159, 162 (Fla. Dist. Ct. App. 2005) (obligation to arbitrate that arose from franchise agreement survived termination); Carpenter v. Pomerantz, 634 N.E.2d 587, 589 (Mass. Ct. App. 1994) (duty to arbitrate dispute under employment contract survived termination).

8. *E.g.*, Exprezit Convenience Stores, LLC v. Transaction Tracking Technologies, Inc., 2005 WL 2704891 at *5 (N.D. Fla. 2005).

9. Pierson v. Empire State Land Associates, LLC, 886 N.Y.S.2d 411, 412 (App. Div. 2009) (indemnification agreement omitted from "survival upon termination" provision of contract).

10. *E.g.*, Pierson v. Empire State Land Associates, LLC, 886 N.Y.S.2d 411, 412 (App. Div. 2009) (indemnification agreement omitted from "survival upon termination" provision of contract); *In re* Rio Grande Xarin II, Ltd., 2010 WL 2697145 at 5–6 (Tex. App. 2010), *review dismissed* (Oct. 1, 2010) (arbitration provision omitted from survival clause).

11. *See, e.g., In re* Rio Grande Xarin II, Ltd., 2010 WL 2697145 at 5–6 (Tex. App. 2010), *review dismissed* (Oct. 1, 2010) (arbitration provision omitted from survival clause nevertheless enforced); Pierson v. Empire State Land Associates, LLC, 886 N.Y.S.2d 411, 412 (App. Div. 2009) (indemnification agreement omitted from "survival upon termination" provision of contract).

12. *E.g.*, Johnson Lakes Dev., Inc. v. Central Nebraska Pub. Power & Irrigation Dist., 576 N.W.2d 806, 817 (Neb. 1998); Avatar Dev. Corp. v. De Pani Constr., Inc., 834 So.2d 873, 875 (Fla. Dist. Ct. App. 2002); Sugar Cane Growers Co-op. of Florida, Inc. v. Pinnock, 735 So.2d 530, 537 (Fla. Dist. Ct. App. 1999) (fact that a contract may under in certain definite circumstances be terminable at a party's option does not as a matter of law render contract unenforceable for lack of mutuality).

13. Johnson Lakes Dev., Inc. v. Central Nebraska Pub. Power & Irrigation Dist., 576 N.W.2d 806, 817 (Neb. 1998).

14. *See generally* Gulf Liquids New River Project, LLC v. Gulsby Eng'g, Inc., 356 S.W.3d 54 (Tex. App. 2011)), *reh'g overruled* (Nov. 10, 2011).

15. *See* Roof Sys., Inc. v. Johns Manville Corp., 130 S.W.3d 430, 442 (Tex. App. 2004).

16. *See* Gulf Liquids New River Project, LLC v. Gulsby Eng'g, Inc., 356 S.W.3d 54, 68 (Tex. App. 2011), *reh'g overruled* (Nov. 10, 2011)

17. *See* Greenwood Sch. Dist. v. Leonard, 285 S.W.3d 284, 288 (Ark. Ct. App. 2008).

18. *E.g.*, Fisherman Surgical Instruments, LLC v. Tri–Anim Health Services, Inc., 502 F. Supp. 2d 1170 (D. Kan. 2007); *see* Acceleration Nat'l Serv. Corp. v. Brickell Fin. Services Motor Club, Inc., 541 So.2d 738, 739 (Fla. Dist. Ct. App. 1989).

19. *See, e.g.*, Boat Dealers' Alliance, Inc. v. Outboard Marine Corp., 182 F.3d 619, 621 (8th Cir. 1999); Fisherman Surgical Instruments, LLC v. Tri–Anim Health Services, Inc., 502 F. Supp. 2d 1170, 1182 (D. Kan. 2007).

20. If parties agree to termination requirements, courts typically require compliance: *e.g.*, Dover Elevator Co. v. Rafael, 939 S.W.2d 474, 476 (Mo. Ct. App. 1996); Szatmari v. Rosenbaum, 490 N.Y.S.2d 97, 99 (N.Y. Justice Ct. 1985); O'Reilly v. NYNEX Corp., 693 N.Y.S.2d 13, 15 (App. Div. 1999); Fargo Foods, Inc. v. Bernabucci, 596 N.W.2d 38, 41 (N.D. 1999).

21. *E.g.*, Szatmari v. Rosenbaum, 490 N.Y.S.2d 97, 99 (N.Y. Justice Ct. 1985) (during period from notice of termination until date when termination becomes effective, contract remains in force and must continue to be performed).

22. Helmerich & Payne Int'l Drilling Co. v. BOPCO, L.P., 357 S.W.3d 801, 803 (Tex. App. 2011).

23. Check state law regarding elements of an action for breach: *e.g.*, Western Distrib. Co. v. Diodosio, 841 P.2d 1053, 1058 (Colo. 1992); Zirp–Burnham, LLC v. E. Terrell Associates, Inc., 826 N.E.2d 430, 439 (Ill. App. Ct. 2005); Shumate v. Lycan, 675 N.E.2d 749, 753 (Ind. Ct. App. 1997);

Thomas B. Olson & Associates, P.A. v. Leffert, Jay & Polglaze, P.A., 756 N.W.2d 907, 917–18 (Minn. Ct. App. 2008); Martha's Hands, LLC v. Rothman, 328 S.W.3d 474, 479 (Mo. Ct. App. 2010); Guinn v. Wilkerson, 963 So.2d 555, 558 (Miss. Ct. App. 2006); RD & J Properties v. Lauralea–Dilton Enterprises, LLC, 600 S.E.2d 492, 497 (N.C. Ct. App. 2004); JP Morgan Chase v. J.H. Elec. of New York, Inc., 893 N.Y.S.2d 237, 239 (App. Div. 2010); Awada v. Univ. of Cincinnati, 680 N.E.2d 258, 262 (Ohio Ct. Cl. 1997); Branche Builders, Inc. v. Coggins, 686 S.E.2d 200, 202 (S.C. Ct. App. 2009); Guthmiller v. Deloitte & Touche, LLP, 699 N.W.2d 493, 498 (S.D. 2005).

24. *E.g.*, GuestHouse Int'l, LLC v. Shoney's N. Am. Corp., 330 S.W.3d 166, 206 (Tenn. Ct. App. 2010), *appeal denied* (Sept. 23, 2010) Quigley v. Bennett, 227 S.W.3d 51, 56 (Tex. 2007).

25. Sharabianlou v. Karp, 105 Cal.Rptr.3d 300, 310 (Ct. App. 2010), *review denied* (May 12, 2010), *as modified on denial of reh'g* (Mar. 3, 2010).

26. In breach of contract cases, courts typically award compensatory damages: *e.g.*, Thompson Pac. Constr., Inc. v. City of Sunnyvale, 66 Cal.Rptr.3d 175, 188 (Ct. App. 2007); Curran v. Barefoot, 645 S.E.2d 187, 193 (N.C. Ct. App. 2007); Totaro, Duffy, Cannova & Co., LLC v. Lane, Middleton & Co., LLC, 921 A.2d 1100, 1107 (N.J. 2007); Aquaplex, Inc. v. Rancho La Valencia, Inc., 297 S.W.3d 768, 774 (Tex. 2009).

27. *E.g.*, GuestHouse Int'l, LLC v. Shoney's N. Am. Corp., 330 S.W.3d 166, 206 (Tenn. Ct. App. 2010), *appeal denied* (Sept. 23, 2010). Expectation or benefit-of-bargain damages is the standard measure for a breach and should not be a windfall, but should be a sum equivalent to expected benefit of performance. *E.g.*, Paul v. Deloitte & Touche, LLP, 974 A.2d 140, 146 (Del. 2009); Munro v. Beazer Home Corp., 2011 WL 2651910 at *8 (Del. Com. Pl. 2011) (unreported case); Columbia Park Golf Course, Inc. v. City of Kennewick, 248 P.3d 1067, 1078 (Wash. Ct. App. 2011), *reconsideration denied* (Apr. 11, 2011).

28. Sharabianlou v. Karp, 105 Cal.Rptr.3d 300, 310 (Ct. App. 2010), *review denied* (May 12, 2010), *as modified on denial of reh'g* (Mar. 3, 2010).

29. LaPoint v. AmerisourceBergen Corp., 2007 WL 2565709 (Del. Ch. 2007) *aff'd sub nom.*, AmerisourceBergen Corp. v. LaPoint, 956 A.2d 642 (Del. 2008) (unreported case). *E.g.*, regarding awards of expectation or benefit-of-bargain damages: Fecteau Benefits Group, Inc. v. Knox, 890 N.E.2d 138, 143 (Mass. Ct. App. 2008).

30. Aronovitz v. Fafard, 934 N.E.2d 851, 859 (Mass. Ct. App. 2010) *review denied*, 939 N.E.2d 785 (Mass. 2010).

31. Sterling Chemicals, Inc. v. Texaco Inc., 259 S.W.3d 793, 798 (Tex. App. 2007).

32. *E.g.*, Castigliano v. O'Connor, 911 So.2d 145, 148 (Fla. Dist. Ct. App. 2005).

33. *E.g.*, Sokoloff v. Harriman Estates Dev. Corp., 754 N.E.2d 184, 188 (N.Y. 2001).

34. *See, e.g.*, Sokoloff v. Harriman Estates Dev. Corp., 754 N.E.2d 184, 188 (N.Y. 2001).

35. Absent extraordinary circumstances, court will not order specific performance of personal service contract since doing so results in involuntary servitude or forces parties into hostile relationship with resulting social costs: *e.g.*, Mercado–Salinas v. Bart Enterprises Int'l, Ltd., 2012 WL 1097687 at *10 (D.P.R. 2012); In re Mitchell, 249 B.R. 55, 59 (Bankr. S.D.N.Y. 2000); Navab–Safavi v. Broadcasting Bd. of Governors, 650 F. Supp. 2d 40, 74 (D.D.C. 2009) *aff'd sub nom.* Navab–Safavi v. Glassman, 637 F.3d 311 (D.C. Cir. 2011); Bilut v. Northwestern Univ., 645 N.E.2d 536, 541–42 (Ill. App. 1994): J.H. Renarde, Inc. v. Sims, 711 A.2d 410, 413 (N.J. Super. Ch. Div. 1998); Metropolitan Sports Facilities Comm'n v. Minnesota Twins P'ship, 638 N.W.2d 214, 228 (Minn. Ct. App. 2002).

36. California case law, for example, sets out requisites for obtaining specific performance—*e.g.*, Blackburn v. Charnley, 11 Cal.Rptr.3d 885, 891 (Ct. App. 2004) (contract terms must be sufficiently definite; consideration must be adequate; must be substantial similarity of requested performance to contract terms; must be mutuality of remedies; and legal remedy must be inadequate). Check the applicable law.

37. Cal. Civ. Code § 3390 (West).

38. Medical Staffing Network, Inc. v. Connors, 722 S.E.2d 370, 375 (Ga. Ct. App. 2012). Rescission and restitution is alternative remedy to damages action and the plaintiff will at some point have to make an election: *e.g.*, Akin v. Certain Underwriters at Lloyd's London, 44 Cal.Rptr.3d 284, 287 (Ct. App. 2006); Shotkoski v. Denver Inv. Group Inc., 134 P.3d 513, 515 (Colo. App. 2006); Wallenta v. Moscowitz, 839 A.2d 641, 660 (Conn. Ct. App.2004).

39. Wallenta v. Moscowitz, 839 A.2d 641, 660 (Conn. Ct. App.2004); Collins v. McKinney, 871 N.E.2d 363, 370 (Ind. Ct. App. 2007) (rescission of a contract is the annulling, abrogating, or unmaking of a contract).

40. State v. Jones, 271 P.3d 1277, 1281 (Kan. Ct. App. 2012). Rescission requires either substantial and fundamental breach defeating purpose of contracting OR mutual and dependent promises so that failure of one party authorizes other to rescind: Vidalia Outdoor Products, Inc. v. Higgins, 701 S.E.2d 217, 219 (Ga. App. 2010); Borah v. McCandless, 205 P.3d 1209, 1215 (Idaho 2009); Browning–Ferris Indus., Inc. v. Casella Waste Mgmt. of Massachusetts, Inc., 945 N.E.2d 964, 975 (Mass. Ct. App. 2011); Asamoah–Boadu v. State, 328 S.W.3d 790, 793–94 (Mo. Ct. App. 2010), *reh'g and/or transfer denied* (Mar. 1, 2011); Turbines Ltd. v. Transupport, Inc., 808 N.W.2d 643, 652–53 (Neb. App. 2012); Brazell v. Windsor, 682 S.E.2d 824, 826–27 (S.C. 2009).

41. CC Disposal, Inc. v. Veolia ES Valley View Landfill, Inc., 952 N.E.2d 14, 20 (Ill. App. Ct. 2010), *reh'g denied* (Jan. 24, 2011), *appeal denied*, 949 N.E.2d 1096 (Ill. 2011).

42. For plaintiff to get restitution, defendant must have received some benefit. *E.g.*, Sharabianlou v. Karp, 105 Cal.Rptr.3d 300, 310 (Ct. App. 2010), *review denied* (May 12, 2010), *as modified on denial of reh'g* (Mar. 3, 2010); Wallenta v. Moscowitz, 839 A.2d 641, 660 (Conn. Ct. App. 2004); Medical Staffing Network, Inc. v. Connors, 722 S.E.2d 370, 375 (Ga. Ct. App. 2012).

43. *See* Wallenta v. Moscowitz, 839 A.2d 641, 661 (Conn. App. Ct. 2004), *cert. denied*, 845 A.2d 414 (Conn. 2004).

44. Wallenta v. Moscowitz, 839 A.2d 641, 660 (Conn. App. Ct. 2004); *see* GuestHouse Int'l, LLC v. Shoney's N. Am. Corp., 330 S.W.3d 166, 207 (Tenn. Ct. App. 2010), *appeal denied* (Sept. 23, 2010).

45. *E.g.,* Fecteau Benefits Group, Inc. v. Knox, 890 N.E.2d 138, 143 (Mass. App. Ct. 2008) (restitution damages is an amount corresponding to any benefit conferred by plaintiff on defendant in performance of breached contract).

46. GuestHouse Int'l, LLC v. Shoney's N. Am. Corp., 330 S.W.3d 166, 207 (Tenn. Ct. App. 2010), *appeal denied* (Sept. 23, 2010).

47. C & J Vantage Leasing Co. v. Wolfe, 795 N.W.2d 65, 77 (Iowa 2011), *reh'g denied* (Mar. 30, 2011).

48. *E.g.*, Zuver v. Airtouch Communications, Inc., 103 P.3d 753, 766–67 (Wash. 2004).

49. "Mutuality of obligation" does not require "mutuality of remedies" in the sense that both parties must have the same remedies for breach. *E.g.*, Ex parte McNaughton, 728 So.2d 592, 598 (Ala. 1998); Grubb & Ellis Co. v. Bello, 23 Cal.Rptr.2d 281, 285 (Ct. App. 1993); DeBauge Bros., Inc. v. Whitsitt, 512 P.2d 487, 490 (1973); Walther v. Sovereign Bank, 872 A.2d 735, 748 (Md. 2005); Blue Paper, Inc. v. Provost, 914 So.2d 1048, 1052 (Fla. Dist. Ct. App. 2005).

50. *See* Mining Inv. Group, LLC v. Roberts, 177 P.3d 1207, 1211 (Ariz. Ct. App. 2008).

51. *See, e.g.,* Savin Gasoline Properties, LLC v. CCO, LLC, 2011 WL 726110 at *8–9 (Conn. Super. Ct. 2011) (unreported case).

52. If the contract sets out prerequisites to cancellation, the parties must comply: *e.g.*, Dunkin' Donuts Franchised Restaurants LLC v. Sandip, Inc., 712 F. Supp. 2d 1325, 1329 (N.D. Ga. 2010); New Image Constr., Inc. v. TDR Enterprises Inc., 905 N.Y.S.2d 56, 58 (App. Div. 2010).

53. "Liquidated damages clause" is defined as a provision permitting parties to agree at outset of contract on the amount of damages in order to avoid extensive litigation over amount if breach occurs: Hot Developers, Inc. v. Willow Lake Estates, Inc., 950 So.2d 537, 542 (Fla. Dist. Ct. App. 2007); Antonios v. Gwinnett Clinic, Ltd., 668 S.E.2d 531, 533 (Ga. Ct. App. 2008); Barrie Sch. v. Patch, 933 A.2d 382, 388 (Md. 2007); Woodkrest Custom Homes Inc. v. Cooper, 24 So.3d 340, 346 (Miss. Ct. App. 2009); Shin–Con Dev. Corp. v. I.P. Investments, Ltd., 270 S.W.3d 759, 767 (Tex. App. 2008).

54. *E.g.*, Hot Developers, Inc. v. Willow Lake Estates, Inc., 950 So.2d 537, 542 (Fla. Dist. Ct. App. 2007); Carrothers Constr. Co., LLC v. City of S. Hutchinson, 207 P.3d 231, 241 (Kan. 2009).

55. St. Clair Med., P.C. v. Borgiel, 715 N.W.2d 914, 921 (Mich. Ct. App. 2006).

56. *See* RESTATEMENT (SECOND) OF CONTRACTS § 356 (1981). According to a Maryland decision, a liquidated damages clause may be unreasonable if either (a) the total amount of damages is sufficiently disproportionate to damages that can be proved as to require inference that agreement resulted from fraud, oppression or mistake or (b) contract uses *in terrorem* agreement to obtain performance instead of fair compensation. Willard Packaging Co., Inc. v. Javier, 899 A.2d 940, 948 (Md. Ct. Spec. App. 2006).

57. *See* RESTATEMENT (SECOND) OF CONTRACTS § 356 (1981). *E.g.*, Lake Ridge Acad. v. Carney, 613 N.E.2d 183, 187 (Ohio 1993).

58. Whether provision is liquidated damages or unenforceable penalty is question of law for court: Antonios v. Gwinnett Clinic, Ltd., 668 S.E.2d 531, 532 (Ga. Ct. App. 2008); Berggren v. Hill, 928 N.E.2d 1225, 1229 (Ill. App. Ct. 2010); Willard Packaging Co., Inc. v. Javier, 899 A.2d 940,

946 (Md. Ct. Spec. App. 2006); St. Clair Med., P.C. v. Borgiel, 715 N.W.2d 914, 921 (Mich. Ct. App. 2006); Lake Ridge Acad. v. Carney, 613 N.E.2d 183, 187 (Ohio 1993) ("virtually the unanimous rule of all jurisdictions"); TXU Portfolio Mgmt. Co., L.P. v. FPL Energy, LLC, 328 S.W.3d 580 (Tex. App. 2010), *reh'g overruled* (Jan. 14, 2011).

59.   Carrothers Constr. Co., LLC v. City of S. Hutchinson, 207 P.3d 231, 236 (Kan. 2009).

60.   Berggren v. Hill, 928 N.E.2d 1225, 1229 (Ill. App. Ct. 2010). If the contract provides for liquidated damages, why is proof of actual damages precluded? *See* Ecology Services, Inc. v. GranTurk Equip., Inc., 443 F. Supp. 2d 756, 774 (D. Md. 2006).

61.   Berggren v. Hill, 928 N.E.2d 1225, 1231 (Ill. App. Ct. 2010).

Endnotes for Chapter 10: Contract Components: Winding-Up, Non-Compete, Severance ...

1.   Examples of such statutes include: ALA. CODE § 8–1–1 (West 2012); ALASKA STAT. § 45.50.562 (West 2012); CAL. BUS. & PROF. CODE § 16600 (West 2012); CONN. GEN. STAT. ANN. § 35–28 (West 2012); FLA. STAT. ANN. § 542.18 (West 2012); GA. CODE ANN. § 13–8–2 (West 2011); MD. CODE ANN., COM. LAW § 11–204 (West 2012); MASS. GEN. LAWS ANN. ch. 93, § 4 (West 2012); MINN. STAT. ANN. § 325D.51 (West 2012); MO. ANN. STAT. § 416.031 (West 2012); NEB. REV. STAT. § 59–801 (West 2011); N.H. REV. STAT. ANN. § 356:2 (West 2012); N.M. STAT. ANN. § 57–1–1 (West 2012); N.C. GEN. STAT. ANN. § 75–1 (West 2012); OKLA. STAT. ANN. tit. 15, § 217 (West 2012); TEX. BUS. & COM. CODE ANN. § 15.05 (West 2011).

2.   *E.g.,* regarding factors that determine whether covenant is reasonable and not in violation of public interest: Premix, Inc. v. Zappitelli, 561 F.Supp. 269, 274–75 (N.D. Ohio 1983); Hilb, Rogal & Hamilton Co. of Arizona v. McKinney, 946 P.2d 464, 467 (Ariz. Ct. App. 1997); Intermountain Eye & Laser Centers, P.L.L.C. v. Miller, 127 P.3d 121, 131 (Idaho 2005); Gleeson v. Preferred Sourcing, LLC, 883 N.E.2d 164, 172 (Ind. Ct. App. 2008); Robert W. Clark, M.D., Inc. v. Mt. Carmel Health, 706 N.E.2d 336, 340 (Ohio Ct. App. 1997); CBM Geosolutions, Inc. v. Gas Sensing Tech. Corp., 215 P.3d 1054, 1059 (Wyo. 2009).

3.   *E.g.,* regarding fact that to be enforceable, a restrictive covenant must be ancillary to a lawful contract, supported by adequate consideration, and consistent with public policy: Freiburger v. J–U–B Engineers, Inc., 111 P.3d 100, 104 (Idaho 2005); McCart v. H & R Block, Inc., 470 N.E.2d 756, 763 (Ind. Ct. App. 1984); Varney Bus. Services, Inc. v. Pottroff, 59 P.3d 1003, 1014–15 (Kan. 2002); Reddy v. Community Health Found. of Man, 298 S.E.2d 906, 910 (W.Va. 1982).

4.   *E.g.,* regarding necessity of a legitimate business interest generally: Del Monte Fresh Produce, N.A., Inc. v. Chiquita Brands Int'l Inc., 616 F. Supp. 2d 805, 817 (N.D. Ill. 2009); Medtronic, Inc. v. Hughes, 2011 WL 134973 at *5 (Minn. Ct. App. 2011) (unpublished decision); Wrigg v. Junkermier, Clark, Campanella, Stevens, P.C., 265 P.3d 646, 650 (Mont. 2011); 1 Model Mgmt., LLC v. Kavoussi, 918 N.Y.S.2d 431, 432 (N.Y. App. Div. 2011).

Montana courts have stated that an employer lacks a legitimate business interest in a covenant if the employer chooses to end the employment relationship. Wrigg v. Junkermier, Clark, Campanella, Stevens, P.C., 265 P.3d 646, 65 (Mont. 2011).

5.   *E.g.,* regarding legitimate business interest in protecting customer relationships and goodwill: Environmental Services, Inc. v. Carter, 9 So.3d 1258, 1265 (Fla. Dist. Ct. App. 2009); Intermountain Eye & Laser Centers, P.L.L.C. v. Miller, 127 P.3d 121, 128 (Idaho 2005); Lifetec, Inc. v. Edwards, 880 N.E.2d 188, 196 (Ill. App. Ct. 2007); Medtronic, Inc. v. Advanced Bionics Corp., 630 N.W.2d 438, 456 (Minn. Ct. App. 2001); Sisters of Charity Health Sys., Inc. v. Farrago, 21 A.3d 110, 114 (Me. 2011); ACAS Acquisitions (Precitech) Inc. v. Hobert, 923 A.2d 1076, 1084–85 (N.H. 2007); Century Bus. Servs., Inc. v. Urban, 900 N.E.2d 1048, 1058 (Ohio Ct. App. 2008); Peterson v. Jackson, 253 P.3d 1096, 1107 (Utah Ct. App. 2011),

6.   *E.g.,* regarding legitimate business interest in protecting against disclosure of proprietary or other confidential business information: Roberson v. C.P. Allen Const. Co., Inc., 50 So.3d 471, 475 (Ala. Civ. App. 2010); Intermountain Eye & Laser Centers, P.L.L.C. v. Miller, 127 P.3d 121, 128 (Idaho 2005); Lifetec, Inc. v. Edwards, 880 N.E.2d 188, 196 (Ill. App. Ct. 2007); Medtronic, Inc. v. Advanced Bionics Corp., 630 N.W.2d 438, 456 (Minn. Ct. App. 2001); ACAS Acquisitions (Precitech) Inc. v. Hobert, 923 A.2d 1076, 1084–85 (N.H. 2007); Shepherd v. Pittsburgh Glass Works, LLC, 25 A.3d 1233, 1244 (Pa. Super. Ct. 2011).

7.   *E.g.,* regarding legitimacy of business interest in preventing competition: Sysco Food Services of E. Wis., LLC v. Ziccarelli, 445 F. Supp. 2d 1039, 1043–44 (E.D. Wis. 2006) ("prima facie suspect"); Roberson v. C.P. Allen Const. Co., Inc., 50 So.3d 471, 475 (Ala. Civ. App. 2010); Freiburger v. J–U–B Engineers, Inc., 111 P.3d 100, 105 (Idaho 2005); Century Bus. Servs., Inc. v.

Urban, 900 N.E.2d 1048, 1058 (Ohio App. 2008); Washburn v. Yadkin Valley Bank & Trust Co., 660 S.E.2d 577, 583 (N.C. Ct. App. 2008).

8. *E.g.*, regarding legitimate business interest in preventing party from luring away employees: U3S Corp. of Am. v. Parker, 414 S.E.2d 513, 517 (Ga. Ct. App. 1991).

9. *E.g.*, Freiburger v. J–U–B Engineers, Inc., 111 P.3d 100, 105 (Idaho 2005).

10. Regarding strict construction against employer of restriction on competition between former employee and employer: *E.g.*, Sysco Food Services of E. Wis., LLC v. Ziccarelli, 445 F. Supp. 2d 1039, 1043–44 (E.D. Wis. 2006) ("prima facie suspect); Global Link Logistics, Inc. v. Briles, 674 S.E.2d 52, 54 (2009) quoting Orkin Exterminating Co. v. Walker, 307 S.E.2d 914 (1983); Intermountain Eye & Laser Centers, P.L.L.C. v. Miller, 127 P.3d 121, 127 (Idaho 2005); Gleeson v. Preferred Sourcing, LLC, 883 N.E.2d 164, 172 (Ind. Ct. App. 2008); Green Clinic, LLC v. Finley, 30 So.3d 1094, 1097 (La. Ct. App. 2010); Softchoice, Inc. v. Schmidt, 763 N.W.2d 660, 666 (Minn. Ct. App. 2009); Healthcare Services of the Ozarks, Inc. v. Copeland, 198 S.W.3d 604, 613 (Mo. 2006); Washburn v. Yadkin Valley Bank & Trust Co., 190 N.C.App. 315, 323, 660 S.E.2d 577, 583 (N.C. Ct. App. 2008); Cranston Print Works Co. v. Pothier, 848 A.2d 213, 219 (R.I. 2004); Murfreesboro Med. Clinic, P.A. v. Udom, 166 S.W.3d 674, 678 (Tenn. 2005); Preston v. Marathon Oil Co., 277 P.3d 81 (Wyo. 2012).

11. In re Mktg. Investors Corp., 80 S.W.3d 44, 47–48 (Tex. App. 1998).

12. *E.g.*, Hilb, Rogal & Hamilton Co. of Arizona v. McKinney, 946 P.2d 464, 467 (Ariz. Ct. App. 1997) (an anti-piracy agreement is an agreement not to solicit an employer's former customers or reveal confidential information; a court might apply less restrictive standards to an anti-piracy agreement); In re Mktg. Investors Corp., 80 S.W.3d 44, 47 (Tex. App. 1998) (non-disclosure agreement does not violate public policy).

13. Central Indiana Podiatry, P.C. v. Krueger, 882 N.E.2d 723, 729 (Ind. 2008).

14. Bybee v. Isaac, 178 P.3d 616, 624 (Idaho 2008).

15. *E.g.*, ILCS S Ct Rules of Prof. Conduct, RPC Rule 5.6. Regarding regarding unenforceability of covenant not to compete that applies to attorneys: *e.g.*, 211 So.2d 805, 811–12 (Ala. 1968); Stevens v. Rooks Pitts & Poust, 682 N.E.2d 1125, 1131 (Ill. App. Ct. 1997); Murfreesboro Med. Clinic, P.A. v. Udom, 166 S.W.3d 674, 682 (Tenn. 2005).

16. Statutes may restrict availability of non-compete covenant in agreement between or involving physicians: *e.g.*, Colo. Rev. Stat. Ann. § 8–2–113 (West 2012); Del. Code Ann. tit. 6, § 2707 (West 2012); Mass. Gen. Laws Ann. ch. 112, § 12X (West 2012).

Some courts may hold such covenants to be unenforceable: *e.g.*, Bosley Med. Group v. Abramson, 207 Cal.Rptr. 477, 482 (Ct. App. 1984); Spectrum Emergency Care, Inc. v. St. Joseph's Hosp. & Health Ctr., 479 N.W.2d 848, 852 (N.D. 1992); Murfreesboro Med. Clinic, P.A. v. Udom, 166 S.W.3d 674, 683 (Tenn. 2005).

Some cases do not hold such covenants to be unenforceable, but may on public policy grounds more strictly scrutinize them: *e.g.*, Valley Med. Specialists v. Farber, 982 P.2d 1277, 1285 (Ariz. 1999); Karlin v. Weinberg, 390 A.2d 1161, 1169–70 (N.J. 1978). Robert W. Clark, M.D., Inc. v. Mt. Carmel Health, 706 N.E.2d 336, 340 (Ohio Ct. App. 1997)

17. *E.g.*, Freiburger v. J–U–B Engineers, Inc., 111 P.3d 100, 105 (Idaho 2005) (covenants not to compete that preclude employees from working in the same business as employers' for certain periods of time are strictly construed against employers; however, anti-piracy agreements that restrict terminated employee from soliciting customers of former employer or making use of confidential information from previous employment held to less stringent test of reasonableness than blanket prohibitions of competition since not nearly as oppressive and unreasonable).

18. Freiburger v. J–U–B Engineers, Inc.,111 P.3d 100, 105 (Idaho 2005).

19. *E.g.*, stating that covenant upheld only to extent not broader than necessary to protect interest: Freiburger v. J–U–B Engineers, Inc., 111 P.3d 100, 105 (Idaho 2005) (covenant not to compete); Team IA, Inc. v. Lucas, 717 S.E.2d 103, 107 (S.C. Ct. App. 2011) (covenant not to compete).

20. Discussion of provision limiting duration: *e.g.*, Compass Bank v. Hartley, 430 F. Supp. 2d 973, 979–80 (D. Ariz. 2006); Smallbizpros, Inc. v. Court, 414 F. Supp. 2d 1245, 1249 (M.D. Ga. 2006) (Georgia and Michigan law); Gleeson v. Preferred Sourcing, LLC, 883 N.E.2d 164, 174 (Ind. Ct. App. 2008); Sutton v. Iowa Trenchless, L.C., 808 N.W.2d 744, 750–51 (Iowa Ct. App. 2011); Medtronic, Inc. v. Hughes, 2011 WL 134973 (Minn. Ct. App. 2011); Techworks, LLC v. Wille, 770 N.W.2d 727, 734–35 (Wis. Ct. App. 2009).

Regarding nondisclosure clause: U3S Corp. of Am. v. Parker, 414 S.E.2d 513, 517 (Ga. Ct. App. 1991) (nondisclosure clause with no time limit was unenforceable).

21.   *E.g.*, discussion of provision limiting geographic scope: Thiesing v. Dentsply Int'l, Inc., 748 F. Supp. 2d 932, 950 (E.D. Wis. 2010) (Wisconsin law); Del Monte Fresh Produce, N.A., Inc. v. Chiquita Brands Int'l Inc., 616 F. Supp. 2d 805, 817 (N.D. Ill. 2009) (Illinois law); Compass Bank v. Hartley, 430 F. Supp.2d 973, 980 (D. Ariz. 2006) (Arizona law); Smallbizpros, Inc. v. Court, 414 F. Supp. 2d 1245, 1249 (M.D. Ga. 2006) (Georgia and Michigan law); Environmental Services, Inc. v. Carter, 9 So.3d 1258, 1264 (Fla. Dist. Ct. App. 2009); Central Indiana Podiatry, P.C. v. Krueger, 882 N.E.2d 723, 730 (Ind. 2008); Sutton v. Iowa Trenchless, L.C., 808 N.W.2d 744, 751 (Iowa Ct. App. 2011); Action Revenue Recovery, L.L.C. v. eBusiness Group, L.L.C., 17 So.3d 999, 1003 (La. Ct. App. 2009); Team IA, Inc. v. Lucas, 717 S.E.2d 103, 107 (S.C. Ct. App. 2011); Techworks, LLC v. Wille, 770 N.W.2d 727, 735 (Wis. Ct. App. 2009).

22.   *E.g.*, Regarding persons to whom access is restricted: Sysco Food Services of E. Wis., LLC v. Ziccarelli, 445 F. Supp. 2d 1039, 1048–49 (E.D. Wis. 2006); Techworks, LLC v. Wille, 770 N.W.2d 727, 735 (Wis. Ct. App. 2009); Lockhart v. McCurley, 2010 WL 966029 at *3 (Tex. App. 2010).

23.   *E.g.,* regarding limits on nature of business activities in which party is prevented from engaging: Smallbizpros, Inc. v. Court, 414 F. Supp. 2d 1245, 1249–50 (M.D. Ga. 2006) (Georgia and Michigan law); Sysco Food Services of E. Wis., LLC v. Ziccarelli, 445 F. Supp. 2d 1039, 1054 (E.D. Wis. 2006); American Control Sys., Inc. v. Boyce, 694 S.E.2d 141, 146 (Ga. Ct. App. 2010); Akhter v. Shah, 456 N.E.2d 232, 235–36 (Ill. App. Ct. 1983); Gleeson v. Preferred Sourcing, LLC, 883 N.E.2d 164, 175 (Ind. Ct. App. 2008); Scanline Med., L.L.C. v. Brooks, 259 P.3d 911, 914 (Okla. Civ. App. 2011); Lockhart v. McCurley, 2010 WL 966029 at *3 (Tex. App. 2010); Home Paramount Pest Control Companies, Inc. v. Shaffer, 718 S.E.2d 762, 765 (Va. 2011).

24.   Some courts allow application of "blue pencil" to covenants (to extent of excising offending language): *e,g.,* Palmer & Cay, Inc. v. Marsh & McLennan Companies, Inc., 404 F.3d 1297, 1303 (11th Cir. 2005) (covenant ancillary to sale of a business); Deutsche Post Global Mail, Ltd. v. Conrad, 292 F. Supp. 2d 748, 754 (D. Md. 2003) *aff'd on other grounds*, 116 F. App'x 435 (4th Cir. 2004); Thiesing v. Dentsply Int'l, Inc., 748 F. Supp. 2d 932, 947 (E.D. Wis. 2010) (discussing Minnesota law); Sunny Isle Shopping Ctr., Inc. v. Xtra Super Food Centers, Inc., 237 F. Supp. 2d 606, 614 (D.V.I. 2002); Gleeson v. Preferred Sourcing, LLC, 883 N.E.2d 164, 177 (Ind. Ct. App. 2008); Kegel v. Tillotson, 297 S.W.3d 908, 913 (Ky. Ct. App. 2009); WellSpan Health v. Bayliss, 869 A.2d 990, 996 (Pa. Super. Ct. 2005).

25.   Many courts that allow "blue penciling" do not permit use of "blue penciling" to *add* terms (only to excise them); if adding a term would be required to make a covenant reasonable, the court will not enforce the covenant: *E.g.,* Technology Partners, Inc. v. Hart, 298 F. App'x 238, 243 (4th Cir. 2008) (North Carolina law); Zimmer, Inc. v. Sharpe, 651 F. Supp. 2d 840, 843 (N.D. Ind. 2009) (applying Indiana law); Deutsche Post Global Mail, Ltd. v. Conrad, 292 F. Supp. 2d 748, 754 (D. Md. 2003) *aff'd on other grounds*, 116 F. App'x 435 (4th Cir. 2004) (Maryland law); (Varsity Gold, Inc. v. Porzio, 45 P.3d 352, 355 (Ariz. Ct. App. 2002)); Freiburger v. J–U–B Engineers, Inc., 111 P.3d 100, 107–08 (Idaho 2005); Kegel v. Tillotson, 297 S.W.3d 908, 913 (Ky. Ct. App. 2009).

26.   *See, e.g.*, Palmer & Cay, Inc. v. Marsh & McLennan Companies, Inc., 404 F.3d 1297, 1303 (11th Cir. 2005).

27.   *See, e.g.,* Smallbizpros, Inc. v. Court, 414 F. Supp. 2d 1245, 1249 (M.D. Ga. 2006).

28.   *See* Central Adjustment Bureau, Inc. v. Ingram, 678 S.W.2d 28, 39 (Tenn. 1984).

29.   *E.g.*, FLA. STAT. ANN. § 542.335(c) (West 2012); Tex. Bus. & Com. Code Ann. § 15.51(c) (West 2011).

30.   Regarding prohibition of "blue penciling" by court: JT Packard & Associates, Inc. v. Smith, 429 F. Supp. 2d 1052, 1054 (W.D. Wis. 2005) (Wisconsin law); Poynter Invs., Inc. v. Century Builders of Piedmont, Inc., 694 S.E.2d 15, 18 (S.C. 2010).

31.   *E.g.*, regarding the mere fact that a promise fails for illegality or other cause does not necessarily result in unenforceability of the entire contract if the contract is otherwise based on sufficient legal consideration but also contains multiple promises that are divisible. Jackson v. Cintas Corp., 425 F.3d 1313, 1317 (11th Cir. 2005); Asbury Auto. Used Car Ctr. v. Brosh, 314 S.W.3d 275, 278 (Ark. 2009); Circle Appliance Leasing, Inc. v. Appliance Warehouse, Inc., 425 S.E.2d 339, 340 (Ga. Ct. App. 1992) quoting Roberts v. H.C. Whitmer Co., 169 S.E. 385 (1933); Alterra Healthcare Corp. v. Bryant, 937 So.2d 263, 270 (Fla. Dist. Ct. App. 2006); In re Poly–Am., L.P., 262 S.W.3d 337, 360 (Tex. 2008).

32.   *E.g.,* regarding invalid provisions that are central to agreement, preventing severance: Nino v. Jewelry Exch., Inc., 609 F.3d 191, 206 (3d Cir. 2010) ("If the unconscionable aspects of the clause do not comprise an essential aspect of the arbitration agreement as a whole, then the unconscionable provisions may be severed and the remainder of the arbitration agreement enforced.").

33. *E.g.,* regarding severance of a provision *tainted* with an invalidating defect: Pokorny v. Quixtar, Inc., 601 F.3d 987, 1005 (9th Cir. 2010); In re OCA, Inc., 552 F.3d 413, 423–24 (5th Cir. 2008).

34. *E.g.,* regarding contract *permeated* by the invalidating defect: Gadson v. SuperShuttle Int'l, 2011 WL 1231311 at 9 (D. Md. 2011); Superior Vending, Inc. v. Dick's Bar of Hudson, Inc., 2010 WL 4386663 at 10 (W.D. Wis. 2010); Trivedi v. Curexo Tech. Corp., 116 Cal.Rptr.3d 804, 812 (Ct. App. 2010).

35. Lhotka v. Geographic Expeditions, Inc., 104 Cal.Rptr.3d 844, 853 (Ct. App. 2010), *review denied* (Apr. 14, 2010), *cert. denied*, 131 S.Ct. 288 (U.S. 2010) (If court finds as a matter of law that the contract or a clause was unconscionable at the time it was made, court may refuse to enforce the contract, may enforce the remainder of the contract without the unconscionable clause, or may limit the application of any unconscionable clause to avoid any unconscionable result; trial court has discretion not to enforce it if the agreement is "permeated" by unconscionability).

36. *E.g.,* Nino v. Jewelry Exch., Inc., 609 F.3d 191, 206 (3d Cir. 2010); Superior Vending, Inc. v. Dick's Bar of Hudson, Inc., 2010 WL 4386663, at 10 (W.D. Wis. 2010).

37. *E.g.,* some courts emphasize importance of severability clause in decision to sever: Santiago–Sepulveda v. Esso Standard Oil Co. (Puerto Rico), Inc., 643 F.3d 1, 8 (1st Cir. 2011) (applying Puerto Rican law); Grove v. Sugar Hill Inv. Associates, Inc., 466 S.E.2d 901, 906 (Ga. Ct. App. 1995); Toledo Police Patrolmen's Ass'n, Local 10, IUPA v. Toledo, 641 N.E.2d 799, 804 (Ohio Ct. App. 1994); City of Brownsville v. Golden Spread Elec. Coop., Inc., 192 S.W.3d 876, 880 (Tex. App. 2006).

38. City of Brownsville v. Golden Spread Elec. Coop., Inc., 192 S.W.3d 876, 881 (Tex. App. 2006) ("Such severability provisions may serve to preserve contracts so long as the invalidated portions of the contract do not constitute the main or essential purpose of the agreement.").

39. *E.g.,* courts discussing merger as extinguishing prior and contemporaneous negotiations, understandings, and verbal agreements, absent fraud or mistake: Rainey v. Travis, 850 S.W.2d 839, 841 (Ark. 1993); J & B Steel Contractors, Inc. v. C. Iber & Sons, Inc., 617 N.E.2d 405, 409 (Ill. App. Ct. 1993) *aff'd*, 642 N.E.2d 1215 (Ill. 1994); New Life Cleaners v. Tuttle, 292 S.W.3d 318, 322 (Ky. Ct. App. 2009); Evenson v. Quantum Indus., Inc., 687 N.W.2d 241, 244 (N.D. 2004); First Nat'l Bank in Durant v. Honey Creek Entm't Corp., 54 P.3d 100, 103 (Okla. 2002). Abercrombie v. Hayden Corp., 883 P.2d 845, 850 (Or. 1994). Flower v. T.R.A. Indus., Inc. 111 P.3d 1192, 1200 (Wash. Ct. App. 2005).

40. *E.g.,* regarding application of the parol evidence rule to bar evidence of prior negotiations or agreements to vary or contradict terms of an integrated agreement adopted by the parties: Lower Kuskokwim Sch. Dist. v. Alaska Diversified Contractors, Inc., 734 P.2d 62, 63 (Alaska 1987); Casa Herrera, Inc. v. Beydoun, 83 P.3d 497, 501–02 (Cal. 2004); Jenkins v. Eckerd Corp., 913 So.2d 43, 53 (Fla. Dist. Ct. App. 2005); J & B Steel Contractors, Inc. v. C. Iber & Sons, Inc., 617 N.E.2d 405, 409 (Ill. App. Ct. 1993) *aff'd*, 642 N.E.2d 1215 (Ill. 1994); Williams v. Spitzer Autoworld Canton, LLC, 913 N.E.2d 410, 416 (Ohio 2009); Gish v. ECI Services of Oklahoma, Inc., 162 P.3d 223, 231 (Okla. Civ. App. 2006); Town Bank v. City Real Estate Dev., LLC, 793 N.W.2d 476, 484 (Wis. 2010).

41. Jenkins v. Eckerd Corp., 913 So.2d 43, 53 (Fla. Dist. Ct. App. 2005); *see* Flower v. T.R.A. Indus., Inc., 111 P.3d 1192, 1200 (Wash. Ct. App. 2005) ("The rule forbids the use of parol evidence to add to, subtract from, modify, or contradict the terms of a fully integrated contract.").

42. *See, e.g.*, Abercrombie v. Hayden Corp., 883 P.2d 845, 850 (Or. 1994); Morgan Buildings & Spas, Inc. v. Humane Soc'y of SE Texas, 249 S.W.3d 480, 488 (Tex. App. 2008); Olsen Media v. Energy Sciences, Inc., 648 P.2d 493, 497 (Wash. Ct. App. 1982).

43. *E.g.,* regarding admission of parol evidence to assist court in construing the contract and determining intent or elucidating the meaning of a term: Casey v. Semco Energy, Inc., 92 P.3d 379, 383 (Alaska 2004); Anderson v. Preferred Stock Food Markets, Inc., 854 P.2d 1194, 1199 (Ariz. Ct. App. 1993); Weber v. Pascarella Mason St., LLC, 930 A.2d 779, 787 (Conn. App. Ct. 2007); Wheelhouse Marina Real Estate, LLC v. Bommarito, 284 S.W.3d 761, 770 (Mo. Ct. App. 2009); First Nat'l Bank in Durant v. Honey Creek Entm't Corp., 54 P.3d 100, 103 (Okla. 2002); Lopez v. Reynoso, 118 P.3d 398, 400 (Wash. Ct. App. 2005).

44. *E.g.,* regarding presumption that a written document is fully integrated: Jenkins v. Eckerd Corp., 913 So.2d 43, 53 (Fla. Dist. Ct. App. 2005); Brewer v. Devore, 960 S.W.2d 519, 522 (Mo. Ct. App. 1998); Fontbank, Inc. v. CompuServe, Inc., 742 N.E.2d 674, 678 (Ohio Ct. App. 2000); Lenzi v. Hahnemann Univ., 664 A.2d 1375, 1379 (Pa. Super. Ct. 1995); Barker v. Roelke, 105 S.W.3d 75, 83 (Tex. App. 2003); Bennett v. Huish, 155 P.3d 917, 925 (Utah Ct. App. 2007).

45. *E.g.*, regarding conclusiveness of a valid merger clause: Hamade v. Sunoco Inc. (R & M), 721 N.W.2d 233, 249 (Mich. Ct. App. 2006); UAW–GM Human Res. Ctr. v. KSL Recreation Corp., 579 N.W.2d 411, 418 (Mich. Ct. App. 1998).

In addition, *see* Magnus v. Lutheran Gen. Health Care Sys., 601 N.E.2d 907, 914 (Ill. App. Ct. 1992); Optimal Interiors, LLC v. HON Co., 774 F. Supp. 2d 993, 1003 (S.D. Iowa 2011); Atlantic Pier Associates, LLC v. Boardakan Rest. Partners, 647 F. Supp. 2d 474, 489 (E.D. Pa. 2009); Peterson v. Cornerstone Prop. Dev., LLC, 720 N.W.2d 716, 725 (Wis. Ct. App. 2006).

46. *E.g.,* regarding non-conclusiveness of merger clause in establishing that the parties intended the contract to be fully integrated, but as supporting a presumption or providing a "clear sign" that the writing is integrated and complete: e.g., Ritter v. Grady Auto. Group, Inc., 973 So.2d 1058, 1062 (Ala. 2007); Carlson v. Hallinan, 925 A.2d 506, 523 (Del. Ch. 2006); Morgan Buildings & Spas, Inc. v. Humane Soc'y of Se. Texas, 249 S.W.3d 480, 486 (Tex. App. 2008).

47. *E.g.*, Betaco, Inc. v. Cessna Aircraft Co., 32 F.3d 1126, 1133 (7th Cir. 1994); Fontbank, Inc. v. CompuServe, Inc., 742 N.E.2d 674, 678 (Ohio Ct. App. 2000); Olsen Media v. Energy Sciences, Inc., 648 P.2d 493, 497 (Wash. Ct. App. 1982).

48. *E.g.*, Jenkins v. Eckerd Corp., 913 So.2d 43, 53 (Fla. Dist. Ct. App. 2005).

49. C & J Vantage Leasing Co. v. Wolfe, 795 N.W.2d 65, 85 (Iowa 2011), *reh'g denied* (Mar. 30, 2011).

50. Lopez v. Reynoso, 118 P.3d 398, 403 (Wash. Ct. App. 2005) ("Although an integration clause is a strong indication that the parties intended complete integration of a written agreement, … a boilerplate clause will not be given effect if it appears that the provision is factually false").

51. M/S Bremen v. Zapata Off–Shore Co., 407 U.S. 1, 17, 19, 92 S.Ct. 1907, 1917–18 (1972).

52. M/S Bremen v. Zapata Off–Shore Co., 407 U.S. 1, 17, 19, 92 S.Ct. 1907, 1917–18 (1972).

53. Kubis & Perszyk Associates, Inc. v. Sun Microsystems, Inc., 680 A.2d 618, 624 (N.J. 1996) (New Jersey Supreme Court remarked that "[t]he *Bremen* approach generally has been applied by federal and state courts confronted by jurisdictional choices involving forum-selection clauses."); *see, e.g.,* America Online, Inc. v. Superior Court, 108 Cal.Rptr.2d 699, 707 (Cal. Ct. App. 2001) (favorable treatment follows from the important practical effect such contractual rights have on commerce generally).

54. Phillips v. Audio Active Ltd., 494 F.3d 378, 383 (2d Cir. 2007). *E.g.*, regarding presumptive validity of clause: Slater v. Energy Services Group Int'l, Inc., 634 F.3d 1326, 1331 (11th Cir. 2011); Archer v. Darling, 2011 WL 861201 at *3 (D. Colo. 2011); Luz v. HNTB Corp., 2006 WL 3734669 at *2 (Mich. Ct. App. 2006); Adler v. 20/20 Companies, 919 N.Y.S.2d 38, 39 (App. Div. 2011); Caperton v. A.T. Massey Coal Co., Inc., 690 S.E.2d 322, 348 (W.Va. 2009).

55. *E.g.*, regarding the need for a strong showing that enforcement would be unfair and unreasonable: Slater v. Energy Services Group Int'l, Inc., 634 F.3d 1326, 1331 (11th Cir. 2011); Adler v. 20/20 Companies, 919 N.Y.S.2d 38, 39 (App. Div. 2011); Caperton v. A.T. Massey Coal Co., Inc., 690 S.E.2d 322, 348 (W.Va. 2009).

56. Gilman v. Wheat, First Sec., Inc., 692 A.2d 454, 462 (Md. Ct. App. 1997).

57. *E.g.,* regarding language expressly dictating an *exclusive* forum for dispute resolution (i.e., by making it clear through use of unequivocal mandatory language that the selected forum is to be the *only* forum for dispute resolution versus language authorizing parties to sue in forum but not prohibiting litigation elsewhere): Slater v. Energy Services Group Int'l, Inc., 634 F.3d 1326, 1330 (11th Cir. 2011); K & V Scientific Co., Inc. v. Bayerische Motoren Werke Aktiengesellschaft ("BMW") 314 F.3d 494, 498 (10th Cir. 2002); Plaza Realty of Rio Piedras, Inc. v. Selcer, 755 F. Supp. 2d 376 (D.P.R. 2010); Bentley v. Mut. Benefits Corp., 237 F. Supp. 2d 699, 701 (S.D. Miss. 2002); Animal Film, LLC v. D.E.J. Productions, Inc., 123 Cal.Rptr.3d 72 (Ct. App. 2011); Travel Exp. Inv. Inc. v. AT & T Corp., 14 So.3d 1224, 1226 (Fla. Dist. Ct. App. 2009); Bohl v. Hauke, 906 N.E.2d 450, 456 (Ohio App. 2009); Caperton v. A.T. Massey Coal Co., Inc., 690 S.E.2d 322, 338 (W.Va. 2009).

58. *E.g.,* Wells Fargo Fin. Leasing, Inc. v. NCH Healthcare Sys., Inc., 756 F. Supp. 2d 1086, 1100 (S.D. Iowa 2010) (permissive clause is not dispositive); Animal Film, LLC v. D.E.J. Productions, Inc., 123 Cal.Rptr.3d 72 (Cal. Ct. App. 2011) (inclusion of permissive clause is one factor court takes into account in determining forum non conveniens analysis).

59. State ex rel. Cordray v. Makedonija Tabak 2000, 937 N.E.2d 595, 601 (Ohio Ct. App. 2010).

60. *E.g.*, regarding the use of "shall," "will," "must," "may," and other auxiliary verbs: Slater v. Energy Services Group Int'l, Inc., 634 F.3d 1326, 1330 (11th Cir. 2011) ("shall" expresses a requirement); Florida State Bd. of Admin. v. Law Eng'g & Envtl. Services, Inc., 262 F. Supp. 2d

1004, 1009 (D. Minn. 2003) (generally, "may" and "should" signify permissive clauses, while "shall," "will" or "must" signify mandatory clauses"); Polk County Recreational Ass'n v. Susque-hanna Patriot Commercial Leasing Co., Inc., 734 N.W.2d 750, 758 (Neb. 2007) (provision that action "shall be brought" in Pennsylvania is mandatory; provision that parties consent and submit to jurisdiction of Pennsylvania is permissive).

61. *E.g.,* Effect of context on use of "may" or "shall"; Fear & Fear, Inc. v. N.I.I. Brokerage, L.L.C., 50 A.D.3d 185, 188, 851 N.Y.S.2d 311, 313 (App. Div. 2008); AGR Fin., L.L.C. v. Ready Staffing, Inc., 99 F. Supp. 2d 399, 402 (S.D.N.Y. 2000).

62. *E.g.,* Celistics, LLC v. Gonzalez, 22 So.3d 824, 826 (Fla. Dist. Ct. App. 2009) (general rule is that a forum selection clause will be considered permissive if it lacks words of exclusivity).

63. *E.g.,* Celistics, LLC v. Gonzalez, 22 So.3d 824, 826 (Fla. Dist. Ct. App. 2009).

64. Yakin v. Tyler Hill Corp., 566 F.3d 72, 76 (2d Cir. 2009) cert. denied, 130 S.Ct. 401 (U.S. 2009).

65. *E.g.,* Yakin v. Tyler Hill Corp., 566 F.3d 72, 76 (2d Cir. 2009) *cert. denied,* 130 S.Ct. 401 (U.S. 2009); Rihani v. Team Exp. Distrib., LLC, 711 F. Supp. 2d 557, 559–560 (D. Md. 2010).

66. *E.g.,* Electroplated Metal Solutions, Inc. v. American Services, Inc., 500 F. Supp. 2d 974, 976 (N.D. Ill. 2007); Caperton v. A.T. Massey Coal Co., Inc., 690 S.E.2d 322, 336 (W.Va. 2009) (first inquiry is whether the clause was reasonably communicated to the party resisting enforcement).

67. In re TCW Global Project Fund II, Ltd., 274 S.W.3d 166, 169 (Tex. App. 2008).

68. *E.g.,* TriState HVAC Equip., LLP v. Big Belly Solar, Inc., 752 F. Supp. 2d 517, 536–37 (E.D. Pa. 2010), *amended on reconsideration,* Tristate HVAC Equip., LLP v. Big Belly Solar, Inc., 2011 WL 204738 (E.D. Pa. 2011).

69. Omron Healthcare, Inc. v. Maclaren Exports Ltd., 28 F.3d 600, 601–02 (7th Cir. 1994) (forum-selection clause that required party to submit disputes "arising out of" the contract to England's High Court of Justice applied to a trademark infringement claim that required interpretation of the contract for its resolution).

70. John Wyeth & Bro. Ltd. v. CIGNA Int'l Corp., 119 F.3d 1070, 1074 (3d Cir. 1997) (forum-selection clause that applied to all disputes "arising in relation to" the contract required only some sort of logical or causal connection between the dispute and the contract).

71. Caperton v. A.T. Massey Coal Co., Inc., 690 S.E.2d 322, 341 (W. Va. 2009) (phrase "in connection with this agreement" is very broad in scope, indicating an intention to have the clause apply equally to contract claims, tort claims, and statutory claims so long as they are brought "in connection with" agreement).

72. Roby v. Corporation of Lloyd's, 996 F.2d 1353, 1359 (2d Cir. 1993) (phrase "relating to" is no less broad than broad phrases "arising from" or "in connection with").

73. John Wyeth & Bro. Ltd. v. CIGNA Int'l Corp., 119 F.3d 1070, 1075 (3d Cir. 1997) (phrase "arising *under* the contract" less broad than "arising in relation to").

74. U.C.C. § 1–301 (Territorial Applicability; Parties' Power to Choose Applicable Law.)

75. Farb v. Superior Court, 94 Cal.Rptr.3d 586, 592 (Ct. App. 2009), *review denied* (Aug. 12, 2009), *reh'g denied* (Cal. 2009). *E.g.,* decisions that have adopted or applied the Restatement Rule (either the 1981 or 1971 version) include: Swanson v. Image Bank, Inc., 77 P.3d 439, 441 (Ariz. 2003); Elgar v. Elgar, 679 A.2d 937, 943 (Conn. 1996); Vaughan v. Nationwide Mut. Ins. Co., 702 A.2d 198, 200 (D.C. Ct. App. 1997) Abry Partners V, L.P. v. F & W Acquisition LLC, 891 A.2d 1032, 1049 (Del. Ch. 2006); Carroll v. MBNA Am. Bank, 220 P.3d 1080, 1084 (Idaho 2009); Old Republic Ins. Co. v. Ace Prop. & Cas. Ins. Co., 906 N.E.2d 630, 636 (Ill. Ct. App. 2009); Hodas v. Morin, 814 N.E.2d 320, 324 (Mass. 2004); Tomran, Inc. v. Passano, 862 A.2d 453, 461 (Md. Ct. Spec. App. 2004) aff'd, 391 Md. 1, 891 A.2d 336 (2006); Chrysler Corp. v. Skyline Indus. Services, Inc., 528 N.W.2d 698, 703 (Mich. 1995); Burchett v. MasTec N. Am., Inc., 93 P.3d 1247, 1249 (Mt. 2004); Armstrong Bus. Services, Inc. v. H & R Block, 96 S.W.3d 867, 872 (Mo. Ct. App. 2002); In re Scott, 999 A.2d 229, 238 (N.H. 2010); Torres v. McClain, 535 S.E.2d 623, 625 (N.C. Ct. App. 2000); Nexen Inc. v. Gulf Interstate Eng'g Co., 224 S.W.3d 412, 419 (Tex. Ct . App. 2006).

76. *See* Restatement (Second) of Conflict of Laws § 187 (1971).

77. *See* Restatement (Second) of Conflict of Laws § 187 (1971).

78. *See* Or. Rev. Stat. Ann. § 15.350 and § 15.355 (West).

79. *See generally* Restatement (Second) of Conflict of Laws § 186 (1971) (comment b.)

80. *E.g.,* Finance One Pub. Co. Ltd. v. Lehman Bros. Special Fin., Inc., 414 F.3d 325, 332–33 (2d Cir. 2005) (validity of a contractual choice-of-law clause is threshold question that must be decided not under law specified in clause, but under the relevant forum's choice-of-law rules governing effectiveness of such clauses).

81. Finance One Pub. Co. Ltd. v. Lehman Bros. Special Fin., Inc., 414 F.3d 325, 333 (2d Cir. 2005).

82. *See* Finance One Pub. Co. Ltd. v. Lehman Bros. Special Fin., Inc., 414 F.3d 325, 334–35 (2d Cir. 2005) New York courts are "reluctant" "to construe contractual choice-of-law clauses broadly to encompass extra-contractual causes of action. Under New York law tort claims are outside the scope of contractual choice-of-law provisions that specify what law governs construction of the terms of the contract, even if the contract also includes a broader forum-selection clause. The Second Circuit said that "presumably" a contractual choice-of-law clause could be drafted broadly enough to reach tort claims, but that no reported New York cases present such a broad clause. Id.

83. *E.g.,* regarding unavailability of attorney's fees to the prevailing party unless authorized by contract or statute: Ilshin Inv. Co., Ltd. v. Buena Vista Home Entm't, Inc., 195 Cal.App.4th 612 (Ct. App. 2011) *modified,* B208839, 2011 WL 2139891 (Cal. Ct. App. 2011); Gen. Motors LLC v. Bowie, 58 So.3d 934, 936 (Fla. Dist. Ct. App. 2011) quoting General Motors Corp. v. Sanchez, 16 So.3d 883, 884–85 (Fla.App. 2009); Ward v. Ward, 710 S.E.2d 555, 557 (2011); Horn v. Messamore, 2011 WL 1344567 at *2–3 (Ky. Ct. App. 2011); In re Estate of Elias, 946 N.E.2d 1015, 1035 (Ill. App. Ct. 2011); Richard v. Broussard, 482 So.2d 729, 734 (La. Ct. App. 1985) *writ granted,* 488 So.2d 190 (La. 1986) *aff'd as amended,* 495 So.2d 1291 (La. 1986); Martha's Hands, LLC v. Rothman, 328 S.W.3d 474, 482 (Mo. Ct. App. 2010); Intercontinental Group P'ship v. KB Home Lone Star L.P., 295 S.W.3d 650, 653 (Tex. 2009).

84. *See, e.g.,* Ariz. Rev. Stat. Ann. § 12–341.01(A)(2012) as amended by 2012 Ariz. Legis. Serv. Ch. 305 (H.B. 2544) (West).The Arizona statute provides that "[i]n any contested action arising out of a contract, express or implied, the court may award the successful party reasonable attorney fees." As recently amended, it is not to be construed as altering, prohibiting or restricting present or future contracts or statutes that may provide for attorney fees.

85. *E.g.,* regarding contractual provisions for attorney's fees: Greystone Equip. Fin. Corp. v. Motion Imaging, Inc., 910 N.Y.S.2d 405 (Sup. Ct. 2010); Twin Creek Estates, L.L.C. v. Tipps, 251 P.3d 756 (Okla. Civ. App. 2011); Menasha Forest Products Corp. v. Curry County Title, Inc., 249 P.3d 1265, 1268 (Or. 2011),

86. *E.g.,* regarding review and control of the fee by the court and a court's inquiry into the fee's reasonableness: Richard v. Broussard, 482 So.2d 729, 734 (La. Ct. App. 1985) *writ granted,* 488 So.2d 190 (La. 1986); *aff'd as amended,* 495 So.2d 1291 (La. 1986); Greystone Equip. Fin. Corp. v. Motion Imaging, Inc., 910 N.Y.S.2d 405 (Sup. Ct. 2010).

87. Cracker Barrel Old Country Store, Inc. v. Epperson, 284 S.W.3d 303, 310 (Tenn. 2009). *But see* Reizfeld v. Reizfeld, 40 A3d. 320, 325 (Conn. App. Ct. 2011) (in a case involving an antenuptial contract, court concluded that the word "liabilities" included attorney's fees.)

88. Pandelis Const. Co., Inc. v. Jones–Viking Associates, 734 P.2d 1236, 1238 (Nev. 1987).

89. *Id.*

90. *E.g.,* regarding lack of mutuality as no bar to enforcement of attorney's fees provision: Butler v. Lembeck, 182 P.3d 1185, 1190 (Colo. Ct. App. 2007); David R. Rykbost Corp. v. O'Connor, 2004 Mass. App. Div. 75 (2004) (not reported in Northeastern Digest).

91. *See, e.g.,* regarding statutes that impose a prevailing party standard on attorney's fees provisions favoring only one party: *see* Cal. Civ. Code § 1717(a) (West 2012) (if contract provides for award of attorney's fees to either one of the parties or to prevailing party, party who prevails in action *shall be entitled* to reasonable attorney's fees in addition to other costs): and Hsu v. Abbara, 891 P.2d 804, 809 (Cal. 1995) (statute applies in favor of prevailing party on contract claim whenever party would have been liable under contract for attorney fees if other party prevailed); *see* Fla. Stat. Ann. § 57.105(7) (West 2012) (if contract allows attorney's fees to *one* of the parties when he or she is required to take action to enforce contract, then court *may* allow reasonable attorney's fees to the party if that party prevails in any action with respect to contract, whether as plaintiff or defendant) and Florida Hurricane Prot. & Awning, Inc. v. Pastina, 43 So.3d 893, 895 (Fla. Dist. Ct. App. 2010) (since contract provided for attorney's fees to one of parties in event of collection action, reciprocity would allow other party to receive attorney fees only if she prevailed in a collection action). *See* Utah Code Ann. § 78B–5–826 (West) (court may award costs and attorney fees to either party that prevails in a civil action based upon any promissory note, written contract, or other writing when provisions allow one party to recover attorney fees).

92. *E.g.,* Spectraserv, Inc. v. Middlesex County Utilities Auth., 7 A.3d 231, 242 (N.J. Super. Ct. App. Div. 2010) (to determine propriety of award of attorney fees, court must first determine whether party qualifies as a "prevailing party").

93. Whipps, L.L.C. v. Kaufman, Vidal, Hileman & Ramlow, P.C., 156 P.3d 11, 13 (Mt. 2007).

94. Global Travel Mktg., Inc. v. Shea, 908 So.2d 392, 403 (Fla. 2005).

95. United Steelworkers of Am. v. Warrior & Gulf Nav. Co., 363 U.S. 574, 581, 80 S.Ct. 1347, 1352 (1960).

96. Ortega v. Contra Costa Cmty. Coll. Dist., 67 Cal.Rptr.3d 832, 840 (Cal. Ct. App. 2007).

97. Buckeye Check Cashing, Inc. v. Cardegna, 546 U.S. 440, 443–444, 126 S.Ct. 1204, 1207–08 (2006).

98. Volt Info. Sciences, Inc. v. Board of Trustees of Leland Stanford Junior Univ., 489 U.S. 468, 109 S.Ct. 1248 (1989).

99. Citizens Bank v. Alafabco, Inc., 539 U.S. 52, 123 S.Ct. 2037, 2040 (2003).

100. Southland Corp. v. Keating, 465 U.S. 1, 104 S.Ct. 852, 858 (1984).

101. Buckeye Check Cashing, Inc. v. Cardegna, 546 U.S. 440, 443–44, 126 S.Ct. 1204, 1208, 163 L.Ed.2d 1038 (2006).

102. Vaden v. Discover Bank, 556 U.S. 49, 59, 129 S.Ct. 1262, 1271 (2009) (the Act is binding on state as well as federal courts); Buckeye Check Cashing, Inc. v. Cardegna, 546 U.S. 440, 445, 126 S.Ct. 1204, 1208–09 (2006).

103. Volt Info. Sciences, Inc. v. Board of Trustees of Leland Stanford Junior Univ., 489 U.S. 486, 477–479, 109 S.Ct. 1248, 1255–56 (1989).

104. Volt Info. Sciences, Inc. v. Board of Trustees of Leland Stanford Junior Univ., 489 U.S. 486, 109 S.Ct. 1248 (1989).

105. *See, e.g.*, Arizona (Title 12, §§ 12–3001 through 12–3029); Arkansas (Title 16, subtitle 7, chapter 108, §§ 16–108–201 through 16–108–230); Colorado (Title 13, Article 22, Part 2, §§ 13–22–201 through 13–22–230); Delaware (Title 10, Part IV, §§ 5701 through 5725); Hawaii (Div. 4, Title 36, Chapter 658A, §§ 658A–1 through 658–29); Kansas (Chapter 5, Article 4, §§ 5–401 through–422); Maine (Title 14, Part 7, chapter 706, §§ 5927–5949).

106. Volt Info. Sciences, Inc. v. Board of Trustees of Leland Stanford Junior Univ., 489 U.S. 468, 479, 109 S.Ct. 1248, 1256 (1989).

107. *Id. E.g.,* Volt Info. Sciences, Inc. v. Board of Trustees of Leland Stanford Junior Univ., 489 U.S. 468, 479, 109 S.Ct. 1248, 1256 (1989) (arbitration under the Act is a matter of consent, not coercion, and parties are generally free to structure their arbitration agreements as they see fit); Peterson & Simpson v. IHC Health Services, Inc., 217 P.3d 716, 720 (Utah 2009); State v. Philip Morris USA Inc., 945 A.2d 887, 892 (Vt. 2008).

108. *E.g.,* Volt Info. Sciences, Inc. v. Board of Trustees of Leland Stanford Junior Univ., 489 U.S. 468, 479, 109 S.Ct. 1248, 1256 (1989) (parties may specify by contract the rules under which arbitration will be conducted; where the parties have agreed to abide by state rules of arbitration, enforcing those rules according to the terms of the agreement is consistent with the goals of the FAA).

109. Mastrobuono v. Shearson Lehman Hutton, Inc., 514 U.S. 52, 62, 115 S.Ct. 1212, 1218 (1995).

110. Mitsubishi Motors Corp. v. Soler Chrysler–Plymouth, Inc., 473 U.S. 614, 626, 105 S.Ct. 3346, 3354 (1985). *E.g.*, regarding courts' "liberal" or "generous" construction of arbitration agreements and their resolving doubts in favor of arbitration: Bechtel do Brasil Construcoes Ltda. v. UEG Araucaria Ltda., 638 F.3d 150, 154 (2d Cir. 2011); Industrial Wire Products, Inc. v. Costco Wholesale Corp., 576 F.3d 516, 520 (8th Cir. 2009); Jorge–Colon v. Mandara Spa Puerto Rico, Inc., 685 F. Supp. 2d 280, 283 (D.P.R. 2010); Dillard's, Inc. v. Gallups, 58 So.3d 196, 200 (Ala. Civ. App. 2010); Saguaro Highlands Cmty. Ass'n v. Biltis, 229 P.3d 1036, 1037 (Ariz. Ct. App. 2010), *review denied* (Oct. 26, 2010); Wattenbarger v. A.G. Edwards & Sons, Inc., 246 P.3d 961, 968 (Idaho 2010), *reh'g denied* (Dec. 23, 2010); Coast Auto. Group, Ltd. v. Withum Smith & Brown, 995 A.2d 300, 304 (N.J. Super. Ct. App. Div. 2010); State ex rel. Masto v. Second Judicial Dist. Court ex rel. County of Washoe, 199 P.3d 828, 832 (Nev. 2009); Ellison v. Alexander, 700 S.E.2d 102, 106 (N.C. Ct. App. 2010); Morris v. Morris, 939 N.E.2d 928, 941 (Ohio App. 2010); Yakima County v. Yakima County Law Enforcement Officers Guild, 237 P.3d 316, 325 (Wash. Ct. App. 2010).

111. *See* Volt Info. Sciences, Inc. v. Board of Trustees of Leland Stanford Junior Univ., 489 U.S. 468, 479, 109 S.Ct. 1248, 1256 (1989) (parties may determine what claims are covered by arbitration agreement). Addressing courts' ability to compel arbitration regarding only claims within the clause's scope: *e.g.*, LRN Holding, Inc. v. Windlake Capital Advisors, LLC, 949 N.E.2d 264 (Ill. App. Ct. 2011): Nw. Chrysler Plymouth, Inc. v. DaimlerChrysler Corp., 168 S.W.3d 693, 696 (Mo. Ct. App. 2005); Council of Smaller Enterprises v. Gates, McDonald & Co., 687 N.E.2d 1352, 1355 (Ohio 1998) (arbitrators derive their authority to resolve disputes only because the

parties have agreed to submit such grievances to arbitration.)

112. Peerless Importers, Inc. v. Wine, Liquor & Distillery Workers Union Local One, 903 F.2d 924, 927 (2d Cir. 1990).

113. *E.g.*, regarding narrow interpretation of exclusionary clauses: Chelsea Family Pharmacy, PLLC v. Medco Health Solutions, Inc., 567 F.3d 1191, 1197 (10th Cir. 2009); Nilsen v. Prudential–Bache Sec., 761 F.Supp. 279, 286 (S.D.N.Y.1991); Molecular Analytical Sys. v. Ciphergen Biosystems, Inc., 111 Cal.Rptr.3d 876, 886 (Cal. Ct. App. 2010).

114. Northwest Chrysler Plymouth, Inc. v. DaimlerChrysler Corp., 168 S.W.3d 693, 696 (Mo. Ct. App. 2005).

115. Coast Auto. Group, Ltd. v. Withum Smith & Brown, 995 A.2d 300, 305 (N.J. Super. Ct. App. Div. 2010).

116. *E.g.*, stating that the clause should be set out in clear and unequivocal language: Gebhardt & Smith LLP v. Maryland Port Admin., 982 A.2d 876, 900–01 (Md. Ct. Spec. App. 2009).

117. *E.g.*, Gebhardt & Smith LLP v. Maryland Port Admin., 982 A.2d 876, 901 (Md. Ct. Spec. App. 2009).

118. *E.g.*, MACTEC, Inc. v. Gorelick, 427 F.3d 821, 827 (10th Cir. 2005);' Uhl v. Komatsu Forklift Co., Ltd., 512 F.3d 294, 300–01 (6th Cir. 2008); Scharf v. Kogan, 285 S.W.3d 362, 372 (Mo. Ct. App. 2009).

119. *See* Freedman v. Comcast Corp., 988 A.2d 68, 78 (Md. Ct. Spec. App. 2010) *cert. denied*, 415 Md. 39, 997 A.2d 790 (2010).

Endnotes for Chapter 11. Contract Components: Modification, Execution, and Effective Date

1. *E.g.*, regarding the right of parties to modify a contract by mutual assent provided that there is a meeting of the minds: Moss v. Allstate Ins. Co., 776 S.W.2d 831, 833 (Ark. Ct. App. 1989); Shelton v. Olowosoyo, 10 A.3d 45, 49 (Conn. App. Ct. 2010); St. Joe Corp. v. McIver, 875 So.2d 375, 381 (Fla. 2004); Richard W. McCarthy Trust Dated September 2, 2004 v. Illinois Cas. Co., 946 N.E.2d 895, 902 (Ill. App. Ct. 2011); Okerman v. VA Software Corp., 871 N.E.2d 1117, 1125 (Mass. App. Ct. 2007); Kloian v. Domino's Pizza LLC, 733 N.W.2d 766, 771 (Mich. Ct. App. 2006); Heritage Bldg. Prop., LLC v. Prime Income Asset Mgmt., Inc., 43 So.3d 1138, 1143 (Miss. Ct. App. 2009), *reh'g denied* (June 22, 2010), *cert. denied*, 49 So.3d 106 (Miss. 2010); G. Adrian Stanley & Associates, Inc. v. Risk & Ins. Brokerage Corp., 473 S.E.2d 345, 348 (N.C. Ct. App. 1996).

2. *E.g.*, regarding the fact that a party typically cannot modify a contract unilaterally: Zuelsdorf v. University of Alaska, Fairbanks, 794 P.2d 932, 935 (Alaska 1990); Crain Indus., Inc. v. Cass, 810 S.W.2d 910, 915 (Ark. 1991); Colowyo Coal Co. v. City of Colorado Springs, 879 P.2d 438, 443 (Colo. App. 1994); St. Joe Corp. v. McIver, 875 So.2d 375, 382 (Fla. 2004); Yellowpine Water User's Ass'n v. Imel, 670 P.2d 54, 57 (Idaho 1983); Solar Motors, Inc. v. First Nat'l Bank of Chadron, 545 N.W.2d 714, 721 (Neb. 1996); United States v. Public Utilities Comm'n, 635 A.2d 1135, 1144 (R.I. 1993).

3. *E.g.*, Guidry v. Charter Communications, Inc., 269 S.W.3d 520, 528 (Mo. Ct. App. 2008) ("When the parties modify an existing contract they are making a new contract; it is only enforceable if there is mutual assent and consideration").

4. *E.g.*, regarding the requirement that modification satisfy the criteria for a valid contract: Honolulu Fed. Sav. & Loan Ass'n v. Murphy, 753 P.2d 807, 813 (Haw. Ct. App. 1988); All Am. Roofing, Inc. v. Zurich Am. Ins. Co., 934 N.E.2d 679, 689 (Ill. App. Ct. 2010); Hinkel v. Sataria Distribution & Packaging, Inc., 920 N.E.2d 766, 770 (Ind. Ct. App. 2010); Roy v. Danis, 553 A.2d 663, 664 (Me. 1989); Heritage Bldg. Prop., LLC v. Prime Income Asset Mgmt., Inc., 43 So.3d 1138, 1143 (Miss. Ct. App. 2009), *reh'g denied* (June 22, 2010), *cert. denied*, 49 So.3d 106 (Miss. 2010); GuestHouse Int'l, LLC v. Shoney's N. Am. Corp., 330 S.W.3d 166, 190 (Tenn. Ct. App. 2010), *appeal denied* (Sept. 23, 2010); Arthur J. Gallagher & Co. v. Dieterich, 270 S.W.3d 695, 702 (Tex. App. 2008); Duncan v. Alaska USA Fed. Credit Union, Inc., 199 P.3d 991, 1002 (Wash. Ct. App. 2008).

E.g., regarding "meeting of the minds:" Esa Services, LLC v. South Carolina Dep't of Revenue, 707 S.E.2d 431 (S.C. Ct. App. 2011); In re Larue, 934 A.2d 577, 581 (N.H. 2007); U.S. Bank Trust Nat. Ass'n v. Bell, 684 S.E.2d 199, 204 (S.C. Ct. App. 2009), *reh'g denied* (Nov. 2, 2009); Arthur J. Gallagher & Co. v. Dieterich, 270 S.W.3d 695, 702 (Tex. App. 2008); Duncan v. Alaska USA Fed. Credit Union, Inc., 199 P.3d 991, 1002 (Wash. Ct. App. 2008).

5. *E.g.*, regarding the effect of modification: Richard W. McCarthy Trust Dated September 2, 2004 v. Illinois Cas. Co., 946 N.E.2d 895, 902 (Ill. App. Ct. 2011) (if modification is inconsistent with a term of a prior contract between same parties, modification is interpreted as including an agreement to rescind inconsistent term in prior contract; modified contract is regarded as creating new single contract consisting of such terms of prior contract as parties have not agreed to change, in addition to new terms on which parties have agreed).

6. *See, e.g.*, Quinn Bros., Inc. v. Whitehouse, 737 A.2d 1127, 1129 (N.H. 1999) (record revealed conflicting testimony regarding whether the terms of contract were modified and, if modified, whether contract was completely performed by defendant).

7. *E.g.*, regarding oral modifications to contracts that prohibit oral modifications: Coral Reef Drive Land Dev., LLC v. Duke Realty Ltd. P'ship, 45 So.3d 897, 901–02 (Fla. Dist. Ct. App. 2010) *reh'g denied*, 60 So.3d 1054 (2011); Martin v. Centre Pointe Investments, Inc., 712 S.E.2d 638, 642 (Ga. Ct. App. 2011); Seneca Waste Solutions, Inc. v. Sheaffer Mfg. Co., LLC, 791 N.W.2d 407, 412–13 (Iowa 2010); 600 N. Frederick Rd., LLC v. Burlington Coat Factory of Maryland, LLC, 19 A.3d 837, 852 (Md. 2011), *reconsideration denied* (June 16, 2011); Services, LLC v. South Carolina Dep't of Revenue, 707 S.E.2d 431, 438 (S.C. Ct. App. 2011); Glenn v. Reese, 225 P.3d 185, 191 (Utah 2009), *reh'g denied* (Feb. 18, 2010).

8. *E.g.*, regarding oral modifications to written contracts: ESA Services, LLC v. South Carolina Dep't of Revenue, 707 S.E.2d 431, 438 (S.C. Ct. App. 2011) (modification of written contract must satisfy all fundamental elements of a valid contract for it to be enforceable, including meeting of the minds between parties with regard to all essential terms).

9. *E.g.*, Schwenk v. Auburn Sportsplex, LLC, 483 F. Supp. 2d 81, 86 (D. Mass. 2007) ("The purpose of a signing a contract is to demonstrate mutuality of assent, which may also be shown by the conduct of the parties").

10. Rocky Creek Ret. Properties, Inc. v. Estate of Fox *ex rel.* Bank of Am., N.A., 19 So.3d 1105, 1108 (Fla. Dist. Ct. App. 2009) citing D.L. Peoples Group, Inc. v. Hawley, 804 So.2d 561, 563 (Fla. Dist. Ct. App. 2002)).

11. Rocky Creek Ret. Properties, Inc. v. Estate of Fox *ex rel.* Bank of Am., N.A., 19 So.3d 1105, 1108 (Fla. Dist. Ct. App. 2009) citing Mandell v. Fortenberry, 290 So.2d 3, 7 (Fla. 1974).

12. All State Home Mortg., Inc. v. Daniel, 977 A.2d 438, 446 (Md. Ct. Spec. App. 2009), *reconsideration denied* (Sept. 1, 2009), *cert. denied*, 979 A.2d 707 (2009) (issue of whether agreement to arbitrate exists governed by contract principles).

13. *Id.* at 448.

14. Uniform Electronic Transactions Act §§ 1 through 21 (1999).

15. 15 U.S.C. §§ 7001–7031 (2012).

16. Regarding contract becoming effective *preceding* the day of signing: *e.g.*, American Cyanamid Co. v. Ring, 286 S.E.2d 1, 3 (Ga. 1982). *See also,* Viacom Int'l Inc. v. Tandem Productions, Inc., 368 F.Supp. 1264, 1270 (S.D.N.Y. 1974) *aff'd*, 526 F.2d 593 (2d Cir. 1975).

17. *See, e.g.*, cases in which substantial rights turned on the effective date: DynCorp Info. Sys., LLC v. United States, 58 Fed. Cl. 446, 458–59 (Fed. Cl. 2003); Schwenk v. Auburn Sportsplex, LLC, 483 F. Supp. 2d 81, 86 (D. Mass. 2007); Suffolk Constr. Co., Inc. v. Lanco Scaffolding Co., Inc., 716 N.E.2d 130, 131–32 (Mass App. Ct. 1999).

18. *E.g.*, regarding conditions precedent to contract formation: Stanwood Boom Works, LLC v. BP Exploration & Prod., Inc., 2012 WL 1428907 at *3 (5th Cir. 2012); Newton v. American Debt Services, Inc., 2012 WL 581318 at *14 (N.D. Cal. 2012); Edelman Arts, Inc. v. Art Int'l (UK) Ltd., 841 F.Supp.2d 810, 824 (S.D.N.Y. 2012). *See also* Evatt v. Steele, 783 P.2d 959, 960–61 (N.M. 1989) (consent not a condition precedent to contract formation).

Endnotes for Chapter 12: How Courts
Read and Construe Contracts

1. *E.g.,* regarding application of rules of contract construction to deeds: Nesbitt v. Wilde, 703 S.E.2d 389, 391 (Ga. Ct. App. 2010); Conservatorship of Estate of Maryland Agric. Land Pres. Found. v. Claggett, 985 A.2d 565, 575 (Md. Ct. App. 2009); Conservatorship of Estate of Moor ex rel. Moor v. State, 46 So.3d 849, 852 (Miss. Ct. App. 2010); Motion Motors, Inc. v. Berwick, 846 A.2d 1156, 1160 (N.H. 2004); Holladay Duplex Mgmt. Co., L.L.C. v. Howells, 47 P.3d 104, 105 (Utah Ct. App. 2002).

2. *E.g.,* regarding application of rules of contract construction to promissory notes: Sunset Mortg. v. Agolio, 952 A.2d 65, 68 (Conn. App. Ct. 2008); RBS Citizens, Nat. Ass'n v. RTG–Oak Lawn, LLC, 943 N.E.2d 198, 205 (Ill. App. Ct. 2011), *reh'g denied* (Feb. 23, 2011), *reh'g denied*

(Feb. 25, 2011); Blair Const., Inc. v. McBeth, 44 P.3d 1244, 1252 (Kan. 2002); Cranberry Fin., L.L.C. v. S & V P'ship, 927 N.E.2d 623, 624 (Ohio Ct. App. 2010); DeClaire v. G & B Mcintosh Family Ltd. P'ship, 260 S.W.3d 34, 43 (Tex. App. 2008); WebBank v. American Gen. Annuity Serv. Corp., 54 P.3d 1139, 1144 (Utah 2002).

3. *E.g.,* regarding application of rules of contract construction to mortgage contracts: Blair Const., Inc. v. McBeth, 44 P.3d 1244, 1252 (Kan. 2002); Archer v. Skokan, 897 N.Y.S.2d 127, 129 (App. Div. 2010); Starcrest Trust v. Berry, 926 S.W.2d 343, 351 (Tex. App. 1996); In re Holmdahl, 439 B.R. 876, 881 (Bankr. W.D. Wis. 2010).

4. *E.g.,* regarding rules of contract construction to deed of trust: Dunn v. GMAC Mortg., LLC, 2011 WL 1230211 (E.D. Cal. 2011); Estates in Eagle Ridge, LLLP v. Valley Bank & Trust, 141 P.3d 838, 842 (Colo. Ct. App. 2005); Sunset Mortg. v. Agolio, 952 A.2d 65, 67 (Conn. App. Ct. 2008); Gilroy v. Ryberg, 266 Neb. 617, 623, 667 N.W.2d 544, 552 (2003); Robinson v. Saxon Mortgage Services, Inc., 240 S.W.3d 311, 313 (Tex. App. 2007); Arnold v. Palmer, 686 S.E.2d 725, 733 (2009).

5. *E.g.,* regarding application of rules of contract construction to assignments: DeVenney v. Hill, 918 So.2d 106, 113 (Ala. 2005); Schoonmaker v. Lawrence Brunoli, Inc., 828 A.2d 64, 79 (Conn. 2003); Amalgamated Transit Worker's Union v. Pace Suburban Bus Div. of Reg'l Transp. Auth., 943 N.E.2d 36, 41 (Ill. App. Ct. 2011); Spellman v. Shawmut Woodworking & Supply, Inc., 840 N.E.2d 47, 52 (Mass. 2006); Crawford Cent. Sch. Dist. v. Commonwealth, 888 A.2d 616, 623 (Pa. 2005); Rancho La Valencia, Inc. v. Aquaplex, Inc., 297 S.W.3d 781, 783 (Tex. App. 2008); Comet Energy Services, LLC v. Powder River Oil & Gas Ventures, LLC, 239 P.3d 382, 386 (Wyo. 2010).

6. *E.g.,* regarding application of rules of contract construction to insurance policies: W3i Mobile, LLC v. Westchester Fire Ins. Co., 632 F.3d 432, 436 (8th Cir. 2011); Employers Reinsurance Co. v. Superior Court, 74 Cal.Rptr.3d 733, 744 (Cal. Ct. App. 2008); Shelter Mut. Ins. Co. v. Mid–Century Ins. Co., 246 P.3d 651, 662 (Colo. 2011); Hanson v. Lumley Trucking, LLC, 932 N.E.2d 1179, 1182 (Ill. App. Ct. 2010); Employers–Shopmens Local 516 Pension Trust v. Travelers Cas. & Sur. Co. of Am., 235 P.3d 689, 694 (Or. Ct. App. 2010) *review denied*, 249 P.3d 542 (2011); Allemand v. State Farm Ins. Companies, 248 P.3d 111, 112 (Wash. Ct. App. 2011).

7. *E.g.,* regarding application of rules of contract construction to suretyship and guaranty agreements: Tenet Healthsystem TGH, Inc. v. Silver, 52 P.3d 786, 788 (Ariz. Ct. App. 2002); McHenry Sav. Bank v. Autoworks of Wauconda, Inc., 924 N.E.2d 1197, 1205 (Ill. App. Ct. 2010); Grabill Cabinet Co., Inc. v. Sullivan, 919 N.E.2d 1162, 1165 (Ind. Ct. App. 2010); Insurance Co. of Pittsburgh v. David A. Bramble, Inc., 879 A.2d 101 (Md. 2005); Fidelity & Guar. Ins. Co. v. Blount, 63 So.3d 453, 460–61 (Miss. 2011), *reh'g denied* (June 30, 2011); Dobron v. Bunch, 215 P.3d 35, 37 (Nev. 2009).

8. *E.g.,* regarding application of rules of contract construction to various types of licenses, including licenses relating to trademark and copyright: Automation By Design, Inc. v. Raybestos Products Co., 463 F.3d 749 n. 6 (7th Cir. 2006); Geneva Int'l Corp. v. Petrof, Spol, S.R.O., 608 F. Supp. 2d 993, 998 (N.D. Ill. 2009); Reinhardt v. Wal–Mart Stores, Inc., 547 F. Supp. 2d 346, 352 (S.D.N.Y. 2008); Trace Minerals Research, L.C. v. Mineral Res. Int'l, Inc., 505 F. Supp. 2d 1233, 1239 (D. Utah 2007); Intel Corp. v. Broadcom Corp., 173 F. Supp. 2d 201, 210 (D. Del. 2001); Intersport, Inc. v. National Collegiate Athletic Ass'n, 885 N.E.2d 532, 538 (Ill. App. Ct. 2008); Monsanto Co. v. Garst Seed Co., 241 S.W.3d 401, 406 (Mo. Ct. App. 2007).

9. *E.g.,* regarding application of rules of contract construction to various types of leases: Sung v. Hamilton, 710 F. Supp. 2d 1036, 1062 (D. Haw. 2010); North Pac. Processors, Inc. v. City & Borough of Yakutat, Alaska, 113 P.3d 575, 579 (Alaska 2005); Chesapeake Bank of Maryland v. Monro Muffler/Brake, Inc., 891 A.2d 384, 390–91 (Md. Ct. Spec. App. 2006); ASP Properties Group v. Fard, Inc., 35 Cal.Rptr.3d 343, 350 (Ct. App. 2005); Pope v. Lee, 879 A.2d 735, 740 (N.H. 2005); Wal–Mart Stores, Inc. v. Ingles Markets, Inc., 581 S.E.2d 111, 115 (N.C. Ct. App. 2003); Cheek v. Jackson Wax Museum, Inc., 220 P.3d 1288, 1291 (Wyo. 2009).

10. *E.g.,* regarding application of rules of contract construction to oil and gas lease or lease of mineral rights: HS Res., Inc. v. Wingate, 327 F.3d 432, 442 (5th Cir. 2003); Alyce Gaines Johnson Special Trust v. El Paso E & P Co., L.P., 773 F. Supp. 2d 640, 644 (W.D. La. 2011) *aff'd*, 438 F. App'x 340 (5th Cir. 2011); Jacobs v. CNG Transmission Corp., 332 F. Supp. 2d 759, 772 (W.D. Pa. 2004).

11. *E.g.,* regarding rules of contract construction to powers of attorney: Grabowski v. Bank of Boston, 997 F.Supp. 111, 125 (D. Mass. 1997); Estate of Smith v. United States, 979 F.Supp. 279, 282 (D. Vt. 1997); In re Doerfer, 2006 WL 3253482 at *3–4 (Bankr. M.D.N.C. 2006); Schock v. Nash, 732 A.2d 217, 226 (Del. 1999); James v. James, 843 So.2d 304, 308 (Fla. Dist. Ct. App. 2003).

12. *E.g.,* regarding rules of contract construction to declaration of covenants and restrictions: College Book Centers, Inc. v. Carefree Foothills Homeowners' Ass'n, 241 P.3d 897, 901 (Ariz. Ct.

App. 2010); Christian v. Flora, 78 Cal.Rptr.3d 892, 900 (Ct. App. 2008); Harbour Pointe, LLC v. Harbour Landing Condo. Ass'n, Inc., 14 A.3d 284, 288 (Conn. 2011); DLY–Adams Place, LLC v. Waste Mgmt. of Maryland, Inc., 2 A.3d 163 (D.C. 2010); Creveling v. Ingold, 132 P.3d 531, 533 (Mt. 2006); Wise v. Harrington Grove Cmty. Ass'n, Inc., 584 S.E.2d 731, 736 (N.C. 2003); Hill v. Lindner, 769 N.W.2d 427, 430 (N.D. 2009), *reh'g denied* (Aug. 20, 2009); Halls v. White, 715 N.W.2d 577, 580 (S.D. 2006); TX Far W., Ltd. v. Texas Investments Mgmt., Inc., 127 S.W.3d 295, 302 (Tex. App. 2004); South Ridge Homeowners' Ass'n v. Brown, 226 P.3d 758, 759 (Utah Ct. App. 2010).

13. *E.g.,* regarding application of rules of contract construction to arbitration agreements: Welborn Clinic v. MedQuist, Inc., 301 F.3d 634, 639 (7th Cir. 2002); Hodson v. Javitch, Block & Rathbone, LLP, 531 F. Supp. 2d 827, 830 (N.D. Ohio 2008); Giordano ex rel. Estate of Brennan v. Atria Assisted Living, Virginia Beach, L.L.C., 429 F. Supp. 2d 732, 735 (E.D. Va. 2006); Chris Myers Pontiac–GMC, Inc. v. Perot, 991 So.2d 1281, 1284 (Ala. 2008); BFN–Greeley, LLC v. Adair Group, Inc., 141 P.3d 937, 940 (Colo. Ct. App. 2006); Ikalina v. City of Pembroke Pines, 972 So.2d 962, 964 (Fla. Dist. Ct. App. 2007); Kilcher v. Dale, 784 N.W.2d 866, 870 (Minn. Ct. App. 2010); Kunzie v. Jack–In–The–Box, Inc., 330 S.W.3d 476, 480 (Mo. Ct. App. 2010); Buice v. WMA Sec., Inc., 668 S.E.2d 430, 434 (S.C. Ct. App. 2008); In re Wachovia Sec., LLC, 312 S.W.3d 243, 247 (Tex. App. 2010).

14. *E.g.,* regarding application of rules of contract construction to corporate by-laws: In re Color Tile Inc., 475 F.3d 508, 515 (3d Cir. 2007); Matanuska Elec. Ass'n, Inc. v. Waterman, 87 P.3d 820, 823 (Alaska 2004); Meshel v. Ohev Sholom Talmud Torah, 869 A.2d 343, 361 (D.C. 2005); Truck Fin. Specialists, Inc. v. W & S Leasing, Inc., 911 N.E.2d 612, 615 (Ind. Ct. App. 2009); Kansas Heart Hosp., L.L.C. v. Idbeis, 184 P.3d 866, 883 (Kan. 2008); Tackney v. U.S. Naval Acad. Alumni Ass'n, Inc., 971 A.2d 309, 318 (Md. 2009); Okelberry v. West Daniels Land Ass'n, 120 P.3d 34, 39 (Utah Ct. App. 2005); Save Columbia CU Comm. v. Columbia Cmty. Credit Union, 139 P.3d 386, 389 (Wash. Ct. App. 2006); Mueller v. Zimmer, 124 P.3d 340, 359 (Wyo. 2005).

15. *E.g.,* regarding application of rules of contract construction to articles or certificates of incorporation: Coury v. Moss, 529 F.3d 579, 585 (5th Cir. 2008); Heritage Lake Prop. Owners Ass'n, Inc. v. York, 859 N.E.2d 763, 765 (Ind. Ct. App. 2007); Okelberry v. West Daniels Land Ass'n, 120 P.3d 34, 39 (Utah Ct. App. 2005); Ferrill v. North Am. Hunting Retriever Ass'n, Inc., 795 A.2d 1208, 1211 (Vt. 2002).

16. *E.g.,* regarding application of rules of contract construction to corporate charters: Airgas, Inc. v. Air Products & Chemicals, Inc., 8 A.3d 1182, 1188 (Del. 2010); Truck Fin. Specialists, Inc. v. W & S Leasing, Inc., 911 N.E.2d 612, 615 (Ind. Ct. App. 2009); Kansas Heart Hosp., L.L.C. v. Idbeis, 184 P.3d 866, 883 (Kan. 2008); Tackney v. U.S. Naval Acad. Alumni Ass'n, Inc., 971 A.2d 309, 318 (Md. 2009).

17. *E.g.,* regarding application of rules of contract construction to pre-or post-nuptial agreements: Stewart v. Combs, 243 S.W.3d 294, 298 (Ark. 2006) (post-nuptial agreement); Murley v. Wiedamann, 25 So.3d 27, 29 (Fla. Dist. Ct. App. 2009), *reh'g denied* (Jan. 21, 2010), *review denied*, 36 So.3d 657 (Fla. 2010) (prenuptial agreement); Spencer v. Estate of Spencer, 313 S.W.3d 534, 538 (Ky. 2010) (prenuptial contract); Reed v. Reed, 693 N.W.2d 825, 837 (Mich. Ct. App. 2005) (prenuptial agreement); Smith v. Smith, 597 S.E.2d 250, 254 (Va. Ct. App. 2004) (prenuptial agreement); Gamache v. Smurro, 904 A.2d 91, 95 (Vt. 2006) (prenuptial agreement).

18. *E.g.,* regarding application of rules of contract construction to separation agreements: Krapf v. Krapf, 771 N.E.2d 819, 822 (Mass. App. Ct. 2002) *aff'd*, 786 N.E.2d 318 (2003); Ritter v. Mantissa Inv. Corp., 864 A.2d 601, 607 (R.I. 2005); Nicholson v. Nicholson, 663 S.E.2d 74, 79 (S.C. Ct. App. 2008); Auten v. Snipes, 636 S.E.2d 644, 646 (S.C. Ct. App. 2006).

19. *E.g.,* regarding application of rules of contract construction to settlement agreements: Hartley v. Hartley, 205 P.3d 342, 346 (Alaska 2009); Artman v. Hoy, 257 S.W.3d 864, 869 (Ark. 2007); Giordano v. Giordano, 14 A.3d 1058, 1062 (Conn. App. Ct. 2011); Knoll v. Knoll, 937 So.2d 1163, 1165 (Fla. Dist. Ct. App. 2006); Shorter v. Shorter, 851 N.E.2d 378, 382 (Ind. Ct. App. 2006); MacInnes v. MacInnes, 677 N.W.2d 889, 891 (Mich. Ct. App. 2004); West v. West, 891 So.2d 203, 210 (Miss. 2004); Crispo v. Crispo, 909 A.2d 308, 312 (Pa. Super. Ct. 2006); Bryant v. McDougal, 636 S.E.2d 897, 900 (Va. Ct. App. 2006); Cellers v. Adami, 216 P.3d 1134, 1137 (Wyo. 2009).

20. *E.g.,* regarding application of rules of contract construction to a divorce decree: Cohen v. Frey, 157 P.3d 482, 486 (Ariz. Ct. App. 2007); In re Marriage of Gray, 66 Cal.Rptr.3d 87, 102 (Ct. App. 2007); Grecian v. Grecian, 97 P.3d 468, 470 (Idaho Ct. App. 2004); Dewbrew v. Dewbrew, 849 N.E.2d 636, 645 (Ind. Ct. App. 2006); Overholtzer v. Overholtzer, 884 N.E.2d 358, 361 (Ind. Ct. App. 2008); Smith v. Smith, 748 N.W.2d 258, 260 (Mich. Ct. App. 2008); Fucito v. Francis, 622 S.E.2d 660, 664 (N.C. Ct. App. 2005); Chapman v. Abbot, 251 S.W.3d 612, 616 (Tex. App. 2007); Mitchell v. Mitchell, 248 P.3d 65, 66 (Utah App. 2011).

21. *See, e.g.,* regarding tests for determining whether a letter of intent is contractually binding: In re Heigle, 401 B.R. 752, 767 (Bankr. S.D. Miss. 2008); Midtown Realty, Inc. v. Hussain, 712 So.2d 1249, 1251 (Fla. Dist. Ct. App. 1998); Gurley v. King, 183 S.W.3d 30, 42 (Tenn. Ct. App. 2005); Kelly v. Rio Grande Computerland Group, 128 S.W.3d 759, 767 (Tex. App. 2004).

22. *E.g.,* the following use intent as their "polestar" in contract construction: Century 21 Real Estate, LLC v. Gateway Realty, Inc., 2011 WL 1322006 at *3 (D.N.J. 2011) (unpublished case applying New Jersey law); Global Ground Support, LLC v. Glazer Enterprises, Inc., 581 F. Supp. 2d 669, 675 (E.D. Pa. 2008) (applying Pennsylvania law); TECO Barge Line, Inc. v. Hagan, 15 So.3d 863, 865 (Fla. Dist. Ct. App. 2009).

23. *E.g.,* the following use intent as their "touchstone" in contract construction: Randall & Blake, Inc. v. Metro Wastewater Reclamation Dist., 77 P.3d 804, 806 (Colo. Ct. App. 2003); Pine Ridge Realty, Inc. v. Massachusetts Bay Ins. Co., 752 A.2d 595, 601 (Me. 2000); Tanner Elec. Co-op. v. Puget Sound Power & Light Co., 911 P.2d 1301, 1310 (Wash. 1996).

24. *E.g.,* the following use intent as their "cornerstone" in contract construction: La Quinta Corp. v. Heartland Properties LLC, 603 F.3d 327, 336 (6th Cir. 2010) (applying Wisconsin law); Stamm v. Holter, 797 N.W.2d 935 (Wis. Ct. App. 2011).

25. *E.g.,* regarding the relevant intent expressed in the contract: Cachil Dehe Band of Wintun Indians of Colusa Indian Cmty. v. California, 618 F.3d 1066, 1073 (9th Cir. 2010) (applying California law); Kingsly Compression, Inc. v. Mountain V Oil & Gas, Inc., 745 F. Supp. 2d 628, 634–35 (W.D. Pa. 2010) (applying Pennsylvania law); Ryko Mfg. Co. v. Nationwide Wash Sys., Inc., 736 F. Supp. 2d 1226, 1234 (S.D. Iowa 2010); DeRyke v. Teets, 702 S.E.2d 205, 207 (Ga. 2010); Town of Plainfield v. Paden Eng'g Co., Inc., 943 N.E.2d 904, 909 (Ind. Ct. App. 2011); Desautels v. Desautels, 915 N.Y.S.2d 337, 341 (App. Div. 2011).

26. Central States, Se. & Sw. Areas Pension Fund v. Waste Mgmt. of Michigan, Inc., 674 F.3d 630, 634 (7th Cir. 2012).

27. *E.g.,* regarding the definition of "ambiguity" as applicable to a provision that has more than one *reasonable* and *plausible* meaning: Okeechobee Landfill, Inc. v. Republic Services of Florida, Ltd. P'ship, 931 So.2d 942, 945 (Fla. Dist. Ct. App. 2006); Pub. Relations Bd., Inc. v. United Van Lines, Inc., 373 N.E.2d 727, 728 (Ill. App. Ct. 1978); Cadleway Properties, Inc. v. Bayview Loan Servicing, LLC, 338 S.W.3d 280, 286 (Ky. Ct. App. 2010); Ubom v. SunTrust Bank, 17 A.3d 168, 173 (Md. Ct. Spec. App. 2011); Am. Bank of St. Paul v. Coating Specialties, Inc., 787 N.W.2d 202, 205 (Minn. Ct. App. 2010), *review denied* (Oct. 27, 2010); Burrus v. HBE Corp., 211 S.W.3d 613, 617 (Mo. Ct. App. 2006); Mark V, Inc. v. Mellekas, 845 P.2d 1232, 1235 (N.M. 1993); Hall v. Cherokee Nation, 162 P.3d 979, 984 (Okla. Civ. App. 2007); Tyco Valves & Controls, L.P. v. Colorado, 365 S.W.3d 750, 766 (Tex. App. 2012); Virginia Elec. & Power Co. v. Norfolk S. Ry. Co., 683 S.E.2d 517, 526 (Va. 2009); Lee v. Lee, 721 S.E.2d 53, 56 (W.Va. 2011); Town Bank v. City Real Estate Dev., LLC, 793 N.W.2d 476, 484 (Wis. 2010).

28. *E.g.,* Allstate Life Ins. Co. v. BFA Ltd. P'ship, 948 A.2d 318, 323 (Conn. 2008); In re Lock Revocable Living Trust, 123 P.3d 1241, 1247 (Haw. 2005); Ubom v. SunTrust Bank, 17 A.3d 168, 173 (Md. Ct. Spec. App. 2011); Tyco Valves & Controls, L.P. v. Colorado, 365 S.W.3d 750, 766 (Tex. App. 2012); Virginia Elec. & Power Co. v. Norfolk S. Ry. Co., 683 S.E.2d 517, 526 (Va. 2009).

29. Young Dental Mfg. Co. v. Engineered Products, Inc., 838 S.W.2d 154, 155–56 (Mo. Ct. App. 1992)

30. Peterson v. Sykes–Peterson, 37 A.3d 173, 176 (Conn. Ct. App. 2012), *cert. denied*, 42 A.3d 390 (Conn. 2012).

31. *See, e.g.,* Bettis v. Hall, 2012 WL 487044 at 6 (D. Kan. 2012) (under Kansas law, if a contract is clear and can be carried out as written, there is no room for construction).

32. *E.g.,* regarding admission of extrinsic evidence to clarify an ambiguity: J & M Associates, Inc. v. Callahan, 753 F. Supp. 2d 1183, 1205 (S.D. Ala. 2010) (applying Alabama law) citing Marriott Intern., Inc. v. deCelle, 722 So.2d 760, 762 (Ala.1998); ExxonMobil Oil Corp. v. Amex Const. Co., Inc., 702 F. Supp. 2d 942, 963 (N.D. Ill. 2010); Allstate Ins. Co. v. Watson, 195 S.W.3d 609, 611–12 (Tenn. 2006); Williams v. Williams, 246 S.W.3d 207, 211 (Tex. App. 2007); City of Grantsville v. Redevelopment Agency of Tooele City, 233 P.3d 461, 470 (Utah 2010); John D. Stump & Associates, Inc. v. Cunningham Mem'l Park, Inc., 419 S.E.2d 699, 707 (W.Va. 1992); King v. Rice, 191 P.3d 946, 951 (Wash. Ct. App. 2008).

33. Okeechobee Landfill, Inc. v. Republic Services of Florida, Ltd. P'ship, 931 So.2d 942, 945 (Fla. Dist. Ct. App. 2006).

34. *E.g.,* Belager–Price v. Lingle, 28 So.3d 706, 711 (Miss. Ct. App. 2010).

35. Houston v. Willis, 24 So.3d 412, 419–20 (Miss. Ct. App. 2009).

36. *See* Restatement (Second) of Contracts § 210 (1981). *E.g.,* regarding meaning of "integrated agreement": Casey v. Semco Energy, Inc., 92 P.3d 379, 383 (Alaska 2004); Anderson v. Preferred Stock Food Markets, Inc., 854 P.2d 1194, 1197 (Ariz. Ct. App. 1993); Abercrombie v. Hayden Corp., 883 P.2d 845 (Or. 1994); Town Bank v. City Real Estate Dev., LLC, 793 N.W.2d 476, 486 (Wis. 2010).

37. *E.g.,* regarding application of the parol evidence rule to bar evidence of prior negotiations or agreements that would *vary* or *contradict* the terms of an integrated written contract: Lower Kuskokwim Sch. Dist. v. Alaska Diversified Contractors, Inc., 734 P.2d 62, 63 (Alaska 1987); Casa Herrera, Inc. v. Beydoun, 83 P.3d 497, 501–02 (Cal. 2004); Schilberg Integrated Metals Corp. v. Continental Cas. Co., 819 A.2d 773, 794 (Conn. 2003); Jenkins v. Eckerd Corp., 913 So.2d 43, 53 (Fla. Dist. Ct. App. 2005); J & B Steel Contractors, Inc. v. C. Iber & Sons, Inc., 617 N.E.2d 405, 409 (Ill. App. Ct. 1993) *aff'd,* 642 N.E.2d 1215 (1994); Williams v. Spitzer Autoworld Canton, L.L.C., 913 N.E.2d 410, 415–16 (Ohio 2009); Gish v. ECI Services of Oklahoma, Inc., 162 P.3d 223, 231 (Okla. Civ. App. 2006); Town Bank v. City Real Estate Dev., LLC, 793 N.W.2d 476, 484 (Wis. 2010).

38. Jenkins v. Eckerd Corp., 913 So.2d 43, 53 (Fla. Dist. Ct. App. 2005). *E.g.,* Flower v. T.R.A. Indus., Inc., 127 Wash.App. 13, 28, 111 P.3d 1192, 1200 (2005) ("The rule forbids the use of parol evidence to add to, subtract from, modify, or contradict the terms of a fully integrated contract."

39. See note 32, *supra.*

40. *E.g.,* Italian Cowboy Partners, Ltd. v. Prudential Ins. Co. of Am., 341 S.W.3d 323 (Tex. 2011).

41. *E.g.,* regarding admission of evidence concerning the parties' circumstances to resolve an ambiguity: Clark v. Hectus & Strause PLLC, 345 S.W.3d 857, 860 (Ky. Ct. App. 2011), *review denied* (Sept. 15, 2011); Birch Broad., Inc. v. Capitol Broad. Corp., Inc., 13 A.3d 224, 228 (N.H. 2010); Township of White v. Castle Ridge Dev. Corp., 16 A.3d 399, 404 (N.J. Super. Ct. App. Div. 2011).

42. Spectrum Glass Co., Inc. v. Public Util. Dist. No. 1 of Snohomish County, 119 P.3d 854, 858 (Wash. Ct. App. 2005).

43. *Id.*

44. Mark V, Inc. v. Mellekas, 845 P.2d 1232, 1235 (N.M. 1993).

45. *Id.*

46. Township of White v. Castle Ridge Dev. Corp., 16 A.3d 399, 404 (N.J. Super. Ct. App. Div. 2011).

47. *E.g.,* regarding use of recitals in determining the proper construction of the contract and the parties' intent: Farouki v. Petra Int'l Banking Corp., 811 F. Supp. 2d 388, 407–08 (D.D.C. 2011); County Com'rs of Charles County, Md. v. Panda–Brandywine, L.P., 663 F. Supp. 2d 424, 430 (D. Md. 2009) *aff'd sub nom.* County Com'rs of Charles County, Maryland v. Panda–Brandywine, L.P., 401 F. App'x 831 (4th Cir. 2010); KMS Fusion, Inc. v. United States, 36 Fed. Cl. 68, 78 (1996) *aff'd,* 108 F.3d 1393 (Fed. Cir. 1997); Gwaltney v. Russell, 984 So.2d 1125, 1135 (Ala. 2007); Burch v. Premier Homes, LLC, 131 Cal.Rptr.3d 855, 867 (Ct. App. 2011); Hagene v. Derek Polling Const., 902 N.E.2d 1269, 1274–75 (Ill. App. Ct. 2009); Andersen ex rel. Andersen, Weinroth & Co., L.P. v. Weinroth, 849 N.Y.S.2d 210, 219 (App. Div. 2007); All Metals Fabricating, Inc. v. Ramer Concrete, Inc., 338 S.W.3d 557, 561 (Tex. App. 2009).

48. *E.g.,* regarding courts' preference for a reading favoring validity of the contract: Laeroc Waikiki Parkside, LLC v. K.S.K. (Oahu) Ltd. P'ship, 166 P.3d 961, 981 (Haw. 2007); Rabius v. Brandon, 257 S.W.3d 641, 646 (Mo. Ct. App. 2008); Credit Suisse First Boston v. Utrecht–Am. Fin. Co., 915 N.Y.S.2d 531, 535 (N.Y. App. Div. 2011); Hicks v. Castille, 313 S.W.3d 874, 880 (Tex. App. 2010), *reconsideration en banc denied* (June 30, 2010), *review denied* (Jan. 14, 2011).

49. Town of Kearny v. Discount City of Old Bridge, Inc., 16 A.3d 300, 316 (N.J. 2011) (court interprets the words chosen by the drafter not in isolation, but as a whole; in construing any *part* of the contract, the court looks to the entire document and will read the contract as a whole and read every part with reference to every other).

50. *E.g.,* regarding reading the contract as a whole to give effect to all provisions: Southern Wine & Spirits of Nevada v. Mountain Valley Spring Co., LLC, 646 F.3d 526, 531 (8th Cir. 2011); Engelhard Corp. v. N.L.R.B., 437 F.3d 374, 381 (3d Cir. 2006); Sparveri v. Town of Rocky Hill, 656 F. Supp. 2d 297, 309 (D. Conn. 2009); KLLM, Inc. v. Watson Parma, Inc., 634 F. Supp. 2d 699, 704 (S.D. Miss. 2009); Hallingby v. Hallingby, 693 F. Supp. 2d 360, 365 (S.D.N.Y. 2010); McNeil Eng'g & Land Surveying, LLC v. Bennett, 268 P.3d 854, 857 (Utah Ct. App. 2011); Rimov v. Schultz, 253 P.3d 462, 466 (Wash. Ct. App. 2011).

51. Wintermute v. Kansas Bankers Sur. Co., 630 F.3d 1063, 1068 (8th Cir. 2011).

52. *E.g.,* regarding the requirement that courts "harmonize" provisions and give reasonable meaning to all parts: NVT Technologies, Inc. v. United States, 370 F.3d 1153, 1159 (Fed. Cir. 2004); Coldwell Banker Roth Wehrly Graber v. Laub Bros. Oil Co., Inc., 949 N.E.2d 1273 (Ind. Ct. App. 2011); Bunnell Farms Co. v. Samuel Gary, Jr. & Associates, 47 P.3d 804, 806 (2002); In re Estate of Harris, 840 So.2d 742, 745 (Miss. Ct. App. 2003); State ex rel. Missouri Highway & Transp. Comm'n v. Maryville Land P'ship, 62 S.W.3d 485, 492 (Mo. Ct. App. 2001).

53. Gillmor v. Macey, 121 P.3d 57, 65 (Utah Ct. App. 2005).

54. *E.g.,* regarding reading language in its plain and ordinary sense: Metropolitan Dist. Comm'n v. Connecticut Res. Recovery Auth., 22 A.3d 651, 655 (Conn. App. Ct. 2011); Pearson v. Caterpillar Fin. Services Corp., 60 So.3d 1168, 1172 (Fla. Dist. Ct. App. 2011); Coldwell Banker Roth Wehrly Graber v. Laub Bros. Oil Co., Inc., 949 N.E.2d 1273 (Ind. Ct. App. 2011); DeRossett v. Duke Energy Carolinas, LLC, 698 S.E.2d 455, 460 (N.C. Ct. App. 2010); Hunter v. Reece, 253 P.3d 497, 502 (Wyo. 2011).

55. McCarty v. Montgomery, 290 S.W.3d 525, 532 (Tex. App. 2009). *E.g.,* Peterson v. Sykes–Peterson, 37 A.3d 173, 176–77 (Conn. Ct. App. 2012), *supra* note 30; Greene v. City of Waterbury, 12 A.3d 623, 627 (2011).

56. Lindskov v. Lindskov, 2011 SD 34, 800 N.W.2d 715, 718 (S.D. 2011).

57. *See* 11 Williston on Contracts § 32:6 (4th ed.).

58. State ex rel. Goddard v. R.J. Reynolds Tobacco Co., 75 P.3d 1075, 1080 (Ariz. Ct. App. 2003).

59. Sacks v. Rothberg, 569 A.2d 150, 157 (D.C. 1990) ("While the same words appearing in different parts of a contract should generally be given consistent meaning, that consistency alone does not erase an ambiguity arising from differing contexts when the words serve a different purpose.")

60. *E.g.,* regarding preference for rational meaning: Southern Wine & Spirits of Nevada v. Mountain Valley Spring Co., LLC, 646 F.3d 526, 531 (8th Cir. 2011); Southern Wine & Spirits of Nevada v. Mountain Valley Spring Co., LLC, 646 F.3d 526 (8th Cir. 2011); Hallingby v. Hallingby, 693 F. Supp. 2d 360, 365 (S.D.N.Y. 2010) *aff'd*, 453 F. App'x 121 (2d Cir. 2012); KLLM, Inc. v. Watson Parma, Inc., 634 F. Supp. 2d 699, 704 (S.D. Miss. 2009); Sparveri v. Town of Rocky Hill, 656 F. Supp. 2d 297, 309 (D. Conn. 2009); Farrington's Owners' Ass'n v. Conway Lake Resorts, Inc., 878 A.2d 504, 507 (Me. 2005); McCarty v. Montgomery, 290 S.W.3d 525, 532 (Tex. App. 2009); Rimov v. Schultz, 253 P.3d 462, 466 (Wash. Ct. App. 2011).

61. *E.g.,* applying doctrine of last antecedent: Johnson v. Manpower Prof'l Services, Inc., 442 F. App'x 977, 984–85 (5th Cir. 2011); J.C. Penney Life Ins. Co. v. Pilosi, 393 F.3d 356, 365 (3d Cir. 2004); Tarsitano ex rel. Twp. of High Sch. Dist. 211 v. Board of Educ. of Twp. of High Sch. Dist. 211, 896 N.E.2d 359, 363–64 (Ill. App. Ct. 2008); Duane Reade, Inc. v. Cardtronics, LP, 863 N.Y.S.2d 14, 17 (App. Div. 2008); McGarry v. Hansen, 120 P.3d 525, 527 (Or. Ct. App. 2005)

A court might decline to apply doctrine of last antecedent if result would be contrary to the meaning of the sentence: Marler v. U–Store–It Mini Warehouse Co., 416 F. App'x 49, 51–52 (11th Cir. 2011); Love Terminal Partners, L.P. v. City of Dallas, Tex., 527 F. Supp. 2d 538, 558–59 (N.D. Tex. 2007); Miller v. Kase, 789 So.2d 1095, 1098–99 (Fla. Dist. Ct. App. 2001); Stewman Ranch, Inc. v. Double M. Ranch, Ltd., 192 S.W.3d 808, 812–13 (Tex. App. 2006); Estate of Fisher v. Fisher, 645 N.W.2d 841, 845 (S.D. 2002).

62. *E.g.,* explaining doctrine of last antecedent: Marler v. U–Store–It Mini Warehouse Co., 416 F. App'x 49, 51–52 (11th Cir. 2011); Red River Holdings, LLC v. United States, 87 Fed. Cl. 768, 794–95 (2009); J.C. Penney Life Ins. Co. v. Pilosi, 393 F.3d 356, 365 (3d Cir. 2004); Miller v. Kase, 789 So.2d 1095, 1098–99 (Fla. Dist. Ct. App. 2001); Tarsitano ex rel. Twp. of High Sch. Dist. 211 v. Board of Educ. of Twp. of High Sch. Dist. 211, 896 N.E.2d 359, 363–64 (Ill. App. Ct. 2008); Duane Reade, Inc. v. Cardtronics, LP, 863 N.Y.S.2d 14, 17 (App. Div. 2008). Stewman Ranch, Inc. v. Double M. Ranch, Ltd., 192 S.W.3d 808, 812 (Tex. App. 2006) McGarry v. Hansen, 120 P.3d 525, 527 (Or. Ct. App. 2005); Estate of Fisher v. Fisher, 645 N.W.2d 841, 845 (S.D. 2002).

63. *E.g.,* regarding priority of specific over general language: Holland v. Holland, 700 S.E.2d 573, 575 (Ga. 2010); Barkley Estate Cmty. Ass'n, Inc. v. Huskey, 30 So.3d 992, 998 (La. Ct. App. 2010); Andersen v. Andersen, 892 N.Y.S.2d 553, 555 (App. Div. 2010); Mark VII Transp. Co., Inc. v. Responsive Trucking, Inc., 339 S.W.3d 643, 648 (Tenn. Ct. App. 2009), *appeal denied* (Mar. 15, 2010); Condominium Services, Inc. v. First Owners' Ass'n of Forty Six Hundred Condo., Inc., 709 S.E.2d 163, 170 (Va. 2011); Trinder v. Connecticut Attorneys Title Ins. Co., 22 A.3d 493, 500 (Vt. 2011); Scherer, II v. Laramie Reg'l Airport Bd., 236 P.3d 996, 1003 (Wyo. 2010).

64. *E.g.,* regarding decisions that have followed the principle of giving priority to the earlier provision: Glenn Const. Co., LLC v. Bell Aerospace Services, Inc., 785 F. Supp. 2d 1258, 1297 (M.D. Ala. 2011); Copacabana Records, Inc. v. WEA Latina, Inc., 791 So.2d 1179, 1180 (Fla. Dist.

Ct. App. 2001); Coker v. Coker, 595 S.E.2d 556, 557–58 (Ga. Ct. App. 2004); Honigsbaum's, Inc. v. Stuyvesant Plaza, Inc., 577 N.Y.S.2d 165, 166 (App. Div. 1991); Park Place Ctr. Enterprises, Inc. v. Park Place Mall Associates, L.P., 836 S.W.2d 113, 116 (Tenn. Ct. App. 1992); Nevarez v. Ehrlich, 296 S.W.3d 738, 742 (Tex. App. 2009).

65. *E.g.,* regarding decisions that have followed the principle of giving priority to provisions of greater importance: National City Bank v. Engler, 777 N.W.2d 762, 765 (Minn. Ct. App. 2010), *review denied* (Apr. 20, 2010); Israel v. Chabra, 601 F.3d 57, 63 (2d Cir. 2010) (in reconciling conflicting provisions under New York law that cannot be harmonized, the court should first inquire which clause was more principal to the contract; if this approach does not resolve the question, the first clause governs).

66. *E.g.,* regarding decisions stating that a provision that contributes to the dominant purpose of the contract takes priority over a conflicting subsidiary provision: Golden Peanut Co. v. Bass, 563 S.E.2d 116, 120 (Ga. 2002); Wheatly v. Sook Suh, 525 A.2d 340, 344 (N.J. Super. App. Div. 1987).

67. Israel v. State Farm Mut. Auto. Ins. Co., 789 A.2d 974, 977 (Conn. 2002).

68. United States v. Seckinger, 397 U.S. 203, 216, 90 S.Ct. 880, 887–88 (1970) (contract construed against Government).

69. New Castle County, Del. v. National Union Fire Ins. Co. of Pittsburgh, Pa., 174 F.3d 338, 343–44 (3d Cir. 1999).

70. Valley Realty Co. v. United States, 96 Fed. Cl. 16, 31–32 (Fed. Cl. 2010).

71. Premier Title Co. v. Donahue, 765 N.E.2d 513, 517 (Ill. App. Ct. 2002); Baker v. America's Mortg. Servicing, Inc., 58 F.3d 321, 327 (7th Cir. 1995) (discussing Illinois' application of doctrine).

72. *E.g.,* some courts have said that *contra proferentum* is a rule of last resort to be applied only if all other rules of construction fail to resolve ambiguity: FabArc Steel Supply, Inc. v. Composite Const. Sys., Inc., 914 So.2d 344, 358 (Ala. 2005); Moland v. Indus. Claim Appeals Office of State, 111 P.3d 507, 511 (Colo. Ct. App. 2004); ConAgra Foods, Inc. v. Lexington Ins. Co., 21 A.3d 62, 72 (Del. 2011), *reh'g denied* (June 17, 2011); Farnsworth v. Dairymen's Creamery Ass'n, 876 P.2d 148, 152 (Idaho Ct. App. 1994); Premier Title Co. v. Donahue, 765 N.E.2d 513, 517 (Ill. 2002); U.S. Life Ins. Co. in City of New York v. Wilson, 18 A.3d 110, 121 (Md. Ct. Spec. App. 2011); Pacifico v. Pacifico, 920 A.2d 73, 78 (N.J. 2007).

73. *E.g.,* Anglo–Dutch Petroleum Int'l, Inc. v. Greenberg Peden, P.C., 267 S.W.3d 454, 469 (Tex. App. 2008); Klapp v. United Ins. Group Agency, Inc., 663 N.W.2d 447, 454–55 (Mich. 2003).

74. *E.g.,* some courts might not apply the doctrine of *contra proferentem* against the drafting party when both parties were sophisticated: The Sch. Bd. of Broward County v. The Great Am. Ins. Co., 807 So.2d 750, 752 (Fla. Dist. Ct. App. 2002) Cummins, Inc. v. Atlantic Mut. Ins. Co., 867 N.Y.S.2d 81, 83 (App. Div. 2008).

75. Colgan v. Agway, Inc., 553 A.2d 143, 145 (Vt. 1988).

76. *E.g.,* regarding strict construction of restrictive covenants in favor of free and unrestricted use of land: Chick–Fil–A, Inc. v. CFT Dev., LLC, 652 F. Supp. 2d 1252, 1260 (M.D. Fla. 2009) *aff'd*, 370 F. App'x. 55 (11th Cir. 2010); LEG Investments v. Boxler, 107 Cal.Rptr.3d 519, 528 (Ct. App. 2010); City of Indianapolis v. Kahlo, 938 N.E.2d 734, 742 (Ind. Ct. App. 2010), *reh'g denied* (Feb. 23, 2011); Wills Grove Homeowners Ass'n v. Yaeckel, 702 S.E.2d 556 (N.C. Ct. App. 2010); Hill v. Lindner, 769 N.W.2d 427, 430 (N.D. 2009), *reh'g denied* (Aug. 20, 2009); Ashley v. Kehew, 992 A.2d 983, 989 (R.I. 2010); Hardy v. Aiken, 631 S.E.2d 539, 542 (S.C. 2006).

77. *E.g.,* regarding strict construction of insurance policies: In re Katrina Canal Breaches Litig., 495 F.3d 191, 207 (5th Cir. 2007); TRB Investments, Inc. v. Fireman's Fund Ins. Co., 145 P.3d 472, 477 (2006); Hale v. State Farm Florida Ins. Co., 51 So.3d 1169, 1171 (Fla. Dist. Ct. App. 2010), *reh'g denied* (Feb. 15, 2011); Western Pac. Mut. Ins. Co. v. Davies, 601 S.E.2d 363, 369 (Ga. Ct. App. 2004); JAM Inc. v. Nautilus Ins. Co., 128 S.W.3d 879, 893 (Mo. Ct. App. 2004); Jordan v. Allstate Ins. Co., 245 P.3d 1214, 1219 (N.M. 2010), *reh'g denied* (Dec. 3, 2010); Penna v. Federal Ins. Co., 814 N.Y.S.2d 226, 228 (App. Div. 2006); Change, Inc. v. Westfield Ins. Co., 542 S.E.2d 475, 478 (W. Va. 2000).

78. *E.g.,* regarding strict construction of power of attorney: Stafford v. Crane, 382 F.3d 1175, 1183 (10th Cir. 2004); In re Porter, 2008 WL 114914 (Bankr. N.D.W. Va. 2008); Smith v. Wachovia Bank, N.A., 33 So.3d 1191, 1195 (Ala. 2009); Archbold v. Reifenrath, 744 N.W.2d 701, 708 (Neb. 2008); Mountjoy v. Smith, 78 Va. Cir. 152 (Va. Cir. Ct. 2009) (unreported case) *aff'd*, 694 S.E.2d 598 (Va. 2010).

But see Estate of Smith v. United States, 979 F.Supp. 279, 286 (D. Vt. 1997) (stating that in Vermont, power is construed neither strictly nor liberally but so as to carry out the intention of the principal) quoting Conger v. Gruenig, 117 Vt. 559, 561, 96 A.2d 821, 822 (1953).

79. *E.g.,* regarding strict construction of a guaranty or suretyship contract: Mauna Loa Vacation Ownership, L.P., a Hawaiian limited partnership v. Accelerated Assets, L.L.C., an Arizona limited liability company, 2005 WL 2410676 at *5 (D. Ariz. 2005); Fielbon Dev. Co., LLC v. Colony Bank of Houston County, 660 S.E.2d 801, 806 (Ga. Ct. App. 2008).

Endnotes for Chapter 14: Introduction to Legislative Drafting

1. *E.g.,* regarding authority that "shall" is mandatory and "may" is permissive: State v. Rogers, 251 P.3d 1042, 1044 (Ariz. Ct. App. 2010), *review denied* (May 24, 2011); State v. Mosqueda, 252 P.3d 563 (Idaho Ct. App. 2010), *reh'g denied* (Mar. 8, 2011), *review denied* (June 13, 2011); Illinois Dept. of Healthcare & Family Services ex rel. Wiszowaty v. Wiszowaty, 942 N.E.2d 1253, 1256 (Ill. 2011); In re Cierra L.,13 A.3d 209, 211 (N.H. 2010); Puckett v. Norandal USA, Inc., 710 S.E.2d 356, 362 (N.C. Ct. App. 2011); State ex rel. Stewart v. City of Salem, 251 P.3d 783, 786 (Or. Ct. App. 2011); In re K.R.P., 247 P.3d 491, 495 (Wash. Ct. App. 2011); Heritage Farms, Inc. v. Markel Ins. Co., 793 N.W.2d 896, 899 (Wis. 2010), *review granted*, 797 N.W.2d 523 (2011).

2. In re Rufus T., 949 N.E.2d 277, 281 (2011).

3. West v. McDonald, 18 A.3d 526, 534–35 (R.I. 2011).

4. West v. McDonald, 18 A.3d 526, 534–35 (R.I. 2011).

5. *See* note 1, supra, and accompanying text.

6. *E.g.,* regarding commentary by courts on verb tense: Matus v. Board of Admin. of California Pub. Employees' Ret. Sys., 99 Cal.Rptr.3d 341, 348 (Ct. App. 2009), *review denied* (Dec. 17, 2009); Pfeiffer v. City of Tampa, 470 So.2d 10, 16–17 (Fla. Dist. Ct. App. 1985); Martinez v. State, 24 S.W.3d 10, 16 (Mo. Ct. App. 2000); State ex rel. Miller v. Anthony, 647 N.E.2d 1368, 1373 (Ohio 1995); State v. Root, 123 P.3d 281, 284 (Or. Ct. App. 2005) quoting Martin v. City of Albany, 880 P.2d 926 (Or. 1994).

7. Matus v. Board of Admin. of California Pub. Employees' Ret. Sys., 99 Cal.Rptr.3d 341, 348 (Ct. App. 2009), *review denied* (Dec. 17, 2009).

8. Martin v. City of Albany, 880 P.2d 926, 930 (Or. 1994).

9. *See* Texas Legislative Council, Texas Legislative Council Drafting Manual at 100 (2011).

10. *See, e.g.,* Manual of Legislative Drafting for the Use of Legislative Staff, Pt. 2, Ch.2 at 57–59 (Alaska 2007); Manual for Drafting Legislation (The Florida Senate 2009), Ch. 2 at 16; Texas Legislative Council, Texas Legislative Council Drafting Manual, at 109 (2011).

11. *See, e.g.,* Arizona Legislative Council, Bill Drafting Manual, page 82 (2009); Hawaii Legislative Drafting Manual 27–28 (9th ed., 2007); Counsel to the Senate and Counsel to the House of Representatives of Massachusetts, Legislative Drafting Manual Pt. 2 at 15 (5th ed. 2010); Montana Legislative Services Division, Bill Drafting Manual, 24–26 (2010); Texas Legislative Council, Texas Legislative Council Drafting Manual, 104–05 (2011); State of Washington Statute Law Committee, Bill Drafting Guide 2011, Part IV(1)(j).

12. *E.g.,* Bank Bldg. & Equip. Corp. of Am. v. Georgia State Bank, 209 S.E.2d 82, 84 (Ga. Ct. App. 1974); Cochrane v. Florida E. R. R. Co., 145 So. 217, 218 (1932).

13. *See, e.g.,* Arizona Legislative Council, The Arizona Legislative Bill Drafting Manual, page 83 (2009); Legislative Drafting Manual for the State of Arkansas, Pt. 4 at 46 (Non–Appropriations Bills Only); Kentucky General Assembly, Bill Drafting Manual, page 36 (2011); Maine Legislative Drafting Manual, Pt. III, Ch. 1 at 100 (2009); Texas Legislative Council, Texas Legislative Council Drafting Manual, page 104 (February 2011).

Endnotes for Chapter 15: Drafting Private Rule–Making Documents

1. Patch v. Springfield Sch. Dist., 989 A.2d 500, 504 (Vt. 2009).

2. *Id.*

3. Ostayan v. Nordhoff Townhomes Homeowners Assn., Inc., 1 Cal.Rptr.3d 528, 533 (Ct. App. 2003).

4. City of Indianapolis v. Kahlo, 938 N.E.2d 734, 742 (Ind. Ct. App. 2010), *reh'g denied* (Feb. 23, 2011).

5. *E.g.,* regarding disfavored status of use restriction: Bickford v. Yancey Dev. Co., Inc., 574 S.E.2d 349, 351 (Ga. Ct. App. 2002) *aff'd,* 585 S.E.2d 78 (2003); Rodeheaver v. State, 917 A.2d 1122, 1125 (Md. Ct. Spec. App. 2007); Schneider v. Forsythe Group, Inc., 782 S.W.2d 139, 143 (Mo.

Ct. App. 1989); Agua Fria Save The Open Space Ass'n v. Rowe, 255 P.2d 390, 394 (N.M. Ct. App. 2011); National Urban Ventures, Inc. v. City of Niagara Falls, 914 N.Y.S.2d 801, 802 (App. Div. 2010); Hill v. Lindner, 769 N.W.2d 427, 430 (N.D. 2009), *reh'g denied* (Aug. 20, 2009); Farrell v. Deuble, 888 N.E.2d 514, 516 (Ohio Ct. App. 2008); Penny Creek Associates, LLC v. Fenwick Tarragon Apartments, LLC, 651 S.E.2d 617, 620 (S.C. Ct. App. 2007); Lakewood Racquet Club, Inc. v. Jensen, 232 P.3d 1147, 1150 (Wash. Ct. App. 2010); Vargas Ltd. P'ship v. Four H Ranches Architectural Control Comm., 202 P.3d 1045, 1050 (Wyo. 2009).

6. Penny Creek Associates, LLC v. Fenwick Tarragon Apartments, LLC, 651 S.E.2d 617, 620 (S.C. Ct. App. 2007)

7. Farrell v. Deuble, 888 N.E.2d 514, 516 (Ohio Ct. App. 2008).

8. Schwartz v. Banbury Woods Homeowners Ass'n, Inc., 675 S.E.2d 382, 388 (N.C. Ct. App. 2009) *review denied*, 694 S.E.2d 391 (2010).

9. *Id.* at 389.

10. *Id.*

11. *See* Colo. Rev. Stat. Ann. § 38–33.3–201(1) (West 2012).

12. Abril Meadows Homeowner's Ass'n v. Castro, 211 P.3d 64, 67 (Colo. Ct. App. 2009).

13. CTS Corp. v. Dynamics Corp. of America 481 U.S. 69, 89–90, 107 S.Ct. 1637, 1649–50 (1987) quoted in State Farm Mut. Auto. Ins. Co. v. Superior Court, 8 Cal.Rptr.3d 56, 63 (Cal. Ct. App. 2003).

14. State by Humphrey v. Delano Cmty. Dev. Corp., 571 N.W.2d 233, 236 (Minn. 1997).

15. *E.g.*, regarding construction of articles of incorporation as a contract: Airgas, Inc. v. Air Products & Chemicals, Inc., 8 A.3d 1182, 1188 (Del. 2010); Truck Fin. Specialists, Inc. v. W & S Leasing, Inc., 911 N.E.2d 612, 615 (Ind. Ct. App. 2009); Brennan's House of Printing, Inc. v. Brennan, 924 So.2d 1067, 1072 (La. Ct. App. 2006) *writ denied*, 930 So.2d 33 (2006); Executive Bd. of Missouri Baptist Convention v. Windermere Baptist Conference Ctr., 280 S.W.3d 678, 687 (Mo. Ct. App. 2009), *transfer denied* (May 5, 2009), *reh'g and/or transfer denied* (Mar. 31, 2009); Okelberry v. West Daniels Land Ass'n, 120 P.3d 34, 39 (Utah Ct. App. 2005).

16. Harbison v. Strickland, 900 So.2d 385, 389 (Ala. 2004).

17. Del. Code Ann. tit. 8, § 109 (West 2012).

18. *E.g.*, regarding construction of corporate by-laws as contracts: Rushing v. Gold Kist, Inc., 567 S.E.2d 384, 387 (Ga. Ct. App. 2002); Heritage Lake Prop. Owners Ass'n, Inc. v. York, 859 N.E.2d 763, 765 (Ind. Ct. App. 2007); Kansas Heart Hosp., L.L.C. v. Idbeis, 184 P.3d 866, 883 (Kan. 2008); Tackney v. U.S. Naval Acad. Alumni Ass'n, Inc., 971 A.2d 309, 318 (Md. 2009); Adams v. Christie's Inc., 880 A.2d 774, 783 (R.I. 2005); Shuler v. Tri–County Elec. Co-op., Inc., 649 S.E.2d 98, 101 (S.C. Ct. App. 2007) *aff'd sub nom.* Shuler v. Tri–County Elec. Co-op, Inc., 684 S.E.2d 765 (2009); In re Aguilar, 344 S.W.3d 41, 49–50 (Tex. App. 2011); Okelberry v. West Daniels Land Ass'n, 120 P.3d 34, 39 (Utah Ct. App. 2005); Save Columbia CU Comm. v. Columbia Cmty. Credit Union, 139 P.3d 386, 389 (Wash. Ct. App. 2006); Mueller v. Zimmer, 124 P.3d 340, 359 (Wyo. 2005).

19. Abraham v. Diamond Dealers Club, Inc., 896 N.Y.S.2d 848, 851 (Sup. Ct. 2010) *aff'd*, 914 N.Y.S.2d 152 (App. Div. 2011).

20. Fla. Stat. Ann. § 608.423(1) (West 2012).

21. Conn. Gen. Stat. Ann. § 34–101 (West 2012).

Endnotes for Chapter 16: Drafting Public Legislation

1. *See, e.g.,* North Dakota Legislative Drafting Manual, Pt. 1 at 5 (2011).

2. *See, e.g.,* Maine Legislative Drafting Manual Pt. 1 at 7 (2009).

3. *See, e.g.,* State of Oregon Bill Drafting Manual, Chapter 2 at 2.4–.5 (2008 ed.)

4. S.C. Const. art. III, § 17 (2011).

5. *E.g.,* Ky. Const. § 51 (2011); Alaska Const. art. II, § 13 (2012); Fla. Const. Art. III, § 6 (2010).

6. Sea Cove Dev., LLC v. Harbourside Cmty. Bank, 691 S.E.2d 158, 161 (S.C. 2010).

7. Wirtz v. Quinn, 942 N.E.2d 765, 771 (Ill. App. Ct. 2011).

8. Croft v. Parnell, 236 P.3d 369, 372 (Alaska 2010).

9. *E.g.*, Pierce County v. State, 185 P.3d 594, 613 (Wash. Ct. App. 2008) (court presumes that a statute is constitutional; person challenging it bears heavy burden to establish its unconstitutionality beyond a reasonable doubt).

10. Nova Health Sys. v. Edmondson, 233 P.3d 380, 380 (Okla. 2010).

11. Smith v. Guest, 16 A.3d 920, 929–30 (Del. 2011), *reargument denied* (Apr. 12, 2011) (if bill contains multiple subjects or its title would "trap the unwary into inaction," bill violates Delaware Constitution); People v. Brown, 866 N.E.2d 1163, 1169 (Ill. 2007) (provisions of a statute that violate the single-subject rule are void *ab initio* and have no force or effect as if they had never been passed).

E.g., regarding unconstitutionality of statutes that violate the single-subject-rule: Pierce County v. State, 185 P.3d 594, 613 (Wash. Ct. App. 2008) (violation of single subject rule sufficient to render provisions unconstitutional).

12. *E.g.* regarding differing standards of compliance with the single-subject rule:

In Illinois courts liberally construe the word "subject" in favor of the legislature. *See* Wirtz v. Quinn, 942 N.E.2d 765, 771 (Ill. App. Ct. 2011). However, while legislative acts "are afforded a considerable presumption of constitutionality," that presumption is not without limits. The subject can be as broad as the legislature wants, so long as the provisions have a "natural and logical connection." Id.

The Ohio Supreme Court states that for the court to conclude that an act violates the one-subject rule, a court must find a "disunity" of subject matter to the extent that the court concludes that there is no discernible reason (practical, rational, or legitimate) for combining the provisions in a single act. Riverside v. State, 944 N.E.2d 281, 295–96 (Ohio App. 2010) *appeal not allowed*, 944 N.E.2d 696 (2011).

The Alaska Supreme Court balances the rule's policy against the policy favoring an efficient legislative process. The court states that if the rule is applied too narrowly, statutes might be unduly restricted in scope and permissible subject matter, thereby multiplying and complicating the number of enactments necessary and their relationships. Croft v. Parnell, 236 P.3d 369, 372 (Alaska 2010). The Alaska court therefore requires only that the act embrace some general subject, meaning that all matters covered must fall under some one general idea and be so related to each other "either logically or in popular understanding" that they are parts of or germane to one single subject. *Id.* at 372–73.

The South Carolina Supreme Court has stated that the legislature complies with the rule if the title states the general subject and the provisions in the act are germane to the title as means to accomplish the objectives stated in the title. Sea Cove Dev., LLC v. Harbourside Cmty. Bank, 691 S.E.2d 158, 161 (S.C. 2010).

On the other hand, a Pennsylvania decision points out that virtually all legislation, however diverse in substance, would meet the single-subject requirement if the "germaneness" concept is too broadly applied since no two subjects are so separate that they cannot be brought into "a common focus" so long as the point of view is "carried back far enough." Commonwealth v. Neiman, 5 A.3d 353, 355–56 (Pa. Super. Ct. 2010) quoting Payne v. School Dist. of Coudersport Borough, 31 A. 1072, 1074 (1895) *appeal granted in part* 27 A.3d 984 (2011). Even so, Pennsylvania law indicates that the single-subject rule should not become a license for the judiciary to undermine the legislature's actions, given that few bills cannot be subdivided under several topics. *Id.* In Pennsylvania, a person who challenges the constitutionality of an enactment based on the single-subject clause must show either (1) that the legislators and the public were actually deceived as to the act's contents at the time they were passed, or (2) that the title on its face is such that no reasonable person would have been on notice as to the act's contents. *Id.*

Florida regards its single-subject rule as imposing three requirements: first, each law can embrace only one subject; second, it can include any matter "properly connected" with the subject; third, the subject must be "*briefly* expressed in the title." Franklin v. State, 887 So.2d 1063, 1072 (Fla. 2004).

13. *E.g.*, Legislative Drafting Manual for the State of Arkansas, Pt. 2 at 9 (Non–Appropriations Bills Only 2010); North Dakota Legislative Drafting Manual, Pt. 2 at 11 (2011)

14. *E.g.*, Legislative Drafting Manual for the State of Arkansas, Pt. 2 at 9 (Non–Appropriations Bills Only 2010); North Dakota Legislative Drafting Manual, Pt. 2 at 11 (2011)

15. *E.g.*, Legislative Drafting Manual for the State of Arkansas, Pt. 2 at 9 (Non–Appropriations Bills Only 2010); North Dakota Legislative Drafting Manual, Pt. 2 at 11 (2011)

16. Beshear v. Haydon Bridge Co., Inc., 304 S.W.3d 682, 694–95 (Ky. 2010), *as corrected* (Mar. 17, 2010), quoting Bowman v. Hamlett, 166 S.W. 1008, 1009 (Ky. 1914).

17. *E.g.,* Pierce County v. State, 185 P.3d 594, 613 (Wash. Ct. App. 2008) (violation of the "expressed in the title" requirement is sufficient to render relevant provisions of the bill unconstitutional). *But see* Tex. Const. art. III, § 35 (2011) (a law cannot be held void on basis of insufficient title) and Garay v. State, 940 S.W.2d 211, 216 (Tex. App. 1997).

18. *E.g.,* Commonwealth ex rel. Armstrong v. Collins, 709 S.W.2d 437, 443 (Ky. 1986) (Section 51 of Kentucky constitution has always been liberally construed, with any doubt resolved in favor of validity of legislative action) quoted in Beshear v. Haydon Bridge Co., Inc., 304 S.W.3d 682, 694 (Ky. 2010), *as corrected* (Mar. 17, 2010).

19. Missouri State Med. Ass'n v. Missouri Dept. of Health, 39 S.W.3d 837, 841 (Mo. 2001).

20. New Mexico Legislative Drafting Manual, Chapter 3 at 21 (2004 update).

21. The Kentucky Supreme Court held that a title is sufficient if it adequately expresses a general subject; any provision in the Act "germane to or reasonably embraced within that general subject" must be considered to be within the scope of the notice of subject given by the title. Beshear v. Haydon Bridge Co., Inc., 304 S.W.3d 682, 694–95 (Ky. 2010), *as corrected* (Mar. 17, 2010). It is sufficient if it furnishes general notice of the general subject of the act and furnishes a clue to the act's contents, in which case it passes constitutional muster. *Id.*

In Washington, a court requires that the title give notice that would lead to an inquiry into the body of the act or indicate the scope and purpose of the law "to an inquiring mind"; in Washington, a title does not have to be "an index to the contents of the bill" or give details contained in the bill. Pierce County v. State, 185 P.3d 594, 615 (Wash. Ct. App. 2008). Furthermore, for a person to succeed in challenging a title on constitutional grounds, any objections to a title must be "grave," and the conflict between it and the constitution must be "palpable." *Id.*

The Georgia Supreme Court said that if what follows the enacting clause is definitely related to content of the title, has a natural connection, relates to the main object of legislation, and does not conflict with it, there is no infringement of the constitutional inhibition. Sherman Concrete Pipe Co. v. Chinn, 660 S.E.2d 368, 370 (Ga. 2008).

In Iowa, courts give greater weight to a constitutional challenge based on the subject/title requirement when *both* are implicated in the challenge, since while the subject and title requirement rules are separate constitutional principles, they operate together to prevent greater harm than if the only claimed violation is the single-subject requirement. Godfrey v. State, 752 N.W.2d 413, 428 (Iowa 2008).

22. North Dakota House of Representatives, House Measure No. 1080, Sixty-second Legislative Assembly of North Dakota (2011).

23. New Mexico Legislative Drafting Manual, Chapter 3 at 21 (2004 update).

24. Manual for Drafting Legislation (The Florida Senate 2009), Ch. 3 at 37.

25. Manual for Drafting Legislation (The Florida Senate 2009), Ch. 3 at 38.

26. Ark. Const. art. V, § 19 (2012).

27. *See* Legislative Counsel of the State of California, A Guide for Accessing California Legislative Information the Internet (2009) http://www.%1Fleginfo.%1Fca.gov/%1Fguide.html [last visited March 14, 2012].

28. *See* Manual for Drafting Legislation (The Florida Senate 2009), Ch. 3 at 38. The Florida drafting manual indicates that even though preambles are not published in the Florida statutes or considered part of the enactment, courts sometimes do consider them.

29. *See* Legislative Drafting Manual for the State of Arkansas, Pt. 2 at 10 (Non–Appropriations Bills Only 2010); State of Oregon Bill Drafting Manual, Chapter 5 at 5.7 (2008 ed.).

30. Legislative Drafting Manual for the State of Arkansas, Pt. 2 at 10–11 (Non–Appropriations Bills Only 2010); State of Oregon Bill Drafting Manual, Chapter 5 at 5.7 (2008 ed.)

31. *E.g.,* State of Oregon Bill Drafting Manual, Chapter 5 at 5.7 (2008 ed.).

32. 2012 Florida House Bill No. 1013, Florida One Hundred Fourteenth Regular Session, 2012 Florida House Bill No. 1013, Florida One Hundred Fourteenth Regular Session.

33. North Dakota Legislative Drafting Manual, Pt. 5 at 91 (2011)

34. *Id.*

35. Manual for Drafting Legislation (The Florida Senate 2009), Ch. 3 at 41.

36. State of Oregon Bill Drafting Manual, Chapter 7 at 7.4 (2008 ed.)

37. *Id.*

38. 2011 Georgia House Bill No. 642, Georgia One Hundred Fifty–First General Assembly—2011–2012 Regular Session, 2011 Georgia House Bill No. 642, Georgia One Hundred Fifty–First General Assembly—2011–2012 Regular Session.

39. 2011 California Assembly Bill No. 1831, California 2011–2012 Regular Session, 2011 California Assembly Bill No. 1831, California 2011–2012 Regular Session.

40. City of Portland v. Tidyman, 759 P.2d 242, 247 (Or. 1988).

41. Hawaii Legislative Drafting Manual, Chapter 2 Part 1 at 8 (2011)

42. 2011 Maine House Paper No. 1109, Maine One Hundred Twenty–Fifth Legislature—First Regular Session, 2011 Maine House Paper No. 1109, Maine One Hundred Twenty–Fifth Legislature—First Regular Session.

43. 2011 West Virginia House Bill No. 2210, West Virginia Eightieth Legislature—Regular Session, 2011, 2011 West Virginia House Bill No. 2210, West Virginia Eightieth Legislature—Regular Session, 2011.

44. *See* Manual for Drafting Legislation (The Florida Senate), Ch. 3 at 40.

45. *See* New Mexico Legislative Drafting Manual, Chapter 3 at 26 (2004 update).

46. *See* Minnesota Revisor's Manual, Ch. 4 at 36.

47. *See* New Mexico Legislative Drafting Manual, Introduction at 4 (2004 update).

48. Phuong Thai Than v. State, 918 S.W.2d 106, 107 (Tex. App. 1996) discussing Act effective Sept. 1, 1994, 73rd Leg., R.S., ch. 900, § 1.18, 1993 Tex.Gen.Laws 3586, 3705.

49. *See* Manual for Drafting Legislation (The Florida Senate 2009), Ch. 3 at 60.

50. 2011 Pennsylvania Senate Bill No. 967, Pennsylvania One Hundred Ninety–Fifth General Assembly—2011–2012, 2011 Pennsylvania Senate Bill No. 967, Pennsylvania One Hundred Ninety–Fifth General Assembly—2011–2012.

51. 2011 Texas Senate Bill No. 647, Texas Eighty–Second Legislature, 2011 Texas Senate Bill No. 647, Texas Eighty–Second Legislature.

52. 2012 Florida Senate Bill No. 642, Florida One Hundred Fourteenth Regular Session, 2012 Florida Senate Bill No. 642, Florida One Hundred Fourteenth Regular Session.

53. *See, e.g.,* Manual for Drafting Legislation (The Florida Senate 2009), Ch. 3 at 60; North Dakota Legislative Drafting Manual, Pt. 2 at 17 (2011).

54. 2011 Arkansas House Bill No. 1545, Arkansas Eighty–Eighth General Assembly.

55. 2012 New Jersey Assembly Bill No. 2095, New Jersey Two Hundred Fifteenth Legislature—First Annual Session, 2012 New Jersey Assembly Bill No. 2095, New Jersey Two Hundred Fifteenth Legislature—First Annual Session.

56. 2011 Rhode Island House Bill No. 5943, Rhode Island 2011 Legislative Session, 2011 Rhode Island House Bill No. 5943, Rhode Island 2011 Legislative Session.

57. Or. Const. art. IV, § 28 (West 2010).

58. 2011 Oregon Senate Bill No. 378, Oregon Seventy–Sixth Legislative Assembly, 2011 Oregon Senate Bill No. 378, Oregon Seventy–Sixth Legislative Assembly.

59. Legislative Drafting Manual for the State of Arkansas, Pt. 2 at 74 (Non–Appropriations Bills Only).

60. 2011 Maine Senate Paper No. 550, Maine One Hundred Twenty–Fifth Legislature—Second Regular Session, 2011 Maine Senate Paper No. 550, Maine One Hundred Twenty–Fifth Legislature—Second Regular Session.

61. *Id.*

62. 2011 Maine House Paper No. 1293, Maine One Hundred Twenty–Fifth Legislature—Second Regular Session, 2011 Maine House Paper No. 1293, Maine One Hundred Twenty–Fifth Legislature—Second Regular Session.

63. *E.g.,* stating that municipalities are creatures of the state and have no inherent powers of their own, possessing only the powers that are granted to them: Fross v. County of Allegheny, 612 F. Supp. 2d 651, 654 (W.D. Pa. 2009) *aff'd and remanded*, 438 F. App'x 99 (3d Cir. 2011); City of Leeds v. Town of Moody, 319 So.2d 242, 246 (Ala. 1975); City of Hollywood v. Mulligan, 934 So.2d 1238, 1246 (Fla. 2006); Spahn v. Zoning Bd. of Adjustment, 922 A.2d 24, 29 (Pa. Commw. Ct. 2007) *aff'd*, 977 A.2d 1132 (2009); Bailey v. Jones, 81 S.D. 617, 623, 139 N.W.2d 385, 388 (S.D. 1966).

64. *See* Fla. Stat. Ann. § 166.041 (West 2012)(defining ordinance as "an official legislative action of a governing body, which action is a regulation of a general and permanent nature and enforceable as a local law.").

E.g., regarding nature of ordinance as a local law enacted by a governing body: Snow v. Ruden, McClosky, Smith, Schuster & Russell, P.A., 896 So.2d 787, 791 (Fla. Dist. Ct. App. 2005) (ordinance is enacted by body such as county commission or city council); McKenzie v. City of Omaha, 708 N.W.2d 286, 292–93 (Neb. App. 2006) (ordinance prescribes general, uniform, and permanent rules of conduct); Wilkins v. Guilford County, 582 S.E.2d 74, 79 (N.C. App. 2003) (like statutes, ordinances are binding on all concerned); O'Connell v. Bruce, 710 A.2d 674, 679 (R.I. 1998) (ordinance prescribes some permanent rule of conduct or government).

65. *E.g.,* regarding challenge to ordinance due to failure to comply with requisite procedures: J.L. Spoons, Inc. v. City of Brunswick, 18 F. Supp. 2d 782, 786 (N.D. Ohio 1998) (ordinances enacted contrary to the procedural requirements of city charter "null and void"); Wilkins v. Guilford County, 582 S.E.2d 74, 79 (N.C. App. 2003) (enacting ordinance requires compliance with procedures such as record vote, public hearing, and published notice); Kimbrell v. Village of Seven Mile, 469 N.E.2d 954, 957 (Ohio Ct. App. 1984) (statutory requirement as to reading ordinances mandatory; noncompliance renders ordinance unenforceable); Drummond v. Oregon Dept. of Transp., 730 P.2d 582, 585 (Or. Ct. App. 1986) (ordinance invalid because state law required two readings of amended version); O'Connell v. Bruce, 710 A.2d 674, 679 (R.I. 1998) (ordinance different from resolution because ordinance must be adopted with formalities required for ordinance).

66. Fla. Stat. Ann. § 166.043 (West 2012).

67. *E.g.,* Wilkins v. Guilford County, 582 S.E.2d 74, 79 (N.C. App. 2003).

68. Smith v. City of Papillion, 705 N.W.2d 584, 598 (Neb. 2005) (courts presume that legislative or rulemaking bodies, in enacting ordinances or rules, acted within their authority; burden rests on those who challenge their validity).

69. *E.g.,* City of Lake Forest v. Evergreen Holistic Collective, 138 Cal.Rptr.3d 332, 353 (Ct. App. 2012), *as modified* (Mar. 29, 2012) (ordinance conflicting with state law would be preempted); City of Hollywood v. Mulligan, 934 So.2d 1238, 1246 (Fla. 2006) (municipal ordinances inferior to state law and must not conflict with controlling provisions); State v. Veolia Envtl. Waste, 2012 WL 1123585 at *3 (N.J. Super. Ct. App. Div. 2012) (in assessing validity of municipal ordinance, court must consider whether local regulations are preempted by state law).

Endnotes for Chapter 17: How Courts Construe Statutes and Other Public Rule-making Documents

1. *E.g.,* regarding application of principles of statutory construction to administrative regulations and rules: Williams v. Chu, 641 F. Supp. 2d 31, 38 (D.D.C. 2009); Roberto v. Dep't of Navy, 440 F.3d 1341, 1350 (Fed. Cir. 2006); Price v. Thomas Built Buses, Inc., 260 S.W.3d 300, 303 (Ark. 2007); Planned Parenthood of Indiana v. Carter, 854 N.E.2d 853, 866 (Ind. Ct. App. 2006); Alliance for Kentucky's Future, Inc. v. Environmental & Pub. Prot. Cabinet, 310 S.W.3d 681, 687 (Ky. Ct. App. 2008); Biogen IDEC MA, Inc. v. Treasurer & Receiver Gen., 908 N.E.2d 740, 752 (Mass. 2009); Silver State Elec. Supply Co. v. State ex rel. Dept. of Taxation, 157 P.3d 710, 712 (Nev. 2007).

2. *E.g.,* regarding application of rules of statutory construction to rules of court: Lopez v. Kearney ex rel. County of Pima, 213 P.3d 282, 285 (Ariz. Ct. App. 2009), *review denied* (Jan. 5, 2010); Conservatorship of Coombs, 79 Cal.Rptr.2d 799, 801 (Ct. App. 1998); Garrigan v. Bowen, 243 P.3d 231, 235 (Colo. 2010), *as modified on denial of reh'g* (Dec. 20, 2010); Barco v. School Bd. of Pinellas County, 975 So.2d 1116, 1121 (Fla. 2008); Roberts v. Richardson, 109 P.3d 765, 766 (N.M. 2005); UAG W. Bay AM, LLC v. Cambio, 987 A.2d 873, 877 (R.I. 2010); State v. Mercier, 164 S.W.3d 799 (Tex. App. 2005); Debry v. Goates, 999 P.2d 582, 585 (Utah Ct. App. 2000).

3. *E.g.,* application of statutory construction principles to local rules: Lang v. Superior Court, 200 Cal.Rptr. 526, 530 (Ct. App. 1984); Kyle v. Johnson, 818 So.2d 979, 981 (La. Ct. App. 2002); Mabe v. White, 15 P.3d 681 (Wash. Ct. App. 2001).

4. *E.g.,* regarding application of principles of statutory construction to ordinances: New Orleans City v. BellSouth Telecommunications, Inc., 728 F. Supp. 2d 834, 846 (E.D. La. 2010); Zubarau v. City of Palmdale, 121 Cal.Rptr.3d 172, 184 (Ct. App. 2011), *reh'g denied* (2011), *review denied* (2011); Paff v. Byrnes, 897 A.2d 1136, 1139 (N.J. Super. Ct. App. Div. 2006); W. Land & Cattle, Inc. v. Umatilla County, 214 P.3d 68, 72 (Or. Ct. App. 2009); Wesco, Inc. v. City of Montpelier, 739 A.2d 1241, 1245 (Vt. 1999).

5. *E.g.,* regarding application of construction principles to a local government's resolutions: MDC Holdings, Inc. v. Town of Parker, 223 P.3d 710, 717 (Colo. 2010); County of Humboldt v. McKee, 82 Cal.Rptr.3d 38, 48 (Ct. App. 2008).

6. Grayson v. AT & T Corp., 15 A.3d 219 (D.C. 2011).

7. *E.g.,* regarding ascertainment and effectuation as legislative intent as primary goal of construction: State v. Leonardo, ex rel. County of Pima, 250 P.3d 1222, 1224 (Ariz. Ct. App. 2011); Minnesota Bd. of Chiropractic Examiners v. Cich, 788 N.W.2d 515, 519 (Minn. Ct. App. 2010); Gardner v. State, 20 A.3d 801, 806 (Md. 2011); Hardy Companies, Inc. v. SNMARK, LLC, 245 P.3d 1149, 1153 (Nev. 2010); City of Oklahoma City v. Int'l Ass'n of Fire Fighters, Local 157, AFL–CIO/ CLC, 254 P.3d 678, 683 (Okla. 2011).

8. *E.g.,* legislative intent was the "polestar" for the following: Arthur v. Bolen, 41 So.3d 745, 749 (Ala. 2010); People v. Fogarty, 126 P.3d 238, 240 (Colo. Ct. App. 2005); Borden v. E.–European Ins. Co., 921 So.2d 587, 595 (Fla. 2006); Parsons v. Mississippi State Port Auth. at Gulfport, 996 So.2d 165, 167 (Miss. Ct. App. 2008); Board of Educ. of City of Sea Isle City v. Kennedy, 951 A.2d 987, 994 (N.J. 2008); Maes v. Audubon Indem. Ins. Group, 164 P.3d 934, 938 (N.M. 2007); Poland v. Ott, 278 S.W.3d 39, 58 (Tex. App. 2008).

9. *E.g.,* legislative intent was the "touchstone" for the following: Sheet Metal Workers Int'l Ass'n Local Union No. 27, AFL–CIO v. E.P. Donnelly, Inc., 673 F. Supp. 2d 313 (D.N.J. 2009); United States v. Jahedi, 681 F. Supp. 2d 430 (S.D.N.Y. 2009); People v. Garcia, 124 Cal.Rptr.3d 886, 891 (Ct. App. 2011), *review denied* (July 27, 2011); In re Det. of Hawkins, 238 P.3d 1175, 1179 (Wash. 2010).

10. *E.g.,* regarding legislature's awareness of the law as a fundamental tenet of statutory construction: Ex parte Ford Motor Co., 73 So.3d 597, 603 (Ala. 2011); Henrichs v. Chugach Alaska Corp., 250 P.3d 531, 538 (Alaska 2011); Mason v. State, 712 S.E.2d 76, 78 (Ga. Ct. App. 2011), *reconsideration denied* (Nov. 7, 2011), *reconsideration denied* (June 17, 2011), *cert. denied* (Oct. 3, 2011); State v. Divis, 589 N.W.2d 537, 541 (Neb. 1999); Dandomar Co., LLC v. Town of Pleasant Valley Town Bd., 924 N.Y.S.2d 499, 506 (App. Div.2011); Hotze v. City of Houston, 339 S.W.3d 809, 814 (Tex. App. 2011).

11. State v. Herbert, 601 N.W.2d 210, 212 (Minn. Ct. App. 1999).

12. State v. Nash, 339 S.W.3d 500, 508 (Mo. 2011) *cert. denied*, 132 S.Ct. 421 (2011).

13. *E.g.,* regarding intention of legislature that provision be constitutional and valid and to act within its constitutional authority: Sandlin v. Criminal Justice Standards & Training Comm'n, 531 So.2d 1344, 1346 (Fla. 1988); M.J. Farms, Ltd. v. Exxon Mobil Corp., 998 So.2d 16, 31 (La. 2008); New Jersey Ass'n of Health Plans v. Farmer, 777 A.2d 385, 393–94 (N.J. Super. Ch. Div. 2000); Peoples Nat. Bank of Greenville v. South Carolina Tax Comm'n, 156 S.E.2d 769, 771 (S.C. 1967); State v. Edmond, 933 S.W.2d 120, 125 (Tex. Crim. App. 1996).

14. *E.g.,* ambiguity arises if provision susceptible to two or more reasonable interpretations: In re Condor Ins. Ltd., 601 F.3d 319, 321 (5th Cir. 2010); D'Andrea Bros. LLC v. United States, 96 Fed.Cl. 205, 219 (Fed. Cl. 2010); DCX, Inc. v. Dist. of Columbia Taxicab Comm'n, 705 A.2d 1096, 1098–99 (D.C. 1998); Dewey Beach Enterprises, Inc. v. Bd. of Adjustment of Town of Dewey Beach, 1 A.3d 305, 307 (Del. 2010); Hand v. City of New Orleans, 892 So.2d 609, 613 (La. Ct. App. 2004) *writ denied*, 897 So.2d 603; Department of Corr. v. Public Utilities Comm'n, 968 A.2d 1047, 1050 (Me. 2009); State v. Stevenson, 656 N.W.2d 235, 238 (Minn. 2003); Waxman v. Waxman & Associates, Inc.,198 P.3d 445, 449 (Or. Ct. App. 2008); S. Carolina Dept. of Soc. Services v. Lisa C., 669 S.E.2d 647, 652 (S.C. Ct. App. 2008); State v. Powers, 101 S.W.3d 383, 393 (Tenn. 2003); Pett v. Brigham City Corp., 246 P.3d 758, 763, *reh'g denied* (Utah Ct. App. 2011); Estate of Bunch ex rel. Bunch v. McGraw Residential Ctr., 248 P.3d 565, 567–68 (Wash. Ct. App. 2011); Marotz v. Hallman, 734 N.W.2d 411, 418 (Wis. 2007).

15. *E.g,* Fountain Place Cinema 8, LLC v. Morris, 707 S.E.2d 859, 863 (W. Va. 2011) (statute open to construction only where language used requires interpretation because of ambiguity either rendering it susceptible to two or more constructions or of such doubtful or obscure meaning that reasonable minds might be uncertain or disagree as to its meaning).

16. *E.g.,* Southern Union Co. v. Department of Pub. Utilities, 941 N.E.2d 633, 640 (Mass. 2011); Marotz v. Hallman, 734 N.W.2d 411, 418 (Wis. 2007).

17. Burton v. Lehman, 103 P.3d 1230, 1234 (Wash. 2005).

18. Connecticut Nat. Bank v. Germain, 503 U.S. 249, 254, 112 S.Ct. 1146, 1149 (1992). *See, e.g.,* Bank of Am. Nat. Ass'n v. Colonial Bank, 604 F.3d 1239, 1244 (11th Cir. 2010); Avendano– Ramirez v. Ashcroft, 365 F.3d 813, 818 (9th Cir. 2004).

19. *E.g.,* Glaze v. Deffenbaugh, 172 P.3d 1104, 1107 (Idaho 2007) (court assumes the Legislature means what it says in a statute unless the result is "palpably absurd"); Bowie v. Washington Dept. of Revenue, 248 P.3d 504, 508 (Wash. 2011) (plain language does not require construction).

20. J.E.M. Ag Supply, Inc. v. Pioneer Hi–Bred Int'l, Inc., 534 U.S. 124, 156, 122 S.Ct. 593, 611 (2001).

21. *See* Karl N. Llewellyn, *Remarks on the Theory of Appellate Decision and the Rules or Canons About How Statutes Are to be Construed,* 3 Vand. L. Rev. 395 (1950).

22. Connecticut Nat. Bank v. Germain, 503 U.S. 249, 254, 112 S.Ct. 1146, 1149 (1992). *E.g.,* Bank of Am. Nat. Ass'n v. Colonial Bank, 604 F.3d 1239, 1244 (11th Cir. 2010); Avendano–Ramirez v. Ashcroft, 365 F.3d 813, 818 (9th Cir. 2004).

23. Title 1, Chapter 1, "Construction of Code and Statutes," Ala.Code 1975 § 1–1–1 through 1–1–16; Title 1, Chapter 10, Article 2, "General Definitions, Residency, and Rules of Construction," Alaska Stat. § 01.10.020–01.10.065; Me. Rev. Stat. Ann. tit. 1, § 71 through 74.

24. Conn. Gen. Stat. Ann. § 1 through 2z (West 2012).

25. *E.g.,* regarding presumed validity of legislative enactments: Schiavo ex rel. Schindler v. Schiavo, 403 F.3d 1223, 1227 (11th Cir. 2005); State v. Manzanares, 152 Idaho 410, 272 P.3d 382, 390 (2012); Murrell v. State, 960 N.E.2d 854, 858 (Ind. Ct. App. 2012); Kansas One–Call Sys., Inc. v. State, 274 P.3d 625, 631 (Kan. 2012); Nader v. Maine Democratic Party, 41 A.3d 551, 558 (Me. 2012); City of Starkville v. 4–County Elec. Power Ass'n, 909 So.2d 1094, 1112 (Miss. 2005); Schatz v. Interfaith Care Ctr., 811 N.W.2d 643 (Minn. 2012); Estate of Overbey v. Chad Franklin Nat'l Auto Sales N., LLC, 361 S.W.3d 364, 372 (Mo. 2012); State v. Green, 724 S.E.2d 664 (S.C. 2012), *reh'g denied* (May 3, 2012); Ultrasound Technical Services, Inc. v. Dallas Cent. Appraisal Dist., 357 S.W.3d 174, 177 (Tex. App. 2011), *review denied* (Apr. 13, 2012); State v. Gresham, 269 P.3d 207, 217 (Wash. 2012).

26. *E.g.,* regarding burden of party to demonstrate unconstitutionality beyond a reasonable doubt: Estate of McCall v. United States, 663 F. Supp. 2d 1276, 1297 (N.D. Fla. 2009) *aff'd in part, question certified sub nom.* Estate of McCall ex rel. McCall v. United States, 642 F.3d 944 (11th Cir. 2011) (Florida law); Verizon Wireless (VAW) LLC v. Kolbeck, 529 F. Supp. 2d 1081, 1093 (D.S.D. 2007) (South Dakota law); Schatz v. Interfaith Care Ctr., 811 N.W.2d 643 (Minn. 2012); Ultrasound Technical Services, Inc. v. Dallas Cent. Appraisal Dist., 357 S.W.3d 174, 177 (Tex. App. 2011), *review denied* (Apr. 13, 2012). *Compare*: Estate of Overbey v. Chad Franklin Nat'l Auto Sales N., LLC, 361 S.W.3d 364, 372 (Mo. 2012) (party must show that the statute clearly and undoubtedly violates the constitution).

27. *E.g.,* regarding court's obligation to adopt a reading that would uphold constitutionality of statute: United States v. Kernell, 667 F.3d 746, 752–53 (6th Cir. 2012); Velazquez v. Legal Services Corp., 164 F.3d 757, 769 (2d Cir. 1999) *aff'd,* 531 U.S. 533, 121 S.Ct. 1043 (2001); Garner v. U.S. Dept. of Labor, 221 F.3d 822, 826 (5th Cir. 2000); Honulik v. Town of Greenwich, 980 A.2d 845, 849–50 (Conn. 2009); People v. Ortiz, 919 N.E.2d 941, 949 (Ill. 2009); Kansas One–Call Sys., Inc. v. State, 274 P.3d 625, 631 (Kan. 2012); M.J. Farms, Ltd. v. Exxon Mobil Corp., 998 So.2d 16, 31 (La. 2008); State v. Letalien, 985 A.2d 4, 12 (Me. 2009); McFee v. Nursing Care Mgt. of Am., Inc., 931 N.E.2d 1069, 1075 (Ohio 2010).

28. People v. Zambia, 254 P.3d 965, 971 (Cal. 2011) (construction of statute must be consistent with apparent purpose and intention of lawmakers and practical rather than technical in nature; when applied, construction must result in wise policy rather than absurdity).

29. Perrelli v. Pastorelle, 20 A.3d 354, 358 (N.J. 2011) (matter of statutory construction does not justly turn on "literalisms, technisms, or the so-called formal rules of interpretation"; instead, construction turns on objectives of legislation and commonsense of situations).

30. Kewalo Ocean Activities v. Ching, 243 P.3d 273, 284 (Haw. Ct. App. 2010).

31. In re United Parcel Serv. Wage & Hour Cases, 192 Cal.App.4th 1425 (2011), *review filed* (Apr. 4, 2011), *reh'g denied* (Mar. 16, 2011).

32. State v. Nash, 339 S.W.3d 500, 508 (Mo. 2011) *cert. denied*, 132 S.Ct. 421 (2011).

33. *E.g.,* regarding courts' reading of statutes in a way that is consistent with underlying goal and purpose of statute: United Pub. Workers, AFSCME, Local 646, AFL–CIO v. City & County of Honolulu, 244 P.3d 604, 606 (Haw. Ct. App. 2010); George v. National Collegiate Athletic Ass'n, 945 N.E.2d 150, 154–55 (Ind. 2011); South Carolina Energy Users Comm. v. South Carolina Pub. Serv. Comm'n, 697 S.E.2d 587, 590 (S.C. 2010).

34. *E.g.,* regarding construction to achieve a rational outcome: Bright v. Calhoun, 988 So.2d 492 (Ala. 2008); State v. Herbert, 601 N.W.2d 210, 212 (Minn. Ct. App. 1999); Great–W. Life & Annuity Ins. Co. v. Texas Atty. Gen. Child Support Div., 331 S.W.3d 884, 893 (Tex. App. 2011); State ex rel. Z.C., 165 P.3d 1206, 1209 (Utah 2007); Tingey v. Haisch, 152 P.3d 1020, 1026 (Wash. 2007); Estate of Osborne, 525 A.2d 788, 793 (Pa. Super. Ct. 1987).

35. Gardner v. State, 20 A.3d 801, 806 (Md. 2011). *E.g.,* regarding construction of the statute as a harmonious whole: People v. Williamson, 249 P.3d 801, 803 (Colo. 2011); State v. Geiss, 70

So.3d 642, 648 (Fla. Dist. Ct. App. 2011), *reh'g denied* (2011), *review granted*, 70 So.3d 587 (Fla. 2011) and *review dismissed*, 88 So.3d 111 (Fla. 2012); Hardy Companies, Inc. v. SNMARK, LLC, 245 P.3d 1149, 1153 (Nev. 2010).

36. *E.g.,* regarding court's reading statute to avoid rendering any part "superfluous" or "meaningless": Collins v. Sutter Mem'l Hosp., 126 Cal.Rptr.3d 193, 202 (Ct. App. 2011); Richardson v. Phillips, 711 S.E.2d 358, 361–62 (Ga. Ct. App. 2011), *cert. denied* (Oct. 17, 2011), *reconsideration denied* (Nov. 30, 2011); People v. Marshall, 950 N.E.2d 668, 673 (Ill. 2011); State v. Keutla, 798 N.W.2d 731, 734 (Iowa 2011); Arguello v. Sunset Station, Inc., 252 P.3d 206, 209 (Nev. 2011); Cortez–Kloehn v. Morrison, 252 P.3d 909, 911 (Wash. Ct. App. 2011) *reconsideration denied* (July 2011), *review denied*, 268 P.3d 941 (2011) (quoting Whatcom County v. City of Bellingham, 909 P.2d 1303, 1308 (Wash. 1996)).

37. *See* Stead v. Swanner, 52 So.3d 1149, 1152 (La. Ct. App. 2010), *reh'g denied* (Jan. 19, 2011), *writ denied*, 61 So.3d 684 (2011).

38. *E.g.,* regarding specific provision or statute controlling a more general provision or statute if they overlap: Arthur v. Bolen, 41 So.3d 745, 749 (Ala. 2010); Town of Branford v. Santa Barbara, 988 A.2d 221, 227 (Conn. 2010); Springs v. City of Charlotte, 704 S.E.2d 319, 328 (N.C. Ct. App. 2011); In re Jackson, 895 N.Y.S.2d 633, 639 (Sup. Ct. 2010); State v. Baber, 240 P.3d 980, 984 (Kan. Ct. App. 2010); Wright v. Kellogg Co., 795 N.W.2d 607, 609 (Mich. Ct. App. 2010).

39. *See generally* Uniform Stat. & Rule Constr. Act § 10 (irreconcilable statutes or rules).

40. Generation Realty, LLC v. Catanzaro, 21 A.3d 253, 259 (R.I. 2011).

41. *E.g.,* regarding importance of reading together statutes enacted at same time as part of same act: United States v. Gallenardo, 579 F.3d 1076, 1083 (9th Cir. 2009); Sempre Ltd. P'ship v. Maricopa County, 235 P.3d 259, 262 (Ariz. Ct. App. 2010); People v. Osorio, 81 Cal.Rptr.3d 167, 178 (Ct. App. 2008); Marino v. Marino, 981 A.2d 855 (N.J. 2009).

42. United Rentals Nw., Inc. v. Yearout Mech., Inc., 237 P.3d 728, 735 (N.M. 2010).

43. *E.g.,* regarding statutes enacted at the same session: Miller v. LaSalle Bank Nat. Ass'n, 595 F.3d 782, 787 (7th Cir. 2010) (when legislature passes several statutes during same session, they should be interpreted in harmony in order to give effect to each).

44. *E.g.,* State v. District Court of Oklahoma County, 154 P.3d 84, 87 (Okla. Crim. App. 2007).

45. *E.g.,* regarding use of title as an aid to construction of statute: State ex rel. Romley v. Hauser, 105 P.3d 1158, 1161 (2005); Jefferson County Bd. of Equalization v. Gerganoff, 241 P.3d 932, 936 (Colo. 2010), *reh'g denied* (Nov. 30, 2010); Com. v. Baker, 295 S.W.3d 437, 443 (Ky. 2009) *cert. denied*, 130 S.Ct. 1738 (2010); In re Estate of Davis, 308 S.W.3d 832, 839 (Tenn. 2010); State v. Gallegos, 171 P.3d 426, 430 (Utah 2007); Dufrene v. Video Co–Op, Louisiana Workers' Comp. Corp., 843 So.2d 1066, 1073 (La. 2003).

46. *E.g.,* Evoy v. Amandio, 932 N.Y.S.2d 874, 878 (Sup. Ct. 2011).

47. Cape Hatteras Elec. Membership Corp. v. Lay, 708 S.E.2d 399, 403 (N.C. Ct. App. 2011).

48. California Retail Portfolio Fund GmbH & Co. KG v. Hopkins Real Estate Group, 122 Cal.Rptr.3d 614, 621 (2011).

49. Motor Vehicle Admin. v. Aiken, 12 A.3d 656, 665 (Md. 2011).

50. *E.g.,* regarding weight accorded to incorporated findings or declarations: Clean Water Coal. v. The M Resort, LLC, 255 P.3d 247, 255 (Nev. 2011).

51. Spalding County Bd. of Elections v. McCord, 700 S.E.2d 558, 560 (Ga. 2010).

52. 1 Pa. Cons. Stat. Ann. § 1924 (West 2012).

53. Cronin v. Sheldon, 991 P.2d 231, 238 (Ariz. 1999) quoted in State v. Rios, 237 P.3d 1052, 1061 (Ariz. Ct. App. 2010).

54. Davis v. County of Fairfax, 710 S.E.2d 466, 468 (Va. 2011). *See* Miranda v. Norstar Bldg. Corp., 909 N.Y.S.2d 802, 806 (N.Y. App. Div. 2010) (legislative intent is to be ascertained from the words and language used, and the statutory language is generally construed according to its natural and most obvious sense, without resorting to an artificial or forced construction).

55. *E.g.,* Microsoft Corp. v. i4i Ltd. P'ship, 131 S.Ct. 2238, 2245 (2011).

56. Microsoft Corp. v. i4i Ltd. P'ship, 131 S.Ct. 2238, 2245 (2011).

57. Oregon Cable Telecommunications Ass'n v. Dept. of Revenue, 240 P.3d 1122, 1126 (Or. Ct. App. 2010).

58. Oregon Cable Telecommunications Ass'n v. Dept. of Revenue, 240 P.3d 1122, 1126 (Or. Ct. App. 2010).

59. *E.g.,* regarding construction of technical words and phrases: People v. Williamson, 249 P.3d 801, 803 (Colo. 2011); In re Nesbitt, 5 A.3d 518, 524 (Conn. App. Ct. 2010); Takacs v. Indian Lake Borough, Zoning Hearing Bd., 18 A.3d 354, 357 (Pa. Commw. Ct. 2011), *reargument denied* (Mar. 10, 2011).

60. School Dist. of Stockbridge v. Evers, 792 N.W.2d 615, 618 (Wis. Ct. App. 2010).

61. *E.g.,* regarding consistent construction of same word or phrase in different parts of same statute: Maksym v. Board of Election Com'rs of City of Chicago, 950 N.E.2d 1051, 1062 (Ill. 2011); City of Rockford v. 63rd Dist. Court, 781 N.W.2d 145, 148 (Mich. Ct. App. 2009) *appeal denied,* 784 N.W.2d 55 (2010); Board of Revision of Taxes, City of Philadelphia v. City of Philadelphia, 4 A.3d 610, 622 (Pa. 2010); Travelscape, LLC v. South Carolina Dept. of Revenue, 705 S.E.2d 28, 34 (S.C. 2011).

62. *See, e.g.,* Jenkins v. Mehra, 704 S.E.2d 577, 583 (Va. 2011) ("It is a common canon of statutory construction what when the legislature uses the same term in separate statutes, that term has the same meaning in each unless the General Assembly indicates to the contrary.")

63. *E.g.,* regarding assumption that different words indicate different meanings: Regional Air, Inc. v. Canal Ins. Co., 639 F.3d 1229, 1238 (10th Cir. 2011); Avila v. Miami–Dade County, 29 So.3d 401, 405 (Fla. Dist. Ct. App. 2010); People v. Santiago, 925 N.E.2d 1122, 1130 (Ill. 2010); Guillen v. Contreras, 238 P.3d 1168, 1172 (Wash. 2010), *reconsideration denied* (Dec. 22, 2010), as amended (Dec. 21, 2010).

64. Mounkes v. Industrial Claim Appeals Office of State, 251 P.3d 485, 487–88 (Colo. Ct. App. 2010), *reh'g denied* (July 8, 2010), *cert. denied,* 2010 WL 4276703 (Colo. 2010).

65. Spicer v. City of Camarillo, 125 Cal.Rptr.3d 357, 360 (Ct. App. 2011), *review denied* (Aug. 31, 2011) *E.g.,* regarding application of the canon *expressio unius est alterius exclusio* (by excluding a matter that it could easily have included, the legislature indicates that it intended to omit it): Fox v. Grayson, 317 S.W.3d 1, 8 (Ky. 2010), *reh'g denied* (Aug. 26, 2010); Sensebe v. Canal Indem. Co., 58 So.3d 441, 451 (La. 2011); Rodgers v. New York City Fire Dept., 915 N.Y.S.2d 724, 727 (App. Div. 2011); Watson v. Price, 712 S.E.2d 154, 156 (N.C. Ct. App. 2011) *review denied,* 718 S.E.2d 398 (2011); Virginian–Pilot Media Companies, LLC v. Dow Jones & Co., Inc., 698 S.E.2d 900, 902 (Va. 2010).

66. *E.g.,* regarding use of extrinsic aids to construction if statute is *ambiguous:* People v. Zambia, 254 P.3d 965, 971 (Cal. 2011); United Pub. Workers, AFSCME, Local 646, AFL–CIO v. City & County of Honolulu, 244 P.3d 604, 606 (Haw. Ct. App. 2010); LaSalle Bank Nat. Ass'n v. Cypress Creek 1, LP, 950 N.E.2d 1109, 1113 (Ill. 2011), *reh'g denied* (May 23, 2011); Phillips v. St. Paul Fire & Marine Ins. Co., 213 P.3d 1066, 1070 (Kan. 2009) quoting 169 P.3d 1025 (Kan. 2007); Commonwealth v. Wynton W., 947 N.E.2d 561, 564 (Mass. 2011); Too Much Media, LLC v. Hale, 20 A.3d 364, 375 (N.J. 2011).

67. *E.g.,* regarding use of previous drafts and wording changes from session to session: Motor Vehicle Admin. v. Aiken, 12 A.3d 656, 665 (Md. 2011); State v. Davies, 330 S.W.3d 775, 785 (Mo. Ct. App. 2010), *transfer denied* (Mar. 1, 2011), *reh'g and/or transfer denied* (Feb. 1, 2011); Montgomery v. City of Dunes City, 236 P.3d 750, 752 (Or. Ct. App. 2010) quoting Krieger v. Just, 876 P.2d 754 (Or. 1994).

68. *E.g.,* explaining that report of a commission that proposed a statute that is subsequently adopted may be given substantial weight, especially if proposed statute is adopted without substantial change: Varshock v. California Dept. of Forestry & Fire Prot., 125 Cal.Rptr.3d 141 (Ct. App. 2011), *review filed* (May 23, 2011).

69. *E.g.,* regarding (differing) uses of records of remarks made on floor of legislative body in statutory construction: Jevne v. Superior Court, 111 P.3d 954, 962–63 (Cal. 2005); Gohel v. Allstate Ins. Co., 768 A.2d 950, 955 (Conn. App. Ct. 2001); Thorson v. Billy Graham Evangelistic Ass'n, 687 N.W.2d 652, 656 (Minn. Ct. App. 2004); Jorling v. Freshwater Wetlands Appeals Bd., 554 N.Y.S.2d 966, 970 (Sup. Ct. 1990).

70. Regarding use of legislative committee hearings to shed light on legislative intent: People v. Rockwell, 125 P.3d 410, 419 (Colo. 2005); State v. Ledbetter, 692 A.2d 713, 724 (Conn. 1997); Burke v. Fleet Nat'l Bank, 742 A.2d 293, 302 (Conn. 1999); First Nat. Bank of Deerwood v. Gregg, 556 N.W.2d 214, 217 (Minn. 1996); Bd. of County Com'rs Clark County v. White, 729 P.2d 1347, 1350 (Nev. 1986).

71. *E.g.,* Haag v. Steinle, 255 P.3d 1016, 1018 (Ariz. Ct. App. 2011) (to determine shared legislative understanding of the relevant language, court may consider minutes of a legislative committee hearing).

72. *E.g.,* regarding use of committee reports to determine intent or resolve ambiguity: Martinez v. The Regents of the Univ. of California, 241 P.3d 855, 865 (Cal. 2010) *cert. denied,* 131 S.Ct. 2961 (2011) (if statutory language is ambiguous, court may turn to legislative history, including committee reports); *see* State v. Vierra, 188 P.3d 773, 779 (Haw. Ct. App. 2008) (while a conference committee report would usually be viewed as providing a better indication of intent than a committee report of the House or Senate, in the particular case, the House Judiciary Committee Report was more probative than the Conference Committee Report).

73. *E.g.,* Walnut Valley Unified Sch. Dist. v. Superior Court, 121 Cal.Rptr.3d 383, 393 (Ct. App. 2011).

74. *E.g.,* Stuto v. Kerber, 910 N.Y.S.2d 215, 216 (App. Div. 2010) *leave to appeal granted*, 910 N.Y.S.2d 215, 216 (App. Div. 20110, *aff'd*, 963 N.E.2d 1267 (2012), (well settled that legislative history of a particular enactment must be reviewed in light of the existing decisional law, which the Legislature is presumed to be aware of and to have accepted to extent legislature left it unchanged).

75. *E.g.,* regarding reference to the historical context and its uses for clarifying meaning of unclear statute: Barber v. Cornerstone Cmty. Outreach, Inc., 42 So.3d 65, 79 (Ala. 2009), *reh'g denied* (Jan. 29, 2010) (permissible for court to look to historical context); Leveraged Land Co., L.L.C. v. Hodges, 249 P.3d 341, 343 (Ariz. 2011); California Sch. Employees Ass'n v. Torrance Unified Sch. Dist., 106 Cal.Rptr.3d 375, 378 (Cal. Ct. App. 2010); State v. Spencer, 248 P.3d 256, 272 (Kan. 2011); Members Choice Credit Union v. Home Fed. Sav. & Loan Ass'n, 323 S.W.3d 658, 663 (Ky. 2010), *reh'g denied* (Nov. 18, 2010); Kinder Morgan Michigan, L.L.C. v. City of Jackson, 744 N.W.2d 184, 191 (Mich. Ct. App. 2007); Hopkins v. Byrd, 146 P.3d 864, 866 (Okla. Civ. App. 2006); In re Hosp. Pricing Litig., King v. AnMed Health, 659 S.E.2d 131, 134 (S.C. 2008).

76. *E.g.,* regarding references by courts to prior case law in interpretation: State v. Soboroff, 798 N.W.2d 1 (Iowa 2011); David N. v. St. Mary's County Dept. of Soc. Services, 16 A.3d 991, 1005 (Md. Ct. Spec. App. 2011); Grenz v. Montana Dept. of Natural Res. & Conservation, 248 P.3d 785, 789–90 (Mont. 2011); Stuto v. Kerber, 910 N.Y.S.2d 215, 216 (App. Div. 2010) *leave to appeal granted*, 944 N.E.2d 657 (2011); State v. Stokes, 248 P.3d 953, 957 (Or. 2011); Smerz v. Delafield Town Bd., 796 N.W.2d 852, 855 (Wis. Ct. App. 2011).

77. *E.g.,* regarding reference to statutes from other jurisdictions on which the statute to be construed was modeled or closely patterned: People v. O'Hara, 240 P.3d 283, 285 (Colo. Ct. App. 2010) *cert. granted*, 2010 WL 4882956 (Colo. 2010); Wittig v. Westar Energy, Inc., 235 P.3d 535, 541 (Kan. Ct. App. 2010); Tally Bissell Neighbors, Inc. v. Eyrie Shotgun Ranch, LLC, 228 P.3d 1134, 1140 (Mt. 2010); Locken v. Locken, 797 N.W.2d 301, 309 (N.D. 2011).

78. *E.g.,* regarding reliance on uniform laws, model acts, their commentaries, or another court's interpretation of a uniform law or model act: Brooks v. Transamerica Fin. Advisors, 57 So.3d 1153, 1159 (La. Ct. App. 2011); Savig v. First Nat. Bank of Omaha, 781 N.W.2d 335, 346 (Minn. 2010); State v. Pennington, 14 A.3d 790, 795 (N.J. Super. Ct. App. Div. 2011); Corum v. Roswell Senior Living, LLC, 248 P.3d 329, 331 (N.M. Ct. App. 2010) *cert. denied*, 243 P.3d 1146 (2010); Vicknair v. Phelps Dodge Indus., Inc., 794 N.W.2d 746, 753 (N.D. 2011).

79. Clarke v. Securities Indus. Ass'n, 479 U.S. 388, 403, 107 S.Ct. 750, 759 (1987) (courts should give great weight to any reasonable construction of a regulatory statute adopted by the agency charged with the enforcement of that statute). *E.g.,* regarding level of deference due to agency opinion: Priority Health v. Commissioner of Office of Fin. & Ins. Services, 803 N.W.2d 132, 135 (Mich. 2011); New Jersey Dept. of Envtl. Prot. v. Exxon Mobil Corp., 22 A.3d 1, 6–7 (N.J. Super. Ct. App. Div. 2011); Held v. State, Workers' Comp. Bd., 921 N.Y.S.2d 674, 679 (App. Div. 2011); Harley H. Hoppe & Associates, Inc. v. King County, 255 P.3d 819, 825 (Wash. Ct. App. 2011) *review denied*, 262 P.3d 64 (2011).

80. *E.g.,* regarding meaning of strict construction: Martel v. Metropolitan Dist. Comm'n, 881 A.2d 194, 207 (Conn. 2005).

81. *E.g.,* regarding statutory ambiguity as "touchstone" of the rule of lenity: Gardner v. State, 20 A.3d 801, 811 (Md. 2011); State v. Dinslage, 789 N.W.2d 29, 36 (Neb. 2010); Such v. State, 950 A.2d 1150, 1158 (R.I. 2008).

82. *E.g.,* State v. Dinslage, 789 N.W.2d 29, 36 (Neb. 2010) (the rule of lenity requires a court to resolve ambiguities in a penal code in the defendant's favor).

83. Regarding broad and liberal construction of remedial statutes: Sheehan v. Oblates of St. Francis de Sales, 15 A.3d 1247 (Del. 2011), *reargument denied* (Apr. 19, 2011); In re Estate of Stoker, 122 Cal.Rptr.3d 529, 534 (Ct. App. 2011), *review denied* (May 18, 2011), *as modified on denial of reh'g* (Apr. 4, 2011); In re Esther V., 248 P.3d 863, 869(N.M. 2011).

84. McKenzie v. Betts, 55 So.3d 615, 622 (Fla. Dist. Ct. App. 2011) *review granted*, 60 So.3d 1055 (Fla. 2011).

85. Dixon v. Walcutt, 787 N.E.2d 1237, 1240 (Ohio Ct. App. 2003).

86. FLA. STAT. ANN. § 501.135(2) (West 2012).

Endnotes for Chapter 23: Background for Drafting a Will

1. *See, e.g.*, Colo. Rev. Stat. Ann. § 15–11–201 (West 2012), Colo. Rev. Stat. Ann. § 15–11–202 (West 2012), Colo. Rev. Stat. Ann. § 15–11–203 (West 2012), Colo. Rev. Stat. Ann. § 15–11–204 (West 2012).

2. *E.g.*, Colo. Rev. Stat. Ann. § 15–11–403 (West 2012).

3. Thompson v. Hardy, 43 S.W.3d 281, 285 (Ky. Ct. App. 2000).

4. *E.g.*, regarding the definition of "will," In re Estate of Waterloo, 250 P.3d 558, 560 (Ariz. Ct. App. 2011); Edmundson v. Estate of Fountain, 189 S.W.3d 427, 430 (Ark. 2004); Candies v. Hulsey, 593 S.E.2d 353, 354 (Ga. 2004); Eagar v. Burrows, 191 P.3d 9, 17 (Utah 2008); In re Estate of Jones, 197 S.W.3d 894, 903 (Tex. App. 2006).

5. *E.g.*, Tex. Prob. Code Ann. § 58(a) (Vernon) (West 2011); N.Y. Est. Powers & Trusts Law § 3–1.2 (McKinney) (West 2012).

6. N.H. Rev. Stat. Ann. § 551:1 (West 2012).

7. W. Va. Code Ann. § 41–1–2 (West 2012).

8. Ga. Code Ann. § 53–4–10(a) (West 2011).

9. *See, e.g.*, Mich. Comp. Laws Ann. § 700.2501 (West 2012) and Cal. Prob. Code § 6100.5 (West 2012).

10. *E.g.*, Cal. Prob. Code § 6102 (West 2012).

11. Tex. Prob. Code Ann. § 58b (Vernon) (West 2011).

12. *E.g.*, Estate of Justesen, 91 Cal.Rptr.2d 574 (Ct. App. 1999); *see* Silverstein v. Laschever, 970 A.2d 123, 129 (Conn. App. 2009) (one of the primary obligations of executor is to effect as speedy a settlement of the estate as reasonably possible).

13. *See, e.g.*, Cadle Co. v. D'Addario, 844 A.2d 836, 850 (Conn. 2004); In re Estate of Kirk, 686 N.E.2d 1246, 1249–50 (Ill. App. Ct. 1997) (in adversarial situation with beneficiaries, primary duty is to estate).

14. *E.g.*, In re Estate of Austin, 666 S.E.2d 73, 75 (Ga. Ct. App. 2008).

15. *See, e.g.*, Ruttenberg v. Friedman, 2012 WL 1650388 at 5 (Ala. 2012); Williamson v. Williamson, 714 N.E.2d 1270, 1273 (Ind. Ct. App. 1999); In re Estate of Carter, 912 So.2d 138, 144 (Miss. 2005); In re Estate of Skelly, 725 N.Y.S.2d 666, 667 (App. Div. 2001); Tsiatsios v. Tsiatsios, 744 A.2d 75, 79 (N.H. 1999); Estate of Justesen, 91 Cal.Rptr.2d 574, 579 (Ct. App. 1999); Matter of Estate of Hessenflow, 909 P.2d 662, 672 (Kan. App. 1995).

16. *See, e.g.*, In re Estate of Kirk, 686 N.E.2d 1246, 1249–50 (Ill. App. Ct. 1997) (though executor owes a fiduciary duty to estate *and* beneficiaries, if an adversarial situation arises, the primary allegiance is to the estate).

17. Matter of Estate of Campbell, 692 A.2d 1098, 1101–02 (Pa. Super. Ct. 1997) quoting In re Estate of Kurkowski, 487 Pa. 295, 409 A.2d 357 (1979).

18. *E.g.*, In re Estate of Waterloo, 250 P.3d 558, 561 (Ariz. Ct. App. 2011); In re Estate of Hendler, 316 S.W.3d 703, 708 (Tex. App. 2010), *reh'g overruled* (Aug. 17, 2010).

19. In re Wilton, 2007 PA Super 72, 921 A.2d 509, 513 (Pa. Super. Ct. 2007); Buchanan v. Buchanan, 698 S.E.2d 485, 488 (N.C. Ct. App. 2010) (the intent of testator is the polar star which guides interpretation of all wills and court will give effect to it unless it violates some rule of law, or is contrary to public policy).

20. In re Estate of Stoker, 122 Cal.Rptr.3d 529, 536 (2011), *review denied* (May 18, 2011), *as modified on denial of reh'g* (Apr. 4, 2011).

21. Swain v. Lee, 700 S.E.2d 541, 543 (Ga. 2010) (quoting Jones v. Habersham, 63 Ga. 146, 157 (1879)).

22. Stevens v. Casdorph, 203 W.Va. 450, 453, 508 S.E.2d 610, 613 (1998).

23. *See* C. Douglas Miller, Will Formality, Judicial Formalism, and Legislative Reform: An Examination of the New Uniform Probate Code "Harmless Error" Rule and the Movement Toward Amorphism, 43 Fla. L. Rev. 167, 259–65 (1991) (discussing the analysis of commentators of the functional purpose served by the formalities).

24. In re Estates of Gates, 876 So.2d 1059 (Miss. Ct. App. 2004).

25. In re Estate of Cote, 848 A.2d 264, 267 (Vt. 2004)

26. *E.g.*, regarding requirements for attested will and requiring a writing: Ala. Code § 43–8–131 (West 2012); Alaska Stat. Ann. § 13.12.502 (West 2012); Ark. Code Ann. § 28–25–103 (West 2012); Conn. Gen. Stat. Ann. § 45a–251 (West 2012); Fla. Stat. Ann. § 732.502(1) (West 2012);

Haw. Rev. Stat. § 560:2–502 (West 2012); IL ST CH 755 § 5/4–3(a) (West 2012); Kan. Stat. Ann. § 59–606 (West 2011); Ky. Rev. Stat. Ann. § 394.040 (West 2011)) Me. Rev. Stat. tit. 18–A, § 2–502 (West 2011) (Uniform Probate Code); Mo. Ann. Stat. § 474.320 (West 2012); N.C. Gen. Stat. Ann. § 31–3.3 (West 2011); N.H. Rev. Stat. Ann. § 551:2 (West 2012); N.J. Stat. Ann. § 3B:3–2(a) (West 2012); N.M. Stat. Ann. § 45–2–502 (West 2012); Ohio Rev. Code Ann. § 2107.03 (West 2011); Or. Rev. Stat. Ann. § 112.235 (West 2012); R.I. Gen. Laws Ann. § 33–5–5 (West 2012); S.C. Code Ann. § 62–2–502 (West 2012); S.D. Codified Laws § 29A–2–502 (West 2011); Tex. Prob. Code Ann. § 59 (Vernon) (West 2011); Utah Code Ann. § 75–2–502(1) (West 2011); Vt. Stat. Ann. tit. 14, § 5 (West 2012); W.Va. Code Ann. § 41–1–3 (West 2012); Wyo. Stat. Ann. § 2–6–112 (West 2012).

27. *E.g.,* requiring at least two witnesses: Ala. Code § 43–8–131 (West 2012); Alaska Stat. Ann. § 13.12.502(a)(3) (West 2012); Ark. Code Ann. § 28–25–103 (West 2012); Conn. Gen. Stat. Ann. § 45a–251 (West 2012); Fla. Stat. Ann. § 732.502(1)(b) (West 2012); Haw. Rev. Stat. § 560:2–502 (West 2012); IL ST CH 755 § 5/4–3(a) (West 2012); Kan. Stat. Ann. § 59–606 (West 2011); Md. Code Ann., Est. & Trusts § 4–102 (West 2012); Md. Code Ann., Est. & Trusts § 4–102 (West 2012); Me. Rev. Stat. tit. 18–A, § 2–502 (West 2012) (Uniform Probate Code); Mo. Ann. Stat. § 474.320 (West 2012); N.C. Gen. Stat. Ann. § 31–3.3(a) (West 2012); N.H. Rev. Stat. Ann. § 551:2(IV) (West 2012); N.J. Stat. Ann. § 3B:3–2a(3) (West 2012); N.M. Stat. Ann. § 45–2–502C (West 2012); Ohio Rev. Code Ann. § 2107.03 (West 2011); Or. Rev. Stat. Ann. § 112.235(3) (West 2012); S.C. Code Ann. § 62–2–502 (West 2012); S.D. Codified Laws § 29A–2–502 (b)(3) (West 2011); Tex. Prob. Code Ann. § 59(a) (West 2011); Utah Code Ann. § 75–2–502(1) (West 2011); Vt. Stat. Ann. tit. 14, § 5 (West 2012); W. Va. Code Ann. § 41–1–3 (West 2012); Wyo. Stat. Ann. § 2–6–112 (West 2012); Vt. Stat. Ann. tit. 14, § 5 (West 2012).

28. *See, e.g.,* Alaska Stat. Ann. § 13.12.505 (West 2012) (individual who is generally competent to be a witness may act as a witness to a will); Ga. Code Ann. § 53–4–22(a) (West 2011) (individual who is competent to be a witness and who is age 14 or older can witness a will); Mich. Comp. Laws Ann. § 700.2505(1) (West 2012) (an individual generally competent to be a witness may act as a witness to a will).

29. Some statutes include an express requirement that the witnesses be "credible": *e.g.*, IL ST CH 755 § 5/4–3(a) (2012); Ky. Rev. Stat. Ann. § 394.040 (West 2011); Md. Code Ann., Est. & Trusts § 4–102 (West 2012); N.H. Rev. Stat. Ann. § 551:2(IV) (West 2012); Tex. Prob. Code Ann. § 59(a) (West 2011); Vt. Stat. Ann. tit. 14, § 5 (West 2012).

30. Tex. Prob. Code Ann. § 59(a) (West 2011).

31. *E.g.*, regarding typical requirement that the person sign in the testator's presence and at the testator's direction: Ala. Code § 43–8–131 (West 2012); IL ST CH 755 § 5/4–3(a) (West 2012); Ky. Rev. Stat. Ann. § 394.040 (West 2011); Me. Rev. Stat. tit. 18–A, § 2–502 (West 2012) (Uniform Probate Code); Mo. Ann. Stat. § 474.320 (West 2012); N.C. Gen. Stat. Ann. § 31–3.3(b) (West 2012); S.C. Code Ann. § 62–2–502 (West 2012); Tex. Prob. Code Ann. § 59(a) (West 2011); W. Va. Code Ann. § 41–1–3 (West 2012).

32. *E.g.*, regarding requirement that the person sign in the testator's *conscious* presence: Alaska Stat. Ann. § 13.12.502(a)(2) (West 2012); Haw. Rev. Stat. § 560:2–502 (West 2012); N.J. Stat. Ann. § 3B:3–2a(2) (West 2012); N.M. Stat. Ann. § 45–2–502B (West 2012); Ohio Rev. Code Ann. § 2107.03 (West 2011); S.D. Codified Laws § 29A–2–502 (b)(2) (West 2011); Utah Code Ann. § 75–2–502(1)(b) (West 2011).

33. *E.g.* stating that the person signing for the testator must do so at the testator's *express* direction: Alaska Stat. Ann. § 13.12.502 (a)(2) (West 2012); Kan. Stat. Ann. § 59–606 (West 2011); Md. Code Ann., Est. & Trusts § 4–102 (West 2012); N.H. Rev. Stat. Ann. § 551:2(III) (West 2012); Ohio Rev. Code Ann. § 2107.03 (West 2011); R.I. Gen. Laws Ann. § 33–5–5 (West 2012); Vt. Stat. Ann. tit. 14, § 5 (West 2012); Wyo. Stat. Ann. § 2–6–112 (West 2012).

34. *E.g.,* regarding requirement that the person signing on testator's behalf sign the will and include a statement that the person was signing on the testator's behalf: Or. Rev. Stat. Ann. § 112.235(2) (West 2012).

35. *E.g.,* stating that the name must be intended as a signature: W. Va. Code Ann. § 41–1–3 (West 2012).

36. *E.g.,* regarding testator's acknowledgment of signature: Ala. Code § 43–8–131 (West 2012); Alaska Stat. Ann. § 13.12.502 (a)(3) (West 2012); Ark. Code Ann. § 28–25–103 (West 2012); Haw. Rev. Stat. § 560:2–502 (West 2012); IL ST CH 755 § 5/4–3(a) (West 2012); Me. Rev. Stat. tit. 18–A, § 2–502 (West 2012) (Uniform Probate Code); N.C. Gen. Stat. Ann. § 31–3.3(c)(West 2012); N.J. Stat. Ann. § 3B:3–2a(3) (West 2012); Ohio Rev. Code Ann. § 2107.03 (West 2011); Or. Rev. Stat. Ann. § 112.235(1)(c) (West 2012); Or. Rev. Stat. Ann. § 112.235(3) (West 2012); R.I. Gen. Laws Ann. § 33–5–5 (West 2012); S.C. Code Ann. § 62–2–502 (West 2012); S.D. Codified Laws § 29A–2–502 (b)(3) (West 2011); Utah Code Ann. § 75–2–502(1) (West 2011).

37. *E.g.*, regarding acknowledgment by testator that the writing is the testator's will: Ala. Code § 43–8–131 (West 2012); Alaska Stat. Ann. § 13.12.502 (a)(3) (West 2012); Haw. Rev. Stat. § 560:2–502 (West 2012); Kan. Stat. Ann. § 59–606 (West 2011); Ky. Rev. Stat. Ann. § 394.040 (West 2011); Me. Rev. Stat. tit. 18–A, § 2–502 (West 2012) (Uniform Probate Code); N.J. Stat. Ann. § 3B:3–2a(3) (West 2012); Utah Code Ann. § 75–2–502(1) (West 2011); W. Va. Code Ann. § 41–1–3 (West 2012).

38. *E.g.*, regarding acknowldgment that witnesses sign "at the request of the testator": Ark. Code Ann. § 28–25–103 (West 2012); N.H. Rev. Stat. Ann. § 551:2(IV) (West 2012).

39. *E.g.*, regarding requirement that witnesses sign in the presence of the testator: Ark. Code Ann. § 28–25–103 (West 2012); IL ST CH 755 § 5/4–3(a) (West 2012); Kan. Stat. Ann. § 59–606 (West 2011); Md. Code Ann., Est. & Trusts § 4–102 (West 2012); Mo. Ann. Stat. § 474.320 (West 2012); N.C. Gen. Stat. Ann. § 31–3.3(d)(West 2012); N.H. Rev. Stat. Ann. § 551:2(IV) (West 2012); N.M. Stat. Ann. § 45–2–502C (West 2012); R.I. Gen. Laws Ann. § 33–5–5 (West 2012); Tex. Prob. Code Ann. § 59(a) (West 2011); Vt. Stat. Ann. tit. 14, § 5 (West 2012); Vt. Stat. Ann. tit. 14, § 5 (West 2012).

40. *E.g.*, regarding requirement that the witnesses sign in the testator's "conscious" presence: Ohio Rev. Code Ann. § 2107.03 (West 2011); S.D. Codified Laws § 29A–2–502 (b)(3) (West 2011).

41. *E.g.*, regarding requirement that witnesses sign within a reasonable time after the signature or the relevant acknowledgment: Alaska Stat. Ann. § 13.12.502(a)(3) (West 2012); Haw. Rev. Stat. § 560:2–502 (West 2012); N.J. Stat. Ann. § 3B:3–2a(3) (West 2012).

42. *E.g.*, regarding requirement that the witnesses sign in each other's presence: Fla. Stat. Ann. § 732.502 (West); Ky. Rev. Stat. Ann. § 394.040 (West); N.M. Stat. Ann. § 45–2–502C (West 2012); R.I. Gen. Laws Ann. § 33–5–5 (West 2012); Vt. Stat. Ann. tit. 14, § 5 (West 2012).

43. Ark. Code Ann. § 28–25–103 (West 2012).

44. Ala. Code § 43–8–131 (West 2012).

45. N.H. Rev. Stat. Ann. § 551:2 (West 2012).

46. *E.g.*, Matter of Will of Ranney, 589 A.2d 1339, 1345 (N.J. 1991) (stating that the provision was enacted to free will execution from "ritualism" of the previous law and to prevent technical defects from invalidating otherwise valid wills; if strict construction would frustrate the purposes of the statute, the spirit of the law should control over its letter).

47. In re Perkins' Estate, 504 P.2d 564, 568 (Kan. 1972).

48. Cal. Prob. Code § 6110 (West 2012).

49. Colo. Rev. Stat. Ann. § 15–11–503 (West 2012). "Although a document, or writing added upon a document, was not executed in compliance with [the requisite formalities], the document or writing is treated as if it had been executed in compliance with that section if the proponent of the document or writing establishes by clear and convincing evidence that the decedent intended the document or writing to constitute … [t]he decedent's will…. [This] section shall apply only if the document is signed or acknowledged by the decedent as his or her will or if it is established by clear and convincing evidence that the decedent erroneously signed a document intended to be the will of the decedent's spouse."

50. *E.g.*, In re Estate of Hendler, 316 S.W.3d 703, 708 (Tex. App. 2010), *reh'g overruled* (Aug. 17, 2010) (to be a codicil, an instrument must be executed with testamentary intent).

51. *See, e.g.*, regarding formality necessary to alter or add to an existing will's provisions: Ga. Code Ann. § 53–4–20(c) (West 2011) (stating that codicil requires same formalities as will); Fla. Stat. Ann. § 732.502(5) (West 2012) (codicil requires the same degree of formality); Nev. Rev. Stat. Ann. § 132.070 (West 2011) (codicil means an addition to the will that is signed with the same formalities).

Refer also to case law dealing with the validity of alleged supplementary writings, indicating that a valid codicil must be executed with full testamentary formalities. *E.g.*, In re Last Will & Testament of Palecki, 920 A.2d 413, 418–19 (Del. Ch. 2007); Parker v. Melican, 684 S.E.2d 654, 656–57 (Ga. 2009); Garrett v. Bohannon, 621 So.2d 935, 937 (Miss. 1993); Matter of Estate of Voeller, 534 N.W.2d 24, 26 (N.D. 1995).

52. Neb. Rev. Stat. § 30–2332 (West 2011).

53. Colo. Rev. Stat. Ann. § 15–11–507(4) (West 2011).

54. R.I. Gen. Laws § 33–5–9.1 (West 2012).

55. Me. Rev. Stat. Ann. tit. 18–A, § 2–508 (West 2011).

Endnotes for Chapter 24: Drafting and Executing the Will

1. In re Estate of Allen, 301 S.W.3d 923, 928 (Tex. App. 2009), *reh'g overruled* (Jan. 20, 2010), *review denied* (June 11, 2010).

2. *E.g.,* stating that court generally gives words in will plain and ordinary meaning (absent indications of a different intent): Harrison v. Morrow, 977 So.2d 457, 459–60 (Ala. 2007); In re Estate of Hope, 223 P.3d 119, 122 (Colo. Ct. App. 2007); Ernest v. Chumley, 936 N.E.2d 602, 606 (Ill. App. Ct. 2010); In re Estate of Owen, 855 N.E.2d 603, 609 (Ind. Ct. App. 2006); Montgomery v. Administrators of Tulane Educ. Fund, 51 So.3d 60, 63 (La. Ct. App. 2010) *writ denied,* 57 So.3d 332 (2011); In re Estate of Ayers, 161 P.3d 833, 835 (Mont. 2007); Holcombe–Burdette v. Bank of Am., 640 S.E.2d 480, 484 (S.C. Ct. App. 2006); In re Estate of Snapp, 233 S.W.3d 288, 291 (Tenn. Ct. App. 2007).

3. *See, e.g.,* Montgomery v. Administrators of Tulane Educ. Fund, 51 So.3d 60, 63 (La. Ct. App. 2010) *writ denied,* 57 So.3d 332 (2011); In re Estate of Musiol, 232 S.W.3d 718, 720 (Mo. Ct. App. 2007).

4. Coleman v. Coleman, 350 S.W.3d 201, 203 (Tex. App. 2011).

5. *See, e.g.,* Estate of Robison v. Carter, 701 S.W.2d 218, 221 (Tenn. Ct. App. 1985) (court could find no reported decisions construing the phrase "closest relative" used in a will, but did find precedent construing "nearest relative," which the court considered "sufficiently synonymous … [to] provide some assistance—i.e., by identifying "the class of persons who have the nearest degree of consanguinity to the testator.").

6. Nev. Rev. Stat. Ann. § 132.055 (West 2011).

7. *E.g.,* regarding characteristics of a general legacy: In re Estate of Lung, 692 A.2d 1349, 1350 (D.C. 1997) (general legacy may be obtained from any source of the estate); Babcock v. Estate of Babcock, 995 So.2d 1044, 1046 (Fla. Dist. Ct. App. 2008) (general devise may be satisfied in cash or in kind out of the general assets of the estate instead of from any specific fund, thing, or things); Cent. Carolina Bank & Trust Co., N.A. v. Wright, 478 S.E.2d 33, 37 (N.C. Ct. App. 1996) (general bequest is a gift of property from the estate that does not specify the exact piece of property the beneficiary shall receive, and may be satisfied from any of estate's general assets); Harris v. Hines, 137 S.W.3d 898, 904 (Tex. App. 2004) (legacy is general bequest if it bequeaths a designated quantity or value of property or money and the testator intended for it to be satisfied out of her or his general assets rather than disposing of, or being charged upon, any specific fund or property).

8. E.g., regarding characteristics of a demonstrative legacy: Smith v. Estate of Peters, 741 P.2d 1172, 1173 (Alaska 1987) (demonstrative legacy is sum of money or some other certain quantity that is satisfied out of a particular fund or property but that remains payable even if the fund fails, so long as the estate contains other property from which it can be satisfied); In re Estate of Lund, 633 N.W.2d 571, 574 (Minn. Ct. App. 2001) (demonstrative legacy is money gift, made a charge on specific fund and directed to be paid out of that fund, but payable even if fund fails); (Estate of Stalnaker, 479 A.2d 612, 615 (Pa. Super. Ct. 1984) (monetary legacy is given with reference to a particular fund, but only as an indication of a convenient source for satisfying such legacy); Hurt v. Smith, 744 S.W.2d 1, 4 (Tex. 1987) (demonstrative legacies are bequests of sums of money, or of quantity or amounts having a pecuniary value and measure, not in themselves specific, which testator intended to be charged primarily to a particular fund or piece of property).

9. *E.g.,* regarding unavailability of cash equivalent or substitute gift if specific item to which specific legacy applies is not available: In re Estate of Lund, 633 N.W.2d 571, 574 (Minn. Ct. App. 2001); In re Estate of Balter, 703 A.2d 1038, 1041 (Pa. Super. Ct. 1997); Polson v. Craig, 570 S.E.2d 190, 193 (S.C. Ct. App. 2002).

10. In re Estate of Balter, 703 A.2d 1038, 1041 (Pa. Super. Ct. 1997).

11. Mont. Code Ann. § 72–2–616 (West 2011).

12. N.M. Stat. Ann. § 45–3–805 (West 2012).

13. *See, e.g.,* Ariz. Rev. Stat. Ann. § 14–3902 (West 2012); Or. Rev. Stat. Ann. § 116.133 (West 2012); 20 Pa. Cons. Stat. Ann. § 3541 (West 2012).

14. *See* Ark. Code Ann. § 28–53–112(a) (West 2012).

15. *E.g.,* Schenebeck v. Schenebeck, 947 S.W.2d 367, 372 (Ark. 1997).

16. *E.g.,* Ark. Code Ann. § 28–53–112(a) (West 2012) and Chalkwater v. Dolly, 672 A.2d 673, 676 (Md. Ct. Spec. App. 1996).

17. S.C. Code Ann. § 62–2–605 (West 2011). *See, e.g.,* Polson v. Craig, 570 S.E.2d 190 (Ct. App. 2002). In that case, the testator's will provided that she was giving her stepdaughter 400 shares in Standard Oil Company. The question was whether the daughter should also receive the enormous increase resulting from stock splits when Standard Oil became Exxon. A lack of clarity as to whether the legacy was general or specific led to a dispute and subsequent litigation that had to be resolved on appeal.

18. *See, e.g.,* Schenebeck v. Schenebeck, 329 Ark. 198, 207, 947 S.W.2d 367, 372 (1997).

19. *See* In re Estate of Lund, 633 N.W.2d 571, 574 (Minn. Ct. App. 2001).

20. In re Estate of Lung, 692 A.2d 1349, 1350 (D.C. 1997). In that case, the testator had provided for legacies to eight enumerated individuals in amounts ranging from from $25,000 to $100,000. *Id.* The testator designated a particular stock fund as the source of funds for these eight sums. *Id.* When he died, however, the stock fund was $460,000 short of what was needed to pay the legacies. *Id.* In addition to those legacies, the testator had created charitable trust for a university that was to be funded out of the residue of his estate." *Id.*

The trial judge applied the presumption against specific legacies, concluding that the eight legacies were demonstrative legacies. *Id.* The University appealed the ruling, since the ruling would require the estate to fund the $460,000 shortfall out of residuary funds. *Id.*

The D.C. Court of Appeals held that the trial judge correctly characterized the legacy as a demonstrative legacy and correctly applied the presumption against specific legacies. "The rationale of this presumption is perfectly suited to this case," the Court of Appeals said. "The presumption against specific legacies exists because such bequests are lost if the designated asset is not part of the estate when the testator dies. Here, if the legacy were found specific, eight individuals would lose over $450,000 because they would be forced to prorate less than $50,000 rather than $500,000." *Id.* at 1351. The D.C. Court pointed out that the language of the legacies did not reflect an intention to create specific legacies. *Id.* Considering the will as a whole, the court concluded that the testator "held bequests to particular individuals in higher regard than the residuary estate." *Id.*

21. Tex. Prob. Code Ann. § 68(b) (West 2011)

22. Tex. Prob. Code Ann. § 68(c) (West 2011).

23. Tex. Prob. Code Ann. § 68(d) (West 2011).

24. Ark. Code Ann. § 28–26–104 (West 2012).

25. Tex. Prob. Code Ann. § 68(a) (West 2011).

26. Ala. Code § 43–8–224 (West 2012); Minn. Stat. Ann. § 524.2–603(1) (West 2012).

27. Neb. Rev. Stat. § 30–2343 (West 2011).

28. Iowa Code Ann. § 633.273 (West 2012) ("If a devisee dies before the testator, leaving issue who survive the testator, the devisee's issue who survive the testator shall inherit the property devised to the devisee per stirpes, unless from the terms of the will, the intent is clear and explicit to the contrary.")

29. *See, e.g.* regarding various approaches: Ala. Code § 43–8–224 (West 2012); Ky. Rev. Stat. Ann. § 394.410 (West 2012).

30. Vt. Stat. Ann. tit. 14, § 621 (West)

31. Mich. Comp. Laws Ann. § 700.2702 (West).

32. *See, e.g.,* Ky. Rev. Stat. Ann. § 394.225 (West 2011).

33. *E.g.,* stating that applicable law is law in effect at the date of testator's death: Will of Boyd, 613 N.Y.S.2d 330, 332 (Sur. 1994).

34. *E.g.,* stating that the court's primary duty is to determine and give effect to the testator's lawful intent:: Howell v. Sykes, 526 S.E.2d 183, 185 (N.C. Ct. App. 2000); In re Estate of Wright, 196 P.3d 1075, 1079 (Wash. Ct. App. 2008)

35. *E.g.,* stating that the court looks for intent within the will's four corners: McKnight v. Way, 58 So.3d 810, 815 (Ala. Civ. App. 2010), *reh'g denied* (Aug. 6, 2010), *cert. denied* (Sept. 10, 2010); Dunn v. Means, 803 S.W.2d 542, 543 (Ark.1991); In re Pike Family Trusts, 38 A.3d 329, 331 (Me. 2012); Collier v. Bryant, 719 S.E.2d 70, 76 (N.C. Ct. App. 2011); Patrick v. Patrick, 182 S.W.3d 433, 436 (Tex. App. 2005); Wendell v. AmeriTrust Co., N.A., 630 N.E.2d 368, 370 (Ohio 1994); In re Estate of Wright, 196 P.3d 1075, 1079 (Wash. Ct. App. 2008).

36. Pickelner v. Adler, 229 S.W.3d 516, 531 (Tex. App. 2007).

37. *E.g.,* stating that the court will not use rules of construction to give an unambiguous will a different meaning from that reflected in its four corners: Lazarus v. Sherman, 10 A.3d 456 (R.I. 2011); In re Estate of Roethler, 801 N.W.2d 833, 842 (Iowa 2011); Hood v. Todd, 695 S.E.2d 31, 33 (Ga. 2010); Bank of Am., N.A. v. Carpenter, 929 N.E.2d 570, 579 (Ill. App. Ct. 2010) *appeal denied*, 237 Ill.2d 552, 938 N.E.2d 518 (2010); Buchanan v. Buchanan, 698 S.E.2d 485, 488 (N.C. Ct. App. 2010); Dantzic v. Dantzic, 668 S.E.2d 164, 171 (W. Va. 2008).

38. *E.g.,* court will not admit extrinsic evidence if the will is unambiguous that would contradict or vary the will's terms:. Matter of Estate of Jenkins, 890 P.2d 188, 190 (Colo. Ct. App. 1994) *aff'd*, 904 P.2d 1316 (Colo. 1995); Cronic v. Baker, 667 S.E.2d 363, 365–66 (Ga. 2008); Flannery v. McNamara, 738 N.E.2d 739, 743 (Mass. 2000); In re Johnson, 190 S.W.3d 469, 475 (Mo. Ct. App. 2006); Lazarus v. Sherman, 10 A.3d 456 (R.I. 2011); In re Estate of Tyner, 292 S.W.3d 179, 182 (Tex. App. 2009).

39. *E.g.,* court will not admit extrinsic evidence to create ambiguity where none is apparent: Bond v. Estate of Pylant, 63 So.3d 638, 647 (Ala. Civ. App. 2010), *cert. denied* (Nov. 12, 2010); Flannery v. McNamara, 738 N.E.2d 739, 743 (Mass. 2000); In re Estate of Harper, 975 A.2d 1155, 1162 (Pa. Super. Ct. 2009).

40. *See, e.g.,* In re Estate of Stanton, 114 P.3d 1246, 1249 (Wyo. 2005).

41. In re Estate of Matthews, 702 N.W.2d 821, 824–25 (Neb. Ct. App. 2005).

42. *E.g.,* Regarding this "general maxim of construction" in favor of testacy: Matter of Estate of Killen, 937 P.2d 1368, 1371 (Ariz. Ct. App. 1996); In re Robinson's Estate, 68 Cal.Rptr. 420, 423 (Ct. App. 1968); Carter v. Succession of Carter, 332 So.2d 439, 442 (La. 1976); Matter of Estate of Bair, 341 N.W.2d 188, 189 (Mich. Ct. App. 1983); New Mexico Boys Ranch, Inc. v. Hanvey, 643 P.2d 857, 859 (N.M. 1982); Wilson Bldg., Inc. v. Baer, 175 N.Y.S.2d 495, 502 (N.Y. Sup. Ct. 1958); Howell v. Sykes, 526 S.E.2d 183, 185 (N.C. Ct. App. 2000); In re Estate of Martin, 635 N.W.2d 473, 476 (S.D. 2001); Dantzic v. Dantzic, 668 S.E.2d 164, 171 (W. Va. 2008); In re Estate of Price, 871 P.2d 1079, 1084 (Wash. Ct. App.1994).

43. *E.g.* stating that the court will prefer a reading of a legacy that makes it valid rather than invalid: deGraaf v. Owen, 598 So.2d 892, 895 (Ala. 1992);. Estate of Blount v. Papps, 611 So.2d 862, 868 (Miss. 1992); Howell v. Sykes, 526 S.E.2d 183, 185 (N.C. Ct. App. 2000).

44. *E.g.,* stating that words are given their ordinary grammatical sense: Click v. Click, 40 A.3d 1105, 1115 (Md. Ct. Spec. App. 2012); Estate of Gill ex rel. Grant v. Clemson Univ. Found., 725 S.E.2d 516 (S.C. Ct. App. 2012).

45. *E.g.,* regarding presumption that testator was aware of the law (including the construction of terminology) at the time of making the will and made the will in conformity with it: Newman v. Wells Fargo Bank, 926 P.2d 969, 977 (Cal. 1996); Noll v. Garber, 784 N.E.2d 388, 392 (Ill. App. Ct. 2003); Lockwood v. Adamson, 566 N.E.2d 96, 98 (Mass. 1991) (testator presumed to know the correct construction of legal terminology); Commerce Bank, N.A. v. Blasdel, 141 S.W.3d 434, 443–44 (Mo. Ct. App. 2004); Matter of Estate of Dunlop, 617 N.Y.S.2d 119, 122 (Sur. 1994); Early v. Bowen, 447 S.E.2d 167, 169 (N.C. Ct. App. 1994); Wendell v. AmeriTrust Co., N.A., 630 N.E.2d 368, 370 (Ohio 1994).

46. *E.g.* Will of Boyd, 613 N.Y.S.2d 330, 332 (Sur. 1994).

47. *See, e.g.,* Noll v. Garber, 784 N.E.2d 388, 392 (Ill. App. Ct. 2003).

48. Click v. Click, 40 A.3d 1105 (Ct. Spec. App. 2012) (stating that in Maryland, if a layperson—rather than an attorney—draws up the will, "the language used may be given the meaning it would commonly have to a person in his situation").

49. *E.g.,* stating that the court can admit extrinsic evidence to clarify an ambiguity: SPCA Wildlife Care Ctr. v. Abraham, 75 So.3d 1271, 1276 (Fla. Dist. Ct. App. 2011); Fifth Third Bank, N.A. v. Rosen, 957 N.E.2d 956, 965 (Ill. App. Ct. 2011); In re Estate of Wicklund, 812 N.W.2d 359, 366 (N.D. 2012); In re Estate of Sherry, 240 P.3d 1182, 1189 (Wash. Ct. App. 2010).

50. *E.g.,* that extrinsic evidence used only to show what testator meant by what testator did say, not what testator intended to say and did *not* say: Matter of Blacksill's Estate, 602 P.2d 511, 513 (Ariz. Ct. App. 1979); In re Estate of Roethler, 801 N.W.2d 833, 842 (Iowa 2011); Matter of Brecklein's Estate, 637 P.2d 444, 451 (Kan. Ct. App. 1981); In re Estate of Cole, 621 N.W.2d 816, 819 (Minn. Ct. App. 2001); In re Estate of Samuelson, 757 N.W.2d 44, 48 (N.D. 2008); Estate of Pegram v. Pegram, 189 S.W.3d 227, 232 (Tenn. Ct. App. 2005); Dalrymple v. Moss, 611 S.W.2d 938, 943 (Tex. Civ. App. 1981).

51. *See* Matter of Brecklein's Estate, 637 P.2d 444, 451 (Kan. Ct. App. 1981)

52. *E.g.,* Matter of Blacksill's Estate, 602 P.2d 511, 513 (Ariz. Ct. App. 1979); Breckner v. Prestwood, 600 S.W.2d 52, 55 (Mo. Ct. App. 1980).

Endnotes for Chapter 26: Choosing Language

1. *E.g.,* F.B.T. Productions, LLC v. Aftermath Records, 621 F.3d 958, 964 (9th Cir. 2010) *cert. denied*, 131 S.Ct. 1677 (U.S. 2011), *reh'g denied*, 131 S.Ct. 2482 (U.S. 2011): in which one of the issues in a dispute over a royalties agreement turned on the meaning of the word "license"; 9th Circuit looked to Webster's Third New International Dictionary of the English Language for the ordinary meaning of the word "license" as well as to the usage of the word in federal copyright law decisions; *see* South Ridge Homeowners' Ass'n v. Brown, 226 P.3d 758, 760 (Utah App. 2010) (court referred to Black's Law Dictionary and two different Webster's dictionaries).

2. *E.g.,* Bliss Mine Rd. Condo. Ass'n v. Nationwide Prop. & Cas. Ins. Co., 11 A.3d 1078, 1083–84 (R.I. 2010) (the court referred to three dictionaries: American Heritage, Random House, and Webster's).

3. South Ridge Homeowners' Ass'n v. Brown, 226 P.3d 758, 760 (Utah App. 2010).

4. See, e.g., Phillips v. AWH Corp., 415 F.3d 1303, 1322 (Fed. Cir. 2005). The court pointed out that a definition from a "general-usage dictionary" cannot override evidence of the meaning of a term that is used in a particular field. Thus, in a patent case, a general-usage dictionary cannot overcome art-specific evidence of the meaning of a claim term. *Id.*

5. United States v. Gonzales, 520 U.S. 1, 5–6, 117 S.Ct. 1032, 1035 (1997) (citing Webster's Third New International Dictionary).

6. W3i Mobile, LLC v. Westchester Fire Ins. Co., 632 F.3d 432, 435 (8th Cir. 2011) (relating to the meaning of an exclusion in an insurance policy); In re SRC Holding Corp., 545 F.3d 661, 665–66 (8th Cir. 2008) (relating to the meaning of an exclusion in an insurance policy).

7. *See* Hoffman v. L & M Arts, 774 F. Supp. 2d 826, 833–35 (N.D. Tex. 2011).

8. Triple–A Baseball Club Associates v. Northeastern Baseball, Inc., 832 F.2d 214, 225 (1st Cir. 1987).

9. E.E.O.C. v. R.J. Gallagher Co., 181 F.3d 645, 652 (5th Cir. 1999).

10. Mark Technologies Corp. v. Utah Res. Int'l, Inc., 147 P.3d 509, 512 (Utah Ct. App. 2006).

11. Grayned v. City of Rockford, 408 U.S. 104, 108–09, 92 S.Ct. 2294, 2298–99 (1972).

12. *Id.*

13. *Id.*

14. United States v. Backlund, 677 F.3d 930, 939 (9th Cir. 2012).

15. *See* Christensen v. Christensen, 176 P.3d 626, 629 (Wyo. 2008); Hot Light Brands, L.L.C. v. Harris Realty Inc., 912 N.E.2d 258, 264 (Ill. App. Ct. 2009) (ambiguity exists where language is obscure in meaning through indefiniteness of expression) quoted in Reserve at Woodstock, LLC v. City of Woodstock, 958 N.E.2d 1100, 1112 (Ill. App. 2011).

16. Farmers Ins. Exch. v. Versaw, 99 P.3d 796, 798 (Utah 2004) (ambiguities typically appear for the following reasons: (1) because of vague or ambiguous language in a particular provision, or (2) because two or more contract provisions, when read together, give rise to different or inconsistent meanings, even though each provision is clear when read alone).

17. *E.g.,* regarding some of the different contexts in which this canon has recently been applied: McCoy v. Commissioner of Pub. Safety, 12 A.3d 948, 957 (Conn. 2011) (meaning of phrase "motor vehicle"); Peak v. Adams, 799 N.W.2d 535, 547–48 (Iowa 2011) (scope of language in contract to rent a truck); Kese Indus. v. Roslyn Torah Found., 940 N.E.2d 530, 533–34 (N.Y. 2010) (whether attorney in tax foreclosure action qualified as a legal representative); In re R.V., 941 N.E.2d 1216, 1220 (Ohio Ct. App. 2010) (meaning of "other relatives" in custody statute) (Grady J., dissenting); Shilling v. Baker, 691 S.E.2d 806, 810 (Va. 2010) (whether scattering cremains on property is a "final disposal" creating a "cemetery"); Barr v. NCB Mgmt. Services, Inc., 711 S.E.2d 577, 581–82 (W.Va. 2011) (meaning of the word "creditor" in a statute).

18. King City Rehab, LLC v. Clackamas County, 164 P.3d 1190, 1194 (Or. Ct. App. 2007).

19. Blue Shield of California Life & Health Ins. Co. v. Superior Court, 120 Cal.Rptr.3d 713, 724 (Ct. App. 2011).

20. *See, e.g.,* Shilling v. Baker, 691 S.E.2d 806, 810 (Va. 2010) ("All the examples listed, however, share a common feature: a permanent resting place either underground or in a confined space or container.... The mere scattering of human remains above ground is not a "final disposal" comparable to a burial underground or in a mausoleum, niche or columbarium.")

21. *See* Ex parte Capstone Bldg. Corp., 2012 WL 887497 at 7 (Ala. 2012) (court found pertinent doctrine of *noscitur a sociis* that if general and specific words capable of an analogous meaning are associated one with the other, they take color from each other so that general words are restricted to sense analogous to less general.)

22. *See* Peak v. Adams, 799 N.W.2d 535, 547 (Iowa 2011) (in most situations, rules produce identical results).

23. Brown v. Saint City Church of God of Apostolic Faith, Inc., 717 So.2d 557, 559 (Fla. Dist. Ct. App. 1998).

24. *E.g.*, State v. Shelton, 363 S.W.3d 183 (Mo. Ct. App. 2012), *reh'g and/or transfer denied* (Mar. 16, 2012), *transfer denied* (May 1, 2012) ("For one thing, *ejusdem generis* ("of the same kind") seems better suited to an "*A, B, C, or other such item*" pattern, a type of which was at issue in [another case], than the word structure here ("*by any means, including but not limited to*" *listed examples*). The meager fruit of our search for cases considering "any means" statutes and *ejusdem generis* suggests, if anything, the same conclusion.")

25. United States v. Migi, 329 F.3d 1085, 1088–89 (9th Cir. 2003) (principle of *ejusdem generis* does not apply here because the statute's plain meaning apparent; application of *ejusdem generis* would narrow Congress's definition of "children"; in addition, *ejusdem generis* not applicable because Congress modified list of examples with phrase "including, but not limited to" which mitigates "sometimes unfortunate results" of rigid application of canon.)

26. *E.g.*, United States v. West, 671 F.3d 1195, 1200–01 (10th Cir. 2012) (courts historically apply *ejusdem generis* to limit general terms followed by specific term ones and statute did not follow this pattern, but used "including, but not limited to"); Cooper Distrib. Co., Inc. v. Amana Refrigeration, Inc., 63 F.3d 262, 280 (3d Cir. 1995) (Alito, J.) (*ejusdem generis* applies only if provision does not express contrary intent and since phrase "including, but not limited to" plainly expresses a contrary intent, *ejusdem generis* is inapplicable).

27. *See* United States v. West, 671 F.3d 1195, 1202 (10th Cir. 2012) (Lucero, J., concurring) (stating that "substantial contrary authority" applies the canon to statutes that use the phrase "including but not limited to"); BNSF Ry. Co. v. Brotherhood of Locomotive Eng'rs & Trainmen, 595 F.Supp.2d 722, 734 (N.D.Tex.2008).

28. Regarding "including but not limited to" as precluding application of the doctrine: E.g., State v. Shelton, 363 S.W.3d 183 (Mo. Ct. App. 2012) ("For one thing, *ejusdem generis ... seems better suited to an* "*A, B, C, or other such item*" *pattern*, a type of which was at issue in William, than the word structure here ("by any means, including but not limited to" listed examples").) *Contra*: Schmidt v. Mt. Angel Abbey, 223 P.3d 399, 407 (Or. 2009) ("Plaintiff next argues that this court need not apply the principle of ejusdem generis because the legislature chose to connect the general term "sexual exploitation" with the specific examples by using the phrase "including but not limited to." Regardless of whether we are constrained by the "rule" of ejusdem generis, we will apply the principle when, as here, it provides useful guidance in interpreting a statutory term.")

29. *E.g.*, State v. Bolin, 662 S.E.2d 38, 39–40 (S.C. 2008) (state constitution expressly permitted legislature to restrict the sale of alcoholic beverage to persons in specified age range but omitted any similar provision allowing restriction on sale of handguns; therefore legislature could not restrict the sale of handguns to those persons); Metzger v. DaRosa, 805 N.E.2d 1165, 1172 (Ill. 2004) (if state Personnel Code provides a private right of action with respect to a specific section of the statute, the court will infer that the legislature did not intend to create a private right of action to enforce other sections of the statute with respect to which no right of action is expressly granted).

30. Mercer v. 3M Precision Optics, Inc., 908 N.E.2d 1016, 1018 (Ohio Ct. App. 2009).

Endnotes for Chapter 27: Drafting Definitions

1. *E.g.*, regarding courts giving plain meaning to words in construing contracts (including insurance contracts): Hamilton v. United Services Auto. Ass'n, 974 A.2d 774, 781 (Conn. Ct. App. 2009); In re Estate of Metz, 256 P.3d 45, 50 (Okla. 2011); Cole v. Wellmark of S. Dakota, Inc., 776 N.W.2d 240, 246 (S.D. 2009); Mathews v. PHH Mortg. Corp., 724 S.E.2d 196, 200–01 (Va. 2012).

2. *E.g.*, regarding courts giving plain meaning to words in statutes: Cahoon v. Shelton, 647 F.3d 18, 22 (1st Cir. 2011); BEPCO, L.P. v. Santa Fe Minerals, Inc., 675 F.3d 466 (5th Cir. 2012); In re Shinnecock Smoke Shop, 571 F.3d 1171, 1173 (Fed. Cir. 2009); Walker v. State, 723 S.E.2d 894, 898 (Ga. 2012); City of Brainerd v. Brainerd Inves. P'ship, 2012 WL 1069947 at *5 (Minn. Ct. App. 2012).

3. *E.g.*, American Tobacco Co. v. Patterson, 456 U.S. 63, 68, 102 S.Ct. 1534, 1537 (1982) (court assumes that the legislative purpose is expressed by the ordinary meaning of the terms used).

4. Caltex Oil Venture v. C.I.R., 2012 WL 95557 at 6 (T.C. 2012).

5. *E.g.*, regarding words in will being given plain and ordinary meaning: Harrison v. Morrow, 977 So.2d 457, 459–60 (Ala. 2007); In re Estate of Hope, 223 P.3d 119, 122 (Colo. Ct. App. 2007); Ernest v. Chumley, 936 N.E.2d 602, 606 (Ill. App. Ct. 2010); In re Estate of Owen, 855 N.E.2d 603, 609 (Ind. Ct. App. 2006); Montgomery v. Administrators of Tulane Educ. Fund, 51 So.3d 60, 63 (La. Ct. App. 2010) *writ denied*, 57 So.3d 332 (2011); In re Estate of Musiol, 232 S.W.3d 718, 720 (Mo. Ct. App. 2007); In re Estate of Ayers, 161 P.3d 833, 835 (Mt. 2007); Holcombe–Burdette v. Bank of Am., 640 S.E.2d 480, 484 (S.C. Ct. App. 2006); In re Estate of Snapp, 233 S.W.3d 288, 291 (Tenn. Ct. App. 2007); Coleman v. Coleman, 350 S.W.3d 201, 203 (Tex. App. 2011).

6. *See e.g.,* stating that certain testamentary language with fixed meaning is construed in that sense: Cheek v. Love, 346 S.W.3d 300, 305–06 (Ky. Ct. App. 2010), *review denied* (Sept. 14, 2011); Click v. Click, 40 A.3d 1105, 1114–15 (Md. Ct. Spec. App. 2012); In re Arnott, 942 N.E.2d 1124, 1135 (Ohio Ct. App. 2010) *motion to certify allowed*, 942 N.E.2d 383 and *appeal not allowed*, 942 N.E.2d 386 (2011).

7. *E.g.,* stating that if will drafted by a layperson, language used may be given the meaning it would commonly have to a person in his or her situation: Friedman v. Hannan, 987 A.2d 60, 67 (Md. 2010); In re Estate of Craigen, 305 S.W.3d 825, 827 (Tex. App. 2010).

Endnotes for Chapter 28: Eliminating Ambiguity

1. *E.g.,* Allstate Ins. Co. v. Howard Sav. Inst., 317 A.2d 770, 778 (N.J. Super. Ct. Ch. Div. 1974); Black v. National Merit Ins. Co., 226 P.3d 175, 182 (Wash. Ct. App. 2010) *review denied*, 238 P.3d 503 (2010).

2. *E.g.,* regarding courts' discussion of "and" and "or": Manor Healthcare Corp. v. Soiltest, Inc., 549 N.E.2d 719 (Ill. App. Ct. 1989); Kansas City Structural Steel Co. v. L. G. Barcus & Sons, Inc., 535 P.2d 419, 423 (Kan. 1975); TAP Pharm. Products Inc. v. State Bd. of Pharmacy, 238 S.W.3d 140, 144 (Mo. 2007); Black v. National Merit Ins. Co., 226 P.3d 175, 182 (Wash. Ct. App. 2010) *review denied*, 238 P.3d 503 (2010).

3. *E.g.,* discussing the possibility that "and/or" can create ambiguity: Leon v. State, 695 So.2d 1265, 1267 (Fla. Dist. Ct. App. 1997); Belz Investco Ltd. P'ship v. Groupo Immobiliano Cababie, S.A., 721 So.2d 787, 788 (Fla. Dist. Ct. App. 1998); Bank Bldg. & Equip. Corp. of Am. v. Georgia State Bank, 209 S.E.2d 82, 84 (Ga. Ct. App. 1974); Manor Healthcare Corp. v. Soiltest, Inc., 549 N.E.2d 719, 724 (Ill. App. Ct. 1989); Victory v. Victory, 399 S.W.2d 332, 338 (Tenn. Ct. App. 1965); Aerospatiale Helicopter Corp. v. Universal Health Services, Inc., 778 S.W.2d 492, 502 (Tex. App. 1989).

4. *E.g.,* D.E. Shaw Laminar Portfolios, LLC v. Archon Corp., 570 F. Supp. 2d 1262, 1268 (D. Nev. 2008); CB & H Bus. Services, L.L.C. v. J.T. Comer Consulting, Inc., 646 S.E.2d 843, 844 (N.C. Ct. App. 2007) *aff'd sub nom.* CB & H Bus. Services, L.L.C. v. J.T. Comer Consulting, Inc., 653 S.E.2d 145 (N.C. 2007);

5. D.E. Shaw Laminar Portfolios, LLC v. Archon Corp., 570 F. Supp. 2d 1262, 1268 (D. Nev. 2008).

6. *Id.*

7. Slottow v. American Cas. Co. of Reading, Pennsylvania, 10 F.3d 1355, 1361 (9th Cir. 1993).

8. Mattison, Inc. v. W. F. Larson, Inc., 529 S.W.2d 271, 273 (Tex. Civ. App. 1975).

9. Interim Healthcare, Inc. v. Spherion Corp., 884 A.2d 513, 555 (Del. Super. Ct. 2005) *aff'd*, 886 A.2d 1278 (Del. 2005)

10. Hill v. State, 488 N.E.2d 709, 710–11 (Ind. 1986).

11. *Id.*

12. *Id.*

Endnotes for Chapter 29: Time Clauses and Conditional Statements

1. *E.g.,* Drummond Co., Inc. v. Walter Indus., Inc., 962 So.2d 753, 774 (Ala. 2006) ("Although the destruction of contracts because of uncertainty is disfavored under the law, if a court cannot discern the intentions of the parties to a contract because the contract is so vague and indefinite, the contract is void on the ground of uncertainty."); Pyeatte v. Pyeatte, 135 Ariz. 346, 350, 661 P.2d 196, 200 (Ct. App. 1982) (terms necessary for the required definiteness frequently include time of performance); Winter Haven Citrus Growers Ass'n v. Campbell & Sons Fruit Co., 773 So.2d 96, 97 (Fla. Dist. Ct. App. 2000) (company failed to prove the existence of an enforceable oral contract because it failed to prove that the parties had agreed upon such material terms as the time for performance); Harmon v. Innomed Technologies, Inc., 309 Ga.App. 265, 267, 709 S.E.2d 888, 890 (2011), *reconsideration denied* (Nov. 7, 2011), *cert. denied* (Oct. 3, 2011) (a promise must be sufficiently definite as to both time and subject matter to be enforceable); Waverly Const. Co., Inc. v. Gold Inv. Co., 60 Or.App. 101, 105, 652 P.2d 880, 882 (1982) (failure to agree on the time of performance can result in a failure to establish a binding agreement).

2. Latinos Unidos de Napa v. City of Napa, 127 Cal.Rptr.3d 469, 473 (Cal. Ct. App. 2011) quoting Ley v. Dominguez 212 Cal. 587, 594–95, 299 P. 713 (1931).

3. *E.g.*, Haw. Rev. Stat. § 1–29 (West 2011); Idaho Code Ann. § 73–109 (West 2011); Idaho Crim. R. 45; N.D. Cent. Code Ann. § 1–02–15 (West); Mo. Ann. Stat. § 1.040 (West 2011).

4. N.Y. Gen. Oblig. Law § 5–903 (McKinney) (West 2011).

5. IL ST CH 815 § 601/10 (West 2011).

6. Vulcan Materials Co. v. Atofina Chemicals Inc., 355 F. Supp. 2d 1214, 1240 (D. Kan. 2005); Dover Elevator Co. v. Rafael, 939 S.W.2d 474, 476 (Mo. Ct. App. 1996).

Endnotes for Chapter 31: Some Basics about Grammar

1. *See, e.g.*, Amway Corp. v. Procter & Gamble Co., 346 F.3d 180, 187 (6th Cir. 2003) (citing *Harbrace* when discussing a coordinating conjunction in a statute); In re Hopkins, 371 B.R. 324, 326 (Bankr. N.D. Ill. 2007) (citing *Harbrace* and *Prentice–Hall* grammar guides when discussing modifier placement in a statutory provision); American Family Mut. Ins. Co. v. Tickle, 99 S.W.3d 25, 30–31 (Mo. Ct. App. 2003) (citing *The Bedford Handbook* regarding a clause in an insurance policy); State v. Sosa, 223 P.3d 348, 352 (N.M. 2009) (citing *Harbrace* to analyze a verb in a court transcript).

2. *See, e.g.*, Allard K. Lowenstein Int'l Human Rights Project v. Department of Homeland Sec., 626 F.3d 678, 681 (2d Cir. 2010) (court used the term "modifier"); Regents of University of Minnesota v. AGA Medical Corp, 835 F.Supp.2d 711, 730 (D. Minn. 2011) (court used the term "prepositional phrase"); Mid–Century Ins. Co. v. Robles, 271 P.3d 592, 595–96 (Colo. Ct. App. 2011) (court used the term "independent clause"); In re Arnott, 942 N.E.2d 1124, 1135 (Ohio Ct. App. 2010) (court used the term "dependent clause"); Leza v. State, 351 S.W.3d 344, 356–57 (Tex. Crim. App. 2011) (court used the term "direct object").

3. *See, e.g.*, Campbell v. District of Columbia, 568 A.2d 1076, 1078 (D.C.1990); Kar v. Nanda, 805 N.W.2d 609, 612 (Mich. Ct. App. 2011); TAC Associates v. New Jersey Dep't of Envtl. Prot., 998 A.2d 450, 456–57 (N.J. 2010).

4. *See, e.g.*, Vaden v. Discover Bank, 556 U.S. 49, 76 (2009); United States v. Weingarten, 632 F.3d 60, 65–66 (2d Cir. 2011); United States v. Reth, 364 Fed. App'x 323, 325 (9th Cir. 2010).

5. *See, e.g.*, U.S. ex rel. Totten v. Bombardier Corp., 380 F.3d 488, 499–500 (D.C. Cir. 2004); Fluor Enterprises, Inc. v. Revenue Div., Dep't of Treasury, 730 N.W.2d 722, 732 (Mich. 2007); City of Portland By & Through Portland Dev. Comm'n v. Smith, 838 P.2d 568, 577 (Or. 1992).

6. Shariat v. County of Orange, No. G034807, 2006 WL 1660576, *1–2 (Cal. Ct. App. June 16, 2006).

7. *Id.*

Endnotes for Chapter 32: Punctuation

1. *See, e.g.*, Bishop v. Linkway Stores, Inc., 655 S.W.2d 426 (Ark. 1983) (discussing a colon in a contract); Baker v. National Interstate Ins. Co., 180 Cal.App.4th 1319, 1330–31 (2009) (discussing a semicolon in an insurance policy); McGrill v. State, 82 So.3d 130, 132 (Fla. Dist. Ct. App. 2012) (discussing commas in a statute); Maxine Co., Inc. v. Brinks's Global Services USA, Inc., 937 N.Y.S.2d 199, 201–02 (2012) (discussing a comma in a contract).

2. North Pointe Cas. Ins. Co. v. M & S Tractor Services, Inc., 62 So.3d 1281, 1283 (Fla. Dist. Ct. App. 2011).

3. Lewis v. Carnaggio, 183 S.E.2d 899 (S.C. 1971).

4. *See, e.g.*, Janvey v. Democratic Senatorial Campaign Comm., 793 F. Supp. 2d 825, 839 (N.D. Tex. 2011) (considering the effect of a restrictive modifier when analyzing a statute); Benson v. City of Birmingham, 659 So.2d 82, 85 (Ala. 1995) (considering a non-restrictive modifier when analyzing statute); Meamber v. Oregon Pac. Bank, Inc., 244 P.3d 901 (Or. Ct. App. 2010) (considering the effect of a restrictive modifier when analyzing a trust deed).

5. "That" is still correct for restrictive modifiers but not for non-restrictive modifiers. However, there seems to be some wiggle room regarding "which": some writers use "which" in either a restrictive or non-restrictive modifier, and the comma (or its absence) determines whether the modifier is restrictive or non-restrictive. *See e.g.*, WILLIAM STRUNK & E.B. WHITE, THE ELEMENTS OF STYLE 59 (50th Anniversary ed. 2009); CHERYL GLENN & LORETTA GRAY, THE HODGES HARBRACE HANDBOOK 90 (17th ed. 2009); DIANA HACKER, THE BEDFORD HANDBOOK 434 (5th ed. 1998).

6. WILLIAM STRUNK & E.B. WHITE, THE ELEMENTS OF STYLE 7 (50th Anniversary ed. 2009); CHERYL GLENN & LORETTA GRAY, THE HODGES HARBRACE HANDBOOK 235–36 (17th ed. 2009).

Endnotes for Chapter 33: Style

1. *See e.g.,* Arizona Legislative Council, The Arizona Legislation Bill Drafting Manual 87 (2009); Florida Senate, Manual for Drafting Legislation 12 (6th ed. 2009); Indiana General Assembly, Bill Drafting Manual, *available at* http://www.in.gov/legislative/2367.htm; Legislative Council of the Maine State Legislature, Maine Legislative Drafting Manual 77 (2009); Texas Legislative Council, Drafting Manual 100 (2011).

2. *See, e.g.,* Stanard v. Nygren, 658 F.3d 792, 798 (7th Cir. 2011) ("At least 23 sentences contained 100 or more words. This includes sentences of 385, 345, and 291 words."); Midland Funding, LLC v. Layton, 2009 WL 6813116 (Fla. Cir. Ct. 2009) ("[C]onsider this 68–word, no-comma sentence from paragraph 19 of the complaint....")

3. *See, e.g.,* North Pointe Cas. Ins. Co. v. M & S Tractor Services, Inc., 62 So.3d 1281, 1284–85 (Fla. Dist. Ct. App. 2011) (finding ambiguity due to, among other things, convoluted sentence structure); Midland Funding, LLC v. Layton, 2009 WL 6813116 (Fla. Cir. Ct. 2009) (criticizing plaintiff's use of "hundred-dollar words" in a pleading); Ramos–Barrientos v. Bland, 2008 WL 474426, at *1–2 (S.D. Ga. 2008) (criticizing convoluted and lengthy sentences in a pleading).

4. *See, e.g.,* Delaware Legislative Council Division of Research, Drafting Delaware Legislation 1 (2009) (advising that drafters (1) use short, simple sentences because complex sentence structures can cause ambiguity; and (2) try to keep sentence length at or below 21 words.); Kentucky Legislative Research Commission, Bill Drafting Manual 23–24 (2011) ((1) stating that simplicity is "highly desirable" if it does not cause loss of meaning; and (2) advising selection of short, familiar words if possible.); Maryland Department of Legislative Services, Legislative Drafting Manual 26 (2012) (advising drafters (1) to avoid long sentences; (2) to use short, familiar words and phrases, and (3) to not use multiple words if one word suffices.).

5. *See, e.g.,* Sabre Int'l Sec. v. Torres Advanced Enter. Solutions, Inc., 2012 WL1476060, at *4 (D.D.C. 2012); Swire Pac. Holdings, Inc. v. Zurich Ins. Co., 845 So.2d 161, 165 (Fla. 2003); District No. 1—Pac. Coast Dist. v. Travelers Cas. & Sur. Co., 782 A.2d 269, 274 (D.C. 2001).

6. *See e.g.,* Patton v. State, 34 So.3d 563, 574–75 (Miss. 2010) (stating that "a properly drafted false pretense indictment is replete with essential legalese, long required by this Court, that would be unfamiliar to most attorneys, even law professors, other than those with significant experience as prosecutors, criminal defense attorneys or judges in Mississippi's criminal courts").

7. *See, e.g.,* Alliance 3PL Corp. v. New Prime, Inc., 614 F.3d 703, 706–07 (7th Cir. 2010) (finding that the use of the word "such" in a contract created ambiguity).

8. *See, e.g.,* Florida House of Representatives, Guidelines for Bill Drafting 95 (2011); Legislative Council of the Maine State Legislature, Maine Legislative Drafting Manual 104 (2009); Texas Legislative Council, Drafting Manual 104 (2011).

9. Sean Flammer, *A New Comprehensive Study Confirms that Judges Find Plain English More Persuasive than Legalese*, 90 Mich. B.J. 50, 50–51 (2011).

10. *See, e.g.,* N.H. Rev. Stat. Ann. § 17–A:6 (West 2012) (encouraging the use of gender-neutral terms in drafting legislation); Ohio Admin. Code 103–3–02 (West 2012) (encouraging agencies to draft rules using gender-neutral language); State of Connecticut, Manual for Drafting Regulations 34 (West 2009) (advising drafters to draft gender-neutrally); Florida Senate, Manual for Drafting Legislation 13 (6th ed. 2009) (advising drafters to avoid gender-neutral pronouns); Texas Legislative Council, Texas Legislative Council Drafting Manual 101 (2011) (stating that drafters should express ideas in gender-neutral terms if possible); Gerald Lebovits, *Ethical Judicial Writing—Part III*, 79 N.Y. St. B.J. 64, 64 (2007) (stating that New York requires that court opinions be gender-neutral).

INDEX

References are to Pages

ACTIVE VOICE
See VERBS

ADEMPTION
See WILLS (Drafting and Execution)

AFFIRMATIVE DEFENSE, see ANSWER

AGREEMENTS TO INDEMNIFY OR DEFEND
Agreement to defend, 139
  Concerns for drafter, 139
  Effect, 139
Agreement to indemnify, 138–39
  Characteristics and purpose, 136–37
    Definition of "indemnify," 136
    Examples,
      Indemnitee indemnified against
        third-party claims due to fault
        of indemnifying party, 136–37
      Indemnitee indemnified against
        liability for own negligence, 137
  Construction and enforceability, 137–38
    Construction, 137
      Indemnification of indemnitee
        against liability for own negli-
        gence, 137
        Nature of fault
        Strict construction often applied,
          137
        Word "negligence" must
          appear in clause in some
          states, 137
    Enforceability
      In commercial settings, 137–38
      Nature of protection
        Against liability for gross negli-
          gence, 137
        Against liability for intentional,
          wanton, or willful acts, 137
        Against liability for punitive
          damages, 137
  Drafting, 138–39
    Attorney's fees, 139
      American rule, 159–60
    Avoiding boilerplate, 138
    Issues to address, 138
    Word choice
      Indemnification against "claims"
        or "demands," 138

AGREEMENTS TO INDEMNIFY OR DEFEND
  —Cont'd
      Indemnification against liability,
        138
      Indemnification against "loss" or
        "damages," 138
      Expressing intended outcome,
        138–39

ALLEGATIONS IN PLEADING
Framing allegations
  Allegations in complaint
    Framing strategically to draw out an
      admission, 28–30
  Allegations in answer
    Allegations in affirmative defense,
      51–53
    Responses to allegations in initial
      pleading, see ANSWER
  Alternative, inconsistent, or hypothetical,
    30, 53
  Expressing time and place, 27–28
Focusing on the parties
  Generally, 26–27
Grounds to strike allegations in pleading, see
  MOTIONS
  Motion to strike allegations, see
    MOTIONS
Incorporation of allegations by reference, 34
Plain, concise, and direct, 26, 53
Re-allegation, 34
Types of Allegations
  Conclusory versus neutral, 29
  Evidentiary, 24, 26
  Extraneous 24, 26
  Legal Conclusion, 24, 25–26[motions]
Ultimate facts, 17, 24, 25

AMBIGUITY
Definition, 335
Sources of Ambiguity
  Inconsistency, 345–46
    Conflicting sentences, 262–63, 345
      Creation of problem, 345

AMBIGUITY—Cont'd
  Sentence overlap, 262–64
  Conflicting sentences in same or different sections, 263
    Examples (problem and resolution), 263, 264
  Each sentence must be true as it stands, 262
    Qualifying conflicting sentences to resolve conflict, 262–63
    Drafting qualified sentences, See CONDITIONAL STATEMENTS
  Same event must not trigger different outcomes, 336
  Inconsistent use of words or phrases, 345–46
    Courts' construction of consistent and inconsistent words and phrases, 171–72
  Modifier placement
    See MODIFIERS
  Plurals, 193–94, 341
  Pronouns, 340–41
    Ambiguous usage
      Exercises, 417
      Generally, 388–89
  Punctuation, 346
    Ambiguous commas, 395–96
  Time terminology
    Ambiguous time terminology
  Words or phrases with more than one meaning, 341–345
    "And" and "or"
      See "AND" AND "OR"
    "Is responsible …" or "Has the responsibility," 345
      Meanings of "responsible for," 100
    "Subject to," 341–42
    "Term," 342–43
    Time terminology, 356–60
      "Between," 357
      "Midnight," 359
      "Month," 358–59
      "To," "Until," and "by," 358
      "Upon," "when," "once," 356–57
      "Week," 359
      "Within" when drafting a due date, deadline, or cut-off, 357–58

AMENDMENT TO PLEADING
Liberal amendment policy in federal court, 52, 62

"AND" AND "OR"
"And/or", 344–45
  Problems created through use, 345
    Illogical use, 344–45
    Needless legal jargon, 412
"And" and "or," 343–44
  Overlapping meanings, 343
    Ambiguity, 343–44
      Resolving ambiguity, 344

ANSWER
Answer,
  Definition, 7
  Purpose, 43
Affirmative defenses, 50–53
  Drafting, 51–53
    Format in document, 53
      Heading, 53
      Numbering, 53
      Motion to strike a defense, 54–55
    Separate statements rule, 33–34
      Re-allegation, 34
    Sufficiency of defense, 51–53
      Applicability of plausibility standard in federal court, 51–53
      Boilerplate defenses, 52
  Special Matters, 54
    Challenge to Capacity, 54
    Defense Based on Fraud or Mistake, 54
    Non–Occurrence or Non–Performance of Condition, 54
  Typical affirmative defenses, 50–51
    Examples, 50–51
    Federal Rule 12(b) defenses raised in answer, 51
  Waiver of affirmative defense, 52
Boilerplate defenses, 52
Caption, see CAPTION
Default, 43–44
  Time for responding, 43
Electronic filing generally, 10
Examples
  Admission and denial, 46
    Partial admission, 47
  Affirmative defenses, 51
  Answer format (text needs revision), 84–86
  Allegation of insufficient knowledge, 46
  Motion to strike affirmative defenses, 55
  Paragraph numbering for responses, 46
Federal Rules Mentioned In Text
  Federal Rule 7(a)(7), 53–54
  Federal Rule 8
    Federal Rule 8(a), 49, 52
    Federal Rule 8(b),
      Admitting in Part, 46–47
      Allowable responses, 44–45
      Evasive responses, 48–49
    Federal Rule 8(c), 50
    Federal Rule 8(d), 51, 53
  Federal Rule 9
    Federal Rule 9(a), 54
    Federal Rule 9(b), 54
    Federal Rule 9(c), 54
  Federal Rule 10(b), 53
  Federal Rule 12
    Federal Rule 12(a), 51
    Federal Rule 12(b), 51
    Federal Rule 12(f), 54–55
  Federal Rule 15, 52
  Federal Rule 55, 43–44
  Federal Rule 60(b), 44
Numbering,
  Affirmative defenses, 53
  Responses, 46–47
Reply to allegations in answer, 53–54

ANSWER—Cont'd
Responses to paragraphs in initial pleading
Allowable responses, 44–45
Drafting allowable responses, 45–47
Alleging insufficient knowledge, 45–46
Drafting admission of paragraph, 45–46
Drafting partial admissions, 46–47
Drafting denial of paragraph, 45–46
Evasive responses to paragraphs, 48–50
Response to allegation regarding another defendant, 49–50
Response to conclusory allegations, 49
Service of Pleadings after initial pleading, 11
Signature, 12–13
Time for responding, 43
Verification, 10

APOSTROPHE
Generally, 401–02
Use
in contraction or omission, 403
in plurals (of numerals, letters, or words), 402–03
in possessive of nouns, 401–02

ARBITRATION AGREEMENTS
Drafting agreement, 161–62
Clear and unequivocal language, 162
Freedom to limit arbitrable issues, 161–62
Broad versus narrow clause, 161–62
If clause is exclusive remedy, 162
Language allowing party to compel arbitration, 162
Liberal construction, 161
Limitation on right to appeal, 162
Freedom to structure agreement as desired, 161
Issues clause might address, 161
Availability of attorney's fees, 161
Choice of law or forum selection
See FORUM–SELECTION AND CHOICE–OF–LAW CLAUSES
Effect (binding or not) of arbitration, 161
Effect of clause (mandatory or not), 161
Mutual agreement to arbitrate, 161
Procedure for arbitration, 161
Effect and purpose of arbitration, 160
Enforceability, 160–61
Under Federal Arbitration Act, 161
Under state laws, 161
Uniform Arbitration Act, 161
Federal Arbitration Act, 160–61
Application to state courts, 161
Nationwide policy favoring arbitration, 160
Uniform Arbitration Act, 161

ATTORNEY'S FEES
American rule, 159–60
Drafting provision, 159
Precisely delineating scope, 160

ATTORNEY'S FEES—Cont'd
Expressly referring to attorney's fees, 159
Enforceability of contract provision, 159–60
Statutes that control effect of one-sided clause, 160

BARGAINING POWER
Disparity
Unconscionability analysis,
See INVALID CONTRACT OR PROVISION
Tunkl factors
See EXCULPATORY CLAUSE

BREACH OF CONTRACT, 144–48
Elements of breach action, 144
Recovery for breach, 144–45
Remedies provided by law, 144–45
Damages, 144–45
Benefit-of-the-bargain, 144
Reliance damages, 144–45
Rescission and restitution, 145
Unavailability if breach not material, 145
Meaning of material breach, 145
Specific performance, 145
Remedies provided by contract, 146
Liquidated damages
See LIQUIDATED–DAMAGES CLAUSE
Non-breaching party's suspension or cancellation of performance, 146
Right of parties to fashion remedies, 146
Mutuality of remedies not required, 146

CANCELLATION AND TERMINATION CLAUSES
Cancellation clause, 146–47
Cancellation or suspension of performance of contract, 146–47
Meaning of "material breach," 145
Definition of "cancellation" under UCC, 140
Distinguished from "termination," 140
Drafting cancellation clause, 147
Requirements for cancellation, 146–47
Termination clause in contract
Termination generally, 140–44
Definition (according to UCC), 140
Drafting termination provision
Requirements for, 142–44
Notice of termination, 143
Termination, 142–43
Termination fee, 143–44
Termination of *specified* provisions versus "termination of contract," 141
Survival of other provisions, 141
Danger of specifying surviving provisions, 141
Effect and purpose of, 140–41

CANCELLATION AND TERMINATION CLAUSES—Cont'd
When right may be necessary, 141
Enforcement of, 141–42
Contract with fixed duration, 142
Drafting to prevent conflict, 142
Termination-for-convenience clause, 142
Unilateral termination right, 141

CANONS OF CONSTRUCTION
See CONTRACT CONSTRUCTION, CRUCIAL CANONS FOR DRAFTER, AND STATUTORY CONSTRUCTION

CAPACITY
Pleading capacity, see ANSWER
Testamentary capacity, see WILL (Background for Drafter)

CAPTION
Components
Case Number, 8
Generally, 8
Application to motions, 8
Party names after initial pleading, 8
Style, 8
Title, 8
Effect of local rules, 9
Format

CAUSE OF ACTION, see INITIAL PLEADING

CHOOSING WORDS
Checking meaning
Definitions from case law, 311
Dictionary meaning, 310–11
Courts' reliance on dictionary, 310
Importance of knowing exact meaning, 310–33
Ordinary meaning unless indicate otherwise, 310
Technical language and terms of art, 311–12
Need for consistency with definitions in case law, 311–12
Need for consistency with word's technical meaning, 311
Choosing the right word, 313–14
Avoid kitchen sink approach, 313
Choose words that effect your precise meaning, 313–14
Omit needless synonyms, 313
Drafting as preventive law, 310

CLAIM, see INITIAL PLEADING

CLIENT
As resource, 3
Client interview or questionnaire and gathering information from client, see CONTENT OF CONTRACT OR RULE–MAKING DOCUMENT
Drafter as advocate, 96–97

CODICIL, see WILLS (Drafting and Execution)

COLON
Exercises, 418–19
Generally, 400–01
Introducing series, list, or quotation, 400–01

COMMA
Comma rules, 396–97
Serial commas, 396
With conjunctions, 396–97
With introductory clauses
With restrictive and non-restrictive modifiers, 397–99
Comma splice, 400
Ways to fix comma splice, 400
Generally, 395–99
Impact on Meaning, 395–96

COMMA SPLICE, see COMMA

COMMENCEMENT
See INITIAL PLEADING

COMPLAINT
See INITIAL PLEADING

CONCISENESS
See STYLE

CONDITIONAL STATEMENTS
Articulating conditional statements, 360–61
Choosing qualifiers: "if," "unless," "except," 360
Avoiding cumbersome or ambiguous substitutes, 360
Pairing statement with parallel conditional statement, 360–61
Placement of conditional clause at beginning of sentence, 361
Placement when sentence also contains a time clause, 361–63
Ambiguity problems from modifier misplacement, 361–62
Removing ambiguity, 362–63

CONTRA PROFERENTEM
Contract construed against drafter
See CONTRACT CONSTRUCTION

CONSISTENCY
Ambiguity caused by inconsistency, 345
Courts' construction of consistent and inconsistent words and phrases, 171–72
Reading consistent terms consistently, 172

CONSTRUCTION OF STATUTE OR OTHER PUBLIC–LAW DOCUMENT
See STATUTORY CONSTRUCTION

CONTENT OF CONTRACT OR RULE–MAKING DOCUMENT
Generating content, 236–250
Assessing client's needs, 237–38

CONTENT OF CONTRACT OR RULE–MAKING DOCUMENT—Cont'd
Public legislation, 238
  Background questions, 238
Impact of negotiating contract, 237
Researching document's factual and legal background, 236–37
Generating master term sheet, 238–41
Creating list of potential content, 218
Steps in preparation, 239
    Use drafting manual for public rule-making document, 240
    Use template for contracts and private rule-making documents (or ordinance), 239
    Contract template, 252–53
    Rule-making document template, 253–54
  Generating preliminary questions, 240, 241
  Preparing client questionnaire, 241–42
    Attributes of useful questions, 242
Types of provisions
  Contracts, see CONTRACT COMPONENTS
  Private rule-making documents (such as bylaws)
    See LEGISLATIVE DRAFTING: PRIVATE RULE–MAKING DOCUMENTS
  Public rule-making documents (such as statutes and ordinances)
    See LEGISLATIVE DRAFTING: PUBLIC RULE–MAKING DOCUMENTS

CONTRACT CONSTRUCTION
Ambiguity
  Definition, 169–70
  Extrinsic evidence admitted to clarify, 170
  Use of recitals to clarify, 171
    Use of recital to forestall application of *contra proferentem*, 174
Approaches to construction, 169–70
  Primacy of parties' intentions, 169
    Determination whether provision is ambiguous, 169–70
  Purpose of construction, 169
    Parol evidence rule, 170
    Definition of extrinsic evidence, 170
Canons of construction, 171–74
  Canons that guide the court in reading the contract, 171
    Reading as a reasonable person, 172
      Refusal to "torture words to import ambiguity," 172
      Terms read in ordinary sense, 172
      Terms read in technical sense, 172
    Reading consistent terms consistently, 172
      Same word or phrase has same meaning throughout, 171
    Reading to give effect to entire contract, 171

CONTRACT CONSTRUCTION—Cont'd
      Giving effect to every word and phrase, 171
        Assumption that parties intend for all provisions to be meaningful, 171
      Harmonizing provisions, 172
        Assumption that parties intend document as a whole to make sense, 171
      Reading to give the contract validity, 171–72
      Reading to produce a rational outcome, 172
        Preference between conflicting interpretations for the rational and probable, 172
    Canons addressing meaning of language
      Modifier placement—doctrine of last antecedent, 173
      See MODIFIERS
      Omissions may be regarded as Intentional, 173
        See CRUCIAL CANONS FOR DRAFTERS
      Words take meaning for associated words, 172–73
    Canons for choosing between conflicting provisions, 173
      Fall-back rules if court cannot harmonize provisions, 173
    Contract construed against drafter (contra proferentem), 174
  Documents courts have construed as contracts, 169
  Extrinsic aids to construction, 218-19
  Strict construction, 174
    Types of provisions typically strictly construed, 174–75

CONTRACT OF ADHESION, 107

CONTRACT COMPONENTS
Arbitration clause
  See ARBITRATION AGREEMENT
Cancellation and termination clauses
  See CANCELLATION AND TERMINATION CLAUSES
Choice-of-law clause
  See FORUM–SELECTION AND CHOICE–OF–LAW CLAUSES
Core obligations, 115–18
  Articulating the basic bargain, 115
    Thing of value exchanged for payment, 115–17
      Client's priorities, 117
      Payment provisions, 115–17
    Thing of value for another thing of value, 118
      Sequencing the provisions, 118
  Covenants that protect business interests after relationship ends
    See COVENANTS RESTRICTING COMPETITION
Execution of contract
  See EXECUTION OF CONTRACT

CONTRACT COMPONENTS—Cont'd
    Exordium (introductory clause) and title,
      108–09
    Forum-selection clause,
      See FORUM–SELECTION AND
        CHOICE–OF–LAW CLAUSES
    Integration (or merger) clause
      See MERGER CLAUSE
    Limitation of liability provisions
      Exclusion of warranty
        See LIMITING OR EXCLUDING
          WARRANTIES UNDER UCC
      Exculpatory clause
        See EXCULPATORY CLAUSE
      Excuse (*force majeure* clause)
        See EXCUSE (*FORCE MAJEURE*
          CLAUSE)
      Indemnity/indemnification
        See AGREEMENTS TO INDEM-
          NIFY OR DEFEND
      Limitation of damages
        See LIMITATION–OF–DAMAGES
          CLAUSE
      Limitation of remedies
        See LIMITATION–OF–REMEDIES
          CLAUSE
    Liquidated damages clause
      See LIQUIDATED–DAMAGES
        CLAUSE
    Merger (Integration) clause
      See MERGER CLAUSE
    Modification of contract
      See MODIFICATION CLAUSE IN
        CONTRACT
    Preliminary matters
      Background recitals, 110
        Drafting recitals, 102–04
        Function of background recitals, 110
      Description of contract's subject-matter,
        110–11
        Articulating description (examples),
          110
        Attachment describing subject-
          matter, 111
      Definitions, 109; see DEFINITIONS
      Duration (of performance), 113–15
      Performance due at or before signing,
        112–13
        Prepayment provisions, 112–13
          Framed as condition, 113
            See CONDITIONAL STATE-
              MENTS
          Framed as recital, 113
            Drafting recitals of fact,
              102–04
    Subsidiary agreements, 118–22
      Duration of subsidiary agreements, 118
      Expressing duration of promise, 113–14
        Examples, 114
      Function of subsidiary agreements, 118
      Types of subsidiary agreements, 118–22
        Assignment and delegation, 122
        Insurance
          Agreement to procure insurance,
            119–20

CONTRACT COMPONENTS—Cont'd
      Types of insurance, 120–21
      Maintenance agreements, 119
        Ambiguous repair provisions
      Other types of subsidiary agree-
        ments
        Compliance with law, 122
        Confidentiality, 122
        Noncompetition, 121–22
      Use of subject matter, 119
        Prohibitions versus restrictions,
          119
    Severance Clause, 152–53
      Invalid Contracts or Provisions
        See INVALID CONTRACT OR PRO-
          VISION
    Signatures, see *Execution of Contract*
      (above)
    Termination and cancellation clauses
      See CANCELLATION AND TERMINA-
        TION CLAUSES
    Winding up the Contractual Relationship,
      149
      Covenants that Protect Business Inter-
        ests after Relationship Ends,
        See COVENANTS RESTRICTING
          COMPETITION

CONTRACT DRAFTING
Applicable law, 97
    Availability of arbitration
      See ARBITRATION AGREEMENTS
    Breach of contract
      See BREACH OF CONTRACT
    Contract of adhesion, 107
    Execution of contract, 164–67
      Effective date of contract, 166–67
      Signatures of parties, 164–66
    Freedom of contract
      Policy favoring freedom of contract, 105
        Preference of courts for enforcing
          contracts, 105
          Severance of unenforceable provi-
            sions, 152–53
    Implied covenant of good faith and fair
      dealing, 97
    Incorporation of existing law, 97
    Integration or merger
      See MERGER CLAUSE
    Modification of contract
      See MODIFICATION CLAUSE IN
        CONTRACT
    Parol evidence rule
      See MERGER CLAUSE
Articulation of provisions
    Drafter as advocate and lawmaker, 96–97
    Drafting style
      Consistency, see INCONSISTENCY
      Grammar, 372–394
      Modifier placement in sentence
        See MODIFIERS
      Preference for active voice
        See VERBS
      Punctuation, 395–406
      Style, 407–414

CONTRACT DRAFTING—Cont'd
    Gender-neutral drafting, 413–414
    Legal jargon, 412
    Sentence structure
        Avoiding sentence overload,
            410–11
        Indented lists, 413
    Organization
        Contract Template, 252–53
        See ORGANIZATION OF DOCUMENT
    Recommended terminology, 98–104
        Stating obligations, 99–100
        "Shall" versus "will," 99
        Stating policies, 100–101
        Stating recitals, 102–04
        Stating requirements, 102
        Stating rights, 101
    Scope of document and provisions
        See DELINEATING SCOPE OF
            PROVISION
Construction of contract
    See CONTRACT CONSTRUCTION
Content of contract
    See CONTENT OF CONTRACT OR
        RULE–MAKING DOCUMENT
Format, see ORGANIZATION OF DOCU-
    MENT
Implied covenant of good faith and fair deal-
    ing, 97
Inability to perform
    See BREACH OF CONTRACT and
        EXCUSE *FORCE MAJEURE*
        CLAUSE
Types of Provisions, see CONTRACT COM-
    PONENTS

CONTRACT ORGANIZATION
    See ORGANIZATION OF DOCUMENTS
Template for contract organization, 252–53

COVENANTS RESTRICTING COMPETITION
Covenants that apply after contractual rela-
    tionship ends, 149–50
Drafting covenant
    Factors affecting enforceability, 151
        Duration, 151
        Geographic territory, 151
        Reasonableness, 151
        Restricted activities, 152
        Restriction on access to persons, 151
Enforcement of restrictive covenants, 150–51
    Covenants other than non-compete cov-
        enant, 150
    Construction of other covenants, 150
    Non-compete between employer and
        employee, 150
        Covenants between professionals might
            violate public policy, 150
        Covenant in sale of business or dissolu-
            tion of partnership, 151
        Strict construction, 150
    Over-broad covenant, 152
Prohibition of restraints on trade, 149

CROSS–REFERENCE
See ORGANIZATION OF DOCUMENTS

CRUCIAL CANONS FOR DRAFTERS
Ejusdem generis and noscitur a sociis, 321–23
    Ejusdem generis, 322–23
    Noscitur a sociis, 321–22
Expressio unius est exclusio alterius, 323–24

DAMAGES
Contract damages
    See BREACH OF CONTRACT
Contract provisions limiting damages
    See LIMITATION–OF–DAMAGES
        CLAUSE
    See LIMITATION–OF–REMEDIES
        CLAUSE
Liquidated damages
    See LIQUIDATED–DAMAGES CLAUSE

DASH [PUNCTUATION], 403-04

DEFAULT JUDGMENT, see ANSWER

DEFENSIVE PLEADINGS, see ANSWER

DEFINITIONS
Courts' interpretation of terms in a document,
    310–12
Determining whether definition is needed,
    325
    In contract or statute, 325–26
    In will, 326–27
    Format and placement, 329–31
    Framing definitions, 327–29
        Common errors, 332–34
            Definition and defined term not
                grammatically parallel, 332
            Strained definition, 333–34
            Substantive rule buried in defini-
                tion, 333

DELINEATING SCOPE OF PROVISION
Canons of construction relating to word choice
    and scope, 321–24
    See CRUCIAL CANONS FOR DRAFTERS
Choosing language to delineate scope
    Achieving definiteness, 320–21
        Using finite general category, 321
        Using specific language (list), 321
    Creating flexible provision, 316–17
        "Best efforts," 319–20
        Circumstances requiring flexibility, 316
        Creation of flexible tests and stan-
            dards, 317–18
        Role of vague language in drafting, 316
            Circumstances in which vagueness
                works, 317
            Distinction between vague and
                ambiguous language, 316
            Downside of vague standard, 318–19
            Over-vagueness, 320
                In contract or private rule-
                    making document, 320
                In public legislation, 320

DELINEATING SCOPE OF PROVISION
—Cont'd
Determining scope of provision, 314–16
   Factors to be considered, 314
      Circumstances that trigger application
        of provision, 314
      Duration of effectiveness, 314
      Persons to whom provision applies, 314
      Rights or interests protected, 314
   Scope reflecting client's priorities, 314

DEMAND FOR JUDGMENT
See INITIAL PLEADING

DURATION OF PERFORMANCE
In contract, see CONTRACT COMPONENTS
   Drafting duration provision, see TIME
      CLAUSES

DUTY
Expressing contractual obligation, see CON-
   TRACT DRAFTING
Expressing duty in statute, see LEGISLA-
   TIVE DRAFTING
Expressing duty in will, WILLS (Drafting and
   Execution)

EFFECTIVE DATE OF CONTRACT, see
   EXECUTION OF CONTRACT

EJUSDEM GENERIS, see CRUCIAL CANONS
   FOR DRAFTERS

ELEMENTS OF A CAUSE OF ACTION, see
   INITIAL PLEADING

**ELECTRONIC FILING (LITIGATION DOCU-
MENTS),** 10

"EXCEPT," "UNLESS," "IF," see CONDI-
   TIONAL STATEMENTS

EXCLUSION OF WARRANTY, see LIMITING
   OR EXCLUDING WARRANTIES
   UNDER UCC

EXCULPATORY CLAUSE
Exculpatory clauses, 126–30
   Characteristics and purpose, 126–27
   Circumstances in which exculpatory clause
      may be necessary, 127
   Common types of exculpatory clauses, 126
   Drafting exculpatory clause to protect a
      party against liability for negligence
      Clear and unequivocal language,
        128–29
        Avoid inconsistency, 129
        Magic words
          Inclusion of the word "negli-
            gence," 129
          Words conveying a similar
            import, 129
      Conspicuousness, 130
      Identifying persons to whom exculpa-
        tory clause applies, 129

EXCULPATORY CLAUSE—Cont'd
      Extending scope to successors,
        assigns, and others, 129
      Identifying by class, 129
   Scope of clause, 129–30
      Circumstances in which it applies,
        130
        Level of specificity required, 130
        Items to which it applies,
          129–30
        Use of catchall language for
          assumption of risk, 130
        Application of ejusdem
          generis, 130
          See also EJUSDEM
            GENERIS
   Enforceability, 127–28
      Circumstances in which enforcement
        sought
        Gross negligence, 127–28
        Intentional, willful, or wanton
          wrong-doing, 127
        Ordinary negligence, 127
          Professional negligence, 128
        Violation of statute, 127
   Conspicuousness, 130
   Nature of harm
      Physical injury, 128
   Public policy considerations, 128
   Unconscionability considerations, 128
      See also INVALID CONTRACT OR
        PROVISION

EXCUSE (*FORCE MAJEURE* CLAUSE)
Excuse, 123–26
   Drafting *force majeure* clause
      Act of God, 124–25
        Actions of third parties, 124–25
        Catastrophic circumstances, 124
        Governmental action, 125
      Articulation
        Addressing actual circumstances of
          client, 125
        Avoiding boilerplate, 125
        Catchall language, 125
        Drafting contract provisions to avoid
          over-reliance on *force majeure*,
          126
   Effect of *force majeure* clause if
      enforced, 124–25
   Reasons for ineffectiveness, 126
   Narrow construction, 125

EXECUTION OF CONTRACT
Effective date of contract, 166–67
Signatures of parties, 164–66
   Effect of signature, 164–65
      Electronic signature, 166
      Imposition of additional formalities,
        164
        Inadvertent imposition of conditions,
          164
   Importance of signature, 164
   Incorporation of exhibits, 9–10
   Use of Exhibits

EXECUTION OF CONTRACT—Cont'd
Effect of exhibits in state and federal courts, 23
Materials "outside the pleadings," 73–74

EXPRESS ASSUMPTION OF RISK, see EXCULPATORY CLAUSE

EXPRESSIO UNIUS EST EXCLUSIO ALTERIUS, see CRUCIAL CANONS FOR DRAFTERS

EXONERATION FROM LIABILITY, see EXCULPATORY CLAUSE

FACT–PLEADING
See INITIAL COMPLAINT and MOTIONS

FEDERAL RULES MENTIONED IN TEXT-BOOK
Federal Rule 4, 11
Federal Rule 5
  Federal Rule 5(a), 11
Federal Rule 6(c)(1), 58
Federal Rule 7
  Federal Rule 7(a)(7), 53–54
  Federal Rule 7(b)(2), 8, 56
Federal Rule 8
  Federal Rule 8(a), 15–16, 49, 52
    Federal Rule 8(a)(1), 17–18
    Federal Rule 8(a)(3), 22
  Federal Rule 8(b), 28, 44–49
    Admitting in Part, 46–47
    Allowable responses, 44–45
    Evasive responses, 48–49
  Federal Rule 8(c), 50
  Federal Rule 8(d), 51, 53
Federal Rule 9 generally, 21
  Federal Rule 9(a), 54
  Federal Rule 9(b), 54
  Federal Rule 9(c), 54
  Federal Rule 9(f), 27
Federal Rule 10
  Federal Rule 10(a), 8
  Federal Rule 10(b), 32, 53
  Federal Rule 10(c), 9, 34
Federal Rule 11, 11–13, 57
  Federal Rule 11(a), 12
  Federal Rule 11(c)(2), 12
Federal Rule 12
  Federal Rule 12(b), 51, 60–67, 72
    Federal Rule 12(b)(6) defense, 61–63
  Federal Rule 12(c), 72
  Federal Rule 12(d), 73
  Federal Rule 12(e), 64–65
  Federal Rule 12(f)
    motion to strike allegations, 66
    motion to strike legal defense, 54–55
  Federal Rule 12(g)
  Federal Rule 12(h), 72
Federal Rule 15, 52, 62
Federal Rule 55, 43–44
Federal Rule 56, 68
  Federal Rule 56(b), 69

FEDERAL RULES MENTIONED IN TEXT-BOOK—Cont'd
Federal Rule 56(c), 69–70
  Federal Rule 56(c)(4), 70
Federal Rule 56(h), 71
Federal Rule 78(b), 58

FLEXIBLE LANGUAGE, see DELINEATING SCOPE OF PROVISION

FORUM–SELECTION AND CHOICE–OF–LAW CLAUSES
Choice-of-Law Clause, 157–58
  Construction of clause, 157–58
  Enforceability and purpose, 157
Forum–Selection Clause, 154–157
  Effect and Purpose, 154–55
  Enforceability, 155
    Drafting presumptively valid clause, 155–57
      Choosing mandatory language, 155–56
      Delineating scope of clause, 156–57
    Presumptive validity, 155
    The Breman v. Zapata Off–Shore Company, 155

FORCE MAJEURE PROVISION
See EXCUSE (*FORCE MAJEURE* CLAUSE)

FORMAT
For pleading or other litigation document
  See ANSWER, INITIAL PLEADING, or MOTIONS
Rule-making document or contract
  See ORGANIZATION OF DOCUMENTS LEAVES

FRAUD OR MISTAKE
Pleading defense based on fraud or mistake, 54

FREEDOM OF CONTRACT
See CONTRACT DRAFTING

GENDER–NEUTRAL LANGUAGE
Drafting gender neutrally, see STYLE

GENERAL LANGUAGE, see DELINEATING SCOPE OF PROVISION

GERUND, 376–77

GRAMMAR
Adjective,
  Compound Adjectives, 405
    Need for hyphen, 405
  Generally, 373
Adverb (definition and examples), 372–73
Antecedent, 373
Clause (definition and examples), 375
Conjunction
  Ambiguous "and" and "or" or "and/or," see AMBIGUITY
  Generally, 374

GRAMMAR—Cont'd
Eight parts of speech (definitions and
    examples), 372–74
Errors, 394
Gerund, 376–77
Interjection, 374
Modifier, see MODIFIERS
Noun (definition and example), 372–73
Object of verb, 375–76
    Direct or indirect object, 376
        Intransitive and Transitive Verbs, see
            VERBS
Parallel structure, 389–90
Participle, 376
Predicate, 375
Preposition, see PREPOSITION
Prepositional phrase, see PREPOSITION
Pronoun, see PRONOUN
Quoted material, see QUOTED MATERIAL
Sentence (definition of), 375
Sentence structure
    Predicate, 375
    Subject, 375
Subject (definition), 375
"That" versus "which"
    Different meanings of "that," 374
    Restrictive and non-restrictive modifiers,
        398–99
Verb, see VERBS

GRAMMATICAL ERRORS
Deal-breaking, 394

GRAMMAR TERMS (MEANING)
Generally, 372–77
    Clause, 375
        Dependent clause, 375
        Independent clause, 375
    Direct and Indirect Objects, 376
    Eight Parts of Speech, 372–74
        Adjective, 373
        Conjunctions, 374
        Noun, 372–73
        Prepositions, 374
        Pronoun, 373
        Verbs, 373
    Gerunds, 376
    Modifiers, 376
    Noun Phrase, 375
    Object, 375–76
    Participle, 376–77
    Phrase, 375
    Subjects and Predicates, 375
    Verb Phrase, 375

HEADING
See ORGANIZATION OF DOCUMENTS

HYPHEN, 404–05

IF, UNLESS, EXCEPT, see CONDITIONAL
    STATEMENTS

**IMPLIED COVENANT OF GOOD FAITH AND
    FAIR DEALING,** see DRAFTING CON-
    TRACTS
See CONTRACTS

INABILITY TO PERFORM
See EXCUSE (*FORCE MAJEURE* CLAUSE)

"INCLUDES, BUT IS NOT LIMITED TO"
Role in drafting, 323

INCONSISTENCY
As cause of ambiguity, 345–46
    Courts' construction of consistent and
        inconsistent words and phrases,
        171–72
    Reading consistent terms consistently,
        172

INDEMNIFICATION, INDEMNITY
See AGREEMENT TO INDEMNIFY OR
    DEFEND

INITIAL PLEADING
Allegations in complaint, 24–33
Cause of action,
    Elements of cause of action
        Generally, 14
            Breach of contract, 144
            Negligence, 14
        Determining elements of statutory
            cause of action, 35–37
        Pleading ultimate facts to establish, 25
    Pleading cause of action in state courts, 17
Claim for relief, 6, 14
    Stating in federal court, 15–16
    Stating in state court, 16–17
Complaint (Initial pleading)
    Purpose of initial pleading, 6
        Notice to defendant of claim, 6; 15–16
        Notice of grounds, 6
    Variations in nomenclature, 6
Demand for Judgment generally, 22
    Placement in multi-count complaint, 34
    Requesting attorney's fees, 22
        Availability of attorney's fees in con-
            tract action
            see ATTORNEY'S FEES
        Requesting relief per statute, 41
Drafting a complaint, 26–42
    Complaint template, 42
    Format of Initial Pleading
        Caption, see CAPTION
        Drafting commencement, 23–24
            Identifying parties, 23–24
            Stipulating party name substitutes,
                23–24
        Effect of Local Rules, 9, 23
        Signature, 12–13
    Framing allegations, 26–30
        Alleging time and place, 27–28
        Alternative, inconsistent, or hypotheti-
            cal pleading, 30
        Focusing on the parties, 26–27
            Active voice, See VOICE
        Framing strategically to draw out an
            admission, 28–30
        Incorporation by reference and
            re-allegation, 34
        Numbering, 33

INITIAL PLEADING—Cont'd
Plain, concise, and direct, 26
Types of Allegations
Conclusory versus neutral, 29
Evidentiary, 24, 26
Extraneous 24, 26
Legal Conclusion, 24,
25–26[motions]
Ultimate facts, 17, 24, 25[motions]
Legal sufficiency of initial pleading,14–17
Federal court
Plausibility standard, 16–17, 61–62
State court
Fact-pleading standards, 17, 64
Notice-pleading standard, 16–17,
63–64
Plausibility standard, 16–17, 64
Organizing allegations into paragraphs, 33
How to create paragraphs, 33
How to number paragraphs, 33
Pleading jurisdiction, see *Jurisdiction and
Venue (below)*
Pleading multiple counts, 33–35
Placement of demand for judgment, 33
Division into counts (when necessary),
33–34
Headings for separate counts, 35
Re-alleging facts from previous counts,
34
Pleading venue, see *Jurisdiction and
Venue (below)*
Statutory pleading, 35–42
Checklist for analysis of statute, 36–37
Elements of cause of action, 14
Pleading the statutory cause of action
Identifying the statute, 38
Identifying the violated sections,
39–41
Tracking the relevant statutory lan-
guage, 38–39
Various examples in textbook
Allegations, framing of
Allegations focusing on parties, 27
Pleading to draw out admissions, 29
Sequence by category, 31–32
Time and place allegations, 28
Caption, 8
Checklist for analyzing a statute, 36–37
Commencement identifying multiple
parties, 24
Complaint to critique, 80–81
Demand for judgment
Negligence case, 22
Statutory cause of action, 22
Headings for separate counts, 35
Multi-count template, 41–42
Paragraph creation, 32–33
Pleading Personal Jurisdiction in fed-
eral court
Application of long-arm statute if
state requires it, 20
Parties section in federal pleading,
20
Pleading Subject–Matter Jurisdiction
Diversity, 18

INITIAL PLEADING—Cont'd
Federal question, 18
Pleading venue, 20
Re-allegation and incorporation, 34
Sequence of allegations (by category),
31
Statutory pleading
Demand for judgment, 41
Sequence,
Chronological, 40
Fact-violation, 40
Tracking statutory language, 39
Summons, 11
Template, 41–42
Types of allegations, 25
Exhibits to Pleading, see EXHIBITS
Federal Rules mentioned in text
Federal Rule 8
Federal Rule 8(a), 15
Federal Rule 8(a)(1), 17–18
Federal Rule 8(a)(3), 22
Federal Rule 8(b), 28
Federal Rule 8(d), 30
Federal Rule 9, 21
Federal Rule 9(f), 27
Federal Rule 10
Federal Rule 10(b), 32
Federal Rule 10(c), 34
Jurisdiction and venue
Jurisdiction, 17–21
Pleading personal jurisdiction, 19–20
Example of allegation, 20
Long-arm statute, 19–20
Pleading application of long-arm
statute, 20
Minimum contacts, 19
Pleading subject-matter jurisdiction,
17–18
Diversity jurisdiction, 18
Example of allegation, 18
Example of allegation, 18
Federal question jurisdiction, 18
Venue, 20–21
Forum-selection clause
See CONTRACT COMPONENTS
Pleading venue, 20–21
Pleading special matters in complaint, 21–22
Service of Initial Pleading, 11
Signature, 12–13
Summons (Example), 11
Verification or Non–Verification, 10

INVALID CONTRACT OR PROVISION, 105–7
Contravening public policy, 105–06
Reluctance of courts to invalidate, 106
Sources of public policy, 106
Illegal contracts or provision, 105
Unconscionable contract or provision, 106–07
Contract of adhesion, 107
Determination of unconscionability, 106–07
Procedural and substantive
unconscionability, 106
Factors indicating procedural
unconscionability, 106

JUDGMENT ON THE PLEADINGS
See MOTION FOR JUDGMENT ON THE PLEADINGS

JURISDICTION
See INITIAL PLEADING

LEGAL DRAFTING
Collaboration with Client, see CONTENT OF CONTRACT OR RULE–MAKING DOCUMENT
Contracts
    Drafter as lawmaker and advocate, 96–97
Focus on Users, Introduction, 2
Goals, Introduction, 1
Skills fostered, Introduction, 1–2

LEGISLATIVE DRAFTING
Attributes, 188
    Private rule-making documents, 188
        See LEGISLATIVE DRAFTING: PRIVATE RULE–MAKING DOCUMENTS
    Public rule-making documents, 188
        See LEGISLATIVE DRAFTING: PUBLIC RULE–MAKING DOCUMENTS
Drafting Rule–Making document
    Articulating legislative statements
        All recommended language, 189 (table)
        Stating a duty or prohibition, 189–90
        Stating a fact, 191
        Stating a legislative policy, 191
        Stating a requirement or a condition precedent, 190
        Stating a right, 190
    Drafting Style, 191–94
        Conciseness, 191–92
        Consistency, 171–72, 345–46
        Grammar, 372–394
        Modifier placement in sentence
            See MODIFIERS
        Preference for active voice
            See VERBS
        Punctuation, 395–406
        Style, 407–414
            Avoiding sentence overload, 410–11
            Gender-neutral drafting, 413–414
            Legal jargon, 412
            Sentence structure
                Indented lists, 413
    Organization of rule-making document, 188
        Contract or private rule-making document, see ORGANIZATION OF DOCUMENTS
        Public rule-making documents, 188
            Legislative drafting manual, 188, 201
    Types of rule-making documents
        See LEGISLATIVE DRAFTING: PRIVATE RULE–MAKING DOCUMENTS and see LEGISLATIVE DRAFTING: PUBLIC RULE–MAKING DOCUMENTS

LEGISLATIVE DRAFTING: PRIVATE RULE–MAKING DOCUMENTS
Construction of document
    Variations in construction, 199
        See STATUTORY CONSTRUCTION
Drafting process, 195
    Organization
        See ORGANIZATION OF DOCUMENTS
    Template for rule-making document, 253–54
Types of documents
    Documents for Property Owner Associations, 195–96
        By-laws for, 197–98
        Declaration of Covenants, 195–96
    Documents relating to corporations, 198–99
        Articles of incorporation, 198–99
        Corporate by-laws, 199
    Documents relating to limited-liability companies, 200
    Other private rule-making documents, 200

LEGISLATIVE DRAFTING: PUBLIC RULE–MAKING DOCUMENTS
Construction of statute or other public rule-making document
    See STATUTORY CONSTRUCTION
Drafter's preparation to draft, 201–02
    Checking legal and factual background, 201–02
    Consulting legislative drafting manuals, 201
    Understanding the legislative process, 201
Drafting Bills, 202–10
    Single subject rule, 202
    Typical components of bill, 203–07
        Body of bill, 207
        Definitions section, 207
        Enacting clause, 204
        Identifying Information and title, 203–04
        Legislative findings section, 205–06
        Preamble section, 204–05
        Purpose or intent section, 205
        Short title section, 206–07
        Technical provisions, 207–10
            Effective date and emergency clause, 209
            Retroactivity of all or part of act, 210
            Saving clause, 207–08
            Severability or non-severability, 208–09
            Sunset clause, 208
Drafting local ordinance, 210–11

LIMITATION–OF–DAMAGES CLAUSE
Limitation-of-damages clause, 131–32
    Characteristics, 131
    Distinguished from liquidated-damages clause, 131
    Effect, 131
    Enforceability, 132

LIMITATION–OF–REMEDIES CLAUSE
Application of UCC to sale or lease of goods, 134
Characteristics, 132–33
Enforceability, 133–134
Exclusive remedy stipulated, 133–34

LIMITING OR EXCLUDING WARRANTIES UNDER UCC
Application of UCC to sale and lease of goods, 134
Characteristics of warranty, 134
Effect of "as is" or "with all faults," 135
    Use of recitals, 135
Exclusion of warranties, 135–36
    Drafting guidance in UCC 2–316, 135
UCC warranties discussed, 134–36
    Express warranties, 134–35
    Implied warranties, 135–36
        Arise by operation of law, 135
        Implied warranty of fitness for a particular purpose, 135
        Implied warranty of merchantability, 135

LIQUIDATED–DAMAGES CLAUSE
Characteristics and purpose, 147
Example (from case), 148
Requirements for Enforceability
    Not a penalty, 147
    Party cannot reject liquidated damages to pursue greater amount of damages, 148
    Reasonable estimate of amount to compensate party, 147

LIST
Indented list, 413

LOCAL RULES OF COURT
Format of pleadings, 9
Motion practice,
    Availability of oral hearing, 58–59
    Documents filed in support of motion, 57–58
    Format requirements for motion, 57
    Signatures, 13

"MAY" (to confer a right)
In contracts
    See CONTRACT DRAFTING
In statutes and rule-making documents
    See LEGISLATIVE DRAFTING
In wills
    See WILLS (drafting and execution)

MERGER CLAUSE
Characteristics and purpose, 153
Integration of writing
    Effect of integration, 153
        Parol evidence rule applies, 153
        Effect of parol evidence rule, 153
    Merger clause
        Conclusive as to integration, 154
        Effect of boilerplate language, 154

MERGER CLAUSE—Cont'd
    Not conclusive, but highly persuasive, 154

MISPLACED MODIFIER
See MODIFIERS

MODIFICATION CLAUSE IN CONTRACT
Right of parties to agree to modification, 163
    Supplementary agreement to modify, 163
        Drafting modification clause, 163–64
            Attempting to preclude oral modification, 164
        Validity, 163
    Unilateral modification not allowed, 164

MODIFIERS
Definition, 374
Generally, 391–94
Problems with modifiers, 391–94
    Dangling modifier, 393–94
    Misplaced modifier, 391–93
        As cause of ambiguity, 335–39
            Cap or maximum, 337
            Percentage sign, 336
            Price and quantity, 338
        Drafting to avoid ambiguity,
            Placement of conditional clause, 361
                At beginning of sentence, 361
                When sentence also contains time clause, 361–63
            Placement of cross-reference, 265
            Placement of time clause, 355–56
    Phrasing of modifiers, 393–94
    Punctuation used with modifiers
        Commas used with restrictive modifier, 397–99
        Dashes used to insert modifier, 494
    Restrictive vs. non-restrictive modifiers, 397–99
        "Which" versus "that," 398–99
    "Squinting" modifier, 339

MOTIONS
Availability of oral hearing, 58–59
    Effect of Local Rules, 58–59
    Effect of Rule 78(b), 58
Baseless or frivolous, 57
    Effect of Rule 11, 11–12
Caption
    See CAPTION
Documents in support of motion, 57–58
    Affidavit, 58
    Brief or memorandum of law, 57–58
    Exhibits
        see EXHIBITS
    Proposed order, 58
Drafting motion, 57
Examples
    Motion for judgment on the pleadings, 73
    Motion for more definite statement, 65
    Motion for summary judgment, 70
    Motion to dismiss complaint, 62
    Motion to strike affirmative defense, 55

MOTIONS—Cont'd
Motion to strike scandalous allegations, 66
Notice of motion, 59
Federal Rules mentioned in text
Federal Rule 6(c)(1), 58
Federal Rule 7(b)(2), 56
Federal Rule 11, 11–13, 57
Federal Rule 12
Federal Rule 12(b) defenses, 60–67, 72
consolidation and waiver, 61
Federal Rule 12(b)(6) defense, 61–63
Federal Rule 12(c), 72
Federal Rule 12(d), 73
Federal Rule 12(e), 64–65
Federal Rule 12(f)
motion to strike allegations, 66
motion to strike legal defense, 54–55
Federal Rule 12(h), 61, 72
Federal Rule 56, 68
Federal Rule 56(b), 69
Federal Rule 56(c), 69–70
Federal Rule 56(c)(4), 70
Federal Rule 56(h), 71
Federal Rule 78(b), 58
Format of motion
Effect of local rules, 58–59
For pleadings and motions, 9
Supporting memorandum, 57–58
Legal sufficiency of complaint, 14
See MOTION TO DISMISS
Motion practice generally, 56–60
Federal motion practice
Availability of hearing, 58–59
Effect of local rules
Baseless motions, 57
Brief or supporting memorandum, 58
Submission of documentary evidence, 58
Preparation of Motion, 56–57
Documents filed in support of motion, 57–58
Notice of Motion, 59
Opposition to Motion, 59
Procedural requisites
Caption
See CAPTION
Signature, 12–13
Verification or Non–Verification, 10
Types of motions
Examples of common types, 56
Motion for summary adjudication, 67–74
See MOTION FOR JUDGMENT ON THE PLEADINGS
See MOTION FOR SUMMARY JUDGMENT
Rule 12 (Pre–Answer) Motions
See MOTION FOR JUDGMENT ON THE PLEADINGS
See MOTION FOR MORE DEFINITE STATEMENT
See MOTION FOR SUMMARY JUDGMENT
See MOTION TO DISMISS

MOTIONS—Cont'd
See MOTION TO STRIKE ALLEGATIONS
See MOTION TO STRIKE INSUFFICIENT LEGAL DEFENSE

MOTION FOR MORE DEFINITE STATEMENT
Federal Court, 64–65
Effect of granting, 65
"Polishing the pleadings," 65
Function of motion, 64–65
Pleading too vague and ambiguous to answer, 65
State court, 65

MOTION FOR JUDGMENT ON THE PLEADINGS
Federal
Comparison to other pre-trial motions
Compared to 12(b)(6) motion, 72
Compared to summary judgment motion, 73–74
Conversion to motion for summary judgment, 73–74
Function, 72
State
Conversion to summary judgment, 74
Unavailability in certain states, 74
Variation in materials considered "outside the pleadings," 74
Determination of motion, 74

MOTION FOR SUMMARY JUDGMENT
Federal court
Availability of summary judgment, 67–68
Function, 67–68
When appropriate, 68
Determination of motion, 68
Effect of competing inferences, 68
Effect of determination, 68
Denial of motion, 68
Grant of motion, 68
Effect of disputed facts, 68
Procedures, 69–71
Availability of discovery, 71
Materials in support of motion, 69–72
Time for filing, 69
State court
Cases not appropriate for summary judgment, 71
Function of summary judgment, 71

MOTION TO DISMISS
Federal court, 61–63
Amendment to dismissed pleading, 52, 62
Effect of exhibits, 63
Example, 62
Federal Rule 12(e), 64
Four corners of complaint, 63
Function of motion, 61
Plausibility standard, 61–62
Pleading oneself out of court, 62
Surviving motion, 61
State equivalents to Rule 12(b)(6), 63–64
Legal sufficiency of complaint, 63–64

MOTION TO DISMISS—Cont'd
Differing standards, 63–64
Fact-pleading standard, 64
Notice-pleading standard, 63–64
Plausibility standard, 64

MOTION TO STRIKE A LEGAL DEFENSE
Disfavored status, 55
Example, 55
Federal Rule 12(f), 54

MOTION TO STRIKE ALLEGATIONS
Federal court, 66–67
Allegations that may be stricken, 67
Requirement of prejudice, 67
Types of allegations
Immaterial, 67
Impertinent allegations, 67
Redundant, 67
Scandalous, 67
Disfavored status, 66
"Polishing the pleadings," 66
Requirement of prejudice, 67
Federal Rule 12(f), 66–67
Function of motion, 66
State court, 67
Sham or frivolous allegations or pleading, 67

MULTI–COUNT PLEADING
Demand for judgment, 33
Division into counts (when necessary), 33–34
Headings for separate counts, 35
Re-alleging facts from previous counts, 34

"MUST" TO EXPRESS A REQUIREMENT
In contracts
See CONTRACT DRAFTING
In rule-documents
See LEGISLATIVE DRAFTING

NOSCITUR A SOCIIS
See CRUCIAL CANONS FOR DRAFTERS

NOTICE PLEADING
See INITIAL PLEADING and MOTIONS

"OR" AND "AND"
"And/or", 344–45
Needless legal jargon, 412
Problems created through use, 344–45
"Or" and "and," 343–44
Overlapping meanings, 343
Ambiguity, 343–44

ORGANIZATION OF DOCUMENTS
Creating outline, 244–57
Creating major sections, 244–45
Creation of issue list and term sheet, 239–41
Grouping issues according to topic, 244–45
Example, 245
"Topic scattering" (avoid), 244
Creating headings, 245–48

ORGANIZATION OF DOCUMENTS—Cont'd
Attributes of headings
Effective heading, 245
Content predictable from heading, 245
Encompasses all content, 245
Excludes topics not covered, 245
Ineffective headings, 245–46
Too narrow or too broad for content, 245–46
Example, 245, 246
Generating effective headings, 246–48
Template for generating headings, 246
3–word minimum, 246
Heading formats, problems, 247–48
Full sentences, 247
Heading and text redundant, 248
Heading replaces omitted text, 248, 261–62
One- or two-word headings, 247
Question or command, 247
Headings *not* based on template, 247
Creating subsections, 244–51
Subdivision errors, 249–51
Organization-by-party error, 250
Avoid organizing based on party "duties", 250
Subdivision scheme creates overlap, 250
Subdivision scheme not reader-friendly, 250
Identify topics based on *issues*, 250
Overlapping-subheadings error, 251
Subsections must name distinct sub-issues, 251
Single-subdivision error, 249
Illogical to subdivide into a single portion, 249
Subdivision of sections, subsections, and sub-subsections, 248–47
Examples of subdivision, 248–49
Guidelines for when subdivision needed, 248–49
At least 2 distinct topics, 248
More than 2–3 manageable sentences, 248
Levels of subdivision, 249
Judgment call for drafter, 249
Example of subdivision to fourth level, 249
Designing format for draft, 255–57
Format examples
Example 1, 256
Example 2, 257
Heading format, 255
Headings that stand out from text, 255
Lettering and numbering all headings, 255
Other tips for designing headings, 255
Indenting subsections, 255–56
Page numbering, 256
Spacing between provisions, 255
Refining drafted document's organization, 244–57
"Displaced text" error, 260–61

ORGANIZATION OF DOCUMENTS—Cont'd
  Heading-replacing-content error,
      261–62
  "Wall of text" section of subsection, 258
  Sentence overlap, 262–64
    Conflicting sentences, 262–63
      Conflicting sentences in same or dif-
          ferent sections, 263
      Qualifying conflicting sentences to
          resolve conflict, 262–63
      See CONDITIONAL STATE-
          MENTS
    Redundant sentences, 262
  Template for contract, 252–53
  Template for rule-making document, 253–54
  Using cross-referencing, 264–65
    Avoid cross-references if possible, 264
    Drafting useful cross-references, 264–65

OUTLINE OF DOCUMENT
See ORGANIZATION OF DOCUMENTS

PARALLEL SENTENCE STRUCTURE
In general, 389–90
Indented lists, 413

PASSIVE VOICE
See VERBS

PERSONAL JURISDICTION
See INITIAL PLEADING

PERSONAL REPRESENTATIVE
See WILLS (Background for Drafter)

PLAUSIBILITY STANDARD
Standard in federal court, 16–17, 64
  Applicability to affirmative defenses,
      51–53

PLEADING
See INITIAL PLEADING or ANSWER

PLEADING SPECIAL MATTERS
See INITIAL PLEADING or ANSWER

**PLEADING REQUESTING AFFIRMATIVE
  RELIEF**
See INITIAL PLEADING

PLURAL
Plurals, 193–94, 341

POLICY STATEMENT
See CONTRACT DRAFTING

PRAYER FOR RELIEF
See INITIAL PLEADING, demand for judg-
    ment

PREPOSITION
Generally, 374
  Introducing indirect object, 378
  Prepositional Phrase, 375–76

PREVENTION DOCTRINE, see EXCUSE
  (*FORCE MAJEURE* CLAUSE)

PROCEDURAL UNCONSCIONABILITY
See INVALID CONTRACT OR PROVISION

PRONOUN
Ambiguous usage, 388–89
Antecedent, 384
Case, 385–87
  Objective case versus subjective case,
      385–86
    "Who" versus "whom," 386
  Possessive case, 386–87
Definition and example, 373, 385
Gender, 387–88
  Drafting gender neutrally, 413–14
Number, 387–88

PUBLIC POLICY, VIOLATION OF
See INVALID CONTRACT OR PROVISION

PUNCTUATION
Ambiguous
  Impact of commas on meaning, 395–96
Apostrophes, 401–03
Colon, 400–01
Dash, 403–04
Hyphen, 404–05
Punctuating quoted material
  Commas, 405
  Colons, 406
  Periods, 405
  Question marks, 406
  Semicolons, 406

QUALIFYING CLAUSE
See CONDITIONAL STATEMENTS

QUESTIONS FOR CLIENT
Drafting client questionnaire
  See CONTENT OF CONTRACT OR
      RULE–MAKING DOCUMENT

REDUNDANCY
In contract or rule-making document
  Overlapping sentences
    See ORGANIZATION OF DOCU-
        MENTS and AMBIGUITY
In pleading

RELEASE
See EXCULPATORY CLAUSE

REPLY
See ANSWER

**RESPONSES TO PLEADING REQUESTING
  AFFIRMATIVE RELIEF**
See ANSWER

"RESPONSIBLE FOR"
See AMBIGUITY

RIGHT
Expressing in a contract
   See CONTRACT DRAFTING
Expressing in a will
   See WILLS (Background for Drafter)
Expressing in rule-making document
   See LEGISLATIVE DRAFTING

RULE 11
Effect of Federal Rule 11, 11–13
   Effect of Presenting a Document to the
      Court, 12
   Safe Harbor, 12
   Sanctions, 12
   State equivalents to Rule 11, 13

SECTIONS AND SUBSECTIONS
See ORGANIZATION OF DOCUMENTS

SEMI–COLON
Avoiding comma splice, 400
In a series, 399–400
Separating independent clauses, 400

SENTENCE OVERLAP, 262–64

SEQUENCE
Allegations in an initial pleading, 31–32, 38,
   40
Provisions in a contract or rule-making docu-
   ment
Templates, 254
   For contract, 252–53
   For rule-making document, 253–54

SERVICE OF PLEADINGS AND MOTIONS
Requirement of Federal Rule 4, 11
Summons (example), 11

SEVERABILITY
Invalid provision in contract
   See CONTRACT COMPONENTS
Severability clause in statute, see LEGISLA-
      TIVE DRAFTING: PUBLIC RULE–
      MAKING DOCUMENTS

SHORT FORM FOR LATER REFERENCE
Commencement
   Identifying parties to a pleading, 24
Definitions
   Creation of short forms using "means"-type
      definition, see DEFINITIONS
Exordium clause in contract,
   Identifying parties, see CONTRACT
      DRAFTING

SIGNATURE
Signing contract
   See EXECUTION OF CONTRACT
Signing pleading or motion, 11–13

STATUTORY CONSTRUCTION
Canons of construction, 215–18
   Canons favoring one reading over another,
      215–16

STATUTORY CONSTRUCTION—Cont'd
   Consistency with related enactments
      intended, 216
      In pari materia doctrine, 216
   Constitutionality and validity pre-
      sumed, 215
   Enforcement of entire statute intended,
      216
   Rational purpose intended, 215–16
   Rejection of reading producing absurd
      or unjust outcome, 216
Consideration of statute's components in
   construction, 216–17
Determination of Term's Meaning or Appli-
   cation, 217–18
   Preference for ordinary meaning, 217
      Circumstances in which words given
         technical meaning, 217
      Effect of definitions, 217
      Rejection of strained or narrow con-
         struction, 217
   Effect of associated words, 217–18
   Effect of consistent and inconsistent lan-
      guage, 217
   Effect of omission or express exclusion,
      218
   See CRUCIAL CANONS FOR DRAFT-
      ERS
Documents to which rules of statutory con-
   struction typically apply, 212
Goal of courts in construing statute, 212–13
   Effectuation of legislative intent, 212–13
   Presumptions concerning legislature that
      enacted statute, 213
Process of statutory construction, 213–14
   Circumstances in which construction
      required, 213
   Primacy of legislative intent, 214
   Strict versus liberal construction, 219
   Use of canons, 214–18
   Use of extrinsic aids, 214
      Types of extrinsic aids used, 218–19
         Case law on same subject, 218
         Historical context, 218
         Legislative history, 218
         Official comments to Uniform Act or
            Model law, 219
         Prior legislation changed or
            accepted by statute, 218
         Reasonable construction of statute
            by enforcing agency, 219

STRICT CONSTRUCTION
Contracts generally
   See CONTRACT CONSTRUCTION AND
      EXCULPATORY CLAUSE

STYLE
Guidance for all drafters, 407–14
   Active voice, 409
   Conciseness, 407–08
   Gender-neutral drafting, 413–14
   Handbooks, 407
   Indented lists, 413
   Legal jargon, 412

STYLE—Cont'd
Passive voice, 409
Sentences, overloaded, 410–11
Simplicity, 411–12

SUBJECT–MATTER JURISDICTION
See INITIAL PLEADING

"SUBJECT TO"
See AMBIGUITY

SUBSTANTIVE UNCONSCIONABILITY
See INVALID CONTRACT OR PROVISION

SUMMARY ADJUDICATION
See MOTION FOR JUDGMENT ON THE
PLEADINGS
See MOTION FOR SUMMARY JUDGMENT

SUMMARY JUDGMENT
See MOTION FOR SUMMARY JUDGMENT

TECHNICAL LANGUAGE
Use in contract, rule-making document, or
will
See CHOOSING WORDS
Use in wills
See WILLS (Drafting and Execution)

TERMINATION CLAUSE
See CANCELLATION AND TERMINATION
CLAUSES

TESTAMENTARY DISPOSITION
See WILLS (Background for Drafters)

"THAT"
Different meanings of "that," 374
Restrictive modifiers, 398–99

TIME CLAUSE
Avoiding ambiguity in time clause
Ambiguous time terminology, 356–60
"Between," 357
"Midnight," 359
"Month," 358–59
"To," "Until," and "by," 358
"Upon," "when," "once," 356–57
"Week," 359
"Within" when drafting a due date,
deadline, or cut-off, 357–58
Placement of clause, 355–56
Placing at beginning of sentence, 355
Placing elsewhere in sentence, 356
Examples of ambiguous placement,
356
Placement when sentence contains a
conditional clause, 361–63
Drafting due date, deadline, or cut-off with
specified dates, 348–49
Drafting due date, deadline, or cut-off with no
specified dates (dates unknown), 349–51
Stating duration period, 351–55
Duration period with specified (known)
dates, 351–52

TIME CLAUSE—Cont'd
Duration period with unspecified (not
known) dates, 352–353
Duration periods with renewable or
extendable performance period,
353–55
Extension by automatic renewal,
354–55
Extension by giving notice, 353–54

**UNCONSCIONABLE CONTRACT OR PROVI-
SION**
See INVALID CONTRACT OR PROVISION

UNIFORM COMMERCIAL CODE
See LIMITATION-OF-REMEDIES CLAUSE
See LIMITING OR EXCLUDING WARRAN-
TIES UNDER UCC

"UNLESS," "EXCEPT," "IF"
See CONDITIONAL STATEMENTS

VAGUE LANGUAGE
Use of vague language
See DELINEATING SCOPE OF PROVI-
SION

VENUE
See INITIAL PLEADING

VERBS
Verbs (discussion), 377–84
(definition and example), 373
Direct and indirect object of, 376
Intransitive or Transitive, 377–78
Mood, 382–384
Imperative, 382
Indicative, 382
Subjunctive, 382–84
Tense, 379–82
Perfect, 380
Progressive (perfect), 381–82
Progressive (simple), 381
Simple, 380
Voice of Verb, 377–79
Transitive verbs, 377
Voices, 378–79
Active voice, 378
Characteristics, 378
Tenses, 380
Passive Voice, 378–79
Characteristics, 378
Strategic use, 379
Tenses, 380
Use in writing, 379

VERIFICATION OF PLEADING, 10

VOICE OF VERB
See VERBS

VOID AS AGAINST PUBLIC POLICY
See INVALID CONTRACT OR PROVISION

WAIVER
Contracts
    See EXCULPATORY CLAUSE
Pleadings
    Affirmative defense
        See ANSWER
    Rule 12 defense, 61

"WHICH" VERSUS "THAT," 398–99

"WHO" VERSUS "WHOM," 386

WILLS (Background for Drafter)
Background, 276–77
    Limited Scope of Discussion, 276–77
Basics, 277–79
    Persons who can benefit from will, 278
    Persons who can make a will, 278
    Property that can pass by will, 278
    Purpose of will, 277–78
        Appointment of representative, 277
        Attributes, 277–78
        Testamentary disposition, 277
    Requirements for valid will, 279–84
        Compliance with formalities, 280–84
        Testamentary intent, 279–80
    Wills act formalities for attested will, 280–84
        Attested will requirements, 280–82
        Changes to will, 284–85
            Codicil, 284–85
                Compliance with wills act formalities, 284
                Drafting to avoid conflict with existing will, 284–85
            Effect of changed circumstances, 285
                Birth of child, 285
                Final divorce decree, 285
                Legal separation, 285
                Marriage, 285
            Replacement will, 285
            Revocation of prior wills, 285
        Compliance with formalities, 282–84
            Strict compliance, 282–83
            Substantial compliance, 283
    Nomination of executor (personal representative), 278–79, 293–94
        Compensation and reimbursement of expenses, 279, 294
        Duties and powers, 278–79, 293–94
        Fiduciary duty, 279
        Identification of successors, 293
        Waiver of bond, 294

WILLS (Construction of Will)
Drafter's need to be aware of presumptions and canons, 303
Primacy of testator's intent expressed in will's four corners, 302
    Ambiguous will construed, 302–03
        Admission of extrinsic evidence, 303
        Definition of ambiguity, 302
        Determination of intent, 302
        Determination of meaning of words, 303

WILLS (Construction of Will)—Cont'd
    Unambiguous will given effect as written, 302

WILLS (Drafting and Executing)
Drafting provisions of will
    Drafting simple dispositive provisions
        Legacies,
            Attributes
                Demonstrative legacy, 295
                General legacy, 295
                Residuary legacy, 295
                Specific legacy, 294–95
            Consequences of characterization
                Abatement, 296–97
                Ademption of specific legacies, 295–96
                Other effects, 297
            Expressing legacies, 297–99
                Demonstrative legacy, 298
                General legacy, 298
                Residuary legacy, 298–99
                Specific legacy, 297
            Preventing lapse of legacies, 299–300
                Crafting provisions, 300
                    Examples, 300
                Effect of anti-lapse statutes, 299
                    Assessing in light of client's intentions, 299
                    Class gifts, 300
            Simultaneous death, 300–01
                Crafting simultaneous death provision, 301
                State statutes, 301
    Drafting provision nominating executor
        See WILLS (Background for Drafter)
Execution Ceremony, 301–02
    Formalities for attested will or codicil
        See WILLS (Background for Drafter)
    Recommended formalities for executing will or codicil, 301
    Self-proving will, 301–02
    Statements in will, 289–290
        Declarations (stating facts), 290
        Expressing disposition of property, 289
        Expressing right or power, 289–90
        Imposing a duty, 290
    Word choice, 290–93
        Achieving requisite clarity, 290
        Checking meaning of words, 291–93
            Checking assumptions about client's terminology, 291–92
            Checking meaning of technical terms, 291
            Checking scope of ordinary words, 291
            Checking usage against statutory terminology, 291
        Drafting definitions, 292–93
Organizing components of will, 286–89
    Approaches to organization, 286

WILLS (Drafting and Executing)—Cont'd
    Division into articles (if desired),
      286
    Outlining
      See ORGANIZATION OF DOCU-
        MENTS
    Organization into sections and sub-
      sections
      See ORGANIZATION OF DOCU-
        MENTS
    Refining organizational scheme
      See ORGANIZATION OF DOCU-
        MENTS
  Components of will, 286–89
    Components set out at beginning,
      286–87

WILLS (Drafting and Executing)—Cont'd
    Definitions, 287
    Preamble and initial declara-
      tions, 286–87
  Components set out at end, 287–88
    Rules regarding dispositions, 287
    Signatures and attestation,
      287–88
  Other components, 286–89
    Dispositive provisions, 288–89
      Residuary disposition, 289
    Nomination of personal represen-
      tative or appointment of
      guardian, 289
    Sequencing other components,
      289

†